S0-AZS-155

New Products Management

The Irwin Series in Marketing
Consulting Editor   Gilbert A. Churchill, Jr.
University of Wisconsin, Madison

New Products Management

Third Edition

C. Merle Crawford
The University of Michigan

Homewood, IL 60430
Boston, MA 02116

©RICHARD D. IRWIN, INC., 1983, 1987, and 1991

All rights reserved. No part of this publication may be reproduced, stored in a retrieval system, or transmitted, in any form or by any means, electronic, mechanical, photocopying, recording, or otherwise, without the prior written permission of the publisher.

Sponsoring editor: Elizabeth S. MacDonell
Project editor: Ethel Shiell
Production manager: Carma W. Fazio
Cover designer: David T. Jones
Compositor: Graphic World Incorporated
Typeface: 10/12 Century Schoolbook
Printer: R. R. Donnelly & Sons Company

Library of Congress Cataloging-in-Publication Data

Crawford, C. Merle (Charles Merle)
    New products management / C. Merle Crawford. — 3rd ed.
        p.   cm. — (The Irwin series in marketing)
    Includes bibliographical references and index.
    ISBN 0-256-08207-3
    1. New products — Management.   I. Title.   II. Series.
HF5415. 153.C72   1991
    658.5'75 — dc20   90–4596
                                                              CIP

Printed in the United States of America

    2   3   4   5   6   7   8   9   0   DO   7   6   5   4   3   2   1

*To the several 3rd-generation "line extensions" of the family—
The Crawfords: Kara Jean, Anna Marie, David Bentley, Steven
Charles, Jane Marie, and Mark Alan. And our new brand, the
Chambers: Rebecca Jane and Megan Elizabeth.*

Preface

New products have always been of interest to both academics and practitioners, but organized, college-level instruction on the subject of new products management traces to the 1950s. As business school enrollments surged during that decade, these schools added many new courses. Some incorporated a major or shared interest on new products.

Depending on the department within which these courses were taught, the emphasis was on marketing, engineering, or economics. Books for those early courses were usually anthologies of articles covering a broad range of technical and marketing topics.

But, by the late 1970s, a new products management discipline was beginning to evolve. There was a small assortment of college texts, the Product Development and Management Association had been founded, and over 100 colleges had courses on new products. The field has continued to grow, and it is estimated that as many as 300 offer such courses as we move into the 1990s.

HOW THIS BOOK VIEWS THE FIELD OF NEW PRODUCTS MANAGEMENT

Such exploding growth means we still take a variety of approaches to the teaching of this subject—technical, creative, economic, marketing science, and so on. This book provides the *management* approach. Every organization (industry, retailing, government, churches, and so on) has a person or group of persons who, knowingly or unknowingly, are charged with getting new goods and services onto the "market." That person or group has to deal with the total task—including strategy, concept generation, and evaluation. So does this book.

Furthermore, this book calls on all the contributing disciplines, stresses recent research findings, and strives for a level of sophistication equal to that of the better practitioners in this field. An instructor wishing to emphasize any of the specialty viewpoints within the general field of new products management will want to supplement the book with specialized material.

On the other hand, this book is not a research report on typical industry practice. It goes well beyond and includes experimental work conducted by the more advanced practitioners.

SOME BASIC BELIEFS THAT GUIDED THE WRITING

People who have used the first two editions of this book know my unique viewpoints on the subject. But for newcomers (and, of course, all students are newcomers), here are some of them:

1. Product innovation is one operation in an organization. It has parts (such as strategy, teams, and plans), but those are all just parts. Any operation that runs as separate pieces misses the strength of the whole.

2. The field is still very new and lacks a systematic language. This makes it very difficult for students, who are accustomed to studying subjects where a term means one thing and only that one thing. I wish this were so in new products. What should we do—slip and slide around over the many terms and their variations? I believe we should not and have proposed a set of terms in this book that seem to fit and deserve consideration. The terms are used consistently, and I urge students to accept them. Some terms will survive, and others will die a quiet death (but, I hope only after losing out to different and better terms that are widely accepted). The Glossary in Appendix D is a testimony to this belief.

3. Ideas learned without application are merely ideas memorized. To become yours, a concept must be applied in little ways or in big ones. Thus, the book is peppered with applications, short cases, and other opportunities for using the concepts studied.

4. As much as I would like them, and have diligently tried to find them, I believe there are no standard sets of procedure for makers of consumer packaged goods, consumer durables, industrial goods, services, and so on. Like a marketing plan and a production plan, there is a best plan for any particular situation. A manager must look at the situation and then compile a set of tools and other operations appropriate to it. All large firms use scores of different approaches, not one. To the extent that generalizations (for example, is there a strategy?) can be made, they will stand out as you work your way through the course. But *what* strategy and exactly *how* to determine it become situational.

5. An example lies in the next belief—should new products strategy rest on a base of technology or of market? These have been argued as options for many years. But, the argument is specious, moot. Strategy should rest on both, all of the time (another generalization, which needs thoughtful application).

6. I believe students should be challenged to think, not just memorize. This book contains lists of things from time to time, but these are a resource for thinking. The above belief about the best approach being situational is based on the need to analyze, consider, discuss, and apply. The great variety in approaches used by businesspeople is not a testimony to their ignorance, rather to their thinking. On a majority of the issues facing us today, intelligent people can have different views. Don't misunderstand—one view *is* better than the other, but it is made better by its defense, not who said it or who used it.

Decisions are often the same—they are not necessarily right or wrong at the time they are made. Instead, the manager who makes a decision then has to work hard to make that decision turn out right. The quality of the work is often more important than the quality of the decision.

7. This leads to the last belief: The "halo effect" hurts the field of new products more than anything else—more than competition, more than government, more than tight budgets. The halo effect shows in the statement "It must be a good thing for us to do—P&G does it." Or, 3M does it, or GE does it, or IBM does it. Those are excellent companies, but one reason they're good is because they spend lots of time and money studying and learning from others. They assume everything they do is wrong and can be improved. You should too. This book does. Citations of their actions are given as examples, not recommendations.

CHANGES IN THE THIRD EDITION

This is an aside to teachers—past and potential adopters of *New Products Management*. Work on the third edition focused on teachability—sharpening the organization, reducing wordiness, getting better and more current examples and applications, generally explaining things better. The book was shortened by about 10 percent. I have tried to make specific recommendations wherever I thought it right to do so. There are more footnotes, thus giving more sources to follow up on, and fewer parenthetical comments in text material. More reference material has been moved to an enlarged appendix.

The last chapter contains a new audit form that can be used by anyone investigating the new product process of a given firm. Students, particularly, will find that with this form, they can hold a challenging discussion with anyone who works in this field.

Applications and the small cases have been updated or replaced. Chapters 1, 2, 3, and 19 have been completely rewritten, based on my own dissatisfaction and the specific suggestions of several excellent reviewers. Chapter 20, on managing the process, was newly created.

Every other chapter was substantially rewritten, terms standardized, conflicts cleared up, and generally made more personal to students. Clutter was dumped — or trashed, as the MAC says.

Chapter 2 now contains a comprehensive product innovation process chart. The original purpose of this chart was to aid in developing a research agenda for the field, but it has been valuable in my classes the past two years in tying this book to the basic Booz, Allen & Hamilton process that we have used for so long. In previous editions, the book used different process steps; but, as one reviewer said, "The BA&H system has faults, but we sure don't need every author making up a new one." Touché.

The book continues to reflect the beliefs stated above and continues to build on several keystones — specifically, the need for strategy to guide operations; the value of an evaluation system into which all evaluation steps are packaged; the role of managerial control; the selective material on marketing planning, which assumes students have had an introductory marketing course; and a two-chapter set on public policy issues.

A new Instructor's Manual reflecting the changes in this edition is available through the Irwin representative.

THE PRACTITIONER

Because this book takes a managerial focus and is updated extensively, it is useful to the practicing new product manager. It has been used in many executive training courses. Great pains have been taken to present the "best practice" of industry.

THE APPLICATIONS

In a break from common practice, the chapters do not conclude with a list of questions. Rather, I have culled from many student conversations those questions and comments they received from business managers on their fly-backs. These comments were structured as a continuing conversation with the president of a conglomerate corporation. Explanation of how to use them is given at the end of Chapter 1.

MULTIFUNCTIONAL FIELD

New products management is multifunctional, a miniaturization of the firm. We pull from all fields of business study, but no one book can be expert in any one of them. Therefore, readers are encouraged to bring specialized, in-depth thinking from those other fields — organization behavior, finance, marketing, manufacturing, R&D, and many more.

ACKNOWLEDGMENTS

Many persons help write a book of this type, and it is impossible to thank them all. Certainly the University of Michigan Business School spent the most time and money on the project, from the excellent services of our Document Processing Center to the highly professional work of departmental secretaries Marilyn Bernhardt and Jackie Bolgos. Great aid came from the staff of the Kresge Business Administration Library here at the university, especially Laura Crawford and Nancy Karp.

From business, hundreds have helped—on field trips and during executive seminars. Scores of wonderful alums have been of fabulous help by telephone calls, campus visits, and the many things they have sent me. Academic colleagues continue making probably the greatest direct contribution by reacting to previous editions. For this edition, I particularly thank Thomas Hustad, Anthony di Benedetto, Richard Robinson, James Tushaus, Jon Freiden, and Thomas Westover.

C. Merle Crawford

Contents

Creative Stimuli Big Winner Competitive Analysis Is
There an Ideal System Combining the Best of the Many
Concept Generation Techniques? Ethics Handling the
Outside Idea *Legal Background Recommended
Procedure The Waiver Acceptable Alternatives Patents
Make a Comeback* Case: Golden Enterprises

PART III
Concept Evaluation

PART V
Structure/Environment

Specific New Products or Types of New Products   Concluding
Matters   *Complaints of CEOs about New Products
Managers   Evaluating an Ongoing Product Innovation
System*

Part I

Overview and Preparation

Chapter 1

The Menu

When someone mentions new products, we often think about technology—fiber optics, 3-lux capability on video cameras, computer graphics, and the like. Other times, we think about far simpler items—caffeine-free colas, "softer-scrub" cleansers, new fall colors, and new flavors of ice cream. Both views are correct—new products run the gamut from the cutting edge of technology to the latest width of masking tape.

How do all these things come about? It would be nice to say they come from an orderly process, managed by experienced persons well-versed in product innovation. But, they do not. Art Fry got his idea for what became Post-it notes when his hymnal page-marking slips kept falling out. And he had a rough time persuading others at 3M that the idea was worth marketing.

If you come from a background in a more established discipline (e.g., engineering, finance, or marketing), you may be confused about the uncertainty prevailing in this book. If so, welcome to the land of creative exploration. In this field, we create new things but often are not sure just what they will be, what they will cost, exactly who will want them, how we will distribute and sell them, and how some regulator in a government office somewhere will react to them.

We do know a lot about how new products should be developed, but the ideal conditions discussed in a textbook are rarely matched in practice. Managers must look at each situation, select from the recommended practice those procedures they feel are appropriate, and then do them the best they can.

Some people call this activity product innovation management, some call it product planning, and some (from a very biased perspective) call it research & development (R&D) or marketing. In this book, it is called the most descriptive term we have: *new products management*.

This opening chapter is entitled "The Menu" because it is built around a series of questions that students of the subject often ask.

WHY DOES THIS FIELD DESERVE STUDY?

First of all, it's big business. Over $100 billion is spent yearly on the technical phase (R&D) in the United States alone (see Figure 1–1). Some industries spend as much as 5 to 10 percent of their sales on technical research (see Figure 1–2). Over 10,000 new products are marketed every year in the United States alone, though no serious effort has ever been taken to find an exact total. Hundreds of thousands of people make their livings producing and marketing new products.

Second, practitioners urge the study of new products management. Business respondents in surveys regularly rank new products management as one of a firm's most important functions.[1] We hear a steady call for more product innovation and claims of its critical nature by top executives. The firm that decides to live on last year's products is courting bankruptcy.

Third, the new products process is exceedingly difficult. Most of the decisions are made with far less information than desired. Hundreds of individuals are involved in the creation of a single product, and many have their own agenda. We will soon see that the complexity of operations and decisions is a characteristic of product innovation. And new products do fail, though at a much lower rate than often quoted.[2] (See Figure 1–3.)

The last reason for studying this field is that it is fun and exciting: so many new things (see Figure 1–4), competitors trying to outguess each other, battlefield promotions when things are going well, midstream terminations when they aren't, huge successes where small clusters of people can honestly claim they made hundreds of millions of dollars for their firms. It's rewarding and stimulating to see an object come into being for the first time, to see a critical consumer or industrial need squarely met, to see a new service performed for the first time, to be invited to a big corporate dinner where the CEO shakes the hands of persons awarded patents during the past year, to have distributors fighting for shipments of your new product, to see your brand make its television debut . . . . New products managers can't be rewarded commensurate with their dollar contributions, for various

---

[1] For example, see Mary L. Wilson and William K. Darley, "The Undergraduate Marketing Core, Marketing Issues, and Other Educator-Related Topics of the 1980s," in *An Assessment of Marketing Thought and Practice: 1982 Educators Conference Proceedings,* ed. B. Walker, W. Bearden, et al. (Chicago: American Marketing Association, 1982). Also, S. W. McDaniel and R. T. Hise, "Shaping the Marketing Curriculum: The CEO Perspective," *Journal of Marketing Education,* Summer 1984, pp. 27–32.

[2] C. Merle Crawford, "New Product Failure Rates: A Reprise," *Research Management,* July–August 1987, pp. 20–24.

FIGURE 1–1 Total Expenditures on Research and Development (in millions of dollars)

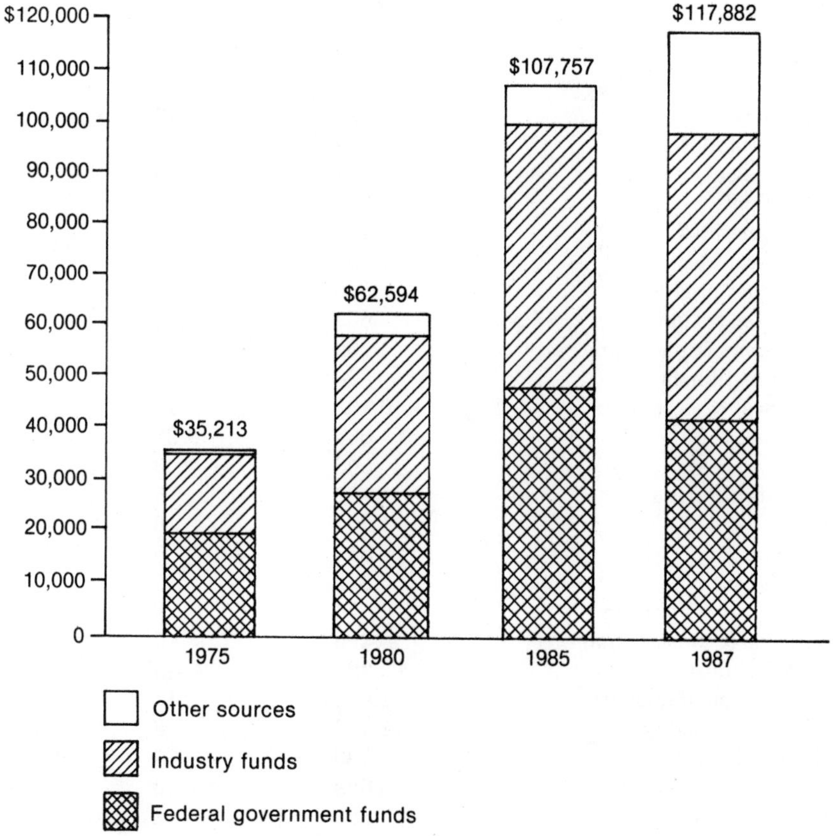

Percent of gross national product:

United States	2.2%	2.3%	2.7%	2.6%
West Germany	2.2	2.4	2.8	2.8
Japan	2.0	2.2	2.8	(NA)
United Kingdom	2.1	(NA)	2.3	(NA)

Note: (NA) = Not available.

The total costs of developing and marketing a new product far exceed research and development expenses; R&D does not include manufacturing and marketing costs, among others.

Source: *Statistical Abstract of the United States*, 1989, pp. 577–68.

FIGURE 1–2 R&D Expenditures by U.S. Firms: Total United States, by Industry, Category, and for Leading Spender in Each Industry Category

	1988 ($ millions)	Percent Change from 1987	Percent of Sales	Percent of Profit
Total United States	$59,377	11%	3.4%	39.4%
Aerospace	3,919	1	4.1	87.3
United Technologies	932	6	5.2	80.0
Automotive	9,528	12	3.2	51.7
General Motors	4,754	9	3.9	70.6
Chemicals	4,454	10	3.6	27.1
Du Pont	1,319	8	4.0	34.5
Conglomerates	3,164	2	2.2	32.4
General Electric	1,155	−3	2.3	24.2
Consumer products	1,595	9	1.6	15.5
Procter & Gamble	652	13	3.4	40.0
Containers & packaging	62	3	1.1	33.8
Owens-Illinois	20	−2	0.6	NEG.
Electrical & electronics	6,108	13	5.3	69.5
Motorola	665	27	8.1	108.7
Food	509	3	0.7	10.1
Ralston-Purina	66	6	1.1	10.8
Fuel	1,704	6	0.7	7.4
Exxon	551	5	0.7	6.4
Health care	6,620	19	8.2	47.7
Johnson & Johnson	674	9	7.5	48.3
Housing & construction	495	0	1.9	22.2
PPG Industries	227	−3	4.0	28.8
Leisure time industries	1,621	12	4.6	56.2
Eastman Kodak	1,147	16	6.7	51.3
Manufacturing	1,083	9	3.3	28.9
3M	689	10	6.5	36.6
Metals & mining	258	−2	1.3	8.7
Aluminum Co. of America	167	−4	1.7	10.2
Nonbank financial	93	27	0.8	5.9
Policy Management Systems	30	22	14.1	98.2
Office equipment/Computers	13,211	18	7.5	66.8
IBM	4,419	11	7.4	48.9
Paper & forest products	422	12	1.0	9.1
Kimberly-Clark	111	0	2.1	17.6
Service industries	179	4	1.2	64.4
Combustion Engineering	56	11	1.6	NEG.
Telecommunications	3,128	6	5.7	NEG.
AT&T	2,572	5	7.3	NEG.

NEG. = Negative earnings.
Expenditures vary slightly from the numbers in Figure 1–1 due to definitions. There are substantial variations by type of product within each industry category; for example, "automotive" includes cars and trucks, parts and equipment, and tire and rubber.

Source: Reprinted from June 16, 1989 issue of *Business Week* by special permission, copyright © 1989 by McGraw-Hill, Inc., pp. 177–232.

FIGURE 1–3 New Product Failure Rates as Reported in Seven Studies Conducted from 1980–1986

	Percent of Products Marketed that Failed		
	All Products	*Consumer*	*Industrial*
The Conference Board[1]	40%	42%	38%
Booz, Allen & Hamilton[2]	35	–	–
Association of National Advertisers[3]	–	39	–
Gallagher[4]	–	36	–
Nielsen (food, drug)[5]	–	61	–
Dancer Fitzgerald Sample (food)[6]	–	98	–
Cooper[7]	–	–	24
Average	38	55	31
Average excluding foods	38%	39%	31%

Sources:
1. David S. Hopkins, *New Products Winners and Losers* (New York: The Conference Board, 1980), pp. 4–9.
2. *New Products Management for the 1980s* (Chicago: Booz, Allen & Hamilton, 1982).
3. *Prescription for New Product Success* (New York: Association of National Advertisers, 1984).
4. *The Gallagher Report,* February 17, 1981, p. 1.
5. "Which Type of Product Is More Successful, New or Me-Too?" *Nielsen Researcher* 2, 1980, pp. 16–17.
6. "New Products: Still Rising . . . Finding a Winner . . . Hassles," *The Wall Street Journal*, November 3, 1983, p. 27.
7. Robert G. Cooper, "New Product Success in Industrial Firms," *Industrial Marketing Management* II, 1982, pp. 215–23.

reasons; but, winners get something more important than immediate income—they get to have a personal imprint on bigger pieces of the corporate charter.

HOW DOES THIS FIELD RELATE TO OTHER COURSES OF STUDY?

The answer depends on what the instructor decides to do. New products management can be taught from many different perspectives—technical, marketing, legal, and so on. It can emphasize the strategic dimension, or the creative task, or the market research tools of concept evaluation, or the marketing planning and commercialization aspects, or the whole ball of wax.

It is usually taught as a marketing course and picks up on the product tool of the marketing mix. Most introductory marketing texts have a chapter or two on new products, touching on some of the key sections of this book.

FIGURE 1–4   The Excitement of Winners from the 80s

Microsoft Excel	Toshiba laptop	Polaroid Spectra	Cherry 7UP
Ford Taurus/Sable	Macintosh computer	SoftSoap	IBM PC
Hyundai Excel	Bartles & Jaymes	JVC camcorder	Acura Legend
Cellular phones	Corona Extra	Laser Tag	Stainmaster carpets
Ultralite batteries	Plax dental rinse	"Springsteen Live"	Borden High-Calcium milk
Coke Classic	Pound Puppy	Nut 'n Honey	Celebrity dirt
Compaq Deskpro 386	Lego blocks	Slice	Cabbage Patch dolls
Metal woods	Dustbuster	TCBY yogurt	*Phantom of the Opera*
Ultra Pampers Plus	Pontiac Fiero	Chrysler minivan	Jarvik-7 artificial heart
Post-it notes	Epcot Center	Citrus Hill juices	Duncan Hines cookies
Premium ice cream	Retin-A creme	Ektar-25 film	Disposable contact lenses
Teddy Grahams	Mazda Miata MX-5	Air pillow sneakers	Lean Cuisine
Tartar Control Crest	SPF sun screens	Oat bran	Nintendo video games

But, several of these winners turned into losers (oat bran, Corona beer, Hyundai Excel, Pontiac Fiero, IBM PC, Laser Tag, Cabbage Patch dolls, Duncan Hines cookies, and perhaps others). Too, many were outright losers, though most of them we may have never heard of or already forgotten: New Coke, Premier cigarettes, Yugo automobile, Kodak Disk camera, RCA SelectaVision, Fab 1 Shot, Holly Farms roasted chickens, IBM PC Jr., home banking systems, Jolt cola, low-alcohol beer, etc.

But even if taught from a marketing perspective, a new products management course cannot deal only with marketing matters, because new products require the cooperation of all departments in the firm. Thus it is a general manager course, and it may even be taught in policy or strategy departments along with such courses as competitive analysis and starting new businesses. Students in engineering or technology schools will study the course from a similar general manager view but will emphasize the technical dimension rather than marketing.

In any event, new products require the expertise of all areas—finance, manufacturing, legal, human resources, strategy, marketing, and so on. New products managers are general managers, without line authority. It's the same with ongoing product managers in consumer-driven companies, who also are general managers for their products, without formal authority over those they must get to work together.

BUT, HOW DOES IT DIFFER FROM THOSE OTHER COURSES?

In many ways, and this is important. The way you study this material will often be new and unlike your study of other fields. For example, you should *begin shaking off any particular functional viewpoint* you may have. New products managers originally came to their jobs from a function (marketing, technical, whatever), and they will often return there. But for now, they are new products people, working with all functions, being biased to none. And biased against none, too. A marketing "type" may not appreciate the thoroughness of a research scientist. And that scientist will not appreciate the marketer's enthusiasm, which sometimes leads to rash and unwarranted conclusions. Now is a good time to begin thinking like a general manager.

Too, this course of study calls for a strong creative contribution. Not only do we create new product concepts; in many firms, that's easy. The tough creativity is process — devising a concept-testing method that works, screening a totally new idea the firm has never faced, figuring out how to integrate scientists into a trade show booth effectively, how to position a product that creates its own new category, how to name it in a way that communicates yet doesn't confuse, and on and on. No answers are found in the back of this book. We never know whether any one decision was right, just whether the total package of decisions worked out.

Being creative means we travel on unmarked roads. Most of our decisions are made on grossly inadequate facts. Not that we don't know what facts we need or how to get them — we usually do. But there's never enough time or money. And what is a fact in January may not be a fact come June, when we actually introduce the new item.

So, we do several things that make lots of people nervous. One, we use heuristics — little rules of thumb that are usually right: "On items such as this, about 30 percent of people who hear of a new brand, try it" or "When the product engineer from R&D disagrees with the process engineer from manufacturing, it's better to go with manufacturing." Heuristics sometimes leave us holding an empty bag; but without them, projects just won't move forward fast enough.

Another technique is to use simple intuition — hunch, gut feel. This explains why most managers want new products people to have spent time in ongoing operations before moving on to new products work.

Another way around the problem is to select people to rely on. Look not to how a recommendation is defended, but to who is making it. This builds close team relationships similar to those often found in sports, politics, or the military — other areas where tough decisions have to be made under impossible conditions.

This suggests another key difference between this course and many of your others. We are *dealing with people under pressure.* Take, for example, the group of 10 to 15 people sent by IBM from Armonk to Boca Raton in 1980. They were given one year to create and market a new product, which eventually became known as the IBM PC. Literally billions of dollars were at stake — the difference between becoming a major player in a new market or missing the boat completely. Virtually every day, someone on that team had to make a decision that could close the show. When studying how strategy shapes decisions that guide teams throughout a project, or how more firms today telescope their market testing into simultaneous regional rollouts, remember that pressure.

The last difference worth noting here is in application. *New products management is an art form.* You can sense that from the above discussion. Actually, some of it is almost accidental; we call it serendipity, which means accidents happen to the prepared mind, as shown in Figure 1–5. So, as with other art forms, we must practice. You cannot learn how to develop a new product concept by reading about attribute analysis or gap analysis. You must do them. The same goes for product use testing, positioning, contingency planning, and many more. Application opportunities appear at the end of every chapter, plus small cases that give you a chance to actually apply what you learned from the reading.

FIGURE 1–5   Not All New Products Are Planned—But, Their Managers Knew Them When They Saw Them

---

A Raytheon engineer working on experimental radar noticed that a chocolate bar in his shirt pocket melted. He then "cooked" some popcorn. The firm developed the first commercial microwave oven.

A chemist at G. D. Searle licked his finger to turn a page of a book and got a sweet taste. Remembering that he had spilled some experimental fluid, he checked it out and produced aspartame (NutraSweet).

A 3M researcher dropped a beaker of industrial compound and later noticed that where her sneakers had been splashed, they stayed clean. ScotchGard fabric protector resulted.

A Du Pont chemist was bothered by an experimental refrigerant that didn't dissolve in conventional solvents or react to extreme temperatures. So, the firm took the time to identify what later became Teflon.

Another scientist couldn't get plastic to mix evenly when cast into automobile parts. Disgusted, he threw a steel wool scouring pad into one batch as he quit for the night. Later, he noticed that the steel fibers conducted the heat out of the liquid quickly, letting it cool more evenly and stay mixed better. Bendix made many things from the new material, including brake linings.

Others? Gor-Tex, dynamite, puffed wheat, Dextro-Maltose, LSD, penicillin, and many more. In each case, a prepared mind.

Sources: Du Pont and Bendix cases, *The Innovators* (New York: Dow Jones, 1968); Raytheon, Searle, and 3M cases, Kenneth Labrich, "The Innovators," *Fortune*, June 6, 1988, p. 56.

BUT, DON'T WE STUDY ABOUT NEW PRODUCTS IN OTHER COURSES, TOO?

Yes, but there are two differences. First, in this course we study all aspects of new products at one time—not just their marketing, financing, or manufacturing. Second, we look mainly at the task of managing the overall process. Someone has to put it all together and keep it together. That person may be called by many different titles, but *new products manager* is becoming more common. This emerging discipline is our focus.

OK, SO WHAT IS A NEW PRODUCT?

Figure 1–6 lists the types of items included as new products. This list is from the developer's view, and may include things you would exclude. For example, can we have a new item just by repositioning an old one (telling customers it is something else)? Arm & Hammer did, several times, by coming up with a new refrigerator deodorant, a new carpet freshener, and a new drain deodorant, all in the same package of baking soda. Even with the same brand name. These may be considered just new uses, but the firm's process of discovery and development are the same. And the new use (particularly in industrial firms) may occur in a completely separate division. Du Pont, for example, uses basic fibers in many different ways, from technical to consumer. Similarly, brand names have long been used as platforms for launching line extensions.

FIGURE 1–6   What Is a New Product?

Commonly accepted categories:
1. *New-to-the-world products:* Products that are inventions; e.g., Polaroid camera, the first car, rayon, the laser printer.
2. *New category entries:* Products that take a firm into a category new to it. Products are not new to the world; e.g., P&G's first shampoo, Hallmark gift items.
3. *Additions to product lines:* Products that are line extensions, flankers, etc., on the firm's current markets; e.g., Tide Liquid detergent, Chrysler K cars, Sears Discover card.
4. *Product improvements:* Current products made better; virtually every product on the market today has been improved, often many times.
5. *Repositionings:* Products that are retargeted for a new use or application; classic case is Arm & Hammer baking soda, which was repositioned several times as drain deodorant, refrigerator deodorant, etc.

FIGURE 1–7   Classic Brand Names

Long-time brands, some with estimated dates of origination:

Budweiser (1880s)	Kleenex (1924)	Gorham
Ivory (1882)	Zippo (1930)	Domino
Coca-Cola (1890)	Ford	Lipton
Maxwell House (1892)	Fruit of the Loom	Knox
Kodak (1900)	Steinway	Colgate
Camel (1913)	Hamilton	Hershey
Oreo (1921)	Grape Nuts	Goodrich

Which of these have the most value today as launch pads for new products?

Source: Larry Wizenberg, *The New Products Handbook* (Homewood, Ill.: Dow Jones-Irwin, 1986), p. 218.

The familiarity of leading brands, such as those shown in Figure 1–7, indicates how easy this is.

Another question mark is the imitation product, a strictly "me-too." If a firm introduces a brand of aspirin tablets that is identical to those already on the market, how is it a new product? It is new to the firm, and it again requires the new products process. It is a new product, managerially.

As an aside, people often get the idea that to imitate is bad and to innovate is good. This idea is incorrect. The best strategy for any situation is the one that maximizes company goals.

That the other types of new products (new to the world, additions, and improvements) are included in Figure 1–6 is no surprise. Generally speaking, the farther down the list, the less expensive and difficult they are to make. A very hot idea in the late 1980s was the improved-quality product, especially keyed to better design or manufacture. But these distinctions are of interest to us only temporarily. The strategic dimension is much more meaningful to us and to managers; we will get to it in Chapter 3. In the meantime, Figure 1–8 shows some of the many variations on the basic set proposed from time to time.

DOES THIS BOOK COVER SUCH THINGS AS NEW SERVICES, NEW INDUSTRIAL PRODUCTS, AND NEW INTERNATIONAL PRODUCTS?

Professionals in all fields often use terms differently than the public uses them. We do too, and a clear example is the term *product*. The public talks about products and services. New products professionals talk about goods and services, both of which are products. The reason is simple:

FIGURE 1–8   Variations on the List of New Products

Types that are not accepted as standard categories, actually fit into one of the categories in Figure 1–6.

Solution to a new problem; new solution to an old problem
New technologies: Product improvements involving a technical change
New to a country: Exportations of a new-to-the-world product
New brand: Usually considered a flanker or line extension
Products for new distribution channels
Appearance or form improvement
Revival of outmoded category
Performance difference
Packaging improvement
Resource difference

---

almost anything marketed today has a tangible component and an intangible component. Automatic tellers are tangible machines that render a service, which is intangible. Automobiles must be serviced, both before and after the sale. So must shoes. Insurance companies provide a carefully written policy. In fact, some service marketers believe it is important to force a tangible component, something for the user to see and hold.

So, the simplest approach is to talk about new products, whether goods or services. Banks, for example, commonly organize their marketing and service innovation around "product" managers.

Note that because they are intangible, pure services cannot be field tested in the usual way. But, all products are intangible at the concept-testing stage. Some people say services are different because their creation involves the user; but, many industrial goods are developed in partnerships with users. Others point out that services cannot be inventoried and thus do not have a distribution system. But the means of creating those services can be inventoried and must be distributed (for example, window-washing franchises or motel beds).

The distinction between industrial products and consumer products is equally vague. A spectrum from, say, a nuclear power installation on one end to a package of chewing gum on the other end has no middle dividing point. Individuals buy computers for use in their homes, whether insurance agents or parents interested in helping their children. So, is the computer an industrial product or a consumer product? Businesses buy Post-it notes, as do homemakers, and often from the same store. Similarly, are Post-its an industrial or consumer product?

Sometimes the distinction is based on who buys the product: industrial products by groups of people and consumer products by individuals. In fact, billions of dollars' worth of industrial goods are bought by individuals, often by computerized reordering systems based on inventory levels. And, most consumers buy houses, cars, $10,000 trips, and retirement plans as groups.

On the international front, it doesn't really matter whether a new product is being developed for customers nearby or around the world. The farther away the customers are and the more they differ in customs and preferences, the more difficult the innovation task will be. So, the key lies in doing what is appropriate for the situation, much as a carpenter's choice of materials and tools depends on the job. A particular saw or piece of sandpaper has no merit in the generic but may be perfect for a particular piece of work. The same applies to the new products process, in which we package up different programs from the same assortment of tools.

The point is, the methods used for different types of product innovation differ. But that difference is of little interest to the manager. The manager's task is to decide what that set of methods should be in the first place. Much as we would like them, there are no generic packages called "tool kit for industrial product innovators" or "tool kit for services developers."

Incidentally, the same thinking applies to so-called high-tech products and to nonprofit organizations as well. Many religious, art, musical, and social service organizations send people to the same executive new product programs used by Kimberly-Clark and 3M.

ON WHAT BASIC IDEAS OR CONCEPTS IS THIS FIELD OF ACTIVITY BUILT?

Several basic ideas have already been mentioned (for example, the role of creativity and the vexing problem of risk and reward). However, the complexity of operations and decisions is the most dramatic hallmark of product innovation. New products managers must be orchestrators. There has never been a simple new products operation. Scores, or even hundreds, of individuals are involved; for most of them, a new product just means more work. One new products manager recently said, "We've got fine people working at this company, so my job is to see that no ball hits the ground." He meant it is easy for slipups to occur, even when capable people are doing the work.

There are other hallmarks, one being the critical key to success: Start with an important customer need or problem, *then* use creative application of technology to solve it. As many businesspeople say, we create "solutions," not products. And we have been doing so for a long time (see Figure 1–9).

FIGURE 1–9 Top 10 New Products of All Time

Over 1,000 new products people were asked to vote for their top 10 new
products of all time.

1. Wheel	9. Paper	17. Printing press
2. Bow and arrow	10. Flush toilet	18. Radio
3. Telegraph	11. Gunpowder	19. Canned food
4. Electric light	12. Antiseptic	20. Airplane
5. Plow	13. Automobile	21. Weaving
6. Steam engine	14. Stone axe	22. Atomic power
7. Vaccine	15. Electric motor	23. Television
8. Telephone	16. Internal combustion engine	24. Computer

How would you rank those 24 inventions?

Source: Jim Betts, *The Million Dollar Idea* (Point Pleasant, N.J.: Point Publishing, 1985), p. 94.

Scores of studies show that new products fail for many reasons: poor market research, poor timing, inability to lower costs, delays, and so on. But these can all be traced down to three final difficulties: (1) the customer had no recognizable need, (2) the new item didn't solve a problem (fill the need), or (3) the solution wasn't communicated or made available properly.

Many inventors spend years trying to convince people that they have a problem, which, of course, the inventor's creation will solve. Other inventors do find solutions to current problems, but their solutions introduce other problems that are worse than the ones being solved (an example is the fingernail puller, designed to solve the problem of having to trim fingernails). And we all know that the better mousetrap won't sell itself, and only solutions like cancer cures will cause the world to beat a path through the forest to the inventor's door.

Don't misunderstand the task of finding customer problems. Some people think this means doing more market research, and that can be a valid recommendation. But, in many industries (perhaps most industrial ones), smart manufacturers work closely with their customers. Salespeople know their customers' businesses as well as they do their own. For them, the ideal is reached when a customer problem or need is filtered through the minds of experienced sales and managerial people and then to the technical people. Many firms go this one better and have their technical people work directly with customers' technical people. This doesn't work for many consumer products, of course, where we need market research to do the gathering.

So, the answer is to begin with a clearly identified problem, one that the customer knows about and agrees is a problem. Then, the solution must be new, effective, and free of baggage that negates its value. Technology can, and does, do this. (See Figure 1–10 for technology examples in the field of dentistry.) We are now being told that technology in the next 35 years will have perhaps 20 times the impact on our lives that technology has had in the past 35 years.

We cannot overstress the role of technology. Problem solutions originating within the marketing department can be successful and once were quite common. But not today. Instead, we see consumer companies building technical laboratories and technical companies building new contacts with the market. When we study strategic planning for product innovation, we will come back to this pairing of problem and technology.

Another hallmark of this field is the regrettable fact that product innovation (like all innovation) must be pushed. Innovation is an unnatural human event. As individuals and as organizations, we build roadblocks against it. So, new products managers have to spend a major share of their energy just opening doors to change. By the way, fear of change, and thus resistance to it, is called *kainotophobia,* a word as complicated as is the phenomenon it describes. See Figure 1–11 for some types of resistance to innovation.

This (1) resistance to change and (2) innovators' need to have a better handle on the customer's problem and possible solutions to it have given the field yet another hallmark. Few companies do product development alone. Today we couple, in every direction. By coupling a "reluctant" person with a willing changer, the reluctant person is more likely to

---

FIGURE 1–10   How Technology Offers Opportunities in the Field of
Dentistry

---

1. *Implants:* Artificial teeth anchored in the gums or jawbone, using screws of titanium.
2. *Bonding:* Etching the surface of unhealthy teeth and applying a liquid resin, which can be shaped and polished when hardened.
3. *Sealing:* Using the same process as bonding, but on children's teeth prophylactically; retreatment every five years or so.
4. *"TMJ" treatment:* Using surgery, bite plates, splints, orthodontic appliances, selective tooth grinding, and biofeedback to relax joint muscles suffering from temporomandibular joint disorder.
5. *Rebuilding jaws:* Using bone putty to rebuild jaws under dentures when they shrivel over time; mineral granules simulate ground bone.
6. *Odds and ends:* Clear plastic braces; device for spraying an acid that eats decay but not the healthy part of the tooth; and possibly anticavity vaccine in pill form!

Source: "Reprinted from April 14, 1986 issue of *Business Week* by special permission, copyright © 1986 by McGraw-Hill, Inc., pp. 114-115.

FIGURE 1–11   Resistance to Innovation of All Types

Why do people resist innovation?

1. The desire to hold onto something worthwhile that appears threatened (e.g., social status or a job).
2. The desire to avoid making a major expenditure to facilitate the innovation; change often costs money.
3. The desire (based on custom, fashion, taste) to perpetuate a general lifestyle or way of doing things; the flywheel of life.
4. The inherent tendency of a group to force conformity on all its members.

Stereotypes: The *ritualist* likes innovation but won't work for it. The *retreatist*, or passive cynic, wants things to stay the same but remains inactive. The *Neanderthal*, or active cynic, resists innovations and works against them.

---

accept change. For example, upstream coupling occurs when General Motors works with Bose Company to develop a new sound system for automobiles, downstream coupling when Dow Chemical works with a housewares firm to improve plastic housewares, and horizontal coupling when computer chip manufacturers jointly fund and manage research laboratories. This cooperative activity will continue to grow.

IS NEW PRODUCTS MANAGEMENT AN ART OR A SCIENCE?

I believe very strongly that new products management is a combination of art and science. Art, of course, is essentially based on intuition, experience, hunch, or gut feel. Therefore, when managers lack the experience or information to make a reasoned decision, they must go with what they feel is right. In other situations, managers simply reject analytical offerings and go with hunch. Many times, managers are under the gun and make whatever decision keeps the project moving. I have heard executives say that a particular project was "something never done before, so there's no book on this one."

Yet, the pressures on new products people are sometimes unkind. Often they are unjustified, denying the chance to do what would make a much better product. Specifically, three tests are critical in product innovation: the concept test (to determine if the intended user really needs the item), the product use test (to see if the new item meets that need), and the market test (to see if we have an effective marketing plan).

These three tests are the most difficult to rationalize under day-to-day pressures. They are too often skipped.

Another example concerns marketing science—the many new techniques (for example, trade-off analysis, financial sensitivity testing, and sales forecasting via mathematical models) developed by marketing academics. These methods are not academic playthings. Today they are operational in some of the best firms in the world, yet they are not used nearly as much as they should be.

This book tries to compromise these views, always looking at various options as the manager would look at them. There are no criticisms of art; the intuitive greats in this field are cited for their success. More analytical methods are right there, too, for those with the time, money, and inclination to use them.

DOES THIS FIELD OF ACTIVITY HAVE A UNIQUE VOCABULARY?

Yes, it does, for two reasons. One, it is an expanding field, taking on new tasks and performing them in new ways. Second, it is a melting pot field, bringing in the language of scientists, lawyers, advertisers, accountants, marketing planners, corporate strategists, organizational behaviorists, and many more. Because many of these people talk about the same event but use different phrases to describe them, communication problems occur. The solution is to force a common acceptance of terms and to urge acceptance of one term for each new idea as it arises.

This has helped, but the study of product innovation will be complicated by the unresolved problems. For example, any new products manager should understand NPV, dual ladders, intrapreneurship, positioning, strict liability, and flexible manufacturing. Many do not, and many students do not. This book introduces such phrases as product innovation charter, protocol, and launch control plan. People who have not studied with this book may not understand these terms. And, the problem becomes much worse from a global perspective. Take, for example, the term *design*. In U.S. new product work, *design* means essentially industrial design or engineering (premanufacturing) design; in Europe, however, *design* means the entire technical creation function from initial specs to the shipping dock. To some design people, it means the entire product innovation function.

The new products field has no definitional authority, as the accounting and legal professions have. The American Marketing Association now has a new set of definitions, and that helps. But for now, we just have to slog along, the best we can. Appendix D is a glossary based on American Marketing Association definitions, plus scores of nonmarketing terms. All are consistent with how they are used in this book.

WHAT PRIOR TRAINING IS PRESUMED?

The material in this book presumes the reader has previously taken a basic marketing course. The marketing stage (Chapters 16 and 17) focuses on aspects of marketing planning that are especially critical for new products. For example, many students have not actually seen the detailed outline of a marketing plan. Too, special attention will go to selecting the target market and positioning the product, because these decisions are made from scratch, not burdened with targetings and positionings from previous product managers.

The discussion of marketing mix tools will be more complete on product aspects (branding and packaging) and on management of the others. Thus, the book presumes the student has knowledge of the product life cycle, how to make a situation analysis, and so on.

DOES THE FIELD OF NEW PRODUCTS OFFER CAREERS?

It does indeed, though not many are entry positions for people right out of college. Generally, managements want new products people to really know the industry involved (that customer focus mentioned earlier) and the firm's various operations (that multidimensional, orchestration task also mentioned). So, most new products managers get assigned to new products work from a position in a single department. For example, a scientist finds working with marketing and manufacturing people interesting, a cost accountant begins costing out new products, a market researcher specializes in running focus groups, a salesperson earns a reputation for good new product concepts, a manufacturing engineer takes a liking to designing new systems, or a management development specialist finds personal satisfaction in training people to accept change. Each of these people is a candidate for full-time work on new products.

Of course, if a new graduate already has had the necessary job experience, direct assignment to a new product job is likely, especially if coming out of a business degree program.

The specific jobs in this field are three. First is functional representative on a team, sometimes full time, more often part time. An example is a marketing researcher or a production planner. These people may be representatives on many teams or on just a few. They are often project managers in training, but many functional people want to stay in their functions. The second job is project manager or team leader. This role, sometimes called "little president," is leader of a team of people representing the functions that will be required. The third position is supervising a group of project leaders. This rare job is necessary where new product activity is heavy.

GIVEN ALL OF THIS, WHAT WILL WE BE DOING IN THIS BOOK?

Chapter 2 shows the road map—the entire product innovation system. It begins somewhere back in the organization's strategic planning; for example, Henry Ford wanted the lowest priced Model T possible, Dan Gerber wanted better products for babies, and the Bell companies wanted customers to buy time on their wires and glass fibers. These goals help drive the new products program.

The end point of a new program is sometimes a surprise—a project is finished when it achieves its objectives. Now, many students think the program is done when the new product is marketed; so do many businesspeople, and they talk about turning a new product over to the "regular" people. But, the project is done only when the new product has sold enough, made enough profit, established a strong toehold in a new market, effectively thwarted a particular competitor . . . whatever the goal was at the time the new product project was initiated. And, in a recent turn of view, no one who worked on that new product should be permitted to "finish early." No one signs off. The team is finished when the team's objectives are reached.

Imagine a track team's relay race—but with a long baton onto which all four runners place their hands at the start and onto which all four hold as they run the four parts of the race. A new products mile race is a four-person mile, not four people running quarter miles. When a customer buys a new item and says it arrived in bad shape, someone from manufacturing and distribution had better be on hand to take care of that problem. In firms that still think of product innovation as a linear process (a relay), the salesperson has to address that problem, often alone. The support people are busy on other projects. But this no longer happens in the better-managed new products operations.

After the overview in Chapter 2, we will take up the task step by step. First is strategy, for the overall product innovation program and for each project or team assignment. Second, we look at concept generation, how we come up with new concepts. Third, we move into evaluation, trying to decide just how good those concepts are, both now and later as they evolve through the development process and into marketing. Fourth is commercialization, the broad stage of activity in which plans become reality, manufacturing processes become factories, and sales plans become sales calls.

Then, knowing the entire process, we can address three other aspects. One is organization, or how to put together an effective work force. Second, how to manage them and manage the project. Third, how to handle the products that some members of society think we shouldn't have—from unsafe cars to 60 sizes of potato chip packages.

At the end of each chapter are four applications, most of which came from job interviews students had after studying this field. The conversational questions came from top managers who wanted answers, not smiles or evasions. If you read an application and have no idea what the president is talking about, glance back through the chapter for clues.

Last, if your course is built around some form of application (individual or team projects and other such assignments), each chapter may offer some challenge for that. If not, try to come up with your own new product concept during your study of Chapters 4 through 7, and then work that idea down through the course. You can do your own concept testing, your own strategic market planning, and so on.

SUMMARY

This chapter has introduced you to the general field of product innovation. You read how the activity is (or should be) found in all organizations, not just business. You read how this course of study relates to others, what a new product actually is, and that services and industrial products are covered, not just cake mixes, videos, and cars. You got a feeling for where the field stands today, the concepts on which our operation is founded, our problems with vocabulary, and possible careers.

APPLICATIONS

At the end of each chapter are four questions that arose sometime or another in a job interview. The candidate was a student who took a course in new products management, and the interviewer was a high-ranking person in the firm. The questions came up naturally during discussion, and they are tough. Often, the executive didn't intend them to be answered so much as talked about. Occasionally, the executive just made a comment and then paused for the applicant's reaction. Each question or comment relates to something in the chapter.

Imagine you are the person being interviewed. You do not have the option of ducking the question or saying, "I really don't know." If, in fact, you really don't know, then glance back over the reading to see what you missed. It's also a good idea to exchange answers with another student taking the course, given that most of the applications involve opinions or interpretations, not recitation of facts.

1. "I'm a great believer in serendipity. We've gotten several big winners that way. I've always wondered, though, how to manage an operation to get more of it. Any ideas?"

2. "You may have read that research shows there are certain causes for new product failures, but I'll tell you why we have them — pure and simple incompetence on the part of individual managers. I could eliminate failures completely if I could just eliminate incompetence. You agree?"

3. "Funny thing, though, it sure does frustrate me when I hear a division general manager's strategy is to imitate other firms. Now, I know some firms might reasonably use imitation, but none of my divisions should. Should they?"

4. "I would like to be sure as many of our people as possible support innovation, but I know some people in the firm just can't react positively to proposed innovation, no matter how much we need it. Tell me, how do you think I should go about spotting the worst offenders, and what should I do with them when I find out who they are?"

The New Products Process

SETTING

Chapter 1 gave us a good feeling for today's new products situation. We discussed the general field of study, how it differs from others, and what we will be doing as we go through the book. Now, it is necessary to identify the process by which an organization creates and markets new products (goods and services). We will first look at a simple scenario to get the overall picture and identify several key activities. This will lead into the full process and an explanation for each step. The chapter will end with a discussion of how the process varies in different types of organizations. Early in the new product process, most firms will also make an organization decision to staff up for the particular task at hand. However, we will defer this subject until Chapter 19, because it's easier to talk organization when we know the full scope of the work.

IT DOESN'T WORK THAT WAY

Businesspeople often look at designs of the overall new product process and say, "It doesn't work that way in our firm." And they are right. A carpenter doesn't use all the tools in the toolbox when building any particular door. Some of the tools may never be used, given that no carpenter builds all types of doors. Some work in firms specializing in heavy church doors. Some work in firms about to go bankrupt, where everything is done as cheaply as possible. And, some carpenters have tricks of their own.

But, we're talking about the tool kit and the procedure that covers all types of situations, in the most desirable way. Any manager using this generic system must cut and fit it to the situation at hand. And if the president says, "No concept testing," then no concept testing—but that doesn't make it right.

THE HIGHLIGHTER SAGA

The following story introduces the new products process.

Betty Wall had been covering Omni's college market for three years, selling, among other office supplies, a line of highlighting products. They were the usual collection of colors, widths, sizes, and shapes. This was an important market for Betty's firm, and Omni shared the lead in this market with Trion. But Betty knew the market was mature, the life cycle far past the dynamic growth stage with no real excitement for several years. Moreover, she had heard from the purchasing agent at Kinsville College that Trion was developing a new concept in highlighters. Apparently, it involved a clear liquid that reacted with ink to give each letter a broader, deeper, and more shiny appearance. Trion was having trouble with the concept, but Betty was worried about her commissions from the Omni line.

So, she called David Raymond, the newly appointed product manager for office supplies, and told him her story and her fears. David asked the market research department to make a quick scan of the highlighter situation — sales, shares, profits, rumors of innovation, and so on. Sure enough, the market was very mature, competitors and customers were complacent. Market research also uncovered the Trion test product, which sounded impressive.

David then discussed the situation with the vice president of marketing, who agreed there was a significant problem. When Omni's president agreed, David was asked to come up with another solution to the combined problem of maturity and competitive innovation.

Fortunately, some brainstorming, combined with astute thinking on the part of a couple of technical people, led to the concept of a solid highlighter. No one was sure it would work (pulling liquid from the air); but, the basic idea seemed sound, interviews with office workers and students were positive, technical people reaffirmed it should be feasible, a scan of its fit with the rest of the firm (safety, production facilities, and so on) scored highly, and preliminary financial analysis gave it an OK.

So, David, as product manager, took over leadership on the project. He decided to put together a team of four people to run the operation, ordered more market research, and laid out a tentative time schedule. Technical people went to work on the solid material concept, and David began thinking about how he would market the item. When Phyllis Chaterji, the technical member of the team, came over with the first prototype, David arranged to show it to some potential customers. They liked the idea very much. So, Phyllis continued her work, final specifications were written, some semifinished product was produced for David to place in offices and dorms to see if it worked in practice, and manufacturing went on to plan the facilities change and a new process.

With this information, David was able to make a financial analysis, with solid product cost estimates and a marketing budget. Management approved, and the product was headed for market. Further product testing was undertaken to get users' full reactions, the product's formulation was fine-tuned, manufacturing locked in on a process and bought the equipment, and marketing fleshed out the marketing plans with an advertising agency and help from the sales department.

When everything looked good, David got approval to make the final product and put it on sale in four college towns in the central part of the country. He and a market research analyst practically lived in those towns for two months. They had anticipated some misunderstanding of how the product was to be used, so they were ready to run off some rather expensive in-store displays that gave better instructions. As it turned out, the displays were needed, the problem was overcome, sales took off, and the product was released to the market. Fortunately for Omni, too, because Trion was ready with its product at about the same time. Suddenly, a very mature market was exciting again.

WHAT HAPPENED IN THAT SAGA?

We just read a whole year's activity in a few minutes. The story, of course, was unreal, but the situation was typical. The story began with an ongoing operation that faced a problem. The problem was studied, and the solution was checked against ongoing new product strategy and then approved for action. Various developmental and evaluative steps followed, along with gradual development of the marketing plan. Launch was on a limited basis, and the manager had anticipated a problem that he was able to handle quickly and successfully.

New products management does not usually begin with an idea. It may, if an idea walks in through the door, but it usually begins with a situation that prompts innovation. Too, development does not take place behind the closed doors of a research lab—there are many interim tests of fit and progress. And, marketing doesn't start when the product is finished—it often starts before ideation, as it did here.

Last, the process is not over when the new product is launched. It ends when the new product is successful, usually after some in-flight corrections (such as with the special in-store display piece).

Let's now look at the full process, including many steps and options that didn't appear in the highlighter story. Incidentally, the new product concept in that story may have seemed crazy, or dumb, or impossible. Most great ideas look pretty bad when they first appear, but we have good methods for sorting them out.

THE NEW PRODUCTS PROCESS

Figure 2–1 (Parts A–E) shows the entire new products process. Please stop at this time to study those charts. Read them as you would a road map, to see where we are going. Think about the highlighter saga. And

FIGURE 2–1 The Product Innovation Process, Part A: Strategic Planning

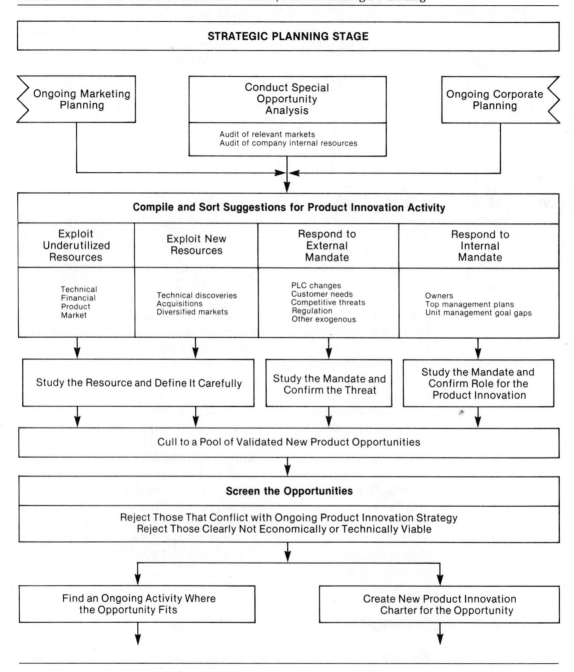

remember, we are looking at the full set of steps and options, from which a new products manager must craft a specific process to fit a given situation.

But, note that the new products process sits within a much larger set of activities within the firm that keeps the ongoing operation alive and well. This process does not stand alone, nor does it dominate the ongoing business. One of the biggest problems in new products management is that preferred plans must be altered to fit with established activities.

Every box in Figure 2–1, every decision, and every person sits in the two worlds of new and ongoing, which makes the charted process more a goal than an operational fact. But it is a worthy goal, and many times the new product's importance makes the process the dominant force.

Where It Starts

The process can get started in four ways. (See Figure 2–1, Part A.) Three are deliberate, and one is opportunistic. The latter happens when someone (most commonly, consumers or the sales force) sends in an idea. It may happen anywhere, and good ideas have been found in the newspaper. The step for this shows up later in Figure 2–1 under ideation. It doesn't take much management, mainly an alert, open system that scans the huge quantity of noise from which, occasionally, a good idea comes.

The other three starting sources are shown at the start of the process in the strategic planning stage. One is ongoing marketing planning, where a product manager or other marketing planner sees a need for product innovation. Such was the case in the highlighter saga; a sales rep convinced a product manager that the mature stage of the life cycle represented a problem, as did rumored competitive activity. Remember that the great majority of new products are improved products; line extensions are second. This is the domain of ongoing management.

Another source is ongoing corporate management, or long-range planning. This work involves resource auditing or evaluation, finding company strengths that are not being capitalized. Any such strength can lead to product innovation.

The fourth source is a special, deliberate situation analysis, often on a scheduled basis, where managers seek opportunities otherwise overlooked.

Opportunity Identification. The outgrowths of these action stimulants are shown on the process chart (Part A) under the heading "Compile and Sort Suggestions for Product Innovation Activity." There are four:

1. *Underutilized resources* — (a bottling operation, for example, or a strong franchise with dealers).

2. *New resources* — particularly technical discoveries (for example, Du Pont's discovery of Kevlar triggered analyses that still haven't stopped).
3. *External mandate* — something outside the firm dictates or strongly suggests a new line of innovation (recall the highlighter).
4. *Internal mandate* — managements make the suggestion. Most common is the growth gap, where management draws a sales or profit line to the point where it wants the line to be in, say, five years. Someone then extends the sales line of current products and shows the gap that almost always exists between the two lines. That gap is the product innovation (and/or acquisition) gap.

These four types of output are called *opportunities* (though managers often see them as problems), and the process of creatively recognizing them is called *opportunity identification*.

Next, these suggestions must be carefully and thoroughly described, then analyzed to confirm that an opportunity does, indeed, exist. (Recall that one of the first things David Raymond did was order a scan of the highlighter market.) And, of course, no firm wants to exploit all opportunities; some are better than others. Some may not fit with company skills, some are too risky, some require more money than the firm has. So, most firms have ongoing, or standing, strategies about product innovation, against which the opportunities must be checked.

These strategies also help guide the process, suggesting certain goals, desirable levels of innovativeness, and many other aspects. For example, Waterford had a strategy that no new product would jeopardize the firm's great image. Cincinnati Milicron's strategy demanded any new product be highly innovative, not a me-too. So, each opportunity must find a strategy, either standing or specially written for it.

The strategy also ensures resource availability, because management must be sure there are enough money, people, and facilities to do the job.

Opportunity identification and strategic planning for new products are covered in Chapter 3.

Ideation

In some cases, merely identifying an opportunity pretty well spells out what is wanted (for example, an opportunity to add a small size of a toothpaste for travelers). Most times, however, it's not so clear, and the ideation process will be demanding. (See Figure 2–1, Part B.)

Ideation involves finding either new ways to capitalize on the available resource or potential solutions to the problems. This problem-solving activity has become quite sophisticated; it's no longer the caricature of a group sitting around a table, spitting out ideas.

FIGURE 2–1   *(continued)*, Part B: Ideation

IDEATION STAGE

↓

Prepare for Ideation
Identify or Establish a Team or Nucleus for the Ideation and Screening Stages Train and Otherwise Prepare the Ideation Team Identify Whether a Specific Problem Has Been Identified

Problem Identification
Routine market contacts Problem analysis Scenario analysis

Ongoing Nonstrategic Ideation by Product Management That Relates to This Project

Problem Solving
Product team ideation Engineering and R&D Group creativity

Ideas Submitted by Employees, Customers, and Other Outsiders That Relate to This Project

Fortuitous Scanning
Attribute analysis Relationships analysis Lateral search

Pool of New Concepts

↓

In the meantime, unsolicited ideas are coming in over the phone and in the mail from customers, erstwhile customers, employees (especially sales and technical), and every other source imaginable. These ideas are reviewed briefly by whomever receives them to see if they are even relevant to the firm and its strategies. They are then put with the ideas that came from problem-solving activities.

Concept generation (problem solving, as well as the more fortuitous type of ideation) is covered in Chapters 4 through 7.

Screening

All of these ideas, problems, and opportunities receive a cursory preliminary evaluation, because it is impossible for a person to think of, or hear about, a new product idea without giving it at least some evaluation.

But what happens next is the first formal type of evaluation, usually called *screening*. (See Figure 2–1, Part C.) Specific people are charged with reacting to the ideas, just as you may have done with the highlighter concept earlier. Reactions of marketers and technical people are usually wanted.

Ideas that pass this entry evaluation are then given a more serious screening called *concept testing*, in which potential buyers are asked for their reactions to the idea and suggestions for improvement. This step may take quite a while if first reactions are negative. In the highlighter saga, Omni did a concept test on its new solid product idea.

By the time concept testing is concluded, technical people are ready to assess technical feasibility.

Ultimately, these views all come together in what is often called THE screen, the final screen. It uses a scoring model of some type and results in a decision to either undertake development or quit. If the decision is to go ahead, the people involved now sometimes write out a statement of what the new product is to do for the customer (the new product's benefits) as a clear guide for those doing the developing.

The various screening steps are covered in Chapters 9 and 10.

Development

Resource Preparation.   Often overlooked by new products managers is a step called *resource preparation*. (See Figure 2–1, Part D.) For product improvements and some line extensions, this is OK, because a firm is already up and going in a mode that fits products that are close to home. The culture is right, market data is good, and ongoing managers are ready to do the work. But, innovation often introduces some problems of fit, and changes are needed. If a firm wants "discontinuous" products (that is, products quite different than what is now available), then new reward systems, revisions in the firm's

FIGURE 2–1   *(continued)*, Part C: Screening

SCREENING STAGE

Entry Screen

Spell out preliminary concept statement
Fit with PIC confirmed
Check technical feasibility
Check marketing feasibility

Customer Screen

Preparation: Concept boards, Prototype
Define criteria, hurdles
Detail concept test plan
Implement concept test plan
Iteration, Conclusion

Technical Screen

Final technical assessment
on latest version of concept

Final Screen

Scoring model process

(Optional)
Business Analysis

Preliminary marketing plan
Preliminary technical plan
Preliminary operations plan
Financial review and approval
Project budgets established

usual project review system, and special instructions to the team may be needed. Without adequate preparation of the ball field, many new product projects are destined to ground out.

The Major Body of Effort.   We can now begin what all of the previous steps have been leading up to—the actual technical and marketing development. But note the three vertical sets of boxes in this part of the process. The set on the left is technical; it involves bench work (goods) or systems design (services), prototypes, product specifications, and so on. It culminates in actual product—produced, tested, and costed out.

FIGURE 2–1 *(continued)*, Part D: Development

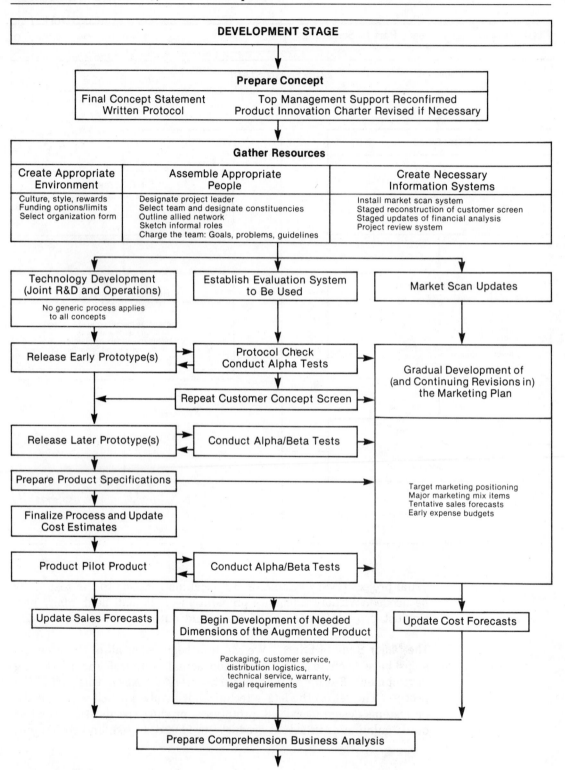

The right-hand set of boxes describes concurrent marketing work, from updated market research (because market needs change over time, and some developments take more than a year) through marketing strategy to sales forecasts.

But going to market requires more than a product and a marketing plan. It requires profit, and that means evaluation. Down the middle of the process chart is a third set of boxes, from setting up an evaluation system through what is here called the *Gamma test*. The product is real, and the Gamma proves it works to the market's satisfaction.

Comprehensive Business Analysis.   If the product is real and customers like it, we are ready to wrap it all up in a comprehensive business analysis (with a business plan) and head for the market. The full financial analysis as well as other evaluation steps are covered in Chapters 11 through 14.

Commercialization

Traditionally, the term *commercialization* has described that time or that decision where the firm decides to market a product. We associate this decision with building factories or authorizing agencies to proceed with multimillion-dollar advertising budgets.

It's a bit more subtle than that now. (See Figure 2–1, Part E.) The commercialization decision is more attitude than anything else. A firm can always pull out, even during a test market, so commercialization should not mean the Go in a Go/NoGo decision. It tends to come just prior to some very expensive step; so, on consumer products, the decision is sometimes made just days before TV contracts are signed. In the pharmaceutical business, in which 8 to 10 years of technical work are required, the commitment to market is really made prior to undertaking the years of technical work; the results of such a program must, by law, meet medical needs and work effectively and safely. Little is left to decide. And then other firms, especially on noncapital-intensive product improvements, just slide along the development trail until they are in the market. They see no dramatic commercialization point.

The commercialization phase often has a pressure cooker character. Everything is rush, everything is critical. Manufacturing is in scale-up mode, and marketing is putting the hundreds of tactical details onto the strategy skeleton written earlier. The critical step—if a company takes it—is the market test, the first time the marketing program and the product dance together. This step is pure dress rehearsal, and managers hope any problems discovered are fixable between dress rehearsal and opening night. If they aren't, the opening has to be delayed; General Foods and Procter & Gamble have kept products in market test for years.

FIGURE 2–1 *(concluded)*, Part E: Commercialization

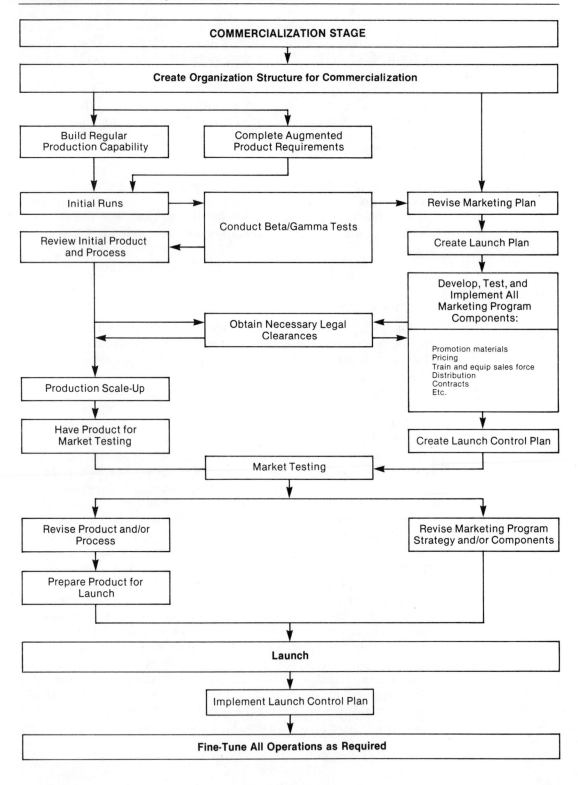

This final preparation phase is sometimes accompanied by too much managerial change, variations in overall priorities and funding, unmet technical goals, and personal failures on little things that grind the project to a halt. We will talk a bit later about the type of management needed during this stage.

Another key activity during the commercialization stage is planning for launch control. Everyone knows that when space shuttles leave the launch pad, a plan of control has been carefully prepared. "Houston Control" runs it, seeking to spot every glitch that comes up during launch and hoping it was anticipated so that a solution is on board, ready to use.

New products managers do the same thing, some formally and some very informally.

Launch.   With everything go, the launch takes place. But, let's not lose sight of reality. Remember most new products are improvements or minor line extensions. They may attract almost no attention. Other new products (for example, a major cancer breakthrough or a potential AIDS cure) are so important they get top TV news coverage. We will see later that the launch period involves several clearly identifiable stages, ending when the new product moves into its own orbit of continued growth.

The commercialization stage, including launch, is covered in Chapters 15 through 18.

PRODUCT DEFINITION

You may have noticed by now that the new products process essentially turns an opportunity into a profit flow. It begins with something that is not a product (the opportunity) and ends up with another thing that is not a product (the profit). The product comes from a situation and turns into an end.

What we have, then, is an "evolving" product. Here are some of the steps, like individual frames in a movie film:

Opportunity—a resource or a problem.

Concept—a form or a technology, plus a clear statement of benefit.

Tested concept—customer screened; need is confirmed.

Protocol—a statement of benefits sought, plus any mandatory features.

Prototype—a tentative physical product or system procedure, including features and benefits.

Specifications — exactly what the product is to be, including features, characteristics, and standards.

Pilot — the product produced by the first process.

Production — the product produced by the scale-up process.

Market — the product actually marketed, in either market test or launch.

Success — the product meets the goals set for it, usually profit.

Some firms have as many as three production models or four prototypes. So, the idea that a new product "emerges" from R&D — like a chicken from an egg — is simply incorrect.

DIFFERENCES BY TYPE OF ORGANIZATION

The above process varies at the operating level in different firms. Let's discuss a few of these variations. First, Chapter 1 indicated goods and services are both products, and each situation requires its own process. The same is true of industrial (or business-to-business) products compared to consumer products.

But, the need for company-specific new product processes is evident even in the same industry. The Miller, Anheuser-Busch, Strohs, and Coors brewing companies have quite different new product strategies. Their new product activities and results also differ greatly.

Similarly, a firm's new product objective could be to gain entry into a new market, or to dominate that market, or to use the new market to test a new technology, or to enter the new market to keep its distributive structure loyal and cooperative. The process would differ for each.

The greatest variation in the new products process, however, is caused by management skill. Successful new product companies are more likely to have a formal new products process (unless they are very small, in which case their process is apt to be created as it unfolds). Successful firms are guided by clearly understood strategies. More research and testing occur up front, so only worthwhile ideas enter their careful and thorough evaluation systems. Firms that skip steps in the process are either (1) run by strong and eccentric individualists, (2) under the tremendous pressure of imminent bankruptcy or acquisition, or (3) unskilled in how to do the job.

SOME COMMENTS ABOUT THE NEW PRODUCTS PROCESS

Product innovation is a developing field with different perspectives on the task.

The Process Is Hard to Identify in Practice

Visitors who ask to see a firm's new products process won't see much. The process is so intertwined with the ongoing operation that it has little separate identity. In small firms, for example, where much innovation originates, the ongoing and the new are essentially the same. All players on one team are players on the other. Even in large firms, where many people specialize full time on new products, most of the players work both games.

Furthermore, the process is fluid, changing. Many iterations may be needed if a failure at one stage forces the play to return to an earlier stage. If a concept fails its screening test with intended consumers, it heads back to the ideation stage or even farther back to the opportunity identification stage. And if a competitor makes a surprise entry, the project may take a risky skip of several stages right into production. A key problem facing new products managers is to keep all players up to date on just where the project is.

There Are Different Views on What the Process Is

One school of thought holds that the product innovation process begins with ideation, called *concept generation*. Proponents believe opportunity identification and the other parts of the process chart that precede ideation are part of ongoing planning. One danger here is that the new products activity may be constrained. A management staff group may say to the new products staff, "Let's develop a new solid form of our highlighter" rather than "The market has matured, our share has stabilized; we need something that reactivates the market." Another danger is that one function (for example, technical or marketing) may work alone too long, closing off options the other group could bring to the ball game.

Another view holds that the new products process ends with launch. Some even hold that it ends if the new products team turns the new product over to the established group to market. Most people today disagree. Regardless of who markets the product, the innovation team should continue playing the game. Dow has several experienced salespeople handle the initial launch and selling effort during R&D. If the product succeeds, then they turn it over. Consumer firms' product or brand managers manage the innovation project from the beginning, so there is no need to turn anything over to anybody. IBM's PC team went to Florida and handled the entire development and marketing, then stayed on as a new division when the launch was successfully managed.

From time to time, some people urge us to focus especially on the most critical steps. Figure 2–2 shows one observer's key steps; read the list

---

FIGURE 2–2   20 Clues to New Product Success

---

1. Has the product been in development for a year?
2. Does your company now make a similar product?
3. Does your company now sell to a related customer market?
4. Is research and development at least one third of the product budget?
5. Will the product be test marketed for at least six months?
6. Does the person in charge have a private secretary?
7. Will the ad budget be at least 5 percent of anticipated sales?
8. Will a recognized brand name be on the product?
9. Would the company take a loss on it for the first year?
10. Does the company "need" the product more than it "wants" it?
11. Have three samples of advertising copy been prepared?
12. Is the product really new, as opposed to improved?
13. Can the decision to buy it be made by only one person?
14. Is the product to be made in fewer than five versions?
15. Will the product not need service and repair?
16. Does the development team have a working code name?
17. Will the company president (or division general manager) see the project leader without an appointment?
18. Did the project leader make a go of the last two projects?
19. Will the product be on the market for more than 10 years?
20. Would the project leader quit and take the item along if the company said it wouldn't back it?

Note: According to the developer of this list (New Product Development, a newsletter firm in Point Pleasant, New Jersey), 11 to 14 yes answers indicates probable success, 8 to 10 yes answers indicates a coin toss, and below 8 says to forget it.

Source: Reprinted by permission of *The Wall Street Journal*, © Dow Jones & Company, Inc., September 24, 1981. All rights reserved.

thoughtfully, because the author is not as tongue-in-cheek as it appears. But this text stresses the entire process, because a text should prepare students to be selective, not be selective for them.

Multifunctionality

The entire new products process rests on a merger of two key areas of activity, technical and marketing, supported in that merger by all other firm functions. There was a time when a firm could interview customers, find what they wanted, and start producing it. Other firms could stand by while their scientists were cooking up a new concept, take it when ready, and market it successfully. These still work sometimes; but the best strategy by far is to ensure the new product embodies a solid customer need or desire combined with a technologically superior way of fulfilling it: dual drive, not market drive or technology drive.

But even the two key disciplines are not enough. A few years ago, Xerox overhauled its entire new products process and, for the first time, put manufacturing people on teams with technical and marketing people. Prior to that time, manufacturing was presented with a new product and told to figure out how to manufacture it. Other functions have now earned early involvement—legal (product liability), design (ergonomics, etc.), finance (risk analysis), packaging (sometimes the essence of the innovation), and vendors (upstream coupling). The name of the game is *teamwork,* and the most critical skill is project or team management.

Managerial Control

The previous point needs to be expanded. Management of a new products project differs from any other type of management with the exception of traditional brand (packaged goods) management. Because all functions are involved, the head of a new products team is, in effect, a general manager, but without authority. A president without line power.

Moreover, the players are all specialists, usually very good ones. A project manager who makes decisions is not needed nearly as much as one who orchestrates the team to work effectively together. The analogy sometimes cited is to the coach of a professional sports team.

We use the term *managerial control* to mean that the project comes out on time with the desired results, not that the manager constrains or restricts or dominates anything. Houston has "control" over a Discovery flight but doesn't do the preparation, blast off, or flying.

In business, this calls for the utmost in managerial skill, and the new products process is partly influenced by the task.

Practice Seems to Fail Prescription

Two new studies have demonstrated again a common fear—business firms do not follow the new products process very well.[1] Figure 2–3 shows some data from one of the studies. There are several reasons why four or five percentages seem low, but two stand out. First, many firms skip steps because they feel they have to—they're short on funds or short on time. Competitors don't wait, and neither do top managements.

---

[1] Robert G. Cooper and Elko J. Kleinschmidt, "An Investigation into the New Products Process: Steps, Deficiencies, and Impact," *Journal of Product Innovation Management,* June 1986, pp. 71–85; and William L. Moore, "New Product Development Practices of Industrial Marketers," *Journal of Product Innovation Management,* December 1987, pp. 6–20.

FIGURE 2–3   Rates of Use of Selected New Product Process Steps

Step	Percent of Firms Using
Initial screening	92%
Preliminary market assessment	77
Preliminary technical assessment	85
Detailed market study	25
Business/financial analysis	63
Product development (technical work)	89
In-house product testing (Alpha)	89
Customer tests of product (Beta)	66
Market testing	23
Trial production setup	49
Precommercialization business analysis	35
Special production start-up	56
Separate marketing plan	68

Source: Robert G. Cooper and Elko J. Kleinschmidt, "An Investigation into the New Product Process: Steps, Deficiencies, and Impact," *Journal of Product Innovation Management*, September 1986, p. 75.

Second, the field of new products management is young, and many managers simply haven't yet been exposed to the various steps or how they can be taken.

Implications for Aspiring New Products Managers

The preceding discussion suggests various attitudes, training, and experience guidelines for people who would like to become managers in the new products process. Here are several:

1. Be multifunctional, not functionally parochial. That is, new products people should have experience in more than one function (marketing, manufacturing, and so on). The broader the education, the better.
2. Be risk takers, willing to do whatever is necessary to bring a product to market. It may be necessary to risk management wrath or make decisions with little knowledge of what should be done.
3. Be general manager types—more interested in managing than in doing. Be able to build and manage networks of trained specialists. Scientists and sales managers can lead new products teams, but they must cease being scientists and sales managers.
4. Be a combination of optimist and realist, aggressor and team player, leader and follower. New products managers are required to play each role at one time or another.

5. Have a strong creative bent to achieve better product characteristics and to carve out new ways of doing things.
6. Be comfortable in unstable environments where chaos and confusion often reign. Be able to work with depressives, euphorics, and those who seem to have no emotion whatsoever.

Fortunately, such managers do exist — and in increasing numbers. I hope you become one of them.

SUMMARY

In this chapter, we studied essentially one thing: the system of steps and activities used in the process of developing and marketing new products. We looked at a simplistic version of this process in a hypothetical situation with highlighter pens. We then went through the process step by step, talking about each one. In that explanation, we noted actions taken or not taken by the people in the office supplies firm.

Following that discussion, we looked at some special viewpoints on the subject, including how the specific steps are difficult to see in an operating environment. Some people see the process differently; the process is multifunctional; and it requires a special application of managerial control. One disappointing dimension is the limited use of this system as a whole. Few steps were practiced by over 70 percent of the firms in one study.

We now turn to Chapter 3, where we will study how firms perform the opportunity identification function and how they build various forms of strategy to guide the evaluation of those opportunities and the specific products they yield. That will prepare us to begin the study of concept generation.

APPLICATIONS

More questions from that interview with a company president:

1. "I've got to make a speech down in Dallas next month. It's part of a conference SMU is having on the general topic of opportunity identification (OI). They want me to explain why OI is sometimes more important than brainstorming and other techniques of concept generation. Seems to me it isn't. What do you think?"
2. "You were telling me a moment ago about a three-pronged development process for new products (technical, marketing, and evaluation). Well, I disagree. We develop a new product first; we have to. When we know what the product will be, then we can estimate its costs, prepare advertising for it, and so on. We simply couldn't do all of these things at one time."

3. "I appreciate that little story you told me about the highlighter pens. Sure would be nice if everything went as smoothly as that one did. But, I'll tell you this, if two of my staff spent most of two months in a market test area, I'd have them up for reprimand. What a waste of time!"

4. "One of our scientists told me the other day that he actually has to be involved in developing at least six different products for every one we market. He said they were "precursors," I think it was, of the final product. He even said he didn't know what product we would ultimately end up marketing. What in the world did he mean by all that?"

Case: Aziza Polishing Pen

In early 1985, Chesebrough-Pond's Inc. began marketing the Aziza Polishing Pen in the Prince Matchabelli line of cosmetic products. This item closely resembled a marking pen, and it was used to apply nail polish quickly and neatly.

The idea of polish in a pen was not new, but the company had to solve the problem of how to get correct polish flow. The solution resulted in part from the firm's policy of free time, whereby its technical research scientists could use Friday afternoons for whatever research activity they wished, so long as it related to a C-P business.

One of the scientists, John D. Cunningham, saw another lab employee with a large marking pen made by Pilot Pen Company, and he thought that if Pilot could solve some of the flow problem, perhaps he could too. And he did—through cooperation with Pilot, some solid creative thinking, and use of other C-P technology. Free time was a controversial program, and this was the first tangible output since its installation at C-P.

The pen was an attractive metal tube about the size of a cigar. The container color matched the polish color. Two or three coatings were required. A metal ball mixed the contents when the tube was shaken vigorously for 30 seconds, and the tube had to be stored on its side.

The product was marketed with other Prince Matchabelli items and had a retail price of about $3.50. It received considerable publicity when it was introduced, including a special section on the CBS morning news program. The newsworthiness came primarily from the free time angle, but one newsperson applied the product on all 10 fingers while another newsperson narrated how the product was developed.

The product sometimes smudged, and the pen tip eventually lost its shape. But, despite these problems, the ease of application was thought to appeal to working women who don't have time for lengthy manicures. The market for this product category was $130 million annually, and the Prince Matchabelli division wanted an 8 percent share of market in 1985.

The firm did not announce its entire product development procedure. Use the material in Chapter 2 to point out (1) which steps in the new product development process would be critical for such a product and (2) what type of testing you would propose for the product.

Chapter 3

Strategic Planning for New Products: The Product Innovation Charter

SETTING

Chapter 2 discussed creating and marketing new products, from strategy to post-launch tracking and evaluation. Chapter 3 examines the first step in that process. Strategy is the foundation for product development and serves as a loose harness for the integration of all the people and resources used in generating new products. We will look first at the purpose of strategy, then at what it should cover, what form it takes, and how it is developed. The chapter concludes with a look at some interesting special aspects of strategy.

WHY HAVE STRATEGIC PLANNING?

Here is a real-life story:

A large manufacturer of nutritional specialties tried to develop a specialty food product (in liquid or powder form) that would be inexpensive and tasty, yet nutritious. But the development process suffered from false starts, iterations, failed tests, frustrations, accusations, and the spending of money that eventually produced nothing—there wasn't even a product to market. The project was abandoned.

Such stories are commonplace. Products don't work, people don't want them, they take too long to develop, they are too costly, they are marketed incorrectly, and so on. A major cause of such failures lies in the program's overall direction. The food company's team members had conflicting ideas about what was needed; without good direction, they could not function as a team.

New products strategy has four purposes. First is to focus team effort. People involved in new products projects suffer many diversions – other projects, emergencies, customer problems, and so on. With today's pressure on product innovators to speed up the process, focus is critical. A specific example is Rubbermaid, a firm that has successfully fought a worldwide collection of lower-cost competitors by cutting costs and focusing almost entirely on finding the needs of consumers.[1]

Second, strategy brings about integration. Scores or hundreds of people are involved in any project, each with their own agenda and departmental pressures. New products managers are expected to make the group work as a team, consistently, and with synergy, not divisiveness. But managers can't be in all places at all times. Strategy statements can be, and they help. Boats can be rowed by several people at one time, but it helps if they agree in advance on where and how they are going. If new product strategy is not offered, individuals make up their own.

Third, strategy is a tool of delegation. All players can't check with the new products manager every time they make a decision or spend some money. So, strategy lets them operate independently, effectively, and efficiently while still integrated with the rest of the team.

Fourth, preparing strategy requires proactive management, not reactive. If it is necessary to state what a project's focus will be, chances are the investigation of the opportunities will be more thorough. And, if the strategic statement must include all critical guidelines, then its author had better study the selected opportunity thoroughly. In other words, having to write out strategy helps create better managers. Bausch & Lomb almost lost its market position when its managers concentrated for too long on improving old products and thus almost missed new products like extended-wear contact lenses. Being forced to review their strategy, they found many more opportunities and are now successfully capitalizing on them.[2]

Though these purposes sound rather academic, the unique nature of the new products process makes them real. Let's look in on a team of people developing a small, portable computer printer. One member is thinking of using a new battery-based technology, while another team member is concentrating on potential customers who work in environ-

---

[1] Alex Taylor III, "Why the Bounce at Rubbermaid?" *Fortune,* April 13, 1987, pp. 77–78.

[2] "Bausch & Lomb Is Correcting Its Vision of Research," *Business Week,* March 30, 1987, p. 91.

ments where wall plugs are available! One department plans to pretest the product extensively, while another department assumes time is critical and is building finished production capability from the beginning! A vendor picked to supply the tractor mechanism has to check with the team leader almost every day because the team has not settled on such guidelines as the function the printer will serve or the target user! And the team is being guided by requests from the sales department, which is currently calling on smaller firms although, in fact, the biggest potential may be in large firms (or governments, or schools)! This team has not developed strategy.

WHAT FORM DOES PRODUCT INNOVATION STRATEGY TAKE?

It's now time to get more specific, but, as stated in the preface, the field of new products management is still young, still evolving. Many firms hardly recognize product innovation as a specific entity, others are only beginning to build a system for it, and still others have theirs already in operation.

Strategy statements, therefore, take almost as many forms as there are firms preparing them. Dan Gerber ran his small firm for many years with a very simple statement: Babies are our business, our only business. This declaration didn't solve every employee's problems, but it helped. Many firms have an even simpler credo: We don't innovate, period.

But, as we move through the 1990s, strategy statements need to be much more definitive. Fortunately, some studies of corporate new product strategies have been conducted.[3] Based on these studies, we can say that a pro forma strategy statement would be like the one shown in Figure 3–1. Before we discuss its parts, several things can be said about it:

1. In this book, it is called a product innovation charter (PIC). The term *charter* suggests a positive direction, a challenge, as well as a permit.
2. The product innovation charter can be for an entire firm (if very small or very narrowly conceived), or for a standing program of activity within a firm (for example, power saws at Black & Decker), or for a specific project (for example, the Saturn or Taurus automobiles). A PIC fits any product innovation activity that is homogeneous within that charter.

---

[3] See C. Merle Crawford, "Defining the Charter for Product Innovation," *Sloan Management Review,* Fall 1980, pp. 3–12; R. G. Cooper, "How New Product Strategies Impact on Performance," *Journal of Product Innovation Management,* March 1984, pp. 5–18; and W. L. Moore, "New Product Development Practices of Industrial Marketers," *Journal of Product Innovation Management,* December 1987, pp. 6–19.

FIGURE 3–1   Standard Form for Product Innovation Charter

PRODUCT INNOVATION CHARTER

Background

Key ideas from the situation analysis; special forces, such as managerial dicta; special reasons for preparing a new PIC at this time, etc.

Focus

Have at least one clear technology dimension (such as a science, a material, or a process skill) and one clear market dimension (such as a user, a use, or an activity). Without both the focus is weak.

Goals — Objectives

Be as specific as possible. Think about what a PIC team should really be held for accomplishing. Don't forget the miscellaneous goals.

Guidelines

This section usually speaks to any special source of the innovativeness that will sell the product. It also may stipulate market precedence if that is important, and it usually gives some suggestions about how unique the items should be (innovativeness). It is also a catchall for the miscellaneous aspects.

---

3. PICs rarely appear as clear-cut as this form suggests. Most product innovation today is undertaken without the benefit of strategies stated as clearly as the PIC outline in Figure 3–1. But research indicates the form is, in fact, what most firms are using — if they are using strategic thinking at all.
4. The PIC often is not written down, partly for reasons of difficulty and partly for security. This is unfortunate, because it will not do its job that way.

Background Section

This section of the PIC answers the question "Why did we develop this strategy, anyway?" The situation is abbreviated and focuses mainly on one of the four opportunities discussed later: underutilized resource, new resource, external mandate, or internal mandate. To the extent necessary, it recaps the analysis behind this particular PIC.

The Focus

The most controversial part of a product innovation charter is unquestionably that of focus. Focus seems contrary to the essence of innovation — creative freedom, open expression, break with the ordinary, and so on. But focus alone can unlock the innate power of innovation. Just as a laser can take a harmless light and convert it into a deadly ray, so can a commitment to, say, the pizza business or to the xerographic process convert limited resources into a strong competitive thrust.

Marketers have known this aspect of market targeting for many years, so it comes easily to them. Technical people, all too often fenced in by time, laboratory facilities, and money, don't relish yet another focus mechanism.

But focus is growing anyway — managed, of course, in a way that is constructive, not harmful. The focus is achieved almost entirely by use of four dimensions, as shown in Figure 3–2. However, there are variations and exceptions in actual practice in different lines of business.

Which dimension to use is determined through the opportunity identification phase, discussed in Chapter 2. An organization has several types of resources: technical, financial, product, or market. Financial strength needs other dimensions to give it focus, but the others can stand alone (for example, Xerox's xerographic technology; Scott's paper mills; Anheuser-Busch's knowledge of the beer business; current market position, such as that of Scotch tape or Campbell soups; and potential markets, such as baby boomers or videotape watchers.)

You read in Chapter 1 that product innovation is a merging of technical strength and market strength. In years past, a firm could be so strong technically that it could ignore the market, produce to its heart's content, and let the sales department sell whatever the labs produced. Edwin Land did this for many years, until he came up with something his salespeople could not sell — Polavision.[4]

Similarly, market-oriented firms (especially consumer packaged goods firms in food, drug, and toiletry categories) used to just survey consumers, find they wanted green biddies rather than yellow ones, and tell the lab people to make them up. This too worked pretty well, as long as there were significant unmet needs and competitors who reacted slowly.

Today, either approach is a big gamble. Frito-Lay and P&G have major laboratory research facilities, for example, and Hewlett-Packard has

---

[4] For an interesting story about what can happen to product innovation strategies built solely on technology, see Lawrence Ingrassia, "How Polaroid Went from Highest Flier to Takeover Target," *The Wall Street Journal*, August 12, 1988, p. 1.

FIGURE 3–2   Options for Specific Content in PICs

Focus

Technology:	Customer group:
Scientific	User status (current, new)
Engineering	Demographic dimensions
Operations	Psychographic dimensions
Marketing	Distribution status
Product type or class	End-use application/activity

Goals/Objectives	*Special Guidelines*
Profit:	Innovativeness:
Total dollars	Pioneering:
ROI, ROAI	State of the art
Payback	Leveraged creativity
Growth:	Applications engineering
Rapid growth	Adaptive:
Controlled growth	Quick second
Maintenance	Second but best
Controlled decline	Imitative/emulative
Market status:	Quick reactive
Enter a market	Segment franchise
Increase share	Price aggressive
Hold share	Other:
Yield share slowly	Function avoidance
Other:	Regulatory avoidance
Diversification	Product quality level
Avoid being acquired	Patentability
Complete a line	Systems or no systems
Alter an image	Growing markets only

announced that it wants a strong market commitment behind every new product program. Whereas we used to talk about a technologically driven firm or a market-driven firm, we now talk about dual-driven firms—increasingly, the winners.

Technology Drivers.   The most common technological strengths are in the laboratories. Large firms throughout the world spend billions of dollars on technical research, all the way from very basic projects that yield the Kevlars and Teflons, through applied projects that result in electronic typewriters, to development projects that produce the many improved products and near line extensions. Moreover, many leading firms (for example, Johnson & Johnson, Du Pont, and Upjohn) systematically search for still other technologies that can be appropriated from outside their own labs.

Corning used to say it would develop those products—and only those products—that exploited the firm's fabulous glass technology. Today's global competition makes it tougher for Corning (and others) to hold a superior position in a technology defined so broadly.[5]

Many times, a firm finds it has a valuable technology outside its laboratories. Avon has an efficient small-order-handling technology. Other operations technologies include soft-drink distributed bottling systems and White Consolidated's efficient appliance production lines.

Even harder to see are technologies in marketing. For example, some packaged goods firms view their product management departments as technologies. Other examples include physical distribution systems, customer technical service, or creative advertising departments.

We also know that product specialization can offer bodies of knowledge that are capable of doing work, if focused and strengthened. Kellogg's takes great pride in its profits from the "cereals business," and most of that firm's product innovation projects focus only on cereals, not on toys, restaurants, and the like. A rapidly growing Korean manufacturer says, "I want to be the Toyota of furniture."[6] Note that this focus is free of restrictions on materials, or markets, so the firm makes all types, for all people, whether residential or office, whether in Korea, or the United States, or (eventually) wherever.

Firms with strategies built on product knowledge feel they can sense better than others what a market needs or what is possible in technical development and manufacturing.

Market Drivers. The other half of the dual-drive strategy also comes from two sources: customer group and end use. The best new product ideas are based on customer input; but, as mentioned above, we can't just ask consumers (home or industry) what problems they have. If we do, they usually just tell us about a problem we're well aware of and have already worked on. The problems we're interested in are problems consumers don't know they have or the ones they are going to have. These still offer potential.

But to find these, a lot of knowledge about particular consumers—how they think and act—is needed. This requires focus. So, the Hoover Company once had a strategy of developing new vacuums for "people

---

[5] The issue of core technologies, and their importance, is discussed by Marc H. Meyer and Edward B. Roberts, "Focusing Product Technology," *Sloan Management Review,* Summer 1988, pp. 7–16.

[6] Wee Sang-sik, as quoted in an article by that name in *Forbes,* May 16, 1988, p. 92.

who already had one"—the two-vacuum home concept. Other firms have relied on demographic dimensions for focus, for example, Consolidated Cigar's "young men," Toro's "young couples," NCR's "banks and retailers," and Olivetti's "banks and law offices." As examples of more abstract dimensions, Hallmark concentrates on "people who care enough," and Helena Rubenstein targets "real women."

All of these are customer groups. Occasionally, a firm can concentrate on one single customer; for example, an auto-parts firm may build new approaches for Ford or General Motors. And still another variation is the focus on a noncustomer. Focusing on current customers helps hold markets; focusing on noncustomers grows volume. Cullinet focused successfully on its customer base and made lots of money, until IBM focused on its noncustomers and ended up sideswiping Cullinet with a new language (SQL).[7]

A different way of focusing on the market side is on a particular activity, say, sports, or even skiing. General Instrument Corporation's new products program concentrated exclusively on wagering. The two approaches (user and use) may appear to be the same (skiers and skiing, for example) but usually have significant differences. For example, focusing on skiing would provide new equipment, but also new lodges, new slopes, new travel packages, and services for lodge owners (who may not even be skiers).

The distinction is clearer in the industrial world. For example, Carborundum focused for a long time on metal removal (an outgrowth of its line of grinding wheels), wherever that removal took place. Even though users differed greatly, their metal removing had a lot in common.

Sometimes the end-use activity is very broad, especially when managements use environmental scanning to spot trends that hold potential. For example, if a cosmetics firm sees increasing concern over allergic reactions to skin chemicals, a PIC might focus on this concern as its market driver.

Combinations. Now, putting one technical driver together with a market driver yields a clear and precise focus. The major new products program of University Microfilms International (now part of Bell & Howell) was oriented to the technology of microfilming and the market activity of education. Microfilm readers for libraries were just one new line. UMI's early use of this strategy would have rejected photocopiers for schools or microfilm readers for law offices.

---

[7] Esther Dyson, "Don't Listen Too Hard," *Forbes,* May 16, 1988, p. 112.

The Signode Corporation set up a series of seven new product venture operations and asked each group to select one company technology and one market opportunity that matched company strengths. The first team chose plastics extrusion (from Signode's primary business of strapping materials) and food manufacturing. This team's first new products were plastic trays for packaging foods; the whole package can be put into a microwave oven for warming.[8]

This reasoning has been carried further, as might be expected. Levi Strauss, for example, had several three-dimensional programs. A profitable one was (1) denim technology, (2) in making clothing, (3) for active people. Figure 3–3 shows a four-column display of potential strategic focuses for an office furniture manufacturer. The first three columns are technology, and the fourth combines end use and customer group. Their strategies are displayed graphically so that changing any item in any column will expose a new and potentially useful one (for example, fabrication of panels for use in factories, whether of plastics or whatever). This approach calls each strategic option (line) a strategic technical arena (STA).[9]

FIGURE 3–3   Multiple-Focus Dimensions—Hypothetical Applications to an Office Furniture Manufacturer

	Dimensions			
Strategy	*Technical skill*	*Application*	*Product*	*Function*
Current business	Fabrication	Steel	Furniture	Offices
New option	Metallurgy	Steel	Furniture	Offices
New option	Fabrication	Plastics	Furniture	Offices
New option	Fabrication	Plastics	Panels	Offices
New option	Fabrication	Plastics	Panels	Factories
Other dimensions	Chemistry, physiology, ergonomics	Materials, forms, fabrics	Floors, machines, packaging	Laboratories, schools

---

[8] For more information on the Signode program, see "The Team Captain," *Business Marketing,* August 1986, pp. 8ff.

[9] For an explanation of the STA line of thinking, see Graham R. Mitchell, "New Approaches for the Strategic Management of Technology," *Technology in Society* 2/3, 1985, pp. 227–39.

Goals and Objectives

Anyone working on product innovation ought to know the purpose, because work can change in so many ways if the purpose changes. The PIC uses the standard definition that *goals* are longer-range, general directions of movement, whereas *objectives* are short-term, specific measures of accomplishment. Thus, a PIC may aim for market dominance (as a goal) and 25 percent market share the first year (as an objective).

Both goals and objectives are of three types (see Figure 3–2 for a listing of the options): (1) profit, stated in one or more of the many ways profit can be stated; (2) growth, usually controlled, though occasionally a charter is used defensively to help the firm hold or retard a declining trend; and (3) market status, usually increased market share. General Foods, for example, insisted that new product teams entering new markets plan to dominate them. But the American Regitel Corporation, marketers of point-of-sale machines, aimed to be number three in its markets, even though the parent firm wanted to be number one as a general policy.

Figure 3–2 also gives some miscellaneous goals uncovered by research. They are not trivial to the firms using them, however. For example, the firm that had to "avoid acquisition" didn't.

Special Guidelines

To this point, we have filled out three sections of the PIC form shown in Figure 3–1. Three sections may be enough—background, focus, and goals or objectives. But research shows that almost every new product strategy has other, sometimes very important, dimensions.

Degree of Innovativeness. An important guideline found in many product innovation charters relates to how innovative a management wants a particular group to be. The options range from first-to-market (whether a new nylon or a Frisbee) to strict imitation.

First-to-market is a risky strategy. It goes by several other names, including pioneering and state-of-the-art breakthrough. Pharmaceutical firms seek it most of the time. Edwin Land once told his researchers at Polaroid that they should "not undertake a program unless the goal is manifestly important and achievement is nearly impossible."[10] Other

---

[10] Lawrence Ingrassia, "How Polaroid Went from Highest Flier to Takeover Target," *The Wall Street Journal,* August 12, 1988, p. 1.

products that came from such programs include bubble memory, the Apple personal computer, the pacemaker, Stainmaster carpets, Simplesse, compact discs, the credit card, and television. Most first-to-market products do not extend the state of the art. They apply technology in a new way, sometimes called *leveraged creativity*. And even less demanding for being first, technically, is *applications engineering,* where the technology may not be changed at all, but the use is totally new. Loctite has done this scores of time, for example, by using glue to replace metal fasteners in electronics and automotive products.

Far more common than pioneering is the strategy of adaptation. Being adaptive means taking a competitive product and improving it in a significant way. The improvement may be technical (a double-sided floppy disk versus a single-sided one, the Lotus 1-2-3 improvement on predecessor VisiCalc) or nontechnical (new flavors of soda).

Adaptation has several interesting aspects, the main one being how adaptive the follower wants to be. Some seek almost trivial change, anything that can be used in advertising. Others follow what is called "second but best"; the improvement is to be major, and the follower intends to take over the market, if possible. GE followed this strategy for many years prior to 1980. Harris Corporation differs slightly; it usually enters markets where others have pioneered and uses its great technical know-how to create a niche with a slightly improved product. The firm's chairman says Harris tries to be strong in technology and to enter a product in a timely manner.[11]

Adaptation is risky. The pioneer often obtains a permanent advantage; if other things are equal, the first product in a new market gains an average market share of around 40 percent. The second firm in (with a substantially similar product) gets around 25 percent, and latecomers (again with similar products) share the rest. So, a big profit swing comes from whether the market thinks any particular adaptation is important or trivial: if trivial, the product gets 25 percent or less; but if important, the product can take over the market and get the 40 percent.[12]

---

[11] AM International employs another example of a noninnovating strategy that works. Its president, Merle H. Banta, said, "We'll wait until new technologies are proven, then use our sales and services organization to get and hold market share." See "AM International: Profits Are In, High Tech's Out," *Business Week,* July 17, 1986, pp. 77–78. Note that product innovation tends to flow over time within an expanding product line, so a firm can begin a line by being first-to-market, and then follow with increasingly less innovative line extensions, even up to putting in some straight imitations to hold against competitors. For more information about this idea, see Steven C. Wheelwright and W. Earl Sasser, Jr., "The New Product Development Map," *Harvard Business Review,* May–June 1989, pp. 112–25.

[12] Glen L. Urban, Theresa Carter, Steven Gaskin, and Zofia Mukcha, "Market Share Rewards to Pioneering Brands: An Empirical Analysis and Strategic Implications," *Management Science,* June 1986, pp. 645–59.

The third level of innovativeness is imitation, or emulation. In late 1979, *Advertising Age* quoted S. W. Lapham, the new products director of Sterling Drug's subsidiary Lehn & Fink, "Replicate, don't innovate." Imitation was a surefire way to succeed.[13] Lapham cited several products that had been successfully copied—Jell-O Pudding followed My-T-Fine; Country Time lemonade mix followed Wyler's; and Stayfree feminine napkins followed Kotex. After recommending that any imitator be careful to sufficiently research the right entry to copy, Lapham described how his firm copied Airwick's Carpet Fresh. Love My Carpet was "developed" and marketed in less than six months. He said, "Trying to innovate as the only way to success is one of the greatest myths of new products ever invented. I have to believe it was created by a marketing research company." A few weeks later, another *Advertising Age* article announced that Lehn & Fink was being sued by Airwick for infringing on the Carpet Fresh patents.[14] Imitation has its risks, too!

Timing. The next category of variation—timing—has three options: quick second, slower, and late. A quick second tries to capture that 25 percent second-share position, perhaps making no significant improvement, but rather just enough to promote. The strategy is very demanding, because such a firm has to make the decision to enter the market before the pioneer is successful or has even come to market. Waiting risks letting the second spot go to other aggressive competitors.

Striving for a slower entry is safer in the sense that a firm knows the outcome of the pioneer's efforts and has time to make a more meaningful adaptation. But, the good market opportunities may be taken.

The last timing alternative, late entry, is usually a price entry keyed to manufacturing skills. In some cases, the late entrant is capitalizing on franchise with a particular segment of the market (like local banks often do). The strategy, while not a big money-maker, can be useful to the smaller or specialized firm.

Miscellaneous. Innumerable specialized guidelines can be found in product innovation charters. Because of today's push to get new items fast—and cheap—one popular guideline relates to brand franchise. A brand is like a charged battery, easy to hook up a new line to. Jell-O-this

---

[13] "Different Strokes," *Advertising Age,* December 17, 1979, p. 4.

[14] "Lehn & Fink Philosophy Draws Suit by Airwick," *Advertising Age,* February 11, 1980, p. 71.

and Jell-O-that . . . instant respectability and demand, if the franchise is strong and carries the right message. Murjani International said it would sell more than $200 million of apparel in 1988 emblazoned with the Coca-Cola logo.[15]

Brand equity describes the value of an established brand. Market research can measure the value of any brand for any particular market (for example, Duracel if put onto wall switches). The measurements actually tell the amount of "free" promotion and integrity the brand equity yields to a new item that uses it.

Pierre Cardin recently said, "I have the most important name in the world. I give my name only to the best products."[16] He knows the brand-franchise strategy is not without its dangers. A bad product can "short" the battery badly. Or, conversely, the new product can be so successful it takes over the main brand (think of Miller Lite and the formerly famous Miller High Life). How to find the right fit is discussed in Chapter 17, "Tools of the Marketing Mix."

In contrast to a strong brand, some firms have a weak marketing arm. For example, a large mining firm told its product innovators to come up with products that didn't require strong marketing; the firm didn't have it and didn't want to invest in getting it. Another firm said to "avoid regulation" in its assignment. A jewelry firm demanded all new items meet or raise its current quality image level. August Busch III said, "You have to have the best. Sooner or later the customer will recognize quality."[17] A pharmaceutical firm said, "It must be patentable." A small computer firm said all new products must be parts of systems, while an even smaller computer firm said, "Nothing that must be part of a system"! Cosmetics firm B required its new products to not threaten Avon seriously, while cosmetics firm C required new items to not step into firm B's backyard! A food firm said, "Don't put anything in a can that Frito-Lay can put in a bag." And on and on. Diversify, avoid diversification; help smooth out seasonals; make us less open to acquisition. Each statement was important to the people involved—both management and product innovators.

Another unusual approach is *repositioning,* a strategy of not changing the product but changing its use or its "positioning" relative to competition. The Linde Corporation, for example, built a major program around repositioning its products into a service component.[18]

---

[15] "The Battle of the Brands," *Forbes,* February 9, 1987, p. 111.

[16] Richard C. Morais, "What Is Perfume but Water and a Bit of Essence?" *Forbes,* May 2, 1988, pp. 90–95.

[17] "August Busch Brews up a New Spirit in St. Louis," *Fortune,* January 15, 1979, p. 92.

[18] Tom Eisenhart, "Breaking away from the Faceless Pack," *Business Marketing,* June 1988, pp. 74–78.

Arm & Hammer is famous for a series of successful repositionings of its baking soda.

Most firms use many different strategies at the same time. For example, a few years back, Texas Instruments was concurrently using R&D as its strength in MOM memories, manufacturing as its base for low-priced watches, and consumer studies for its line of games.

Examples of Product Innovation Charters

Now, let's put these options together and see how a product innovation charter actually looks. Figure 3–4 shows two abbreviated examples. The chemical firm's PIC contains:

Background: The firm was stymied in its present markets and needed to find new opportunities.

Focus: R&D skills (technology), specialty chemicals (product type), in metal finishing (end-use).

Goals/objectives: Market share leader, 35 percent ROI, three-year payout, recognition.

Guidelines: Adaptation (demonstrably superior products), in-house, willing to invest, patents, increase safety. No panic.

The computer firm's PIC has the following points:

Background: The firm had been having trouble servicing small offices that had bought its new systems. The customers were not getting the type of service that the computer firm wanted them to have.

Focus: The small offices (customer group) and two sets of company skills (technologies).

Goals/objectives: Overcome objections, increase net operating revenues.

Guidelines: Be innovative, protected product, and not use much time or money.

Both firms had other options, and various people in their product innovation functions had argued for them. For example, some people in the computer firm said this problem customer group wasn't worth the cost of innovation. They argued that the company should just wait: if no competitor came up with a better method of field service, little would be lost; and if one did, this firm had the skills to copy it quickly. In each case, a written PIC settles the argument but does not guarantee each solution was the correct one. And, PICs are sometimes revised during implementation, though strategy gains strength from duration.

One question frequently asked is "Do we have to develop our own PIC, or are there standard ones to choose from?" Standards do exist

---

FIGURE 3–4   Two Partially Hypothetical Product Innovation Charters

---

A PIC for a Tangible Product

The XYZ Company is committed to a program of innovation in specialty chemicals, as utilized in the automobile and other metal-finishing businesses, to the extent that we will become the market share leader in that market and will achieve at least 35 percent ROI from that program on a three-year pay-out basis. We seek recognition as the most technically competent company in metal finishing.

These goals will be achieved by building on our current R&D skills and by embellishing them as necessary so as to produce new items that are demonstrably superior technically, in-house, and have only emergency reliance on outside sources. The company is willing to invest funds, as necessary, to achieve these technical breakthroughs, even though 1987 and 1988 IATs may suffer the next two years.

Care will be taken to establish patent-protected positions in these new developments and to increase the safety of customer and company personnel.

A PIC for a Service

A major growth opportunity for a new field service is the smaller office that over the past three years has bought one of the new computer systems designed for such offices. Because they are found in every conceivable location and because they purchase computer equipment with the intention that it last a long time, they offer a unique service problem. This opportunity will be addressed using (1) our systems analysis skills and (2) our field service capabilities.

The goals of the activity are (1) to overcome all reasonable objections about service levels by this group and (2) to increase our net operating revenues from the sale of these new services by at least $18 million per year.

These goals will be achieved by creating unique service approaches that are based on current field service resources, hopefully protected from quick competitive emulation, without extensive development expenditures either inside the firm or outside, and with an absolute minimum of development time.

---

but only in general outline. The PIC should reflect the situation for which it is written, otherwise it loses most of its purpose. From a study of Canadian industrial firms, the following five types of strategies evolved:

1. *Balanced strategy* (16 percent of the sample): Technologically sophisticated, oriented, and innovative, but with a strong market orientation. Sought high-potential products, in growing markets, with good fit to current products. (This strategy was the most common winner in the study.)
2. *Technologically driven strategy* (26 percent): Technologically sophisticated, oriented, and innovative. Strong technological focus, and took

markets wherever the technology led. Thus, little product line focus or fit with present products. Aggressive R&D.

3. *Defensive, focused, technologically deficient strategy* (16 percent): Defensive, aimed at current markets, fairly focused product lines, but sought innovative products.

4. *Low-budget, conservative strategy* (24 percent): Low R&D spending, lacked technological capabilities, high product line focus, ho-hum products, but with tight synergy among technical, operations, and marketing functions.

5. *High-budget, diverse strategy* (19 percent): High levels of R&D spending; little focus on products, technologies, or markets; shotgun approach. Usually ended up in highly competitive new markets.[19]

PICs can, and do, take many forms, but form is not the point. The real issue is whether the PIC guides the innovation program effectively and efficiently.

THE PROCESS FOR DEVELOPING CHARTERS

Chapter 2 described the overall process of product innovation, including the early strategic planning stage. This stage is reproduced in Figure 3–5 and expanded to include more details.

Remember the PIC says, "Go in this direction and the chances are good that you will find something interesting." So, the challenge is to find those directions. To do so, we use the three inputs shown at the top of Figure 3–5.

Three Sources of Opportunities

The first input is ongoing marketing planning. Product managers and other planners look at markets, current standings, competitive strategies and strengths, what has been done, and so on. Their problems and opportunities feed directly into product innovation. For example, a product manager sees market share slipping; market research indicates the reason is competitive product superiority. Up comes a request for product improvement. Another product manager sees very rapid growth in an overall market and fragmentation into clear market segments. Up comes a request for product line extensions, one for each market

---

[19] Robert G. Cooper, "New Product Strategies: What Distinguishes the Top Performers?" *Journal of Product Innovation Management*, September 1984, pp. 151–64.

FIGURE 3–5 Strategic Planning Stage of the New Products Process

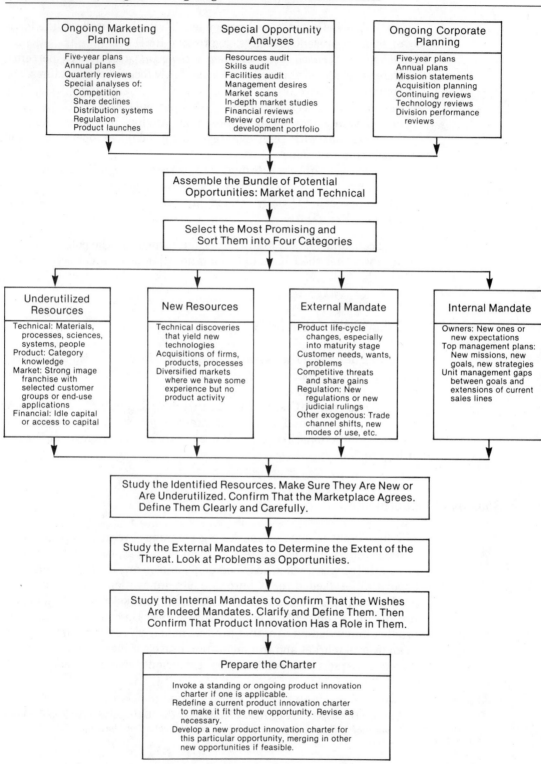

segment. Still another product manager notices how current customers also purchase in a nearby category that does not include the company. The strong franchise of the firm with those customers indicates ease of entry for a new product.

Some marketing planning techniques overlap with the analysis done by new products people. For example, consider the product/market matrix. For marketing people, it indicates options for improving present products for present markets or for expanding one or both of those dimensions. So, the new products people have altered the standard matrix to read "technologies/applications" matrix. We see products as only one type of technology (as discussed above) and market as only one mode of application (use, user, distribution, etc.). Use of this matrix leads to applying strong technologies to new applications in areas where the firm is strong. Just as marketers shy away from the new product/new market cell in the matrix, so do product innovators shy from the new technology/new application cell.

Other special techniques of marketing planning are also useful on new products. The market share/profitability analysis has led to share being a key goal or objective in most PICs. And the investment intensity/profitability relationship directs managements in evaluating the expected investment in any particular PIC. Portfolio analysis has shown how a PIC can help support a star product, help continue the harvesting of a cash cow product, and improve a question mark to where it can become a star. Every product in a portfolio analysis should fit in an appropriate charter, unless it is an abandoned dog. Last, the well-known tools of competitive analysis lead directly to new product opportunities.

Some of the new product action requests from marketing will fit into current PICs, because a firm should have at least one PIC for each market it serves, if for no other reason than one should have been written when the first entry in that market was developed and marketed. If it wasn't, what really amounts to a PIC can be found in the marketing strategy given in the annual marketing plan for that product. Figure 3–6 shows the forms that market opportunities usually take – the dimensions talked about earlier in the section on focus. Distribution franchises have been listed separately from users, but they are the same. These opportunities feed into one of the four boxes in Figure 3–5. Here are some hypothetical examples for a firm making hand tools:

Underutilized resource: We have the best line of small tools in the home repair market today, and dealers prefer us over any other manufacturer.

New resource: Research shows that owner repair of automobiles is growing rapidly. This market will now support product development research.

FIGURE 3–6 Market and Technology Opportunities

Market Opportunities	Technology Opportunities
User (category)	Product type
User (for our product)	Specific product
Customer (buyer)	Primary packaging
Influencer	Secondary packaging
Potential user	Design process
Nonuser	Production process
Demographic set	Distribution process
Psychographic set	Packaging process
Geographic set	Patent
Retailer	Science
Wholesaler	Material
Agent	Individual
Use	Management system
Application	Information system
Activity	Analytical skill
Franchise	Expert system
Location	Project control
Competitor	Quality attainment
Regulator	Project design

External mandate: Competitor C has just launched a new line of tools like ours but made with a new alloy from the space program. Consumers are excited about it.

Internal mandate: Division management has decided it needs $20 million of new products within three years. They reached this conclusion after studying the annual marketing plans.

New product opportunities also come from the other ongoing type of planning shown at the top of Figure 3–5—corporate planning. For example:

Underutilized resource: Company planners decide the corporate image is not being capitalized on and thus ask for new products that might be marketed under that brand.

New resource: Planners ask division A to develop products utilizing the strong market position of division B.

External mandate: Planners decide the firm is being too negative on a particular aspect of federal regulation and so ask all consumer divisions to come up with products that build on the regulation, rather than fight it.

Internal mandate: New corporate owners ask planners to coordinate a companywide program to clean up a hodgepodge of packages and brands.

You may ask, if a firm does good strategic corporate planning, why does it need PICs; isn't the necessary guidance in those corporate plans? The answer is yes, companies do make product innovation strategy decisions at the top as part of ongoing planning, and these decisions feed into new products management as shown in the process chart in Chapter 2 and in Figure 3–5. But, corporate strategic thinking does not give the help needed at the working level of new products. Teams of people (operating as a microcosm of the firm, formally or informally) need their own strategies, which is exactly what the PIC does. Corporate decisions and pronouncements cannot apply to all teams and be complete. The PIC interprets corporate strategy and blends it with other guidance for the team.

The third source of opportunities from the marketing perspective resembles the first two, but the search is done by persons charged with a new product focus. Most teams, in one way or another, take their own look at the marketplace. Many teams are simply given the boost of a background problem or concern and then asked to develop an appropriate new products program. Such opportunity identification programs are far superior from a new product perspective, and they should be encouraged.

Figure 3–5 shows some of the work involved in this special analysis, and most of it is self-evident. Auditing a firm's strengths and weaknesses, however, is not. Critiquing other people, while always touchy, is doubly so here because the people (marketing or technical) being audited are so often the very people touting their own favorite strategic directions. Yet, it does little good to build a new product strategy on weak foundations. A recent report on the PICs of movie producers disclosed that (1) Warner Bros. spends lavishly on its top stars and depends on them to make successful movies; (2) Paramount Pictures takes star courting a step further by luring top directors and producers as well and giving them lucrative contracts; and (3) Walt Disney Studios, on the other hand, elevates the story over the stars and has "made its mark by conceiving a genre of slapstick, class-warfare comedies."[20] Each strategy can be traced to a strength of the company involved.

Nor should the personal wishes of top managers be ignored. Strategic planning has always had room for the personal preferences of CEOs and division GMs; there is no exception in new product strategy.

---

[20] Christopher Knowlton, "Lessons from Hollywood Hit Men," *Fortune*, August 29, 1988, pp. 78–82.

While all of these market-oriented analyses are being made, another set of opportunities relates to technology. Recall the options in the area of focus — technology and product versus use and user. Again, they can come from any of the three sources, though they tend to come more often from corporate planning and special investigations.

Technology is the capability for doing work, know-how that can be used to produce or sell a product. It is potential. Many more types of technologies exist than people realize, as shown in Figure 3–6. That list is only suggestive; there are many more. In fact, one of the most valuable creative skills in product innovation is the ability to look at a building, an operation, a person, or a department and visualize how it could be used in a new way. This skill can be developed — and should be practiced.

And again, the technology identified can be underutilized, new to the firm, forced on it by something outside the firm, or mandated by management. One example of each:

Underutilized resource: The McDonald's system. It could be used in scores of additional ways.

New resource: The technical accomplishment of the 64-bit computer chip.

External mandate: The European Economic Community will be pressuring thousands of firms to standardize technologies, as the costs of resisting (or the rewards of cooperating) surge upward in the next few years.

Internal mandate: Management asks new products management to develop new programs that will generate quick cash flow by exploiting as many company standing technologies as possible, as quickly as possible, to help avert takeover.

Evaluating Opportunities

The next step is to evaluate the opportunities identified, whether marketing or technology, and whether from market planning, corporate planning, or special investigation. All opportunities that came from others (for example, external mandate, sales force report on competition, top-management request) have not been fully studied. They are someone else's opinion on what is worth developing.

Before any opportunity is converted into a specific product innovation charter, it should be investigated from the new products perspective, which usually means new research, at least on secondary sources and expert opinion. The factors that can be used for this evaluation are shown in Figure 3–7. There will always be other factors peculiar to the opportunity being evaluated, but these lists are sufficient for most

FIGURE 3–7 Evaluation Forms for Market and Technology Opportunities

Factors for Judging a Market Opportunity	*Score 1–5 Points*		*Factors for Judging a Technology Opportunity*
How large is the demand in this area? Is it, for us, a major source of new business or a minor one?	—	—	How unique is this technology? Are we the only ones who have it?
What is the current degree of felt need or unrest in this area? Do potential customers agree?	—	—	What is the value of things it does or permits us to do?
How well will our new product solve the customer's problem?	—	—	In what stage of the technology life cycle is this technology? (The earlier the better.)
How unique, relative to competition, will our product be?	—	—	How controllable is it? Do we have it tied up with a patent, with licensing, as a trade secret?
How easy will it be for us to explain and demonstrate our new products?	—	—	Can we extend the technology by further work?
What is the life-cycle stage of the marketplace activity involved with this opportunity?	—	—	Is it going to be inexpensive for us to use, or will it take major investments?
Is there a ready technology that would match this opportunity?	—	—	Is it going to take a long time to use?
Is this market free of any entrenched competitors?	—	—	Will it take us into new, risky ball games?
Do we have a trade channel that fits this opportunity?	—	—	Are products of this technology marketable by us alone?
Is this opportunity easy for us to study?	—	—	Are products of this technology manufacturable by us alone?
Will this market opportunity stir controversy within the firm?	—	—	Will this technology receive the support of company people who must support it?
Total Score	—	—	(Over 35 in each column = Good.)

situations. For example, Du Pont looks to see if the technology will be a necessity in the application and if the firm has previously demonstrated special expertise in it. Dow asks, "Can we own that market?" Celanese asks whether the development can expect costs to be manageable. Other firms ensure the presence of someone high enough in the firm to help the technology weather annual budget revisions. PQ and Reichhold want to concentrate on core product lines and thus make sure the selected technologies fit.[21]

The end results of the evaluation, of course, are the three conclusions indicated in the process chart of Figure 3–5: definition, confirmation of threat, or confirmation of role for product innovation. If the opportunity is real, and relevant, it is ready for writing a PIC.

INTERESTING ASPECTS

By now, students usually have many questions. Let's try to anticipate them.

• **Now that a new products manager has written a PIC, is that it?** Hardly, though the manager wishes it were so. Because PICs authorize ideation and spending money, managements must approve them. Moreover, projects must usually share resources (R&D, process development, market research, and so on), so they must be coordinated. And they must fit together as a product innovation portfolio, in the usual financial sense.

• **Are there differences in all this when the firm has a global perspective?** Only in amount, not kind. The more countries in which a firm operates, the more options and opportunities it has, and the tougher the analyses are prior to conclusion. But, the procedure doesn't vary. In the product realm, the biggest global issue is in what countries to market what products, not whether to develop a new product for other countries. We do know, of course, that how we develop products for world markets is key; but getting to know the markets and working closely with them applies in all phases of product innovation.[22]

• **How about the "strategic window"?** The concept of strategic windows does apply to new product strategic planning. So much so, in fact, that much desirable market analysis is skipped. Timing is critical on new products because being first or second has such large rewards.

---

[21] These and other special views are discussed in W. David Gibson, "A Maze for Management: Choosing the Right Technology," *Chemical Week*, May 7, 1986, pp. 74–78.

[22] See Kenichi Ohmae, "Planning for a Global Harvest," *Harvard Business Review*, July–August 1989, pp. 136–45.

Yet, being too early has also cost many firms dearly, so the window shouldn't dominate common sense.

• **Where does licensing or acquisition fit in here?** This book concerns internal product innovation, or management of the new products process. Acquiring products from outside is not covered here, though that source does substitute for internal innovation. Similarly, firms can license a technology or joint venture a market opportunity, so new products are not the only choice on the selling side, either.

• **You haven't mentioned fads, yet millions of dollars are made this way.** Yes, it seems to happen every day, but very few firms have a strategy of capitalizing on fads. And few fad-based innovators succeed time and again. The inventor of the Pet Rock tried several other ideas and then went back to the advertising business. Many firms in such industries as clothing, films, and TV programming watch fads closely and prepare to capitalize on them when there is a fit. But this is just what we've been talking about (opportunities); the only difference is the time the window is open.

• **Will the trend toward regional marketing affect product strategy?** Yes, and probably for the worse. Regionalizing product lines makes them more attractive to consumers, but splintering the effort is bound to retard breakthrough innovation. The problems in having many regions in one country are almost the same as the problems in having many countries in a global strategy.

• **Are there problems in implementing strategy?** Some people say writing new product strategy is easy, but sticking to it is impossible. This is incorrect. But, it is correct to say that circumstances put heavy pressure on PICs, the same as they do with all important strategies. Some managements abort a strategy at its first failure. Yet some of our most respected product innovators have announced strategies and stayed with them for many years. We will return to the issue of implementing strategy in Chapter 20.

• **Is strategic planning all good, or are there legitimate criticisms of the approach discussed in this chapter?** A cartoon often shown around this field has a senior executive standing beside a person sitting at a drawing board. The executive says, "Panelli, we've completed our market analysis. Design something domestic and electrical."[23]

Technical people, in particular, often object to PICs. They have good reasons. Unplanned product innovation should be permitted. Too many good things have resulted from nonstrategic modes. Could Edwin Land

---

[23] This cartoon is by "Nelson," but its origin is undocumented.

have been successful at Kodak? Could Thomas Edison have worked for GE, the firm he founded? Quite a few top firms rejected xerography when Chester Carlson offered it to them.

The answer is to have planned—as well as unplanned—innovation. Texas Instruments and 3M both have programs specifically designed to aid the bootlegger or moonlighter. One 3M scientist received an Oscar for his method of increasing the reflectiveness of movie screens, but he had to develop the process at night and on weekends because his (strategically driven) superior had to deny him time for it.[24] Many firms have a policy of free time in the labs, and Chapter 2's Aziza Polishing Pen was one result.

So, there is a trade-off. Let strategies guide, but listen to anyone who thinks there should be a variance. And then, treat variances like you would investing in oil wells—big potential, but don't do it if you will miss the money.

SUMMARY

Chapter 3 dealt with the most important and difficult step in the entire new products process: developing a sound strategy to guide the subset of people and resources charged with getting new products. Strategy turns such a group into a miniature firm, a microcosm of the whole.

We first looked at the reasons for strategic planning. Next we got into the heart of the matter, the product innovation charter, and examined its content and some examples. This led into the process by which a PIC is developed, introduced in Chapter 2. The chapter ended by looking at other aspects of the topic through the eyes of former students.

We can now begin the study of concept generation—the subject of four chapters in Part II.

APPLICATIONS

More questions from the interview with the president:

1. "I'm afraid I don't follow your reasoning very well when it comes to this matter of innovativeness—being a pioneer, an adapter, quick second, and so on. Seems you've always got to come up with something new, or it simply won't sell. I believe we agreed on that earlier when we discussed the failure rate of new products. Further, if you've got something new, why in the world would you ever want

---

[24] The fabulously successful new product system used at 3M has been described many times, but a good presentation is in "Masters of Innovation," *Business Week,* April 10, 1989, pp. 58–63.

to be less than first to market with it? You'll lose your uniqueness that way. Sounds like you've taken a simple practice and made it complex."

2. "I didn't like what you said a minute ago about that internal mandate. I take it you were referring to top management. Well, the implication is that you new products people study markets and technical skills, make rational decisions, and come up with sound strategy, while presidents just shoot from the hip with a 'Do this' or 'Do that.' Is that what you really mean?"

3. "Somewhere along the line, R&D gets the short end of the stick. Now, I know about the arguments for strategy, but I really do feel that R&D deserves a better shake than to simply be told to do this or that. Some of our top people are in R&D—our electronics division has a couple of the world's best in their areas. If I were doing it, I think I would have R&D prepare the first draft of a PIC, at least their areas of a PIC, and then have other areas like manufacturing add to it. When all of the interior departments have their sights properly set, I would ask marketing to reconcile the PIC with the marketplace. Otherwise, we'd have the tail wagging the dog when it comes to the new products function."

4. "On the other hand, I must admit to being rather antiproclamations when it comes to strategy and policy. Some things are just as well left unstated—that gives a manager more leeway to change a position if it turns out wrong, without embarrassment, and more opportunity to exploit situations that come up. No, I guess I really don't agree that new products strategy should be written down, and it certainly shouldn't be shown around where it might get to a competitor."

Case: Apple Computer Co.

Apple Computer entered the 1990s on a roll. Sales were rising steadily at close to a 50 percent rate, international market shares were rising, and profits were good (with some occasional glitches, of course).

The Macintosh was its strategic base, and because Apple controlled all parts of the architecture (hardware, software), it could achieve superior integration. Macintosh applications covered every conceivable computer use, from aerospace to education, and exploited its excellent graphics, user-friendliness, and networking capabilities.

Apple felt it needed to concentrate on that technology, seeking evolution (not revolution), line extensions to the Macintosh, advances in networking and communication, and filling out the line with new offerings in education, publishing, electronic mail, and software programming.

The Macintosh was supported by an almost endless set of software covering almost every application. Apple's factories were extremely efficient though not highly automated. Because labor represented less than 1 percent of the cost of producing a Macintosh, the firm could not afford to automate them. Component plants were next door to assembly plants, and management considered the firm's manufacturing to be a competitive advantage. They relied very little on outside programming and tooling.

Upper management was often in the headlines, as John Sculley continued his overhaul of the firm in its transition from the start-up, "California cool" days of Steve Jobs. The right-brained firm was going left brain. Two second-level aspirers to the throne competed vigorously—one in new products was from France, very creative, and committed to that freedom; the other was a new, tough-manager type, looking for ways to cut costs. The two made for a strange, two-personality management culture.

Competition was vigorous, including IBM's PS/2 and the Micro-Channel bus architecture, DEC's strong networking capabilities, advances by clone-makers, and workstation manufacturers such as Sun Microsystems and NeXt, Inc.

All of this gave the firm certain strengths and weaknesses at retail, in the plant, in R&D, in financing, in its worldwide sales force and distribution structure, its Macintosh trademark, and so on.

To apply the ideas from Chapter 3, especially the product innovation charter, see if you can define two specific strengths that would have made a good PIC focus. One should be in technology, and one in market. Given that focus, try to spell out the rest of the PIC, including goals and objectives and guidelines.

Your PIC, of course, would be only one of perhaps several score that Apple would have had at any one time, so clearly differentiate it from the others.

Part II

The Ideation Stage

Chapter 4

Concept Generation: Goals, Process, and People

SETTING

Chapter 2 stated that the various steps in the product innovation process are rarely sequential, identifiable, or unique. Proof begins to unfold in this chapter, because ideation is not simply a stage that takes place after strategy is determined and before evaluation begins. Ideation goes on constantly, and some of the strategic analysis is actually ideation—for example, dreaming up a new way of segmenting a market to spot a group of people with a unique need. And, ideation certainly goes on after evaluation begins, if no more than changing the concept to overcome an objection.

Following a brief review of the overall process and how ideation fits in, we will spell out what the ideators are trying to find—this thing called *concept*. Many people in this field call it an *idea;* still other people use *concept* and *idea* interchangeably. In this book, the primary term is *concept;* but even here, the term *idea* will sometimes be used.

Next, we will study the process of ideation and see the several options from which an ideator can choose. Finally, we will concentrate on the people who do this creative thinking: what are they like, can we spot them, and how are they best managed?

WHERE CONCEPT GENERATION FITS IN THE PROCESS

Before defining a concept, let's take another look at the overall product innovation process. The process chart described in Chapter 2 shows that strategic planning comes first. The rationale is to seek ideas that are best for the firm. Believing a new type of soup or running shoe is a good new product for Ford Motor Company would take quite a stretch of the imagination. Conversely, as the 1988 movie *Tucker* showed, a person without very deep pockets has no business trying to develop a new car.

Ideally, then, ideation should follow the strategic analysis that involves seeking underutilized resources, new resources, external mandates, and internal mandates. These are all opportunities, and ideating on them ensures that the concepts so generated will be useful and potentially profitable.

Of course, as revealed in the process chart, some *non*strategic ideation usually occurs (for example, a product manager spots a way to change a current product and make it more useful).

Once an idea appears, it enters evaluation. The overall process chart indicates what is involved in the evaluation stage. It is the subject of Part III.

THE CONCEPT

At this point, we need some definitions. Commonly heard statements include "I'm trying to think up a new product" or "Let's do some brainstorming and see what new products we can come up with." The fact is, a new product doesn't even come into existence until it is successful in meeting whatever objectives (sales, profit, market share, and so on) were set for it. Prior to that time, it is only a hopeful product, a proposed product, or (in our language) a concept. What is thought up first is a far cry from what is later marketed, and what we market is, unfortunately, often a far cry from what we eventually succeed in selling.

The Sequence

Recall from Chapter 2 that a new product is actually an evolving thing, that it goes from opportunity to concept to tested concept to protocol to prototype concept to specifications to pilot product concept to production product concept to marketed concept to successful new product. From the third step to the last, the effort is concept *fulfillment* — actually accomplishing what was visualized throughout the process. Rarely, if ever, does the final product match the original concept, and most of the difficulties stem from having to make adjustments.

Benefit plus Either Form or Technology

Figure 4–1 helps clear up this fulfillment aspect. Recall that we talked about merging technology and market, and we provided focus on a PIC by seeking at least one technology dimension and at least one market definition.

FIGURE 4–1   The New Product Concept

Form ⟋Technology
 ↘ Attribute(s) + Benefit(s) = Product concept

Complete concepts:
  Slager beer: A new brewing technique brings a completely different enjoy-
   ment to beer. (This is technology plus benefit, with form unstated.)
  Slager beer: A double-strength beer that recaptures the taste enjoyment of
   the 1800s. (This is form plus benefit, with technology unstated.)
Incomplete concepts (cannot be evaluated):
  Slager beer: A beer that tastes good. (Benefit only.)
  Slager beer: A beer that is darker than other beers. (Form only.)
  Slager beer: A beer made by a totally new process. (Technology only.)

The market aspect is based on need or benefit. People with no teeth need more comfortable and aesthetic chewing devices. You will see in a moment that the first step in the best ideation approach (problem analysis) calls for interviewing target market participants to learn what, if any, important unmet needs or difficulties they have.

Therefore, a product concept (the first one) must have a clear statement of benefit. There is no market drive if there is no benefit worth seeking.

The technology side, however, is a bit more difficult. The original concept, if it is to do its job at that stage, must also have something from the technical drive—in most cases, either a product form or a technology. For example, in Figure 4–1, a new beer concept might be "a double-strength beer that recaptures the taste enjoyment of the 1800s." The market need or benefit is old-time taste enjoyment. The technical side is double-strength beer. This is *form*. No one knows yet how we're going to produce such a beer, but we can visualize it, and so can the customers whose reactions we seek.

The beer concept might have been "recapture the old-time taste of beer by using sonic technology." We have no idea yet what the beer will look like, but we have focused on the technology.

Figure 4–1 contains statements that are not product concepts. Simply stating the idea of a better-tasting beer (without either specific form or technology) tells nothing. Might as well say the idea is "A product that can cure cancer." These are opportunities, not concepts. How are you going to make the beer taste better? How are you going to cure cancer?

The Bubble Gum Example.   Because it's easy to get confused about this idea of "benefit plus either form or technology," let's look at a specific example: soft bubble gum. Many years ago, bubble gum was sold in small chunks, rolls, or sheets. The gum was quite hard and difficult to soften enough so that bubbles could be blown. Let's imagine we worked at a bubble gum company in those years. Imagine also three different people walked into the new product office one week, each with an "idea" for a new product. One person said, "Our most recent survey showed that consumers would like a bubble gum that doesn't take five minutes to soften up" (a benefit). A second person came by to say, "I have just finished an attribute analysis of bubble gums and noted that the texture of bubble gum could be changed from hard to flexible" (form). Still a third person announced, "I have just returned from a scientific meeting where I heard discussion of a new chemical that keeps foods from drying out; maybe it would be useful in our business" (technology).

None of those people had a product concept yet. Each had part of one—the first person had that cancer cure mentioned above. The second didn't know if consumers wanted a soft texture or how it could be made. The third didn't know what the technology would do to traditional bubble gum or whether consumers would want it.

A new product concept would result if the first person met up with either the second or the third. If the second, they would ask the lab for a technology that would produce the sought form and benefit. If the third, they would undertake lab work to find the exact form of the new technology (for example, how soft). Of course, if all three met at the same time, the development period would be shortened greatly, but this doesn't happen very often.

Getting a Testable Concept

Knowing benefit and either form or technology permits us to talk to potential buyers. They can visualize enough about the new product to see its drawbacks, in addition to telling us whether it fulfills their need.

Proposing a "no-calorie beer" is not researchable. Asking for beer drinkers' opinions about this "idea" will only result in questions about how we intend to accomplish it. If we ask taxi company owners whether they would like a cab with a 10-cents-per-mile operating cost, their answers would be quite positive; but if we clarify that the cabs would use the technology of a Caterpillar tractor, their responses would change.

Several years ago in a Du Pont laboratory, Stephanie Kwolek developed a superstrength fiber (later named Kevlar). Her fantastic, well-rewarded accomplishment was a "product" that Du Pont sold, but it was not a product concept. For all the manufacturers who might use it in their products, Kevlar was just a technology. Du Pont had to find some uses for it.

Semantics are not perfect, and this benefit-form-technology distinction sometimes collapses. But keep in mind that we need to know enough about the idea to ask consumers and technologists for their reactions. Until that time, we do not have a concept.

The Task of Concept Fulfillment

Once the concept has passed its early tests, technical work begins—to find either a technology giving the desired form or attributes yielding the desired benefit.

Skipping Some of the Stages

Even though most new products come from the 10-step sequence discussed above (opportunity to successful product), they can originate at any of the points. For example, an inventor walks in the door with a "product," in physical form, even fully tested in the marketplace. The firm is thus ready for step seven. Or, a successful, marketed product is reached directly via acquisition. Or, a bootlegging scientist, after working nights and weekends, pops out of R&D with a "product" in hand. It is a prototype concept, ready for testing.

And, incidentally, we reiterate a lot. Loops abound. When we fail to produce a prototype, we may have to alter the original concept. Or, if the prototype fails the use tests, we may have to go back to the lab.

THE PROCESS OF IDEATION

Figure 4–2 shows the ideation stage of the overall process. Understanding what happens during this phase helps make sense of the material in the next three chapters.[1]

First, much of the ideation comes out of the strategic planning activity. It's not always as formal as the diagram implies, however. For example, a manager may talk about a really great idea dreamed up on a recent trip. Further discussion reveals that the manager had been concerned about a falling market share in the South, so he had taken a trip through that

---

[1] What follows is a classification of the many techniques for getting new product ideas. Other classifications and lists are available for those who want more than what is contained in Chapters 5, 6, and 7 and Appendix B. One such source is A. B. VanGundy, *108 Ways to Get a Bright New Idea and Increase Your Creative Potential* (Englewood Cliffs, N.J.: Prentice-Hall, 1983). Another is Trevor Sowrey, *The Generation of Ideas for New Products* (London: Kogan Page, 1987).

FIGURE 4–2   The Ideation Stage of the Product Innovation Process

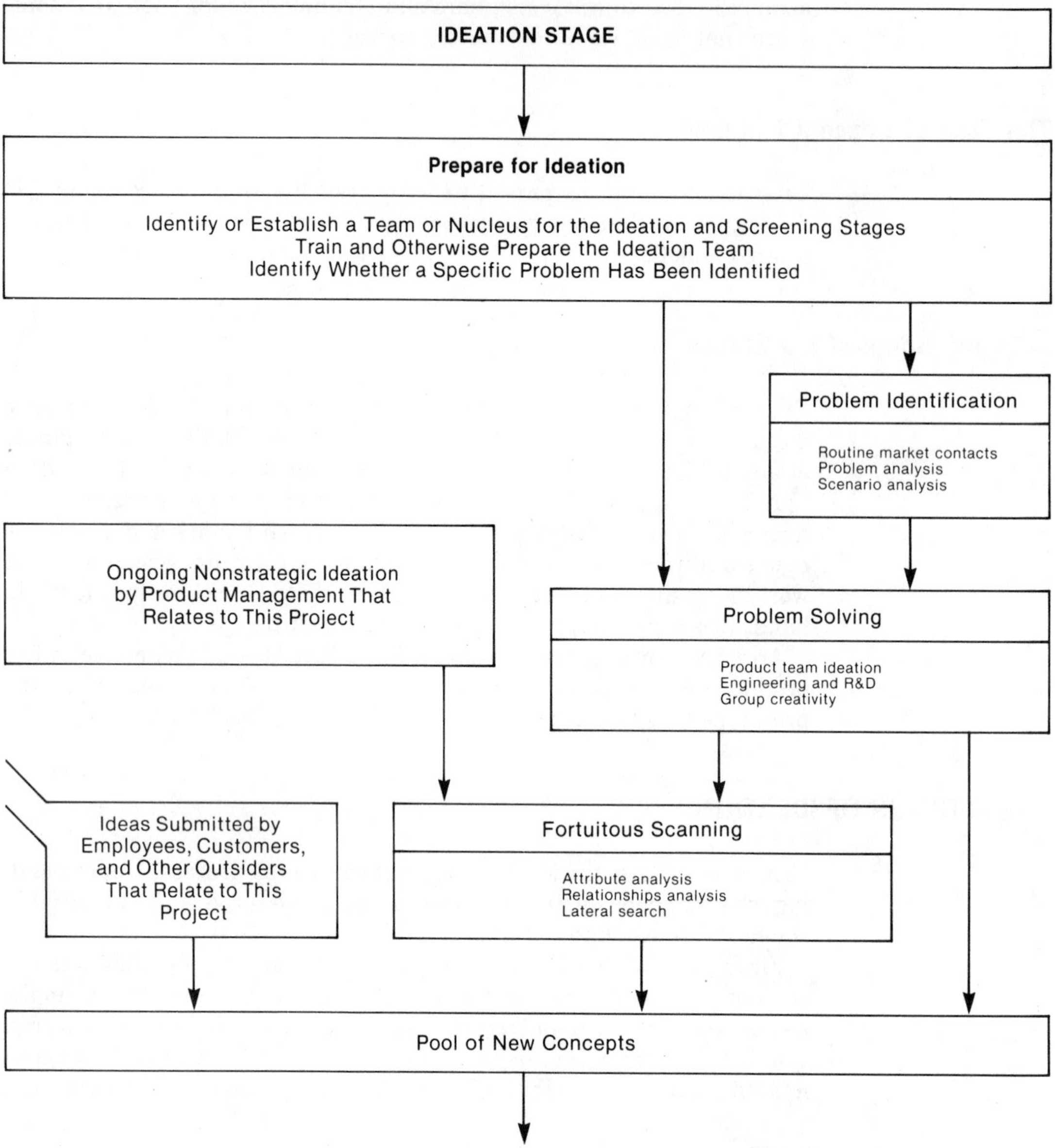

area last month to talk to dealers and customers firsthand. The ideation
that took place on the more recent trip was actually a serious mental
attempt to solve a key problem brought out in those interviews.

In new products language, the manager was doing ongoing marketing planning and landed on an external mandate. The mandate received special study, some problems were identified, and the manager then decided the situation was important, realized something should be done (a PIC existed), figured out the real problem in that situation, and solved the problem by coming up with the new product concept, which would now be screened.

In the language of Figure 4–2, this manager, with a new competitive action, came down through external mandate, into finding new ways to address it, into problem identification and then problem solving, and finally out with a concept for screening.

But, this route may vary. For example, the manager may not have found a ready solution to the problem using customary problem-solving tools. So, he used what we call *fortuitous scanning tools*. These powerful techniques are not problem oriented per se; but, they produce scores or hundreds of ideas, and in those ideas, managers often find solutions to their problems. This route is shown in Figure 4–2 where activity goes from problem solving (unsuccessful) into fortuitous scanning.

Nonstrategic Ideation

Three other routes are, unfortunately, used a great deal. The first two are called *nonstrategic ideation* in Figure 4–2. Coming in on the left and bypassing the strategic planning stage, one route makes use of the fortuitous scan techniques and the other doesn't. For instance, an engineer studying a firm's stapler (using a technique called *attribute analysis,* though unaware of it) notes that staplers are all metal or plastic; why not make the tops out of a soft rubber for comfort and safety? In an unrelated activity, the stapler product manager draws a "map" of the market (plots each product in relation to the others) and finds a hole in the market — no staplers are tiny and designed specifically for the advertising market. Voilà!

This nonstrategic planning route is easy, fun, and often creative. Several fortuitous scan techniques were specifically developed to force divergent thinking, and they do. However, bypassing the marketplace usually leads to ideas that no one wants. Bypassing the product innovation charter leads to concepts that are not appropriate for the firm (skills, money, and so on). Some people say this often results in solutions running around looking for a problem. And, if the solution happens to come from a powerful person in the firm, there will be a problem found.

The second way managers and other team members skip the problem identification step is the pure technology-driven concept. Sometimes this is serendipitous, as when a spilled chemical gave 3M Scotchguard. Other times, the ideas come from deliberate scientific investigation; for example, a scientist comes up with a way to imbed electrical conductor material in a sheet of adhesive tape. Whether basic research or serendipity, the scientist is usually working with at least a general problem in mind. The pharmaceutical chemist who discovers a new chemical to lower blood pressure knows full well that a blood pressure problem exists. So does the person who authorized the laboratory work.

The fact is, scientists rarely discover a new product "out of the blue." Thomas A. Edison said when Congress turned down his idea for a device that would electrically tabulate votes taken during sessions: "There and then I made a vow that I would never again invent anything that was not wanted." The point is, he said *wanted,* not *needed.* Although we usually use the term *need,* it assumes the potential user can be made aware of the need (which Congress couldn't be) and convinced that the proposed solution is a good one. This is easier to do if users are consulted prior to ideation.

The third route around strategic planning and problem solving is the gathering of ideas already created, and this route warrants some thought.

Gathering Ideas Already Created

Some managers opt not to use the more expensive and time-consuming proactive methods of ideation. They choose, instead, to contact persons who may already have interesting new product ideas. Figure 4–3 shows that in one study, some 40 percent of new product ideas came at least partially from suppliers, users, and published information.

Gathering ideas already created should not be viewed as an alternative to seeking them yourself. Some firms do essentially no ideation, but they are rare. The typical pattern is to do both; for example, Pillsbury uses its annual Bake-Off Contest to supplement the vigorous ideation going on in the firm. Of course, some leading food companies get so many ideas from consumers that they have to refuse them all. And, legal problems may arise with ideas created outside the firm, as we will see in Chapter 7.

Consumers gave General Foods the idea for more-compact cereal boxes, which fit better on cabinet shelves. Kimberly-Clark got the idea for Man-Size Kleenex from its combination panel/focus group. American Home Foods got the suggestion for a frozen veal parmigiana from consumers. Many industrial firms have evolved ways (seminars, visits to customers' plants, and so on) to more systematically involve user groups because these groups have been so productive. ARCO actually ran full-page *Wall Street Journal* ads that reproduced good suggestions sent in by the public and encouraged more.

Appendix A lists and discusses the most common sources of ideas already created. They are many, diverse, and of varying quality.

FIGURE 4–3   Sources of New Product Ideas

	Industrial	*Consumer*
Insiders		
Internal other	36%	32%
Analysis of competitors	27	38
Internal R&D	24	14
Total	58%	57%
Outsiders		
Users	26%	30%
Suppliers	13	4
Published information	8	11
Total	47%	45%

Conclusion: Industrial firms rely more on internal and upstream sources, while consumer firms rely more on downstream sources.

Note: Some ideas originated from more than one source, so the percentages total over 100.

Source: Leigh Lawton and A. Parasuraman, "So You Want Your New Product Planning to Be Productive," *Business Horizons*, December 1980, p. 31.

However, one of those sources deserves special attention — the customer, consumer, user. People who use a product would have ideas for improving it, but unfortunately, their ideas are usually common and rather obvious. Black & Decker reportedly received over a thousand suggestions for a new product that would be a Dust-Buster type bug catcher.

Even if new, consumer users' ideas are usually for product improvements, not significant line extensions or new-to-the-world products. In some industries, however, the end user plays quite a different role.[2] For example, manufacturers of scientific instruments and plant process equipment report the majority of their successful new products came originally from customers. (In contrast, manufacturers of engineering polymers and of chemical additives for plastics report no projects coming from customers.)

Customers and users tend to play more of a key role in industries where individuals can tinker around with equipment and actually prototype new pieces in their places of business. For example, dentists and medical technicians develop many new product concepts.

---

[2] The best summary of findings and recommendations in this area can be found in Eric von Hippel, *The Sources of Innovation* (New York: Oxford University Press, 1988). Research in this area clearly shows how much industries vary; some find users absolutely invaluable, while others never find specific new product concepts, let alone prototypes.

The latest development in use-oriented ideation involves identifying the *lead* users associated with a significant current trend (for example, fiber optics in telecommunications). These firms (or individuals) are at the leading edge of the trend, have the best understanding of the problems faced, and expect to gain significantly from solutions to those problems. Although usually fairly easy to identify, they may also be outlanders, or not established members of that trade. And, if they are really leaders, they may think they have already solved their problems. But in an evolving trend, their solutions will not hold up; product developers can work with them to anticipate their next problem.[3]

CREATIVE PEOPLE AND THEIR MANAGEMENT

Organizations known for their innovative product programs are also known for being staffed with highly creative people and for managing those people so as to maximize their creativity. Deciding which people are the creative ones, however, is not easy. Psychologists' theories help but are not the real test. Probably more important than their selection is their management—environment, motivation, and the like.

Creative People: Which Ones Are They?

Being creative means having a capacity for frequently generating ideas with a high degree of usefulness. Mental patients frequently have ideas, but these ideas are not very useful in the new product sense. Conversely, the inventor of the Frisbee had a great idea, but it was apparently his only invention. We want people who are "quality prolific."

Psychologists have been trying to discover ways to identify such persons for most of this century. Their many studies have identified a long list of traits associated with creativity, as shown in Figure 4–4. But the items in the list are varied and conflicting. For example, creative people are self-disciplined yet show bohemian unconcern; they are emotional and less inhibited, yet introverted.

The list suggests two different groups of creative people: those with artistic creativity and those with scientific creativity. The new products field needs both, as depicted in Figure 4–5. Inventors (persons with new product creativity) are high in both artistic and scientific cre-

---

[3] Eric von Hippel, "Lead Users: A Source of Novel Product Concepts," *Management Science,* July 1986, pp. 791–805.

FIGURE 4–4　Traits Associated with Creativity

Personality:

Dissatisfied	Less conversational
Self-assertive	Thorough
Little interpersonal	Feminine interests
Constructively critical	Less self-critical
Anxious	Single-minded
Self-disciplined	Broad orientation
Emotionally unstable	Perseverant
Shows evangelical zeal	Independent
Nonconformist	Willing to take risks
Unsociable	Impulsive
Paranoid over potential idea loss	Aggressive
Counterconformist	Low in economic values
Dominant	Autonomous
Introverted	Lacks masculine aggressiveness
Shows bohemian unconcern	Loves his or her work

Cognitive:

Analytical	Suspends judgment
Well-stocked mind	Observant
Intuitive	Conceptual fluency
Intense restless curiosity	Likes complexity
Thoughtful	Need for order

Source: Morris I. Stein, *Stimulating Creativity,* vol. 1 (New York: Academic Press, 1974), pp. 58–61; and various other sources published since 1974.

ativity. Engineers without the touch of the artist and artists without scientific strength are, perhaps, less successful in new products ideation.

Note we are discussing traits, not jobs. A marketing person may well be an artist, a scientist, or a combination; creativity may (and often does) appear anywhere in an organization. But the inventive talent, if psychological studies are correct, utilizes both artistic and scientific traits.

Dr. Bryant Tiep (former director of Prescott College, the unique school of technological innovation in Prescott, Arizona) frequently pointed out that the good inventor was a mix of artist and mechanic. Dr. James Adams, acclaimed innovation educator at Stanford University, taught a course combining art and engineering. And the field of industrial design is so closely a merger of art and engineering that controversy exists over which school in a university should house it. The inventor is not inconsistent if sensitive and analytical, intuitive and observant, impulse-sensitive and persevering.

FIGURE 4–5   The Three Forms of Human Creativity

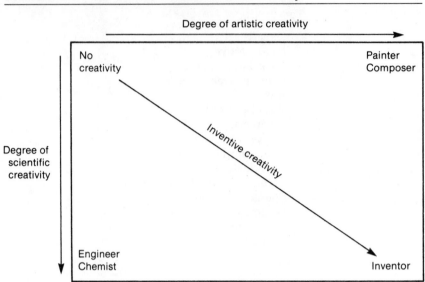

Oddly, creativity does not correlate with general education or intelligence. Past an IQ level of around 120, intelligence does not appear to enhance creativity.

Some great creative talent has been labeled eccentric. For example:

Schiller kept rotten apples in his desk; Shelley and Rousseau remained bareheaded in the sunshine; Bossuet worked in a cold room with his head wrapped in furs; Milton, Descartes, Leibniz, and Rossini lay stretched out; Tycho Brahe and Leibniz secluded themselves for very long periods; Thoreau built his hermitage, Proust worked in a cork-lined room, Carlyle in a noise-proof chamber, and Balzac wore a monkish working garb; Grety and Schiller immersed their feet in ice-cold water; Guido Reni could paint and de Musset could write poetry only when dressed in magnificent style; Mozart, following exercise; Lamennais, in a room of shadowy darkness; and D'Annunzio, Farnol, and Frost, only at night.[4]

Most creative persons are not eccentric, but they do announce themselves by leaving a lifetime trail of creative accomplishments.[5] They are creative in their early years and never become uncreative. A longtime chief executive of Procter & Gamble used to ask applicants, "Have you

---

[4] H. B. Levey, "A Theory Concerning Free Creation in the Inventive Arts," *Psychiatry* no. 3 (1940), pp. 280–91.

[5] A great deal of research supports this statement about lifetime trails; but, like everything in the area of creativity, there are exceptions!

ever invented anything?'' People without that lifetime trail usually blame unfamiliar environments, overpowering bosses, limited opportunities, and the like.

How to Manage the Creative Function

Education cannot make a person creative, but giving creative people a good environment and management can markedly enhance their creative output. Figure 4–6 shows how genetic barriers prevent people from changing their creative potential.

Roadblocks. Management is responsible for creating situations where creative people can throttle up to high output. They can, and they want to, but many managements won't let them. Figure 4–7 compiles well-known roadblocks to creativity; most can be relieved by smart management.

Some roadblocks are less obvious and, perhaps, more insidious:

The dummy task force: Seemingly directed to innovation but—carefully—without concrete goals or a time schedule; often staffed with people known not to be wave makers.

The task force as a setup: Hatched when the executive already has a new new product idea and wants a task force to find the right problem for it.

Rock-hard controls: Those 14 approvals that the initiative requires.

FIGURE 4–6   Creative Performance as a Two-Factor Consequence

Effect of Environment	*Amount of Creative Potential*		
	None	*Some*	*Great*
Negative	No creative performance	Low creative performance	Some creative performance
Positive	No creative performance	Some creative performance	Very high creative performance

Barriers

Comment: The environment (including management) can markedly increase an individual's creative performance but only within the limits of the individual's basic creative potential.

The no-special-treatment reflex: Asking for entrepreneurship, risk taking, and unrelenting pursuit of the dream, but all within the current compensation system, of course.[6]

Synectics, Inc., a leading creativity training organization in Cambridge, Massachusetts, has a key element called *itemized response.* All trainees must practice it personally. When an idea comes up, listeners must first cite all of its advantages. Then they can address the negatives, but only in a positive mode. The recommended language is "OK. Now

---

FIGURE 4–7   Roadblocks to Creativity in the Generation of New Product Concepts

Roadblock statements
1. "It simply won't work."
2. "Are you sure of that?"
3. "Don't be ridiculous" or "You can't be serious."
4. "It's against our policy."
5. "Let's shelve it for the time being."
6. "That won't work in our market."
7. "Let's think about that some more."
8. The nonstatement: Sneer, shrug, lifted eyebrow, silence.

Cultural roadblocks
1. Too much faith in reason and logic.
2. Desire for the safety of the known or the familiar.
3. Desire for conformity to adopted patterns or to belong.
4. Belief that indulging in fantasy is a waste of time.
5. Desire to be practical and economical.

Emotional roadblocks
1. Fear of making mistakes, of ridicule, of looking foolish.
2. Fear or distrust of supervisors.
3. Fear of the risks of pioneering.
4. Strong desire for security.
5. The inflexibility of a closed mind, of strong opinion.
6. A general negativism toward things or people.
7. Overconfidence in one's own judgment.
8. No sense of humor.

Perceptual roadblocks
1. Difficulty in isolating the real problem.
2. Failure to use all the senses of observation.
3. Difficulty in seeing remote relationships.
4. Failure to distinguish between cause and effect.

---

[6] Walter Kiechel III, "The Politics of Innovation," *Fortune,* April 11, 1988, pp. 131–32.

let's see what would be the best way to overcome such-and-such a problem." Note that this constructive comment assumes the problem can be overcome. Itemized response replaces the negative blast that so often follows ideation.

A book entitled *Failure of Success* has a section presenting the most famous rejections of all time, one of which was by a journal editor to rocket pioneer Robert Goddard: "The speculation . . . is interesting, but the impossibility of ever doing it is so certain that it is not practically useful." And 18 months before the Wright brothers flew their first plane, an eminent astronomer said, "Flight by machines heavier than air is unpractical and insignificant, if not utterly impossible."[7]

Management Styles.   Research has disclosed three alternative styles of managing new product operations.[8] Here they are, along with their attributes:

Entrepreneurial

Autonomous	Reports higher up
Entrepreneurial people	Top-management support
Incentives for risk taking	Little formal planning

Collegial

Clear functional commitments	Strong senior management
Strong management support	participation
for risk taking	Formal process to follow

Managerial

Hierarchical	Strong top–down direction
Functions are stressed	Business planning orientation
Inflexible formal processes	Formal financial criteria

The entrepreneurial management style is by far the most conducive to creativity, though Chapter 19 points out that entrepreneurial is not without difficulties. All three styles are good, given appropriate strategies (for example, managerial is fine for near line extensions involving almost no risk). But such dimensions as formal processes, top–down direction, business planning, and formal criteria are the bane of creative types.

Generally, we look for other constructive dimensions too — nondirective management, participatory decision-making style, an environment in which idea generators are not monitored too closely, and higher management's willingness to share in the riskiness of creativity.

---

[7] Alfred J. Marrow, ed., *The Failure of Success* (New York: AMACOM, 1972), pp. 76–93. This section is subheaded "Rejection" and offers many examples.

[8] *New Products Management for the 1980s* (Chicago: Booz Allen & Hamilton, 1982), p. 19.

Telling people it is OK to fail is easy, but getting them to believe it is tough. John Cleese of "Monty Python" fame is now a training consultant for industry. He jokes, "No more mistakes and you're through!"[9]

Motivation.   Creative people also need personal motivation. Managements do several things to get it. First, they recognize that innovators are apt to be "different" and need special treatment. Innovators can't be allowed to violate rules at will, but managements need to recognize individuality, be tolerant of some aberrations, and be supportive under stress. Apple CEO John Sculley said, "I would worry if there weren't always a little bit of anarchy in the organization. It's like arsenic: A little is medicinal, but a lot can kill you."[10]

Second, managements should allow innovators freedom to associate with others in similar positions. This freedom extends to all functional areas and to outside the firm as well—no locked cells.

Third, management should permit innovators to help select projects for development, though this is often difficult.

Fourth, management should recognize achievement. Creative people are usually unimpressed by group rewards. They believe group contributions are never equal, especially if the group is company employees, for many of whom creatives have great disdain. (On this issue, creatives are unfair; today a large portion of successful creativity is set in groups.) But they do like personal accolades—preferably immediately. The famous Thomas Watson of IBM commonly carried spare cash in his pockets so he could reward persons with good ideas when he heard them. Campbell Soup has Presidential Awards for Excellence. A chemical company manager said, "We are going to make you rich . . . 10 percent of everything that comes in the door."[11]

Fifth, job assignments should be challenging. Creative people don't lack confidence and, in fact, often consider their present assignments a waste of time. This means they will determine whether an assignment is worthy—no one can tell them.

Sometimes, pressure to produce can assist a creative activity, though usually it does not. Some firms deliberately create competitive teams and

---

[9] "No More Mistakes and You're Through," *Forbes,* May 16, 1988, pp. 126–28.

[10] "Sculley's Lessons from Inside Apple," *Fortune,* September 14, 1987, p. 117. This article speaks directly to the matter of managing creative people productively. Another source that contains many experience-based suggestions is Michael K. Badawy, "How to Prevent Creativity Mismanagement," *Research Management,* July–August 1986, pp. 28–35.

[11] Michael G. Dever, *The Commercial Development of New Products* (New York: The Conference Board, 1986), p. 14. Unfortunately, Dever tells of other cases where the threat of job loss was used, effectively, to motivate creative people.

have them race to a deadline. Ford Motor Company's Mustang design came from such competition. Bell & Howell's management once faked the news of an impending competitive breakthrough to urge a scientific group to speed up. Managing the new products creative activity is an extremely difficult and delicate matter often left to the discretion of the individual manager.

Special Techniques.   Managements constantly experiment with new ways to motivate creative people, and this experimentation has produced a bundle of helpful special techniques.

1. *Customer visitations.* Many firms use this highly regarded technique even though it risks disclosure of unfavorable data or experience.
2. *Free time for creative personnel.* Though free time is usually associated with R&D personnel, free time for creatives runs as high as 20 percent in several departments. The 3M Company is a major follower of this technique, and another example was the Aziza case in Chapter 2.
3. *Piece of the action.* Much more controversial is the question of whether employers should reward employee idea generators with more than symbolic dollar prizes. Although most firms vociferously oppose major cash rewards or royalty payments for employee inventors, some firms have used these devices successfully. The practice is more common in Europe than in the United States, and there is occasional government pressure to recognize some actual "right" of employees to their inventions. Moreover, employee views are changing; and although inventor "equity" systems may create more dissension and unfairness than benefits, practices will probably change.
4. *Contests.* Though used occasionally, contests have a rather high cost and do not produce appreciable, lasting benefits.
5. *Flexibility in hours.* This is not flextime but rather such extreme flexibility as letting employees take work home or work evenings whenever they wish. Although such flexibility is difficult in some settings, marketing departments' experiences with this approach have been strongly favorable.
6. *Transferring creative personnel.* The transfer opportunity is sometimes offered because the highly creative person seems to be most useful when he or she is a relative newcomer to a project or area. Creative people have a "need for novelty" and prefer to change situations occasionally.[12]

---

[12] Donald C. Peltz and Frank M. Andrews, Scientists in Organizations (Ann Arbor: University of Michigan Institute for Social Research, 1976).

7. *An idea collection point.* Some firms use an idea solicitator – an employee who circulates around the firm and picks up ideas that have not gotten into the system. Others use a posted source (person or number) to which ideas can be routed.

8. *Training in creativity.* The continued commercial and noncommercial success of various creativity centers amply demonstrates industry's belief that creativity can be substantially enhanced by training. However, the few well-known centers (Synectics, Inc.; University of Buffalo; and University of North Carolina) with firm track records should not be confused with a seemingly endless stream of individuals and new firms claiming expertise in this area.

9. *Special funding.* This rare approach is exemplified by the Texas Instruments IDEA (identify, develop, expose, and action) program.[13] Sixty IDEA representatives throughout TI can dole out funds (without higher approval) for projects proposed by personnel who do not have enough influence to get funds through normal channels. Speak & Spell and Magic Wand are two notable recipients of such funds.

10. *A technical forum.* The 3M Company integrates more than two dozen employee chapters and committees to provide almost continuous dialogue among technical innovators throughout the company. The company's chairman said, "We do expect mistakes as a normal part of running a business, but we expect our mistakes to have originality."[14]

11. *Tolerance of tinkerers.* 3M also has a tolerance of tinkerers and offers this proof:

> Another young lab worker was experimenting with tiny glass beads, more a novelty than a product. He was told to get back to his regular work. And he did. But, fortunately, because he was a bachelor, he could return to his lab and his pet bead project after normal working hours. This he did, and many nights he burned the midnight candle. Today those tiny beads are on reflective road bridges and bridge safety signs all over the world. Just a few years ago, no longer a bachelor, he took his wife to an Academy Awards presentation where he received an Oscar for a bead-based front screen projection system for moviemakers.[15]

Physical Environment.   In general, creative operations should be in areas conducive to exchange of ideas, office arrangements should make people comfortable, and distractions should be held to a minimum.

---

[13] Lawrence Ingrassia, "There's No Way to Tell If a New Food Product Will Please the Public," *The Wall Street Journal,* February 26, 1980, p. 1.

[14] L. W. Lehr, "The Role of Top Management," *Research Management,* November 1979, pp. 23–25.

[15] Ibid., p. 24.

SUMMARY

Chapter 4 introduced concept generation for new products. First we looked to see where ideation fits into the overall product innovation process (from Chapter 2), and then we explored the idea of concept. This exploration included what a new product concept is, the stages it goes through, and how to prepare for testing it with intended users. Following that came the actual process of ideation, both the strategic form and the nonstrategic form (fortuitous scan methods), and the approach of gathering already-created ideas from persons around the firm or outside it. Creating ideas firsthand requires creative people. Fortunately, creative types are fairly easy to spot—they have been creative all their lives. But management can either stimulate their creative activity or stunt it, and we looked at styles, environments, and techniques that firms have found useful in this area.

Given an understanding of the creative process, the people, and their management, we can now turn to the specific techniques people use in this activity. These techniques are discussed in Chapter 5, Chapter 6, and part of Chapter 7.

APPLICATIONS

More questions from that interview with a company president:

1. "Competitive espionage is something I have always been leery of. Most of it is probably illegal, yet I know there is quite a bit of it in several of our industries. I even read recently where some chap in Australia is what some call a professional espionage agent. He employs a network of stewards and air hostesses to gather tidbits of information overheard in the first-class compartments of international flights. Sells this information for over a million dollars a year! I wonder what suggestions I should put in a memo for employees to minimize the chances that key new product information will be stolen by competitors."

2. "In these days of intensive ideation, it sure surprised me to read that a man named Reuben Ware, a retired furniture upholstery restorer in Savannah, Georgia, had to reactivate a successful business he had shut down—producing and selling a special formulation of carpet shampoo. Seems that he had invented a formulation that removed almost anything (blood, lipstick, doggie stains, whatever) from your carpets, your laundry, or even your windshield. Sold it for a while, then dropped it. People clamored for it, so Rich's department store has bankrolled him for more product. He's quite a jokester; he even wrote a popular song about former

governor Lester Maddox getting caught in a speed trap, and he says he chose the product's name, Aunt Grace's, because he was paying his trademark attorney by the hour, so he accepted the first name that got through. When people ask him about his not being a chemist, he answers, 'Was Edison an electrician?' Seriously, how in the world, in these days of expensive R&D laboratories, could someone out there come up with a formulation that seems to be better than anything industry can come up with? And after first marketing his formulation in 1965, how was he able to keep his lead?"

3. "In-house inventors are tough to deal with. Right now we have this Ph.D. in physics, a really great person, bright as they come, and terribly creative. Has had no less than 11 ideas go to market since she joined the firm four years ago. But she feels we don't reward her properly, even though she is on a good salary, shares an annual bonus with all the other persons in research, and even got a special bonus of $5,000 last year. Frankly, I think she will leave us if I don't find some way to let her have an equity position in some of her ideas. What do you think of her argument, and how might I arrange something if I wanted to?"

4. "We've got a shoe division that is supposedly trying to be creative and innovative, but they haven't had a good new idea in years. I've got my eye on a good consultant to go in there and review their environment, their motivating systems, and so on, but first I want to know if they have creative people. How could I find that out?"

Case: The Kids Wise Up*

Here are some sad tales from 1989:

- Educational toy chain Enchanted Village carried chemistry sets, computers, and the like — and went out of business after five years.
- Video Technology, Inc., marketed a new educational video system called Socrates. But after lackluster sales, the firm turned to noneducational toys to increase its business.
- Chemistry and biology sets in 1988 were down 27 percent from 1987.
- The Master Scientist and Monster Lab series was discontinued by Mattel early in 1989.

---

* Source: Based partly on Joseph Periera, "Educational Toys Receive a Failing Grade as Kids Wise Up to Their Parents' Game," *The Wall Street Journal,* April 11, 1989, p. B1.

• Talking Toby, a 10-pound plastic robot that Coleco created to play word games with eight-year-olds, was withdrawn from the market after a year.

What was going on? Some people thought the educational toy market had hit its peak and was a typical mature market. A stock market analyst said calling a toy "educational" was the kiss of death. The term *edutainment* was dead. Enthusiastic parents who liked to flash cards in front of crib children had apparently slacked off, or gone to other devices. The demise of specialty retailers like Enchanted Village resulted.

Marketing research showed that about two thirds of educational toy sales came from electronic toys and building sets. Staple lines (such as puzzles, word games, and flash cards) made up the rest.

Some of the reasons were thought to be known: some educators had been less than enthusiastic, the developers had sometimes created confusion about what exactly their products were, and child development experts sometimes told parents to just let their children play. Worst of all, perhaps, the basic idea—parents should use toys to con their children into more school when they thought they were playing—hadn't worked. The kids caught on fast. And, of course, many of these edutainment toys were not entertaining. Toby, for example, was a one-trick robot.

Not all educational toy producers were willing to throw in the towel. Video Technology was focusing its attention on preschoolers, and others were tying toys that actually were more fun to educational characters like Big Bird and Cookie Monster. The founder of Enchanted Village was about to open a new chain of mom-and-pop stores in academically oriented neighborhoods.

Some toy makers felt the problem was that they hit a really good idea only rarely; when they did, sales were fine, and even the 1988 market share of 5 percent yielded sales of around $750 million for all educational toys. So, one issue seemed to be how they should go about getting new product concepts.

They knew they got hundreds of ideas each year, with no end of inventors in garages and basements around the world. Maybe these ideas should have been studied more carefully. Too, they knew their own staffs had literally thousands of ideas, generated from spending their time making and selling the current lines.

But these approaches had always been available, and as one said, "Look where we are!" One toy developer said she wanted to get into a new dimension of creativity—something that would produce toys that were genuinely fun, so much fun that kids would want to play with them as such. Yet these toys would be almost secretly educational. But how to do *that,* she didn't know.

Concept Generation: The Problem/Solution Route

SETTING

Chapter 4 gave us the structure for new product ideation. After management selects appropriate strategic arenas in which to seek ideas, and after intense study of those arenas, ideation proceeds through several tracks, one of which is called the *problem/solution route.*

Problem/solution is a rational, market-based approach, while fortuitous scan is based on the product improvement model — altering what is available in some novel way. As shown in the overall product innovation process chart in Figure 2–1, the problem/solution method can also utilize fortuitous scan if other problem-solving methods won't do the job.

Chapter 5 looks at the many special techniques that help in the problem/solution process, while Chapters 6 and 7 cover those for fortuitous scan. There are too many of these techniques to cover them all in Chapters 5 through 7. Instead, the best will be presented in enough detail to make them useful, while the less important ones are given in Appendix B. Those in Appendix B are not bad techniques but, rather, the specialized inventions of individuals who found them effective. Most are for special situations or are slight modifications of the major ones.

REVIEW

A couple things should be kept in mind. One, we are looking for concepts — or ideas that lead to concepts. A *concept* is defined as a *benefit* for which we have either a *form* or a *technology* that promises to yield the benefit. Thus benefits, forms, and technologies all offer routes to ideation.

For example, Eddy Goldfarb, a famous toy inventor, was asked how he did it. He replied, "Notice what things your child plays with, and try to spot what's lacking."[1] He also said he likes to look for new processes and materials and "for holes—you know, a lack of a certain item on the market." These statements cite need, technology, and form, in that order.

Second, the importance of these three dimensions varies by industry. In most industries, one of the three often needs no attention because of general knowledge within the industry. Pharmaceutical new products people do not have to check out the desirability of reducing blood pressure, or of stopping body fluid buildup, or of eliminating cancer. Furthermore, pharmaceutical expertise is available to "package," or form, virtually any new drug, so technology is the only unknown and thus the focus of attention.

The leading food companies presume the kitchens and factory can put together anything the customer wants, so benefit (ascertained through taste tests, for example) becomes the prime variable.

In the automobile industry, car manufacturers so dominate the new products process that components suppliers are told what benefit is wanted and then work with either technology or form for its innovation.

In all three cases, discussion with new products people quickly indicates the critical avenue of innovation for their firm or industry. And the distinctions are not moot—they provide the direction for the idea stimulation process.

Third, in Chapter 3 we discussed the idea of market-driven firms versus technology-driven firms. The distinction oversimplifies the three-part benefit-technology-form position presented above. People with a functional or departmental position speak of R&D versus marketing as sources for new product ideas. In this view, benefits are presumably marketing sourced and attributes are R&D sourced. Although others talk about "supply-pushed innovation" and "demand-induced innovation," the distinction is essentially departmental. Demand-induced innovation is usually on some minor line of technology, so scientists sometimes call it "micro-invention" and say it has minor impact.

Necessity causes more innovations, but the best innovations come from desire. The most basic technological breakthroughs are discovery based, but most innovation has less value and is need based.[2]

---

[1] Fran Carpentier, "Can You Invent a Toy?" *Parade,* December 1981, pp. 14–15.

[2] Several of the better studies of innovation sources are S. Globe, G. W. Levy, and C. M. Schwartz, "Key Factors in the Innovation Process," *Research Management,* July 1973, pp. 8–15; J. Langrish, M. Gibbons, G. Evans, and J. R. Jerons, *Wealth from Knowledge* (New York: Macmillan, 1972); and S. Myers and D. Marquis, *Successful Industrial Innovations* (Washington, D.C.: U.S. Government Printing Office, 1969).

Ironically, because a concept must have three dimensions, the department on the "wrong" end of the above appellations may make the most critical contribution, and if a project aborts, it may be the fault of the department with the "easy" task. For example, a television manufacturer's marketing research may show that consumers want a television set that will increase in volume as room noise picks up and decrease in volume as room noise subsides. This research is presumably the creative act that engenders the idea for the new product, so the process would be demand induced. But, in reality, the technical side of the business has the toughest task.

A similar situation existed when a small Michigan firm attempted to find markets for a new development in retriculated vitreous carbon. The situation was clearly "product to need," with technology providing the breakthrough; but, again ironically, the pressure was on marketing to find applications to yield adequate volume for a profit. It couldn't, and the firm folded.

One study among Canadian firms found that 44 percent of the key thrust came from market needs (alone or in combination) and that 34 percent of the key thrust was a new technology.[3] Other new products were simply line extensions or complete concepts offered by customers. Another study reported a similar situation among U.S. firms in the chemical, drug, petroleum, and electronics industries — 75 percent of R&D projects were demand induced. Furthermore, technology-pushed projects were costlier, riskier, and less likely to succeed than demand-induced projects.[4]

In practice, however, the process of generating concepts for new products is frequently so iterative that it becomes essentially circular. Thus, for instance, the television manufacturer referred to above might find after considerable technical work that the new automatic volume control cannot be made to *reduce* volume though it can indeed *increase* volume as room noise increases. This limited solution is taken back to the market, where studies show that consumers would accept this contribution if a remote device permitting *manual* lowering of the volume could be added. Back in the lab, scientists report that they can provide such a hand control but ask, "Why not add channel selection?" Back to the market, back to the lab. Which source of new product concepts is more operative in such cases is both unknown and moot, and, for this reason, the need versus product and supply versus demand argument has more academic than managerial value.

---

[3] Blair Little, "New Focus on New Product Ideas," *Business Quarterly*, Summer 1974, pp. 62–68.

[4] Edwin Mansfield, J. Rapoport, J. Schnee, S. Wagner, and M. Hamburger, *Research and Innovation in the Modern Corporation* (New York: W. W. Norton, 1971).

The remainder of this chapter will be devoted to finding problems that market players have and to finding solutions for those problems.

DETERMINING NEEDS AND PROBLEMS

The number one cause of new product failure is that the intended user did not need what the product offered. So, it is logical to begin with need as a source of new product concepts. Three of the many techniques for the needs approach will be discussed here (see Figure 5–1).

Routine Market Contacts

The most common source of needs and problems is an organization's contacts with customers and others in the marketplace. Daily or weekly sales call reports, findings from customer or technical service departments, and tips from resellers are examples. Many people have direct or indirect contact with end users, and all of these contacts should be pumped for leads on what needs are unmet and what problems are being dealt with.

Industrial and household consumers misuse and misunderstand products and erroneously project into their use of products what they are seeking rather than what the products are offering. A complaint file thus

---

FIGURE 5–1 Approaches Used to Discover Unmet Needs and Problems

A. *Routine Market Contacts.*
　　1. Sales call reports.
　　2. Service department records.
　　3. Complaint files.

B. *Problem Analysis.*
　　1. Determine the product or activity category that will be studied.
　　2. Gather a list of user problems.
　　　　a. Expert opinion.
　　　　b. Published sources.
　　　　c. Direct inquiry of heavy users, individually or in focus groups.
　　　　d. User panels.
　　　　e. User observation.
　　　　f. Role playing.
　　3. Score the problems by degree of annoyance and frequency of occurrence.

C. *Scenario Analysis.*
　　1. Scenario-extend.
　　2. Scenario-leap (static and dynamic).

---

becomes a psychological projective technique. One approach to handling use complaints is the hot line or toll-free number. It helps defuse criticism and can lead to new products. P&G claims to get over 200,000 calls per year on its many hot lines. And at least one firm's R&D employees actually work at customer sites to hear their problems firsthand.

Unfortunately, these needs and problems are usually seen in their traditional construct; for example, if a user normally has a particular problem and has had it for years, the problem becomes "part of the wallpaper" and thus forgotten. A fresh approach to user needs is better because we can often see a need that the user doesn't recognize. This leads to the other methods of ideation shown in Figure 5–1.

Problem Analysis

Determining the problems that users associate with various products and activities is the most logical place to begin explorations on possible new products, and it seems that every history of an industry, a business firm, or a famous businessperson cites some key time when a new product or service capitalized on a problem that others didn't sense or appreciate. Studying user problems has become the *most widely used* technique for generating new product ideas.

The approach has been so widely used, in fact, that it almost defies typology. One difficulty is that it is known by various names. For instance, General Electric calls it discrepancy analysis; some call it benefit deficiency or need confrontation; one person jokingly refers to it as developing a bug list. Moreover, the essential idea is often confused by the number of research techniques available to implement it. These techniques will be classified after the basic idea of problem analysis has been explained.

Problem analysis is much more than a simple compilation of user problems. Although the term *problem inventory* is sometimes used to describe this category of techniques, taking the inventory is only the beginning—analysis is the key.

As one executive recently said,

> If you ask people what they want in a new house and also ask them what are their problems with their current house, you will get distinctly different subject matter on each list. If you then observe their subsequent behavior, it becomes clear their problem list is a far better predictor than the want list.[5]

---

[5] Tom Dillon, then chairman of the advertising agency BBD&O, as reported in Claes Fornell and Robert D. Menko, "Problem Analysis—A Consumer-Based Methodology for the Discovery of New Product Ideas," *European Journal of Marketing* 15, no. 5 (1981), pp. 61–72.

This peculiarity occurs because users verbalize their wants in terms of current products, whereas problems are not product specific. Thus, if you ask what a person needs or wants from a shampoo, the answers will be clean hair, manageable hair, and so on—replies reflecting recent promotions of product benefits. But if you ask, "What problems do you have with your hair?" the answers may range into areas (for example, style or color) unrelated to shampoo. Product development can then establish new relationships through new creations. See Figure 5–2 for an example of problem analysis.

The General Procedure. There are several approaches to problem analysis. One is essentially a focus group approach. Another is a quite different method called *benefit structure analysis;* this method is really

---

FIGURE 5–2   Problem Analysis Applied to the Telephone

The telephone is hard to clean.
The telephone is too big.
The cord tangles easily.
The dial can't be seen in the dark.
The other room noises make it difficult to hear.
The style doesn't match the room.
The cord is too short.
Do not like recording messages on answering machines.
The colors are poor.
Hard to find (or remember) telephone numbers.
Waiting for busy lines is inconvenient.
Difficult to move while on the phone.
The phone is too heavy.
The cord is easy to trip on.
Telephone directories are not available for other cities.
The telephone can only be used in the room it's installed in.
Would like to know who called while not at home.
A phone cannot be installed in the garage easily.
Would like to have easy way of providing a second phone line.
Too many nuisance calls.
The receiver is uncomfortable on the ear.
The phone does not have modern styling.
The sound of the bell is unpleasant.
The bell is too loud (or soft).
The phone interrupts other important things.
The conversation (or important information) cannot be recorded.

Note: The problem analysis method yields lists much like those obtained from the attribute analysis weaknesses method. But they are usually much more focused on problems in using the device than on the device per se. The problems are also quite personal, suggesting why heavy users (and thus presumably better analysts) are commonly used.

---

closer to relationships analysis than to problem analysis and will be discussed later. But the best approach is the following:

Step One: Determine the appropriate product or activity category for exploration. This has already been done if the product innovation charter has a use, user, or product category dimension in the focus statement.

Step Two: Identify a group of "heavy" product users or activity participants within that category, because heavy users are apt to have a better understanding of the problems and they represent the bulk of the sales potential in most markets. For example, 20 percent of adult females account for 70 percent of all regular shampoo usage. A variation here is to study *non*users to see if a solvable problem keeps them out of the market.

Step Three: Gather from these heavy users or participants a set of problems associated with the category. This is the inventory phase mentioned earlier, but far more is involved than just asking respondents to list their problems. A good method of doing this is the market or benefit structure study, in which respondents are asked to rate the benefits they want from a set of products and the benefits they are getting. The differences indicate problems.

Step Four: Sort and rank the problems according to their severity or importance. Various methods can be used for this, but the common one shown in Figure 5–3 utilizes (1) the extent of the problem and (2) the frequency of its occurrence. This "bothersomeness" index is then adjusted by users' awareness of currently available solutions to the problem. This step identifies those

---

FIGURE 5–3   The Bothersomeness Technique of Scoring Problems

The following is an abbreviated list of pet owners' problems found by manufacturers of pet products.

	A *Problem Occurs* *Frequently*	*B* *Problem Is* *Bothersome*	*C* *A × B*
Need constant feeding	98%	21%	.21
Get fleas	78	53	.41
Shed hairs	70	46	.32
Make noise	66	25	.17
Have unwanted babies	44	48	.21

Source: Burton H. Marcus and Edward M. Tauber, *Marketing Analysis and Decision Making* (Boston: Little, Brown, 1979), p. 225.

problems that are important to the user and for which the user sees no current solutions.

The information shown in Figure 5–3 indicates why pet manufacturers have worked so hard to come up with flea collars and other devices.

Georgena Terry made a special study of women's bicycle needs and came up with a line of bikes that have shorter tubes to permit easier reaching of handlebars, smaller brake levers and toe clips, and wider seats. An interesting feature of her bikes is a smaller front wheel, which gives better stability.[6]

Another unmet need that had existed for years was the noisy candy wrapper in the theater. Gene Shalit, of NBC's "Today Show," complained one morning about crackling candy bars. An executive at Hercules, Inc., overheard his comment and asked the laboratory for a "silent candy wrapper." Polypropylene provided the answer, though not without tricky effort on heating, waterproofing, and air-proofing.

Problem analysis is especially appropriate for entering foreign markets. For example, bathroom fixture makers completely missed Japanese women's special need for an oversize sink. Because the Japanese typically bathe in the evening, and young women like to wash their hair in the morning, the larger sink marketed in 1988 was very welcome.

Methodologies to Use.   The generalized structure of problem analysis still contains the question of how to gather the list of consumer problems. Many methods have been used.

The first is *expert opinion* — simply canvassing the opinions of persons experienced in the category under study. These experts include sales personnel, retail and wholesale distribution personnel, and professionals who support an industry — architects, doctors, accountants, and the staffs of government bureaus and trade associations. Though quite product oriented, they constitute an inexpensive and easy-to-reach source.

Second, *published sources* are frequently useful — industry studies, the firm's own past studies on allied subjects, government reports, investigations by social critics, scientific studies in universities, and so on.

A third method is to ask *household or industrial consumers directly.* The most popular technique is the focus group, because the focus group is designed to yield the exploratory and depth-probing type of discussion required and is also easy and inexpensive to set up and use.

Although the focus group technique is common, the outcome is not always, or even usually, successful. Many product planners have been misled by the seeming simplicity of this research. There are several

---

[6] Mary Guterson, "A Bicycle Built for Women," *Venture,* April 1987, p. 15.

key difficulties. One is that the consumer/user often does not perceive problems well enough to verbalize them. Second, if the problems are known, the user may not agree to verbalize them. Much of the sophistication in newer technologies was developed specifically to deal with these problems. For example, several of the newer technologies, including factor analysis and trade-off analysis (conjoint measurement), don't require the user to be articulate on precise attributes. This will be discussed in the section on gap analysis.

The focus group is a qualitative research technique. Unlike the traditional survey, it depends on in-depth discussions rather than the power of numbers. A problem analysis focus group should be asked:

1. What is the real problem here—that is, what if the product category did not exist?
2. What are the current attitudes and behaviors of the focus group members toward the product category?
3. What product attributes and benefits do the members of the focus group want?
4. What are their dissatisfactions, problems, and unfilled needs?
5. What changes occurring in their lifestyles are relevant to the product category?[7]

Other suggestions for helping guarantee the usefulness of focus group findings are:

- Invite scientists to the sessions, even encourage them to bring an idea or two along. This will stimulate conversation and help the scientist get a firsthand feel for how users think.
- Be sure management attends some of the sessions. Reading summaries of the discussions is not enough.
- Avoid what some people call:

    T-groups: doing statistical analysis on what is clearly not statistical data.

    Prayer groups: the manager sits behind the mirror and prays for the comments wanted rather than really listening to what users are saying.

    Tour groups: the only reason for holding the session was to get to Phoenix in February (otherwise known as the boondoggle).

    Right-to-life groups: the moderator and/or the participants are blamed for suggesting the wrong thing or not suggesting the thing wanted. The desired idea must live on.

---

[7] "When Using Qualitative Research to Generate New Product Ideas, Ask These Five Questions," *Marketing News*, May 14, 1982, p. 15.

- Be sure the focus groups are large enough for the interactions and synergy that make them successful, yet not so large that significant minority opinions are repressed. From 8 to 12 members is a popular range.
- Don't expect focus group members to like your firm or its products, and don't expect them to care about the activity being studied the way you do. They won't necessarily be consistent, they won't look like you, they will be uncomfortably candid at times, they will have erroneous preconceptions, and yet they expect perfect honesty from you.[8]

A fourth method for gathering the list of consumer problems is the *user panel.* A steel company created an advisory panel of 200 steel users who were contacted quarterly on many matters, including their need for new products; and an office products firm maintained a panel of secretaries whose reactions to new products and user problems were requested. Mead Johnson & Co. long maintained panels of physicians and hospital and trade personnel. Maintaining panels is easier than conducting separate surveys, and the participants often take their assignments more seriously than do survey respondents, but they also suffer from panel fatigue and from the erosion of their independence. They are certainly not an ideal source for serious problem analysis.

A fifth method is *user observation,* which utilizes the technology of work simplification and methods analysis. One firm studied the maintenance and cleaning of hospital floors by setting up a special motion study laboratory where hospital personnel were brought in to clean floors under observation by company personnel.[9] Other firms have used simulated kitchens whose observers watch from behind one-way mirrors. Purchase behavior in stores is frequently studied by the observation method; and an extreme — but highly useful — application of the method is the filming of surgical operations in hospitals. The method's obvious drawback for new product development is that it permits only problem identification because it excludes verbalization of users' feelings and attitudes.

---

[8] Judith Langer, "Personal Encounters with Buyers the Key to Successful New Products," *New Product Development* (newsletter), February 1988, p. 5. For other good advice on the running of focus groups, see Raymond Rowe Johnson, "Focus Groups Are Divided into Four Distinctive Categories," *Marketing News,* October 24, 1988, p. 21. A more complete source is Edward F. McQuarrie and Shelby H. McIntyre, "Focus Groups and the Development of New Products by Technologically Driven Companies," *Journal of Product Innovation Management,* March 1986, pp. 40–47. A comprehensive source on all aspects of the subject is Jane Farley Templeton, *Focus Groups* (Chicago: Probus Publishing, 1987).

[9] Knut Holt, *Product Innovation: A Workbook for Management in Industry* (London: Newnes-Butterworth, 1976).

A sixth method attempts to meet that objection and yet retain actual consumer product usage. This method is *role playing*. Though role playing has long been used in psychology to enhance creativity, there is little evidence of its successful use in generating ideas for new products. Presumably, it would be valuable in instances where product users are unable to visualize or verbalize their reactions. It should also be valuable where consumers are emotionally unable or unwilling to express their views—in areas of personal hygiene, for example.

An interesting variation on role playing asks users to describe in detail exactly how they go about doing some task. For example, have them write out each step in preparing a frozen pizza or in starting up the car in the morning and getting it out onto the expressway. Problems tend to come up naturally, often ones the user didn't think worth mentioning in direct questioning.

Unfortunately, though users are the best single source of ideas and problem analysis is the most widely used method of concept generation, most firms still do not have organized systems to exploit this source. Considering that Levi Strauss got the idea for steel-riveted jeans from a Nevada user in 1873, one must wonder why not.

Scenario Analysis

So far, we have talked about routine market contacts and problem analysis as two techniques for finding problems. The third method— scenario analysis—comes into play because end users often need help in knowing what problems they *will* be having in the future. Today's problems they know, but they are usually unable to paint a logical picture of their future.

Scenario analysis does this for us. For example, if we were to describe apartment life 20 years from now, we would probably see lots of windows and sunlight coming in. If a furniture manufacturer were doing this scenario analysis, the analyst could immediately see two problems: those apartment dwellers will need (1) new types of upholstery that are more resistant to the sun and (2) new types of chairs that will let them continue such activities as conversing and eating but also let them gain exposure to all that sunlight.

The procedure is evident: first, paint a scenario; second, study it for problems and needs; third, evaluate those problems in some way to rank order them; and fourth, begin trying to solve the most important ones. Painting a scenario does not yield a new product concept directly; it is only a source of problems, which still must be solved.

Scenarios take several different forms. First, we distinguish between (1) *extending* the present to see what it will look like in the future and (2) *leaping* into the future to pick a period that is then described. Both use current trends to some extent, of course, but the leap method is not constrained by these trends. For example, an extend study might be: Currently, homeowners are converting from individual housing to condominium housing at an annual rate of 0.9 percent. If this keeps up for 20 years, there will be XXX condominium units in use, which will offer a market of ZZZ for special "visitors" motels in major condominium areas to house visitors who cannot stay in the smaller units with their hosts.

By contrast, a leap study might be: Describe life in the year 2010 in a major urban area of the United States contrasted with life in a similar setting in Europe. Apple Computer's John Sculley said,

> Most corporate planners decide where the company should go in the next year or two by peering into the company's past, making judgments and extrapolations based on their experiences. We ask ourselves, What will 1992 be like? We create in our minds a portrait of the economy, our industry, and our company. Then we move back into the present, envisioning what we have to do to get to the future."[10]

This is precisely what new product managers do, only they use market behavior and practice, not company operations.

Leap studies can be *static* or *dynamic*. In dynamic studies, the focus is on what changes must be made between now and then if the leap scenario is to come about—the interim time period is the meaningful focus. In static leaps, there is no concern about how we get there. Figure 5–4 shows a dynamic leap scenario—a period in which the auto dealer service problem no longer exists is broken down to yield the technical breakthroughs needed soon to reach that ideal condition. The leap scenario needn't be high probability—it can be a forecast or a goal or anywhere in between.

Edwin Land used the dynamic leap scenario to develop the instant camera. ARCO also uses the dynamic leap scenario technique.[11] A group of managers were told they had fallen asleep and just now awakened five years later. They were shown a dummy newspaper article stating they had just won the Nobel prize for opening the Arctic to worldwide economic development. They were asked how they did it, and their answers led to several worthwhile ideas.

Most scenarios are in the extend form simply because we can easily spot current trends and because forecasting by extrapolation is easier than forecasting by speculative leaps.

Static leap is the type of futures forecasting that gave scenario its name. A period of time and a category of activity are selected (for

---

[10] "Sculley's Lessons from Inside Apple," *Fortune*, September 14, 1987, p. 117.

[11] "One Office the MAC Has Conquered," *Fortune*, November 9, 1987, p. 60.

FIGURE 5–4   The Relevance Tree Form of Dynamic Leap Scenario

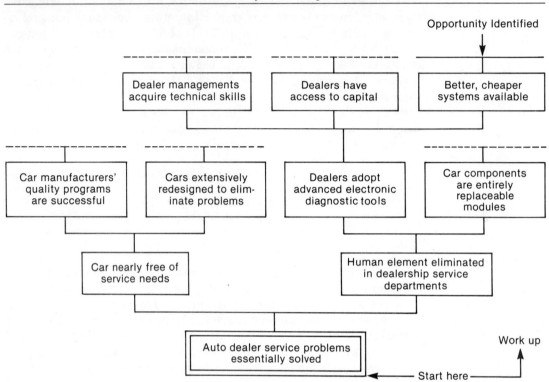

The analysis begins at the bottom of the chart (the ideal future condition that is the expected end). Working back, each level shows the necessary conditions for the item below it. All branches of the tree are worked back to conditions that already exist. Somewhere in the analysis, on one of the branches, a condition that does not exist offers someone today an opportunity for product innovation. In this case, with only a few of the branches completed, there appears to be an opportunity for some firm to develop better, cheaper diagnostic systems for ultimate use in reaching the goal at the bottom of the tree. (The analysis is for demonstration only.)

example, trucking in 1998 or elementary schools in 2000). A team of experts is assembled to paint a total picture of the chosen topic. Then, new product managers study the predicted scene for ideas of the needs and problems people will have at some future time, even though they don't know it now.

A variation on the leap scenario method is hypothetical scenarios. Creativity needs a genuine push sometimes, so why be constrained to forecast reasonable futures? Simply spell out any future, but do not overlook the basic laws of nature. There must still be gravity, friction, and so on. But beyond that, all is open. For example, a bicycle manufacturer might imagine a city built entirely on pillars, steel-mesh roadways, people wearing virtually no clothing at all in air-conditioned hothouse environments, and so on. What implications would these conditions have for new bicycles?

Seed Trends.   Seed trends, the best extend scenario, involves extending whatever current trends have meaning to the firm doing the analysis. The secret is to pick the trends with major lateral impact. Environmental scanning came from this method of creating scenarios, and the business literature is replete with various persons' and organizations' perceptions of the most important seed trends. However, Figure 5–5 gives you a chance to see how perceptive *Business Week* editors were in early 1990 when they predicted what would be "in" and "out" during the coming year (and, presumably, somewhat later). Would these predictions have made good scenarios for developing new goods and services?

One way to separate temporary fads from meaningful trends is to ask the following questions:

- Does the new development fit with the lifestyle and value system of society?
- Are several different types of satisfaction involved with the new development?
- Can the new development be modified or adapted by different people in different uses?
- Who started the development, and who will adopt it next?
- Are there some strong underlying themes in the development?
- Are there related trends that give it strength?[12]

Other methods of ascertaining meaningful trends to extend include studying trendy people and trendy places; these other approaches are included in Appendix B.[13]

SOLVING THE PROBLEMS: GROUP CREATIVITY

Once a set of user problems—properly qualified by frequency and importance—has been compiled, we can begin solving them. Naturally, much solving is done by new products team members' thinking and analysis. In fact, some problems essentially suggest their own solutions.

---

[12] "Distinguishing Fads from Trends with Six Research Guidelines," *Marketing News,* January 21, 1983, p. 3.

[13] For more on using scenarios, see Harold S. Becker, "Developing and Using Scenarios—Assisting Business Decisions," *The Journal of Business and Industrial Marketing,* Winter/Spring 1989, pp. 61–69.

FIGURE 5–5   Seed Trends as an Extend Scenario

What Was In for 1990	*What Was Out for 1990*

Politics and Economics

Peace dividend	Defense spending
Atlantic Basin	Pacific Rim
Berlin	Beijing
Vaclav Havel	Margaret Thatcher
White House secrecy	White House show biz
Speeches about ethics	The Keating Five
Invasions	Wimpy leadership
Universal health insurance	Catastrophic health insurance

Management

Simplicity	Bells and whistles
Ma Bell	Big Blue
'Global integration'	'Competing internationally'
Early retirement	Corporate loyalty
Mommy track	Super Moms
Touchy-feely MBAs	Number-crunching MBAs
Michael Moore	Roger Smith
Micro-marketing	Mass-marketing
CNN	CBS
Team effort	Direct orders

Finance

Morgan Stanley	Henry Kravis
Energy and utility stocks	Banking and high-tech stocks
Deutsche mark	Yen
Bank of America	Bank of Boston
Debt restructuring	LBOs
Rentals	Condos
Bonuses	Salary hikes
Treasury bonds	Junk bonds

Social Trends

Volunteerism	Narcissism
Seattle	Boston (still)
Car phones	Digital dashboards
Bifocals	Suspenders
Russian watches	Designer watches
PPOs	Family doctors
Michelle Pfeiffer	Meryl Streep (temporarily)
Consumer Reports	*Spy*
Billiards	Health clubs
Customer service	Rudeness

FIGURE 5–5 *(concluded)*

What Was In for 1990	What Was Out for 1990
Social Trends (continued)	
Diaper services	Disposable diapers
Mail order	Bloomingdale's
Roller blades	Skateboards
The rain forest	Ozone
Mashed potatoes	Sushi
Faux fur	Mink
Carnivores	Vegetarians

Source: Reprinted from January 15, 1990 issue of *Business Week* by special permission, copyright © 1990 by McGraw-Hill, Inc., p. 31.

Engineering and other research laboratories also try to solve problems. But the new products manager can also use group creativity for this purpose.

The secret of group creativity is that two heads are better than one. Though some scientists loudly protest that this is not true, most people accept the synergism that takes place in group sessions.

Alex Osborn developed what he called *brainstorming* in 1938. All of the group ideation techniques developed since that time are spin-offs of his process and embody one idea: One person presents a thought, another person reacts to it, another person reacts to the reaction, and so on. This presenting/reacting sequence gives group creativity its meaning, and the various techniques developed simply alter how ideas are presented or how reactions take place.

Group creativity differs from individual creativity in four ways:

1. Groups offer a broader range of interests and capabilities by joining persons of diverse backgrounds.
2. Conflicting points of view arise more easily in groups.
3. Groups usually have more complex criteria for accepting problem solutions.
4. Ideas must be more clearly and completely thought out to be communicated in groups.

Individuals can handle really new ideas and find radical solutions to problems better than groups can. Some feel that one reason small firms are more innovative than large firms is that they do not often use group creativity.

Group homogeneity enhances group cohesion and members' willingness to submit to group rules and goals, while group heterogeneity does the opposite. Unfortunately, new product ideation groups need group heterogeneity, so special care must be taken to direct and control the natural conflicts that arise.

These observations indicate (1) the importance of building groups according to the kind of creativity needed, (2) the need to alter the structure of a creativity group over the life cycle of ideation, and (3) the critical nature of group leadership.

Brainstorming

Osborn's approach includes two basic principles and four rules of conduct. The two principles are:

1. *Deferral of judgment.* This requires participants to be free to express any idea that comes to mind without having to worry about criticism from others in the group. The judicial mind weighs evidence, but it discourages the free flowing of ideas.
2. *Quantity breeds quality.* According to associationist psychology, our thoughts are structured hierarchically; the most dominant are the habitual thoughts with which we are most comfortable. To have really new ideas we must break through these conventional ideas, and Osborn felt this would follow from attempts to achieve the largest quantity of ideas possible.[14]

These two principles led to the following four rules for conducting a brainstorming session:

1. *All criticism is ruled out,* and the leader must ensure this. Even chuckles or raised eyebrows are banned.
2. *Freewheeling is welcomed* — the wilder the better, with no inhibitions whatsoever. Not only is divergent or lateral thinking desired, but it should be forced by the leader.
3. *Quantity is wanted,* so nothing is permitted to slow the session down (such as taking time to record an idea clearly or completely).
4. *Combination and improvement are sought* by leadership that encourages each person to hear the idea of another person and then to carry that idea to another stage of development or application.

Many persons who express disappointment with brainstorming have violated those rules. For example, session participants should have experience in the general field with which the problem is concerned — product experience, in our case. They should be trained in brainstorming method; they should be told the precise problem being attacked; they

---

[14] Alex Osborn, *Applied Imagination,* 3rd ed. (New York: Charles Scribner's Sons, 1963).

should be a diverse group but not so diverse that they cannot readily communicate (they can be co-workers or strangers); and they should not be particularly adept at the normal methodology of problem solving.

The group should have one or more leaders who combine the skill of stimulating discussion with that of controlling behavior. The leaders see that the rules are obeyed without inhibiting the group. Fast, cryptic notes are made without elaboration and without credit to individuals.

Preparation is critical. A good brainstorming session cannot be arranged on the spur of the moment. A department manager should not be the leader of a discussion group consisting of the department's employees, though many new product brainstorming sessions have gotten started just that way.

We know that deferral of judgment leads to an increased *quantity* of ideas but not necessarily to a higher average *quality* of ideas.[15] We also know that people working in groups produce more ideas than do comparable individuals working in isolation (synergism is real); but, again, the evidence suggests no superiority in the quality of their ideas. And, most important, despite the many testimonials to brainstorming and the many anecdotal reports about its successes, the question of whether brainstorming leads to successful solutions of real-life problems remains unanswered. These conclusions are consistent with the very irregular, sporadic use of brainstorming by business and with the many attempts to improve its output, as represented by the following modifications:

Phillips 66 groups.   To increase participation, Dr. J. Donald Phillips broke Osborn's 12-person groups into subgroups of six members each, sending the subgroups to break-off rooms for six minutes each, rearranging the subgroups, sending the new subgroups off for another six minutes, and so on. Rearrangement was Phillips's key to eliminating the problem of dominant or conflicting personalities. The Phillips 66 groups are sometimes called buzz groups, free association groups, and discussion 66 groups.

Brainstorming circle.   This approach forces the conversational sequence around a circle, and each person expands or modifies the idea expressed by the prior person in the circle. The brainstorming circle is more orderly and forces all persons to participate equally.

Reverse brainstorming.   This approach concentrates on a product's weaknesses or problems rather than on solutions or improvements.

---

[15] See Morris I. Stein, *Stimulating Creativity,* Vol. 2 (New York: Academic Press, Harcourt Brace Jovanovich, 1975) for a full discussion of brainstorming, including a review of the literature.

The discussion attempts to ferret out every criticism of, say, a vacuum cleaner. Later, attempts are made to eliminate the weaknesses or solve the problems.

Tear-down.   The rule of suspended judgment is reversed in this approach. Instead of avoiding criticism, tear-down requires it, and participants must find something wrong with the previous idea to get a talking turn.

And also.   In this approach, each speaking participant enlarges or extends the previous idea. No lateral moves are permitted unless the chain runs dry. The approach has been called idea building and modification.[16]

Gordon method.   Prior to developing synectics, W. J. J. Gordon used groups that were not told what the problem was. In this method, if a discussion is to develop new ideas for recording musical performances, the group is encouraged to discuss opera. Eventually the leader turns the discussion toward the problem but still without divulging it.

Disciplines Panel

Several of today's leading new products consulting firms believe group ideation is essential but reject brainstorming. They believe the group should actually work on a problem, not just talk about it for 20 minutes. Their approach is to assemble experts from all relevant disciplines and have them discuss the problem as a panel. There may be just one meeting of the panel, but usually there are several lengthy meetings (see Figure 5–6).

A panel on new methods of packaging fresh vegetables might include representatives from home economics, physics, nutrition, canning technology, marketing, plastics, chemistry, biology, industrial engineering, agriculture, botany, and agronomy. Panels of 30 or 40 have been used, and the use of subpanels and one overall panel has sometimes been required.

Sometimes the panel consists of both company personnel and outside expert personnel. Sometimes the panel is entirely in-house with leadership or support from an outside new products consulting firm or a nearby university. Outside leadership avoids some of the people problems encountered when company persons also serve as discussion leaders.

---

[16] Charles S. Whiting, *Creative Thinking* (New York: Van Nostrand Reinhold, 1958).

FIGURE 5–6   The Disciplines Panel for Group Ideation

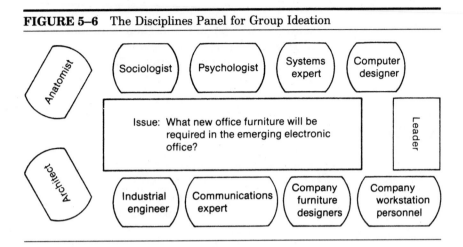

The disciplines panel approach seeks and expects synergism, but the panel members meet as experts and are expected to perform as experts. As various ideas are proposed, the panel members evaluate and modify them. Panel leadership is essential to maintain a focus on the problem at hand.

The disciplines panel approach is growing as an alternative to brainstorming. Its applications are primarily in situations calling for significant innovation, not line extensions.[17]

SUMMARY

Chapter 5 began our study of the many specific techniques developed by concept creators to aid them in their work. The most common approach is based on the paradigm of "find problem, solve problem," so we looked first at the many techniques developed to spot problems. These included (1) routine market contacts, (2) problem analysis as a way to discover present problems, and (3) scenario analysis to predict future problems.

Once problems are discovered, efforts at solution can begin; most efforts are individual thinking and analysis, whether in the office or in the lab. One major group of techniques under the label of group creativity includes a great variety of approaches, but most are variations of brainstorming.

[17] The disciplines panel is part of the approach used by a leading creativity consultant, Innotech, Inc. For a good description of its operation, see Robert A. Mamis, "The Gang that Doesn't Think Straight," *INC,* October 1985, pp. 108–11.

This completes our study of the purposive approach—logically seeking out problems and their solutions as ideas for new products. Next we will turn to techniques that scan the general situation and seek accidental or fortuitous ideas, primarily as improvements to current products.

APPLICATIONS

More questions from that interview with the company president.

1. "Our electronics division has become increasingly interested in the home as a market for new products. Recently, I read where some experts are forecasting that the average home is in for some fantastic changes in the years ahead—using the computer to order merchandise and plan menus, playing chess and checkers as well as other games on the computer, writing 'letters' to people who also own computers, and so on. They say we'll have home repair instructions stored on disks and there will be new synthetic foods, creative garbage disposal systems, and so on. Could you show me how that scenario might be used to create ideas for new electronic devices in the home—that is, new ones not already available or described in the scenario?"

2. "I personally love to watch for a trend and predict some new product from it. For example, just to see how good you are at creative thinking, here are some trends I noted recently in the press. Can you think of two possible products suggested by each?
    a. Lofty goals are giving way to very personal wants; there is less social globalism.
    b. There has been great growth in bulk foods, items in barrels that we dish up ourselves.
    c. AT&T tells us that the very idea of long-distance calling will soon disappear. All calls will be charged by distance and time, even within a city.
    d. Formal weddings are back in style."

3. "I believe in problem analysis—that's at the heart of things. But I sure don't like those focus groups. I sat in on a couple last year, and all the people did was chat. And the chatting never seemed to lead to anything. After the second one was over, I quizzed the moderator, and she agreed that there had been a lot of rambling. She kept talking about the gems of knowledge we found—common threads, I believe she said. Now, honestly, isn't that pure bunk? And a good reason to go one-on-one with users,

where there can be a meaningful exchange on that person's real problems."

4. "You know a lot about rental or formal wear, like tuxedos, I imagine. Can you take me through a problem analysis, using the formal wear rental market as an example? Several of our divisions are involved in the retail business, and I'm curious to see what problems you come up with that we haven't solved yet."

Case: Six Key Trends*

In late 1989, the editors of *Business Week* reviewed the world around them and came up with six trends that they felt would have a significant impact in the 1990s. Here they are.

• *Boomers at fortysomething.* In the 1990s, 75 million baby boomers will move through or approach their 40s. Knowing that people in their pre-40s are usually concerned about their jobs, their families, college education for their kids, and the like, the editors believed scenarios could be predicted of how these baby boomers will be living.

• *A nation within a nation.* The second trend they believed vital was that of the increasing population of Hispanics. About 20 million people of Latin American background were living in the United States in late 1989. With high levels of immigration and high birthrates, their 8 percent of total population was growing rapidly. Hispanics were rapidly becoming more prominent in advertising, politics, and life in general. Their incomes were rising, and they were speeding up their move out of the barrios.

• *Forget the rocking chairs.* The third condition pertained to the elderly. It was a "good time to be old." Social Security was solvent, and national incomes were high. The editors looked at the elderly as a group, and although they saw many fighting illness and infirmity and living on small social security checks, they also saw an emerging new cohort. These they called the "young old." They enjoyed early retirement, better health and wealth, and higher expectations. Some intergenerational scuffling was going on, but not much and not seriously. Arguments occurred over who should pay for health care for the elderly; but, at the same time, the baby boomers made it clear they did not want their parents to move in with them. The elderly seconded that motion, and politicians were listening.

• *Moving out to the city.* Turn-of-the-century Americans wanted small towns. Post–World War II veterans wanted subdivisions. Baby boomers, seeking

---

*Source: "How the Next Decade Will Differ," *Business Week,* September 26, 1989, pp. 142–56.

their own new setting, were heading toward metropolitan areas. They didn't select the biggest central cities, however. They sought newly energized regional centers—Charlotte, North Carolina; Burlington, Vermont; Salt Lake City; and Nashville. These areas offered more yet were more livable than the previous large centers. Meanwhile, the traditional suburbs were themselves becoming urbanized. And, movement of people from the North to the South and West continued with no signs of weakening.

• *The password is flexible.*   The corporation has always been adaptable, and 1989 was no exception. There were two big changes in process. One concerned productivity, stemming from new technologies and new methods of production. The second involved needing fewer people to achieve that higher productivity—getting them, keeping them, helping them be productive. This involved increased child care, drug treatment, literacy programs, and the like. New organizational formats were being adopted (to replace the hierarchical), and companies sought flexibility in everything to meet the increasing competition from all quarters. They made greater use of computers, teams, and projects.

• *Putting the earth first.*   Environmentalism was back. Several key disasters (Chernobyl, Alaskan oil spill) were putting strength back into environmental groups, and polls showed Americans cared more about environmental issues. The editors believed this was more than Earth Day thinking. It was broad based, grass roots. And the feeling among the populace was that this was too serious to depend on Washington for leadership. Groups like the Sierra Club, National Wildlife Foundation, and even the EPA were attacking everywhere. Corporations did not escape, but they were no longer the only scapegoat. People quoted the Pogo classic: "We have discovered the enemy, and it is us."

The editors faced the task of drawing up scenarios that extended and blended these six major trends. It was a good assignment for them—and perhaps for you, too.

Chapter 6

Attribute Analysis

SETTING

In Chapter 5, we studied the purposive approach to concept generation. The first step isolates users' problems, and the second tries to find solutions to those problems. This approach is the best because product concepts found by the problem/solution route are most likely to have value for the user.

However, earlier we saw another approach—the fortuitous scan. This approach is not nearly as purposive; it is almost a random, though thorough, search of present products on the market and their relationships with each other and with users. We look logically for what is almost an accidental discovery—adding a third stocking to a package, quick-drying inks, clocks combined with TVs, adding colors to things, making things colder, and so on.

The fortuitous scan approach uses three classes of techniques: attribute analysis, relationships analysis, and lateral search. The many variations in these categories have been developed by some of the world's leading experts in creative thinking. Some of the techniques are widely used, some hardly at all.

Chapter 6 focuses on attribute analysis, while Chapter 7 covers relationships analysis and lateral search.

ATTRIBUTE ANALYSIS

Attribute analysis techniques are generally intended to discover product improvements and line extensions. They are not meant for new category or product discoveries, though such discoveries have occurred.[1] All of

---

[1] See Michael D. Johnson, "Consumer Similarity Judgments: A Test of the Contrast Model," *Psychology & Marketing*, Spring 1986, pp. 46–60.

this is for the good, because most new product managers are looking for improvements and extensions, and most new entries are of these types. The flow is needed to sustain growth and to hold market shares.

The basis of attribute analysis is that any future change in a product must involve one or more of its current attributes. Therefore, if we study those attributes, particularly if we change each one in all the ways it could be changed, we will eventually discover every change that could ever come about in that product.

Much of what we do in this chapter is no more complicated than that, although a few of the techniques are difficult. But, most products have many attributes, and each attribute has a preference structure among users, so combining them expands the options exponentially.[2]

Figure 6–1 shows the different approaches covered in this chapter and identifies others discussed briefly in Appendix B.

ATTRIBUTES

First, we need to talk about what attributes are. Figure 6–2 shows the structure of attributes. A product is really nothing but attributes, and any product (good or service) can be described by citing its attributes. Incomplete descriptions result from forgetting one or more attributes.

Attributes are of three types: features, functions, and benefits. For example, a spoon usually has a wide surface that is concave upward. That concavity enables the spoon to function as a holder and carrier of liquids.

FIGURE 6–1   Typology of Attribute Analysis Techniques

Those Discussed in Chapter 6	*Those Discussed in Appendix B*
1. Dimensional analysis	1. Function analysis
2. Checklists	2. Attribute extension
3. Gap analysis	3. Relative brand profile
4. Trade-off analysis	4. Pseudoproduct test
	5. Systems analysis
	6. Unique properties
	7. Hierarchical design
	8. Weaknesses
	9. Achilles' heel

---

[2] Attribute measurement and assessment is not the exact science its techniques suggest. For a rather distressing but enlightening report, see James Jaccard, David Brinberg, and Lee J. Ackerman, "Assessing Attribute Importance: A Comparison of Six Methods," *Journal of Consumer Research,* March 1986, pp. 463–68.

FIGURE 6–2   A Typology of Attributes

Product attributes are of three types:
  Features
  Functions
  Benefits

Functions are rarely used and often are treated as features or benefits, depending on the case.

Features can be many things:
  Dimensions
  Esthetic characteristics
  Components
  Source ingredients
  Manufacturing process
  Materials
  Services
  Performance
  Price
  Structures
  Trademarks
  And many more, tangible or intangible, real or perceived.

Benefits can be many things:
  Uses
  Sensory enjoyments
  Economic gains
  Savings, such as time and effort
  Nonmaterial well-being, such as health.
  They are direct (clean teeth) and indirect (romance following from clean teeth).

Attribute analysis methods use different attributes:
  Dimensional analysis uses features.
  Other analysis methods in Appendix B use functions and benefits.
  Checklists use all attributes.
  Gap analysis uses some attributes (the determinant ones).
  Trade-off analysis also uses determinant attributes.

The holding function enables the user to bring the held material easily and neatly to the mouth. Of course, the spoon has many other features (including shape, material, reflection, and pattern). And many other functions (it can pry, poke, project, and so on, as junior high school cafeteria managers know all too well). And many other benefits (such as pride of ownership, status, or table orderliness).

Theoretically, the three types of attributes occur in sequence. A feature permits a certain function, which in turn leads to the benefit. The metal or solid paper and plastic feature of a spoon permits the carrying (holding) function, which permits the material carried to reach the mouth. A shampoo may contain certain proteins (feature) that coat the hair during shampooing (function), which leads to more shine on the hair (benefit).

But the three often aren't that obvious or necessary. Concept generation mainly concerns features and benefits, either alone (as in the first attribute analysis method, below) or in many different combinations (for example, gap analysis).

Dimensional Analysis

One of the earliest (pioneered in 1950) techniques developed for idea stimulation was dimensional analysis.[3] The name is misleading because the method uses any and all *features,* not just those normally considered measurements (such as spatial—length, width, and so on). The task involves listing all of the features of a product type. Because it only lists them, the technique is sometimes called *attribute listing.* The almost limitless set of features includes methods of fabrication, materials, parts, shape, size, and hardness. Just being able to think of the features is creative.

Product concept creativity is triggered by the mere listing of every such feature, enhanced by the questions "Why is it this way?" and "How could it be changed?" Note, however, that rarely is anything worthwhile found in dimensional analysis until the list is long. The easily seen features have been "seen" by thousands of other persons, usually for many years. The challenge is to push beyond the ordinary—to see a product in a way others have overlooked.

Some of the most interesting features are those a product doesn't seem to have. For example, the spoon discussed above has aroma, sound, resilience, bendability, and so on. Granted, the aroma may be hard to detect, the sound may be zero, and the resilience may be only when pushed by a vice. But each feature offers something to change. How about spoons that play musical notes as children move them to the mouth? How about spoon handles that can be squeezed to play notes? How about spoons that smell like roses?

---

[3] For more information on this technique, see Robert P. Crawford, *How to Get Ideas* (Lincoln, Neb.: University Associates, 1950). Other good sources on dimensional analysis (as well as many other techniques) are J. H. McPherson and D. A. Guidici, *Advances in Innovation Management* (Palo Alto, Calif.: Stanford Research Institute, 1978); Morris I. Stein, *Stimulating Creativity,* vols. 1 and 2 (New York: Academic Press, Harcourt Brace Jovanovich, 1974); and Charles S. Whiting, *Creative Thinking* (New York: Van Nostrand Reinhold, 1958).

Listing hundreds of features is not uncommon. Figure 6–3 shows a list for the common flashlight, and it can be extended even further.

Engineers have long used dimensional analysis for another purpose and under a different name—value analysis. They list each attribute but then ask, "Can that attribute be changed in any way to reduce its cost?"

General Electric calls the approach "deliberate induction," which alludes to the rather mechanical nature of the task (the inherent power of the method is that merely listing and observing leads to new perspectives). Dimensional analysis in the form of reverse engineering has recently been popularized in the computer chip arena.

Checklists

Early use of the various attribute analyses naturally gave way to combinations. From these combinations evolved one of today's most widely used idea-generating techniques—the checklist.

The most widely publicized checklist was given by the originator of brainstorming:

Can it be adapted?	Can something be substituted?
Can it be modified?	Can it be magnified?
Can it be reversed?	Can it be minified?
Can it be combined with something?	Can it be rearranged in some way?[4]

Another source urges use of the following principles:

Association	Sensory appeal
Subtraction	Symbols
Doing the unexpected	Addition or combination
Other forms	Timing or frequency
Adaptation	Other uses
Reversal	Competitive demonstration[5]

The usual consumer product list can be converted into a much longer one that would fit industrial goods by stressing form of energy, materials,

---

[4] Alex F. Osborn, *Applied Imagination,* 3rd ed. (New York: Charles Scribner's Sons, 1963).

[5] George J. Abrams, *How I Made a Million Dollars with Ideas* (Chicago: Playboy Press, 1972).

FIGURE 6–3 Feature Attributes of a Flashlight

Using dimensional analysis, here are 156 dimensions. A change in any one of them may make a new flashlight.

Weight
Number of bulbs
Hollowness
Number of batteries
Width of strap
Spring size
Size of batteries
Number of switches
Use of attachments
Filament shape
Bulb shape
Rust resistance of body
Balance
Lamp protective material
Reflector depth
Gripability
Shock resistance of case
Lens material
Rechargeability
Shear force of joint
Heat tolerance
Rattle of batteries
Warmth of material
Strap fastener type
Type of solder/bulb
Metal wire type
Wire weight
Insulation material
Wire fastener type
Battery terminal type
Use in outer space
Elasticity of strap
Opacity of lens
Bulb sealant material
Thread size of stem
Adhesion of label
Gas resistance
Automatic flasher
Distance visible
Length
Lens color
Freestanding ability

Hangability
Strength of strap
Material of spring
Wearability of case
Switch type
Attachment material
Filament material
Stain resistance
Switch texture
Size of lamp protector
Reflector shape
Reflector durability
Texture of grip
Lens strength
Type of metal liner
Thread type
Total number of pieces
Cold tolerance
Safety of corners
Shatter point of bulb
Strap fastener material
Number of screws
Wire gauge
Flexibility of body
Insulation color
Melting point of solder
Number of terminals
Texture of lenses
Number of closures
Direction of batteries
Color of bulb sealant
Material of wire fastener
Registration or patent number
Color of metal fastener
Manual flasher
Translucence of body
Shape of cylinder
Focus of beam
Closure type
Strap handle

Color of strap
Spring strength
Material of lining
Noise of switch
Wand bouyancy
Bulb glass color
Spring length
Conical bulb connection
Toxicity of material
Flammability
Reflector material
Reflector surface
Hardness of body
Malleability of metal
Thread depth
Ease of battery change
Glow in dark
Compressibility
Amperage required
Reflectiveness of body
Head type of screws
Wire resistance
Tensil strength/wire
Heat tolerance of solder
Number of springs
Picture directions
Removability of tag
Volume of accessories
Translucence of bulb
Color of wire fastener
Number of reflective surfaces
Accidental on/off prevention
Surface area/color
Aesthetic appeal
Flashing of lights
Handle type
Security of closure
Length of strap
Resistance to rust
Texture of strap

Material of case
Light wand attachment
Color of body
Bulb size
Bulb gas type
Protect rusted batteries
Switch pressure
Number of seams on body
Reflector color
Reflector temperature limit
Water resistance
Melting temperature of metal
Thread strength
Diameter
Washability
Mode of bulb replacement
Ease of assembly
Bulb fastener type
Melting point of screws
Wire length
Wire insulation type
Number colors of wire
Weight of metal used
Explosiveness
Smell of unit
Number of tags
Storage of accessories
Length of bulb stem
Part numbers
Language of directions
Snagability (catch)
Number of flat surfaces
Power requirements of bulbs

ease of operation, subassemblies, and substitutable components. (See Figure 6–4 for an abbreviated list of these industrial checklist questions.)

Marvin Small created one of the most complete checklists developed to date. His 112-question list covers dimensions commonly used for consumer items. The full list is in Appendix C, with an example for each stimulator.[6]

Checklists produce a multitude of potential new product concepts, but most of these concepts are worthless, and much time and effort can be spent culling them down to the best. The technique is frequently used in conjunction with one of the other methods, especially some form of group creativity.

Gap Analysis

Gap analysis, a newer technique, has immense power under certain circumstances. Like the approaches used in problem analysis, it studies users and nonusers to determine how various products are perceived relative to each other. Various "gaps" are determined from these measurements. Gap analysis also relates directly to new product

---

FIGURE 6–4   Checklist of Idea Stimulators for Industrial Products

Have I pinpointed the problem?
Have I considered the physical, thermal, electrical, chemical, and mechanical properties of this material?
Have I looked for electrical, electronic, optical, hydraulic, mechanical, or magnetic ways of doing this?
Have I looked at analogues for parallel problems?
Is this function really necessary?
Could I construct a model?
What other forms of power would make it work better?
Could standard components be substituted?
What if the order of the process were changed?
Can it be made more compact?
What if it were heat-treated, hardened, alloyed, cured, frozen, plated?

Source: Abbreviated list from D. W. Karger and R. G. Murdick, *Managing Engineering and Research* (New York: Industrial Press, 1963), p. 142.

---

[6] The source for Small's checklist is given in Appendix C, where it is displayed in full. A more current version of a complete checklist is PICL (product improvement check list), where the creator adds major categories of stimulations (for example, who, what, where, try to, or make it) — over 900 stimulations, in total. PICL, developed by Arthur VanGundy, comes on one large foldout sheet or in a wheel format and can be obtained from Point Publishing Company, P.O. Box 1309, Point Pleasant, NJ 08742.

positioning—a critical issue in the marketing stage of new products. Several levels of sophistication will be cited, because many firms prefer to use the technique in a simple form, while others have achieved their greatest success with the more complex versions.

Three gap procedures are used:

1. Determinant gap map (by manager).
2. Perceptual gap map (by users, factor analysis).
3. Perceptual gap map (by users, similarities data).

As it is sometimes put, determinant maps use our factors and our scores, perceptual maps (factor analysis) use our factors and customers' scores, and perceptual maps (similarities) use customers' factors and customers' scores.

Determinant Gap Maps.   Figure 6–5 shows a map of snacks prepared by a new products manager seeking to enter the snack market. Remember that concept generation follows decisions on new product strategy (product innovation charter) and thorough market research of the selected target areas for ideation. This research tries to determine such things as how customers look at products, how they tell them apart, and what determines how much they prefer or dislike specific competitive products in that market.

This information permits all product attributes to be categorized as differentiating or not, and important or not. Figure 6–6 shows how these distinctions are used to spot *determinant* attributes (attributes that actually determine what products customers buy). Determinant attributes differentiate competitive offerings and are important to the buyer. Examples of determinant attributes for cars are given in Figure 6–6.

Then, taking the determinant attributes two at a time, maps can be prepared like that shown in Figure 6–5 for snacks. (Incidentally, as with almost every technique in this book, gap analysis applies to industrial products and to all types of services, even though examples here are usually consumer items.)

Students will probably disagree with some of the placements on that snack map. They would probably also disagree if the positions came from customer research (see perceptual gap maps, below). But, experienced managers using solid market knowledge can get pretty close, usually close enough to permit identification of the gaps where there are no products currently. Such gaps are shown in Figure 6–5. Each gap is a new product concept; for example, a snack that is crunchy and has nutritional value, but less so than an apple or a granola bar. Too, a new snack product with the values of raisins might be interesting.

Some analysts like to use three determinant attributes at a time and make three-dimensional maps, but such maps are difficult to interpret.

FIGURE 6–5 Gap Map for Snack Products

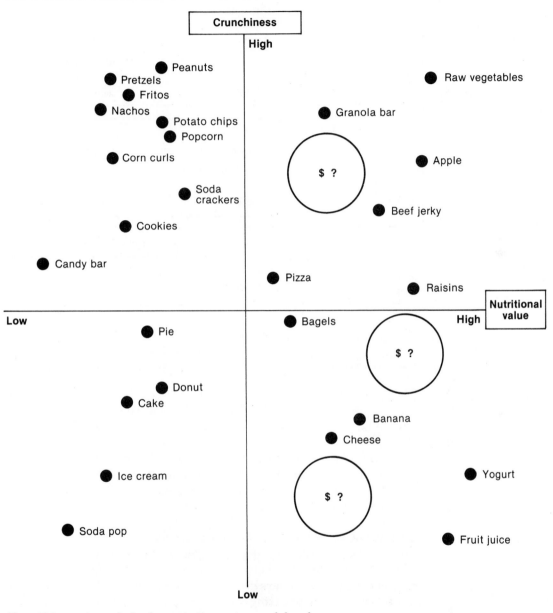

Note: This map is purely for demonstration, not research-based.

FIGURE 6-6 The Definition of Determinant Attributes

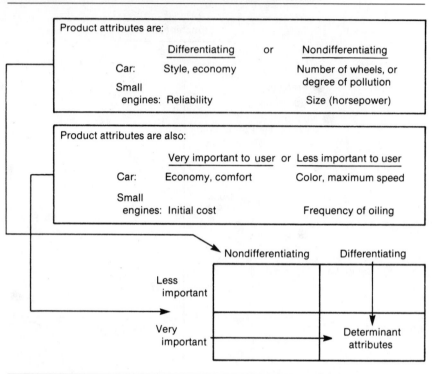

A technique discussed in Chapter 7 (morphological analysis) shows how to use a large number of attributes via computer printout rather than mapping.

Although determinant gap maps are speedy and cost efficient, the method misses customer perceptions that, though inaccurate, may nevertheless be the ones driving their decisions. For customer perceptions, we turn to the next two techniques.

Perceptual Gap Maps. Unlike the previous method, perceptual gap mapping asks market participants (buyers and users of the products) to tell what attributes they believe products have. For example, product users may think candy bars are high in nutrition—doubtful, but if this were so, then any map putting candy bars low in nutrition is incorrect for seeking gaps. Determinant maps are based on "real" reality, and perceptual maps on what one might call "marketplace" reality.

Usual methods of market research are used to gather people's perceptions, including focus groups and individual interviewing. The basic procedure (with many variations in practice) asks consumers what attributes are important in their purchases of products in the subject category. Factor analysis sorts the full list of attributes down to a set of composite factors that reflect the full decision process.

Next, users score each product on each of the final factors (the determinant attributes). From these data, perceptual gap maps are drawn. They look like the snack map in Figure 6–5, and selecting of gaps proceeds as before.[7]

Perceptual Gap Maps with Similarities Data. Perceptual maps early on suffered a criticism that led to a variation preferred by some product innovators. The problem was that users sometimes made purchase decisions using attributes they could not identify. These "phantom" attributes didn't show up on the maps, and their absence distorted the analysis. Too, some users have difficulty scoring attributes, even when they are aware of them, because of various aspects of focus group settings, privacy, and so on.

Du Pont offered an early example of the phantom problem. The company sold filler material for pillows and wanted to find the best type and form of filler to enhance its sales to pillow manufacturers. But Du Pont market analysts found that consumers could not clearly describe the attributes of pillows and could not communicate the attributes they wanted in pillows.

So, the firm created several different types of pillows and then gave them to consumers three at a time, along with the question "Which two are most similar, or which one is least like the other two?" Du Pont's research was much more complex than this question implies; but, in essence, Du Pont was now able to use a computer algorithm to convert the "similarities" data into a map showing closeness of products, regardless of which attributes created that closeness.

Let's look at an analogy that helps explain the process. If residents of any country were given three of that country's cities at a time and asked which two are closest together, they would be doing what Du Pont asked sleepers to do. If enough sets of three cities were used, if a reliable sample of users were studied, and if the country's residents knew their geography, the computer program would print out an accurate map of the country.

Figure 6–7 shows a similarities map of European cheeses. Note there are no dimensions; people were not asked to score the cheeses on different attributes, but only how similar each was to others. Analysts

---

[7] For more information on this use of factor analysis, see Uwe Hentschel, "On the Search for New Products," *European Journal of Marketing* no. 5 (1976), pp. 203–17; and for full development of the mathematics, see Edgar E. Pessemier, *Product Management,* 2nd ed. (New York: John Wiley & Sons, 1981).

FIGURE 6–7   Nonmetric Perceptual Map of the U.K. Cheese Market (without dimensions)

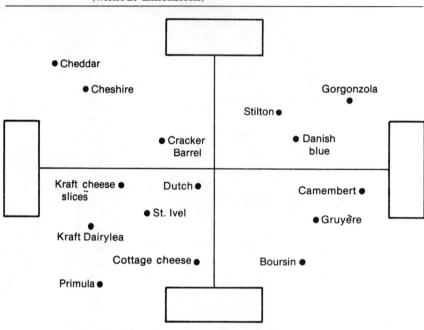

Source: Gordon Douglas, Philip Kemp, and Jeremy Cook, *Systematic New Product Development* (London: Halsted Press, 1978), p. 74.

studied the map carefully, did some regression analysis, and hypothesized that the vertical dimension was popularity. They felt that a horizontal dimension might be mildness/pungency. A third dimension was found to run from northwest to southeast on the map, as products seemed to line up with native cheeses on the upper left and foreign cheeses on the lower right. Again, a reader familiar with the U.K. cheese market might disagree.

Comments on Gap Analysis.   The more advanced forms of perceptual and preference mapping are quite controversial. Here are some criticisms of gap analysis:[8]

1. The input data come entirely from responses to questions about how brands differ. Nuances and shadings are necessarily ignored.

2. All brands comprise a finite set of attributes. Thus totalities, interrelationships, and synergisms are overlooked, as are creations requiring a conceptual leap. In the early 1800s, for example, gap analysis

---

[8] Stephen King, *Developing New Brands* (New York: John Wiley & Sons, 1973), p. 96.

might have led to breeding faster horses or to wagons with larger wheels, but it probably would not have suggested the automobile.

3. The analysis of brand attributes and mappings is history by the time the data are gathered and analyzed. Most of the consumer packaged goods markets in which the advanced techniques have been developed are very fast moving.

4. The advanced mathematical approaches suffer the same difficulty here as in other aspects of marketing research—acceptance of the findings by persons turned off by the calculations. Fortunately, the physical nature of maps themselves greatly alleviates this problem.

5. Perhaps the most damaging aspect of all gap analysis is that it discovers gaps, not demand. Gaps usually exist for good reasons (for example, fish-aroma air freshener). New products people still have to go to the marketplace to see if the gaps they discovered represent things people want. This has led to *preference maps*—three-dimensional diagrams from the technology of computer-aided design, where dimensions matching those on a gap map are the *x*- and *z*-axes, but the *y*-axis shows preference levels. The result resembles a blanket laid down over objects of various sizes; high levels show where preferences lie, and low levels of preference lie between the humps of high preference. New products people hope a gap in product availability matches the peaks in preference. It isn't that simple, of course, so most new products people will use their own knowledge of the market to make quick assessments of whether a gap is any good, and then back that up by concept testing (discussed in Chapter 9.)[9]

And, as in all of ideation, new products people must avoid being bound by what is now "impossible." For example, for years gap maps on analgesics showed a big hole in the map where strength was paired with gentleness. The strong/gentle part of the map was always empty, and everyone knew why—an over-the-counter analgesic could not be made that was potent yet didn't irritate the stomach. Of course, Extra-Strength Tylenol proved everyone wrong.

Many forms of gap analysis have been used in industry, and our discussion here merely introduces the subject. Except for determinant gap maps, the work should be done by professional market research people. And, the advanced systems are only used in firms with the internal sophistication, time, and money to handle them. Most firms settle for the simpler versions.

---

[9] Further information on using preference data in conjunction with gap maps can be found in Samuel Rabino and Howard R. Moscowitz, "Detecting Buyer Preferences to Guide Product Development and Advertising," *Journal of Product Innovation Management,* September 1984, pp. 140–50.

Trade-Off Analysis

The next technique is more a tool of concept evaluation than of concept generation, and we will meet it again in Chapter 9. But it is clearly a method of attribute analysis. *Trade-off analysis* (originally, and often still, called *conjoint measurement*) is actually a continuation of gap analysis.

Recall that after finding the determinant attributes (important attributes on which the available products differ), gap analysis plots them on maps. Trade-off analysis instead puts the determinant attributes together in new sets, which offer a variety of possible products.

For a simple example, presume coffee has three determinant attributes: flavor, strength, and aroma. If we could find five different flavors, three different strengths, and four different aromas, these attributes could be put together in 60 different combinations. Consumers could then be asked their preference (although 60 possible new products are too many for a consumer to handle). One favorite would emerge from this array, and unless that particular combination was already on the market, we would have our new product.

Given that a serious study of this type may turn up 10 determinant attributes (not 3), and that each attribute may have 5 to 8 possible measurements (for example, flavors), the number of possibilities gets completely out of hand.

Enter trade-off analysis. Using the principles of experimental design, mathematicians can array, say, 10 proposed new products including the full range (though not every step) of attribute variations. But now, most consumers won't be able to find the exact combination they want. So they must choose the combination that most closely meets their desires by trading off attributes wanted most against those wanted less.

What happens next demonstrates the real power of trade-off analysis. A computer program calculates a utility function for each of the 10 attributes. The analyst can then order up the one new product (perhaps never thought of before) that optimizes the 10 variables—so much of this, so much of that, and so on. If that product already exists in the market, the next best product can be derived. Trade-off analysis does actually generate new products. Some people have called the method *product optimization* because of how it works.

Let's look at a couple of examples. First, the Sunbeam Corporation wanted to expand its kitchen mixing appliances sales in various countries around the world. But what variations did each country want? The company identified three types of attributes—silhouette, features, and benefits. The key attributes for each appliance were identified, and the range for each selected. For instance, silhouettes had about 10 combinations—low versus high, strong versus stylized, and so on.

Cards representing new products that combined specific silhouettes, features, and benefits were prepared. Consumers in the various countries were asked to sort the cards by preference from top to bottom. If a person wanted a low, strong silhouette, a large number of variable speeds, a very quiet motor, and the ability to use on semiliquids, one card may have had the right silhouette, speed, and noise but couldn't be used on liquids. Another could be used on liquids and had the right silhouette and noise but had only three speeds. To choose one, the consumer would have to trade off speed variety against use on liquids. With hundreds of consumers doing this, a good picture for each attribute can be obtained and the optimization process begun.[10]

Another example concerned an industrial service of information retrieval for sale to financial institutions.[11] Twelve attributes were considered important, and each was given a range for the test. Here are three of many examples:

Nature of output:	Speed of delivery:	Output format:
Citation only	Within hours	Photocopy
With documentation	Within days	Microform
With interpretation		

The research procedure was the same one that Sunbeam used. The research firm put together a set of cards representing many different versions of the proposed service and covering all characteristics of the 12 attributes. Financial firms were approached, rankings of the cards were made, utility functions were determined, and the ideal service was calculated and returned to the financial institutions for evaluation.

Remember that the key concept generation contribution here is when the respondents, in effect, create a product by telling us how they score attributes. In fact, the above variation on trade-off analysis, called product optimization by its creators, will do essentially that. For example, if an available data set tells which attributes are wanted and how much of each attribute is considered the best amount, then any good cook could put together the ideal (optimized) new product—so

---

[10] The Sunbeam example is described in Albert L. Page and Harold F. Rosenbaum, "Redesigning Product Lines with Conjoint Analysis: How Sunbeam Does It," *Journal of Product Innovation Management,* June 1987, pp. 120–37.

[11] The financial information example is discussed in detail in Yoram Wind, John F. Grashof, and Joel D. Goldhor, "Market-Based Guidelines for Design of Industrial Products," *Journal of Marketing,* July 1978, pp. 27–37.

much of this attribute, so much of that one. The supposedly ideal composite is then taken back to the customer to see if the mix still looks good.[12]

Because business buyers tend to make a more rational analysis of product features, trade-off analysis is becoming increasingly valuable for industrial product innovation.

SUMMARY

We have now finished a review of the first fortuitous scan category— attribute analysis. The techniques varied from the very simple yet challenging dimensional analysis to some very complex methods. Gap analysis and trade-off analysis are more complex, although simplified versions of both can be used by a manager without help from a skilled marketing research department or advertising agency.

The essence of attribute analysis, in every case, is to force us to look at products differently—to bring out new perspectives. We normally have fixed ways of perceiving products, based on our sometimes longtime use of them, so forcing us out of those ruts is difficult.

Many different approaches are available now, and any particular situation will respond to several of them. Some trial and error is recommended; keep early trial simple until a successful output is achieved. Some new products managers use several techniques, saying any one technique will bring perspectives that the others don't. This is particularly true when user perspectives are sought.

We can now move to two more sets of fortuitous scan techniques— relationships analysis and lateral search.

APPLICATIONS

1. "Thanks for telling me about some of those attribute analysis methods you've been studying. I must confess, however, I'm slightly confused by the terminology. Wish fewer experts had been at work here. But tell me, what is the difference again between dimensional analysis and the checklist method? Seems to me they are essentially the same."

2. "As you can probably tell by now, I am an engineer by training and have always enjoyed playing around with what you call attribute

---

[12] For more on product optimization, see Rabino and Moscowitz, "Detecting Buyer Preferences to Guide Product Development and Advertising." For an update on recent usage of the trade-off technique, see Dick R. Wittink and Philippe Cattin, "Commerical Use of Conjoint Analysis: An Update," *Journal of Marketing*, July 1989, pp. 91–96.

extension (see Appendix B). In fact, I recently asked our personal computer division to take five dimensions of the standard PC and extend each out as far as they can see it going and tell me what ideas they get from it. For example, I specifically mentioned the amount of memory as one of those dimensions. Could you do something like this for me now . . . that is, take five dimensions and extend them? It would help me get ready for their presentation Thursday.''

3. "Another method you say you studied is of great interest to me, for reasons I'll not go into. It is gap analysis, especially the idea of maps. Could you please take, say, the beer market and draw up a product map for that market? I understand it can be done by a manager at a desk, although, of course, it wouldn't be nearly as accurate as if we had all the technical data, and so on. But could you try?''

4. "I guess I really like checklists best — they're easy for me to understand and use. I've never seen this one by Small that you mentioned — wow, four pages of ways. Is all that really necessary? Sounds almost boring. Couldn't just as good a job be done with, say, one page?''

Case: Sound*

The field of recorded music has always been driven by technology. Though Edison thought people would need the first phonograph, so far as we know he did no market research to find problems and unmet needs. We have seen 78s, 33⅓s, long-play, and long-long play. Cassette tapes, eight-track tapes, and more. Compact disc players, videotape recorders and players, video disks. Stereo sound and quadriphonic sound. Head sets, belt sets, bathroom versions, and underwater versions. Probably few, if any, of these were market-sourced concepts. Even a device as user-friendly as the Walkman came about because Sony's chairman saw a former chairman wearing a homemade version.

Attributes of products can be features, functions, or benefits. The features are usually physical, though in service industries, they are procedures and actions. Functions are actions of the product, sometimes thought of as performance attributes. Benefits are direct and indirect, measurable and perceived, functional and emotional, real and false. Just what do people get from listening to recorded music?

The question is, do our many techniques of attribute analysis contain anything that would help this industry be more consumer oriented? Dimensional

---

*Source: Some of the information for this case came from Herb Brody, "It Seemed Like a Good Idea at the Time," *High Technology Business*, October 1988, pp. 38–41.

analysis is technology based, really. But benefit analysis (Appendix B) is not. Nor need gap analysis be. If the determinant attributes operating in the field of recorded music could be found, and those having a base in customer needs and desires selected, and then two or three pairs of them used in developing gap maps, a new opportunity might be discovered. Think through the attribute techniques you have just studied, select one or two that appear useful, and give them a try.

As assistance, here are the sad facts about two innovations in recorded music that failed. Quadraphonic sound was stereo music split again—four ways. If two-dimensional was better than one, surely four would be better than two. But the premise was false. Hooking up four speakers in a typical room was almost impossible without tripping over wires every other step. Experts thought the actual quality improvement was marginal. No industry standards existed, so CBS records would not play on RCA equipment. And, the CB radios that were very popular about that time created too much interference in radio waves based on quad-broadcasting.

Another failure was the eight-track tape, a victim that appeared in the 1960s. At that time, high-fidelity sound came from records, FM radio, and reel-to-reel tapes. But FM radio was weak, and the records and tapes of that day wouldn't work in cars. Nor in planes—so Learjet developed a four-track system for use in private aircraft. Later, in conjunction with Motorola, Learjet developed the eight-track device. Unfortunately, though car makers provided the playing device, the tapes were too complex mechanically. The arrival of audio cassettes and better FM signals doomed the eight-track tape to extinction.

Chapter 7

Other Fortuitous Scan Methods and Outside Ideas

SETTING

Attribute analysis was the first of three major categories of fortuitous scan methods. We can now look at the other two. *Relationships analysis* methods are based on the idea that creativity comes essentially from relating things that have something in common. A "shave and a haircut" must have spurred many new product ideas. And now that we have nail polish pens (Aziza Case, Chapter 2), before long someone will notice that the polish tube and the lipstick tube have a lot in common. Here comes the piggyback lipstick/nail polish in matching colors.

But we can also relate the unrelated, an approach even closer to the hearts of the creative purists who claim all genuine creativity must do just that. So, we will look at a few of the many *lateral search* approaches, some of which are fairly frustrating to use.

Near the end of the chapter, we will arrange the many techniques studied so far into an overall concept generation system. This ideal, generic system would have to be adapted to fit a particular firm. Last, we will deal with the legal aspects of handling ideas from nonemployees.

RELATIONSHIPS ANALYSIS

Several concept-generating methods *compare* things: perceptual maps compare attributes, and group creativity is stimulated by reasoning from a known to an unknown, for example. But the comparisons are incidental to a larger issue in those methods. We will now look at three fortuitous scan techniques that go right to the point — forcing things together for examination. These three techniques are the two-dimensional matrix, the morphological matrix, and analogy.

About the Dimensions Used in Relationships Analysis

Recall that Figure 6–2 said attributes are features, functions, and benefits of products. They include dimensions (such as length), operations (such as coating hair with protein), and benefits (such as economy and health). We also distinguished between determinant (important) and nondeterminant attributes.

But other aspects of products are not attributes per se — for example, different places of use, occupations of users, or other items the product is used with. These may be translated into features, functions, and benefits, but relationships analysis techniques use them directly.

Actually, finding different ways to think of products is key to these techniques. For example, the second figure in this chapter will show a study of household cleaners, and one column is "Cleaning Instrument." This is not an attribute of the product, rather an attribute of cleaning systems in which cleaners are used. In relationships analysis, we seek any and all dimensions that help, and those cannot be stipulated in advance. Hopefully the examples shown in this chapter will suggest the view you should take in creating the matrixes.

Two-Dimensional Matrix

The simplest format for studying relationships is seen in Figure 7–1, where two attribute sets are combined in a matrix to force the existence of many cells. Only two dimensions (food form and packaging) are used, but just these two give 377 cells to consider. Notice that only with a technique like this could we expect to come up with aerosol ice cream, bottles of pancakes, or velcro hot dog buns!

The number of two-dimensional matrixes that can be prepared is almost unlimited. Keep looking at different ones until satisfied with the list of new possibilities found, or convinced that the technique "just isn't for me."

Morphological or Multidimensional Matrix

The next method, morphological analysis, simultaneously combines more than two dimensions. The matrix can include many dimensions, and the technique originated many years ago when a

FIGURE 7–1 Relationships Analysis: Sample Grid of Two-Dimensional Foods

Food Forms	Aerosol	Bag	Boil in Bag	Bottle	Box	Can	Envelope	Flow-Through Bag	Jar	On a Stick	Pan	Sack	Tube
Biscuit	1	2	3	4	5	6	7	8	9	10	11	12	13
Bread	14	15	16	17	18	19	20	21	22	23	24	25	26
Burger	27	28	29	30	31	32	33	34	35	36	37	38	39
Butter	40	41	42	43	44	45	46	47	48	49	50	51	52
Cereal	53	54	55	56	57	58	59	60	61	62	63	64	65
Cocktail	66	67	68	69	70	71	72	73	74	75	76	77	78
Cookie	79	80	81	82	83	84	85	86	87	88	89	90	91
Crust	92	93	94	95	96	97	98	99	100	101	102	103	104
Custard	105	106	107	108	109	110	111	112	113	114	115	116	117
Dip	118	119	120	121	122	123	124	125	126	127	128	129	130
Dressing	131	132	133	134	135	136	137	138	139	140	141	142	143
Fish	144	145	146	147	148	149	150	151	152	153	154	155	156
Fondue	157	158	159	160	161	162	163	164	165	166	167	168	169
Frosting	170	171	172	173	174	175	176	177	178	179	180	181	182
Fruit	183	184	185	186	187	188	189	190	191	192	193	194	195
Glaze	196	197	198	199	200	201	202	203	204	205	206	207	208
Ice cream	209	210	211	212	213	214	215	216	217	218	219	220	221
Jelly	222	223	224	225	226	227	228	229	230	231	232	233	234
Juice	235	236	237	238	239	240	241	242	243	244	245	246	247
Meat	248	249	250	251	252	253	254	255	256	257	258	259	260
Pancake	261	262	263	264	265	266	267	268	269	270	271	272	273
Pie	274	275	276	277	278	279	280	281	282	283	284	285	286
Pizza	287	288	289	290	291	292	293	294	295	296	297	298	299
Salad	300	301	302	303	304	305	306	307	308	309	310	311	312
Sandwich	313	314	315	316	317	318	319	320	321	322	323	324	325
Soup	326	327	328	329	330	331	332	333	334	335	336	337	338
Tea	339	340	341	342	343	344	345	346	347	348	349	350	351
Vegetables	352	353	354	355	356	357	358	359	360	361	362	363	364
Waffle	365	366	367	368	369	370	371	372	373	374	375	376	377

Source: Edward M. Tauber, "HIT: Heuristic Ideation Technique—A Systematic Procedure for New Product Search," *Journal of Marketing*, January 1972, p. 61.

scientist was trying to further development on what became the jet engine.[1]

The more recent example shown in Figure 7–2 covers household cleaning products. Consumers were surveyed and asked to provide the following information about their recent use of such items:

1. The cleaning instruments used.
2. The basic ingredients in the cleaners used.
3. The objects cleaned.
4. The type of package or container the products came in.
5. The substances removed with the cleaners.
6. The textures or forms of the cleaners.[2]

Figure 7–2 shows the six categories and the items reported within each category. The new product manager's task now is to link up combinations of those items. One common technique is to have a computer print out all possible combinations, which are then scanned for interesting sets.

Other analysts just use a simple mechanical method of reading the rows across; the top row says, how about a cream substance, in an aerosol package, to be applied to a broom, whereby the alcohol in the cream would clean blood from shoes? The second row asks about a bag of ammonia crystals to be applied with a brush so that body odors can be removed from skis! After going through the rows, the analyst systematically alters one item in each row with one from another, and so on. Many fortuitous scan techniques produce noise from which good ideas must be picked; but what at first appears to be noise may simply be a great new idea no one could have thought of logically.

In any event, the structure shown in Figure 7–2 should be followed. Creation of the columns was discussed at the beginning of this section of the chapter. The number of items in each column is either (1) the entire set, as in the survey above, or (2) a selection representing the full array. For example, a study of play wagons might have a column headed number of wheels, and the rows would be two, three, four, five, and six; but the height column might just have rows of 6 inches, 8 inches, and 12 inches (low, medium, and high).[3]

---

[1] The scientist used 11 parameters (dimensions), each of which had between two and four alternatives; that set yielded 36,864 combinations (possible engines). Incidentally, that matrix also yielded two combinations that became the German V-1 and V-2 rockets in World War II. See Fritz Zwicky, *Discovery, Invention, Research: Through the Morphological Approach* (New York: Macmillan, 1969).

[2] C. L. Alvord and J. B. Mason, "Generating New Product Ideas," *Journal of Advertising Research*, December 1975, pp. 27–32.

[3] For a recent report of several applications of this technique, see Simon Majaro, "Morphological Analysis," *Marketing Intelligence and Planning* no. 2 (1988), pp. 4–11.

FIGURE 7–2   Relationships Analysis: Morphological Technique—Dimensions Relevant to a Household Cleaner

Dimension 1: Cleaning Instrument	Dimension 2: Ingredients	Dimension 3: Objects to Be Cleaned		Dimension 4: Package	Dimension 5: Substance to Be Removed	Dimension 6: Texture
Broom	Alcohol	A/C filters	Glass	Refrigerators	Aerosol	Blood	Cream
Brush	Ammonia	Air	Glasses (eye)	Screens	Bag	Body odors	Crystals
Damp mop	Deodorizing	Aluminum	Grill	Shoes	Bottle	Bugs	Gaseous
Dry cleaning	agent	Boats	Jewels/	Skis	Box	Burns	Gel
Dry mop	Disinfectant	Brooms	jewelry	Stainless	Can	Dirt	Liquid
Hose	Pine oil	Brushes/	Leather	steel	Easy-carry	Dust	Powder
None	Scenting	combs	Linoleum	Stoves	Easy-pour	Food	Solid
Rag	agents	Cabinets	Mops	Synthetics	Jar	Germs	Wax
Sponge		Carpet	Motorcycles	Tiles	Spray	Glue	
Steel wool		Cars	Ovens	Toilets	See-through	Grass stains	
Vacuum		Cement	Paint	Tools	Tube	Grease	
Wet mop		China/crystal	brushes	Toothbrushes	Unbreakable	Mildew	
		Clothes	Pans	Toys	Unspillable	Mud	
		Corfam	Pets	Upholstery		Odors	
		Curtains/	Pictures/	Vinyl		Oil	
		draperies	paintings	Walls		Paint	
		Diapers/pails	Pillows/	Water		Rust	
		Dog houses	mattresses	Windows		Spots	
		Fences	Plastic	Wood		Streaks	
		Floors	Pool	Wool			

Interpretation: Using only the top item from each of the six dimensions, we could get a cream substance packaged in an aerosol package, to be applied to a broom, whereby the alcohol in the cream would clean blood from shoes. This is only one of many thousands of combinations the morphological approach would generate from the above lists.

Source: Charles L. Alvord and Joseph Barry Mason, "Generating New Product Ideas," *Journal of Advertising Research*, December 1975, p. 29.

Analogy

A relationship needn't be direct; it can also be only partially direct. We can often get a better idea of something by looking at it through something else—an analogy.

A good example of analogy was the use of airplane feeding systems by a manufacturer of kitchen furniture and other devices. Preparing, serving, and consuming meals in a plane is clearly analogous to doing so in the home, and the firm created several good ideas for new processes (and furniture) in the home kitchen.

An analogue for bicycles might be driving a car—both incorporate steering, moving, slowing, curving, and so on. But the auto carries more passengers, has four wheels for stability, variable power, built-in communications, and the like. Each difference suggests another new type of bicycle; some of these types are already available. The bicycle could also be compared to the airplane, to skating, to the submarine, to swimming, and at the extreme (for illustration) to a mouse in a maze.

The secret, of course, is finding a usable analogous situation, which is often difficult if not impossible. The analogy should meet four criteria:

1. The analogy should be vivid and have a definite life of its own.
2. It should be full of concrete images.
3. It should be a happening—a process of change or activity.
4. It should be a well-known activity and easy to visualize and describe.[4]

Airplane feeding systems and driving a car qualify easily.

LATERAL SEARCH

As indicated earlier, one school of thought holds that all "nearby" creativity produces only insignificant line extensions and modifications. These people have only disdain for matrixes, analogy, and attribute analysis. They insist the mind must be pushed beyond where it wants to go. See Figure 7–3 for a typology of the novel lateral search techniques.

Lateral Thinking—Avoidance

Some people have stressed the use of avoidance techniques to keep an idea from dominating thinking as it has in the past or to prevent the

---

[4] Edward DeBono, *Lateral Thinking for Management* (New York: American Management Association, 1971), p. 107.

FIGURE 7–3 Typology of Lateral Search Methods

In Chapter 7:
  a. Lateral thinking—avoidance: deliberately searching for uncommon approaches.
  b. Forced relationships: forcing relationships between totally unrelated things.
  c. Creative stimuli: applying the goal of a particular analysis to a set of stimulating words.
  d. Big winner: extrapolating commonalities in a set of popular products, activities, or people.
  e. Competitive analysis: legal espionage.

In Appendix:
  a. Free association: intensely associating the subject with another specific thing.
  b. Stereotype activity: how would so-and-so do this thing we are studying?
  c. Cross-field compilation: scientific inquiry entirely outside the scientific field of the inquiry subject.
  d. Key word monitoring: seeking popular terms in the general press.
  e. Use of the ridiculous: deliberately attempting to do ridiculous things, after which the result is studied for any logical tips.

---

usual reaction to an idea from shutting off original thinking. They cite many ways of achieving avoidance:

Keep asking, "Is there another way of looking at this?"

Keep asking, "Why?"

Deliberately rotate attention to a phase or aspect of the problem other than the logical one.

Find an entry point into the problem other than the one habitually used.

List all possible alternatives to every aspect of the analysis.

Deliberately seek out nonstandard concepts other than those inherent to the problem. Try "unconcepting" or "disconcepting," or try dropping a concept.

Fractionalize concepts and other aspects of the problem.

Bridge two or more concepts to form still other concepts.[5]

Other people call the approach disparate thinking, zigzag, and divergent thinking. This method was claimed to have partially solved a long-standing problem of light bulb theft in the Boston subway—light bulbs were made to screw in counterclockwise.

---

[5] Ibid.

Forced Relationships

The two-dimensional matrix and the morphological matrix are based on *relevant* product or market characteristics. Sometimes, however, interesting viewpoints are achieved by forcing relationships between normally *unrelated* (or even opposed) things.

The forced relationships technique has spawned many preferences; the most quoted is the catalog method. In this method, a catalog, journal, or magazine is selected, and then a relationship is forced between everything in it and something else (perhaps a product or a consumer group). Some suggest using the table of contents in magazines or the Yellow Pages in telephone directories. Other names for the forced relationships approach are pick-a-noun and random walk.

Creative Stimuli

Another unique approach is called *creative stimuli*. The idea subject is specified first—the problem, the product, and so on. Then the tangible goal is stipulated—the desired result or what the specified idea should accomplish. Last, a long list of words, names, and phrases is studied for ideas that accomplish the tangible goal. Figure 7–4 gives a selection of these stimuli. The stimuli seem simplistic but are effective. The technique is easily incorporated into such overall systems of idea stimulation as group creativity and need assessment.[6]

Big Winner

Some product developers believe many successful firms, teams, or individuals in sports, politics, television, and so on are uniquely in tune with the thinking of society. Studying these big winners may lead to principles that can be generalized to new products. At the end of the 1980s, for example, something might be found by studying Michael Jackson, the San Francisco 49ers, Leonard Bernstein, small sport convertibles, cellular phones, flavored soda water, George Bush, the fax

---

[6] For a complete set of the stimuli words and phrases, see Donald Cantin, *Turn Your Ideas into Money* (New York: Hawthorn Books, 1972). A much newer version that combines stimulating terms with variations on the more familiar checklist discussed in Chapter 6 is the product improvement check list (PICL) by Arthur VanGundy. It is available from new Product Development Newsletter, P.O. Box 1309, Point Pleasant, NJ 08742.

FIGURE 7–4   Selections from a List of Creative Stimuli

Guest stars	Charity	Family
Photography	Alphabet	Education
Timeliness	Interview	Inert ingredients
Truth	His and hers	Videotape
Testimonials	Outer space	Style
World	Stunts	Decorate
Chart, diagram	Nation	Legalities
Birth	Showmanship	Gauge, scale
Weather	Ethnic	Floor, wall
Zipper	Habit, fad	Push button, lever
Participation	Fantasy	Transportation
Snob appeal	Music	Folklore, magic
Symbolism	Romance	Direct mail
Subconscious need	Calendar	Parody, lampoon, satire
Summer, fall	Hobbies	Rhinestones
Graphics	Holidays	Curiosity
Sketch, doodle	Security	Telephone

Procedure: Think of the product or use area; then look at each of the above words and wait for an idea.

Source: Donald Cantin, *Turn Your Ideas into Money* (New York: Hawthorn Books, 1972), condensed from pp. 34–41.

machine, and Roseanne. One consulting firm compiled a list of the 20 all-time best-selling packaged goods; from this list, the firm generalized principles to transfer to clients' new products.[7]

Competitive Analysis

Many firms claim that by studying the strategic plans and actions of competitors, they can detect new product approaches, especially defensive ones. Figure 7–5 lists methods used in the competitive information arena. The first eight are generally considered legal and ethical; the remainder are not. Three particular competitor analyses for new product development are:

1. Life-cycle models help a firm estimate when competitors will take over any of its markets and thus stimulate new products to defensively cannibalize sales.

---

[7] Robert Danielenko, "Those New Products Wizards," *Product Management*, September 1976, pp. 40–44.

FIGURE 7–5   Methods of Competitive Espionage

Published material and public documents, such as court records.
Disclosures made by competitors' employees and obtained without
  subterfuge.
Market surveys and consultants' reports.
Financial reports and brokers' research surveys.
Trade fairs, exhibits, and competitors' brochures.
Analysis of competitors' products.
Reports from salespeople and purchasing agents.
Legitimate employment interviews with people who have worked for
  competitors.
Camouflaged questioning and "drawing out" of competitors' employees at
  technical meetings.
Direct observation under secret conditions.
False job interviews with competitors' employees (that is, where there is no
  real intent to hire).
False negotiations with competitors for license.
Hiring a professional investigator to obtain a specific piece of
  information.
Hiring an employee away from a competitor to get specific know-how.
Trespassing on competitors' property.
Bribing competitors' suppliers or employees.
"Planting" your agent on competitors' payroll.
Eavesdropping on competitors (for example, via wire tapping).
Theft of drawings, samples, documents, and similar property.
Blackmail and extortion.

Note: The methods are listed in descending order of ethics and legality. The first eight are
usually considered legal and ethical.

Source: Knut Holt, *Product Innovation: A Workbook for Management in Industry* (London:
Newnes-Butterworth, 1976), p. 65.

2. Technological mapping is a form of relevance tree forecasting in
   which the competitive capability of each competitor is predicted. It
   lays the groundwork for decisions to push or play down certain
   technologies in the home firm.
3. Strategic analysis permits direct forecasting of probable future
   changes in competitors' technological commitments by studying mer-
   gers, acquisitions, sell-offs, patent applications, patent sales, and so
   on. A keen analyst can predict major market swings and thus suggest
   new product opportunities (or lack of opportunities) for the firm.[8]

---

[8] On the matter of technologies, see James Brian Quinn, "Technological Forecasting,"
Harvard Business Review, March–April 1967, p. 101. For more current views on the
overall matter of how (and how not) to gain competitive information, see Doug Stewart,
"Spy Tech," *Discover*, March 1988, pp. 58–65; and Gregory L. Miles, "Information
Thieves Are Now Corporate Enemy No. 1," *Business Week*, May 5, 1986, pp. 120–25.

IS THERE AN IDEAL SYSTEM COMBINING THE BEST OF THE MANY CONCEPT GENERATION TECHNIQUES?

Having now spent most of three chapters discussing the various approaches ideators take in seeking new product concepts, students may wonder which ones to use in each situation. The answer is twofold. First, every ideation situation is different and varies by:

- The urgency.
- The skills of the individuals involved.
- The expertise (and thus helpfulness) of the end user.
- The nature of the product, because some (such as small appliances) are much better for, say, attribute analysis than are others.
- The resources available (because problem analysis is more expensive than most of the others).

Second, however, one general approach can be modified to fit the situation. The steps are as follows:

1. Do thorough research into company sources of market needs, problems, and suggestions for new products.
2. Make an extensive problem analysis, including focus groups, followed by one-on-one survey quantification of the findings from the focus groups.
3. Do a scenario analysis to add whatever problems are seen for the future, even though users do not know of them now.
4. Select from the above set the few problems worthy of further development effort now. Hold the others.
5. Assemble a group or groups (either brainstorming or disciplines panel) to attack the chosen problems, while at the same time seeking appropriate technical help from the firm's engineering and R&D groups.
6. While the problem solving is under way, try out two or three fortuitous scan methods that fit the situation. For example, one good start is to do a thorough checklist attack on current products to seek improvements. Another good step is to put together a morphological analysis (similar to the one of household cleaning earlier in this chapter) to really push the imagination. This activity will generate possible additional products, perhaps some short-term entries to help hold you off until the problem-oriented items are ready to go.

The productivity of concept generation does not depend on how systematic or scientific the approach is. Considerable leeway is required, and the method's personal "fit" is always the best indicator of its effectiveness.

ETHICS

Any set of concept generation techniques contains some potential ethical problems. Many persons, for example, believe a firm has a right to an exclusive field of privacy and one firm should not be permitted to hire an employee or rent an airplane to invade the privacy of another. Others make the same objection on behalf of the individual. Some ideators fail to explain that the mirror on the focus group wall is actually a one-way window. In-store observations are normally from a hidden spot; and psychological projective techniques are designed to get us to verbalize thoughts that we would not (or could not) say. Fortunately, marketing research has recently avoided blatant invasions of personal privacy.

HANDLING THE OUTSIDE IDEA

In almost any system, nonemployees are asked to give information that directly or indirectly may lead to a successful new product. And, even if not asked, they often submit it anyway (letters, suggestions to field salespeople, comments made at trade show booths, and many more). When they do, a potential problem arises that most firms are now trying hard to avoid.

For example, a short time after 3M marketed its fabulously successful Post-it notes, the firm received word from Colorado businessman Thomas N. Garland that in 1971 he had written to it suggesting such a product.[9] He had been told that 3M "was not interested at the present time." The company said it forgot about his suggestion after rejecting it and considered the idea of nontight adhesive only after employee Art Fry found in it the solution to his problem of holding notes in a choir hymnal. Whatever the outcome of that disagreement (3M says there was no suit, but will not comment beyond that), the implication for other managements is clear; all involved (inventor, developing firm) want to have clear and firm ground on which to stand.

Fortunately, a system exists for dealing with suggestions from nonemployees. Unfortunately, one study showed that some companies aren't aware of it or fail to enforce it (see Figure 7–6). We will look first at the legal background and then at the generally accepted system.

---

[9] Bill Abrams, "Minnesota Mining and Manufacturing Co.," *The Wall Street Journal*, June 9, 1983, p. 33.

FIGURE 7–6 Methods Used by American Firms in Handling New Product Ideas Suggested by Outsiders

	Foods	*Household*	*Clothing*	*Personal*	*Misc.*	*Total*
Legally sound						
Waiver	7.0%	22.2%	21.4%	16.7%	22.5%	17.5%
Patents only	4.7	0	0	14.1	2.5	2.4
Reject outside	27.9	0	0	25.0	7.5	12.6
Total	39.6	22.2	21.4	55.8	32.5	32.5
Dangerous						
No response	25.6	42.2	35.7	25.0	15.0	28.3
Evaluated	34.9	35.6	42.9	29.2	52.5	39.2
No good	9.3	17.9	28.7	4.2	10.0	12.7
On market	9.3	4.4	7.1	12.5	25.0	12.0
Known to us	14.0	4.4	0	8.4	10.0	8.5
Not our area	2.3	8.9	7.1	4.1	7.5	6.0
Total	60.5%	77.8%	78.6%	54.2%	67.5%	67.5%
Number of firms	43	45	14	24	40	166

Foods: Cookie, sandwich, candy, vegetable, cracker, coffee, wine, soft drink, pet food.
Household: Tool, appliance, carpet, television, air freshener, oven tray, cooking bag, bug killer, sound system.
Clothing: Shirt, dress, shoes.
Personal: Hair care, after-shave, shampoo, jewelry, tobacco.
Miscellaneous: Photography, sports, banking, game, auto part, motor additive, office tape dispenser, pen.

Source: C. Merle Crawford, "Unsolicited New Product Ideas: Handle with Care," *Research Management*, January 1975, p. 22.

Legal Background

A new product concept (if really new) is a trade secret — something that due to its secrecy gives one firm or person economic advantage over others. If that secrecy is lost, the concept loses much of its value.

If the creator can get a patent on the concept, most of the difficulty is eliminated. But some concepts won't patent, and even simple patents take time and money (which inventors often don't have).

The firm receiving an outside suggestion faces a tricky dilemma: how to handle the idea without letting it be exposed to an employee (engineer, marketer) who might now or later forget having seen the suggestion and suggest the firm use it.

Of course, the legal system holds that the firm is still protected, no matter who sees an idea, if it has proof it had the idea earlier. And if the concept is actually well known or even already on the market, the firm is again protected.

Unfortunately, these scenarios are full of potential judgment problems. How good is the proof of prior knowledge? Who in the firm actually knew of the suggestion? Could a scientist have come to the same idea independently of the suggester, and at about the same time? (This is not at all unknown in scientific circles.)

Recommended Procedure

Recognizing all of this, most corporate legal departments have a specific procedure to follow on the receipt, by any employee, of a new product suggestion from an outside person (a nonemployee). The steps, with modifications to fit individual industries and persons, are:

1. If the suggestion is oral, have the suggester put it in writing.
2. Whoever receives the idea is to send it (including any accompanying document, such as drawings) directly to the legal department. The suggestion is not to be read or evaluated in any way. If the outside address on the envelope indicates the envelope contains a suggestion (for instance, if the envelope is addressed to the new products department), the envelope is not even to be opened until it reaches the legal department. If the opener of the letter has not been forewarned, he or she should stop reading as soon as it is clear that the letter contains a suggestion.
3. In the legal department, the idea letter is given a number or an identification of some other type, and the suggester is sent a form letter that expresses the firm's thanks, indicates the conditions under which the company considers outside suggestions, and (usually) includes a waiver form that the suggester is to sign and return. The waiver form stipulates, among other things, that the offer is made free of any obligation on the part of the firm except as stated in the form. Some waiver forms even stipulate that the firm may use the idea and pay only what it determines is reasonable.
4. If the waiver form is returned by the suggester, the original suggestion is taken from its place of restricted storage (a safe or a securely locked file) and sent to the proper party (engineer, marketing, R&D) for evaluation. What happens afterward depends on the perceived value of the idea.
5. Along the way:
   a. No acknowledgement of idea receipt is given by anyone outside the authorized department.

    b. No one asks for more information from the suggester until a waiver form is signed. (Whether more information is needed could not be known unless the suggestion was read by someone who understood it, and that shouldn't have happened.)

    c. Even if the employee receiving the suggestion thinks it is obviously not new or completely lacking in merit, the suggestion is handled in the prescribed manner.

This procedure clearly handles the legal issues. First, the firm readily concedes that the idea is a trade secret and that it may have value. After the firm has obtained the waiver form, it can claim that the idea is not new (secret) because the suggester has agreed to this. Second, the procedure clearly forestalls accidental premature use of the idea by any employee who is unaware of the legal problems. An outsider's idea cannot be used if there is no exposure to it. Third, the procedure provides absolutely safe conditions under which the idea can be fairly and completely evaluated. There is no need to use a rush system or to engage in any clandestine operations, which, in turn, frees the firm on the matter of motive and gives any court a clear indication of the procedure that the firm thinks proper.

The procedure is not fraudproof, of course, as various persons would still be in a position to cheat the suggester, but it is difficult to do this and still deceive the legal department.

The Waiver

Figure 7–7 shows a waiver form used by AMF, Inc., that is representative of the better ones available. It discloses without confidentiality; it calls for no obligation from the firm; it admits the firm accepts no liability other than that coming from a patent; it admits the submission of the idea was not requested by the company; and it agrees that any benefits of a nonpatented idea will be solely within the discretion of the firm. In lay terms, the company says, "We'll look at it if you want us to, but the idea is no secret, and it is not worth anything unless we say it is."

Though such a system seems severe, it allows courts to ensure the suggester's rights as well as protect the company from unreasonable accusations. Needless to say, a company that attempts to make a totally unreasonable payment for an idea it decides to accept will probably be given a chance to explain its decision to the courts. Moreover, an honest estimate of low value will not be binding if it later turns out that the invention was worth much more. Sears lost a case on this

FIGURE 7–7 Waiver Form Used by AMF, Inc.

Submitting ideas to AMF, Incorporated, and its subsidiary corporations

To avoid any possible future confusion between your ideas and those already acquired by AMF and its subsidiaries from the efforts of their own employees and others, and to prevent any misunderstanding as to your rights and the obligations of AMF and its subsidiaries, your submission can be considered only under the following conditions:

1. AMF and its subsidiaries do not solicit suggestions, and sending this form does not constitute an invitation to disclose an idea.
2. No suggestion will be considered unless it is submitted in writing. Material submitted will not be returned, so retain a duplicate.
3. No suggestion will be accepted by AMF or its subsidiaries on the basis of a confidential relationship or under a guarantee that the idea shall be kept secret, or on condition that AMF or any subsidiary shall agree to terms of compensation before they know the idea.
4. A patented idea, or one on which a patent application has been filed, will be considered only on the basis that the submitter will rely exclusively on the rights granted under the Patent Statutes. (In the case of a patentable idea, it is suggested that the submitter file a patent application before submitting an idea.)
5. Where an idea has not been patented, and no patent application is pending on it, payment, if any, for the use of the idea shall be in an amount solely within the discretion of AMF or its subsidiary.
6. Neither AMF nor its subsidiaries shall be obligated to give reasons for their decision or to reveal their past or present activities related to the submitted idea. Negotiating or offering to purchase an idea shall be without prejudice to AMF or its subsidiaries and not be an admission of the novelty, priority, or originality of the idea.

To AMF Incorporated and its subsidiaries:

I have read the conditions outlined above and agree to them. In addition, I warrant that the idea submitted is my own and that I am free to offer it.

My idea is _____

_____

_____

_____

_____

_____

_____

Signature _____

Date _____   Street address _____

City and state _____ Zip _____

point in the late 1970s. Munsingwear faced a similar situation when it actually signed a license with a girdle inventor and then informed the inventor that his idea was without merit. When Munsingwear later marketed a similar item, the inventor went to court and won a $31 million award.

The system keeps substantial rights with the inventor, which is certainly socially desirable. Yet it also protects companies from unreasonable charges by outside idea sources. It avoids expensive legal suits—if used properly—and yet protects all interests.

Acceptable Alternatives

There are two acceptable alternatives to the waiver system if the firm wishes to avoid the complexity and costs of that better system.

1. *Reject all outside ideas.*   This is the policy of many firms that are the targets of thousands of ideas. Both General Foods and General Mills get thousands of such ideas each year, and a waiver system would be totally impractical for them. Of course, the firm must not violate the policy when it thinks it sees a good idea.
2. *Evaluate only patented ideas.*   This method is also quite safe, but it obviously causes the firm to lose out on good unpatented ideas.

Both alternatives compel the firm to handle ideas carefully to prevent the well-meaning or uninformed employee from considering or even using an occasional outside idea. The firm's response to the suggester, for example, should be rapid; otherwise, there is reason to suspect that time is being taken for evaluation.

Patents Make a Comeback

The strategy of being willing to evaluate outside ideas only if they are patented has been criticized for the last 10 to 15 years. Most new products people, especially in electronics industries, have felt patents are so weak—so poorly enforced—that they are almost irrelevant. Such people have opted to rely on trade secrets instead.

However, the picture has changed in recent years. In 1982, Congress created the Court of Appeals for the Federal Circuit, which handles all patent appeals. Formerly, litigants searched through the various appeals courts to find one where they had reason to think they would find judges sympathetic to their situation. The new court has called for easier requirements from holders of patents (in court proceedings) and heavier burdens of evidence from infringers. It has ruled for patents in over half of its cases.

Patent holders now get quicker injunctions and can expect their rights to run all the way to the end of the patent. They also are getting bigger damages and damages that include lost profits. Once again, patents are worth considering.[10]

SUMMARY

This chapter concludes the subject of concept generation. We looked at the other two categories of fortuitous scan methods—relationships analysis and lateral search. Relationships analysis essentially prompts new ideas by comparing a product, an attribute, or a situation with a similar thing from an allied setting. Each relationship offers a new perspective with the chance for ideation. On the other hand, lateral search is less intentional and reaches for comparisons that seem to make little sense. Of course, those unlikely stimuli may contain more ideation possibilities.

The numerous techniques for these scans should be studied and sampled. When one fits and works, it should be used more intensively. The less logic there is in a technique, the less likely it is to work for a particular individual.

Chapter 7 also addressed the important question of how organizations should handle an idea from a nonemployee. Because it is easy to have a slipup and court suits have been very costly, many managements have adopted a tough waiver procedure recommended by their legal departments. Weaker alternatives are to (1) refuse all outside ideas and (2) accept patented ideas only. And any of the techniques used should be part of an overall proactive system of concept generation developed for each situation. No two people or firms have quite the same system, but the general outline for them all was given in this chapter.

New ideas are fragile, which argues for their need to have an incubatorlike environment to mature—which leads us to the next subject. Part III covers the phase of innovation called evaluation. Here the basic concept further evolves through evaluation, implementation,

---

[10] For more on the patent revival, see Steven A. Meyerowitz, "Protection through Patents: New Power for an Old Remedy," *Business Marketing*, July 1988, pp. 63–67; and Norm Alster, "New Profits from Patents," *Fortune*, April 25, 1988, pp. 185–90.

and marketing. Remember, the concept is fully developed only when it is marketed successfully.

APPLICATIONS

More questions from that interview with the company president.

1. "One of our divisions, the result of an acquisition, runs a chain of car washes in the Jacksonville, Florida, area. About 10 units, I believe. Anyway, that business is tired — no innovation except some cute tricks in pricing and some added waxing and cleaning services. But I was intrigued with that creative stimuli method you mentioned earlier. I'd sure like to see what that method would do on car washes, particularly to see if it can come up with some really innovative new services those businesses could offer."

2. "Now that you have studied the legal situation on outside ideas, you might be able to help me with a problem our foods division has. We're being sued by a lady in Austin, Texas, who claims we took her suggestion for a new type of cookie, marketed it, and pocketed the profits without paying her anything. Says she sent it to us in a letter about a year before we marketed the new cookie, knows we made a lot on it, and now is demanding no less than $100,000! I'm told we will probably come out OK, but I'm not so sure. Just as a reminder, exactly what should I look for when I visit the foods division next month, that is, to see if we did the right thing in that case and if we are all right in general?"

3. "You may recall that I mentioned earlier a new bubble gum idea — where the bubble gum would be in the shape of a 3-inch record, packaged in a tiny record jacket with a label for a top-40 number. The idea is that the record jackets would change and become collector's items — like bubble gum cards. I wonder if you could show me how the two-dimensional matrix idea would apply to bubble gum. I'd sure like to get a better idea than the recording one, and I'm curious as to how that method works anyway."

4. "Heard recently about a man named Frederick G. Gosman who invented a parlor board game featuring Christmas. He found that we had Monopoly-type board games on many subjects but none on Christmas. Unfortunately, the industry didn't like the idea at all, so he had some made up, ordered 25,000, quit his job, and with an expense budget of $5,000 a month, hit the road, calling on stores. It worked. Big department stores bought out the 25,000, and he has now produced another 30,000. Tell me, why did his approach work? Why does that industry accept so

few ideas from inventors? Cadaco, for example, gets 8 to 10 suggestions every day and has accepted just 1 idea from 6,000 received in recent years. Other firms have about the same experience."

Case: Golden Enterprises*

In 1984, Golden Enterprises, Inc., of Birmingham, Alabama, had sales topping $100 million and an aftertax margin of 8.6 percent. That's a higher rate than Nabisco Brands, a leading competitor. Golden was less profitable than Frito-Lay and considerably smaller than Lance, Inc., a $337 million firm it was frequently compared with. Golden, known in the Deep South for its Golden Flakes potato and corn chips and fried pork skins, had doubled sales every five years since 1960. The stock was selling well, and the firm was 51 percent controlled by one man—Sloan Bashinsky.

The firm had 800 company-owned trucks that plied 666 routes. They sold supermarkets, convenience stores, and other vendors over a 12-state area. The company's new product strategy was strictly imitative/emulative. For example, Frito-Lay introduced O'Grady's cheese chips, and Golden introduced Au Gratin chips a year later. Bashinsky claimed Frito-Lay spent over $50 million developing the O'Grady's line, while he spent nothing.

He even farmed out early production of a new item to avoid investing in manufacturing facilities until he was sure he had a winner. In recent years, he invested in some corn-processing facilities because he wanted to emphasize corn products over potato—they were cheaper and less dependent on the weather. Revenue in 1984 was 45 percent from potato chips, 30 percent from corn chips, and 15 percent from fried pork skins.

To date, the strategy had paid off, but new management was taking over from the 65-year-old Bashinsky and would soon review the standing imitation strategy. The technologies of Frito-Lay and Nabisco Brands would increasingly threaten the industry's main imitators.

So the issue was: What would be the best approach for the firm to use in coming up with new snack ideas? Was the firm set up for the problem/solution approach, or was fortuitous scan better? No decisions had been made about a new strategy to replace imitation, so some thinking was needed there. If you feel problem/solution would be best, which approach(es) in that category would be most fitting? If fortuitous scan, which technique(s) would work the best? In other words, what type of systematic concept generation program would you have recommended for Golden Enterprises as it attempted to become less dependent on imitating Frito-Lay?

---

* Source: Some information in this case came from "Copycat," *Forbes*, May 20, 1985, pp. 126–28.

Part III

Concept Evaluation

Chapter 8

The Concept Evaluation System

SETTING

We have just finished studying the various methods of generating new product concepts. The next step is to evaluate these concepts. Evaluation takes place at many different times and in different ways, by different people, for different reasons. Therefore, a system of evaluations is needed, an idea explained in Chapter 8. Then, beginning in Chapter 9, we will look at the different phases in that system. Concept testing is the first major tool and will be discussed there.

Chapter 10 covers the activity generally called a *full screen,* a step where the concept is judged by how well it fits the company and its marketing strengths. Chapter 10 also covers some work needed before the concept can be turned over to the technical departments for development.

Chapter 11 picks up the evaluation task after prototypes begin appearing. The principal tool is product use testing, or field testing. Chapters 12 and 13 cover market testing, the evaluation that takes place as the firm tests its ability to put the product together with its marketing plan.

Chapter 14 concludes Part III and explains the financial analysis used on new products.

All of these evaluations are important, and certainly the financial summary is critical. However, new products people tend to spend most of their time and energy on three steps tied to the three major causes of new product failure. New products fail because (1) there was no basic need for the item, as seen by intended users, (2) the new product did not meet its need, net, considering all disadvantages, and (3) the new product idea was not properly communicated (marketed) to the intended user. In sum, they didn't need it, it didn't work, they didn't get the message.

The three key evaluation steps in Part III, therefore, are concept testing (reconfirms need), product use testing (it works), and market testing (communication).

WHAT'S GOING ON IN THE NEW PRODUCTS PROCESS?

New products actually build up the way rivers do. Great rivers are systems with tributaries that have tributaries. Products that appear complex are just collections of metal shapes, packaging material, fluids, prices, and so on. Another good analogy is the production of automobiles, with a main assembly line supported by scores of subsidiary assembly lines scattered around the world, each of which makes a part that goes into another part that ultimately goes onto a car in that final assembly line.

If you can imagine the quality control people in auto parts plants evaluating each part before releasing it to the next step, you have the idea of a new product evaluation system. The new product appears first as an idea, a concept in words or pictures, so that must be evaluated first. As workers turn the concept into a formed piece of wood or metal or software, those forms are then evaluated. When a market planner puts together a marketing plan, its parts are evaluated separately (just as minor car parts are) and then evaluated again in total, after it is added to the product.

Purposes of Evaluation

Although the overall purpose of evaluation is to guide us to profitable new products, each individual evaluation step has a slightly different purpose, keyed primarily to what happens next. For example, the very first evaluation precedes the product concept. (See Figure 8–1, which shows graphically where evaluation takes place relative to other activities.) The first judgment or assessment is made on an opportunity. Someone decided the firm had a strong technology, or an excellent market opportunity, or a serious competitive threat— whatever. As discussed in Chapter 3 on strategy, a judgment was made that if the firm tried to develop a new product in a given area, it would probably succeed.

This early evaluation step (direction) is shown in Figure 8–2 as part of the overall evaluation system. Where should we look, what should we try to exploit, what should we fight against? The tool is opportunity identification and evaluation, also discussed in Chapter 3. This tool keeps us out of developments where we stand a poor chance of winning; in other words, it makes sure we play the game on our home field.

FIGURE 8–1 Timing of the Product Innovation Activity Sequence

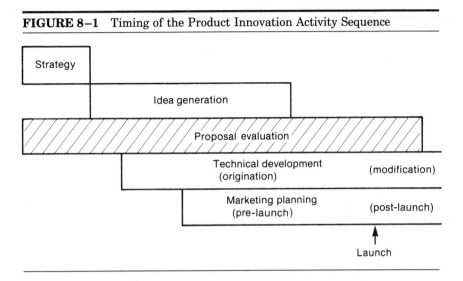

After ideas begin to appear, the purpose changes: to avoid the big loser or the sure loser. We want to cull them out and spend no added time and money on them. We're sometimes wrong, of course, but usually we're right, and this step is essential if we are to focus limited resources on the worthwhile concepts.

Early evaluation also tries to spot the potential big winners. Most good concepts are just that—good. A few are great, and we want to recognize them as soon as possible. These get added effort, special attention, top priority.

Other evaluations key more directly to the following step. A protocol check tells whether we are ready to develop a product for serious field testing. A customer use test tells whether we are ready to get serious about marketing. A market test tells whether we are ready to roll out the product on a national or international basis.

These points appear through further study of Figure 8–2. The second step in the system is prescreening (initial review)—deciding whether an idea is worth screening. Today's complex screening processes are a far cry from the simple checklists of 10 to 15 years ago. Undertaking a full screen is not advisable without first developing the specific concept or without early impressions of the market and buyers.

Marketing decisions are not made during the next step (full screen)—the central question there is whether the firm will try to execute the concept being evaluated. Whether to market it will be decided when the firm has a clearer idea of what it has developed; only rarely does the marketed product closely match the screened idea. More on this later.

The fourth step (progress reports) in Figure 8–2 is actually a set of evaluations for two reasons. One, a firm often develops several different

FIGURE 8–2   The Evaluation System

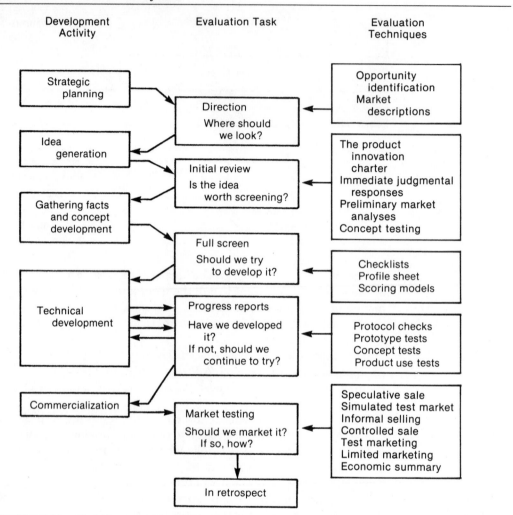

forms of products—precursors of new products—and it needs to know certain things about each form before going on to the next. (See Figure 8–3 for a list of the forms required to develop a Xerox copier.) Two, technical development is naturally iterative: one new discovery leads to another; directions are changed; specific attempts fail, and we have to back up. At Hollingsworth & Vose, an industrial specialty paper company, gaskets are tested five times in this stage—in-house lab test, customer lab test, customer engine test, car manufacturer engine test, and fleet test.

FIGURE 8–3   Xerox Standard Development Model Definitions

Model	Number	Relation to Final Configuration
1. Laboratory bench fixture	1–2	No relation to product concept in size, configuration, or input-output optimization. Emphasis on function.
2. Process feasibility breadboard; semi-integrated	1	Little or no relation to product concept. Functional in purpose. Flexibility process capability to explore limitations. Repeated design changes.
3. Product feasibility breadboard; integrated	1–2	Begins to approach product concept configuration. Not all features incorporated. Industrial design mock-up separate. Basic consideration of manufacturing service and maintenance.
4. Engineering model (optional)	2–6	Simulates final product design. Incorporates nearly all features and functions. Preliminary consideration of industrial design. Human factors. Plus serviceability and maintainability. May be adopted for early field test or latent market probe.
5. Preprototype model (optional)	1–12	Configuration aimed at final product. Configuration complete with covers and control panels.
6. Prototype model	1–12	Models used for TAD, engineering evaluation. Critical design review for maintainability, serviceability, and reliability.
7. Preproduction model (prototype built by manufacturing)	12–24	Final configuration design subject to modification from results of field test and TAD evaluation.
8. Initial production units	50–100	Final product configuration. Units utilized for initial machine observation, market introduction, and Xerox Service Center tests.
9. Production units	1,000s	National launch model. Full-scale sales, service, and consumables support.

Note: TAD = Technical assurance department.

Source: Adapted with permission from Raymond C. Zoppoth, "The Use of Systems Analysis in New Product Development," *Long-Range Planning*, March 1972, p. 25. © Copyright 1972, Pergamon Press, Ltd.

Commercialization follows successful technical development. This decision says, "Our product is OK; can we market it?" Market testing answers this question and, if successful, leads into full-scale marketing. Complete financial analyses are built into the market testing.

The last step (the postmortem or "in retrospect") in the evaluation process is often overlooked. The question is, "Should the development have been undertaken and carried to conclusion?" This often creates a political squabble, but it shouldn't. The purpose is not to find the guilty party for a product that bombed but, rather, to study the evaluation process to prevent a repetition.

Balanced Product Innovation Portfolio

The evaluation system keeps the new product operation efficient, and we will talk more about this in a minute. Keep in mind, however, that any one product being evaluated is not alone. Most organizations have several products under development, sometimes scores or even hundreds of them. Managements would like to think that every project will yield a big profit. They won't, so managements think in terms of a portfolio of new product projects.

Different firms put together different portfolios of new product projects. The stable, healthy firm usually has a mix of projects from low-risk, short-term ones to high-risk, longer-term ones. The portfolio of a conservative firm avoids the high-risk projects. A firm in trouble seeks only higher-risk projects of a short-term nature. Of course, a firm that hasn't heard of product innovation portfolio strategy will have no focus and will accept anything that comes along and looks good. In any event, the system of evaluation steps must reflect the firm's strategy.

THE TWIN STREAMS CONCEPT

Figure 8–4 shows an abbreviation of part of the overall new products process chart that appeared in Chapter 2. It emphasizes that two main streams of activity take place during most of this process. Instead of just preparing the new product, we also prepare its marketing plan. The marketing plan may actually start first, as, for example, when strategists identify an emerging group of people or firms with a new type problem. They become part of a product innovation charter, so we have a target market – the first part of the marketing plan – before we have anything resembling a product.

Evaluation integrates and coordinates the two streams of activity. Every effort is made to avoid a product that marketing can't sell, of

FIGURE 8–4 The Twin Streams of Development

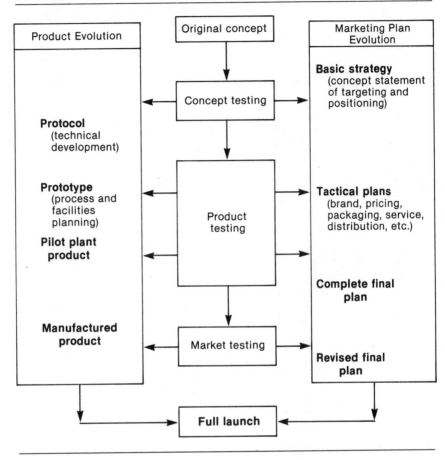

course, but marketing also must have a product to sell. According to an often repeated—perhaps apocryphal—story about an Alberto Culver shampoo, television ads were filmed and at the networks ready for showing before the chemist could find an appropriate formulation!

THE CUMULATIVE EXPENDITURES CURVE

As mentioned earlier, the new product evaluation system flows with the development of the product. What evaluation occurs at any one point (how serious, how costly) depends greatly on what happens next. Figure 8–5 shows a key input to the design of any evaluation system: in the middle of that figure, a gradually upward-sloping curve represents the

FIGURE 8–5   Cumulative Expenditures–All-Industry Average Compared to Occasional Patterns

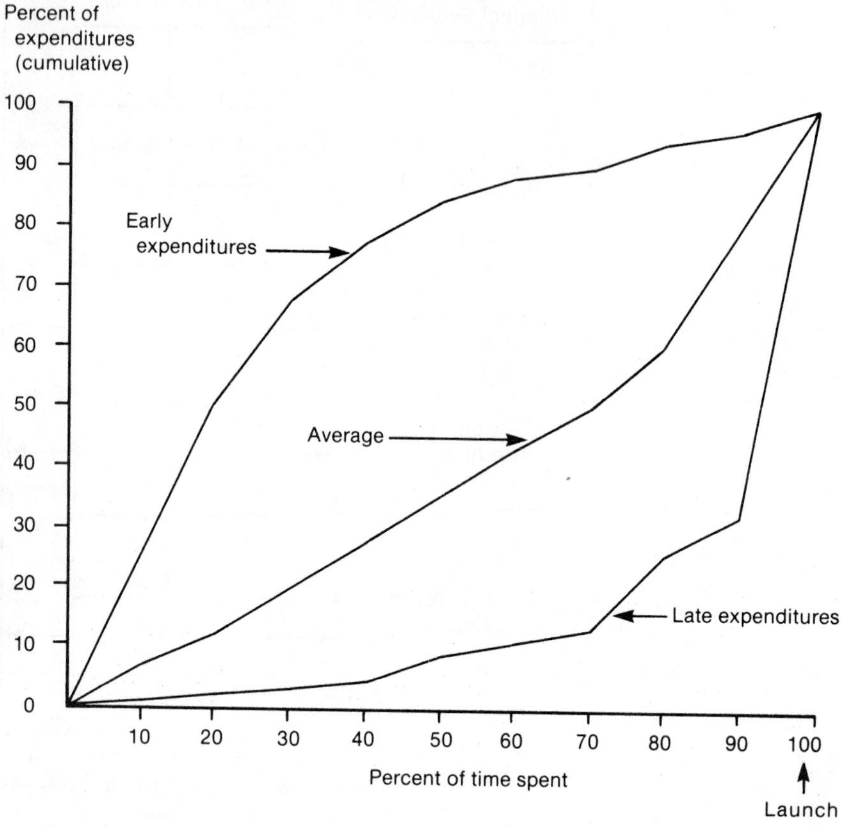

Percent of
expenditures
(cumulative)

accumulation of costs or expenditures on a typical new product project from its beginning to its full launch.

This generalized curve, taken from various studies over the years, is just an average. It probably reflects no one firm or, perhaps, no one project. Shown with the average curve are two others. The early expenditures curve is representative of product development in technical fields, such as pharmaceuticals, optics, and computers. R&D is the big part of the cost package, and marketing costs are relatively small. The other curve in the figure shows the opposite type of firm, say, a consumer packaged goods company. Here the technical expenditures may be small, but a huge TV advertising program is needed at introduction.

Concept evaluation activities vary accordingly. An ethical pharmaceutical firm does its market evaluation of a new product concept early and then spends years on technical development. When it receives Food & Drug Administration (FDA) approval to market the item, little money will be spent on positioning studies, package design, price, and the like. The consumer products company, on the other hand, must make those TV expenditures efficient, so it devotes large sums to market testing.

These are generalizations, and individual exceptions do occur, such as when Procter & Gamble spends years developing a fat substitute called Olestra or Upjohn markets a line of generic drugs. The point is, whoever develops a concept evaluation system needs to know what situation it is for. No evaluation decision is independent of considerations on what will be done next, how much will be spent, or what points of no return are passing. An old Chinese proverb says, "Spend your energy sharpening the edge of the knife, not polishing the blade."

The Risk Matrix

Figure 8–6 applies the ideas just discussed. At any single point in the evaluation process, the new products manager faces the four situations shown. Given that the product concept being evaluated has two broad ultimate outcomes (success or failure) and that there are two decision options (move on or abort the project), there are four cells in the matrix.

The AA cell and the BB cell are fine; we abort a concept that would ultimately fail, or we continue on a concept that would ultimately succeed. The managerial problem arises in the other two cells. AB is an error: a winner is discarded. But BA is also an error: a loser is continued to the next evaluation point.

FIGURE 8–6   Matrix of Risk/Payoff at Each Evaluation

Decision is to: → *If the product were marketed*	A Abort the project now	B Continue to next evaluation
A. It would *fail*	AA	BA
B. It would *succeed*	AB	BB

Comment: Cells AA and BB are "correct" decisions. Cells BA and AB are errors, but they have different cost and probability dimensions.

Which error does the manager most want to avoid? The answer depends on the dollars. First, throwing out a winner is very costly, because the ultimate profits from a winning product are bound to be much greater than all of the development costs combined, let alone those in just the next step. So error AB is many multiples of BA.

Except, of course, for opportunity costs. What other project is standing by waiting for funding? When good candidates wait in the wings, the losses of aborting a winner are much less.

The point is, a manager must think of these matters when deciding what evaluation to do. If the net costs in any situation are low, then a decision will probably be made to go ahead, perhaps with very little information. For example, when IBM had just one year to develop and market the original PC computer, it felt the losses from delay greatly exceeded the gains from concept tests, lengthy field use tests, market tests, and so on. The company didn't do any. On the other hand, General Foods kept Brim coffee in market test for several years, because it wanted to make sure the market plans were correct before undertaking the very expensive national launch.

A good example of what the risk matrix can lead to came when Pillsbury announced that it had, in one year:

1. Failed with Appleeasy because it had, at the last minute, cut the amount of apples in reaction to increasing apple prices.
2. Failed with vegetable yogurt because people simply didn't like the idea.
3. Failed with presweetened baked beans because people liked to sweeten their own.
4. Succeeded with Totino's Crisp Crust Frozen Pizza. Sales of the frozen pizza were over $60 million the first year, while none of the losers cost the company as much as $1 million.[1]

The Decay Curve

The risk matrix decisions lead to the idea of a decay curve, as shown in Figure 8–7. That figure depicts the percentage of any firm's new product concepts that survive through the development period, from the 100 percent starting out before concept testing to the 2 percent (estimated from various studies) going to market. The discarded 98 percent dropped off at various times during the process, and when they drop off is primarily determined by the analysis of the risk matrix.

---

[1] Lawrence Ingrassia, "There's No Way to Tell If a New Product Will Please the Public," *The Wall Street Journal*, February 26, 1980, p. 1.

FIGURE 8–7   Mortality of New Product Ideas – The Decay Curve

---

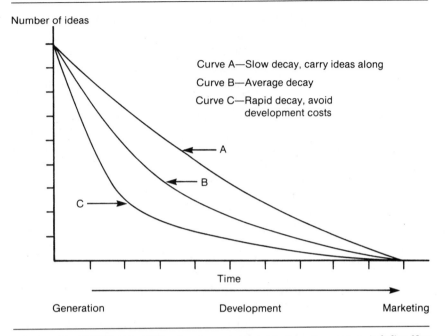

Number of ideas

Curve A—Slow decay, carry ideas along

Curve B—Average decay

Curve C—Rapid decay, avoid development costs

A

B

C

Time

Generation   Development   Marketing

Source: Hypothetical representation based on empirical data in various sources, including *New Products Management for the 1980s* (Chicago: Booz Allen & Hamilton,1982), p. 14.

Though hypothetical, the curves represent real firms. Decay curve C is for a company in the paper industry that wanted to kill off all possible losers early and spend time developing only those proposals worthy of marketing. Decay curve A is for a service firm that had very low development costs and wanted to kill a project only when it had solid evidence that the product should be killed.

But, note the decay curve is a result, not a plan. It comes from the scores of individual evaluation decisions made on all projects over their entire lives. Its value as a managerial concept lies in helping the manager see the need for thinking through the risk matrix (above) for each new product concept as it starts its journey through development.

PLANNING THE EVALUATION SYSTEM

The previous considerations help set the tone for management decisions on an appropriate evaluation system for any particular new product concept. But the individual manager has many specific things to think about when deciding whether to concept test, how long to run a field use test, whether to roll out or go national immediately, and how thorough a financial analysis to demand.

Everything Is Tentative

It's easy to imagine that building a new product is like building a house — first the foundation, then the frame, then the first floor, and so on. Unfortunately, product aspects are rarely locked in that way. Occasionally they are, as when a technical process dominates development, or when a semifinished product is acquired from someone else, or when legal or industry requirements exist.

We usually assume everything is tentative, even up through marketing. Form can usually be changed, and so can costs, packaging, positioning, and service contracts. So can the marketing date and the reactions of government regulators. So can customer attitudes, as companies with long development times have discovered.

This means two long-held beliefs in new product work are actually untrue. One is that everything should be keyed to a Go/No Go decision. Granted, one decision can be decisive — at times for example, when a firm must invest millions of dollars in one large facility or when a firm acquires a license that commits it to major financial outlays. But, many firms are finding ways to avoid such commitments (for example, by having another supplier produce the product for a while before a facilities commitment, or by negotiating a tentative license, or by asking probable customers to join a consortium to ensure the volume needed to build the facility).

The other "untrue truism" is that financial analysis should be done as early as possible to avoid wasting money on poor projects. This philosophy leads firms to make net present value analyses shortly after early concept testing, although the data is inadequate. The paper products firm whose decay rate was presented in Figure 8–7 rejected hundreds of ideas before realizing that early financial analysis was killing off ideas that would have looked great after further development. The financial analysis is best built up piece by piece, just like the product itself. We will see later how this works.

Still another tentative matter is the marketing date. Marketing actually begins very early in the development process (for example, when purchasing agents are asked in a concept test whether they think their firm would be interested in a new item). Roll-outs (limited marketing devices, discussed in Chapter 13) are now so common it is hard to tell when all-out marketing begins. General Electric once invested in a small, $20 million facility for a new heat-resistant plastic for circuit boards. After IBM and some other customers approved the product, GE announced it would build a full-scale, $50 million plant. Dr. Roland W. Schmitt, chief of research in the lab where the product was invented, put it this way: "Marketing people are wrong as often as technical people. It is important to approach markets as well as science in an experimental fashion."[2]

Another GE division for some time was "marketing" its line of factory automation systems to its own plants and using them as showcases for customers to visit. Apple Computer's Steve Jobs wasn't kidding when he said that one of Apple's early marketing steps was to give new products to employees to use. Some might call this product testing, but Jobs was thinking marketing.

Often no one pulls a switch and marketing instantly begins. We more often "sneak up" on it, which clearly affects the evaluation system.

Potholes

One critical skill of product developers is the ability to anticipate major difficulties, the potholes of product innovation. In automobile travel, potholes are always a problem, but they only become costly when we fail to see them coming in time to slow down or steer around them. The same thinking applies to new products: we should carefully scan for potential problems and keep them in mind when we decide what evaluating we will do.

For example, when Campbell Soup Company undertakes the development of a new canned soup, odds are in its favor. But experience has shown two points in the process when it may fail, and if it does, the product won't sell. The first is manufacturing cost—not quality, that's one of the company's key strengths—whether the chosen ingredients can be put together for a given target cost. The second is whether consumers think it tastes good. The company's evaluation system cannot overlook these two points.

The People Dimension

Product developers also have to remember they are dealing with people, and people cause problems. For example, although R&D workers are quite enthusiastic early in the life of a new product, the idea has little support outside of R&D; it is fragile and easy to kill. Late in the development cycle, more people have "bought in" on the concept and are supportive. The fledgling product already has their input, so they want it to succeed; consequently, the now strong proposal is tough to stop.

---

[2] Stratford P. Sherman, "Eight Big Masters of Innovation," *Fortune,* October 15, 1984, p. 80.

This means evaluation systems should have supportive testing early on. (We will see later that concept testing is sometimes called concept development, to reinforce the idea of helping the item, not just killing it off.) Later in the cycle, hurdles should usually be tough and demanding, not easily waved aside. One firm designated its market research director as an absolute screen for a 70 percent preference on new food products against their respective category leaders. If less than 70 percent of the testers preferred the new item, it was stopped, period.

Another people problem relates to personal risk. All new product work has a strong element of risk—risk to jobs, promotions, bonuses, and so on. Consequently, some people shy away from product innovation. And, new products people are always under the gun from someone—an ambitious boss, a dedicated regulator, an aggressive competitor, a power-hungry distributor, an early critic who was overruled within the company, and more. These people compound the risk.

So, evaluation systems should be supportive of people—they should anticipate problems of this type and offer the reassurance that players need.

Surrogates

The timing of factual information does not often match our need for it. For example, we want to know customer reactions early on, even before we develop the product, if possible. But we won't actually get that information until we make some of the product and give it to them to try out. So, we look for surrogates, or pieces of information that can substitute for what we want to learn but can't.

Here are four questions to which we badly need answers and four other questions that can be answered earlier (thus giving clues to the real answer):

Real Question	*Surrogate (Substitute) Question*
Will they prefer it?	Did they keep the prototype product we gave them at the end of the concept test?
Will cost be competitive?	Does it match our manufacturing skills?
Will competition leap in?	What did they do last time?
Will it sell?	Did it do well in field testing?

Note each response has little value except to help answer a critical question that cannot be answered directly.

Surrogates often change at different times in the evaluation process. For example, let's go back to one of the questions just above: Will cost be competitive? At different times, surrogates might be:

Time 1: Does it match our skills?

Time 2: Are the skills obtainable?

Time 3: What troubles are we having in making a prototype?

Time 4: How does the prototype look?

Time 5: Does the manufacturing process look efficient?

Time 6: How did the early production costs turn out?

Time 7: Do we now see any ways we can cut the cost?

Time 8: What is the cost?

Time 9: What is the competitive cost?

Only when we know our final cost and the competition's cost can we answer the original question. But the surrogates helped tell us whether we were headed for trouble.

SUMMARY

Each step in a proposed new product evaluation must be done well, of course. But deciding what evaluations to do, and when to do them, is also critical—maybe even more so.

So, we think in terms of an evaluation system for new products. The system's distinct purposes are more involved than a simplistic "Will it sell?" primarily because we usually don't know if it will sell until late in the process, if then.

Several descriptors of the general situation are most important. They guide us to the system appropriate for each situation. For example, the product itself is tentative until it sells successfully, the actual date of marketing is increasingly unclear as firms adopt limited marketing approaches, evaluation actually begins well before ideation with the innovation charter, and a product is an assemblage of many parts, each requiring its own evaluation.

Six broad questions need to be asked and answered in the general evaluation sequence. But how and when they are asked is determined by those descriptors. For example, because we can't ask people whether they will buy a product whose actual characteristics are still unknown, we must adopt surrogate questions. These are questions consumers probably can answer, and from these questions we can surmise what we want to know. As another example, because the product is evolving simultaneously with its evaluation, we are always working with a tentative product format. So we choose evaluation techniques accordingly; for example, early in the process we use concept tests because a verbal concept statement is all we have.

This chapter also looked at the other restraints complicating the situation: the risk matrix, the decay curve, and the many pressures acting on the people doing the evaluating.

The net result is a new products manager who knows the purposes of evaluation, the descriptors of the situation, the specific decisions to be made, and who is aware of the surrounding pressures and can thus select the specific evaluation tools for a particular system. The system should be unique because no two situations are alike.

What are the specific tools, what can each do, and what are their weaknesses? These are the topics of the next five chapters. You may want to follow Figure 8–2, which indicates the different decision stages.

APPLICATIONS

1. "During a recent management meeting, two of my division managers got into quite a tussle over the programs they use to evaluate new product ideas. One of them said he felt evaluation was very important; he wanted to do it quite completely, and he certainly didn't want anyone working to further the development of an item unless the prospects for it looked highly promising. The other manager objected to this, saying she wanted products to move rapidly down the pike, saving the serious evaluation for the time when she had the data to make it meaningful. Both persons seemed to have a point, so I just let it ride. What do you think I should have said?"

2. "Recently I was reading an article about Xerox, and its president was saying how he wanted to drive the costs down earlier, freeze the specs earlier, eliminate duplication of effort, and get new products into customer hands earlier in order to learn more about performance and costs. Using the idea of an evaluation system, can you tell me what you would say to that president about what he wants to do?"

3. "I don't know what your profs would say, but it often seems to me that we might be just as well off if we didn't do any evaluation on new products. Just produce the ones we're convinced will sell the best and really support those. Let's face it—we never have reliable data anyway, and everyone is always changing minds or opinions. Never knew so many people could say I told you so."

4. "Funny thing about evaluation—seems as though the folks involved in it never use the facts or data that they should and instead use some sort of surrogate data. I don't see why you have to beat around the

bush. Why not just gather the real facts in the first place and not use those substitutes?''

Case: Concept Development Corporation

Late in 1985, three bridge-playing friends in a southern college town decided to start their own firm. One, Bob Stark, worked for General Motors as a planning manager in a local assembly operation. The second, Betsy Morningside, was a speech and theater professor at the college. The third, Myron Hite, was a CPA who worked for one of the Big Eight accounting firms.

All three were exceptionally creative and especially enjoyed their bridge sessions because they had a chance to brag about their new creations and to hear the creations of the others. It was all for fun until one evening it struck them that it was time to stop the fun and start making some money from their many ideas. So, they quit their jobs, pooled their savings, rented a small, three-room office, hired a couple of people, coined the name Concept Development Corporation, and started serious work.

A professor from the college was asked to help set up a system to evaluate their ideas. They fully realized they were better at thinking up things than evaluating them. They also were aware of their deficiencies: little staff, little money, little experience in making things like the ones they created, and little time before their meager savings disappeared completely.

They began with two product areas. One was toys, broadly defined as things children played with, especially educational activities. The other area was writing services, as temporary spin-offs from their own abilities and those of the two people they hired. These services primarily involved designing and writing instruction sheets for area firms (training manuals, copy for package inserts, instruction signs—anywhere words were used to instruct people in doing things). They each had some background in instructions, and one of the people they hired was a man experienced in writing and layout work.

Their strategy was to develop unique toys that required little up-front expenditures (for example, dies and packaging equipment). They were too creative for imitation. Most toys would have some game or competitive aspect, be educational, and involve paper, color, numbers, and the like. They figured "most of the stuff would be for children under 12."

The writing services would be partly reactive in that they would do whatever clients asked them to do. But, being creative, they also planned to create innovative services—new ways of meeting industry and business needs. For example, they wanted to offer a special test/training service, whereby after developing a training manual or instruction sheet they would have some employees for whom the piece was developed come to a special room where they would read the material, apply it in some fashion, be tested on it, and so on. What they delivered to the client would be proven to work. They had many such ideas.

The professor went back to the college and decided to let a new products class assist in the assignment. They were asked to think about the new firm's situation, the general evaluation system in Figure 8–2, and the various purposes and special circumstances discussed in Chapter 8 and then come up with one general guideline statement of evaluation policy for the toy ideas and another for the new services. They hadn't yet studied specific techniques (such as concept testing), but they could clearly indicate which of the six major stages were the most critical, where the toughest decisions would be, and so on. The professor was especially interested in what the students felt the differences were between the evaluation of toys and the evaluation of services.

Chapter 9

Charter and Prescreening

SETTING

This chapter is the first of six spelling out the various tools for evaluating new products (goods and services). Chapter 9 will cover (1) the charter and market analysis activities, which occur before the idea appears, and (2) the initial reaction and the concept testing, which occur immediately after the idea appears. These steps precede the full screen, which generally kicks off the primary R&D or other technical work. The full screen is the subject of Chapter 10.

Many of the evaluation tools discussed in these six chapters have a long history and are themselves major topics, so our discussions must be selective. Unfortunately, industry uses many of the tools in different ways, so they tend to blend together at the edges. When, for example, does a prototype concept test become a product use test? When does a minimarket test become a test market?

Likewise, industry often combines two or even three of the tools. For example, many firms like to do an early customer survey that is partly market analysis, partly concept test, and partly prototype test, particularly when the idea first emerged in prototype form.

Finally, industry developers have been all too willing to invent terminology. Therefore, we have had to do some standardizing of terms, and some of the decisions won't be acceptable to all people. Appendix D contains a glossary of terms as used in this text.

THE PRODUCT INNOVATION CHARTER

The earliest evaluation that a firm makes is of itself and its situation. That evaluation yields a priori conclusions about new product proposals. The firm reaches these conclusions while making basic strategic decisions, as discussed in Chapter 3. These decisions decree what types of new products fit best. For example,

Smith & Wesson wanted items to sell to law enforcement agencies.

Remington sought new uses for powered metal technology.

Nabisco sought technological breakthroughs in snack foods.

Iroquois Brands wanted items to fill specialized niches.

The dimensions covered by the basic strategic decisions are shown in Figure 9–1. The figure shows that of all possible new product concepts, the firm decides to reject (in advance and without knowing the concepts) those requiring technologies the firm does not have, or those sold to customers about whom the firm has no close knowledge, and so on. These directions exclude most new product ideas. If they do come up, they can be dismissed immediately in the initial reaction stage (where a second use of the PIC will be discussed in a moment). For example, a few years ago the business press told us that all low-quality gift items had already been negatively evaluated by Hallmark management, and all items not related to oil wells had been prerejected by Rucker.

The charter given to new products management thus eliminates more product ideas than all the other tools combined; and, by coming at the beginning of the new products system, it precludes the unfortunate practice of having unwanted proposals eat up valuable development funds before they are detected.

FIGURE 9–1   The Exclusion Power of a Product Innovation Charter

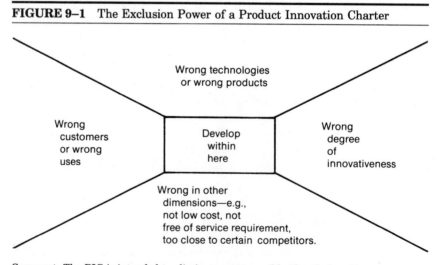

Comment: The PIC is intended to eliminate most possible ideas before they come up.

MARKET ANALYSIS

The second pre-concept emergence tool is an in-depth study of the market area that the product innovation charter has selected for focus. The study takes place immediately after the PIC is approved, and the depth of the study depends on how well the firm already knows the market selected. Ongoing ideation in support of present product lines takes place within a standing type of PIC, and no special study is necessary (assuming current product managers do their jobs correctly).

But, in most cases, the PIC-designated market is not thoroughly understood. In the Rucker Company example above, new products people knew the oil industry well, but they didn't know everything about it. Moreover, their new products would probably be developed for specific new uses within that industry, about which the firm perhaps knew very little.

This preliminary study of markets has received dramatic attention in recent years. The increase in time and dollars spent up front has been the most significant change in the overall process during the past two decades. Whereas in 1968 industry put 58 ideas into R&D for every 1 idea that went to market successfully, that number is now down to 7.[1] Eliminating the 51 unsuccessful ideas is the purpose of all evaluations prior to screening. Further, whereas in 1968 roughly 10 percent of all new product cost was incurred prior to R&D, industry now allocates over 20 percent to that phase.[2] Thus, despite the tenuousness and difficulty of prescreening market research, its use has increased greatly.

The information gathered in preevaluation market analysis is comprehensive, and the general coverage is suggested by the items in Figure 9–2. Greater detail is added as the list is made industry specific. Thus, a market analysis for the shoe industry also covers colors, styles, materials, sizes, joint purchase, joint consumption, the international supplier situation, mass merchandiser trends, and the like. A study of the cough syrup market adds details on seasonal deals, in-store retail displays, competitive product formulations and claims, FDA regulations, and so on.

Both primary and secondary sources are used, and at least one field survey is essential, but most of the information is available in secondary sources or from a small number of in-depth interviews with respected persons active in the market. Like all techniques used in this step, the

---

[1] *New Products Management for the 1980s* (Chicago: Booz Allen & Hamilton, 1982), p. 6.

[2] Ibid.

FIGURE 9–2 Basic Market Description

Market size

Definition: By nature of product, by supplier, by user.

Sales: Dollars, units, by total and subgroups.

Trends: Growth total and rate by subgroups.

Key segments: Demographic, attitude, behavior.

Special aspects where appropriate: Cyclicality, seasonality, erratic fluctuations.

International variations and trends.

Distribution structure available

Retailers: Types, shares, demands, activities, current margins and profits, trends and forecasts, attitudes.

Wholesalers: Distributors, jobbers, agents, types used, functions performed, policies, compensation, attitudes, trends, variances, by segments.

Bargaining power and channel control.

Degree of and trends in vertical integration.

Variations by geographic area.

Use of multiple or dual channels.

Competition

Current brands.

Manufacturer source for each.

Sizes, forms, materials, etc. All variations, temporary and permanent. Quality levels.

Prices: Final discounts, special, changes.

Market shares: Dollars, units, by segments, using various definitions of "market."

Changes: Trends of entries and exits, reaction times.

Profits being achieved: Sales, costs, ROIs, paybacks, trends.

Promotional practices: Types, dollars, effectiveness.

Manufacturing and procuring practices.

Financial strengths.

Special vulnerabilities, instabilities.

Possible new entrants, current R&D activities, skills, track records.

Inventory policies and conditions.

Excess capacity trends and effects.

Special unique strengths: Patents, source controls, images, personnel, economies of scale, experience effect, essential keys to success.

Consuming units

Consumers: Users, influencers, buyers—household, industrial, or commercial.

Purchasing behavior: Sources, reasons, information processing, postpurchasing behavior, biases and prejudices, price and quality sensitivities, interest in new products, past acceptance rates.

Full demographic description of all participants—age, sex, size, etc.

Segmentation variations: Usage rates, usage reasons, location.

Product usage description: When used, how used, how discarded or replaced, special concerns, trends.

FIGURE 9–2 *(concluded)*

Full description of derived demand aspects.
Industry life cycle analyzed by segments.

Special aspects

Government and regulatory restrictions, especially trends and
expectations.

Third-party influences: Scientists, institutions, research centers,
associations, standards, pressure groups.

Effects of inflation, labor rates, union activity.

Upstream participants: Supplier manufacturers, importers, technology
control.

General social attitudes and trends.

Industry productivity and efficiency in use of personnel and other
resources.

Trends in industry costs: Materials, labor, transportation.

Sources: The above list was compiled from many sources, but particularly helpful and worthy of further study are E. Patrick McGuire, *Evaluation of Product Proposals* (New York: Conference Board, 1973); Edgar E. Pessemier, *Product Management* (New York: John Wiley & Sons, 1972), chap. 3; Burton H. Marcus and Edward M. Tauber, *Marketing Analysis and Decision Making* (Boston: Little, Brown, 1979), chap. 1; Robert G. Cooper, *Winning at New Products* (Reading, Mass.: Addison-Wesley Publishing, 1986), pp. 135–49; and Frank R. Bacon, Jr., and Thomas W. Butler, Jr., *Planned Innovation* (Ann Arbor, MI: University of Michigan Industrial Development Division, 1981), chaps. 10 and 11.

purpose is to explore current attitudes, awareness, practices, frustrations, and so on, not to gather reactions to specific proposals. The basic analysis is rather standard, and most marketing research directors know what needs to be done. The procedure is routine in many firms, as shown by the following:

	Use of Basic Market Studies		
	For Line Extensions	*For New Brands*	*For New Categories*
Firms who			
Never use	21%	9%	4%
Occasionally use	45	34	22
Use more than half of the time	34	57	74
Total	100%	100%	100%

Source: *Prescription for New Product Success* (New York: Association of National Advertisers, 1984), p. 17.

INITIAL REACTION

The ideation stage follows the market analysis just discussed. Concepts begin flowing in, usually very fast. Most firms have evolved some special technique to handle this deluge, and, for want of an established term, we call it *initial reaction.*

Chapter 8 noted that new product development expenditures grow continuously over the life of the project. Accordingly, the evaluation program starts out simple and gets more serious as the expenditures mount. In the 1960s, Dow Chemical Company's early expenditures on new chemical specialties were:

Cost to react to idea	$ 100
Cost to screen idea	1,000
Cost to prototype idea	10,000

Because Dow spent only $1,000 to screen a proposed new chemical, any evaluation prior to that had to be inexpensive, and it was — $100. This evaluation was essentially a set of thoughts and a brief discussion of the idea by two to four professionals.[3]

At Oster, each idea that came from the marketing or administration departments went to the sales vice president first, and each idea from the technical departments or production went to the engineering vice president first. If one of these vice presidents approved the idea, it was sent to the other. If both approved, the idea went to a committee and the system became more formal. The two people making the initial reaction primarily used their experience of many years in the small-appliance industry.

Every company wants a quick and inexpensive initial reaction type of evaluation, but several provisos apply:

1. *The idea source does not usually participate in the initial reaction.* A person who has an idea may want to explain it and argue for it, but this person should probably not have a vote in the decision to advance the idea or drop it.
2. *Two or more persons are involved in any rejection decision,* based on the "fragility of new ideas" concept discussed in Chapter 8. The rejection percentage is much higher here than at any other stage, but involving two or more persons dilutes the biases of a single person.

---

[3] Personal communication with Robert Williams, then director of consumer research for the Dow Chemical Company.

The Oster system did not have this safeguard because either vice president could kill the suggestion.

3. *The initial reaction, though quick, is based on more than a pure intuitive sense.* The evaluators are trained and experienced; records are kept and reviewed; and objective aids are sought.

One of several techniques used in this very early evaluation is the product innovation charter. Knowing such things as whether a firm wants to be first or last, high risk or low risk, internally or externally developing, and stay in shoes or add handbags leads to quick and decisive action.

A few factors from the scoring models discussed in Chapter 10 offer help here. Some of the more powerful factors can be brought forward and used as heuristics (rules of thumb) for rough screening at this point. For example, scale (is it in our league?), competition, state of the art, and fit are particularly useful. Persons who make early evaluations certainly think about such things.

Some managers prefer to use a small-scale informal survey at this point, particularly when some aspect of the proposal extends beyond the evaluator's experience. But unless such a survey is held to the level of telephone checks with professional colleagues, it violates the essence of this step — to decide whether more dollars should be spent in preparing for the full-screen review.

In summary, the most prevalent initial reaction is personal; reasonably subjective; aided by training, experience, strategy statements, and some quantitative and nonquantitative heuristics; and carefully structured with personnel and procedures that will pass along an appropriate stream of ideas.

CONCEPT TESTING AND DEVELOPMENT

While Alan Ladd, Jr., reigned as top judge of new movie scripts at Twentieth Century-Fox Film Corporation, he revealed that his product proposal evaluation system ended about as soon as it began. He would just read a script and decide whether to make the movie. He and his small staff knew their markets well, had a guiding product innovation charter, and combined their knowledge and the charter with personal judgment to reach decisions. They did not use concept testing, full screening, or product use testing. Ladd said, "It's based on my intuition and experience. There's no way to put it on a chart or graph or formulate it."[4]

Perhaps. Some agree with Mr. Ladd, but most do not, preferring instead to move to the next prescreening activity — the concept test. This

---

[4] Earl C. Gottschalk, "How Fox's Movie Boss Decides that a Script Is a Powerful Winner," *The Wall Street Journal,* May 17, 1979, p. 1.

step should be called concept *development* because its enhancement aspect is as valuable as the evaluation.

Most major firms make frequent use of concept development. It is a mandatory part of the process for makers of consumer packaged goods. Use of concept testing is growing in industrial firms, which actually invented it. Business-to-business firms have always spent much time talking with users about their needs and problems, what suggestions they have, what they think about various ideas, and so on. They just never called it concept testing.

But before looking at the specifics, we should recognize that concept testing is not appropriate at times, and managers must decide when these times are. When the prime benefit is a personal sense, such as the aroma of a perfume, concept testing usually fails. The idea cannot be communicated short of actually having some perfume there to demonstrate. And when the concept embodies some new technology that users cannot visualize, it is also a weak tool. Kodak realized this when it tried to concept test its new disc camera. So did Alberto-Culver when it first tested the concept of hair mousse. Women used to sprays could not imagine putting "stuff like that" on their hair. Only after the company developed the product and set up training classes in salons did women agree to try the mousse.

But, concept testing is useful in most cases; far too often, a situation arises like that faced by the Suga Test Instruments Company of Tokyo when it marketed its $1.3 million artificial snow machine. Designed for utilities, car manufacturers, battery makers, outdoor clothing makers, and others, the snow machine met with almost zero adoption. True, it made more and better snow than any other machine, and it did the work inside a five-story building. But every target market already had methods for product testing and did not need the new machine. No one had bothered to ask them.[5]

What Is a New Product Concept?

Chapter 4 introduced the concept idea, and review of that material might be in order now. *Webster's* says a concept is an idea or an abstract notion. The *Random House Dictionary* agrees. Businesspeople use the term *concept* for the product promise, the customer proposition, and the real reason why people should buy. It is a stated relationship between product attributes (form or technology) and consumer needs or values—claim of proposed satisfactions.

---

[5] Marc Beauschamp, "Cold Shoulder," *Business Week*, October 6, 1986, p. 168.

This promise is open to four interpretations:

1. The producer's perception of the attributes of the new product.
2. The consumer's perception of that attribute set.
3. The producer's estimate of the value delivered by that attribute set.
4. The consumer's estimate of the value delivered by that attribute set.

These are only forecasts, or guesses, at this time—not reality, even with a prototype in hand. They rest on expectations.

Thus a complete new product concept is *a statement about anticipated product features that will yield selected benefits relative to other products or problem solutions already available.* An example is "A new electric razor whose screen is so thin it can cut closer than any other electric razor on the market."

Sometimes the concept can be assumed; for example, saying "a copier that has twice the speed of current models" assumes the benefits of speed can go without saying. However, spelling out the features and the benefits is safer.

The Purposes of Concept Testing

Recall that concept testing is part of the prescreening process, preparing a management team to do the full screening of the idea just before beginning serious R&D. We are looking for information to help the screeners use the scoring models we meet in Chapter 10. This information will also be the primary determinant of *protocol*—the agreement with R&D as to what they are expected to accomplish.

Therefore, the *first* purpose of a concept test is to identify the very poor concept so it can be eliminated. If beer drinkers, for example, cannot conceive of a one-calorie beer and reject it out of hand, the concept is probably a poor one. If pharmacists say round-bottomed drug bottles fall over in a busy pharmacy, that's it.

If the concept passes the first test, a *second* purpose is to estimate (even crudely) the sales or trial that the product would enjoy—a sense of market share or a general range of revenue dollars. Some people believe this buying prediction is worthless. Others claim a clear, positive correlation between intention and purchase. One longtime practicing market researcher claimed to have confidential data showing correlations of 0.60 and well above.[6]

The buying intention question appears in almost every concept test. Even if replies fail to forecast sales, they do help confirm stated preferences. The most common format for purchase intentions is the

---

[6] Personal communication with Anthony Bushman, then Professor of Marketing, Drexel University.

classic five-point question: How likely would you be to buy a product like this, if we made it?

1. Definitely would buy.
2. Probably would buy.
3. Might or might not buy.
4. Probably would not buy.
5. Definitely would not buy.

The number of people who definitely would buy or probably would buy are usually combined and used as an indicator of group reaction. This is called the *top-two-boxes* figure.

Whether this many people actually purchase the item is not important. Researchers have usually calibrated their figures, so they know, for example, that if the top two boxes total 60 percent, the real figure will be say 25 percent. They do this from past experience. Direct marketers can do the best calibration, because they will later be selling the tested item to market groups they surveyed; they can tell exactly how actual behavior matches stated intentions. The data banks of Burke Marketing Services, the largest supplier of concept tests, literally let the company calibrate all of its concept test questions, by product type. For a price, Burke translates a client's raw intentions data into probable intentions.

Incidentally, sometimes experience calibrates the probable intention *higher* than the respondents say now. On complex products, people often use caution at concept testing time but end up buying the product when they have a chance to see the final item and hear all about it.

The *third* purpose of concept testing is to help develop the idea, not just test it. Concepts rarely emerge from a test the way they went in. Moreover, a concept statement is not enough to guide R&D. Scientists need to know what attributes (especially benefits) will permit the new product to fulfill the concept statement. Because the attributes frequently oppose or conflict with each other, many trade-offs must be made. When better to make them than when talking with people for whom the product is being developed? Some firms use the same analytical device discussed in Chapter 6 for concept generation—trade-off (or conjoint) analysis.

RESEARCH PROCEDURE

The sequence of steps in a concept test varies in practice, but the general pattern is as follows. Note the decisions are not as isolated as this list suggests; for example, the format of the concept statement and the choice of respondents is a chicken-and-egg question.

Prepare Concept Statement

Concepts are usually presented to potential buyers in one of three formats:

1. Narrative (verbal).
2. Drawing, diagram, sketch.
3. Model or prototype.

Figure 9–3 shows an example of the narrative format. Some people prefer a very brief presentation, giving only the minimum of attributes and letting the respondent offer additional ones. Others prefer a full description, approaching what a diagram or prototype would provide. In the pure narrative, the concept is totally intangible, though there are ways to provide some measurements of intangibles.[7]

Figure 9–4 demonstrates the use of a drawing. Drawings and diagrams usually must be supplemented by a narrative statement of the concept.

Prototypes, or models, are an extreme form of concept statement, because many decisions had to have been made about the new product to get to this point. They are useful only in special situations, as, for example, with simple-to-prepare food products or, at the other extreme, with concepts so complex that the buyer cannot react without more knowledge than a simple narrative would give. A firm in Canada was trying to get reactions to a traveling medical examining unit that would be driven to various corporation offices where examinations would be given. The answer was to build a small model of the unit, showing layout, equipment, and so on.[8]

The real question is "What does it take to communicate to the buyer what we have in mind?" For office furniture, most buyers want lots of details, so prototypes would probably be necessary. But for turnip-flavored yogurt, one sentence would probably work.

If we only want reaction to part of the concept (say, size, cost, or function), then simple formats are acceptable; but if we must have solid indication of purchase intentions, then we must provide most of the information buyers want for that decision. The latter usually calls for more complex formats.

The other aspect is cost and inconvenience to us. The non-narrative formats usually cost more and take longer to prepare and to administer. They are OK only if not called for too often.

---

[7] An example of how services can be somewhat quantified is shown in a study of retail service by A. Parasuraman, Valarie Ziethaml, and Leonard L. Berry, *Servqual: A Multiple-Item Scale for Measuring Customer Perceptions of Service Quality* (Cambridge, Mass.: Marketing Science Institute, 1986).

[8] Robert G. Cooper, *Winning at New Products* (Reading, Mass.: Addison-Wesley Publishing, 1986), p. 59.

FIGURE 9–3   Mail Concept Test Format – Plain Verbal Description of the Product or Service and Its Major Benefits

---

A major soft-drink manufacturer would like to get your reaction to an idea for a new diet soft drink. Please read the description below before answering the questions.

New Diet Soft Drink

Here is a tasty, sparkling beverage that quenches thirst, refreshes, and makes the mouth tingle with a delightful flavor blend of orange, mint, and lime.

It helps adults (and kids too) control weight by reducing the craving for sweets and between-meal snacks. And, best of all, it contains absolutely no calories.

Comes in 12-ounce cans or bottles and costs 16¢ each.

---

1. How different, if at all, do you think this diet soft drink would be from other available products now on the market that might be compared with it?

   ☐ Very different
   ☐ Somewhat different
   ☐ Slightly different
   ☐ Not at all different

2. Assuming you tried the product described above and liked it, about how often do you think you would buy it?

	Check one
More than once a week	☐
About once a week	☐
About twice a month	☐
About once a month	☐
Less often	☐
Would never buy it	☐

Source: National Family Opinion, Toledo, Ohio.

Commercialized Concept Statements.   A special variation, regardless of format, concerns whether to make the statement in commercialized (promotional) mode. Compare these two concept statements:

Light Peanut Butter, a low-calorie version of natural peanut butter that can provide a tasty addition to most diets.

FIGURE 9–4   Mail Concept Test—Sketch

Aerosol Hand Cleanser

A large-size can of hand cleanser concentrate that completely eliminates those lingering unpleasant odors that come from handling fish, onions, garlic, furniture polish, etc. Not a covering odor! Just press the button and spray directly on the hands, rub for a few seconds, and rinse off under the faucet. 24-ounce aerosol can will last for months and can be easily stored. Costs 69¢.

1. How interested would you be in buying the product described above if it were available at your supermarket?

	Check one
I would definitely buy	☐
I would probably buy	☐
I might or might not buy	☐
I would probably not buy	☐
I would definitely not buy	☐

Source: National Family Opinion, Toledo, Ohio.

A marvelous new way to chase the blahs from your diet has been discovered by General Mills scientists—a low-calorie version of ever-popular peanut butter. As tasty as ever and produced by a natural process, our new Light Peanut Butter will fit most weight-control diets in use today.

Those statements show little substantial difference, yet they will draw different reactions. Commercialized formats produce "more realistic" evaluations (that is, greater acceptance), but they risk the bias of good or poor advertising copy writing. Proponents say noncommercialized statements won't provoke typical market reactions in this commercial world. Critics answer, why evaluate the advertising when all we want at this time is reaction to the concept?

Neither form is *better* than the other. The choice should be determined by the situation. Relatively simple items, often almost impulse purchases, seem to work very well in commercialized form. The commercialized concept statements in Figures 9–3 and 9–4 are even in rough advertising layouts, though not finished copy. But, many products are not normally thought of in commercial form, and these are better kept noncommercialized. As before, the key question is, "Which form best communicates what the respondent must have to give a reaction at this time?"

Offering of Competitive Information.   Customers of all types know much less about their current products and other options than we would like. A new concept may well offer a benefit that the customer doesn't realize is new. One solution is to provide a full data sheet about each competitive product. The issue was researched (on dog food), and results showed no significant difference, though most of the data did bend slightly in favor of the new product when there was full information.[9]

Price.   Another issue turns on whether to put a price in the concept statement. The examples in Figures 9–3 and 9–4 both mention price. Burke Marketing Services insists on price in its concept tests. Some people object, saying reaction to the concept is wanted, not to its price. Yet price is part of the product, and buyers can't be expected to tell purchase intentions without knowing price. An exception occurs for those complex concepts (for example, the medical examinations van, above) requiring many decisions before the cost is known.

One solution to the price issue, and to the commercialization and prototype issues discussed earlier, is to "do both." If time permits, concept tests can be phased (done in waves), with a simple narrative, noncommercialized, nonprice statement for the first round, followed later by a prototype or model in commercialized form with full pricing information.

Define the Respondent Group

In all cases, we would like to interview any and all persons who will play a role in deciding whether the product will be bought and how it might

---

[9] James B. Miller, Norman T. Bruvold, and Jerome B. Kernan, "Does Competitive-Set Information Affect the Results of Concept Tests?" *Journal of Advertising Research*, April/May 1987, pp. 16–24.

be improved. When the New Zealand Wool Testing Authority recently came up with a new wool testing service, it had to test the concept with three levels in its channel — brokers who sell the raw wool, scourers who scour the wool and prepare it for shipment, and exporters who sell the wool to manufacturers.[10] Some industrial products may involve 10 to 15 different people at each buying point. Yet that peanut butter mentioned above could probably be tested with just one person — the homemaker who does the buying.

This decision is usually not difficult, though getting money to do the full set may be. Some people try to seek out a smaller number of potential buyers who are "lead users," or influencers, or large users.[11] This approach saves some money and gets more expert advice but often fails to reflect key differences in the marketplace. Of course, we should always watch out for critics, people who have a reason for opposing the concept. A developer came up with a device for reading electrocardiograms and needed the reactions of cardiologists; but the obvious conflict of interest made the interviewing tricky.

Select Response Situation

There are two issues in the response situation: (1) the mode of reaching the respondent and (2) if personal, whether to approach individually or in a group.

Most concept testing takes place through personal contact — direct interviewing. Survey samples typically run about 250 to 400 people, though industrial samples are usually much smaller. Personal contact allows the interviewer to answer questions and to probe areas where the respondent is expressing a new idea or is not clear.

One research firm uses personal interviews to evaluate a set of product concepts on a shared-cost basis. Each periodic wave of interviewing yields 1,000 interviews, and the cost per idea evaluated is around $1,000. Other research firms use pseudo stores in vacant locations at shopping malls.

The high costs of personal contact have led developers to try other methods, especially the mail and the telephone. Portfolios of concepts can be mailed to potential users, though problems occur with sample selection and response cooperation. The method only works for items

---

[10] Arch G. Woodside, R. Hedley Sanderson, and Roderick J. Brodie, "Testing Acceptance of a New Industrial Service," *Industrial Marketing Management,* 1988, pp. 65–71.

[11] The lead-user recommendation is explained in Glen L. Urban and Eric von Hippel, "Lead-User Analyses of New Industrial Product Concepts," *Management Science,* May 1988, pp. 569–82.

that will be heavily promoted. Consequently, the firm that offers the mail examples in Figures 9–3 and 9–4 also offers videotape presentations in conjunction with the mail forms.

The telephone has also been used a great deal, especially to reach consumers who are rarely in the malls and businesspeople deep within large companies. The call often uses a mailed concept statement, giving the respondent a chance to study and understand the proposal.

The second issue concerns individual versus group. Both are widely used. Groups (usually just called focus groups) are excellent when we want respondents to hear and react to the comments of others. Individual situations are better when we don't want that type of influence. Focus groups are also good when we want respondents to think about the concept—how it would be used, problems that would come up, what other people would think, how it would affect what is being done now, and so on. Focus groups are much more expensive, so they are usually used when smaller samples satisfy.

Prepare the Interviewing Sequence

Simple interviewing situations simply state the new product concept and ask about believability, buying intentions, and any other information wanted. The whole interview may take only two or three minutes per product concept, if the item is a new packaged good and all we really want is a buying intention answer.

Usually we want more than that, however, particularly if the concept is something other than a consumer packaged good. In these cases, we first explore the respondent's current practice in the area concerned, asking how people currently try to solve their problems, what competing products they use, and what they think about those products. How willing would they be to change? What specific benefits do they want? What are they spending? Is the product being used as part of a system?

This background information helps us understand and interpret comments about the new concept, which is presented next. The immediate and critical question is, "Does the respondent understand the concept?" Given understanding, we then seek other reactions:

• Uniqueness of the concept.
• Believability of the concept.
• Importance of the problem being addressed.
• Extent to which the concept is interesting.
• Extent to which it is realistic, practical, useful.
• Extent to which it solves a problem, or meets a need.
• How much they like the concept.
• How likely they would be to buy the product.
• What problems they see in using the product.

Other information occasionally sought includes perceived negatives in the concept (the baggage it carries), comparisons with other products in the category, further information wanted about the idea, and the expected degree of use disruption. We are especially interested in what changes they would make in the concept, exactly what it would be used for and why, what products or processes would be replaced, and who else would be involved in using the item.

In all this interviewing, remember we are not taking a poll but, rather, exploring what people are doing and thinking. Only a few questions will be in standard form, for tabulation. Each new concept addresses a very specific problem (or at least it should), and we need to know what people think about that problem in the context of the new concept.

Trial Interviewing

As in all research work, it is important to do some trial interviews with people in the target respondent group. Trial interviews are especially needed on concept testing, given the communication problems inherent in new things.

Interview, Tabulate, Analyze

The analysis of standard products is quite standard and may be summed up in one statistic—the top two boxes. But we usually want much more. Some surprise findings will require further thought and even further interviewing. The analysis stage differs from that in other surveys—it is a group activity, product managers and technical people are involved, it is a creative session, and numbers are not as important as general confirmation of earlier thoughts.

CONCLUSIONS

The advantages of concept testing and development prior to full screening are:

1. It can usually be done quickly and easily, well before prototypes are available.
2. It gives the screeners invaluable information for the many ratings they must make—applications, user types, preferred attributes, design parameters, marketing applications, and so on.
3. Proven market research technology exists.
4. It is reasonably confidential because small samples are typical and most concept particulars can be kept elusive.

5. The truly bad idea is easily detected, particularly if it is bad for one clear reason.
6. The research permits further orientation to buyer thinking, misunderstandings, misperceptions, prejudices, and so on.
7. Segments and positionings can be developed in tandem with the concept.

All those advantages notwithstanding, concept testing has weaknesses. Some new product managers will have nothing to do with it for the following reasons.

1. Communication is treacherous. Opportunities for misunderstanding abound—new items, new uses, multiple attributes, some secrecy desired, no product available, and so on. There have been classic flops, most of which passed concept tests—dry soups, white whiskey, and so on. For example, General Foods reported that only 40 percent of the items that passed concept tests later went to test market. The original chewable antacid tablet floundered because the concept test missed the idea that people then wanted water with antacids. One firm studied executions of a single new product idea by three copywriters and found that the most important determinant of high scores in the concept test was the skill of the copywriter.[12]
2. Researchers can never be sure exactly what is being measured by any particular statistic. For example, a recent study reported 31 percent of the people understood the main benefit, and only 10 percent found some aspect of the concept hard to believe. Unfortunately, further analysis revealed almost all of those 10 percent were among the 31 percent, thus sharply deflating the value of the positive response.[13]
3. People find reacting to entirely new concepts difficult without a learning period. The stimulus of a concept statement is very brief.
4. Testing occurs long before marketing, and many situation variables will change by the time the product is marketed.
5. Although interviewing looks simple, considerable skill is required, especially in focus groups. Too, technical people need to be involved in the work of focus groups, especially if a champion is involved because a champion won't accept rejection secondhand.
6. Certain attributes cannot be measured in a concept test—for example, rug texture, shower nozzle impact, and what color will be "in" next season.

---

[12] Russel I. Haley and Ronald Gatley, "Trouble with Concept Testing," *Journal of Marketing Research,* May 1971, pp. 230–35.

[13] David A. Schwartz, "Concept Testing Can Be Improved," *Marketing News,* January 6, 1984, p. 22.

7. Establishing the validity or reliability of a concept test is very difficult.
8. The entire testing procedure is unreal — it lacks a full environment; people are asked to be judges; courtesy endorsements are common.

Strong differences of opinion will continue, but concept testing methodology has now reached the point where the burden of proof is on those who recommend not doing it in any case.

SUMMARY

This was the first chapter covering the tools used to evaluate new product proposals. Because evaluation actually begins prior to ideation (that is, deciding where to seek ideas), we first looked at the product innovation charter. By focusing the creative activity in certain directions, the charter automatically excludes all other directions and thus, in effect, evaluates them negatively.

Once the strategic direction is clear, most firms undertake a market analysis of the opportunity described by it. The customer should be a major input to any product innovation program, and immediately after strategic decisions have been made is an excellent time to seek this input. Then, as the ideas begin to roll in, an initial response is made — highly judgmental, quick, and designed primarily to clean out the worthless ideas.

Once an idea passes that test, more serious evaluation begins. The tool at this point is concept testing or concept development, which now has a lengthy history of successful use, although some managers won't touch it.

The chapter gave the overall procedure for concept testing, including its purposes, options in concept format, respondent selection, and the interviewing procedure.

An immediate benefit of concept testing is that it gives management the information needed to make the judgments required by the scoring models used in the following step — the full screen of the concept, which is the subject of Chapter 10.

APPLICATIONS

1. "You know, most of our new products people do a great deal of marketing research — concept testing, attitude surveys, and the like. But let me read something that one automobile designer thought about marketing research:

   Market research is probably the greatest single deterrent to excellence in modern business. It's a crutch for managers with no vision and no conviction. On the surface, it sounds sensible enough: Find out exactly what the buyers want before you come to a design. But in practice, it's impossible. The public doesn't know what it wants without being shown the choices, and even then, preference is apt to veer off in the direction of K mart. Market research gives you Malibus with Mercedes grilles, refrigerators in avocado hues, and Big Macs with everything. You do not, however, produce greatness with this technique.[14]

Perhaps you would comment on that statement."

2. "Last year, a firm in New York called Telesession Corporation claimed that it had perfected a system of conference calling where telephones could be used for a focus group. Telesession claims to have used it on specialized groups as well as homemakers – for example, hospital lab directors and electrical engineers. It even has a deal whereby packages are mailed to the persons to be interviewed (after they agree to participate) with instructions not to open the package until told to do so during the conference call session. Which of our many divisions do you think might be able to use this system of concept testing?"

3. "A food company competitor is trying to speed up its new product process by a system that uses (1) brainstorming to create ideas (392 in a recent session); (2) evaluation of those ideas by the same group of people, down to only the best 50 ideas; and then (3) focus group sessions for concept testing those ideas down to the few that should be developed rapidly. Do you see anything wrong with this system?"

4. "I would be curious to test your personal judgment on some new ideas from one of our recent idea sessions. What do you think about each of the following?
   a.   A gasoline-powered pogo stick.
   b.   A combination valet stand and electric pants presser.
   c.   Transistorized golf balls and an electric finder.
   d.   An Indian arm wrestling device so you can arm wrestle with yourself.
   e.   An electrically heated bath mat.
   f.   Chocolate candy in an edible chocolate box."

Case: Wolverine Car Wash

In 1968, Jerry Waldrop opened his first car wash, called the Wolverine Car Wash, in Columbus, Ohio. He had never worked for car washes but had run various small businesses as he worked his way through Ohio State University. He was convinced that better ways of running car washes rested primarily on money,

---

[14] "The Best Car in the World," *Car and Driver,* November 1979, p. 92.

which he was fortunate enough to have access to. Given ideas, money, and small business talent, he was sure he could succeed.

And he did. By 1986, he had four establishments, was one of the leading car wash independents in the Midwest, and was still seeking better ways to do things. In 1984, he had put in a car detailing service ($110 for total cleaning of a car, inside and out, motor, under fenders, everywhere), and it was already selling well.

About this time, he participated in a college concept-generating program that the son of his office manager was running in a course he was taking at another university. The subject was "The car wash—how can it be improved?" The experience was interesting—and fun to a guy like Jerry—but now he was giving hard thought to one idea from that session—a portable car wash that offered home or office delivery service. The idea itself wasn't new, of course, but several aspects of this particular proposal were.

The idea was this: Many people would get their cars washed more often (and probably waxed, too) if they didn't have to take the time to drive to the wash facility and chance having to wait in line. The answer to these people was a portable car wash. Somehow, a self-contained car wash unit would be built that could be pulled around town, taken to a home or to a company parking lot on order, set up to a source of water (it would do its own immediate heating of the water), and have the vehicle(s) driven through it. Granted the washing would be less thorough than at the central units, but more personal attention would probably offset the facility size. And the service would be of maximum convenience, for which selected individuals would probably pay a good price.

But Jerry really wondered what to do next. He knew the car wash business and the people who bought the service. He had an immediately favorable reaction to the idea when it came up, impossible as it seemed at first, but now figured he had better do something other than rely on gut feelings.

He had heard of concept testing at a recent Chamber of Commerce meeting and thought this might be the time to try it. So, he called the university marketing department, was referred to the placement office, and ended up with two marketing majors (of whom you are one). He asked each of them to prepare a concept testing proposal. The proposal was to contain a statement of the specific concept, the research format(s) of that concept, and the general research methodology.

He told them that if the idea passed the concept test, he planned to have a unit built and put into service on a limited basis in Columbus. He could start it with businesses, or with homes, or in shopping centers, so he hoped the concept test would help on that decision, too. And, what would he have to tell people about the new service? That is, what questions and problems would they have? And . . . but then he thought he had better let the students get started.

The Full Screen

SETTING

As we saw in Chapter 9, business approaches to the prescreening tasks vary considerably. Use of full screening also varies, because businesses differ so much in what follows the screening. Some firms need very little technical work to come up with a suitable product. For them, the screen is a minor exercise on the way to a much more important step — product use testing.

For other firms, the technological breakthrough is the whole ball game; their R&D may require millions of dollars and many years. The full screen is the last low-risk evaluation, and managers want it done well.

Consequently, this chapter cannot present what any particular firm should do. That's up to the new products manager. But we can present the range of alternatives and a middle ground that actually fits most firms. It can easily be modified.

Chapter 10 also discusses a new step (called protocol) between the screen and serious R&D and prototype concept testing.

PURPOSES OF THE FULL SCREEN

Recall where we are in the product innovation process. After the original idea emerged, we translated it into concept format and then gave it early and intermediate evaluation. The initial reaction of key players was brief. The concept testing, however, was not; it enabled us to add the thoughts of potential users to the set of market and other data collected since the time of the product innovation charter. And along the way, we have been compiling the inputs of key functional people in the firm — technical, financial, operational, and the like.

This work culminates in a step called the *full screen*. It is full in the sense that we now have as much information as we're going to get before actually beginning work on the product. The following material deals with how that step can be made most worthwhile, and the first issue is, why do we do it? What is the purpose? There are several:

1. To decide whether R&D resources should be devoted to the project and, if so, how vigorously.
2. To cycle potentially worthwhile concepts back into concept development where more work may make them acceptable.
3. To rank the available options so some options are on standby when an ongoing project stalls or is canceled.
4. To record appraisals and actions because projects are sometimes resubmitted with or without changes. A record of actions and eventual outcomes also helps in revising the system.
5. To encourage cross-functional communication. Scoring sessions are peppered with such statements as "Why in the world did you score that rachet idea so low on such-and-such a factor?" The screening process is a learning process, particularly in making managers more sensitive to how other functions think.
6. To flush out all basic disagreements about a project and set them up for discussion. Scorers are sometimes so enamored with their own viewpoints that they cannot perceive that others differ. Other times, a scoring model forces discussion of an issue too political to come up otherwise. Major differences should be known as early in the process as possible.
7. Last, conflicts in the scoring process often tip off management that a product innovation charter is wrong. It may be incomplete, or people may disagree on what the firm is really good at.

Many different approaches have been created for this step, and we will now look at them.[1]

SCREENING ALTERNATIVES

Recognize that no established typology of full screen methods exists. It's like making a list of the different types of chili. Each firm seems to have created a unique approach.

---

[1] An expansion of these ideas can be found in Robert G. Cooper, *Winning at New Products* (Reading, Mass.: Addison-Wesley Publishing, 1986), pp. 101–13.

Simple Judgment

This approach essentially takes the process from the initial reaction right into R&D. One or a few people make judgments about the "developability" of a concept and let it go at that. Each person probably has one or, at most, two key factors in mind (for example, would people actually buy this, or is it something we can do?).

Single-Drive Decisions

Back at the time of strategic planning (Chapter 3), we talked about the alternatives of market-driven, technology-driven, or dual-driven focuses. Firms using a single drive often defer the development decision to that source. For example, a consumer products firm may let the concept test be the deciding factor—if the customer wants it, let's make it. Technology-driven firms often depend on the technologists. The decision involves much more than initial reaction, but it is still a single-drive one. No serious consideration is given to factors beyond that.

Portfolio Models

Some firms want to be more thorough than the first two methods but happen to be operating in the old-style method of letting R&D do the project selection. It isn't that they are technology driven, just that they have delegated the product innovation management task to people in R&D. So, they call screening *project selection* and employ a raft of methods for doing it. These methods, called portfolio models, are designed not so much to determine whether any particular proposal is good but rather how good it is *relative to the others*. Selection is a matter of ranking, taking projects from the top of the list as money becomes available.

Most of the methods involve quantitative analysis, often summarizing the data about the proposed projects being evaluated and converting these statistics about each project into an index number for that project. But, these methods are weak relative to the scoring models discussed below. Besides, the screening decision should be made at a nonfunctional level, not in marketing or research.[2]

---

[2] An exception is Glenn D. Lammey, "New Product Portfolio Power," *Business Marketing*, October 1987, pp. 64–70. This article shows how a scoring model (though a simple one) can be used as a portfolio model too. It is geared to evaluating whether a particular project meshes well with the firm's technical and marketing skills.

Financial Model

Some firms like to do their full financial evaluation early, which works if the new product concepts are simple line extensions in current markets. The techniques are quite like those to be discussed in Chapter 14. Unfortunately, using dollars does not dodge the fact that, in most cases, we don't know what the dollars should be—what kind of a price we will be able to get, how expensive it will be to change our distribution structure, what portion of early users will adopt the item after they have tried it, and what product liability dangers exist. We will come back to this problem in a moment.

Checklists

A long time ago, managers began making the above methods more efficient by use of a checklist—a list of factors that contribute to the answer and should not be overlooked. Checklists are still used today, and they look very much like the scoring models we will talk about next if the columns used for weighting are eliminated. But scoring models are easy to work with and do so much more for us.

Scoring Models

The scoring model is used so widely today that it deserves special discussion.

THE SCORING MODEL

Introductory Concept

We will now present a very simple situation to help explain a scoring model. Assume a student is trying to decide what social activity to undertake this weekend. The student has several options, and more options may appear between now and then.

The student could list criteria on several decisions that are personally important, specifically:

1. It must be fun.
2. It must involve more than just two people.
3. It must be affordable.
4. It must be something the student is capable of doing.

These four criteria (here called *factors*) are shown in Figure 10–1. Of course, 20 or 30 factors might be involved in this student's weekend social decisions, but let's stick with the 4. These factors are not absolutes; they can all be scaled—some fun, lots of fun, and so on. Figure 10–1 shows a four-point scale for each factor.

Next, each scale point needs a number so we can rank the options. With that done, the student can proceed to evaluate each option (as indicated in the figure) and total up the score for each. The final answer is to go boating—even though it isn't quite as much fun—primarily because it can involve lots of people, it is cheap, and the student is a capable rower.

But, suppose the student protests at this point and says, "There's more to it than that. If I go hiking, I'll get more exercise; but if I go skiing, a certain person is apt to be there." Moreover, the student argues that affordability is more important than the other factors because if money is inadequate, there is really no need to score the other points. Too, "Having fun is really more important than skill, so let's double the points for fun." And then there are objections that "skiing really is not all that much fun, boating is more expensive than you think," and so on.

The student's objections contain the basic problems of new product scoring models. We will see how the criticisms can be handled to keep a system that works pretty well.

FIGURE 10–1   Scoring Model for Student Activity Decision

	Values			
Factors	*4 Points*	*3 Points*	*2 Points*	*1 Point*
Degree of fun	Much	Some	Little	None
Number of people	Over 5	4 to 5	2 to 3	Under 2
Affordability	Easily	Probably	Maybe	No
Student's capability	Very	Good	Some	Little
Student's scorings:	*Skiing*		*Boating*	*Hiking*
Fun	4		3	4
People	4		4	2
Affordability	2		4	4
Capability	1		4	3
Totals	11		15	13
Answer: Go boating.				

The Procedure

Fortunately, the scoring model procedure is quite simple. It takes a while to develop a system; but once it is running, the fine-tuning does not require much effort.[3]

What Is Being Evaluated. In the case of the above student, we chose to base the model on four arbitrarily selected factors. Selecting factors in real life is not that easy, however. Actually, if we could, we would use only one factor: net present value of the discounted stream of earnings from the product concept, considering all direct and indirect costs and benefits.

This is shown on level one in the abbreviated graphic of Figure 10–2. As mentioned a moment ago, if we knew that profit figure, none of the others would be needed. But we don't, so we use surrogates for it. Level two in Figure 10–2 shows those surrogates. If we can estimate the likelihood of technical accomplishment (meaning, if we can create something that will do what customers want) and the likelihood of commercial accomplishment (meaning, if we can sell it profitably), there is again nothing left to do.

Experience shows we can't make these estimates directly. So, we reach for more surrogates, this time at level three. The figure shows only those for commercial accomplishment; again, if we know our sales, our margins on those sales, and our marketing and administrative expenses, we have the commercial half of the answer. Alas, again we fall short and have to seek surrogates.

This leads us to level four, which is where the action is. Level-four factors have answers, or at least answers we can estimate better than the factors at higher levels. The figure lists only three of the many factors at this level.

The reasoning goes like this: If you tell me whether the new product will enter a market with which we already have great familiarity, chances are we will be able to communicate with buyers in that market. This raises the chances for good sales, and greater sales make for more likely commercial fulfillment, which, in turn, leads

---

[3] Though quite easy when done in the mode of the scoring model example given later in this chapter, we should note that an immense body of theory lies behind all scoring decisions. For example, our scoring model is technically a linear compensatory model. That model, plus the conjunctive, disjunctive, and lexicographic models, is discussed (and compared in a new product screening exercise) in Kenneth G. Baker and Gerald S. Albaum, "Modeling New Product Screening Decisions," *Journal of Product Innovation Management,* March 1986, pp. 32–39.

FIGURE 10–2   Source of Scoring Model Factors

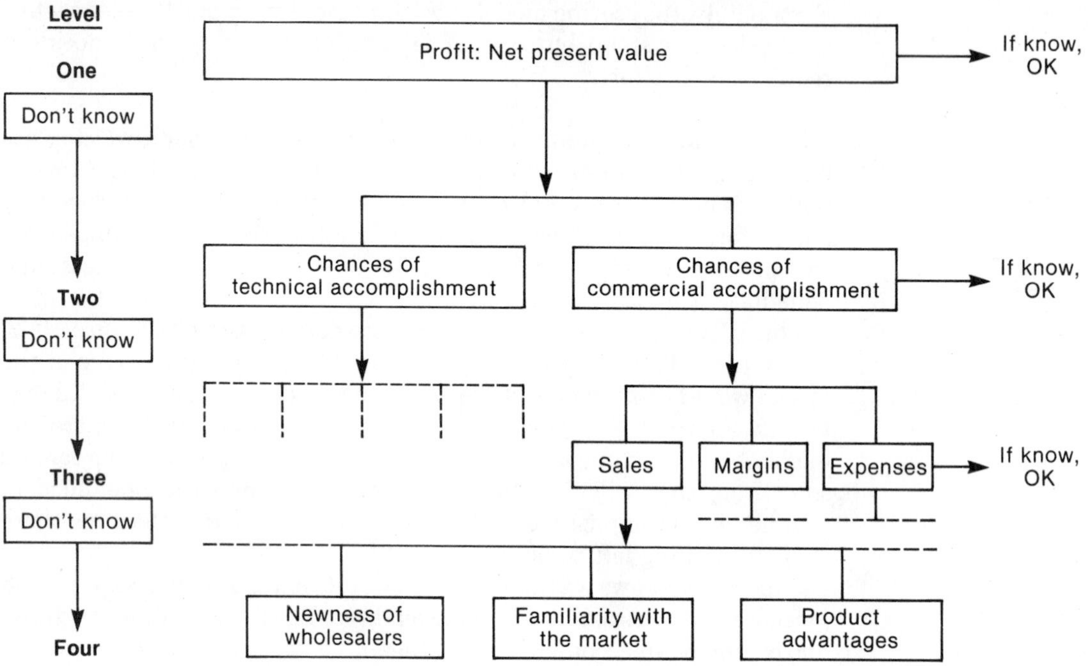

to profit. This takes us to the top of the figure, where we wanted to be in the first place. So, the key is to spot those level-four factors that contribute to the technical and commercial operations in this firm and on this particular product concept. Level-four factors compose the scoring model shown in Figure 10–3. Some firms include profit, sales, and so on as factors even though their surrogates should be there already.

The Scoring.   Given a scoring form such as that shown in Figure 10–3, the team members who will be doing the scoring first undergo a familiarization period during which they get acquainted with each proposal (market, concept, concept test results). Then, each scorer starts with the first factor (in this case, the difficulty of the technical task) and rates each one by selecting the most appropriate point on the semantic differential scales given on the second half of the screening form. These scorings are multiplied by the assigned importance weights, and the factor totals are extended. The scorings continue for the other factors, and the ratings are then totaled to get the overall rating for that concept by each individual.

Various methods are used to combine the individual team member's ratings, an average being the most common. Some firms use the Olympic method of dropping the highest and lowest ratings before averaging. Some firms have an open discussion after the averages are shown, so individuals can make a case for any view that is at odds with the group.

Unusual Factors.   On some factors, a bad score constitutes a veto. For example, in the case of the student seeking to decide what entertainment to pursue this weekend, a money shortage may block anything costing more than $30. This problem should be faced in the strategy, so no time is wasted drumming up options costing more than $30. Industry is the same, and a key role for the product innovation charter is to point out those exclusions. Some call these *culling factors.*[4]

Another problem occurs when the factor being scored has all-or-nothing, yes-or-no answers; for example, "Will this concept require the establishment of a separate sales force?" This type of factor is handled by using the end points on the semantic differential scale, with no gradations. If possible, such factors should be scaled as, for example, "How much additional cost is involved in setting up sales coverage for this concept?" Columns might be None; Under $50,000; $50,000 to $100,000; $100,000 to $300,000; and Over $300,000.

The Scorers or Judges.   Selecting the members of a scoring team is like selecting the members of a new products committee. The four major functions (marketing, technical, operations, and finance) are involved, as are new products managers and staff specialists from systems, distribution, procurement, public relations, personnel, and so on, depending on the firm's procedure for developing new products.

Top business unit managers (presidents, general managers) should stay out of the act, except, of course, in small firms. Such people inhibit the frank discussion and scoring especially needed when assessing the firm's capabilities (for example, in marketing or manufacturing).

Screening experience is certainly valuable. So is experience in the firm and in the person's specialty. Perhaps the best rule is to look at a person's past scoring efforts. Some firms actually weight each evaluator's scores by past accuracy (defined as conformity with the team's scores).

---

[4] See Rodger L. DeRose, "New Products—Sifting through the Haystack," *The Journal of Consumer Marketing,* Summer 1986, pp. 81–84. This article shows some direct connections between product strategy at Johnson Wax and the firm's new product screening; for example, its screening factors include "only safe products," "use existing capabilities," and "reflect the company's position and style."

FIGURE 10–3 Scoring Model for Screening New Product Concepts

Category	Factor	Weight	Score	Weighted Score
Technical Accomplishment	Technical task – difficulty			
	Technical certainty			
	Research skills			
	Development skills			
	Technical equipment			
	Technical processes			
	Rate of technological change			
	Design superiority (assurance)			
	Security of design (patent)			
	Special technical risks			
	Service capability			
	Manufacturing equipment			
	Manufacturing processes			
	Raw materials			
	Vendors			
	Safety in manufacturing			
			Total	
Commercial Accomplishment	Market volatility			
	Current market share			
	Probable market share			
	Cannibalization			
	Probable product life			
	Product line similarity			
	Sales force			
	Advertising and promotion			
	Target customer			
	Distributors			
	Retailers/Dealers			
	Importance of the task to user			
	Degree of unmet need			
	Likelihood of filling need			
	Competition			
	Value added			
	Field service			
	Safety in selling			
	Safety in use			
			Total	
	Concept: _____ Date: _____ Action: _____		Grand Total	_____

FIGURE 10–3 *(concluded)* Scales for Scoring Model Factors

Factor	Scale				
	1	2	3	4	5
Technical task – difficulty	Very difficult				Easy
Technical certainty	Doubtful				Certain
Research skills	Have none required				Perfect fit
Development skills	Have none required				Perfect fit
Technical equipment	Have none required				Have it all
Technical processes	Have none required				Very familiar
Rate of technological change	High/erratic				Stable
Design superiority (assurance)	None				Very high
Security of design (patent)	None				Have patent
Special technical risks	Great				None
Service capability	Have none required				Have it all
Manufacturing equipment	Have none required				Have it all
Manufacturing processes	Have none required				Very familiar
Raw materials	Don't use now				Routine items
Vendors	Unfamiliar				Strong bonds
Safety in manufacturing	Very high risks				No risks
Market volatility	High/erratic				Very stable
Current market share	None				Leader/high
Probable market share	Very low				Leader/high
Cannibalization	High portion				None
Probable product life	Less than 1 year				Extended
Product line similarity	No relationship				Very close
Sales force	No experience here				Very familiar
Advertising and promotion	No experience here				Very familiar
Target customer	Perfect stranger				Close/Current
Distributors	No relationship				Current/Strong
Retailers/Dealers	No relationship				Current/Strong
Importance of the task to user	Trivial				Critical
Degree of unmet need	None/satisfied				Totally unmet
Likelihood of filling need	Very low				Very high
Competition	Very tough				None
Value added	At our lowest margin				At our highest margin
Field service	No current capability				Ready now
Safety in selling	Very high risks				No risks
Safety in use	Very high risks				No risks

Technical people generally feel more optimistic about probable technical success, and marketers are more pessimistic.[5]

Problems with individuals are more specific. Research indicates that (1) some people are always optimistic, (2) some are sometimes optimistic and sometimes pessimistic, (3) some are "neutrals" who score to the middle of scales, (4) some are far more reliable and accurate than others, (5) some are easily swayed by the group, and (6) some are capable but erratic. Scoring teams need a manager to deal with such problems.

Weighting.   The most serious criticism of scoring models is their use of weights, because the weightings are necessarily judgmental (an exception from new research will be discussed in a moment). Let's go back to the student seeking a weekend activity. To a money-cautious student, affordability deserves more weight than the other factors. But how much more? Should it be weighted at two and the other factors at one?

Because of weighting's importance, some firms measure its effect using sensitivity testing. Scoring models are actually just mathematical models or equations, so an analyst can alter the scorings or the weightings to see what difference the alterations make in the final score. Spreadsheet programs handle this easily, and putting scoring models in spreadsheet format is becoming more common.

Profile Sheet

Figure 10–4 presents an alternative preferred by some firms for its graphic capability. The profile sheet graphically arranges the five-point scorings on the different factors. If a team of judges is used, the profile employs average scores. The approach does indeed draw attention to such patterns as the high scores given near the bottom of the profile (in Figure 10–4) compared to those near the top.

A Research-Based Model

Figure 10–5 shows the latest contribution to our collection of scoring models, a study of successful and unsuccessful products.[6] Some 100 Canadian industrial firms cooperated in the study, which correlated

---

[5] A. H. Rubenstein and H. Schreder, "Management Differences in Assessing Probabilities of Technical Success for R&D Projects," *Management Science*, October 1977, pp. 137–48.

[6] Robert G. Cooper, "Selecting Winning New Product Projects: Using the NewProd System," *Journal of Product Innovation Management*, March 1985, pp. 34–44.

FIGURE 10-4   The Profile of a New Product Proposal

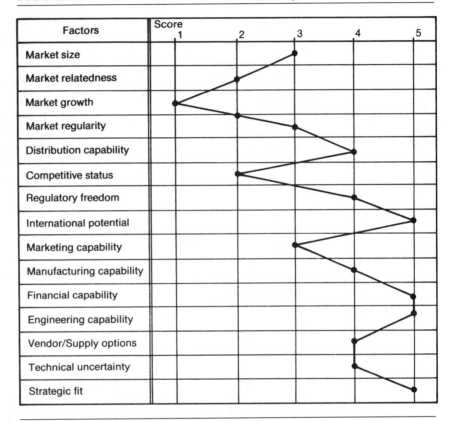

success and failure with the characteristics of the project/product at the time it would have been screened. The firms cited a total of 80 descriptive characteristics when asked why the product failed (or succeeded). From these, 48 that would have been known at the time of the screening (pre–R&D) were selected. Factor analysis reduced this set of 48 to the 13 underlying factors or dimensions that captured the essence of the 48. Next, the regression coefficients were calculated (correlation between each factor's score and the success or failure of the product), and 8 of the 13 were found to be significant. The regression coefficients serve as the weights for the eight factors in the model.

Figure 10–5 shows the results for the eight factors. The figure shows the six variables from which the first—product superiority, quality, uniqueness—was factored. The factor is important (1.744 weight) and positive. What the figure really shows is that the typical industrial firm should use eight factors in the scoring model, with the weights indicated.

FIGURE 10–5   Research-Based Scoring Model

Of 13 Key Factors, 8 Were Significant:	*Weight from the Regression Coefficients*	*48 Variables that Can Be Measured at the Screening Stage of Development and the Factors They Support*
Product superiority, quality, uniqueness	1.744	Product is superior. Product has unique feature. Product is higher quality. Product does unique task. Product cuts user's costs. Product is first of kind.
Overall project/firm resource compatibility	1.138	(See source for the other 42 variables.)
Market need, growth, and size	0.801	
Economic advantage of product to end user	0.722	
Newness to the firm	-0.354	
Technological resource compatibility	0.342	
Market competitiveness	-0.301	
Product scope (mass rather than narrow specialty)	0.225	
Constant	0.328	

Note: This table reads as follows: The most important factor in screening industrial products is the degree of product superiority, quality, or uniqueness. This superiority factor is derived from six specific scorings, the first of which is how superior the proposed product is to its probable competitors. If a score for all six variables is determined and then put into a score for the factor as a whole (see source for method), that factor is then given a weight of 1.744. After all eight factors have been scored, the total is determined and compared with other product proposals.

Source: Robert G. Cooper, "Selecting Winning New Product Projects: Using the NewProd System," *Journal of Product Innovation Management*, March 1985, pp. 34–44.

Unfortunately, a repeat of this study has not been published, though several company applications are still confidential. Too, good correlations may often be gotten by going back into the past, because the judgments scorers make now are influenced by the known outcomes of the concepts being scored. But, time will tell. The users of the approach say that because managers are sometimes reluctant to see their ideas shot down by an equation, it is better to think of using this technique to *guide* the concept, showing where it misses out so that further development work can be done.

Special Aspects

A few other aspects round out our discussion of scoring models. One concerns the product champion (discussed fully in Chapter 19). Champions are sometimes needed to push past normal resistance to change and to see that the concept gets a fair hearing at all turns. They also try to affect the scorings by ensuring the scorers are given all favorable information or by arguing that standard forms don't fit special situations (for example, "The standard forms are wrong in this case"). Champions often try to persuade their firms to override negative results of scoring models. Managements usually want champions to do just this, in the interest of seeing that unusual ideas get genuine consideration.

Another special aspect concerns the computer, which fits the scoring situation well and aids sensitivity testing. Some companies have even combined computerization with display by having all scorings done on electronic input devices, having weightings and averaging done by a standard program, and then presenting the data on visual display devices showing the averages and the distribution of scores. Team members can see how they voted compared to the others and can then make instant changes in their scores. The changes are immediately seen (anonymously) on the screen.[7] Dow Brands uses a computerized approach primarily for this anonymous aspect.

Last, experience shows that managements sometimes misuse scoring models. One report told how a consumer products manufacturer threw out a scoring model system because it:

1. Was rejecting products that would help round out the line.
2. Was rejecting products that would help forestall competitive entry into the market.
3. Was rejecting too many products, according to the sales department.[8]

The first two problems arose from either faulty factor selection or faulty factor weighting and were easily solved. The third arose because the cutoff score was set too high. Thus, scoring models require competent management.

---

[7] The computer approach was first described by William W. Simmons, "The Condenser," *The Futurist*, April 1979, pp. 91–94. A later version from Option Technologies, created for use by focus group participants in voting on product attributes, could probably be converted for use as a scoring model. See Tom Eisenhart, "Advanced Research Finds a New Market," *Business Marketing*, March 1989, p. 60. A different computer-based system is described in Kenneth G. Baker and Gerald G. Udell, *KISS: A Strategy for New Product Screening* (Eugene: University of Oregon Experimental Center for the Advancement of Business Administration, 1977).

[8] E. Patrick McGuire, *Evaluating New Product Proposals* (New York: The Conference Board, 1973), p. 32.

PROTOCOL

The purpose of a scoring model is decision: Discard the concept or send it into technical development. But before the latter can happen, at least one more action is necessary. It involves how the actual request will be sent to R&D.

Currently, most firms that describe the desired product do so in what we call *feature form* — feature attributes, such as color, size, material, and appearance. Many R&D departments are so conditioned to getting specific requests from marketing that they can't operate without them.

Examples

But, R&D should be getting requests in benefit or performance form, not features. For example, a Stride Rite new products manager asked for a new pair of Topsiders that "must not slip on polished wood at 30-degree pitch, must dry overnight," and so on. She didn't ask for any particular sole compound, shape, or color, just performance.[9] Dow-Merrell pharmaceutical developers asked their assigned scientist to develop a new bulk laxative that would (among other things) "dissolve completely in a four-ounce glass of water in 10 seconds." No mention of chemical, size of granules, or other features.

The Process

We'll see a complete example in a moment, but first think about what has to happen here. From the market study, the concept testing, and the many discussions during the scoring process, marketing has gotten a good feel for what the market wants. But, negotiation must take place. For example, marketing asks for a product that "removes all grease in 10 seconds." Technical may respond that because no solvent could do this in a kitchen setting, should they begin basic research? Management answers no, but what time *is* possible? Technical responds that they can't know for sure, but 15 seconds seems to be the best possible within today's state of the art. Do they know how they will achieve this? No, but it seems to be an achievable goal. And so on down through the list.

The end result is a list of attributes — mostly benefits, not features (though some features are always required by the market, such as legal

---

[9] "Setting the Pace in Shoe Design," *The Wall Street Journal,* August 13, 1987, p. 21.

requirements or constraints put on us by distributors' warehouses or rail cars). The technical group promises they will be able to produce those items. Marketing promises that if they do, the product will be sold profitably. This is an agreement, or a *protocol*.

An extreme version of a protocol was reported by a pharmaceutical firm in which a new products manager sent a comprehensive advertising layout to his technical counterpart in R&D with an attached note, "Please prepare an item that will back up this ad." The first reaction was negative, until technical realized they were given carte blanche to do whatever they wanted, so long as the result met the listed claims.

The Recommended Format

Figure 10–6 shows a hypothetical protocol raising most of the issues involved here. Note the introductory paragraph describes the setting, the essence of the product, the level of support, and the target market.

Next comes the specific attributes requested. Note the one possible confusion (item 3), a couple of items in which the request verges on specific features (4 and 5), one item that provides the standard to be used for measurement (7), and one clear violation of the rule that the protocol offer only benefits (item 8).

The Overall System

Figure 10–7 offers an overview of the process, who the players are, when they participate, and so on. What ends up as a specific feature of a new product (say, shape) begins as a thought (usually a problem) in the mind of the buyer. Under the leadership of marketing, the new product team becomes aware of the problem and, after investigation, comes up with a proposed protocol. Negotiation with technical people (within the team) results in a final protocol, which the technical people (in conjunction with marketing) then convert into a statement of design parameters. These design parameters lead to feature specs, to early prototypes, and so on.

The protocol's helpfulness to engineering and scientific people varies with the experience of the product planner, the thoroughness of the concept development work, and the completeness of research on the marketplace. Given good preparation, the protocol can save untold dollars and time; it also increases the likelihood that the first prototype will be the last.

However, the protocol's greatest value probably lies in the new relationship it can produce between marketing people, technical people, and the rest of the team. This functional interface (often called just a

---

FIGURE 10–6   Hypothetical Protocol

This protocol has been written as part of our lawn-and-garden devices project. It describes what we have been calling our snow-blade, a hand device that we visualize homeowners in northern climates would use to push snow off their walks and driveways. The protocol has the support of technical, operations, and marketing departments as being feasible and marketable.

1. Persons using the device must be able to push snow at an accumulation of 8 inches.
2. The device must be usable by all persons over 8 years of age, unless there is physical impairment.
3. There must be flexibility in the device such that the user can push from either direction on the sidewalk and have the snow go off the near side of the walk.
4. In storage, the device must take up no more room than that required by the typical garden hoe.
5. There must be no significant product liability risk in the device. If there is, it must be such that warnings and other instructions can legally protect the company.
6. The device must remove snow at least equal to that done by the leading brands of snow blowers.
7. The device must be considered attractive by its intended users.
8. The handle of the product must be made of a hard rubber.

Comments about the above protocol:
- Most of the items are clearly benefits.
- Item 3 is potentially confusing, but it suggests that persons working on the project understand what is meant.
- Items 4 and 5 verge on specific dimensions. So long as all involved parties understand the focus on a benefit, there is room for negotiation during development.
- Item 5 states an ideal requirement; all persons understand that they may have to take on some product liability risk, but if so, it will be by known exception.
- Item 7 shows how the protocol can provide a standard when dealing with subjective factors.
- Item 8, a clear violation of protocol requirements, is apparently a legal requirement.
- Other requirements could be on a separate sheet as "desirable" but not necessary.

---

marketing/R&D interface because of the difficulty these two groups sometimes have in working together) will be discussed further in Chapter 19, but note here it is real—and costly.[10]

---

[10] One retired scientist creates laughter during his speeches when he refers to such "unalterable laws" as MS = MD. This translates into Monkey See = Monkey Do. "Marketing generally cannot relate to a product or product category that does not already exist." See *Marketing, a Bimonthly Briefing from the Conference Board,* December 1987, p. 4. The scientist, Raymond C. Odioso, presented the total set of "laws" in a Conference Board Research Management Report, according to the cited source.

FIGURE 10–7 Protocol and the Entire Market–Technical–Market Communications Process: Stages of Activity and Progress of Concept

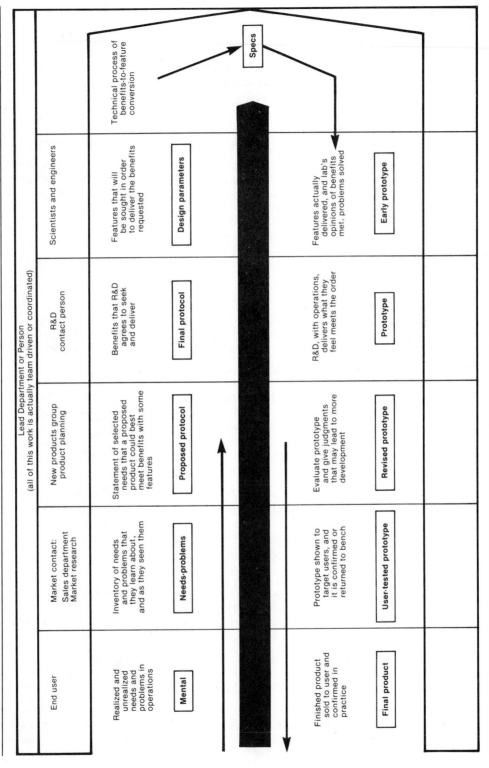

The essence of protocol is focus, or direction of technical strength, but only so much as the situation demands. No arbitrary constraints are put on the work. This focus puts immense pressure on others, particularly marketing, to be thorough in their homework because when R&D comes up with a product meeting the prescribed conditions, marketing must be prepared to market it successfully. No afterthoughts. No new conditions.

Few firms as yet play out the protocol game in such theatrical fashion, but the concept does introduce new discipline immediately after screening, before serious technical work begins. And, most important of all, it forces someone to contact the intended customer, a step still avoided in far too many companies.[11]

TESTING THE PROTOTYPE

One other test of the new product concept often takes place after that concept has been put into physical or service form. When it is easy to prepare prototypes (such as a cake mix, an insurance policy, a revised computer keyboard), developers like to just prepare a few and *then* talk with intended buyers.

A *prototype* is a model of the ultimate production unit. It may be highly synthetic, but it does replicate the essential elements of the production unit while ignoring or bridging extraneous or purely supporting elements. Let's look at some typical prototypes.

Cake mix: The mix ingredients are representative of the finished product. The packaging used is irrelevant.

Automobile: This product has several prototypes because of the size and complexity involved. Small component units (for example, a wheel or a dashboard) are used, if possible; then, on to clay models and fully engineered working models, which are usually adaptations of current cars or amalgamations of parts of several cars. Up to a million dollars has been spent on a new car's models alone.

Electrical measuring instrument: The prototype begins as a breadboard but ends up as a fully handcrafted model. Sometimes these are quite sophisticated, and if previous body parts can be used, the prototype is hard to distinguish from a production model.

Pharmaceutical item: The prototype is a chemical entity, with or without cosmetic elements. Preliminary testing uses a liquid, tablet,

---

[11] A full discussion of protocol can be found in C. Merle Crawford, "Protocol: New Tool for Product Innovation," *Journal of Product Innovation Management,* April 1984, pp. 85–91.

capsule, or injection that is purely functional. Additions to improve acceptance, appearance, or shelf life come later.

Loan service: Pure services (those without a tangible component) can be prepared almost by stipulation. A loan prototype states the conditions of the loan and a plan for how people and process will make it.

Against the Protocol

The first testing of a prototype is with the protocol. Because R&D people used the protocol to produce the prototype, this test is conducted by the marketing department or by a separate new product management team. If marketing people stay close to R&D during development, no surprises happen here. And there shouldn't be any, because the development process provides for continuous checking against the protocol with iterations as necessary until the best approximation is obtained.

Repeat the Concept Test

When the rest of the team is satisfied that the prototype has only acceptable variances from what was wanted, they are ready for the second test—a repeat of the earlier concept test, this time using the prototype.

To some extent, the prototype concept test is the first step in a "series of successive compromises" as various desired attributes stated in the protocol are sacrificed to technical realities and/or production costs.[12]

The compromising that began during the earlier concept testing continues during R&D and even during the prototype checks by marketing personnel. However, it intensifies at this point. The adage is that a product never looks as good as when it was first thought of.

Compromising continues all the way to marketing (for example, a positioning change at the last minute), but the postprototype reconfirming concept test is perhaps the most critical adjustment. Time has passed, people have changed, competition has changed, and the prototype inevitably varies some from the protocol.

Generally speaking, the same research technology is used here as before. The shortage of prototypes is often a limiting factor, but if enough prototypes exist to permit some actual product usage, this step can be called the "concept trial."

---

[12] This feeling about successive compromises is a personal communication from Professor Thomas P. Hustad of Indiana University.

The loan service in the above list of prototypes shows how prototype concept testing merges into product use testing, a subject we will cover in the next chapter. If a prototype can be prepared in some quantity, it can be put through a full field use test, and we are no longer just looking at a prototype. The Fairchild Camera and Industrial Corporation repeated field prototype testing on a movie projector three times before achieving success. The product was called Mark IV even before it went into production.[13]

Prototypes are far more tentative than most field test products, however. They are prepared primarily to see if everyone understands the concept the same way.

Sample selection is perhaps the most controversial here. This research is less exploratory than the earlier concept testing, so participant demographics and psychographics are more important. Yet, simplicity and cost are relevant because this phase of testing may cycle around several times before a prototype is released for implementation by process and manufacturing engineering. And, secrecy is often vital.

A few people feel that innovators (such as opinion leaders or early adopters who will be the first to adopt the innovation) should be used. The theory is that innovators must approve the prototype or it will never receive market acceptance.[14] Most new products managers disagree.

SUMMARY

If an idea progresses through early concept testing and development to the point where it is a full-blown concept ready for technical workup, it must then be screened. Screening is commonly done with scoring models, whereby the firm's ability to bring off the required development and marketing is estimated. If the concept scores well by whatever criteria the firm uses, it is sent into technical development. Just prior to that, however, some firms try to spell out a protocol—an agreed set of benefits that the new item is to deliver to the customer—to guide technical development.

Once R&D feels the protocol has been achieved, the concept is in prototype form. The prototype is not a finished product by any means, but it is a form that others can compare to the protocol and that can be taken to the field for further concept testing. The concept test is much

---

[13] E. Patrick McGuire, *Evaluating New Product Proposals* (New York: The Conference Board, 1973), p. 51.

[14] The principal proponent (and an able advocate) of using innovators for prototype concept testing is David F. Midgley, *Innovation and New Product Marketing* (New York: John Wiley & Sons, 1977).

more productive when the concept is in prototype form, though it may be more expensive because substantial R&D expenditures have already been made.

If the prototype passes the new round of concept testing, the firm can then undertake further technical work that will bring the new item to the stage of use testing, the subject of the next chapter.

APPLICATIONS

1. "Our small electrical engines division recently threw out a screening system that was based on a fairly complete scoring model, as they called it. Seems the model kept rejecting too many of their product ideas, some of which looked like sure winners to them—and to me, incidentally. Now their top-management committee reviews these ideas personally, without all that paperwork, and it looks like things will be better. Do you have any reaction to that?"

2. "In late 1981, the Dow Jones people announced that they had to cancel their plans for a *Wall Street Journal Magazine.* They had spent over a year in planning, but when they showed prototype copies of the new publication to test readers, the readers were somewhat short on enthusiasm. They wanted more information on personal finance and several other areas that the firm had been planning to handle in their regular publications like the *Journal* and *Barron's.* Couldn't something have been done to find this out earlier and save that year of very expensive planning?"

3. "Yet, another new service that tries to give consumers information on TV shows and movies is rather widely criticized. A firm named ASI Market Research, Inc., has a service called Preview House. The service hooks up movie theater audiences (which it gets from telephone lists with promises of free movies) with an instantaneous response machine that has dials for recording likes and dislikes. The firm can test upcoming shows, entire movies (for example, if they had tested *Heaven's Gate,* a bundle might have been saved), records, and so on. Granted, audiences go especially big for sex, puppies, little children, and so on, but if that's what they like, that's what they want. Mr. Magoo goes especially well. What do you think of a service like this?"

4. "I heard a funny one two weeks ago that might interest you. Seems one of our R&D people went to a new products management seminar and heard about a thing called the protocol. They told him it was the device whereby the overall manager of new products communicated to R&D exactly what was wanted from the technical group. R&D even had to "sign on the dotted line" swearing that they thought it could be done. He was really steamed—said no one could tell R&D what they

should come up with, not in advance anyway. And R&D is responsible only to top management, not new products managers, so they don't have to promise anything. He said he considered that concept the most stifling single action imaginable. How would you answer that scientist, or would you?"

Case: *Wilson Sporting Goods**

In mid-1985, the Wilson Sporting Goods Division of PepsiCo, Inc., was trying to bring engineering and other technology to the sporting goods business. Materials-based technologies had already produced easy-to-hit tennis balls and a more responsive softball (which produced games with scores of 50 to 48).

Other firms were also active. Puma produced a running shoe with an electronic device that measured time, distance, and calories expended. AMF had a chemical compound to reduce the shock for tennis rackets.

The reason for Wilson's special interest in technology was its conviction that technology could be used to lure consumers back into the market. Tennis and golf had fallen off rather badly, for example, and many participative sports were suffering in varying degrees. There had been successes, however: better running shoes showed that technology could advance a sport, shoulder pads benefited from space-age technology, baseball centers were now sometimes polyurethane. Computers had already helped tennis rackets, golf ball designs, and more. Of course, there were also failures.

But the present need was for some way to screen through the many ideas that came naturally out of such a campaign. Wilson had the engineers, and the firm knew sports. It had a broad product line, an excellent distribution system, and was one of the leading firms in the athletic goods industry. But money in the industry was short, especially for higher-risk R&D. So, Wilson needed a scoring model to help select the new product ideas most likely to contribute to company profits, especially considering the short-term financial squeeze in the industry.

The firm's considerable experience in new product work enabled it to use a full scoring model (not just a few factors), and it wanted a good weighting system built in. Wilson executives did not indicate whether the firm routinely used concept testing as a prescreening step, but it probably did.

Develop a scoring model for Wilson and give some thought to the problems of implementing the system in this firm. Which department would be the biggest problem, that is, be least likely to live with the results of a scoring session? Would using protocols be reasonable in this situation? Help the firm adopt this new idea by spelling out a five-step protocol for a new set of bowling pins that would exploit technology, enliven the game, and attract new attention to it.

---

*Hal Lancaster, "For the Poor Athletes Who Blame Their Tools, New Ones Are Coming," *The Wall Street Journal*, May 14, 1985, p. 37.

Chapter 11

Product Use Testing

SETTING

Chapter 10 said the output of R&D (or engineering, or systems design) is something in prototype form, preliminary, and suggestive of the product's final attributes. The prototype is checked against the protocol and then perhaps sent to the marketplace for a confirmatory concept test. This latter test compares the intended customers' reactions to the prototype with the results of the original concept test.

This phase usually leads back into some further technical work, and eventually what was a prototype becomes an actual working product. If the prototype was not functional (it didn't actually work), then *considerable* further technical work may have been necessary. A cake mix prototype may have needed little work, but a tractor prototype may have just been a mock-up, totally nonfunctional.

In any event, when the technical people deliver something that can actually do what it was intended to do, we enter an entirely new phase—called *product use testing,* or *field testing,* or *user testing.* Such testing is the topic of this chapter.

IS PRODUCT USE TESTING NECESSARY?

Before we get into the details, we have to face the reality that product use testing is often considered unnecessary. Remember, we have been working on this new product for months, if not years, and have spent lots of money on it. Various experts have done the work, they are naturally optimistic, and early market research said the market wanted a product like this, so why dally around any longer? Management is usually under pressure for the revenues the new item will bring, and there is always the gnawing fear that a competitor will announce a similar product any day now and take the play away from us.

Here are the specific forms this objection takes:

"Time pressure won't let us do it. Everyone is in an up mode, and stopping for testing suggests we don't have faith in what we've been doing."

"We have thoroughly tested the concept, and the product now matches what we talked with people about earlier; what is there to test?"

"Users' reactions are scientifically (or systematically) based, and we can predict them. Everyone knows what's needed here, and we have it."

"We've been in the market for years, and we certainly know what the users want."

"If we take the time to test, competitors will find out what we are doing; even if they don't, we just give them more time to do something else."

"This product really isn't testable because the customer will have to learn some really new ways of doing things, and this would take more time than we have."

"No matter how hard you try, product use tests are fake. They require users to make evaluations isolated from the natural forces in the marketplace, so they just aren't reliable enough to be worth the time and effort."

"Listen, we've already got so much invested in this project there is no way it could be stopped. We didn't spend six years in technical development scattered over three labs just to have some market researcher tell us customers may not like it as well as we thought."

Are These Arguments Correct?

These arguments are persuasive, especially when put forth by the person on the top floor who has funded the work to date. But they are incorrect in the sense that they imply we don't have anything to learn. We have an unknown in our hands; the user whose problem probably started the project still hasn't told us our product solves that problem. The product won't sell unless it does.

So, where does that leave us? It leaves us knowing that all new product testing is a trade-off: (1) additional knowledge that reduces the chances of failure due to having the wrong product, versus (2) the added costs of the testing, including cash outlays and delays. What the firm does is the result of analyzing that trade-off. Unfortunately, many firms still underestimate the risks. They seem to forget that "not meeting customer needs" is one of the top three reasons for new product failure. So, they go ahead, hoping they are right.

Meeting customer needs is a complex matter. It is solving the big problem that users told us they have (for example, does Rogaine actually help some people regrow hair?). But it is also the baggage the product brings along—such as the side effects, the cost, and the learning required. Sulfuric acid will clean out clogged water pipes, but it takes some of the metal with it.

Meeting customer needs also means delivering a quality product. Can we make one? For example, in 1982, Amdahl was an established and successful maker of mainframe computers—big ones. But that year, it rolled out a new line and "offered a convincing demonstration of how to do everything wrong . . . . When [the machines] did arrive, they were infested with so many bugs that Amdahl field engineers had to scurry about doing retrofits . . . . Predictably, the results were devastating . . . . Share slumped to around 12 percent, from 17 percent."

Three years later, Amdahl announced its next generation of computers. It took the time to "do the job right," even though IBM got the jump on it. "By insisting on exhaustive, pre–roll-out testing, President Lewis made sure the machines worked." The result was spectacular, with sales of 250 machines costing between $3 million and $9 million apiece. The following year, share was back up to 15 percent and climbing.[1]

In 1987, IBM marketed the AS/400 minicomputer (called the most successful product launch in IBM history). By the introduction date, potential buyers had tested 1,700 of the computers! A year later, they had bought 25,000 of them.[2]

New product graveyards are littered with unnecessary failures:

- The electric-powered microscope whose electric cord produced shocks.
- In cold weather, a new baby food separated into a clear liquid and a sludge.
- The gas cap on a tractor disengaged because the gas filler spout expanded when the tractor was in use.
- A kitchen mixer was made quiet, which the concept test showed people wanted; but when they turned it on, it was "underpowered and not worth buying."
- A leading chemical company developed and sold a mortar additive for major buildings. The mortar reacted with the steel and gave off free chloride, a salt that caused severe corrosion. Over 2,000 buildings were involved.[3]

---

[1] Marc Beauchamp, "Learning from Disaster," *Forbes,* October 19, 1987, p. 96.

[2] Joel Dreyfuss, "Reinventing IBM," *Fortune,* August 14, 1989, p. 35.

[3] Some of the examples given here came from Glen L. Urban and John R. Hauser, *Designing and Marketing New Products* (Englewood Cliffs, N.J.: Prentice-Hall, 1980), p. 20.

To bypass product use testing is a gamble that should be considered only when there is just cause. The burden of proof is on whoever argues for skipping it.

The Problem of Beta Testing

As if the various dimensions of the trade-off just discussed were not enough, we must also deal a bit further with the management that says, "OK, I'm convinced. Let's put the product out there and see for sure that it works." Computer hardware and software companies have been following this instruction from their beginnings. First, they put their new item into use in-house, in their own ongoing operations, in what they call *Alpha testing*. (A new accounting software package could be tested in the firm's own accounting department.)

If it "works" there, they move into what they call *Beta testing,* or testing to see how the product "works" in customers' operations. The terms *Alpha* and *Beta* are so widely used in the computer industry that they are often picked up and used in other industries.

But both can be misleading, particularly Beta testing. Note the executive just above said, "that it works," not "that it meets the needs of the customer." Amdahl's problem was that its 1982 product "didn't work." Because this can happen so easily in the computer industry, computer firms take their final versions of the product out to users in the target market and sell them on *trying it*. Here is a typical procedure, used recently in a firm that makes computer hardware. Note the words carefully. Of the "80 pilot units made . . . 10 units went to the company's field test department for installation at selected customer sites . . . . While pilot testing was under way, manufacturing completed the pilot run and went into full pro-duction."[4]

No way did those users have time to judge whether the new equipment met their needs, how cost effective it was, how various employees in their firms adjusted to the new item, and so on. Computer industry manufacturers know this, but they usually go ahead and produce and introduce the product.

---

[4] Paul G. Waitkus, "Managing High-Tech Product Development," *Machine Design,* June 20, 1985, p. 95. Don't get the idea that this is exceptional; it is fundamental thinking in a major industry. For example, a software products company, "Cognos, Inc., launched a new concept: an in-house software evaluation center where customers are invited to test products. 'So far we feel we're getting more quality evaluation done in three or four days than we were when people had six weeks to examine the product at their leisure.' " Brian Banks, "Testing, Testing," *Canadian Business,* January 1988, p. 95.

Beta testing does not meet the developer's real needs. A third term just beginning to appear, *Gamma* (Greek for *C*) *testing,* designates the ideal product use test, where the item is put through its paces and thoroughly evaluated by the end user. To pass this test, the new item must solve whatever problem the customer had, even if the solution takes several months.

Even though Gamma testing is the ideal test (and is urged in this chapter), firms anxious to save time, money, and competitive leapfrogging nevertheless opt to ride with the Beta version.

TYPES OF PRODUCT USE TESTING

The two basic classes of methods for product use testing parallel the Alpha and Beta/Gamma testing above. The first, in-house testing, has several forms. One is experimentation by the *developers* themselves. They almost always "try it out" in one way or another. A second is by *professional testers,* best known of which is probably the wine taster. Third is *employees.*

The second class of method involves working directly with persons in the marketplace — *market users.* This testing can be what are called *central location tests* (opportunistic testing of items at trade shows, focus groups, kitchens where customers are brought in to try out new concoctions, and scores of miscellaneous ones). As an example, L'Oréal maintains a 300-seat hair salon, where its products are tested along with competitive items. One hair dye went through 28,000 applications over a three-year period, and Free Style mousse was tested for five years.[5]

Or, the tests can be run *at the point of use.* Most industrial testing fits here, simply because most testing is in ongoing processes that don't fit salons or trade shows. Beta/Gamma tests fit here. Of course, if the potential buyer can make a decision from just one exposure (for example, a candy bar), then all testing can be done at central locations instead.

These different types of testing are often combined into a *system* of testing. See Figure 11–1 for a description of the several tests Gillette used for a new deodorant. The extensive list demonstrates how different types of use testing are done for different purposes at different times. Disappointments need to be cycled back to try something else. The Dry Idea sequence also shows that although the package and the product may be on different testing streams, they must eventually come together, at which time still different problems may arise.

---

[5] Patricia Benjamin, "Sitting Pretty," *Business,* January 1987, pp. 65–67.

FIGURE 11–1   The Product Testing System Used for Gillette's Dry Idea
Deodorant

---

1. Technical lab work in 1975 suggested available technologies to achieve a drier deodorant.
2. A 2,000-person concept study (cost: $175,000) determined that "Yes, roll-ons are good, but they go on wet and make you wait to get dressed." A concept was at hand.
3. Laboratory project assigned to scientist: find a replacement for water as the medium for the aluminum-zirconium salts that did the work.
4. A prototype using silicone was developed, and it wasn't wet or sticky. But it did dissolve the ball of the applicator. (In-house lab test.)
5. Next prototype was tested by volunteers from the local South Boston area. It was oily. (Outside research firm employed to test college students in the area. Gillette often used in-house test of employees too).
6. By late 1976, a later prototype tested well on women recruited to sweat for hours in a 100-degree "hot room." (Test of market users in the Boston area who served on a regular panel.) Unfortunately, though it worked well, it eventually turned into a rock-hard gel.
7. By early 1977, another prototype had passed the "hot room" tests and was then sent to company-owned medical evaluation laboratories in Rockville, Maryland. (In-house test on rabbits and rats.) It passed the test.
8. Packaging was being developed and tested by in-house package design engineers. Early packages leaked.
9. However, the package dispensed a product that test subjects felt was too dry going on! (Test of market users.)
10. They then returned to a conventional roll-on bottle, added a special leak-proof gasket, and enlarged the ball so the antiperspirant could be applied in quantities large enough to be felt. Another test of market users confirmed that people did indeed feel drier. This conclusion, when put with the earlier data that the product did have a good antiperspirant effect, was enough to go to market.

Note: This procedure used several different types of tests, with different objectives and formats, and with reiterations. The product was cycled until successful.

Source: Neil Ulman, "Sweating It Out," *The Wall Street Journal*, November 17, 1978, p. 1; and "For Some Concerns the Smell of Success Isn't Exactly Sweet," *The Wall Street Journal*, December 28, 1977, p. 1.

Devising such a sequence or system of use tests requires new products management to know about the various testing options available. These will be discussed in detail shortly; however, we should review the purposes of product use testing before we specify how to do it.

PURPOSES OF PRODUCT USE TESTING

Product use testing has four purposes, the first of which is far more important than the others.

Fulfill Protocol.   The aim here (as with prototype testing) is to see whether the technical or procurement personnel have produced a product with the attributes called for in the protocol. This means physical features, perceptual features, functional modes, and perceived benefits. We need to prove that claimed attributes exist and to find the causes for missing attributes.

Obtain Ideas for Improvements.   Even at the last minute ways usually appear to improve performance or to reduce cost; use tests suggest many. General Foods, for example, carried to the very last test the issue of the relative proportions of instant coffee and roasted grains for Mello-Roast. It wanted to balance very carefully and accurately the trade-off between the lower cost of the grains and the effect on flavor.

Learn Modes of Use.   Most products can be used in various ways, and these options can be researched during the use tests. Industrial firms often cite this as one of the most important objectives of their use tests.

Verify Claims.   New product developers know they must anticipate criticisms of their claims. The criticisms may come from government, from voluntary self-regulatory groups, or from self-appointed consumer groups. And, the marketing people need verification too, because they are making final selection of target markets (does the item work well for them?) and final positioning (does their experience with the product support the benefit claim?). Marketing planners also have to worry about acceptance of product claims by their own sales force, by the advertising agency, and by others.

TESTING DIMENSIONS

Gillette's testing system involved several separate tests, each of which had to be crafted carefully. To do this, the firm's developers were faced with at least 13 decisions (special cases may call for others). Let's look at those 13 decisions and the options within each. They are identified in Figure 11–2, and the identifying letters and numbers will be used here.

FIGURE 11–2   Decisions that Define Product Use Tests

A. Those concerning what we need to learn.
    1. *This is an open set.*
B. Those concerning contacting test groups.
    2. *User groups.*
        In-house (lab personnel, experts, employees).
        Market users.
        Miscellaneous.
    3. *Mode of contact.*
        Mail versus personal.
        Individual versus group.
        Point of use versus central location.
    4. *Identity disclosure.*
        Branded versus blind.
    5. *Degree of explanation about usage.*
        No comment.
        Commercial.
        Full explanation.
C. Those concerning product usage.
    6. *Degree of control over use.*
        Total control.
        Supervised.
        Unsupervised.
    7. *Singularity.*
        Monadic.
        Paired comparison.
        Triangular.
    8. *Duration of use.*
        Single use.
        Short period (week).
        Extended (up to six months).
D. Those concerning the product itself.
    9. *Source of product.*
        Batch.
        Pilot plant.
        Final production.
   10. *Product form.*
        Best single product.
        Variants (size, color, shape, etc.).
E. Those concerning measurement and analysis.
   11. *Mode of recording reaction.*
        Like/dislike.
        Preference.
        Descriptive.
   12. *Source of norms.*
        Previous studies versus judgment.
   13. *Research service.*
        In-house versus outside firm.

A. Testing Dimensions Concerning What We Need to Learn

1. An Open Set. What we need to learn is totally situation specific. Generally, the list of specific needs includes items from the above statement of purposes—who used it, how it was used, whether it met the need(s) stated in the protocol, and what problems came up. In any particular case, the developers know their concerns full well, and these should be decided first. No one test can cover everything, and most of the other 12 decisions will vary by what is decided in this first one.

B. Testing Dimensions Concerning Contacting Test Groups

2. User Groups. The choice set of specific users for a use test was identified earlier. There are many choices and many nuances. First, some use testing is done with *lab personnel* at the plants where the products are first produced. Most of this work is technical testing, not use testing, but the technicians try things out informally. If it's a hammer, they will certainly drive some nails with it; and if it's a new candy bar, they will certainly be its first tasters. Still, most of their work concerns technical performance testing, shelf-life studies, and the like.

Experts are the second testing group (for example, the cooking staff in a food company kitchen). Car companies have styling professionals; wine companies have tasters; and some manufacturers have panels of particularly astute buyers.[6] A steel company keeps a panel of machine designers. Retailers frequently have expert panels that react to new service proposals. All of these experts will give more careful consideration than will typical users and probably will express more "accurate" reactions. They will not be interested in the same things that interest customers, however, so they are ordinarily used for interim testing before the firm tests typical users. Many industrial firms use their own manufacturing departments at this point if these departments happen to be consumers of the products that the firms produce (for example, materials handling equipment). Dog food firms can easily find experts—in company kennels.

---

[6] A recent article gave interesting insights into the life of a professional taster (actually more of a smeller, as that is where taste tends to originate). One Arthur D. Little sniffer could identify hundreds, if not thousands, of different smells. He once identified the peculiar smell of a comatose child as being due a metabolic disorder linked to certain foods; the diagnosis saved the child's life. See David Stipp, "A Flavor Analyst Should Never Ask, 'What's for Lunch?' " *The Wall Street Journal,* August 3, 1988, p. 1.

The third test group option, *employees,* is widely utilized though the use of this option is often criticized. Obvious problems of possible bias can be overcome to some extent by concealing product identities and by carefully training and motivating the employee panel. The advantages of using employees are many, including convenience, cost, speed, ease of retesting, and secrecy. One manufacturer's marketing research people found little variation between the preferences of employees and those of outsiders.[7] P&G asked 500 employees to do their laundry regularly with new cleaning products. Du Pont frequently asked female employees to wear test hosiery. However, the company environment or the employees' lifestyles and customs may distort their opinions and attitudes.

Market users are the next choice, and if there is enough time and money, they will certainly be included. But what specific ones? The distinctions between customers and noncustomers and between users and nonusers are important. Should they be users of competitive products? What segment of market users was identified as the source of the problems or needs that the test product was developed to solve?

Another issue concerns whether the people (or firms) chosen should be one-time testees or members of panels. Although panels are criticized because their members are said to become panelwise and unrepresentative, the evidence seems to refute this. Many commercial and private panels operate and are regularly endorsed by leading new products manufacturers primarily because of their ease of use, their broad representativeness, and the opportunity for study-to-study comparisons. Corning Glass is an example of a firm with its own (1,500-member) panel. Some firms, in effect, use panels without realizing it because many consumers are used over and over again by the research firms from whom they buy testing service. For example, some organizations' members (such as churches) hire themselves out at one to five dollars a test. Such groups are easy and inexpensive to reach, but their use raises questions of representativeness (both in selection and in modes of product use).

The last test group, the usual *miscellaneous,* is often overlooked. Retailers, wholesalers, agents, repair organizations, technical support, specialists, regulators, consumer pressure groups, and the media are among the groups whose reactions to new products have been sought.

---

[7] E. Patrick McGuire, *Evaluating New Product Proposals* (New York: The Conference Board, 1973), p. 41.

These miscellaneous groups are often called facilitators, and the testing merges into a seeding promotion.

The other relevant issue concerning user groups is sample size. From 3 to 6 experts is a workable number for small groups, and at least 30 employees and market users should be used. This minimum is probably OK for early employee testing, and it does permit some common statistical analysis, but it is *barely* a minimum. Samples of around 300 are much more common, and Gillette used 2,000 in the deodorant case above. As usual, sample size is primarily a function of what is being tested.

Figure 11–3 demonstrates how the concept of sampling error is a simple way to make estimates of sample size. Assume we plan to use test a new popcorn machine for theaters, and we want to be sure at least 70 percent of the theaters prefer our machine. What sample size would ensure random sampling is probably not causing false answers?

FIGURE 11–3   Method for Calculating Use Test Sample Size

What is the expected or desired preference for your product over that of the leading competitor (or other product) it is being tested against? _____%. Call this *Our*.

Thus, the preference for the other product is 100 − *Our*, or _____%. Call this *Their*.

The minimum sample size, accounting for normal sampling error, is:

$$\frac{4\,(Our \times Their)}{(Our - 50)^2}$$

Example: If your next test is expected to produce a victory over the top competitor of 70 to 30 (percent preference), then your sample size should be

$$\frac{4\,(70 \times 30)}{(70 - 50)^2} = \frac{4\,(2{,}100)}{(20)^2} = \frac{8{,}400}{400} = 21 \text{ people or firms}$$

However, if you thought the preference would be less and the race tighter (say, 60 to 40), then calculation will show the sample needs to go up to 96. And if it is even less (say, 55 to 45), then the sample would have to be 396.

The logic of this is simple: The tighter the race, the more likely a fluke could throw it off, so the more people we need to test.

Note: This calculation is based on the theory of the standard error of the proportion and on the "T" test. It presumes a standard error of two is adequate. Other methods for estimating desired sample size are based on other measurements in the use test, but this method is quite adequate for most testing done today.

The number is 21. Testing less than that creates too big a chance that random sampling caused the difference.

Incidentally, the sample should also be representative of the entire population for which the product is targeted. A hair products firm marketed a new tonic for men after use testing, and it flopped primarily because it was tested in more humid areas of the country. In drier areas, the product evaporated too quickly to do the user any good.

3. Mode of Contact.   Many options also exist here. First, there is the *mail* versus *personal* option. The mail method is more limited than personal contact in type of product and depth of questioning, but it is more flexible, faster, and cheaper. The mail method (for example, with well-established opinion panels) has been thoroughly researched and verified. One soap manufacturer mails bars of soap to large samples and asks for volunteers. Burlington Industries uses its WATS line to ask people to serve on special one-time mail panels that evaluate new fabrics.

Second, there is a choice between *individual contact* and *group contact*. Most firms prefer individual contact, especially at this definitive point in the development cycle, but some firms use focus groups. The latter gain in synergism, but they lose statistical quality.

Third, the individual mode of contact brings up the question of *location*. Should the test be conducted at the *point of use* (home, office, or factory), or should it be conducted at a *central location* (test kitchen, shopping center, theater, or van)? This decision varies with the product and with the information sought. The point-of-use location is more realistic and permits more variables to operate. But it offers poor experimental control, permits easy misuse, and may cause the user to lose interest without frequent prodding. Moreover, the realistic quality of such product use may be greatly overstated.

In contrast, the central location offers very complete facilities (such as kitchens, one-way mirrors, eating areas, pseudo stores), good experimental control, speed, and lower cost. But the respondents are less apt to be representative, and they can usually be contacted only once. For consumer products, the central location approach is winning out, but industrial firms will almost certainly stay with on-site studies.

4. Identity Disclosure.   A key issue concerns how much the user should be told about the identity of the product. Some testers prefer to use a product fully identified by *brand,* but some cases call for *blind* tests. It may be that the brand cannot be hidden — as with many cars, some shoes, and typewriters — and it may be that the developer is an industrial firm well known to the user. But the preference runs toward blind testing, if possible, because of halo, image, and similar problems. Most persons have perceptions about various firms and brands. These perceptions color reactions to new products. Even ersatz identity symbols may have an effect (for example, using code letters such as *Q, P,* or *x*). In the late 1970s, Coke and Pepsi had quite an argument over whether the codes that Pepsi used to identify Coke were fair. The tests were blind, but some observers felt the Coca-Cola product was deliberately coded with letters known to be less attractive to Americans. Pepsi later used less controversial code letters.

The key to deciding the issue of blind versus branded testing is to determine exactly what is being tested. Developers often need to know two things. First, they need to know whether the new item is better than the competition. Only blind tests can determine this. But they also need to know whether users *perceive* the new item to be better. In many situations, this can only be learned from branded tests.

Even the results of branded tests cannot be totally certain because a key variable is missing from them—competitive reaction. Some persons, for example, believe P&G's Pringles potato chips suffered sharply when a large Chicago potato chip manufacturer undertook aggressive advertising by telling consumers about taste differences. Some experts now recommend a *series* of use tests in the following order: (1) blind tests (unbranded) of both the new and the established, (2) brand tests of the same group, and (3) overall reevaluation of the new product concept. This sequence generates the least amount of bias.

5. *Degree of Explanation about Usage.* Some people conduct use tests with virtually *no comment* other than the obvious "Try this." But such tests run the risk of missing some of the specific needs discussed in the first decision on this list. The second level of explanation, called *commercial,* includes just the information the customer will get when actually buying the product later. This means at least package and label copy but usually includes other things, such as inserts. The third level is *full explanation.* When fairly complex products are quite new, it may be necessary to include more information than just what the typical customer will get later—just to ensure the product gets used properly. Some people do one round of testing with full explanation, followed by a brief round at the commercial level.

C. Testing Dimensions Concerning Product Usage

6. *Degree of Control over Use.* Manufacturers of medical and dental products find that some of their products can be tested legally only in the hands of physicians and dentists specifically qualified in test work. This almost *total control* is essential when accurate data are required and when patient safety is a concern. Many industrial products also require total control.

But most products do not, so testers opt for one of two other levels of control. They actually want users to experiment, to be free to make some mistakes, and to engage in behavior representative of what will happen later when the product is marketed.

General Foods will forever be cited in connection with the classic Gainesburger test in which dogs got sick from eating the new product because their owners overfed them. The owners thought those "little packets" just weren't enough. This example shows how important it is for the test to be conducted so we get an honest, typical market reaction, not just an ideal experience.

General Foods was not happy to have the test ruined but was happy to learn of the problem. Had the testing been done under carefully controlled conditions, the misunderstandings would have been avoided and perhaps never anticipated.

A new blend of coffee may be tested under conditions of perfect water, perfect measuring, and perfect perking, but it should also be tested in the kitchen the way coffee preparers will do it—right or wrong.

This does not mean, of course, that dangerous forms of misuse should be permitted, so two modes of looser control—*supervised* and *unsupervised*—have developed. For example, if a conveyor belt manufacturer puts out a new type of belting material for testing, company technical and sales personnel will be at the user's plant when the material is installed (supervised mode). After early runs indicate there are no mistakes, the belting people go back home, and the material is left to run in an unsupervised mode for the full testing period. (*Supervised* here means supervision by the producer; user personnel are usually present in any test.)

The key here is the selection of a mode that prevents serious mistakes yet permits natural functioning to take place. Children's toys are usually use tested in central locations—playrooms where the play can be monitored by toy company personnel behind one-way mirrors. Test users of new electrical appliances are usually centrally trained in a place where first use can be watched carefully; when they seem to understand, they are sent home with product for an extended use under real-time conditions.

If there is always a risk (say, as with the original microwave), the developers may have to make do with full control or at least supervised testing.

7. Singularity.   The product may be tested alone in a *monadic* test; it may be tested in a *paired comparison* with one other competitor; or it may be tested in a *triangle* with two competitors (see Figure 11-4). More sophisticated experimental designs exist, but they are only used in

FIGURE 11–4   Variations in Singularity as Applied to a New Toothbrush

Type	Products	Instructions
Monadic	The new product alone.	Try this new toothbrush, and tell me how you like it.
Paired comparison*	The new product and an-other toothbrush— (1) the market leader or (2) one known to be the best or (3) the leader in the segment selected for the new product or (4) the one currently used by the testee.	Try these, and tell me how you like them, which you prefer, etc.
Triangular*	The new product and *two* of the others. A varia-tion is to use two vari-ants of the new prod-uct and one of the others.	Same as on paired comparison.

*These multiple-product techniques can employ either of two product use approaches:
  Side-by-side: Please brush your teeth with this toothbrush, and then brush again with the other one. Then give me your reactions.
  Staggered: Please use this toothbrush for a week, and then switch to the other one for a week. Then give me your reactions.

special situations.[8] The monadic test is the simplest; it represents normal usage of products. The usual *side-by-side* or simultaneous form of *paired comparison* is the most unrealistic test, but it is by far the most sensitive. A variation, the *staggered paired comparison,* is probably the ideal combination, though it takes longer. In the staggered format, a user may try out a toothbrush for one week then change to another for the second week. Food products are commonly tested this way. (Though clearly a pairing of two stimuli, this method is often called *sequential monadic;* the term *monadic* in this usage describes how many products a tester uses *at one time.*)

_____

  [8] For added information on such matters as experimental designs, sequencing of stimuli, and sample design, see Howard R. Moscowitz, *Product Testing and Sensory Evaluation of Foods* (Westport, Conn.: Food and Nutrition Press, 1983). Less thorough, but still useful, is Richard R. Batsell and Yoram Wind, "Product Testing: Current Methods and Needed Development," *Journal of Market Research Society* 22, no. 2 (1980), pp. 115–39.

Even monadic tests usually involve a "silent" competitor—the product being used before the new one appeared. When an established category (such as fax machines) is involved, then it is almost a must to test a new product against the category leader (or perhaps the leader in a segment of the market that the new product is aimed toward). But in the absence of an established category, as was the case with the first fax machine, what does the developer do? That depends on how successful the user has been in finding an answer to the problem. For example, photocopying and overnight delivery were well established and successful; it would pay to test the first fax against them. But where there is no direct predecessor, as was the case with the microwave oven, product developers usually just run a monadic test and then ask the user to compare the new product with whatever procedure was being followed before.

Whether monadic, paired, or triangular, these product use tests are sensitive to seemingly irrelevant effects. The testing record is studded with instances where product developers were fooled. For example, novel products cannot usually be tested in the paired-comparison mode—too much variation precludes use of this highly sensitive test. Consumers approved a soap-impregnated rubber scrubber under the name Buster versus the steel wool pad, 80/20, in a plain paired comparison. And they preferred a wax-impregnated disposable polish cloth to aerosol furniture polish. Both the rubber scrubber and the polish cloth failed to achieve adequate sales. But they shouldn't have been tested only in the comparative mode; asking people if they prefer product X over product Y may yield a yes in the test, but they may not really like *either* product.[9]

An after-shampoo product use test showed that only one variable should be tested at a time. A paired-comparison test found that a new item scored as well as the market leader, Tame. The new item was a colorless, transparent formula. Then another version (with a bit of blue dye added) was soundly trounced by Tame. Both test versions had a new fragrance, and if only the second version had been tested, the success of the fragrance would have been missed.

These examples make the point that the processes for testing products against each other require considerable expertise and should be designed only by persons reasonably proficient in the technology.

8. Duration of Use. Some use tests require a *single* product experience (this may be all that is needed for a taste test); some require use over *short periods* of up to a week; and some require use over *extended periods* of up to six months. A longer period is needed if substantial learning is required or if initial bias must be overcome. A

---

[9] See "Poorly Designed Tests Cause Many New Product Failures," *Marketing News,* December 4, 1979, p. 8.

longer period is also needed if the product faces a full range of variations in use (for example, entertaining in the home, carelessness in the office, or high-pressure overtime in the plant). Again, researchers opt more often to use several modes. The initial, quick test predicts the early reactions of innovators. Failure here, even if perceptions are unjustified, will often doom a good product. On the other hand, favorable initial impressions must be sustained well past the novelty stage. Many products have flared briefly before sputtering to an early death.

Unfortunately, few company situations permit the ideal duration. There is just too much pressure on new product schedules. However, shortening the test means attention should go to how many products are being tested. For example, a quick sensory test in a shopping mall should be paired or trio (not monadic) because there is too much temptation to give the interviewer courtesy endorsements when only one product is being tested. On the other hand, a longer test in a plant, office, or home can narrow down to just one item more easily, especially if effort is made to get each user to give separate reactions.

Tests over a month long are rare and difficult to defend to management. Recall the earlier discussion about Beta testing versus Gamma testing. The decision, as do the others in this chapter, depends on just what the developers need to know. If a new piece of equipment will be positioned on its cost-cutting advantage, the use test had better run long enough to ensure the user sees a significant cost reduction.

D. Testing Dimensions Concerning the Product Itself

9. Source of Product.   Generally speaking, three different sources of the product are employed in a use test—*batch, pilot plant,* and *final production.* If the firm will employ just one type of use testing, then the final production material is far and away the best. Batch product should be used only if the production process is perfectly reproducible in batch mode. In-house, physical, and scientific laboratory testing necessarily use premature product, but those are not *use* testing.

Pilot plant product is better and more reliable than batch, but it can often be faulty too. The process usually shortcuts some problems, uses equipment that is more carefully tested, and is managed by a far more attentive management group. All use testing should employ final production line material unless such is precluded by the situation. And, if final production is too expensive to set up just for product use testing, then confirmatory testing should take place on final-run material even if the firm is now beyond the point of no return in the product's development.

As with many other phases of product development, the decision on source of product is a trade-off between the cost and value of information. Being penny-wise at this point has proven over and over to be pound-foolish.

Often overlooked is the question of what the developer does with the new product after the test is concluded. Usually, the product is collected and perhaps closely examined for clues about user problems and actions during the test. If a patent application will follow soon, it is very important to pick up all of the product; otherwise, developers risk losing the originality requirement of the patenting process.

10. Product Form.   One view favors producing the *best single product,* according to market analyses and concept testing, and then testing that product. The opposing view favors building *variants* into the test situation—colors, speeds, sizes, and so on. The latter approach is more educational but also much more costly. Every variant adds substantially to the total cost.

The decision rests on several factors, the first being how likely the lead variant is to fail. No one wants to elaborately test one form of the product and then have that form fail.

Further, what effect will added variants have on users' understanding of the test? The more they test, the more they understand, and the more they can tell us. For example, a maker of aseptic packaging for fruit juices realized the juice and the package were both new to consumers, so the firm tested orange juice in the new package first and subsequently tested the new apple and cranberry juices. (Incidentally, the firm shipped the orange juice to its European factory for packaging so that it would spend the same time in the box as did the apple and cranberry juices.)

In general, some variants are almost always used, but a good rationale should be given to warrant the added cost.

E. Testing Dimensions Concerning Measurement and Analysis

11. Mode of Recording Reaction.   The options here take us deep into market research methodology, so anyone designing a product use test should consult an authority for assistance. Most marketing research departments can handle the whole matter, as can most research departments of larger advertising agencies and a wide assortment of marketing research firms specializing in product use testing and other new product work.

Essentially, three options are available, as demonstrated by Figure 11–5. First, a five- or seven-point verbal rating scale is generally used to record basic *like/dislike data.* Second, the respondent is usually asked to compare the new product with another product, say, the leader or the one currently being used, or both; this is a *preference* score, which can be obtained several ways. Third, for diagnostic reasons,

FIGURE 11–5 Data Formats for Product Use Tests (samples selected from the many available)

Like/dislike

Product A:

1	2	3	4	5
Dislike strongly	Dislike some	Neutral	Like some	Like very much

Test product:

Which of these words best describes your overall satisfaction with the test product? (circle one)

Happy   Contented   So-so   Unhappy   Angry

Preference

What was your preference between the two products?
- ☐ Much prefer C
- ☐ Somewhat prefer C
- ☐ Don't care either way
- ☐ Somewhat prefer M
- ☐ Much prefer M

Descriptive/diagnostic

For each attribute below, please check your feelings about the test product:

Tastes great |———|———|———|———|———|———|———| Tastes awful

On which of the following applications would you want to use the new material?
- ☐ Floors   ☐ Roofs
- ☐ Ceilings   ☐ Inside cabinets
- ☐ Walls   ☐ Other – please specify: _____

_____

What changes would you like to see made in the test product?

_____

testers usually want *descriptive information* about the product that covers any and all important attributes. Examples include taste, color, disposability, and speed. A semantic differential scale is the most common here.

In addition to gathering reactions to the product, veteran product testers have begun to add variations that tie this step to the concept testing stage. This is consistent with the greatly increased importance of concept testing today. For example, a research firm was involved in studying opportunities for a new sausage and had previously asked consumers to rate the sausage products then available on a variety of attributes, including greasiness and saltiness. The results showed strong aversions to both of those attributes, which were associated with low overall scores for product quality.[10]

The researchers presumed from this that the ideal sausage would have low levels of greasiness and saltiness, and several test products were developed accordingly. Needless to say, use testing proved just the opposite—the two top sausages in the test ranked first and second in saltiness, and they were among the greasiest. Some of the least greasy test products had some of the lowest overall scores.

Another reason for careful marketing research at this point concerns category definitions. The comparative items presented to users are based on what the developer thinks the new item should be compared to and compete against. Users often differ, and if clear-cut category lines were not drawn in earlier research, they should be at this time. It is sometimes necessary to extend the product use test to include items added by users.

Marketing research has spawned a large group of exotic research methodologies found to be useful in new product testing. For example, brain wave measurements have been used, sometimes at the concept stage but principally at the actual product use stage. In addition to what people say they think of something, their inner thoughts can sometimes be helpful, especially if they have a strong emotional reaction to the product being tested.

Voice pitch analysis has also been used. Product testers have always had to look carefully behind what people say is their reaction to a new product. Many people try to be "helpful" or don't want to hurt the tester's feelings. Sometimes, people simply want to get on their way and to avoid a hassle of explanation or argument about their opinion. To help avert such problems, voice pitch analysis has been used to detect emotional negatives or positives behind the spoken word.

---

[10] Howard R. Moskowitz and Barry E. Jacobs, "Combine Sensory Acceptance, Needs/Values Measures When Researching Food Products," *Marketing News,* January 22, 1982, sec. 2, p. 6.

Galvanic skin response has also been used for this purpose. Unfortunately, most of the electronic approaches are very sensitive (they have to be) and thus are affected by many factors in the test environment besides the user's response to the products being tested. Sexist reactions to especially attractive males or females administering a beer test to persons of the opposite sex would probably make most of the electronic approaches unusable. There is also great concern that not enough is known about these approaches to make their use reliable at this time. Some product developers simply try to gauge the excitement evidenced by respondents.

One additional piece of information is very important at this point—intent to purchase. Recall that near the end of the concept test, we asked respondents how likely they thought they would be to buy the product if it became available on the market (the top-two-boxes question). Now is the time to ask this question again, as a confirmation. Granted, we have already asked them how well they liked the product and whether it was preferred to their currently used product. But, put back into concept form, with price, it helps us get a figure we can relate to the earlier ones.

12. Source of Norms. After all of the above decisions have been made, analyzing the results of a product use test would seem simple; but yet another decision must be made. Any one of the above statistics (for example, the percentage who say they like the product) means very little standing alone. We know, for example, that some people try to "like" everything. Others are naturally cautious. Even when they like something in a test doesn't mean they will like it in the real world of competition, garbled messages, and so on.

So, testers have long realized that they want comparative figures, not just absolutes. That is, if 65 percent of the users liked a product, how does that percentage compare with previous tests of somewhat similar items? If previous winners all scored over 70 percent on the "like" question, then our 65 percent isn't very impressive.

The 70 percent figure is a norm. Where we get norms and how we use them is often a serious question. The first source is obvious—the library of past experiences, thoroughly studied and averaged. Norms pulled from the air at committee meetings are virtually worthless. And the norms "bank" should contain data describing market use and attitudes prior to any effects of the new entry.

But, controversy surrounds the question of how norms are developed and used. One leading grocery products manufacturer gave the director of marketing research a "war chest" of $500,000 to conduct whatever studies were necessary to construct hurdles for future test products to surmount. The manufacturer's internal system is confidential, but the hurdles apparently were to involve concept test scores, product use test like/dislike scores, and relative product pref-

erence scores. For example, if "60 percent paired-comparison preference with the leading brand" was the hurdle, no product could go
to the market testing stage until product use tests scored at least 60
percent.

This sounds logical and innocuous, but in practice it forces someone
to play traffic cop by using data that can obviously be inaccurate and
manipulated. Technical people can claim marketing is using a hurdle to
kill a product it dislikes for other reasons. Yet, marketing frequently
needs just such protection from technical and top-management people
who are oversold on an item. Mandatory norms can be a healthy thing
if used with considerable skill, and they certainly help communicate the
risk in any particular situation. If a management wants to run right past
previously agreed barriers, then there is not only a red flag obvious to all;
depending on the amount of discrepancy between the norms and the
facts, the degree of danger is also underscored.

13. Research Service. Although *who* conducts the research
might not seem important, several options deserve note. The first
option is between personnel *within* the company and personnel
outside the company, and this option is usually settled as policy; either
the firm has personnel skilled in conducting product tests or it
doesn't.

If personnel within the company are used, disputes frequently arise
over the matter of department control. The technical people would prefer
to be in charge, but they usually cannot be unless the testing is a matter
of technical or legal confirmation. A popular approach is to have the
development team responsible—the same team that handled the
prototype concept testing.

One industrial firm gave its technical people complete authority up to
the introduction date. A leading food company permitted its R&D
department to set up two focus group facilities and to maintain a
300-person consumer panel to react to various product changes. In this
case, the resources are used prior to presenting a product to the new
products marketing manager, but the system does put product use test
skills in the technical group.

SPECIAL PROBLEMS

Some special ideas holding the attention of veteran new products people
run through all product use testing situations.

Don't Change the Data Just because They Came out Wrong.   One firm
discovered a user problem in a use test but couldn't correct it at that
time, so the firm went ahead with marketing plans. The president said,

"They're just going to have to live with it." Unfortunately, the use test did not ask whether users were *willing* to live with it. They weren't, and the product failed.

Remember Products Are Just Bundles of Attributes. Almost every measurement concerns one or more specific attributes — a feature or a benefit. That's where the questioning should focus. But sometimes the up-front research we talked about in Chapter 9 is skipped or done haphazardly. Testers don't know what attributes people in their new market will use to evaluate products. For example, here are the attributes generic to *services:*

Reliability (consistency)	Responsiveness (readiness)
Competence (skills)	Access (approachability)
Courtesy (respect)	Communication (informed)
Credibility (trustworthy)	Security (safety)
Understandability (knowing)	Tangibles (physical evidence)[11]

Be Alert to Strange Conditions. Use tests are really choreographed, set up, and directed as a whole. The parts we have discussed in this chapter are only their content. For just one example, many testers use means (averages) yet forget that many distributions are bimodal. Some people like spicy foods, and some dislike them. A mean would probably give a false picture in a foods test, just as the proverbial river that averaged three feet deep drowned a person who tried to walk across it. It is frequently necessary to back off, just to make sure the total picture of the test and its progress make sense.[12]

People in different departments of a firm should know what others are doing, but they sometimes don't. For example, a bar soap being tested got an accidental indentation from the top of the new mold. It won all the tests because (they found out later) it was convenient to hold! Researchers for a baby products firm bought competitive nursers from a retail store and were shipping test materials to the field when the product manager noticed that the purchased nursers were improvements over the previous product. These items were no longer right for the test as designed.

---

[11] The list of services was developed by A. Parasuraman, Valarie A. Zietmal, and Leonard L. Berry, *A Conceptual Model of Service Quality and Its Implications for Future Research* (Cambridge, Mass.: Marketing Science Institute, 1984).

[12] This and several other examples of actual field testing in this chapter came from Robert J. Lavidge, "How to Mislead Product Planners, or Marketing Research Mistakes to Avoid," *Marketing Today* no. 2 (1984), p. 1.

A new weighing scale was about to go to the field when someone noticed a change in the display mechanism. The safety manager had read of a possible new regulation on scale readability and thought he should get a jump on it by making the change now. He didn't think the change would be significant to anyone!

One industrial firm noticed that several electrical measuring instruments showed signs of tampering after a field test. On examination, they found users were making a particular change to aid the product's function; after a few telephone calls, they had an improved product design ready to go out for more testing.

SERVICES

Recall we began this book with a definition of product that included goods and services. Lest students think use testing differs from any other part of the overall task, let's take a look at the 13 decisions just discussed. Every decision applies to a service.

What We Need to Learn.   What we need to know for goods and services is the same—do they meet protocol, what problems arise in use, do they solve the customers' problems?

User Groups.   Services don't lend themselves to laboratory testing, but employees can test them. Market users are the most critical group, as is the case with goods.

Mode of Contact.   Potential users can be contacted in any of the ways listed—by mail or in person, by individuals or via groups. But the service must usually be performed individually and in person. Pure services have their value created at the time the customer is "served."

Identity Disclosure.   Services can be tested blind, unless they require the facilities of a current outlet. A bank, for example, could set up a new type of automatic teller incognito in a shopping mall, but usage couldn't be tested in final form apart from the bank premises. This means the service user will usually know the identity of the provider.

Degree of Explanation.   Totally the same for both goods and services: underexplain to test their quickness of understanding, use commercial level as we would do later in marketing, or overexplain to be very sure they understand.

Degree of Control over Use.   Services cannot be bought by or given to users and then taken home for use at their leisure. Therefore, the testing will be at least supervised. Of course, if the service can be sold by mail (for example, a new insurance policy), the process will be unsupervised at the user's end.

Singularity. It is hard to imagine paired-comparison testing of a new surgery procedure and an established one. But it can be done by using pairs of people who are matched in characteristics. A third party makes the comparison (in this case, a surgeon). The same applies to goods, of course (for example, new apartment houses; new cars; even new suits, for most of us). Again, the decision set is situational, whether good or service.

Duration of Use. Services will typically be used for short time spans, often just one use, especially if they are difficult to set up. Yet, many services have the full time option (such as airlines with new promotional packages, TV networks with new shows put on for a summer run). Some goods can be used only once also.

Source of Product. Again, services have a choice of all three types. The automatic teller can be hand assembled and put into the lobby of a bank—totally batch. Or, several can be made up on a pilot line. Where no good is associated with the service (say, a new college degree), the testing must be with final production. Again, the same holds for goods (for example, the auto industry has not been able to field test pilot production cars).

Product Form Variants. The situation is the same for both. The average service probably has more variations than the average good, and multiples can be tested.

Mode of Recording Reaction, Source of Norms, and Research Service. These three are totally the same for goods and services.

Conclusion: Each product use test must be analyzed and then structured to fit its situation, whether the item is a tangible good or an intangible service. In fact, in most cases everything being tested has a tangible component and an intangible component, and the presence of both leads to most of our tough decisions.

SUMMARY

Chapter 11 dealt with the issues of whether a product solves customer problems, how it compares to other products, and what else can be learned about it at this stage. Getting this type of information would seem critical, but strong pressures are exerted to skip product use testing and go ahead with marketing. We talked about the arguments for skipping and showed why they should be followed only when overpowering.

We also talked about several different types of use testing, from the original lab testing by scientists through extended field testing by the target market users.

That paved the way for discussion of the 13 dimensions of product use tests, ranging from "Exactly what do we want to learn from this test?" to "Who should conduct the test?" Each dimension has several options, and selecting from among them usually follows an analysis of the situation.

At the end of the product use testing, given favorable results, we have a product that has been approved. If not, the product is routed back into technical work to resolve the problems, or it is dropped. Otherwise, we now proceed to commercialization and the preparation of finished product and marketing plans. When they are ready, we enter the next phase of evaluation—*market testing,* the subject of Chapters 12 and 13.

APPLICATIONS

1. "Colgate's marketing people apparently had some trouble a while back with a new detergent laced with a dye that turned laundry blue during a test market. Another product of theirs, a dishwasher detergent packaged in waxy cartons like those used for orange juice, was rejected by test market mothers who were afraid their children might think the cartons contained juice. Seems to me those errors were inexcusable. Shouldn't they have discovered both of those things in earlier product use testing? How would you have made sure of that?"

2. "I think some research suppliers oversell a bit—they want us to do too much market research. For example, one of the biggest recently published data on a 'blind' versus 'identified' product test. Here are the results:

Branded		*Unbranded*	
Prefer A	55.5%	Prefer A	45.6%
Prefer B	45.5	Prefer B	54.4
Prefer A	68.0	Prefer A	60.7
Prefer C	32.0	Prefer C	39.3
		Prefer B	64.4
		Prefer C	35.6

I'm told the differences were highly significant statistically. The research firm concluded that there was no choice *between* blind and identified but that both should be used in just about every case where there was any reason to even suspect an effect of branding. Do you agree?''

3. ''I've got to go out to our toys division later this week, and I just know they're going to want to talk up product use testing. Not many things about toys are more important than what the kids think about them. But I understand you have a list of 13 dimensions for product use testing. Could you please take those and give me a general pattern you think those folks should use when use testing new toys?''

4. ''Our pharmaceutical division, of course, develops new pharmaceutical products for use by doctors and hospitals. The technical research department does all the testing (they have different names for the various tests). The last phase is clinical testing, where the drugs are given to humans in a manner that will substantiate claims to the Food and Drug Administration. The clinical tests are conducted by M.D.s in the clinical research section, which is in our R&D department along with all the other technical people. Now it seems to me those clinical tests are designed to satisfy more people than just the FDA— physicians, pharmacists, nurses, and so on. But M.D.s in clinical testing are not too high on marketing research-type thinking, so it dawned on me that I should see that at least one thoroughly trained marketing research person was assigned to clinical research— to help me make sure the clinicals have maximum impact later in marketing. Do you agree?''

Case: The Cat Challenger 65

In 1987, Caterpillar Inc. introduced the Cat Challenger 65, a new farm tractor that it had been working on for seven years. Though the market for farm tractors was soft in 1987, the firm thought its machine was ready. The Challenger was rolled out in 12 introductory states and two Canadian provinces in February. Full market launch followed in late December.

Source: Based partly on Kate Bertrand, ''New Product Success Starts with Homework,'' *Business Marketing*, August 1988, pp. 37–44.

The Challenger traveled on a steel-reinforced rubber track and combined the best of steel-track and four-wheel-drive technologies. It was Caterpillar's first four-wheel-drive tractor. The technology for this product originated in the company's R&D labs in the early 1980s. The first Challengers followed in 1982 and 1983.

In 1983, Caterpillar hired a market research firm to pinpoint customers' tractor needs by mailing 1,000 questionnaires to farmers; 150 were returned. Then the market research firm conducted about 100 personal interviews with U.S. and Canadian farmers. Dealers were also interviewed (25 of them) by members of a joint marketing/technical managers team. The dealers were asked how they would sell and service the new product.

The results of all this research were given to a product development team that had been established to work on the project. The product team used the information to modify the product, while the promotional group got the information to develop advertising, and dealer network managers studied it for clues on dealer training.

This 1983 research showed that farmers wanted certain things, including powershift transmission, no-stop shifting, and greater fuel efficiency. Technical people put these features on a new Challenger produced in 1984, the first true prototype of the 65. Later in 1984 and into 1985, six of these prototypes were tested under "controlled and commercial conditions" (working farms in 12 states and test fields at two agricultural state universities). They used different soils and various ground conditions.

Altogether, the prototypes logged 12,000 test-hours, about the same amount of time six regular tractors would be used in a year. Operations were videotaped at more than 50 locations.

Starting in 1986, a large commercial farm (2,000 acres) was selected as a prototype test site. This farm was owned by a firm that manufactured plows, so Caterpillar was able to get information on the new product's ability to pull large implements. Moreover, because the farm was a large commercial operation, the firm was able to telescope to two weeks the time needed to reach six months' equivalent running time.

The test farm also matched the intended target market—large firms—since the machine would sell for around $100,000 (versus competitive products at $75,000 to $80,000).

The farm used the prototypes for free, on the condition that the owner would share data on the results—costs, fuel use, and so on. Caterpillar kept complete notes on use of the prototype machine and had field personnel on hand every time one was run. Each member of the team of watchers was responsible for one part of the machine, such as the power train. Additional information came in by telephone from the farm.

The prototype testing produced one change—the addition of a quick-change feature for larger implements. Then Challenger was ready to produce commercially. As a last step, the firm conducted two months of "field-follow tests," a normal part of its product development. This testing used actual production models, which farmers were offered on a rent-to-buy basis. This procedure avoided the necessity of refunds, but none of the final testers wanted to return their machines anyway.

Other nonproduct testing involved focus groups on advertising and a regional roll-out, which ensured the company would be able to meet market demand and build the necessary service capabilities before full launch. Fast service is critical on a seasonally used product like a farm tractor.

Early sales returns looked favorable, running above company forecasts. The product testing system used for the Challenger had apparently done its job, but any system can always be improved.

Market Testing:
Pseudo Sale

SETTING

By this point in the development process, we have a physical product (or the complete specifications for a new service). The item (actually an implemented concept) has passed a use test of some type. It may have been recycled a time or two. Early concept testing showed a need, and the use test indicated the emerging product met that need, without serious drawbacks.

Now, we must prove we can communicate to potential users a message that will motivate them to try it. Note the importance of *trial*—we already feel positive that people will like the product once they try it; we proved that in the use test. We must also prove we can get good distribution for the product, provide the necessary service, set an acceptable price—in other words, we can market the item successfully.

This phase of the development, called *market testing*, combines the product and the marketing plan for the first time. Chapter 12 gives the overall picture for market testing and introduces the first of the three types—pseudo sale. Chapter 13 discusses the other two general types of market testing.

A terminology problem arises here because, over the years, one type of market testing has been the most common one and the one people talk about—test marketing. Many people think *market testing* means *test marketing*. Let's try to keep the terms straight, especially because test marketing as a technique has suffered a major loss of ground to newer, faster, and cheaper techniques.

WHERE WE ARE IN THE PROCESS

As stated above, we need to keep in mind where we are to understand what comes next. Look at Figure 12–1, a repeat of a diagram first displayed in Chapter 8, where the concept of an evaluation system was introduced. During all the work to date, we have been coming down the two sides of the "twin streams" diagram. Team members, especially marketers, have been focusing on the marketing plan and settling on various pieces of it at each step. Team members, especially the technical group, have also been putting together the physical items or service steps that will offer a particular bundle of attributes (features and benefits).

If this book followed the steps as they actually occur in business, we would now move into Chapters 15 through 17. That's what the team is doing—finalizing target market, positioning, price, and the like, plus

FIGURE 12–1   The Twin Streams of Development

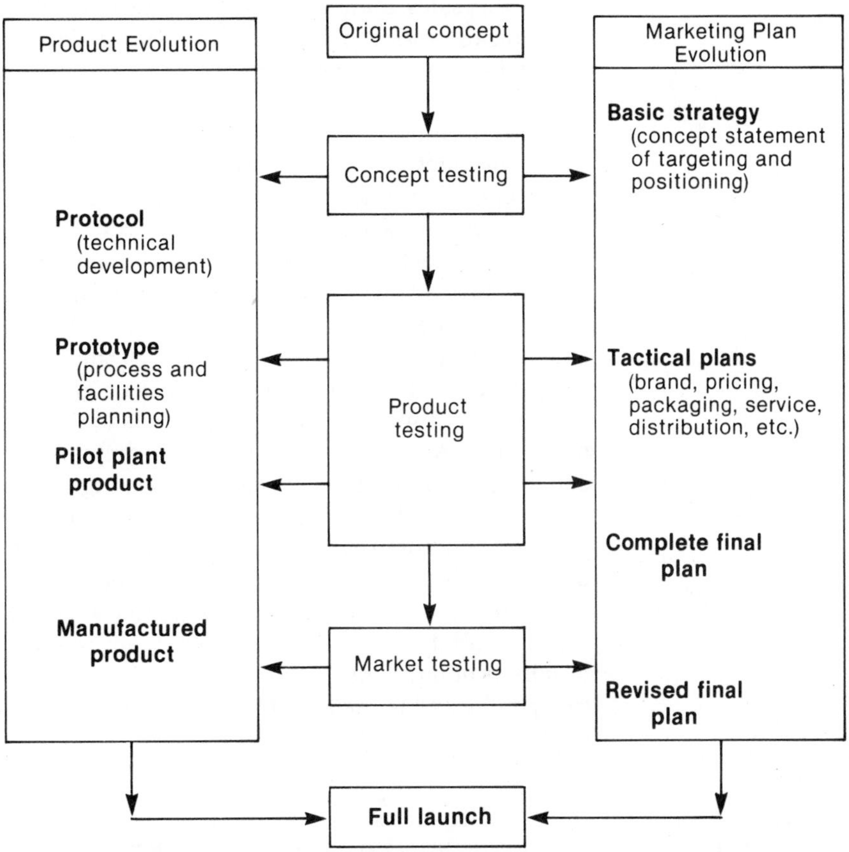

training salespeople and doing many other things. They are doing final market planning and will move into market testing when they're ready.

But we take up the subject of market testing now because it is such an important part of the overall evaluation system and can best be understood in relationship to such procedures as product use testing and concept testing. We did the same thing by discussing the product innovation charter in Chapter 3, whereas, in practice, some of the market research covered later in Chapter 9 is done prior to deciding the charter. That let us deal with the entire evaluation system as one set, although, in fact, it is spread out over the entire process.

So, keep in mind as we go through Chapters 12 and 13 that we have a completed marketing plan, in full detail, ready to go national if necessary. At the pseudo sale test, the plan is sometimes still fragmentary, but the big decisions have already been made. Remember too that the many people who have been making the final marketing decisions are not working in the dark. They have done this many times before and usually have years of experience in the particular business at hand. When the sales manager at Quaker Oats decides to offer a particular stocking allowance to large chains, this decision is not a guess. And when the packaging manager decides to add a foil liner to protect the product inside a package, this too is an experience-based decision.

Even more important, the scores of people doing this final phase of work (product as well as marketing plan) are doing what we call *component testing* while they're at it. The advertising agency often does copy testing, showing target customers the proposed ad layouts and copy to get their reactions.[1] That packaging manager just mentioned tests the foil's ability to hold against various weather conditions. The sales manager makes a few calls on large chain buyers to get a feeling for how anxious (or unanxious!) they are to stock the new item and, thus, a sense of how much stocking allowance must be given.

So, don't think all of the many details of final product and marketing plan arrive at this point untested. Component testing is severe and demanding, even if it's only against the judgment of managers doing the work. Some of the component testing is held for the market testing phase, if the item really tests best in the total setting, and many of the individual decisions are confirmed (or denied) in that phase. We'll talk about this in a moment, when we get to the purposes of market testing.

But—and this is critical—despite all the component testing, the hundreds of individual decisions have not yet been tested *as a group*. We can gamble and launch the product. Or, we can stop and do some market testing.

---

[1] Lots of methods can be used for copy testing the advertising component. One, with numbers to back it up, is discussed in Kirby Andrews, "Communication Imperatives for New Products," *Journal of Advertising Research,* October/November 1986, pp. 29–32.

WHAT MARKET TESTING IS ALL ABOUT

Up to this point in the overall product innovation process, every judgment and test has been at least slightly void of reality. Every question asked, every test of some decision, and every behavior sought required something to happen that was not a true test of the world out there. Product use testing, for example, set up usage experiments separate from the buying process, separate from the advertising that tells consumers about this product they are trying, separate from competitive efforts that are certain to affect their judgments at least a little bit.

For example, the food industry has some of the world's most sophisticated marketing talent and spends huge sums of money on concept and product testing. Yet, it has a poor record on product innovation compared to other industries primarily because people just cannot (or, perhaps, will not) tell food company new products people what they really think and want. Managers can't trust any judgment until it is made under typical market conditions, which only occur during the market testing stage.

Market testing, then, serves as a dress rehearsal to see if the various plans are actually working, whether the different parts fit with each other, and, most of all, to confirm that the product and what we say about it do indeed motivate people to buy it (and that they keep on buying it, if repeat buying is a factor).

The theater has various forms of dress rehearsal. The orchestra has its final run through the music; costumes are displayed for all to see; staging crews run through systems checks on all equipment; actors test themselves on their lines. These production parts are brought together one by one, and a final dress rehearsal is staged.

What form of dress rehearsal they use is a function of how much doubt they have, how much is at stake, and how much time they have. Important productions are taken on the road and kept there until they sell or give evidence that some last-minute changes will make them sell. Only then are they taken to New York City or wherever they are to be marketed. On the other hand, some theatrical productions get no more than the classical one-night dress rehearsal.

Market testing of products and services is much the same. The new products manager's task is to craft an appropriate market testing plan for each new product after thoroughly studying the situation and the available market testing tools.

Before getting into the details, let's deal with some reality. New products managers and their many bosses approach market testing with considerable skepticism. First, many of them have come up through their functions without exposure to the full range of market testing techniques. They think test marketing is the only choice, and, as we will see in Chapter 13, this is often a bad choice. Second, they feel market testing is very expensive, usually again the result of exposure to the costs of test marketing. In fact, some inexpensive market testing methods are available. Third, because they are reluctant to tip their hands to competitors, they want to get to full launch secretly. They do have a point here, but competitive reaction is not a common reason for product failure. A product fails usually because there was no need for it, it didn't meet a need well, or it was marketed unwisely. These issues can be answered in a market test.

Fourth, and perhaps the most difficult to deal with, they are under intense pressure to get the new product marketed, fast. Every innovation project has fallen behind schedule (unless pressure was intense from the start), and lots of money has been spent. It takes a strong manager to say at this point, "I know we have spent a fortune, and we are running late, but I am not at all sure we have made the right decisions, so I want to take a couple of months (or more) to be sure." Will that type of statement inspire confidence from the typical top management? Perhaps we should be surprised market testing ever takes place.

Yet, in other fields, the idea of last-minute testing of the total package is widely accepted. The field of science insists on it. Major parts of the entertainment field do too. Market testing should be a part of the package from the very beginning. It should be assigned specific pieces of the work. And the testing method should be selected to compromise the various needs and intensities.

The basic value of market testing is unquestionable. The burden of proof for skipping the step lies squarely with the person who advocates doing so. IBM marketed the original PC without a market test; but the PC came from a crash 12-month program that had immense risks in it from the start, and billions of dollars were at stake in market positions. These were good reasons. Unfortunately, IBM did not have those good reasons for the IBM Jr., nor did RCA when it marketed the first SelectaVision videodisc player, and nor did literally scores of others. See Figure 12–2 for some familiar examples.[2]

PURPOSES OF MARKET TESTING

The various forms of market testing are rich in information, so many departments use their output. The legal department may want a trademark confusion test, packaging may want some shades of purple checked out, customer services may want to know what testing devices

---

[2] The decision process managers must go through was recently presented as a case study in Steven H. Star and Glen L. Urban, "The Case of the Test Market Toss-Up," *Harvard Business Review*, September-October, 1988, pp. 10-16+.

FIGURE 12–2   Examples of Firms that Wish They Had Not Skipped
Market Testing

New Coke: The Coca-Cola Company had perhaps the most famous example of
a thoroughly tested product marketed without a market test. Allegedly,
some 200,000 people overwhelmingly preferred the New Coke. But, when
offered the chance to buy it, in the total milieu of a market full of publicity, they refused. Coke had to bring back the old formula, branded Coke
Classic, and it is still the leading seller.*

TV-Cable Week: Staffers who developed Time Inc.'s competitor to *TV Guide*
"repeatedly called for a small-scale market test and were repeatedly
turned down." The $100 million investment lasted six months.‡

Treesweet Low-Calorie Orange Juice: "Clinton E. Owens thought he had all
the fixins for success in the juice business . . . industry veteran . . . innovative product . . . jazzy package . . . eye-catching ads . . . ." A year later, after "betting the farm" without market testing, the product had failed, the
juice lines were on the block, and Chapter 11 "was a possibility."‡

Toppels: In a 1986 article about companies getting on the fast track, "Frito-
Lay skipped test marketing for its new Toppels cheese snack so competitors
wouldn't have time to study the ingredients and copy them.§ 'We felt very
strongly we had a winner and didn't want to tip our hand.' " But in 1989,
after noting several failures in new snack products, "The debacle convinced
Frito-Lay that true market testing is a necessity, even for a market leader."‖

Sources:
*The New Coke story is told in many places, one good summary being "Coca-Cola's Big Fizzle," *Time*,
July 22, 1985, pp. 48–52.
†"Time Inc.'s $47 Million Belly Flop," *Business Week*, February 17, 1986, pp. 14–15.
‡"A Juice Maker Squeezes Itself Dry," *Business Week*, August 10, 1987, p. 42.
§Ronald Alsop, "Companies Get on Fast Track to Roll out Hot New Brands," *The Wall Street Journal*,
July 10, 1986, p. 23.
‖"Marketers Blunder Their Way Through the 'Herb Decade,' " *Advertising Age*, February 13, 1989,
p. 3.

---

are used in customer repair departments, and so on. However, these are
really incidental to the two major purposes.

First, the planners need solid forecasts of volume—not the general
market figures or ranges of possible shares that guided earlier planning
decisions. They will soon be making a full financial analysis, and the most
essential unknown on the income statement is sales volume.

Second, the planners need diagnostic information to help them revise
and refine the marketing plan. At this point, there are usually
controversies within the planning group that must be resolved; inevitably, many seemingly minor points must be changed. Examples abound.
Here are a few:

1. Cadbury tested a new fresh cream dessert that it planned to market
   in a tetra package. But retailers claimed that the package wouldn't
   stack, so it had to be changed.

2. A camouflage cosmetic worked well at concealing scars, as planned, but a much greater market opened up when women decided to use it for concealing minor blemishes.
3. An industrial firm developed a very complex new technology, gave it thorough technical testing, and went into a regional market test. Only then did the firm discover that the new system could be blocked by a group of consulting engineers who had not been included in the marketing plan.
4. Makers of dry soups knew their product was technically sound. But they overestimated the willingness of Americans to adapt to new tastes. Even Cadbury failed when it tried to get English people to change the way they made tea.
5. Foremost Foods found an awareness problem on one product, and the simulation results indicated the need for an increase in media weight, so the spending levels were increased successfully.

THE A–T–R MODEL

Running through most of the market testing methodologies is a basic calculation by which market testers utilize the different pieces of information they acquire. The calculation is much like a pro forma income statement, an *array* of figures allowing us to see what the profits will look like based on where we are to date.

The basic formula, shown in Figure 12–3, is based on what is known in the marketing field as the A–T–R concept (awareness–trial–repeat). This is *diffusion of innovation:* for a person or a firm to become a regular buyer of an innovation, there must first be awareness that it exists, then there must be trial of that innovation, and finally there must be the type of happiness with it that leads to adoption, or repeat usage.[3]

We want to use the formula to calculate all the way to profit, so we expand it to include market size, units purchased, and the economics of the operation. But at the heart of the calculation is A–T–R. Market testing is especially designed to tell us about these three variables.

Let's take a simple example to explain how it works. Assume we have developed a new compound for polishing sports cars; it contains ingredients that leave a much enhanced sparkle to the car's finish. To use the paradigm, we need the following data:

1. Number of owners of such sports cars: 3 million.
2. Percentage who become aware of our new polish: 40 percent.

---

[3] The basic A–T–R sequence has been broken down further into many microsteps. One example of this extension is John H. Antil, "New Product or Service Adoption: When Does It Happen?" *Journal of Consumer Marketing,* Spring 1988, pp. 5–16.

FIGURE 12–3 A–T–R Model

Profits = Units Sold × Profit per unit

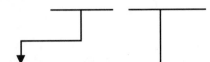

Units sold = Number of buying units
     × Percentage who become aware of the product
     × Percentage who opt to try the product if they can get it
     × Percentage of intended triers who can get the product (it is
       available to them)
     × Percentage of triers who like the item enough to repeat their
       purchase
     × Number of units that repeaters will buy in a year

Profit per unit = Revenue per unit (unit list price less trade margins, promo-
       tional allowances, freight, etc.)
     − Costs per unit (usually cost of good sold plus direct market-
       ing costs)

Therefore:
  Profits = Buying units × Percent aware × Percent trial ×
      Percent availability × Percent repeat × Annual units bought ×
      (Revenue per unit − Costs per unit)

---

3. Percent of aware who decide to try the polish and buy some: 20 percent.
4. Percent of stores stocking the product (potential users will probably not seek beyond one store if they cannot find it there): 40 percent.
5. Percent of triers who like the product and buy more: 50 percent.
6. Number of cans a typical user will buy in a year: 2.
7. Dollar revenue at the factory, per can, after trade margins , and so on: $2.
8. Unit cost of a can, at the intended volume: $.65.

The profit contribution forecast, based on the A–T–R model, would be 3 million × .40 × .20 × .40 × .50 × 2 × ($2 − $.65) = $129,600.

We have prepared a mathematical formula and run it through one set of data. The first purpose of market testing given above was to prepare a solid forecast of volume, and we have done so.

Two things are important about this model's sales and profit forecasts for the polishing compound:

1. Each factor is subject to estimation, and in every market test, we are trying to sharpen our ability to make the estimates. For example, we may be trying to check the promotion's awareness-building capability. We may want to know just how much sampling or price discounting we must do to motivate a trial purchase. We may be mainly concerned with how well the new sparkling appearance is accepted by users after they try the product one time. We may be worried about how we're going to get enough distribution to make the product available when car owners seek it.

2. An inadequate profit forecast can be improved only by changing one of the factors. For example, if the forecast of $129,600 profit contribution is insufficient, we look at each factor in the model and see which ones might be changed and at what cost. Perhaps we could increase the retail discount by 5 percent and get another 20 percent of stores to stock it. On the other hand, perhaps an increase in advertising would produce more awareness. Qualitative changes (such as a new advertising theme) can be made in addition to the quantitative. The proposed changes must then be put back into another market test, which yields another set of results, some more changes, and so on. Sometimes the issue raised is so fundamental that it is more efficient to cycle back to product use testing or even to a concept test before returning to a new market test.

A–T–R is a term that came from consumer products marketing. Industry has traditionally used slightly different language, so a natural question is "Does the model apply to all types of new products, including industrial ones, and services too?" The answer is absolutely, though each term may be defined slightly differently in different settings.

For example, see Figure 12–4 for the definitions of terms that vary. A consumer *buying unit* may be a person or a home. For office furniture, it will perhaps be a facility manager; for industrial products, it will generally be a purchasing or engineering person (part of a team); and for a consumer bank loan, it will once again be a person or a family. Product developers have known which is which since early in the development (for example, since early market research and concept testing).

Without a precise definition there can be no worthwhile measurement. In each case, something about the term tells you how to define it. For *awareness,* we want to know if the buying unit has been sufficiently informed to move to investigate. If it has only heard the product's name, it probably won't. For *trial,* we want a definition that tells us two things:

1. The buying unit went to some "expense" to get the trial supply—if there was no cost, then we can't be sure there was evaluation of the product message and interest created. Anyone can taste some sausage in a supermarket, but that doesn't mean the taste was a true trial.

FIGURE 12–4   Definitions Used in A–T–R Model

Buying Unit means purchase point; may be each person or department who participates in the decision.

Aware means someone in the buying unit hears about the existence of a new product with some characteristic that differentiates it; subject to variation between industries and even between developers.

Available means the percentage chance that if a buyer wants to try the product, the effort to find it will be successful; often "percent of stores that stock it." Direct sellers have 100 percent availability.

Trial is variously defined; may be use of a sample in an industrial setting where such use has a "cost" associated with it; in most situations, means an actual purchase and at least some consumption.

Repeat is also varied; on packaged goods, means to buy at least one (or two or three) more times; on durables, may mean be happy and/or make at least one recommendation to others.

---

2. The buying unit has used enough to have the basis for deciding whether the product is any good.

For *availability,* we want to know whether the buyer can easily get the new product if early investigation is favorable. This factor is more standard, usually the percent of outlets where the firm has stocking of the new item. If the firm sells direct, there is always availability (unless the factory has extended back orders).

Repeat is easy for consumer packaged goods (usually, a repeat purchase), but it really means the trial was successful—the buying unit was pleased. For one-time purchases (industrial or consumer), we have to decide what statistic will tell us that. Some people use the direct one: "Were you satisfied?" Sometimes, an indirect one—such as "Have you had occasion to recommend the product to others?"—is better.

Where Do We Get the Figures for the A–T–R Model?

Figure 12–5 shows where we customarily get the data for the A–T–R model and, thus, how the model ties the entire evaluation process together. Though various evaluation events can help on several of the key factors, we are most interested in the one event that makes the biggest contribution—noted as *Best* in the figure. And, we should know which these are prior to starting the evaluation. That way, we spend our limited funds first on the key steps and then on others if funds are available. Too, if we have to skip a step (for example, the concept test),

FIGURE 12–5 Items in the A–T–R Model Have Multiple Sources: A Rolling Evaluation

A–T–R Item	Various Sources of Estimates for It				
	Basic Market Research	Concept Test	Product Use Test	Component Testing	Market Test
Market units	Best	Helpful	Helpful		Helpful
Awareness*		Helpful	Helpful	Best	Helpful
Trial		Best	Helpful		Helpful
Availability†	Helpful				Best
Repeat (Adoption)			Best		Helpful
Consumption	Helpful	Helpful	Helpful		Best
Price Per Unit	Helpful	Helpful	Helpful	Helpful	Best
Cost Per Unit‡				Helpful	Best

Key: Best = The best source for that item.
Helpful = Some knowledge gained.
*Awareness is often gauged by the agency that develops the advertising.
†Availability is usually estimated by sales management, and doubts about the figure are key to selection among market testing methods.
‡The cost component in profit contribution is internally estimated, usually prior to actual start-up. But, valid figures can only come after some significant production.

we immediately know we are leaving open the question of whether users are likely to try the item when it becomes available. If we are going to do use testing, then it should be set up in a way that lets us go through a concept test in the process of getting people to sign up for the use testing. It's later than we most wanted concept test information, but better now than not at all.

The A–T–R process, in effect, lets the new products manager manage the process of evaluation; building to the final profit figure is like building anything else. Let's take one specific example. Some of the market testing methods we will study allow us to test our ability to convince dealers to stock our item. Some of the cheaper methods do not. You know the A–T–R model needs a figure on distribution. If you happen to be in a leading firm or developing a really dramatic product for which distribution will be easy, then you can use one of the less expensive methods. If your sales department is experienced in this business, they can probably get pretty close without a test; but if you are getting into something new, look out.

METHODS OF MARKET TESTING

The ingenuity of marketers is legendary. They have developed a seemingly endless array of market testing methods for new products.

One firm uses a very large company cafeteria. Another uses small foreign divisions. Still another uses the facilities of a chain of radio stations owned by a sister subsidiary. But the methods tend to fall into one of the following three general categories (see Figure 12–6).[4]

Pseudo Sale

This approach asks potential buyers to do something (such as say they would buy if the product were actually available, or pick the item off the shelf of a make-believe store). The action is distinct and identifiable, and much of the marketing strategy is utilized in the presentation; but the

FIGURE 12–6 Methods of Market Testing, Where Used

Methods	Industrial Goods	Industrial Services	Consumer Packaged	Consumer Durables	Consumer Services
Pseudo sale					
Speculative sale					
Personal selling	X	X		X	X
Advertising				X	
Simulated test market			X		
Controlled sale					
Informal selling	X	X		X	X
Direct marketing	X			X	
Mini market	X	X	X	X	X
Scanner markets			X		
Full sale					
Test marketing	X	X	X	X	X
Limited marketing (roll-out)					
By application	X	X			
By influence	X	X			X
By geography	X	X	X	X	X

The header structure spans: Product Categories Where Useful (over all), with Industrial (Goods, Services) and Consumer (Packaged, Durables, Services).

[4] At the time of this writing, the consumer packaged goods industry is going through a major terminology change caused by technological changes in market measurement. For example, a new term—*electronic test marketing*—may be accepted. Such a term may replace the *scanner market* term used in this book, but it may also replace the *minimarket*. What will happen to the traditional *test marketing* term is totally unclear. Your professor will have more up-to-date information when you read this, but we suspect the uncertainty in packaged goods will remain for several years.

key factor here is little pain for the buyer—no spending, no major risk. It is, as the name says, a pseudo sale.

Controlled Sale

Here the buyer must make a purchase. The sale may be quite formal or informal, but it is conducted under controlled conditions. The method is still research because the product has not been released for regular sale. Some key variable (often distribution) is not opened up but is contrived. Controlled sale is more vigorous than the pseudo sale, however, and much more revealing.

Full Sale

Here the firm has decided to fully market the product (not so in the above methods). But it wants to do so on a limited basis first, to see if everything is working right. Barring some catastrophe, the product will go to full national launch.

SYSTEMS

Each of the 11 methods in the three categories of Figure 12–6 can be used alone, and many firms use the one they think is best in terms of cost and what they can learn. But, some firms want a system of two or more techniques.

Such firms usually begin with a pseudo sale method—the speculative format, if they are industrial or in a business where personal selling is the major marketing thrust; or the simulated test market, if they are in consumer packaged goods. Pseudo sale is cheap and quick. Learning is limited, but it is a good leg up on the problem.

The firm then turns to one of the controlled sale methods, especially informal selling for industrial firms or minimarkets for consumer goods firms. If the second test will be the last, firms tend to slide into a full sale method rather than a controlled sale method. Thus, an industrial firm might use a speculative sale followed by an applications roll-out. A packaged goods firm might start with a simulated test market followed by a geographical roll-out, or a simulated test market followed by a scanner market and then full launch.

These are generalizations; it's up to the new products manager to tailor the right testing package for the product at hand. There are no ready-made suits on the hangers.

PSEUDO SALE METHODS

Industry gets potential users to make some expression or commitment resembling a sale without actually laying out money in two different ways. The *speculative* method asks them if they would buy it, and the *simulated* method creates a false buying situation and observes what they do.

Speculative

Here, a contrast must be made between a question usually asked in concept and product use tests and one asked in speculative market testing. It is, essentially, "Would you buy this product?" In market testing, however, the question is couched in a full explanation of key marketing variables, which are not known at concept and product testing.

Specifically, industrial new products people frequently take a new piece of equipment or a new material, develop a strategy for presenting it, settle on a price, produce a selling visual, and then head for the field. They make pseudo sales calls—presenting the new product as though it were available for purchase, answering all questions, and then asking if the respondent would buy it if actually available.

The distinction between this question and a concept test question about purchase is that in this case, the other marketing decisions have been made. The product is real, as are the price (with a full array of appropriate discounts), delivery schedules, selling presentation, and so on. The target market has been determined (by the interviewing plan), and full commitment has been made to a certain positioning. There is little to guess about. In the setting of a full marketing plan, the buyer has little to do except make a decision. That decision may be just to ask for some samples to try, but because that is what the industrial marketer is seeking, there is "trial."

Although the tool is typically used for industrial products (because sale of most industrial products fits the method so well), it can also be used for certain consumer products. Rubbermaid is an example of such a firm. Rubbermaid sells its products essentially by a push strategy, with some image advertising to consumers but product presentation confined to store counters. This setting can be duplicated easily, so Rubbermaid uses the speculative method in a setting that looks much like a focus group concept test (except using finished product with information on usage, pricing, and so on). The consumer faces a situation much like that in a store and can easily speculate on whether a purchase would be made.

Situations where the speculative method fits include:

1. Where industrial firms have very close downstream relationships with key buyers.
2. Where new product work is technical, entrenched within a firm's expertise, and only little reaction is needed from the marketplace.
3. Where the adventure has very little risk, and thus a costlier method is not defendable.
4. Where the firm has a tight patent, is in no rush, and wants to develop the market and the product together.
5. Where the item is new (say, a new material or a completely new product type) and key diagnostics are needed. For example, what set of alternatives does the potential buyer see, or what possible applications come to mind first.

One variation on speculative sale is with advertising. The technique is not common, but sometimes a product is sold primarily by direct-mail advertising or telemarketing. Though this approach is usually a controlled sale (see below), the buyer can be asked the "Would you buy?" question instead.[5]

Simulated Test Marketing (STM)

Packaged goods firms do a great deal of product development, yet the speculative sale methods (above) don't fit them. They want a cheaper, more confidential, and faster method than controlled sale. They find it in a variation of the A–T–R model discussed earlier.

The essential idea uses a research technique to get the trial percentage and the repeat percentage. Awareness comes from the advertising agency's component testing, and the firm's managers supply the other factors of market units and availability. (This STM method only goes down through the A–T–R model to market volume and share of market, not profit.)

Basic Procedure.   Here is the basic procedure, with modifications from supplier to supplier:

1. Respondents are usually gathered in a *mall intercept* — they are intercepted as they walk through a mall and invited to participate in a marketing study. At least one major supplier selects and invites respondents by telephone. Respondents are qualified both by observa-

---

[5] What is here called *speculative sale* has many variations and many names. Ted Karger calls it *bundle tests,* as explained in "Test Marketing as Dress Rehearsals: Bundle Tests and Test Market Diagnostics," *Journal of Consumer Marketing,* Fall 1985, pp. 49–56.

tion before interviewing (estimates of age, sex, income, family status, and so on) and by questioning (such as product category usage) during a brief interview in the mall corridor. It is important at this point to eliminate persons for whom security would be a problem (for example, employees of other manufacturers). If the respondent qualifies (fits the criteria for sample selection), he or she is invited to step into a nearby research facility (usually one of the empty mall store areas, though occasionally a permanent facility built in one of those areas).

2. In the facility, the procedure varies depending on the client and what is being tested, but generally the respondent will be given a self-administered questionnaire covering base-level attitudes and practices in one or more product categories. Then comes either individual or small-group exposure to advertising stimuli. The advertisements are sometimes couched in a television presentation (for example, a TV pilot program that is itself being tested) or just any TV show that hides the key stimulus. The ads may be presented without pretense of a television show, or they may be in what appears to be a magazine. Several ads are presented so the respondent isn't sure what is being tested. One of the ads, of course, is for the new product being market tested.

3. The respondent is then taken into another room, usually what appears to be a very small convenience store with shelves of products. The test manager gives the respondent some play money (one supplier uses cash), not usually enough to make a purchase but enough to make such a purchase less painful. A respondent so inclined can walk right out without making a purchase, even with actual cash. (The leading seller of simulated test marketing services does not use a pseudo store. Instead, it asks respondents the standard buying intention question we used in Chapter 11 on product use testing and then gives trial product to those who express buying interest.)

4. Hopefully, the respondent will now purchase the new product advertised in the first room—the key variable *trial*.

5. Most of the participants are then free to go. Perhaps 10 percent are taken into another room where a focus group of 8 to 10 is held. Another 10 percent may be asked to fill out another self-administered questionnaire covering post-exposure attitudes, planned product usage, and the like. If our product was purchased, we will be contacting the respondent later; but if it was not, we want to find out why. Nonbuyers are often given trial packages of the product as they leave.

6. Sometime later (time varies with the product category involved), the respondent is contacted by telephone. The call may be identified with the mall experience or it may be camouflaged. Information is sought about such things as product usage, reactions, and future intentions. Many diagnostics are obtained at this time, such as who in the family used the product, how it was used, and products it was used with.

7. At the end of the call, the respondent may be offered a chance to "buy" more of the product. This is the first step in a *sales wave*. Product is delivered to the respondent's home by mail or another delivery system, and the call is later repeated, new information gathered, and another sale opportunity offered. Note the sales wave is designed to get the *repeat* measurement for the A–T–R model.

These simulated test markets usually involve 300 to 600 people, require 8 to 14 weeks, and cost a minimum of $50,000, depending on the number of sales waves. The service is offered in various forms by quite a few firms, the leaders of whom are:

- BASES II, by Burke Marketing Services, Cincinnati.
- ASSESSOR, by M/A/R/C, a market research firm in Chicago.
- LITMUS, by Clancy Shulman and Associates, New York.
- ESP, by NPD Research, Floral Park, New York.[6]

Output.   Many things come from this activity. Users have given their opinions on the product, they have probably bought (or been given) some, they have expressed their reactions to it, and so on. But the key purpose of an STM is to estimate how well the product will sell, so the various services offer trial rate, repeat rate, market share estimates, and volume estimates. The latter comes when they combine their trial-and-repeat rate with the client's assumptions on awareness, retail availability, competitive actions, and the like.

The originator of the method (the predecessor of Clancy Shulman and Associates) and the current leading provider of the service (Burke) take fairly simple approaches to the calculations. They take the raw trial-and-repeat data from the test, calibrate it using the vast data from their past studies, and put it through their version of the A–T–R model to come out with market share or actual sales. The other leading suppliers get into far more complex mathematical models, which we will look at when discussing financial analysis in Chapter 14.

A key aspect of the STM method is simulation. If the client doesn't like the sales forecast from a study, variations are easily tested. For example, the model can be "asked" what amount of trial would be necessary to get to the desired market share. In turn, the cost of getting that trial (for example, by doubling the number of coupons currently planned for the introductory period or by lowering the price for a while) can be evaluated.

---

[6] An excellent contrast and evaluation of these modeling operations can be found in Allan D. Shocker and William G. Hall, "Pretest Market Models: A Critical Evaluation," *Journal of Product Innovation Management,* September 1986, pp. 86–107. Unfortunately, these operations, their methods, and their supplier firms change often, so such listings as those in Chapter 12 and in this article will always be a little out of date.

Usage. A recent survey of leading advertisers (some of the most likely users) showed that only 63 percent used simulated test marketing.[7] A survey of a larger group of firms showed that only 37 percent used this method.[8] Several marketing researchers believe the market penetration of this tool is less than 50 percent, even among firms that are the most logical users.[9] Suppliers, of course, claim much greater usage.[10]

Why would this be? Critics have many arguments, first of which is the mathematics' complexity. STMs have a sense of magic, a mumbo jumbo sometimes encouraged by the sellers of the services. Second, everything in the system is false: the mall intercept creates false conditions at the start, then the stimuli are unrealistically administered, the "store" is obviously fake, and much attention is focused on the behavior of the consumers being tested. Third, the calculations require a set of givens from the client before the formulas can be run (on availability, for example, or on the advertising budget, on how good the advertising will be, and on competitive reaction). Most of these numbers are assumptions.

In sum, complexity, unreality, and assumptions entail quite a charge and explain much distrust. However, the firms supplying the service simply ask, what other method comes close? Besides, their sales forecasts are often accurate. So, usage and controversy continue. But suppliers have been slow to expand the STM service to nonpackaged goods, as they have long intended. At this writing, Assessor service is being offered on some consumer durables, cameras, and cars, though this service is not completely operational and is substantially modified from the packaged goods service due to the lack of a data base for these products.

Leading packaged goods firms have often leapt from the results of a simulated test market directly into national launch. They get to the market fast without the costs of controlled sale or full sale. Other such firms don't even use the simulated test market. Market testing is still something of an art, and strong opinions will probably always exist.

A manager's task is to decide whether the simulation method fits the product under development. Some marketers don't think it will fit if the product:

Is totally new to the market (the first TV dinner, for example, because no category data exist in the data bank).

---

[7] *Prescription for New Product Success* (New York: Association of National Advertisers, 1984), p. 26.

[8] "Many Hesitate to Simulate," *Advertising Age*, February 21, 1983, p. M42.

[9] Ibid.

[10] For some fairly recent opinions, see Howard Schlossberg, "Simulated versus Traditional Test Marketing," *Marketing News*, October 23, 1989, p. 1.

Is a highly seasonal item (test it and then wait a year?).

Is sold by personal selling or point-of-purchase promotion (rather than mass advertising), or requires significant presale service.

SUMMARY

Chapter 12 was the first half of a two-chapter set on market testing. First we had to put market testing in its place in the overall new products process—after use testing and after all marketing planning, but before full national launch. Then we defined market testing and described its purposes.

Because a major purpose of market testing is to make sales forecasts, we had to have a method of tying together the various pieces of information we have been gathering throughout the evaluation process. For this, the A–T–R model was presented and demonstrated.

Then students had a chance to study one of the three types of market testing methods—pseudo sale. It comes in two forms: speculative sale and simulated test marketing. The first is simple and the second is complex, but both meet the needs of certain developers, up to a point. Beyond that, more advanced methods are needed, and they are the subject of Chapter 13. Keep the A–T–R model in mind, and don't forget that we primarily want good forecasts of sales volumes and good ideas on how to fine-tune the marketing plan.

APPLICATIONS

1. "You know, we recently had a food product go through one of those simulated test markets, and it was a disaster. The new products people forgot completely about the possibility that the customers who bought the product in the shopping center pseudo stores might not actually get around to trying it. But it happened. Based on in-store purchases, everything was OK, but a good percentage of the purchasers changed their minds later; and, if they used the product at all, it was limited trial by just one person. Solution, of course: A sales wave test added to the end of the lab test. But that is quite expensive. Could you tell me when we should use the added sales wave and when we shouldn't?"

2. "One of our corporate market researchers the other day was trying to explain how we should forecast sales for new products. She said they were recently working with the small-appliance division and learned that managers there were doing something like this: Homes with a need × Percent of families with incomes over $25,000 × Percent remembering they saw our new product ads in an

advertising pretest (one that was run in a doctor's office with fake magazines). She said that was a weird one, and she wanted to run a seminar to tell everyone that the calculation method should be the traditional one of Awareness × Trial × Repeat. Should I allocate the money for that seminar?''

3. ''I really was confused by something she said later in the session. It concerned our industrial tubing division, which sells extruded aluminum tubing of various smaller sizes for encasing wiring in commercial buildings. She was recommending that they market test their new items by going out to the customers and making what she called fakes—pretending to sell something they wouldn't have yet. This was so silly, it was one of the reasons I doubted her judgment on that sales forecasting matter I just mentioned. Surely you don't agree with her, do you?''

4. ''As I have said before, one of our better divisions is in the toy business. Children's stuff of many kinds and for pretty much all ages. Not educational items, just fun things. I was chatting with them recently about market testing, and they said they don't do any of it! Would you like to guess what they said were the reasons for this policy?''

Case: Electronic Measurements, Inc.

Bill Bergen, executive vice president and chief operating officer of Electronic Measurements, Inc., was on his way back from lunch in the cafeteria when he almost bumped into Ann Toliver. Ann, the head of the SimTest Division new customer department, seemed preoccupied. She invited Bill to stop for a chat, and he found out why. A member of Ann's staff (Chez Tronwath) was preparing for a presentation to the marketing group at Midwest Condiments, and Ann had been helping him.

Midwest was a small- to medium-sized regional producer of a line of catsups, mustards, and other condiments. It had begun in 1974 with a tasty pickle relish and had added other items over the years since then. The company had been advertising from the beginning and held good share in its markets. But early this year, it had been acquired by MasterFoods and was now getting ready to move out nationally. Midwest had been told to sharpen its market research practice and to adopt better ways of market testing its new products. Two MasterFoods brand managers were made available for advice on how to plan better market

---

This hypothetical case is based on realistic business circumstances.

research, and word had gone out to Electronic Measurements and some other firms that Midwest would be interested in learning what they had to offer.

As it happens, they had a lot to offer, and Ann Toliver was preparing a proposal for a simulated test market. Ann and Chez had been out to see Midwest the day before and had learned that a new line of sandwich spices was on its way to market. Apparently, the new line would be marketed in special shakers; so when making a sandwich, the consumer could sprinkle one or more types of spices onto its filling. Ann and Chez couldn't learn the content of the spice bottles, but apparently the combinations were unique and original.

The issue was, should Midwest use Electronic's simulated test market service in market testing the new spice line? The product had passed concept tests and had done well in a limited home placement test involving employees. The testers didn't think the product was the best they had ever heard of, but it did make sandwiches more interesting, was easy to use, and had created lots of talk in the households where used. The price was reasonable. The spice line would be targeted to busy people who ate lots of sandwiches but were bored with them. Positioning was straight to the fun and excitement of more interesting sandwiches.

So far, no one had actually been asked to buy the product. The advertising agency had developed copy for local TV and in-store display use, tasting samples would be made available in most stores, price would be a bit upscale (Poupon?), and the bottles and labels were clearly of upscale design.

Midwest was concerned about two things: (1) Would people take the product seriously enough to actually buy some and try it? and (2) Would they continue using it after the novelty had worn off? (The product use tests had lasted two months, but each bottle lasted longer than that, so users had not run out during the test.)

Ann and Chez had just finished putting together their presentation to Midwest, and Ann asked Bill if he would like to see it. Bill said he would, and a time was set for the following morning.

And then an odd thing happened. On his way on down the hall, he passed the office of CEO Edie Hopkins. Edie had developed the SimTest Division and done so well at it she got the nod to replace Electronic's founder when he took early retirement. She said she had made a visit to MasterFoods earlier in the week and was amazed to find that the MF sales force had absorbed the Midwest Condiment sales force. The condiment line would be sold along with the rest of the MasterFoods items. This surprised her because she had heard stories about the Midwest sales vice president, now just a regional sales manager for MasterFoods. Apparently, he had fantastic rapport with regional food chain buyers, built on his uncanny ability to predict winners and losers in the food business. People said he had never stocked the trade with a loser, either at Midwest or at another food company where he began his career. Edie knew no sales manager had product authority at MasterFoods (except for local, so-called micromarketing promotions). She wondered how he would handle the sell-in of new items he didn't think would be successful.

The SimTest division of Electronic Measurements offered a market modeling service based on consumer reactions to advertising and product display in one of the firm's four mall test centers. The test centers were much like several other research firms' centers. Consumers were found by mall intercepts, screened for market fit, interviewed about product awareness and usage, invited to screen proposed new TV shows, exposed to several TV ads (including the test product), invited to shop the firm's pseudo stores, given the test product if they didn't buy it in the "store," and followed up later to see if they had used it and whether they wanted more.

Electronic had been at this for about nine years, so it had a solid data base and had fine-tuned its sales forecasting models to make accurate forecasts of new product sales and market shares. The models did require some assumptions, however, and Bill was worried that Midwest might not be sophisticated enough to make them. For example, SimTest needed to know what percent of stores would stock the product, what type of awareness the planned advertising and in-store displays would generate, and what were the competitive products.

Bill saw a chance for him and Edie to sharpen presentations to clients and, at the same time, learn a few things about their staffs. He proposed that he and Edie role play Midwest management the following day, and the SimTest group (Ann and Chez) would make a presentation to them. The presentation would aggressively argue that the new spice line should be market tested via the SimTest service.

All the players (including Chez, who would actually make the presentation) knew this was no easy sell. MasterFoods brand people had been using simulated test marketing for several years and were generally satisfied with it. But Midwest had never used it. Word was that if it did anything at all, it had merely put out a new item in a limited area near the plant and watched what happened. Losers were quickly "deep-sixed," as a Midwest product manager put it.

The SimTest Ann and Chez were thinking of would cost about $95,000 and take three months.

Market Testing: Controlled Sale and Full Sale

SETTING

This is the second of a two-chapter set on market testing. Chapter 12 covered the first of the three methods (pseudo sale), so now we move to the other two. First will be controlled sale, followed by full sale. For your convenience, Figure 13–1 repeats the list of methods and where each finds its greatest use.

CONTROLLED SALE

The two pseudo sale methods of market testing discussed in Chapter 12 are unrealistic. They are useful as an early test and occasionally reliable as a final measure when the only issues involve how the customers react to the concept in a commercial setting. Users can argue, for example, that simulated test marketing fits lots of food products well—we see a commercial and then later meet the item on a store shelf. We buy or we don't buy.

Historically, however, we have relied on other market test methods that introduce the matter of cash—real purchasing under some competitive environment. Test marketing was probably the first method invented, but it has major drawbacks. Consequently, marketers have invented several other less expensive market testing methods, all of which have a strong dose of reality but also "control" away one or more dimensions of the situation. For example, test marketing requires fighting a way onto store shelves or warehouse shelves—what we call *getting distribution,* or *sell-in.* Marketers have always wished for a market testing method that assumes distribution, or gets it automati-

FIGURE 13–1   Methods of Market Testing, Where Used

| Methods | Product Categories Where Useful | | | | |
| | Industrial | | Consumer | | |
	Goods	Services	Packaged	Durables	Services
Pseudo sale					
Speculative sale					
Personal selling	X	X		X	X
Advertising				X	
Simulated test market			X		
Controlled sale					
Informal selling	X	X		X	X
Direct marketing	X			X	
Minimarket	X	X	X	X	X
Scanner markets			X		
Full sale					
Test marketing	X	X	X	X	X
Limited marketing (roll-out)					
By application	X	X			
By influence	X	X			X
By geography	X	X	X	X	X

cally, without having to earn it. Then they could test the other things faster and cheaper.

This wishing has resulted in the controlled sale market testing methods.

Informal Selling

In the industrial market, many firms are either too small to want to mess with test markets and other complex market testing methods or find they really don't need to. Much industrial selling is based on clearly identifiable product features. In many cases, there really is no question about target market because the item was developed to meet a particular technical need.

These product developers want potential buyers to see the product and hear the story, to make a trial purchase (or accept the offer of free trial supply), and to actually use the product. Repeat sales should follow unless product use testing was poorly done. Personal selling is the primary promotional tool, and there is little need to assess advertising. Most important is how the customer uses the product, what procedures are replaced, and so on.

So, the obvious approach is to train a few salespeople, give them the product and some selling materials, and have them begin making calls. This informal selling method can even be handled at trade shows, either at the regular booths or in special facilities nearby. The presentations are for real, cash payments are expected, and the innovating firm finds what it needs to know before making a commitment to large-volume production. Often, enough time remains between the order and the expected date of shipment that production can be arranged after sufficient orders are obtained.

Informal selling differs only slightly from the speculative sale method discussed in Chapter 12. There we asked people if they *would* buy; here we ask them *to* buy. And, just as Rubbermaid was mentioned as a consumer products firm using speculative selling, we find consumer firms using informal selling. All products sold primarily by salespeople directly to users, for example, and services of most types, fit informal selling. Though rarely identified as a market testing method, informal selling is actually very popular, perhaps used by more firms than any other method. In use, it phases easily into limited marketing (roll-out), a technique we will discuss in a moment.

Direct Marketing

Another simple method of controlled sale is by direct marketing. Though usage of the term *direct marketing* varies, here it includes the sale of a (primarily) consumer product by the maker directly to the consuming unit by means of mail or telephone. Many variations exist, so terminology becomes slippery. For example, some firms sell house to house or retailer to retailer by van. Others are starting to use fax and computer networks. If used for market testing, these are probably all direct marketing, but each industry tends to adopt its own language.

As examples, L. L. Bean and Lands' End are large direct marketers. They can easily test a new service of some type, or a new product or product line, simply by listing it in *some* of their catalogs and counting the orders. The advantages are several:

- More secrecy than by any other controlled sale method.
- The feedback is almost instant. No need to wait for weeks to get the first word back from the field.
- Positioning and image development are easier because more information can be sent and more variations can be tested easily.
- It is cheaper than the other techniques.
- Target markets can be defined and reached better.
- Product can be sent if desired.

- The technique matches today's growing technologies of credit card financing, telephone ordering, and mail list compilation.

The van can be a convenient substitute for mail and telephone. Several U.S. firms offer the service, and the United Kingdom's Research Bureau Limited does too; one firm in Europe even buys vans, modifies them, and then franchises them to smaller research firms.

Minimarkets

Whereas the informal marketing and direct marketing methods essentially avoid distributors and retailers/dealers, a third method involves outlets on a very limited basis. The new products manager first selects one or a few outlets where sale of the new product would be desirable. In no way a representative sample, these are more likely to be bigger outlets where there is reason to think cooperation could be obtained. Instead of using whole cities (as in test marketing), we use each store as a mini-city or minimarket, thus the name.

Black & Decker, for example, could contact some of its Ace hardware outlets or a couple of mass merchandise outlets and make arrangements to display and sell a new version of its Dustbuster. It could not use local TV or newspaper advertising because the item is available in only one or two outlets, but the stores could list the item in *their* advertising, there could be shelf display and product demonstrations, and sales clerks could offer typical service. Some method (such as offering a rebate or a mail-in premium) could get the names of purchasers for follow-up contact by market research people.

The minimarket situation is more realistic, actual buying situations are created, great flexibility is allowed in changing price and other variables, somewhat more confidentiality is possible than with test marketing, and it is cheaper. Of course, it is still somewhat contrived, store personnel may "overattend" the product, and sales cannot be projected to any national figure.

Several market research firms offer this service to manufacturers, using stores with which they have previously set up relationships and also using their fleet of vans to rapidly get product out to more than just a few stores. At least one of the firms has special new product racks in supermarkets, where the new items are displayed.

Note this method is very unscientific; it is used to catch the first flavor of actual sale and/or to work on special problems the developers are having (such as brand confusion, price, package instructions, product misuse, or different positionings). It is not at all a full test of sale; but, it does give a very good clue to that A–T–R trial factor, and, if enough people buy it, we can get a feeling for repeat.

Scanner Markets

Within the consumer packaged goods business, a spin-off of minimarket testing has resulted in what we call *scanner markets*. At the time of this writing, one firm — Information Resources, Inc. (IRI) — offers such a service called *BehaviorScan*.

IRI uses eight U.S. cities of around 100,000 population. Examples include Marion, Indiana, and Eau Clair, Wisconsin. Around 70 percent of the households contacted in these cities agree to cooperate, and they are used to form two panels of 1,000 families each in each city. Participants agree to (1) have electronic technology installed on their television sets, (2) list their exposure to print media, (3) make all of their purchases of grocery store products in the BehaviorScan stores, and (4) use a special plastic card identifying their family. The families get various incentives (such as lottery participation) to get their initial and sustained cooperation.

The key parts of the scanner system are (1) cable TV interrupt privileges, (2) a full record of what other media (such as magazines) go into each household, (3) family-by-family purchasing, and (4) a complete record of 95 percent of all store sales of grocery items from the check-out scanners IRI provides free to the stores. IRI knows almost every stimulus that hits each individual family, and it knows almost every change that takes place in each family's purchase habits.

For example, assume Kraft wants to market test a new version of cheddar cheese, called Cajun. It contracts with IRI to buy the cheese category in two of the eight cities. It then places Cajun in one of the cities and starts local promotion. The other city is used temporarily as a control. Kraft gets the right to put its commercials (via cable interrupt) into whichever of the homes (for example, younger families) it chooses. Kraft knows whether the families watched TV at the times of the commercials, whether they bought any of the Cajun, whether they bought it again, and so on.

The two panels in each city allow Kraft to use two different positionings in its TV advertising, one positioning for each of the two panels. And so on, and so on. The variations and controls stretch the imagination. Kraft can find out how many of the upscale homes who watched the initial commercial bought some of the product within the next two days. And what they bought on their prior purchase, what they paid, what else they bought at the time, and the like.

Scanner market technology is used for much more than just new products. For example, Johnson & Johnson's problems when one of its products was poisoned were lessened when its scanner market service showed that the item's share of market dropped from 47 percent to a bit over 6 percent in the problem city—but began to revive the very next week.[1]

The scanner market is undergoing a lot of change, with new firms coming and going as the industry tries to find the ideal technology. At the moment, the move is toward lower-cost methods that still achieve the integration of TV viewing and shopping behavior. By the time you read this, other changes will have occurred.

The scanner market method of testing is not without criticism, and its growth has leveled out far faster than predicted in its early years: it relies on cable, which isn't standard in the United States yet; it is offered only for a small number of cities that are not representative of the whole country; it intrudes into the families' lives in a way that probably distorts their representativeness; and participants have indicated their fun and excitement about being in it.[2] Are they therefore more aware of, and think more about, stimuli? We just don't know.

Too, scanner market testing is still a controlled sale technique, with no true market test of the innovator's ability to get stocking at the retail level.

FULL SALE

All of the market testing techniques discussed so far have been created in an effort to cut the time and costs of traditional test marketing. Each has done so, but at a cost in measurement. Now is the time to take a look at test marketing itself, for comparison. After that, we will discuss an innovation in the other direction, a technique *closer* to real launch—limited marketing (roll-out). It is only slightly more expensive than test marketing and offers some clear advantages.

Test Marketing

As the term is commonly used, *test marketing* refers to that type of market testing in which a presumably representative piece of the total market is chosen for a dress rehearsal. The test market is a miniaturization and test of the *total marketing program,* which distinguishes it from the earlier forms of market testing. Here, *all* variables are *go,* including competition and the trade. The test market tests the realities of national introduction.

---

[1] Fern Schumer, "The New Magicians of Market Research," *Fortune,* July 25, 1983, p. 72.

[2] Ibid.

It is interesting to note that the popularity of the test market seems to be cyclical. Prior to 1950, the test market was a rarity. From 1950 to 1965, it enjoyed great and growing popularity. Near the end of that period, the new ways of market testing discussed above were coming into use, and many top researchers spotted the threat to the established technique. The 1970s and 80s saw a resurgence of test marketing, followed currently by a lessening—at least among the big marketers. Smaller firms are taking up the slack, however, as they get more into market testing.[3]

The *purpose* of most test marketing today differs from the original purpose. Test marketing was originally used to predict profits and thus help decide *whether* to go national. Today, a firm has already decided the "whether" question and wants to know *how best* to do it. If the firm cannot find a way, the national activity is canceled, but test marketing is an expensive final exam.

This is a critical distinction, as shown by the market testing traditionally used for Broadway plays and musicals. Some of them *have* to play Detroit or Boston to prove their worth, but these are small, shoestring operations destined for an off-Broadway location. Big-time shows spend the real money getting *to* Detroit, where they fine-tune the operation, confirm volume and cost forecasts, and so on. A major production that fails in Detroit is a rarity. Of course, as in all businesses, lots of managements opt to skip the test market, often to their regret.

Pros and Cons. In contrast to other test methods, test marketing is intended to offer typical market conditions, thereby allowing the best sales forecast and the best evaluation of alternative marketing strategies. This, in turn, helps ensure that the eventual national plan has a good chance to succeed. It certainly reduces the risk of a total or major flop.

The test market offers the most abundant *supply of information* (such as sales, usage, prices, or competitive reactions) and many less important but occasionally valuable by-products. For example, a small firm or a firm producing a questionable new type of product can use successful test market results to help *convince national distributors* to chance stocking the item. Even large firms cite this advantage.[4]

---

[3] Some of the firms currently using test marketing are Monet Jewelry, Sporto/Goldseal Rubber, Progresso Foods, Igloo (ice chests), Ocean Spray, and Tropicana. They find roll-outs too expensive and risky. See Arthur Bragg, "How Smaller Companies Meet the Test," *Sales and Marketing Management*, March 10, 1986, pp. 88–92.

[4] Hans Lopater, vice president of marketing research for Gillette, recently said, "There will always be a place for conventional test marketing because you need it to measure trade acceptance and to get a true reading of [local store] promotional levels." See Rebecca Fannin, "Research's New Know-It-Alls," *Marketing & Media Decisions*, May 1986, pp. 75–88.

The test market also permits *verifying production,* where the ability to do this is an issue. ITT Continental Baking had to withdraw its Continental Kitchens line of prepared entrees from a test market because suppliers of the retort pouch couldn't maintain deliveries. Nabisco had trouble with Legendary Pastries when a seemingly harmless ingredient in the canned topping mix caused the product to explode on kitchen shelves. Both firms saved great sums of money by opting for a test market.

Other firms have been surprised by the effects of *humidity* or *temperature, abuse* by distribution personnel, *ingenious undesirable uses* of the product, and *general misunderstanding* by company or distributive personnel.

Of course, the method is *expensive:* direct costs easily run $300,000 to $500,000 per city; many indirect costs (for preparing product, special training, and so on) must be considered as well.

These costs are often acceptable if the data are accurate, thus allowing the test markets to be projected to a national sales figure. But researchers have known for a long time that *test market results are not really projectable.*[5] We cannot control all *environmental factors,* company people tend to *overwork* a test program, dealers may *overattend or underattend,* and the constant temptation exists to *sweeten the trade package* unrealistically in fear that inadequate distribution will kill the entire test.

In addition, there is the question of *time.* A good test takes a year or more and also gives competition full view of the test firm's strategy, time to prepare a reaction, and even the chance to leapfrog directly to national marketing on a similar item. Kellogg watched the early results of General Foods' Toast-Ems in test market and then went national ahead of General Foods to grab the major market share with Pop Tarts. Though General Foods still uses test markets, it jumped over Carnation's test market entry—Ground Round dog food—and went straight to national with Gaines Complete. Carnation, in turn, skipped test markets and nationally launched Come'n Get It.[6]

The general manager of General Foods' beverage division recently told of test market "informants who live in the town and pay off the supermarket managers to be allowed to hang around. You see these

---

[5] See J. A. Gold, "Testing Test Market Projections," *Journal of Marketing Research,* August 1964, pp. 8–16.

[6] These interesting situations are discussed in John Revett and Larry Edwards, "Carnation Bites Back," *Advertising Age,* June 9, 1980, p. 1. Another firm, Masters Brewing Co., spent three full years developing its marketing plan (including a long time arriving at the name *Masters*) and then opted to skip test marketing and go directly into roll-out. Situations vary tremendously. See Daniel B. Roman, "Brewing up a Name for Masters," *Sales and Marketing Management,* March 10, 1986, pp. 107–10.

mysterious characters watching how fast the Mighty Dog is moving and in what sizes." Other test market participants tell of competitive price cuts to thwart premium-priced new entries and of bulk new product purchases by competitive salespeople to falsely increase sales reports.[7]

Finally, there is an *inevitable* temptation to rationalize away a test market difficulty by citing what the now-known trouble was and how the firm "can take care of it on national launch."

The Decision Mode.   Given these strong benefits and objections, it is fortunate that industry has a good decision process to use when considering test markets. Some firms use oversimplified heuristics: "We test market everything" or "We test market every new product with an expense budget over $800,000." But new product managers more typically look for four factors on which to base the cost/risk decision:

1. Is a great deal of *money at stake?* Have there been high development costs, large potential profits, an expensive introduction, a large investment in production facilities?
2. Will success require a significant *change in consumer purchasing habits or in the consumer's normal mode of product usage?* Will a new cooking or serving routine or a significant educational task be needed?
3. Is there reason to think *we might not be able to bring that change about?*
4. Could our *competition* gain enough time or knowledge during the test to seriously threaten the whole program?

Many market conditions alert developers to the likelihood of trouble with items 2 and 3—for example, a situation where consumers are generally quite satisfied with what they are now doing, or a case where the new product is essentially a me-too, or the existence of a new advertising appeal.

A classic case showing how these factors apply was General Mills' development of a cookie mix line. Great dollars were at stake, but no great behavior change or attitude change was required because Nestlé

---

[7] This comment was made by Robert Sansone in Sandra Salmans, "New Trials in Test Marketing," *New York Times,* April 11, 1982, p. F1. These negatives are echoed by American Express, which feels that "It's hard to confine our products to a test market." So, it tries to use simulated test markets (pseudo sale) and then go national immediately. See Aimee L. Stern, "Test Marketing Enters a New Era," *Dun's Business Month,* October 1985, pp. 86–90.

and Quaker Oats had already established the new category. General Mills successfully skipped test market.

Another case shows how gambling is sometimes worthwhile. Smith, Kline and French (then the name of a typical large ethical pharmaceutical manufacturer) developed a consumer form of its successful delayed-action time capsule for treating colds. The first three items on the above list were negative—dollars, behavior, and inexperience with proprietary products. But, the product was needed, it worked, and (item 4 above) it was patented. Contac cold product was probably the greatest-volume new proprietary ever introduced nationally without a test market, and it was introduced by a firm on its first venture into large-scale consumer promotion. There are no rules in market test decision making!

The issue of competition is difficult. Test marketing does give the maximum advantage to competitors, but it is only one of four factors and must be analyzed. For example, P&G had been an avid user of test marketing for many years, but in the 1970s, the firm began skipping it once in a while. As it turned out, some of its recent new products had lacked the strong technical differentiation that P&G products traditionally had. Because competitors could readily copy them, P&G wanted to capture market position as quickly as possible.

The Test Parameters. A large body of test market literature is available, and most of the leading market research consulting firms stand ready to design tests appropriate to any situation, so no depth of detail is needed here. The most common questions are "Where should we test?" and "How long should the test run?"

Picking Test Markets. Each experienced test marketer has an ideal structure of cities or areas. Figure 13–2 gives a long list of popular places. Picking two or three to use is not simple, but the most common factors are:

1. *Demographics*—population, income, employment, and so on.
2. *Distribution*—the structure of retail and wholesale firms, including any difficulties of getting in.
3. *Competition*—you need enough, but not too much.
4. *Media*—newspapers, radio, and TV covering just that market, not a huge surrounding area.
5. *Category activity*—no strong regional, ethnic, or economic peculiarities in product consumption.

Test areas need to be stand alone, not where there will be a lot of sales leakage into other areas, and yet self-contained and representative of the nation or a big piece of it. And, any areas used should be generally

FIGURE 13–2 Recommended Test Markets, 1987

1. Albany–Schenectady–Troy	24. Milwaukee
2. Atlanta	25. Minneapolis–St. Paul
3. Boise	26. Nashville
4. Buffalo	27. Oklahoma City
5. Cedar Rapids–Waterloo–Dubuque	28. Omaha
6. Charlotte	29. Orlando–Daytona Beach–Melbourne
7. Cincinnati	30. Peoria
8. Cleveland	31. Pittsburgh
9. Colorado Springs–Pueblo	32. Portland–Poland Spring
10. Columbus, Ohio	33. Portland, Oregon
11. Dayton	34. Rochester, New York
12. Denver	35. Sacramento–Stockton
13. Des Moines	36. St. Louis
14. Erie	37. Salt Lake City
15. Evansville	38. Seattle–Tacoma
16. Fargo	39. South Bend–Elkhart
17. Fort Wayne	40. Spokane
18. Grand Rapids–Kalamazoo–Battle Creek	41. Springfield–Decatur–Champaign
19. Green Bay–Appleton	42. Syracuse
20. Greensboro–Winston Salem–High Point	43. Toledo
21. Indianapolis	44. Tulsa
22. Kansas City, KS–Kansas City, MO	45. Wichita–Hutchinson
23. Louisville	

Source: These are the recommendations of the advertising agency Saatchi & Saatchi; DFS Compton.

accepted as representative if the results need to impress distributors and retailers.

Duration of Test. There is no one answer to the question of how long a test market should last, as made clear by Del Monte's U.S. marketing vice president, who said his test markets were conducted to (1) verify prior research on all aspects of the program—for example, pricing, distribution, and repeat rates—and (2) estimate probable volumes. Accomplishing those tasks was expected to take 24 to 36 months for Garden Show, a line of indoor plant care items, but only 6 to 9 months for Fruit Taffy, a candy snack.[8] Figure 13–3 shows some data used in the duration decision; a test should run through at least two buying cycles to get a good fix on repeat.

---

[8] Sally Scanlon, "Zeroing in on Profits," *Sales and Marketing Management,* March 1979, p. 66.

FIGURE 13–3 Purchase Cycles on Selected Product Categories

	Purchase Frequency (weeks)	Average Four-Week Penetration (percent)		Purchase Frequency (weeks)	Average Four-Week Penetration (percent)
Air fresheners	6	12.3%	Fruit drinks	4	27.8%
Baking supplies			Presweetened		
Brown sugar	17	13.6	powdered		
Cake mixes	10	29.6	drinks	8	13.2
Chewable			Laundry care		
vitamins	26	0.8	Heavy-duty		
Cleaners			detergents	5	50.4
All-purpose			Soil and stain		
cleaners	35	3.4	removers	25	4.7
Window			Liquid bleach	6	18.3
cleaners	27	7.1	Margarine	3	71.7
Rug cleaners	52	2.4	Milk additives	9	11.8
Bathroom			Mouthwash	13	9.7
cleaners	25	4.2	Pet food		
Coffee	3	53.1	Cat (total)	2	14.1
Frozen foods			Dog (dry)	4	23.2
Frozen			Dog (total)	2	41.8
entrees	6	19.5	Raisins	18	8.3
Frozen pizza	8	21.1	Salad dressings	6	32.9
Furniture			Salad toppings	8	1.2
polish	27	7.0	Snacks	3	17.7
Hair care			Steak sauce	23	5.4
Hair color	12	4.7	Toothpaste	9	33.1
Shampoo	8	23.4			
Juices/drinks					
Fruit juices	3	33.6			

Note: The first column is the average time between purchases of the category cited, by the households in the ADTEL panel. The second column is the percentage of panel households that made at least one purchase in a four-week period. Both figures contribute to the decision on test market duration.

Source: ADTEL, Inc.

Conclusions on Test Marketing. In some instances, test marketing is virtually mandatory; in others, it is clearly undesirable. Most situations are less clear-cut, but the advantages and disadvantages of the tool are well known, and it does use a four-point decision process. A currently emerging trend is for managers to select test market areas that can be used to merge into limited marketing (roll-out). Distinction between the two is becoming less clear and less necessary.

Another factor that will blur the market testing distinctions in the consumer packaged goods business is the widespread adoption of scanners in food stores. Scanners permitted the BehaviorScan controlled sale method discussed earlier. But the supplier of that service, IRI, now offers a full market measurement service called *InfoScan*. This service reports on all product sales in food stores in some 60 metropolitan areas. The sales data are so complete and so fast (usually one week) that many firms are putting together a modified version of the true test market; they sell into one or more of these markets for a while, then move out.

Figure 13–4 shows some of the turbulence or variation that exists, and Figure 13–5 shows the little we know about how many companies are actually using test marketing and the other market testing devices discussed above. Note the possible bias in the samples for those two studies.

FIGURE 13–4 Recent Actions Indicating the Turbulence in Market Testing Methodology Choices

---

Richardson-Vicks undertook a national launch of Olay Beauty Bar on the basis of simulated test marketing (STM) only. The firm has an extensive background in beauty products and can move quickly. It did the same thing in Australia by going national with Climacel based only on STM. It claims ASSESSOR predictions are quite accurate. Both products succeeded.

S. C. Johnson took Agree cream rinse to simulated test market, where it did well. It then went into test market (type unknown), but success came so clearly that the firm collapsed six months off normal test market time. "We sort of rolled right over and went national."

Zero Corporation — a $44 million (1984) Burbank, California, electronics firm — is moving into test marketing in a major way for the first time.

Sensormatic Corp., a medium-sized firm making electronic surveillance systems for supermarkets, combined product use testing and test marketing by selling Winn-Dixie on a test in its Florida division. The test market was then "rolled out" to several other grocery chains and then to liquor stores.

Several food companies recently took action indicating the extreme competitiveness of that industry. All of the following items were taken directly from simulated test marketing to national launch: Sara Lee's meat-filled croissants, General Foods' new flavors of International Coffees, Quaker's Chewy Granola Bars, and Pillsbury's Milk Break Bars. However, P&G (which also went from STM to national on several items) stayed in test market for three years with Cinch dishwasher detergent and Certain bathroom tissue.

Limited Marketing (Roll–Out)

Test marketing was for a long time the final dress rehearsal. But it had serious drawbacks, and lots of managers realized they might have their cake and eat it too if they could go national in a way that gave them some of the protection of a test market. They found such a way, and it is becoming increasingly popular. Best called *limited marketing,* it more often goes by the nickname *roll-out.*

FIGURE 13–5   Use Frequency of Various Market Testing Methodologies

Survey A: Of 183 of the largest American consumer goods and service companies:

	1978	1983
Percent saying major share of research dollars spent on:		
Own test marketing	15%	11%
Controlled store testing	19	25
Simulated test marketing	10	14
Nonmarket testing research	56	50
Percent using within past year:		
Own test marketing	40	33
Controlled store testing	32	36
Simulated test marketing	32	37

Survey B: Of 138 major national advertisers (all types of products and services) about what they do when entering a market (category) new to the firm:

Use simulated test marketing	34% never had
If do use, the simulations are:	
Concept test only	38%
Concept and product (usual definition)	65
Used alone	6
Used with test marketing	94
Would you go to national launch based on the simulations?	
Yes	14
Possibly	31
Not likely	50
Percent of respondents who use controlled outlet testing of any type (mostly one or a few stores)	68
Percent of respondents who use test marketing	84

Sources: Survey A: "How It's Done," *Advertising Age,* February 20, 1984, pp. M11 and M42. The study was done by Market Facts, Inc., Chicago. Survey B: *Prescription for New Product Success* (New York: Association of National Advertisers, 1984), pp. 24–27.

Let's take an example. McDonald's Corporation wants to add a line of breakfast products, but such an action is risky. So, it puts the products into sale in a couple of areas. When everything goes well (operations, sales, profits), surrounding *(geographical)* areas are added, and sales continue. Eventually, the new line is in all outlets.

Although this may sound like test marketing, it differs in two big ways. First, the starting areas were *not representative areas* but, rather, areas where the company thought it had the right people, and perhaps the right markets, to get the thing going. Second, there was no doubt about what the company was doing: *it was launching the breakfast products.*

Let's take another example. Assume an industrial adhesives firm develops a new adhesive that works on many *applications,* including fastening bricks to steel plates, fastening insulation siding to the two-by-four studs in a house, and fastening shingles onto plywood roofing sheets. It has been field tested in all three applications and has been tested in informal selling (controlled sale) in one use (shingles), where it received a good response. Should the firm offer it for all three applications at once? Arguments against this include (1) the adhesive has not been market tested in the first two applications, (2) such action would strain resources, (3) multiple uses might confuse customers, all of whom are in the construction field and will hear of all three selling efforts, and (4) the new products manager wants to have some successful experience to talk about when entering the brick and siding fields, because they are highly competitive.

Answer: Market the new adhesive in the shingles business first, get it started there, gain experience, build up some cash flow, and establish credibility. Then, gradually begin selling it to the siding firms and make whatever changes are indicated. Still later, move into the brick field.

A third example would be the adhesives firm if there were only one major application and the product (1) was only marginally better and (2) required lots of training for the distributors' reps. The adhesives firm could choose to begin selling the adhesive through one of its best (and friendliest) distributors, a firm willing to go along on the new item. When that went well, it could gradually add other distributors with whom it had increasingly less *influence,* using prior successes to persuade them.

Forms that Limited Marketing Takes. Those three examples indicate three of the leading forms taken by limited marketing—geography, application, and influence. In each case, the form chosen is one where the product should sell. Then, less likely selling efforts are added as the product picks up steam. In its simplest form, the technique has been called "Make a little, sell a little." Anyone entering a cold lake or swimming pool does the same thing, and it's their feet they put in first, not their heads or their torsos.

Contrasts with Test Marketing.   Limited marketing has many advantages. The biggest are that it gives management most of the knowledge learned from a test market, it has an escape clause if things bomb, and yet we are well on our way to national availability when early marketing works. This is important in the competitive battle, because test marketing gives the competition time to launch their products while we are still in test market or getting geared up to go national.

Does this sound like the best of all worlds? What's the catch? In some situations, there isn't any catch, and the technique is justifiably growing in use. But, many firms find limited marketing to be just as big a risk as full launch. Here are some of their reasons:

1. Their biggest investment may be in a new production facility, and to roll out requires the full plant at the start.
2. Their competitors can move very fast (for example, because no patent or new facilities are required), so a slow marketing gives them about as much advantage as would test marketing.
3. Their distributors are powerful, and none are friends willing to trust them.
4. They need the free national publicity that only a full national launch can get them. Roll-outs tend not to be newsworthy.

There are other such situations. What does a firm do? The answer is to go through the same decision process given for test marketing. What are the risks? What do we need to know for sure? What are the costs in research and operations dollars and in terms of competitive response? Many of the answers depend on conditions at the moment — if a firm doesn't want any unfavorable publicity, if it wants fast cash in an acquisitions battle, if the top management is new and wants a couple of successes before the first loss, and so on. There are no recipes here.

Speed of Roll-Out.   Because the purpose of limited marketing is to acquire more information before going all out, the speed or duration of roll-out varies. If a product catches on fast, the roll-out may last just long enough for management to arrange for national distribution, make the product, and schedule promotion. But, problems may stretch it out; P&G kept Charmin toilet tissue in roll-out for several years while working out production and marketing problems.

Other Variations.   There is probably no end to variations on the roll-out theme. Some firms use trade shows, especially in industries with strong seasonal variations. A new item (say, a line of clothing or sporting equipment) can be displayed and sold at the show for delivery six months hence. Ample time remains for adjustments in price, delivery, service, or promotional assistance before true national launch takes place. Yet, such a sale is not a test market because the commitment has been made and full-scale launch preparations are under way.

Another form of limited marketing is country by country. Some Japanese firms, for example, have marketed products first in Europe and then rolled them out to the United States and other areas. Their strategy was based on the need to acquire marketing and manufacturing experience before entering the difficult and critical U.S. market.

SUMMARY

Chapters 12 and 13 covered the market testing phase of the overall evaluation task that involves putting product together with marketing plan. The techniques of market testing vary from the simplistic (and quite unreliable) one of making a sales presentation about the new product to potential buyers and then asking them if they would buy it if available, to a full-scale test market or even a roll-out or other form of limited marketing.

The appropriate market testing methodology for any particular new product cannot be stipulated here. Companies vary tremendously in product confidence, financial capability, competitive pressure, and so on. Some firms have good arguments for doing no market testing of any type. For example:

1. Some manufacturers sell to a small number of buyers (such as car or appliance OEMs) and thus develop an item in conjunction with those buyers. There is very little testing other than product use testing.
2. Some firms are technology based and develop what they feel the customer needs and will want. But they also know it has to be explained (sold) and, thus, distrust any kind of intermediate testing.
3. Some new product innovation is of such low risk that no market testing can be defended.
4. In some patent situations, the innovator firm wants to develop the product and the market simultaneously.

On the other hand, leading consumer packaged goods firms may invest as much as $50 million in marketing. They will sometimes use each of the various market testing techniques and even double back over some of them a second or third time.

Market testing is difficult and easily botched. Competitors make sure the waters are kept at least slightly muddy. The new products manager (1) is putting together the full company team for the first time, (2) is beginning to compete with ongoing marketing effort for resource allocation, and (3) must deal with the persistent foot-dragging of negativists who have doubted the item from the beginning.

Consequently, the results of market testing must be interpreted cautiously. We need to learn how best to market the product, but as market testing continues the most critical issue of all is eventually closed: Can the item be marketed successfully? The answer requires a full financial analysis. Financial work begins early in the new product process (how big is the market, and if we succeed in it, would our volume be enough to make the effort worthwhile?), and it accumulates. The form financial analysis takes and the problems associated with it are the subject of Chapter 14.

APPLICATIONS

1. "I love a good competitive battle, so I was intrigued a couple of years ago when S. C. Johnson went directly national (without a test market or a roll-out) with a product called Complete (furniture polish). What was interesting was that Texize was then in test market with a similar product called Wood*Plus. Why do you suppose a fine, successful firm like S. C. Johnson would take a major risk like that?"

2. "Another firm I remember skipped test markets back in 1977 when R. J. Reynolds marketed Real cigarettes. The firm said the cigarette was so promising that it didn't need to spend time in test markets. It spent $40 million on advertising and promotion—the most ever on a new brand at that time. It used 130 boxcars of display materials and 25 million sample packs. Three years later, the product had a tiny share of market, and rumors were that the product would be dropped. My question is this: Couldn't that product have been taken through one of the other types of market testing? Even if test markets were deemed too expensive and time consuming, couldn't cigarettes be tested by some of the controlled sale methods or in simulated test markets?"

3. "Several of our divisions have lately been using this so-called scanner market service. We had some cold products using BehaviorScan and some food products too. But I am increasingly concerned about the panel members in those test cities. My concern is not that the people become accustomed to the testing or that they overreact to stimuli. These are valid concerns, but there's not much I can do about them. I am concerned, however, that our people do not know the effect of these things on the data we get. How would the results of our tests be affected if people like the testing too much? Or, if they tend to become professional test participants and begin thinking like judges?"

4. "Back in an earlier conversation, I mentioned that New Cookery by Nestlé was awarded mention as a line of products greatly talked about in 1980. Well, it seems the line didn't work out in test market quite as well as expected. In fact, it has been withdrawn with no plans announced for the future. Retailers complained the products in the new line were often priced higher than competitive products. Some said the items lacked a clear-cut reason for being because although advertised as low-calorie items, the catsup line was only marginally lower in calories than Heinz and Del Monte catsups. Other comments were 'People here aren't thinking much about diet and health when they're shopping' and 'The concept was too esoteric and incomprehensible to the ordinary consumer.' Now, this new product line came from a fine firm, and the advertising was by one of the biggest and most successful advertising agencies. Just how could such a disappointment have come about?"

Case: *Square D Remote Lamp Dimmer*

In early 1985, the consumer products division of the Square D Company had completed technical development of a new product designed for the home: a remote dimmer to use on table lamps. The product would soon join other consumer division products (particularly door chimes, weatherproof wiring devices, circuit breakers, and smoke detectors) for sale to the retail market.

The idea for the product had come originally from Ron Rogers, national sales manager of the division, and was based on his previous experience with motor speed controls and on a study of dimmer technology. The development had taken 14 months and cost less than $20,000. The product used a radio frequency that did not interfere with radios, TVs, or other such items. Its signal could penetrate normal walls of plasterboard and/or wood. The remote unit had an on/off control as well as brightness-level control. The control had a 30-foot range.

The U.S. market (the product's major potential at this time) consisted of 75 million households with an average of eight table lamps in each. There was no direct competitor to the new dimmer, although wall switch dimmers had been available for many years. It was not known whether there would be any patent protection, but the likelihood was not strong.

The product had many special uses (with handicapped persons, for example) and could be used from in bed and from room to room. A person returning home could arrive at the garage, open it with the garage opener, drive inside, and then turn on a lamp in the house before even getting out of the car.

This case is compiled from information provided by the firm.

The lamp dimmer retail package consisted of two pieces heat-sealed inside a display hanger. The first piece was a small space-capsule-shaped control that screwed into the lamp; the bulb was screwed into the unit so that the control piece was between the bulb and the lamp socket. The second product piece was the remote control, which was much like a small TV remote control unit. The product was expected to retail for $33.50.

Square D was a large and prosperous firm, although the consumer products division was much younger. The lamp dimmer product had not been use tested in the home, although some engineers and managers had used it in their homes. The principal market study to date was a survey of manufacturers' reps, who endorsed the concept. This division sold through a national force of reps who called on such retail organizations as hardware stores, mass merchandisers, and department stores. Most marketing strategy was push oriented with a minimum of consumer advertising.

The issue for you is, how would you have recommended to Mr. Rogers that the product be market tested? Or, would you have recommended no market testing? Please state your recommendation with supporting logic.

Chapter 14

Financial Analysis

SETTING

Early in the product evolution process, we hit the issue of when to do financial analysis. Firms for which this is a screening task have financial predictions in their scoring models. They like to "know" whether they are going to make any profit before they authorize R&D work. Other firms more wisely feel financial predictions can't be made at such an early date, so they hold off until after the prototype appears, or until after product use testing and market testing are completed.

All firms begin to get a financial picture early on, as we will see in a minute. But, somewhere near the end of the development cycle, this analysis gets serious. Chapter 14 covers what is done at this more final stage. The procedure may seem primarily a matter of accounting practice in the firm, and accounting (as in budgeting or financial analysis) is important. But, we will also see that the real analysis here is far more than that.

WHERE WE ARE AT THE MOMENT

The purpose of financial analysis is clear: Bring the many numbers together and lay the groundwork for decision. That decision is usually to commercialize the product, continue its development some more, or abandon it.

Financial Analysis Is a Continuing Process

In a way, we have been doing financial analysis over the life of the project. For example:

1. In the product innovation charter, we select focus restrictions

(technology or market) on which we are strong; that is, where we should be able to make lots of money.

2. Also in the charter, we often see such guidelines as "Any new product must sell at least $100 million the first full year on the market."

3. In concept testing, we ask about buying intentions, and we translate those buying intentions into sales volumes and market shares.

4. At full screening time, our scoring model asks how close the product concept is to our technical capabilities and to our selling capabilities. Presumably, if we know how to make it and sell it, we can make money on it.

5. At the end of product use testing, we again ask about buying intentions.

And so on. Sales volumes and costs have never been far from our minds. Some managers actually keep a rough income statement in hand—"How much can we sell?" "What kind of trade markup will we be able to get on it?" "What will it cost to make?" They can multiply these figures into an estimated profit or at least into some profit contribution. And the A–T–R model can serve as the "back of an envelope" very well.

When to Finalize It?

But managers don't—or, at least, shouldn't—put these figures into official form. The numbers are primarily estimates of capability; they predict the chances of doing a good job. But, a lot of hands-on management lies between those predictions and the time of full financial analysis.

That's why we like to wait until after use testing before getting serious about profit forecasts. And, questions usually arise even then. For example, prior to market testing:

Edwin Land did not *know* we would pay a large premium for his instant Polaroid pictures.

Apple did not *know* we would buy millions of its Macintosh.

Ford did not *know* we would storm the dealers for its new Taurus.

J&J did not *know* we would consume millions of disposable contact lenses.

They thought we would. And we did. But their financial analyses had to reflect some doubts, which is what makes our job so difficult. Even on simple line extensions, a figure that we think is almost certain can be ruined by a competitive move, by distributors' demands for better margins, or by a regulator's decision.

Recall that a concept doesn't actually change into a product until it is successful. And we won't know that until we have launched it and dealt with the problems that will inevitably come up during that launch. (See Chapter 18 on launch control.) So, the firm has several good choices as to when it makes its serious financial analysis. In general, firms attempt financials around the time technical work is being started. Then, another look is taken as use tests and early, inexpensive market tests indicate a potential winner. This look may be very complete and be the last full analysis, especially if the firm is about to move into launch (either in roll-out form or national). Some firms keep the last premarket analysis alive and updated through the early market period, until success is achieved. And, of course, some desire another complete financial analysis several years later, as a total project review.

After going through traditional financial analysis for new products, we will deal with an even tougher issue — how to factor in such issues as the impact of a successful new product on employee morale. Some experts are demanding a "new accounting."

TRADITIONAL FINANCIAL ANALYSIS FOR NEW PRODUCTS

New products financial analysis requires two separate activities: (1) gathering the full set of data and other "givens" in the situation and (2) using them in calculations to derive whatever final figure is sought. These two tasks are shown in Figure 14–1 (the key data form) and Figure 14–2 (the financial worksheet).

Compiling the Key Data

Let's go through the key data form section by section, realizing each organization has its own preferences and policies.

Economic Conditions.   Most firms have ongoing economic forecasts, but sometimes a team wishes to differ. If so, the difference should be noted here.

The Market or Category.   The "market" for the new product is defined carefully, and the growth rate assumption is noted. Also, the current total market unit and dollar volumes are recorded.

Product Life.   The number of years used in the economic analysis of new products is usually set by company policy, but any particular project may be an exception.

FIGURE 14–1   Key Data Form for Financial Analysis, Part A

Financial Analysis Proposal: <u>Bay City Electronics Closure</u>*
Date of this analysis: _____Previous analyses:_____

1. Economic conditions, if relevant:
   Corporate scenario OK

2. The market (category): Stable – 5% growth	3. Product life <u>5</u> years

4. List price: $ <u>90</u> Distributor discounts: <u>$36</u> Net to factory: $ <u>54</u>	Other discounts: Promotion: <u>$1</u> Quantity: <u>$1</u> Ave. dollars per unit sold: <u>$52</u>

5. Production costs: Explanation of any unique costing procedures being used: None. Experience curve effect.	Applicable rate for indirect manufacturing costs:_____ 20% of direct costs

6. Future expenditures, other capital investments, or extraordinary expenditures:
   Build production facilities: $50,000
   Ongoing R&D: $15,000; $10,000; $15,000; $10,000 for first four years after intro
   Special UL test during the 2d year will cost $5,000
   Expand facilities in 3d year for $45,000

7. Working capital: <u>35%</u> of sales 10% inventory; recover 80% in period 5 15% receivables; all recovered in period 5 10% cash, all recovered	8. Applicable overheads: Corp.: <u>10</u>% of sales Division: <u>–</u>% of sales

9. Net loss on cannibalized sales, if any, expressed as a percent of the new product's sales: <u>10</u>%

10. Future costs/revenues of project abandonment, if that were done instead of marketing:
    Abort now would net $3,000 from sale of machine.

11. Tax credits, if any, on new assets or expenditures: 1% of taxes due to state and federal,
    based on positive environmental effect.

12. Applicable depreciation rate(s) on depreciable assets: 25% on orig. plant and machines;
    33 ⅓% on expansion facilities

13. Federal and state income tax rate applicable: <u>34</u>%
    Comments:

14. Applicable cost of capital: <u>16</u>%
    ± Premiums or penalties: <u>high-risk project</u> <u>8</u>%
    _____ _<u>_</u>%
    Any change in cost of capital anticipated over life of product? No

---

* Note: This key data form is filled in with demonstration data from the Bay City Electronics case, given at the end
of this chapter.

FIGURE 14–1   Key Data Form for Financial Analysis, Part B

15. Basic overall risk curve applicable to the NPV: Standard OK ✓

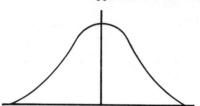

16. Key elements to be given sensitivity testing (e.g., sales, price cuts) (See below)	17. Sunk costs: Expenses to date: Ignore Capital invested to date: $15,000

18. Elements of new product strategy that are especially relevant on this proposal: (e.g., diversification mandate or cash risk):
Strategy calls for us to strengthen company in diversified markets, which this product will do.

19. Basic sales and cost forecasts:

Year	Unit sales	Direct production cost per unit	Marketing expenses
1	4,000	$16	$100,000
2	10,000	12	80,000
3	18,000	11	50,000
4	24,000	9	60,000
5	5,000	14	10,000

20. Hurdle rates:
Must have 40% gross margin after production costs.

21. Any mandatory contingencies: None

22. Other special assumptions or guidelines:
  (1) The total $110,000 of facilities and machines will salvage for $10,000 when production is finished.
  (2) The firm has other income to absorb any tax loss on this project.
  (3) Ignore investment tax credit.

  Sensitivity testing (Calculate the effect on NPV of the following):
  (1) We may have to cut the price to $34 net at start of third year.
  (2) Our direct manufacturing cost estimate may be overoptimistic. What if we never get the cost below the original $16?
  (3) Competition may force much higher marketing costs—what if starting in year 2 the level we have to spend at is just twice what we forecasted above?
  (4) How about a worst-case outcome, in which all of the above three contingencies are tested at one time?

FIGURE 14–2   Financial Worksheet

Product Proposal: _____   Date: _____

Years on the Market

	0	1	2	3	4	5
1. Unit sales						
2. Dollar sales						
3. Production costs:						
4. Direct						
5. Indirect						
6. Total cost of goods sold						
7. Gross profit after CGS						
8. Direct marketing costs						
9. Profit contribution						
10. Overheads (excluding R&D):						
11. Division						
12. Corporate						
13. Total overheads						
14. Other expenses/incomes:						
15. Depreciation						
16. Loss on cannibalization						
17. R&D yet to be incurred						
18. Extraordinary expense						
19. Project abandonment						
20. Total other expenses/incomes						
21. Total overheads and expenses/incomes						
22. Income before taxes						
23. Tax effect:						
24. Taxes on income						
25. Tax credits						
26. Total tax effect						
27. Income after taxes						
28. Cash flow:						
29. Income after taxes						
30. Depreciaton						
31. Production facilities						
32. Working capital—cash +/−						
33. Working capital—inventory +/−						
34. Working capital—receivables +/−						
35. Net cash flows						
36. Discounted cash flows						

37. Net present value: $_____

38. Internal rate of return: _____%

39. Payback: _____ years

Pricing. Start with the end-user list price, work back through the various trade discounts to get a factory net, then deduct any planned special discounts and allowances. The average dollars per unit sold is the price used in worksheet calculations.

Production Costs. Most firms have an established method of estimating production costs. But, we need to know whether anything unusual is being done on this project. We also need the percentage rate by which factory overheads are assigned.

Future Special Expenditures. Typical special expenditures include factory facilities, licensing rights, the one-time introductory marketing cost, up-front payments to suppliers, further R&D on improvements and line extensions, and plant expansions as volume grows. In our calculation, these are all investment outflows.

Working Capital. This estimates cash, inventories, and receivables needed to support the sales volumes. They are as much an investment as are moneys spent for plant and R&D, though recovered at a higher rate when the product is eventually abandoned.

Applicable Overheads. Opinions and practice vary here because some firms prefer to see new products as increments, especially if these products do not extend or alter the basic nature of the business in any way. These firms assign only "direct" overheads—those caused by the new product (such as an expanded sales force or a new quality control function). Other firms believe overheads tend to grow as functions of volume and will eventually go up whether directly related to the new product or not. The latter is probably closer to reality, so overheads should be included.

Net Loss on Cannibalized Sales. Some new products are totally new to current lines, but most are not. This section lists the effects of cannibalization by the new item on the current line. Some experts omit it, believing if they don't take it, a competitor eventually will.

Future Costs/Revenues of Project Abandonment. This section is tricky. A decision to abandon a project does not entirely end the matter. Along the way, the project has usually accumulated facilities, people, patent rights, inventories, and so on. If the project is abandoned now, the disposal of these items will produce revenue, sometimes substantial revenue. Such revenues thus constitute a cost of not abandoning the project. Similarly, any *cost* of abandonment is an added *revenue* of going ahead (for example, disposing of a large supply of radioactive chemicals purchased for product development).

Tax Credits. Occasionally, federal or state incentives arise for new products activity in the public interest.

Applicable Depreciation Rate. Although this rate is sometimes difficult to decide as a policy question, it is usually given to the new products manager for application to any particular project.

Federal and State Income Tax Rate. Again, this figure is a given for new product financial analysis.

Required Rate of Return. This one is not so easy. Usually, the rate of return (or cost of capital) to be used in the calculation is given by someone in the firm's financial operation. But, the percentage is often critical to whether the project is profitable; this means new products managers are very interested in how it is determined and how it might be changed.

Various techniques may be used in any firm. Theoretically, the figure to use is the *weighted average* cost of capital, including the three sources of capital—debt, preferred stock, and retained earnings. If the new product requires new investment capital (and it always does), the firm may feel it has those three choices. Or, it can borrow the money, in which case the cost of capital is *the firm's current borrowing rate.* Another alternative is the opportunity cost concept, which uses the *rate of earnings from current operations*; that is, if a firm is currently averaging an aftertax return of 18 percent on assets, management may use 18 percent as its current cost of capital.

New product managers object to methods that increase the percentage, because a high cost of capital forces higher hurdles for the new product. But, getting into discussions on this subject frequently leads nowhere; so much good theory is applicable, and so many parties are interested, that the actual method used in a firm must be the rather arbitrary preference of its managers.

Whatever the rate, the next step is to decide how the riskiness of the particular project being evaluated compares with the rest of the firm's activities. Look at Figure 14–3—a relationship between risk and rate of return exists for every business. This relationship is revealed in the upward slope of the line, which means that the more the risk, the more the profit must be or the activity won't be undertaken.

The line slopes differently for each firm, depending on its strengths and weaknesses, its industry, and so on. A powerful firm will use a line with great slope because it need not take as much risk to make its gains. Given the current average cost of capital and the level and slope of the line, the manager can mark off the risk of the particular new product, go up to the risk/return line, and then read off the required rate of return. Except in unusual circumstances, that required

FIGURE 14–3   Calculating the New Product's Required Rate of Return

Percent return

Required rate
of return

Cost of
capital

Average
risk
of the firm

Risk
on a
particular
proposed
product

Risk

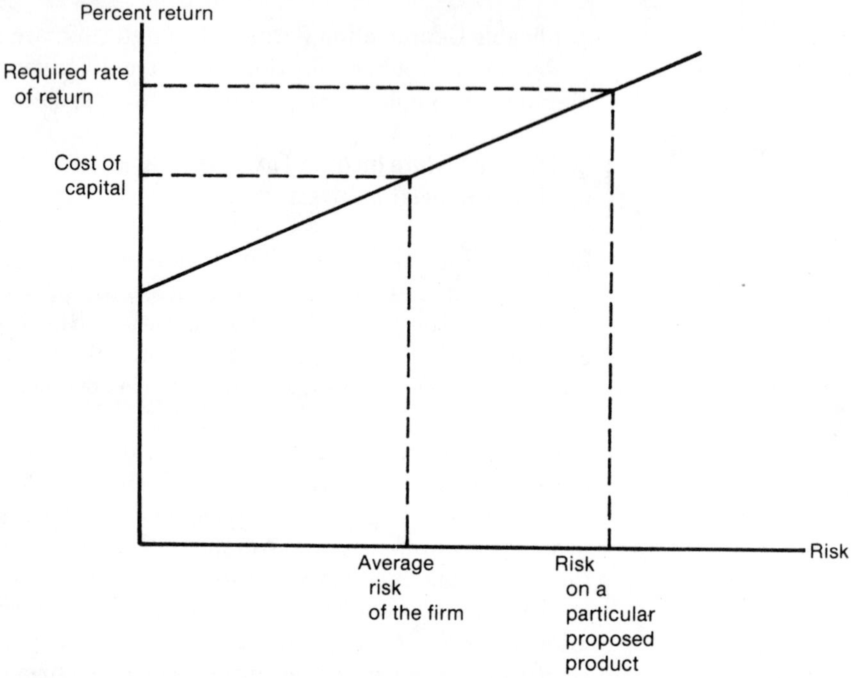

Explanation: Required rate of return (hurdle) = Cost of capital + Risk premium for the new product.

level will represent a premium over the current cost of capital. The premium is entered in section 14 of the key data form. The riskier the new project, the more management will expect as a promised return before giving money to it.

Risk Curve.   Figure 14–4 shows the typical curve of possible profit outcomes from a given new product project. This curve is also shown in the key data form. The other diagrams in Figure 14–4 show other patterns. In the B pattern, chances are the project will have a lower payout, but a very high payout is also possible. Imitative competition is expected; but, if it doesn't come, the profit will be high. The C pattern reverses this—imitative competition is not expected; but, if it comes, most of the profit will be eliminated. In the case of pattern D, no one really knows what the outcome will be.

This risk pattern information is good to keep in mind when making the financial analysis, though few firms undertake the probability-adjusted risk analysis it permits.

FIGURE 14–4   Risk Curves—Frequency Distributions of Outcomes

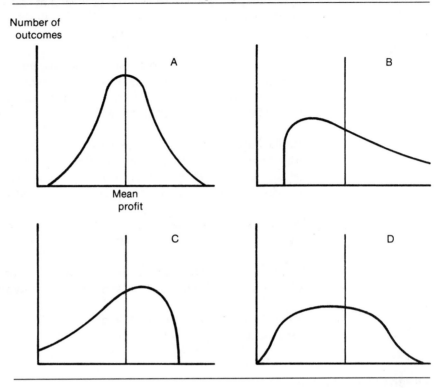

Number of
outcomes

A

B

Mean
profit

C

D

Sensitivity Testing.   Sensitivity testing is a key part of many firms' financial analyses, for good reason. For example, a common contingency relates to price, where, say, $10 is used in the analysis but the developers fear a given competitor will force that price down to $8. After the analysis has been completed using original data, the analyst goes back and recalculates the profit using $8 as the price. Scores of possible scenarios can be anticipated and their effects calculated easily, particularly if the analysis is set up on a spreadsheet, as it should be. A 1982 study showed that 93 percent of firms said they did these "what-if" analyses.[1]

Elements of Strategy.   Each firm's new products strategy, embodied in its product innovation charter, calls for certain types of products. For good reason, some of these products may in themselves be unprofitable; so, when evaluating subsequent new product proposals, it is important

---

[1] The full study is reported in Richard Klein, "Computer-Based Financial Modeling," *Journal of Systems Management,* May 1982, pp. 10–17.

to remember the strategy that prompted them. A leading example is diversification, and another is the provision of short-term assistance on a particular problem (such as cash). Less profitable products may well be warranted under such circumstances.

Basic Sales and Cost Forecasts.   The primary data inputs to the calculation go here. Managers need to know the number of units to be sold, the direct production cost per unit, and the total marketing expenditures. Sales forecasting will be discussed further in a minute.

Hurdle Rates.   A company sometimes has hurdle rates on variables other than rate of return. For example, some firms say they won't even get into a new venture unless they can have at least a 50 percent gross margin after direct production costs. Others may use such hurdles as "no years with a negative cash flow" or "payback in less than three years." Figure 14–5 shows how some common hurdles can also vary by the proposed product's strategic purpose.

Mandatory Contingencies.   A firm may want one or more contingencies worked into the analysis every time, not left optional.

Other Special Assumptions or Guidelines.   This is the typical miscellaneous section, totally situational.

Other Considerations

Summary Form.   Figure 14–6 shows a summary form that can be used for communication both among team members and with higher

---

FIGURE 14–5   Hurdle Rates on Return and Other Measures

		Hurdle Rates		
Product	*Strategic Role or Purpose*	*Sales*	*Return on Investment*	*Market Share Increase*
A	Combat competitive entry	$3,000,000	15%	None needed
B	Establish foothold in new market	$2,000,000	17%	15 Points
C	Capitalize on existing markets	$1,000,000	12%	1 Point

FIGURE 14–6 Financial Analysis Summary Form

Product Proposal:_____   Date:_____
Applicable financial criteria: Division hurdle rates
   Net present value: $_____ $10,000
   Internal rate of return: _____ %   45%
   Payback: _____ years   1.5 years
Comments:
   Explanations of above figures, if needed:

   Re key difficulties or unknowns in this development:

   Re key intangible contribution from this development:

Conclusion:
   ☐Continue as planned.
   ☐Hold for clarification on indicated matter.
   ☐Shelve for now. Reactivate if:
   ☐Abandon project, convert assets.

       Name:_____

---

management. It presents the major points without the full details of the
key data form or the worksheet, and the content varies if the firm prefers
net present value or internal rate of return.

Sunk Costs.   Occasionally, a financial manager will insist on considering
sunk costs in the analysis. Though a space may be given for them on the
worksheet, they should be excluded. Sunk moneys are just that—sunk.
They stay sunk whether we go ahead at this time or abort. Of course, if

something that was bought with sunk moneys still has market value, then this should be treated under section 10 of the key data form, Future Costs/Revenues of Abandonment. And, if the money was a capital investment (say, a building), then it is an asset, not a sunk cost; its depreciation is included.

Salvage.   Five-year capital budgets occasionally contain an item called *salvage.* This usually pertains to some item of equipment that is not worn out or obsolete when the product dies. It can be sold. The amounts are usually small, and it is probably best to omit them because they are so difficult to predict.

Portfolio.   Nowhere on the worksheet is anything mentioned about a portfolio of new product projects. Several times in this book, however, we have referred to portfolios. A firm doesn't want all high-risk or all low-risk projects. It wants some of each, in balance with its financial situation. There is no easy way to put this into the worksheet, but note that even a high-return project may be turned down (or, at least, put on hold) if the portfolio already has too many of this type.[2]

Simplified Version

Most of the steps in the preceding method for analyzing new products are quite routine and traditional. The worksheet takes the form of the traditional income statement or profit-and-loss (P&L) statement. It starts with sales and ends with profit. But, simplifying things further is easy to do. Starting with the worksheet (Figure 14–2), a new products manager can eliminate the following items, in the order listed:

- Internal rate of return and payback (lines 38 and 39).
- Discounted cash flows and net present value (lines 36 and 37).
- Future investments (lines 31 through 35).
- Tax effect (lines 23 through 27).
- Cash flow calculation (lines 28 through 30).
- Other expenses/incomes (lines 14 through 20).
- Overheads (lines 10 through 13).

This leaves unit sales, dollar sales, production costs, and direct marketing costs, resulting in a statement of dollar contribution from the new product.

---

[2] For further information on how the portfolio Beta concept can be applied to new products, see Samuel Rabino and Arnold Wright, "Financial Evaluation of the Product Line," *Journal of Product Innovation Management,* March 1985, pp. 56–65.

Sales Forecasting

As indicated earlier, managers worry about potential sales very early in the product innovation process, starting with the product innovation charter. For example, a large industrial conglomerate in the Midwest will not take on a new product that is not a close line extension unless the item promises annual sales of over $200 million. Getting into a new line of business is expensive.

Likewise, early market analysis measured the sales potential for a new product. Concept testing asked questions about probable purchasing. So did product use testing. Probable sales volume has never been far from managers' minds.

But, by the time a concept has worked its way down to market testing, sales forecasting has become serious indeed. Essentially three different approaches may be used, as shown in Figure 14–7. The right-hand

FIGURE 14–7 Structure of New Product Sales Forecasting Alternatives

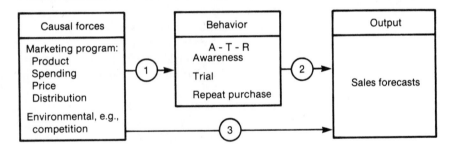

Forecasting modes

1 Forecasting behavior from causal forces:

    A. Averages for past new products.
        1. Judgment of executives.
        2. Statistical norms/models.
    B. Special for this product.
        1. Judgment of executives or sales force.
        2. Attitudes and purchase intention surveys.
        3. Panel in pretest market.
        4. Panel in test market.

2 Forecasting sales from behavior:

    A. Direct relationship (projections).
    B. Equations breaking down A - T - R (models).

3 Forecasting sales from causal forces:

    A. Judgment by executives, sales force, or users.
    B. Model based on past products.

column shows the forecasts, or outputs of the forecasting system. The middle column states the key variables determining how much will be sold. These behavior variables include at least awareness, trial, and repeat. (Recall Chapter 12's discussion of the A–T–R model.) Potential customers go through the A–T–R sequence and, managers hope, complete their journey by demonstrating post-use enthusiasm about the new item. Sales will follow, barring such inhibiting factors as poor distribution or a competitive giveaway.

The left-hand column contains the two sets of factors that determine how many potential customers work their way through the A–T–R sequence and the speed with which they do so. The factors are used in two ways. We can use the left-hand column to predict the A–T–R and then use that to predict sales. Or, we can go directly from the left-hand factors to a sales prediction.

Most of the forecasting modes in Figure 14–7 are self-explanatory, but a few deserve added comment.

Statistical Norms for Behavior from Causal Forces.
In Chapter 12, we talked about how experienced sales managers can usually look at a planned marketing effort and tell us how much distribution we're going to get, how much awareness, and so on. But market research directors also can pull out data from past introductions, showing, for example, that "Whenever we market a general usage software item, we get at least 40 percent trial based on our strong market franchise."

Attitudes and Panels.
Again, think back to concept testing and product use testing. The top-two-boxes question comes in here. If 70 percent of the testers said they would definitely or probably purchase the item, this response can be calibrated from experience into a forecast of, say, 50 percent trial. If buyers are asked to rank our new product along with the market leaders, average rankings of product preference can be calculated. The forecasted market shares can be made equal to the percentage preferences ranking. It's shaky but sometimes done.

Models Based on Past Products.
The A–T–R model that we used when studying market testing (Chapters 12 and 13) was very simple, but it was only a model. Given the data, it can be used to construct a sales forecast (or a profit forecast). Market research scientists long ago pushed the early, simple models into far more powerful forecasting devices.

Here's how. Each factor in the A–T–R model can be taken as a *dependent variable* and a secondary equation constructed for it. For example, *trial* may result from (1) degree of unmet need in the market, (2) economic well-being of the potential users, (3) their risk-taking attitudes, (4) intensity with which competitors are expected to attack our new offering, and (5) ease of purchase. Given all those, we can use the equation to calculate a figure for trial.

Then, going one step further, we can put each independent variable as dependent variables in their own equations. For *ease of purchase* as a *dependent* variable, independent variables could include *(a)* product availability in the marketplace, *(b)* the general price level of this product type, and *(c)* the frequency with which the potential user is in the marketplace where such products are sold.

All of this makes for sophisticated models, but these models (given the data) make good sales forecasts. They are used almost entirely on consumer packaged goods, where firms have lots of new product experience on which to develop the model's parameters and to calibrate the raw percentages they get from consumers. And, they are mainly used early in the process, where real market data are scarce. The chief research tool is simulated test marketing, a pseudo sale method of market testing discussed in Chapter 12, but the models can work with data from other sources as well, even assumptions.

Model makers are rapidly accumulating experience and sharpening their models, which are now readily available to consumer packaged goods innovators, quite inexpensive compared to test markets and roll-outs, and allow diagnostic output as well as sensitivity testing.

Unfortunately, they also require massive amounts of data to work best, are built heavily on assumptions, and are so complex that many managers are wary of them. They are now a mature industry, but a large and profitable one.

It is interesting that the most successful firm by far uses the simplest methodology and requires the least data. In BASES II, Burke staffers combine a concept test and a product use test, calibrate the trial and repeat percentages from their massive files of past studies, and use a set of experience-honed heuristics (rules of thumb) to translate those percentages into market share.

But, product innovators outside of consumer packaged goods still most often use the simple version of the A–T–R model in Chapter 12, if they use any forecasting model at all.

SPECIAL VIEWS

Having covered the traditional methods of financial analysis for new products, from simplified versions to advanced mathematical models, we now come face to face with a very dissatisfied user group. Managements are not at all pleased with the general state of product innovation in most of their firms.

Their criticism is beginning to mount and have effect. Essentially, it goes something like this:

> We have to have more innovation to remain competitive at home and in global markets. But traditional accounting dampens innovation. Its methods

overlook several variables (such as worker attitude and customer happiness) that actually are key to how well we do, and they are too easy to manipulate by persons in the firm who are opposed to this innovation or that innovation. The consequence is that new products people are too often making the wrong decision. We must find better ways to make our financial analyses if we are to win our quest for faster and better product innovation.

Currently, the leading innovations in accounting are being made in the manufacturing area (where managements are also dissatisfied), but what they learn applies directly to the product area.[3] Action is taking place on four fronts, as applied to new products. We cannot say what difference these actions will ultimately make, but traditional financial analysis will probably never be the same again. Here are the four fronts:

The Strong Leader

If we have a strong, dedicated, and capable leader, that person will force the necessary action, even over the opposition of accounting data. These highly motivated people will not accept rejection. We hear over and over about the importance of the new product champion, and many firms go so far as to require a champion for a project to be activated—a volunteer champion, not someone appointed champion.

The Use of Predictors

Instead of judging the estimated output of a given program (the profit, or net present value) this argument says we should judge the input. Judge the people doing the work, the market opportunity, the company's skills in the selected area. These predictors of success are key ideas in the product innovation charter. One manager recently put it this way, "If there is a good trout stream with lots of trout in it, and a good angler with good equipment, we don't need an accountant to tell us how many fish we will catch. Just go ahead, whatever happens will be good, and who cares exactly how good?"

Put Risk back into the Game

Some top managers believe we have analyzed everything to the point where no risk remains. And we have motivated our key functional heads

---

[3] For the manufacturing view on needed changes in accounting, see "The Productivity Paradox," *Business Week*, June 6, 1988, pp. 100–14.

to avoid taking any chance that could ruin their careers or seriously hurt the firm. A famous defense department criticism was "paralysis by analysis." These managers urge going back to the essentials of product innovation. What makes for successful new products? Dissatisfied customers? Acceptable field trials? Supportive distributors? Effective advertising?

Name the essentials, and then concentrate on their analysis. Don't let extraneous items into the calculations.

Other ways mentioned as devices for putting risk back into the game include isolating or neutralizing the in-house critics (a strong reason for setting up project matrixes and spin-outs). Get away from people who have an inherent conflict of interest with the particular new product.

Another device is to depend on the customer, even if it looks like we might lose some money on the project. Manufacturing people find that making a product the way customers want it brings profit, even if not at the very start. Buyers like to deal with firms who understand what the buyers' firms need to prosper. And, salespeople are highly motivated when they have such products to sell.

Another approach defers financial analysis until later in the development process. One firm realized it was consistently killing off good new product ideas by demanding precise financial analyses at the time of screening. It didn't have the data. A variation uses more roll-outs (see Chapter 13). If a financial analysis looks weak, but the idea seems sound, try it out on a limited scale to see where the solution might lie. Or, as one president said, give us the volume and we'll find a way to squeeze a good profit out of it. This thinking violates several popular management theories, but it may be necessary at times.

New Accounting Methods

Manufacturing managers complain about cost accountants' common practice of allocating factory overheads to various products on the basis of the labor-hours in them. But labor today only makes up 8 to 12 percent of product cost. Time is the biggest cost factor in manufacturing today, and accounting is not well equipped to deal with this. New products people are interested in the argument and are trying to find new methods for their items as well.

Threshold.   One approach says the actual profits from a new product are not as critical as whether there will be any profits at all. If sales are high enough and expenses low enough, we will enter the profitable zone—the *threshold of profitability* will be passed. From there on, only time will tell how far we go, given market unknowns.

Creatively Attack the NPV.   This approach takes net present value as a starting point rather than an ending point. Undertake an intense search for ways to shave costs and boost volumes.

Avoid Unnecessary Hurdles.   No matter how well intentioned, many hurdles are deadly roadblocks for the product innovator. The furniture division of a large firm was about to go under. Its last-ditch effort, a new chair, was being brought along; but at the last minute, financial analysis showed only a 48 percent gross margin. Corporate policy demanded 50 percent. Several hours of negotiation failed to break the hurdle. The chair was abandoned, and within six months, the division was folded and its assets sold. We're not saying the division should not have been folded. But perhaps the circumstances called for more risk, which the hurdle had been established to avoid.

Put the Intangibles into the Analysis.   What is a new customer franchise worth? What is the effect on a firm's image of a new product that customers want and need? What is the value of the motivation that comes from having customers actually ask to see our salespeople? How much is worker pride worth?

   Granted, these intangibles are difficult to work into standard financial analysis. Some people add a line to the worksheet entitled Indirect Benefits. Another person proposed a "strategic discount," a percentage used to *lower* the required rate of return, reflecting values that cannot appear in the regular analyses.[4] Whatever the method, it is probably worth trying, especially because intangible benefits are sometimes the primary purpose of the innovation.

SUMMARY

This chapter presented a method for making a financial analysis of a proposed product launch. We began with a key data form, which collects the relevant statistics, policies, and guidelines needed to complete a financial analysis. The top of the worksheet begins with sales, so we looked carefully at ways to make sales forecasts. They vary from the simple judgments all managers make to the somewhat systematic A–T–R calculation and then to the full, complex mathematical models used in some firms today. The models are the same ones cited in Chapters 12 and 13 as used by research companies selling the simulated test marketing service and others selling scanner markets testing. Much of

---

   [4] Gordon Pearson, "The Strategic Discount — Protecting New Business Projects against DCF," *Long-Range Planning* 1, 1986, pp. 18–24.

the development effort for this forecasting technology is done by such firms.

The sales forecasts can next be added to the other data on the key data form, after which calculation on the financial worksheet can be done. This latter calculation is rather straightforward, income statement work tempered by capital budgeting steps near the bottom of the sheet.

We discussed each section of the key data form, including the difficult matter of how best to derive an appropriate required rate of return. We also looked at the hurdle rate and the threshold concept as well as at some nonfinancial (and at times highly relevant) aspects of the process.

Last, we took a look at current managerial concerns about financial analysis in general, as it influences innovation. Many people in business are currently trying to find ways to reconcile financial analysis with the many dimensions of new product innovation that such analysis does not cover. Some of these ways were discussed.

This completes the evaluation process, except, of course, for the ongoing evaluation during the post-launch tracking phase (see Chapter 18) and a final, overall evaluation by higher management looking back from sometime down the road.

If an evaluation after market testing is positive, the firm can then commit to full commercialization and undertake actual production and marketing. This takes us into Part IV, where we will look at the overall control task, various aspects of marketing planning peculiar to new products, and the launch control process.

APPLICATIONS

1. "Lately, I have become very frustrated when evaluating division proposals for new product funding. The proposals have come in all kinds of formats, with different data, and so on. So, I had my finance staff develop the ideal figure and format for this purpose—it's very similar to the one you showed me earlier from your textbook. But I also asked that it be probabilistically determined and include all direct and indirect costs and benefits. That way, I get to see the entire picture before we grant them any major investment or marketing funds. I hope you support my thinking on this."

2. "One thing I know for certain—I don't want any sales managers or technical research people making new product forecasts. I've never seen such lousy forecasting as we get from these people. Sales managers either love a new item so much they think it will outsell everyone, or they think it is a dud and underforecast equally badly. Absolutely no objectivity in them. And the technical people, well, they become so enamored with their inventions that they lose all objectivity too. What I like is forecasting done by independent

people—project managers or new products managers in separate departments. Have you run into any good ways of keeping sales managers and technical researchers out of forecasting? You agree that they should be excluded, don't you?"

3. "I was talking just the other day about our most recent acquisition—a chain of four large general hospitals on the West Coast. These are private hospitals, and we fully intend them to be profitable, but it is a service, I guess, and there are some public service overtones in the deal, whether we want them there or not. My concern, as we talk about evaluating new products, is how would this new division go about evaluating new service proposals? The same as our product division? If so, which product division would be the best model?"

4. "At a party about a month ago, our host reminded me of a classic flop—the Frost 8/80 whiskey that Brown-Foreman marketed in the early 1970s. The company had noted a strong trend to lighter alcoholic beverages—vodka, Scotch, and Canadian. So it did a combined telephone and mail concept test of some 2,400 people, and the research showed clearly that people strongly favored a whiskey that would have a mild whiskey flavor but would be dry and white. Clear. So the company developed one—a whiskey that was as clear as vodka. It also ran consumer tests to see if the name was communicating, and it was. The packaging was also tested. Then, it put out an intensive marketing program—including $2 million of first-year advertising. But, guess what? The new whiskey laid a complete egg. Had to come off the market and never did make a penny. I know you don't know much, if anything, about this case, but I wonder if you could see any reasons why this outcome took place, given the research the company did."

Case: Bay City Electronics

Financial analysis of new products at Bay City Electronics had always been rather informal. Bill Roberts, who founded the firm in 1970, knew residential electronics because he had worked for almost seven years for another firm specializing in home security systems. But, he had never been trained in financial analysis. In fact, all he knew was what the bank had asked for every time he went to discuss his loan and line of credit.

Bay City had about 45 full-time employees (plus a seasonal factory work force) and did in the neighborhood of $18 million in sales. His products all related to home security and were sold by his sales manager, who worked with a group of manufacturers' reps, who in turn called on hardware and department store wholesalers and larger retailers. He did some consumer advertising, but not much.

Bill was inventive, however, and had built the business primarily by coming up with new techniques. His latest device was a remote-controlled electronic closure for any door in the home. The closure was effected by a special ringing of the telephone: for example, if a user wanted to leave a back door open until 9:00 P.M. it was simple to call the house at 9:00 and wait for 10 rings, after which the electronic device would switch the door to a locked position. A similar call would reopen the door.

The bank liked the idea but wanted Bill to do a better job of financial analysis, so the loan officer asked him to use the forms shown in Figures 14–1 and 14–2 of this text. After some effort, Bill was able to fill out the key data form, as shown early in Chapter 14. But his task now was to do the analysis required in the financial worksheet. Interpreting the results would also be difficult because he had no background on hurdle rates, and so on, but he figured he could draw some conclusions.

To date, Bay City had spent $85,000 in expense money for supplies and labor developing the closure and had invested $15,000 in a machine (asset). If the company decided to go ahead, it would have to invest $50,000 more in a new facility, continue R&D to validate and improve the product, and — if things went according to expectations — invest another $45,000 in year 3 to expand production capability.

Part IV

Commercialization

Chapter 15

Control and Launch Cycle

SETTING

Somewhere during the preceding process of evaluation, a decision is made to develop and market the concept being considered. It may have come early in the process or at the very last minute. Management focus now changes from analysis to operations. There will still be opportunities to abort the project, and there are usually people around the shop who think it should be aborted. But the thrust now is upbeat, positive commitment. Marketing and production are in the limelight.

The new phase, called *commercialization,* sees people actually buying machinery rather than estimating its cost, finalizing sales call schedules, registering brands, locking in R&D specifications, and spending money. There are more and more people involved, coordination meetings, massive information accumulation, greatly elevated risks and tempers, euphorias and disappointments, security problems, politics, and a far too attentive top management. Panic has set in, and it will not cease for some time.

The commercialization process has been called the graveyard of product innovation — not because new products die here but because real innovation often dies here. The product concept that seemed so feasible in the beginning now is tarnished and fraught with pressure to compromise. Compromises almost always favor established technology, not high risk.

Time, not technology, is the enemy of innovation, partly because managements are impatient but mainly because time costs money. Consequently:

- Products fall far short of their glowing beginning.
- They are invariably late.
- They inevitably cost more than anticipated.

A creative activity that is more art form than science needs order, and business responds with managerial control. Control and its partner — the launch cycle — are the subjects of this chapter. They will be followed by two chapters dealing with aspects of marketing planning peculiar to new products. The last chapter in Part IV addresses control during the post-launch period.

THE CONCEPT OF MANAGERIAL CONTROL

The essence of managerial control has four parts:

1. Statement of what an activity should accomplish — results, output, goals. (What should be.)
2. Information gathered on progress against this plan. (What is.)
3. Prediction of the operation's ability to meet its objectives, given where we are now. (What will be.)
4. Action to correct the deviation if deemed serious — and if action can be taken. (What to do.)

Figure 15–1 offers an example of managerial control relative to wholesale or retail distribution. The plan includes a plan line, an actual line based on spot checks of distribution after 2 and 4 weeks, a prediction that after 10 weeks we will be well below plan, and a new plan with remedial action. If the analysis is correct and if the action is taken soon enough, it will solve what was about to be a problem.

That's what control is all about — keeping an activity on target and seeing that we get where we want to go. Good managerial control avoids problems. An excellent analogue is space management: the space controllers in Houston don't want to learn later that a flight missed its target planet. They want to know quickly that it is off track while there is still time to get it back on.

The Requirements of Control

A new products manager must be able to do those four things — plan, measure progress, predict, and act. They are more difficult for new products than for ongoing operations. For example, we often don't even know for sure what our planning targets should be: How much distribution is needed, how much awareness, what level of product performance?

Measuring progress entails the usual high costs of marketing research, of course, but excruciating internal problems are also present. How close is engineering to finishing that base plate revision? How far along is legal on getting the trademark registered? If some production people didn't want to do the project in the first place, can they be trusted to give accurate feedback on where they stand today?

FIGURE 15–1   Basic Control Plan for Retail Distribution

Verbal format:
   Retail stocking of the new product is to start at zero, advance to 50 percent of all-commodity volume (A. C. Nielsen) by week 4, and level out at 80 percent by week 10.

Graphic format:

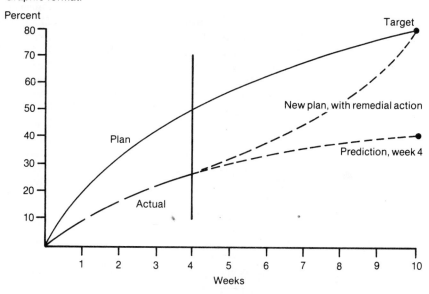

Making predictions in this milieu is even worse. If we can't be sure where we are today, how can we decide when we will be finished? And the problem doesn't concern just the product itself. Figure 15–2 lists things needed for launch of a soft drink in Canada, every one of which could have gone wrong!

Interim measurement and prediction may well be the worst aspects of the job. New product managers must be master network builders and human relations magicians.

Planning and Reporting Systems Used

Five devices are commonly used to help a new products manager keep the situation under "control." The first is a simple *checklist,* which is much like a shopping list. It comes directly from an item list such as the one in Figure 15–2.

The second device is a *milestone events system,* a piece of which is given in Figure 15–3. It can run as long as 50 pages, and it grows

---

FIGURE 15–2   New Product Output List for a Canadian Soft Drink

---

The soft drink itself	Returnable bottles
Gaily striped carton	Sales training movie
Outline of marketing program	Selling instructions
Specially painted trucks	Tailgate announcement banners
In-store POP banners	Mother-daughter display cutout
Motorized trylon	Salesperson uniform crest
"Facts" carton stuffer	Medical/dental letter
Medical/dental ads	Sample coupon—medical/dental
Sample carton—medical/dental	Retail stuffers
Chain buyer flip chart	Free case racks
Co-op ad schedules	One-page fact sheet
Fifty-case display	Two-color ad
Media merchandising folder	Black-and-white ad
Radio spot	TV spot
Outdoor painted boards	Supplement insertions
Dirigible balloon	Market survey
Cooler and door decals	Vending machine ad strips
CARE PR release	Counter CARE card
Piggyback carrier	Kiwanis PR plan
Half-price carton stuffers	Roll-out pallet
Exhibition booth	Bottle cap cash numbers
Bath scale displays	Bath scales
Christmas wreath	Bottle hanger tags
Christmas ads	Throwaway bottles

---

until it breaks down and forces another system. Note the names and dates on the milestone chart: the system offers some accountability, although the charts often start more arguments than they settle.

Third is a very traditional method of project control—the *bar charts* or *Gantt charts*. Each output piece from the milestone chart in Figure 15–3 is given a time line, and then a horizontal bar is drawn to cover the activity time from start to finish. The bar is broken into sections to indicate accountability.

Fourth is *network control,* which is the ideal control approach depicted in Figure 15–4. That figure shows a critical path network listing each job that needs to be done, who is to do it, when it is to be done, and, most important, what jobs had to come before it could begin and what jobs are waiting for it to finish. The name *critical path* comes from finding which path through the network will take the longest time—the critical one that actually sets the total time of the job. A computer-based system called *PERT* (Program Evaluation Review Technique) is a type of network control used for the most complex developments (such as

FIGURE 15–3 Selection from Milestone Events Chart

Code Name: Zippits

Page 2 of 13 pages

No.	Step name	Responsibility of	Scheduled date	Revised date	Actual date
11	Package labels delivered	Mesell	8–3		
Package inserts					
12	Finished art ordered	Tosape	6–22		
13	Finished art received	Tosape	6–30		
14	Requisition and finished art to Purchasing	Neff	7–1		
15	Package inserts delivered	Mesell	8–3		
Blister-Pack sample					
16	Packaging specifications issued	Tonebar	6–10		
17	Visual design layout approved	Bewal	7–1		
18	Finished art ordered	Tosape	7–2		
19	Photostats received	Tosape	7–10		
20	Photostats approved with revisions	Bewal	7–13		
21	Finished art to Production Control	Tosape	7–15		
22	Requisition and finished art to Purchasing	Neff	7–16		
23	Pilot plant scale-up completed	Lane	7–17		
24	Production of initial quantities completed	Jacobs	9–16		
25	Samples of initial quantities received in Control Lab	Jacobs	9–21		
26	Initial quantities released by Control Lab	McCrary	9–24		

FIGURE 15–4 A Time-Based Critical Path Network for New Products

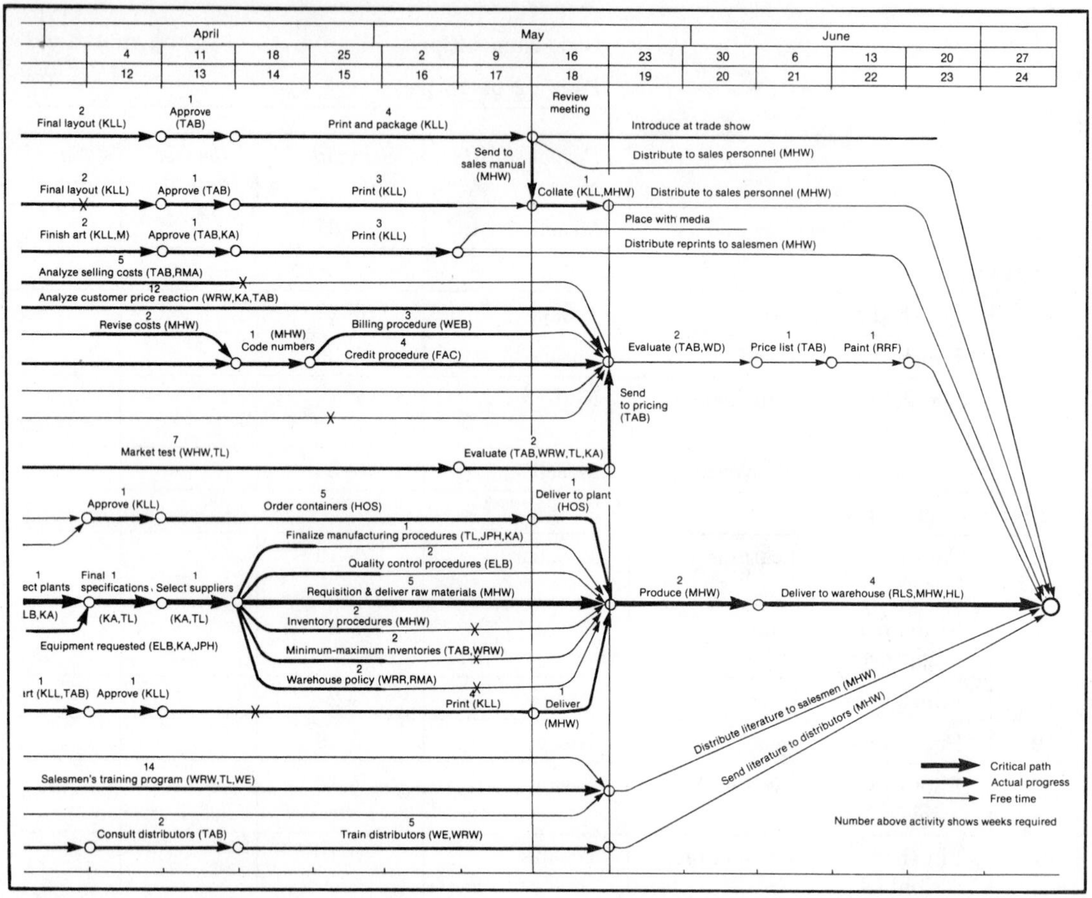

Source: Warren Dusenbury, "CPM for New Product Introductions," *Harvard Business Review*, July–August 1967, p. 130. Reprinted by permission of the *Harvard Business Review*. Copyright © 1967 by the President and Fellows of Harvard College; all rights reserved.

automobiles and military systems), but few product managers face such situations.

The complexity of these systems shows why experienced new products managers rely on eyeball control: they are constantly on the go, they visit every area of the firm every day if possible, they gather their own information, and they become expert enough to sense what is OK and what isn't. They believe the old adage that the best fertilizer in the garden is the footprint of the gardener, and a product manager who depends on complex control charts will soon lose "control."

A fifth device is a monthly reporting form. Figure 15–5 shows a typical one. Note the reporting form contains all four of the managerial control requirements: plan, actual, prediction, and action. In the typical approach, someone on staff prepares these summary forms monthly, and then a meeting is held to discuss the variances. If management really has

FIGURE 15–5 Project Control Form

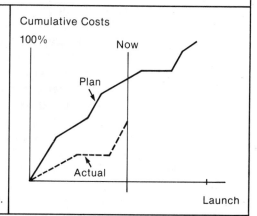

Monthly Project Control Report November 15, 1990

PROJECT: Mongoose. Retail store operations guide. Joint development with Osgood Department Stores. Jenkins is project manager. Development budget = $840,000. Scheduled launch date is May 10, 1991.

☐ Project development on schedule.

☐ Cost development on schedule.

☒ Labor force OK.

The Problem:

Particleboard strike delayed deliveries. Osgood notified and has accepted temporary revision in schedule. Strike now settled, and priority shipments will make up time. Milestone 4 will be on schedule.

Cumulative Costs

100% Now

Plan

Actual

Launch

Milestones:

1. Osgood store management division approves base design.

2. Design converted into procurement formats.

3. Construction materials in hand.

4. Test system installed in Richmond store.

5. Test system accepted by Osgood management.

6. Begin selling to roll-out markets.

control (that is, problems anticipated and remedial actions already planned), then there is little to talk about at these meetings. Otherwise, they can go on for hours.

Inherent Problems

Don't assume managerial control works smoothly. Too many things in a new product's development are simply not known. They can't be timed or estimated. For example, *breakthrough* activities — someone, a scientist perhaps, is trying to find a way to do something never done before — cannot be put on a critical path schedule because they cannot be timed. The work will be done when it is done and not before. This results in the complaint often heard about automotive engineers: "Engineering never releases anything — you have to take it from them!" Japanese manufacturers (such as Honda, Matsushita, and Casio) solve this problem by (1) determining what their customers want, (2) designing that product, and (3) prohibiting further major changes. Late ideas are included in the next product generation.

Change is the second enemy of control. Absolutely nothing stands still during development. A federal regulator changes a standard, a competitor introduces a new product, a supplier comes up with a new material, accounting revises the long-standing product cost estimates, a new division general manager is hired, and so on. One new products manager was recently asked whether his firm used critical path scheduling. He said, "We tried, but the data processing fellow was still trying to get things tied down enough to run off the first network print when we went to market."

Communication is another problem. It is unreasonable to expect people to report negatively on themselves. People in new product work, after all, are like people everywhere: some are incompetent, some are afraid, some are selfish. These traits are sand in the gears of managerial control. But, good new products managers pull it if off somehow. That's what their job is really all about.

THE LAUNCH CYCLE

What we call the *launch cycle* runs from the commercialization decision until the new item is well enough established that it will hold on and grow. How the launch cycle compares to the product life cycle is shown in Figure 15–6. The entire launch cycle includes a short time just prior to launch and continues part way through the growth phase. It contains four phases: pre-launch preparation, announcement, beachhead, and early growth.

FIGURE 15–6 The Launch Cycle

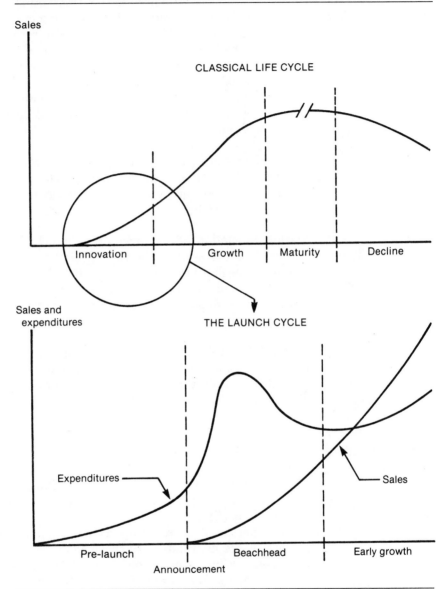

Pre-Launch Preparation

The preparation phase of the launch cycle includes the activities preceding the new product announcement and, as the name suggests, is designed to make that announcement effective. The activities are of four types.

Building Marketing Capability. A new product that is strictly a line extension will have little need for new marketing capabilities. Another product may require a totally new marketing organization.

The sales force is the biggest problem in this regard. A new advertising agency can be hired at a minimum up-front cost, but a complete and functioning sales force isn't just "started," nor can an existing sales force be casually redirected.

But whether the sales force is new, temporary, or regular, special training and motivation are customary. Just as the production head had to plan and build the proper facilities, so must the marketing head.

Service Capability. A second type of preparation involves building a network for presale or postsale service. The network must comprise locations, facilities, equipment, parts, and personnel, all well ahead of the time they are needed.

Presale Promotion. Sometimes, the launch of a new product is shrouded in such secrecy that the market has little or no knowledge of it prior to the first press conference. This often holds true for launches of nonpatented or loosely patented technological advances. Often, however, firms find major opportunities for preannouncement or presale promotional activities.[1]

Stocking/Availability. The last type of preparation entails making the new item available where and when the customers will want it. Good distribution fulfills the demand created by promotion and publicity and also helps encourage promotion.

Announcement

The second phase of the launch cycle — unveiling the new item for public inspection — although usually brief, is also distinct, critical, and managerially demanding.

Many parties have a stake in the announcement — stockholders, potential users, distributors, financial analysts, employees, competitors, regulators, the media, and so on. Polaroid, for example, usually stages its announcements quite dramatically. Polio vaccine was announced in a special midmorning national TV program. Car companies spend millions of dollars on the effort.

---

[1] See Jehoshua Eliasberg and Thomas S. Robertson, "New Product Preannouncing Behavior: A Market Signaling Study," *Journal of Marketing Research,* August 1988, pp. 282–92.

Public relations departments are usually involved in the planning. The setting can be TV, print media, a trade show, a sales force meeting, or a press conference, and it may well be all of those.

Beachhead

Announcement gives way rather promptly to the next phase—beachhead. The expression "get the ball rolling" describes a new product launch. Marketers also talk of priming the pump, getting a fire started, getting off the ground. In each situation, a standstill is followed by movement in a manner similar to that of a kite pulled into the wind, a descending bobsled, or a military invasion force expanding from a small strip of shoreline.

The new products novice almost invariably focuses on announcement as the culmination of the entire new product development process, which it clearly is not.

What Is to Happen?   The objective of the beachhead phase is to trigger trial and repeat purchase. Only repurchase provides the momentum needed to make the expenditure levels profitable.

What Is the Activity Here?   During beachhead, the original position statements, claims, and so on are repeated and reinforced. Within the mix of ads and sales calls, a subtle change in emphasis occurs as initial announcement gives way to "reason why" and then to the rationale of trial and the reinforcement of successful experience.

This shift is probably imperceptible to the target consumer, however, because such a flurry of activity takes place in this intense postannouncement period.

Other activities during this phase include technical efforts to solve the product problems that usually appear, efforts to reduce costs, and efforts to iron out glitches in shipping or service.

How Long Does Beachhead Last?   A New York play can take six months to develop and then close after one or two nights on Broadway. This brief beachhead is certainly not typical of new products, but it does set the minimum time frame. In contrast, General Foods held Maxim in roll-out for two years before enough repurchase was found to support a seminational extension. Microwave ovens, frozen orange juice, instant coffee, and coffee creamers were also very slow to get started.

A true cancer cure would probably catapult from preannouncement publicity directly to full-scale growth. Fortunately, new products managers can usually predict how long beachhead will last. Some experienced consumer product firms can narrow their timetables to just 8 or 10 weeks.

What Decisions Are Made?   The key decision in this phase is to end it — inertia has been overcome, the product has "started to move." This decision triggers a series of actions. Improvements and flankers will now be brought along as scheduled; new budgets will be approved and released; temporary marketing arrangements will be made permanent (such as a temporary sales force, an advertising agency, or a direct-mail arrangement).

One new products manager said he knew this decision had been made when the firm's president stopped calling him every couple of days for the "latest news."

Growth

Beachhead is followed by the growth phase. We will not speak to the problems and activities of the later growth stages (maturity, decline, and demise). These are clearly problems and activities of ongoing products management and, although very demanding, not in the domain of the new products manager.

User Actions.   The users who successfully concluded trial and repurchase during the beachhead phase are now beginning to spread the word about the product and are incorporating the product into their routine activities. They will attempt applications not envisioned by the marketer.

Competitive Actions.   Competitive actions typically fall into two categories. First are the adapters — firms that alter the product in a significant way — and the extenders — firms that find a new use or user segment to which they position their rather similar product. These competitors are the most beneficial because they contribute to market expansion.

Second are the price entries — imitators or simplifiers. These firms have a manufacturing advantage or perhaps an established contact in the price segment of the market (such as agreements with mass merchandisers to make private brands).

Company Strategies.   The firm introducing a new-to-the-world product will continue to press for new primary demand (demand for the generic category) well into the growth phase, just as it did during the beachhead phase. But it will gradually add promotion designed to pick up selective demand (market share).

Firms also add new segments during the growth phase—lower income levels, new psychological dimensions, and so on. Firms often must add channels and make product alterations or additions to reach these segments, just as adapters and extenders do.

Another strategy of the growth phase is product quality improvement. Although efforts were made to find product flaws as early in the beachhead phase as possible, most improvements will not actually become available until the growth phase.

Simultaneously, technical and manufacturing people will be trying to take cost out of the product. The pressure on cost margins stems from the pressure on prices certain to come later in the growth phase or early in maturity.

Pattern of Growth. Each new product evolves into growth by its own pattern, and no one can predict what that pattern will be at the time of launch. In fact, some of the newer thinking in product life-cycle theory has suggested abandoning the fixed product life-cycle concept in favor of an *evolutionary* approach to product growth.

Although the idea of a fixed and predictable life cycle comes from nature and applies to individual organisms like particular animals or trees, it does not apply to *species*. Biologists use the theory of evolution to analyze species, noting that although the individual deer lives and dies predictably, the deer herd prospers or suffers according to unpredictable environmental changes and the herd's ability to make adjustments (such as moving) to soften the effects of those changes. It is now suspected that the evolutionary theory more nearly meets the needs of product analysts than does the fixed life–death theory because the product marketer has such options as product change (genetic mutations in the deer herd) and new segmentation (relocating the herd).[2]

Variations in the Above Phases

No two firms go through the above phases the same way, and we should note what causes the differences.

Degree of Learning Required. The degree to which a new product requires a user to make substantial changes in that product's use will affect the speed with which the product will be accepted. The more changes, the slower the adoption.

---

[2] For a full discussion of this different view, see Gerard J. Tellis and C. Merle Crawford, "An Evolutionary Approach to Product Growth Theory," *Journal of Marketing*, Fall 1981, pp. 125–32.

Several learning requirements are involved. First is variations in physical use—not how the product works, but how the body works. The Frisbee is a classic case, but more recent examples include the lap computer and the fax machine.

Closely allied is the second requirement, a change in how the product works. No-suds detergents were perhaps the classic here—without suds, how could the detergent clean? Other early products that had problems were the "silent" kitchen mixer, pleasant-tasting mouth wash, and colorless iodine. Similar problems have beset the cellular phone, because some people don't trust the openness of the transmission.

The third requirement is a change in role, where any person involved in product use perceives a lessening in their importance. A classic was instant coffee, which homemakers for years felt guilty about using because it (presumably) reduced their creative role in the kitchen. A contemporary example is computer conferencing, because many professional participants refuse to sit at a keyboard.

Fourth is negative value perception, or doubts about the value of what the product does. Body deodorants, for example, were shunned by men for years because they "didn't need them." More recently, the market has rejected the remote car starter and the microwave oven (an item that was for several years called the "most expensive coffee-warmer in town").

Last is where the new product requires change in a strong negative belief. This is much more than value perception; it is vigorous aggression against the product. Early examples include the two-piece swim suit, the birth control pill, hair spray for men, and porno videos. But the best example today would be a new device that makes abortion quick and simple.[3]

Urgency of Launch.   Another variation in the launch cycle's four phases results from management's need for either a faster or slower launch. New products managers are often in a great hurry (due to impending competitive entry or the need to establish product sale to strengthen a patent application), so they use what is called a crash or hurried launch. On the other side of a normal launch is the conditional launch, in which something is not yet clear, so launch is slowed down to allow it to be clarified (one of the learning requirements above, for example, or doubts about the firm's ability to get adequate distribution, or the sales force's need to learn about a complex new market). We may be short of money and unable to afford a full launch. Or, we may be using the roll-out method of market testing. As soon as the condition clears, we resume a normal launch.

---

[3] The subject of learning requirements is best developed in Chester R. Wasson, *Competitive Strategy and Product Life Cycles* (St. Charles, Ill.: Challenge Books, 1974).

Industrial versus Consumer. The industrial firm may market a product requiring a closer relationship between seller and buyer. So, it extends the downstream coupling that developed during concept testing and product use testing. It may have to concentrate as much on market development as on product development. Consumer products do not often require such closeness, but if they do, their launch cycle assumes similar characteristics.

Adoption and Diffusion of Innovation

Another useful concept in planning a new product's launch cycle involves the adoption and diffusion of innovation. New products are innovations, and we call the spreading of their usage *diffusion*. The adoption and diffusion of the microwave oven was slow, but it has been quite rapid for the cellular phone. For a cancer cure, it would be almost instantaneous.

Two things increase the speed of an innovation—the character of the innovation itself and the extent to which early users encourage others to follow. Let's take the innovation first.

Product Characteristics. Over the years, research has derived five factors for measuring how "adoptable" a new product is. Here they are:

The relative advantage of the new product—How superior is the innovation to the product or other problem-solving methods it was designed to compete against?

Compatibility—Does it fit with current product usage and customer activity? (See learning requirements, above.) We say it is a continuous innovation if little change is required, a discontinuous innovation if much is.

Complexity—Will difficulty or confusion arise in understanding the innovation's basic idea?

Divisibility (also called trialability)—How easily can trial portions of the product be purchased? Foods and beverages are quite divisible, but new homes and word processing systems are much less so.

Communicability (also called observability)—How likely is the product to appear in public places where it is easily seen and studied by potential users? It is high on new cars, low on items of personal hygiene.

An innovation can be scored on these five factors, using primarily personal judgment plus the findings from market testing during earlier phases of the development. Launch plans can then be laid accordingly.

The Spreading of the Word. As stated above, two factors determine the speed of a new product's adoption. The first is the nature of the innovation itself. The second is the degree to which early users actively encourage others to adopt a new product; if they do, its spread will be rapid. So, interest has focused on the *innovators* (the first 5 to 10 percent of those who adopt the product) and on the *early adopters* (the next 10 to 15 percent of adopters). The theory of innovation diffusion states that if we could just market our new product to those innovators and early adopters, we could then sit back and let them spread the word to the others. The action has been compared to the spread of ripples around the spot where a stone enters the pond.

Other categories of adopters include the *early majority* (perhaps the next 30 percent), the *late majority* (perhaps another 30 percent), and the *laggards* (the remaining 20 percent). Each group aids previous groups in encouraging others. This encouraging is not necessarily active persuasion; if one person has influence over another, mere adoption is enough. Famous people are active targets of many new product marketers, but they are a difficult group to reach.

The obvious question is "Which specific people will be the innovators and early adopters?" Can we identify them so as to focus our early marketing on them? Researchers have been trying to answer this question for many years, and their work suggests the answer depends on the product category being studied. Still, the following five traits have often emerged from the studies:

1. *Venturesomeness* — the willingness and desire to be daring in trying the new and different; "sticks his neck out"; "deviates from the group social norms."
2. *Social integration* — frequent and extensive contact with others in one's "area," whether work, neighborhood, or social life; a strong industrial counterpart.
3. *Cosmopolitanism* — point of view extending beyond the immediate neighborhood or community; interest in world affairs, travel, reading.
4. *Social mobility* — upward movement on the social scale; successful young executive or professional types.
5. *Privilegedness* — usually defined as being better off financially than others in the group. Thus the privileged person has less to lose if the innovation fails and costs money. This trait tends to reflect *attitude* toward money as much as *possession* of money.

People in the above adopter categories are identified more easily in the abstract than in the marketplace. There does not seem to be one group of innovators that will always be the early users. Early users do come typically from the innovator group, but it is impossible to predict which ones. In the industrial setting, early adopters:

1. Tend to be the largest firms in the industry (though some studies have suggested the opposite).
2. Stand to make the greatest profit from the innovation.
3. Spend more on R&D.
4. Have presidents who are younger and better educated.[4]

Caveat. The theory of diffusion of innovation is a powerful concept that should be used by every new products manager. However, it does have problems, one of which is that we are still not sure the innovators and early adopters actually influence other people. They are the first users, but marketers cannot just market to them and assume they will spread the word to the majorities and laggards. Second, many new products managers will have difficulty identifying specific persons or customer firms as innovators and early adopters ahead of the launch. However, unless such people do indeed adopt the new product early in the beachhead, the battle will be lost right there. Finding ways to entice them into trial is key to the launch strategy.[5]

SUMMARY

Our previous emphasis has been on getting and evaluating product concepts. With this chapter, we moved into the operations phase. First, we met the concept of managerial control, which states where we want to go, where we are now, where it looks like we will end up if nothing is done, and what we can do to get things back on track if they are off.

This is a tough assignment for new products; but, in one way or another, a new products manager is expected to keep in control of the development. Sometimes we can, and sometimes we can't. We looked at various scheduling and reporting formats used to accomplish control.

Next we looked at the launch cycle, which is a subset of the product life cycle. It contains four clearly different phases, each requiring different management. Firms differ, so their needs during the four phases differ too, and we looked at a number of factors causing those

---

[4] Frederick E. Webster, Jr., *Industrial Marketing Strategy* (New York: John Wiley & Sons, 1979).

[5] Still an authoritative source of thinking on the general subject of new products and the theory of innovation is David F. Midgley, *Innovation and New Product Marketing* (New York: John Wiley & Sons, 1977).

differences. The most critical factor is the degree of learning required by the intended product user.

The subject of launch cycle was closed out by showing how the diffusion of innovation affects the marketing of a new product. Unfortunately, the idea is more useful for stimulating thinking than for giving specific direction; we cannot identify change agents as clearly as the theory demands.

We can now turn to the actual marketing planning for new product introduction, the subject of the next chapter.

APPLICATIONS

1. "Product innovation in some of our divisions is so unreliable that it's almost embarrassing. I recently said to one division general manager that he had surely heard of managerial control, and I asked him why he didn't use more of it. He answered, 'Controlling our new product development is a lot like controlling a symphony orchestra.' What in the world did he mean by that?"

2. "Something another division general manager said also has me bothered. She's in the sporting goods business and is doing an above-average job, but she seems to have trouble getting her new items into the stores in time for their seasons. So, I suggested she look into the matter of control systems, but she said, 'All the fancy control charts, the CPM systems, and so forth, won't make for efficient product development unless the people involved want the system to be efficient. Give me the right people, and I won't need all those things. But give me the wrong people, and gimmicks won't make them efficient.' How would you suggest I answer her?"

3. "In my position, I get to see lots of control reports, especially the monthly reports most of the better divisions put out on new product projects. I'm always sort of intrigued by these forms because they're so simple—rarely with more than a dozen key facts on them. Now, I happen to know that hundreds of things could be reported on—so how do they choose just the 12 or so that they use?"

4. "In the material we were given at a new products conference recently, I noticed a strange chart. If I recall correctly, the chart showed that marketing planning began before the project got started. How could that be? Also, the chart showed that 'preparing the product' went on after the item was launched. I presume that was because someone wasn't doing the job right. You think maybe that chart was incorrect?"

Case: The Cyclotron Corp.

Shortly after the microwave oven began to sell at levels indicating its successful move from beachhead to growth, the Electronic Kitchens Corporation moved aggressively into the next phase of its planned new product work. It had not been first with the microwave, but it had the technology and had entered soon enough to get a respectable position in the new market.

Electronic Kitchens Corp. was a wholly owned subsidiary of a large conglomerate; therefore, it had access to large resources and had capitalized on this strength to build a strong capability in all phases of electronics applying to kitchens—residential, commercial, industrial, space, and so on. It had achieved sales of slightly over $400 million with various types of ovens, routine and special freezing appliances, timer-controlled appliances of all types, safety controls for use on its own and other appliances, and the like.

The R&D department was one of the best (if not the best) in the industry, and the new product strategy was to capitalize on that technical strength while staying in the general area of food preparation. The firm intended to be first in each market or a quick second based on technical adaptation. It accepted risks.

However, when a scientist invented what later came to be known around Electronic Kitchens as the black box, it decided to spin out a new organization to handle the product's further development and marketing. Thus the Cyclotron Corp. was born.

The black box was an electronic device that apparently created a flow of heat; that is, it sent heat in a circular pattern around whatever happened to be on the shelf of the device. It went fast and, in effect, echoed the winding patterns around cores in golf balls and baseballs. This high-intensity heat cooked much faster (safely and controllably) than traditional gas and electric ranges.

Chet Vinton, the scientist in charge of the project, said, "People can now do all of their cooking in this new box, though they may still prefer the slightly better speed of the microwave in some cases. But our device is better than anything else, plus it gives better browning and heat control and distribution than the microwaves do." He was very anxious to get the product onto the market and said the field product use testing was going well, although consumers did fuss about not being able to know or see what the central heating unit was. Uncertainty about a patent made the firm very secretive about the technical nature of what it called the Cyclotron Kitchen.

If you were appointed product manager for this new product, what particular concerns would you have about the internal problems of project control? That is, what problems might warrant your close attention? And second,

---

This hypothetical case is based on realistic business circumstances.

when you began putting together the marketing plan for the market test on the residential models, what peculiarities out there would you be concerned with on such a product as this? Don't worry about the legal side (such as liability) just now; the legal department will help you on that. But what about the marketing aspects? Any particular learning requirement problems here? Distributor attitudes?

The Marketing Plan

SETTING

The commercialization process begins with a decision to market the new product (barring some valid reason for an expensive, last-minute abort). But the new products manager has been gathering ideas on marketing planning and strategy for a long time. The product innovation charter gave some ideas (such as a target and a technology commitment), and others have been added at each testing stage. Concept testing clarified target and began positioning. Product use testing began singling out specific claims, and so on.

So, we are now at the point of pulling it all together. Skeleton strategic outlines are fleshed out with full tactical details, and decisions are made on the thousand and one details needed for marketing—including distribution, pricing, branding, packaging, advertising, selling, and sales meetings.

Most firms want a marketing plan (sometimes called a business plan), and we will look at the outline generally approved for this purpose. The plan should clearly state the overall strategy, including the critical matters of target market and competitive positioning for the new item. Then the plan should state what the various marketing tools will be doing—promotion, distribution, pricing, and the product itself.

Chapter 16 will cover the plan and the strategy, around which it is built. Emphasis will be on the target market, positioning of the product for that market, and building a marketing mix appropriate for that target/positioning combination. Chapter 17 will cover the individual tools of the mix, with primary emphasis on the product tool.

These two chapters cannot cover the entire marketing planning task. Instead, they focus on aspects (1) not usually emphasized in introductory marketing courses or (2) especially important to the new products manager. It's assumed that students have had training in the basic ideas of marketing planning—market research, buyer behavior, and strategy, either by experience or in a marketing management course.

Remember that although we covered market testing in Chapters 12 and 13 as part of the evaluation topic, the marketing plan and full implementation are ready prior to market testing. Changes (big or minor) will be made prior to full launch. Look back at the overall product innovation process chart (Figure 2–1) to see where marketing planning fits in.

THE MARKETING PLAN

No two firms approach marketing the same way, and Figure 16–1 gives a marketing plan outline based on the best information we have. The plan generally follows these guidelines:[1]

- Summarize the analysis done for this plan.
- Give overall strategic thinking.
- Give the tactical actions, including those for departments other than marketing.
- Make sure everyone knows the financial situation and how the plan will be measured and evaluated.

The outline should communicate the plans to everyone involved, have built-in control mechanisms, and serve as a permanent record.

Contents

Certain sections of the marketing plan deserve additional comment. But remember: if the new product is a line extension, many of the early sections of the plan are unnecessary because the information is not new.

Consumers/Users/Buyers.   This section addresses the key element in the product's rationale. Data are given on the various buyer categories, the extent to which buying differs from using, the existence of influencers, and the specific process by which users acquire the merchandise. This includes buying motives, brands considered, information sought, product preferences, images, and unmet needs. It also covers how products are actually used and by whom.

This section will help anyone who reads the plan understand the decisions described later—for example, on targeting, positioning, and

---

[1] An excellent source of guidance for writing new product marketing plans is David S. Hopkins, *The Marketing Plan,* Report no. 801 (New York: The Conference Board, 1981).

FIGURE 16–1 Outline of Marketing Plan for a New Product to Be
Adapted to Fit Individual Firms

I. Introduction. This section briefly describes the product, tells who prepared the plan, and its timing.

II. Situation analysis.
   A. Market description.
      1. Consumers, users, and other market participants.
      2. Buying processes pertinent to this plan.
      3. Direct and indirect competitors.
      4. Current competitive strategies.
      5. Market shares on sales, profits, and budgets.
      6. Available distribution structure, plus attitudes and practices.
      7. Key environmental or exogenous factors.
   B. Full description of new product, including all pertinent test data and comparisons with competition.

III. Summary of opportunities and problems.
   A. Key exploitable market opportunities.
   B. Key problems that should be addressed by this plan.

IV. Strategy.
   A. Overall guiding statement, including key actions and their quantitative and qualitative objectives.
   B. Market targets/segments, with positioning for each.
   C. Overall marketing efforts.
      1. General role for product, including planned changes.
      2. General role for advertising, including copy platforms.
      3. General role for personal selling.
      4. General role for such other tools as sampling and trade shows. Copy platforms for any creative units.
      5. General role for distributors (wholesale, retail).
      6. Price policy, including discounts and planned changes.
      7. Any special roles for nonmarketing departments.

V. Economic summary.
   A. Sales forecasts in dollars and units.
   B. Expense budgets by category of activity.
   C. Contribution to profit, with pro forma income statement.
   D. Risk statement: major problems, uncertainties.
   E. Future capital expenditures, with cash flows.

VI. Tactical plans. This section is situational to the firm. It includes each tool, what will be done with it, objectives, people responsible, schedule, creative units needed, etc.

VII. Control
   A. Key control objectives for reporting purposes.
   B. Key internal or external contingencies to watch.
   C. Information generation schedule.

VIII. Summary of major support activities needed, including data processing, warehousing, technical service, R&D, finance, personnel, public relations.

IX. Chronological schedule of activities.

push-pull strategy. It also summarizes the general equilibrium of the market and highlights any instabilities that can be capitalized.

Competition. All plan readers must be told about the competitive situation because many of them are not in a position to have regular contact with it. Specific company and brand names and a description and evaluation of key competitive products should be given first. Figure 16–2 gives a part of a useful and demanding form. If the product manager doesn't know the determinant attributes in this market or how the new product compares on those attributes with products already out there, then the firm isn't ready to market the new item.

The competitors' overall business and marketing strategies are also needed, especially those appearing effective. This includes positioning, pricing, claims, and distribution.

Exogenous Factors and Change. Markets are not static, and everyone involved needs to be apprised of likely changes. No surprises should appear, and none will if the planner has been careful. Some often overlooked changes are government regulations, competitive product improvements, direct selling (skipping a distributive level), price breaks, new competition based on new technologies, and future changes in how this type of product is bought and/or used.

Product Description. In some cases, a product can be described in a few sentences; in others, readers of the plan almost need a seminar. Product

---

FIGURE 16–2 Comparative Product Data

Feature \ Company Brand	Our	Resco	Resco	Flemming	Etc.
	Our New	Ipsi	Zip	Flan	
Size	30 cc	=	=	+	
Color	Red	+	+	+	
Speed	50 sec	–	–	– –	
Etc.					

+ +We are demonstrably superior on a meaningful feature.
 +We are felt to be superior, but the feature is not a key one or our proof is lacking.
 =Essentially the same as that of competitor.
 –We are probably deficient here, but the difference is not critical.
– –We are clearly deficient on a meaningful feature.

complexity cannot be allowed to destroy understanding. The plan should guide other people in doing their parts in the overall marketing effort, so they need to know just how good this new product really is. The plan should summarize the key findings of concept testing, product use testing, and market testing. It should include product strengths and weaknesses, perceptual problems, unusual uses of the product, physical characteristics, costs, and restrictions applied to any applications.

Objectives.   A statement of what is expected from marketing this new product should be included near the start of the strategy section. But, let's differentiate between objective and goal. A *goal* is a long-term direction of movement (sometimes not easily quantified) used for guidance, not internal control (for example, "It is our goal to become a leader in the snacks market"). An *objective* is an intermediate point on the road toward attainment of a goal (for example, "It is our objective to capture a 15 percent share of the snacks market during our first year on the market"). Objectives should be clearly and precisely stated in fairness to the new products manager. A narrative at this point in the plan will help clarify objectives.

Restraints.   Every new product marketing effort has some built-in restraints that should be made clear. For example:

> The new product will be marketed in accordance with the division's customary reliance on its industrial distribution system.
>
> The sales force is currently questioning the ability of the new products department to come up with winners. Because the morale of the sales force is quite important to this division, actions will be taken to ensure the success of this particular product.
>
> The strategy will not introduce potential problems of interpretation by the Federal Trade Commission, nor will it conflict with outstanding consent decrees.

Such restraints as these can have obvious effects on a marketing plan; if they are not stated, readers may not understand why certain actions are being taken.

Support Needed.   Experienced new product marketers never underestimate the contribution of the many nonmarketing departments in the firm, but novice new products people often do. For this reason, some firms want the marketing plan to stipulate the help needed from the nonmarketers. Later, when the engineers, finance people, and others read drafts of the plan (let's hope they have a chance to see *drafts*), they usually will have suggestions to make.

Management of the Task

Putting together a marketing plan is a complex process, filled with grand strategic decisions interspersed with trivia. Everyone is helping us, yet everyone is a problem for us. Each person involved in the new product's marketing has ideas about what that person should do; they differ from what other people think that person should do. And vice versa. All are experienced people, and we have worked with them for some time. We would like to just ask each of them what they want to do and then put their requests into a package and call it a marketing plan. Some plans are actually developed that way.

Such plans don't work very well, however, unless we have a new product that essentially sells itself. Or, unless the new item is a simple line extension, marketed totally as a new member in a line of products. The product line marketing plan captures the new item and tells it what will be done.

And, of course, in rare instances our new item doesn't have to be marketed at all, in the usual sense. For example, we may be making it in response to a military order, where the sale was made at the time our bid was accepted. Or, we may be developing an item for a major producer of complex products (such as automobiles); in such a case, the producer essentially told us what to make, and all we have to do is deliver it and stand by to service it.

But, these are exceptions; in most cases, the new item needs its own strategy, at least in concept. Otherwise, the various players will never come together to make up a team.

Let's distinguish between planning and a plan. Planning yields a strategy; the plan states the strategy, adds the tactical details, and directs the implementation. New products can use both, but the strategy is critical. Once the new products manager begins to concentrate on the plan, with its many budgets, dates, and other details, no strategy in the world can keep the players motivated, integrated, and effective.

Some new products managers (called *champions*) orchestrate the team by dint of personal leadership. These people may miss dates and budgets but market a successful product. A product marketed well over budget—but on time—makes more money than a product marketed within budget but three months late.

This line of thinking does not apply to established products, which need annual or quarterly marketing plans. They already have the infrastructure, the stature, the support base within the firm, and the experienced players that the new product lacks.

So, as we go through these two chapters, keep in mind that we are looking at things that really make a difference. That's all that most new product managers have the time to seriously think about.

One other thought: the team that develops a new product also develops the plan for it and leads the plan's implementation. The team is multifunctional (includes representatives from manufacturing, engineering, and R&D), so formal "sign-offs" from the various departments are not needed. Top-management approval is needed, however. "Whoever pays the fiddler calls the tune," so new products managers must deal with the frustrations caused by highly participative top managements.[2]

STRATEGY

The heart of the marketing plan is the strategy section. The situation analysis culminates in a strategy, and the strategy drives tactical planning and financial analysis.

Most new product strategy sections begin with a general statement of what the new product introduction is all about. They state the objectives (sales volume, market shares, profit contributions) and give the "tone" of the introduction—how aggressive it is—and the speed dimension. They summarize target marketing positioning, and marketing mix, which are discussed next.

TARGET MARKET

When Coca-Cola changed its formula in 1985, marketing observers noticed promotion of the new product was essentially directed to everyone. This contrasted with the firm's promotion of diet Coke a year earlier, which was targeted to men, and also contrasted to Tab, which had established itself primarily with women. This situation dramatizes the three options a firm faces on target marketing: one, make one product (such as Coke) and sell it to everyone *(undifferentiated marketing)*; two, make one product for each of the various groups and sell them as a line *(differentiated marketing)*; three, concentrate on only one segment and go all out for that one, as Pepsi did many years ago when it selected young people as a target in an effort to fight its way into the soft-drink market *(concentrated marketing)*.

Competition forces the overwhelming majority of companies to use concentrated or differentiated marketing. Very few products are so well

---

[2] The general subject of marketing planning, and the analysis integral to it, can be found in all introductory marketing management texts. A good one is Thomas C. Kinnear and Kenneth L. Bernhardt, *Principles of Marketing,* 2nd ed. (Glenview, Ill.: Scott, Foresman, 1986), and later editions.

established that they can profitably orient to everyone—as Coca-Cola found with its reformulation bombshell of 1985. This means companies must market to specific target groups.

Alternatives

The targeting choices facing a new product marketer are few in concept and complex in implementation.

1. *End-use.*   Athletic shoes are now oriented to the type of athletic activity in which the user participates. Vacuum bottles are made separately for work and for school. Plastics are sold for hundreds of different applications.

2. *Geographic.*   Convertibles are not marketed aggressively in Duluth, and parkas are not designed for Mobile. *Grit* is a rural newspaper, and the *New Yorker* is an urban magazine.

3. *Demographic.*   This involves all the vital statistics, social factors, and so on. Right Guard was first a family deodorant and then a male one. Marlboro cigarettes began as a female product (hence the box to keep loose tobacco out of purses) and then changed to a male orientation. Other bases are income, social class, race, life cycle, occupation, education, religion, and nationality.

4. *Behavioral.*   This one is more complicated because behavior is not as easily identified in the market. But, kitchen-model TVs were developed for people who like to cook, Kevlar bullet-proof jackets for people exposed to danger of guns. Some clothing is for people who want to innovate, and other clothing is for those who don't buy until the fashion is passé.

5. *Psychographic.*   Many products relate to lifestyles—tax shelters, clothing, cars. The Pontiac Fiero was psychographically targeted (the yuppie lifestyle) but grew beyond that to include a full sports-loving group. In contrast, the original Mustang was oriented toward working singles (especially female) but soon had to be redirected to a fun-loving market of all ages, sexes, and occupations.

Combinations of Target Dimensions Are Common.   For instance, a very risky new product program for the London Fog Division of Londontown Corp. came about when the firm decided its position in the market was tied too closely to middle-aged and older men. The company formulated a new charter to develop products for younger people, especially those younger people who desired acceptable fashion change without extremism. The program succeeded, though not before management resisted the inclusion of many higher-fashion jackets and short coats that would have been for a different target.

Making the Decision

Given a probable need to segment the market and a wide range of choices, how does a new products manager make the decision? First, the target market may be clear from the original concept generation. For instance, when a food company does a problem analysis of the backyard patio barbecue market and finds that fathers of small children have problems playing catch with them while not letting the food burn, its target market for the resulting product is clear. Ditto when a sales rep notifies management that offices with southern exposure are having problems with the new personal computer screens, and a new display unit evolves.

Second, the firm's method of operation may constrain the choice. A small soft-beverages firm in Texas will have regional or ethnic targets whether desirable or not. Unisys (then Burroughs) corporate strategy oriented it to banks and several other major business segments, and its new product marketing was to follow this orientation. Similarly, if a firm's sales force calls on hospital accounting departments, its new line of tabular records will be so targeted.

Third, many things happened during concept testing, product use testing, and other component testing. The original target market may have rejected the idea when they tried it out. Though it is possible at this point to change to a new target and go ahead, it is far better to cycle back through at least some of the testing, just to be sure the new target is better than the one that just fell by the wayside. Many firms use parallel development, keeping two or three targetings in development.

A twist of great interest to new products people is called *benefit segmentation,* or a variant of it. The theory states that via concept testing (and other research), you have learned a lot about which people see a real benefit in the new item. Correlation with other descriptors of those people (their age, location, buying behavior, and so on) tells you exactly which people like the benefit you offer. What better market target segment than that group, whether demographical, geographical, or whatever?

Another current twist in target market selection is the trend toward smallness. Now that retail stores are putting in scanners for checking out, they know a great deal about very small groups of people. For example, suburban areas, neighborhoods, and even individual stores may have unique purchase patterns. These clusters have been labeled *micromarkets,* and the development of special products and promotions for them is called *micromarketing.*

The ultimate smallness, of course, is the individual, and we are now seeing lots of targeting of individuals. In what is sometimes called *mass customization,* the seller offers each buying unit a chance to order an individual product. For example, some hotels now offer the reserving customer a choice of floor, smoking or not, size of room, view, number and type of beds, and so on. The patron actually stipulates the product wanted. The industrial and commercial worlds have had this individualization for many years, but we often forget it is a form of targeting.

However it comes about, the decision essentially measures (1) how much potential is in each target market option, (2) how well our new product meets the needs of people in each of those markets, and (3) how prepared we are to compete in each — that is, our *capacity* to compete there.

In industrial and business markets, another factor usually arises — the likelihood that the first users will influence others. This influence results in diffusion of the innovation, an activity discussed in Chapter 15. So, these managers often think of four factors, shown graphically in a hypothetical example from the cutting tool industry in Figure 16–3.

Last, the target market decision is complicated by target markets within target markets for most products. The prime target may be an end user (builder, physician, food manufacturer, family food shopper), but most of those cases have at least one major influencer. So, we have to have a strategy for that person too. If we are selling to physicians, we want pharmacists and nurses to support us, but we have to decide which pharmacists and which nurses — same decision, made several times, often with each subtarget getting its own mini marketing plan.[3]

THE "BROADEN THE MARKET" SYNDROME

As we approach the marketing date, intense pressure builds up in the organization to add just a few more buyer groups, a few more store types, a few more uses or applications, because "The product is good for them too, isn't it?" Several specific errors can result. One error, the curse of no decision, goes something like this: "Let's just announce it and begin general selling. Then, when we see which groups think it's a winner, we can narrow in on those." The problem is that the product and its promotion cannot be good for lots of different groups, unless it is so general it doesn't have any zing for any of them.

---

[3] A discussion of this multiple-target problem on a general maintenance product being marketed to the industrial market can be found in Marvin Berkowitz, "New Product Adoption by the Buying Organization: Who Are the Real Influencers?" *Industrial Marketing Management,* February 1986, pp. 33–43.

FIGURE 16–3   Graphic Representation of Target Market Selection Process

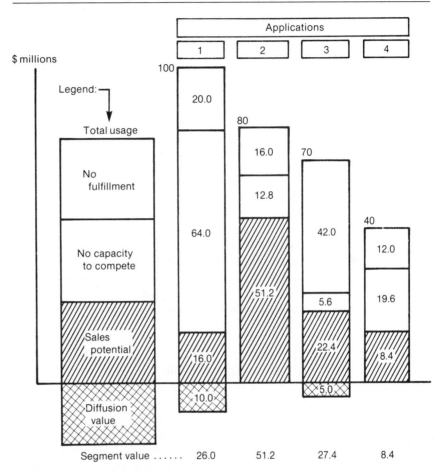

Explanation: Here are four possible applications for a new industrial cutting tool. Application 3 has a total market size of $70 million, but $42 million of that is in uses where our product will not work (no fulfillment), and $5.6 million is in markets where we cannot compete. This leaves $22.4 million potential for us; plus, getting it established there opens up an additional $5 million sales diffusion value through the attention it will get in this newsworthy application. Total value of the segment to us as a target market is $27.4 million.

Targeting the promotion for several specific groups at the same time can be a second mistake because *conflict and dissonance in the promotion* are apt to occur. How can one ad or one selling brochure display the product being used by different types of people in different uses without giving conflicting cues? Does a fourth grader want a peanut butter sandwich like the one shown being eaten by a senior citizen?

A third error is the quick switch, which occurs when management agrees to the recommended targeting but begins to demand a switch shortly after introduction if the product doesn't take off immediately. Chances are the whole marketing program is geared to the first target and cannot be changed quickly. For example, trade show schedules are fixed, as are most print advertising schedules. Packaging, pricing, and even branding are other commitments difficult to change on short notice.

POSITIONING

Once a target market has been selected, the new product marketers must differentiate their item from products already offered to that target group. This differentiating, called *positioning the product,* is now in widespread use.

Positioning originated in advertising and said that a buyer's mind is a memory bank with slots or positions for each competing alternative course of action. Each alternative product was ranked by sales volume like a rung on a ladder, and the top rung was the market leader. Strategists for various products could exploit this idea in several different ways:

1. Create a new market by claiming to be the top rung on a new ladder (light beers and Miller).
2. Outperform the top firm and take over the top rung (what IBM did to Sperry-Rand).
3. Deliberately position relative to the top firm and fight for a better lower rung (Avis slogan "we try harder").
4. Reposition the leader or any occupant of a position being sought—a really dramatic event when one figures out a way (Royal Doulton ads: "Royal Doulton—the china of Stoke-on-Trent, England, versus Lenox, the china of Pomona, New Jersey").
5. Simply differentiate the product from those already on the ladder and thus break the one ladder into two or more ladders, one for each segment. Shampoo manufacturers and car manufacturers have done this for years.

This early concept of positioning has changed. First, positioning is now seen as an ingredient of total strategy, not just an advertising ploy. Product, brand, price, promotion, and distribution are all potential positioning tools, and they must all be consistent.

Second, there is no buyer's perception on a new product. Positioning is a decision for the marketer. The slate of buyer memory is clean. Later there will be buyer perceptions; but in the meantime, the developers have their best chance ever to effect a particular positioning for their item.

Third, the ladders-and-rungs idea has not lasted. We will see later that competitive rank positionings are rarely used. Relative ranking is a valuable concept, but new products today seek unique positions based on many factors other than sales volume or market share. Companies no longer have to position relative to a leader.

The tool can be subtle and complex, and some marketers reject it. However, the concept is a valid step in the new products process that is here to stay.

Alternatives in Positioning

The alternatives used today in positioning fall into two broad categories:

A. Position to an *attribute* (a feature, a function, or a benefit).
B. Position to a *surrogate* that *implies* features, functions, or benefits. Surrogates in use today, in order of popularity, are:
1. Nonpareil.
2. Parentage.
3. Manufacture.
4. Target.
5. Rank.
6. Endorsement.
7. Experience.
8. Competitor.[4]

Feature, function, and benefit are the historical positioning devices and are directly related to the product. Thus, a dog food may be positioned by such *features* as "the one with three flavors" or "the one with as much protein as 10 pounds of sirloin." *Function* is more difficult to use and is used less often, but an example is the advertising for the shampoo that "coats your hair with a thin layer of protein." The *benefits* used in positioning can be direct (such as "saves you money") or follow-on (such as "improve your sex life by using our toothpaste"). A follow-on benefit stems from a more direct benefit—in this case, cleaner teeth or cleaner breath.

Sometimes, positioning combines two or even three attributes. Thus, one may position a hotel as the one that has over 1,000 rooms (feature) and therefore can cater your banquets more efficiently (function), which in turn will make those who attend your meetings very happy (benefit).

---

[4] For more details on this concept, see C. Merle Crawford, "A New Positioning Typology," *Journal of Product Innovation Management,* December 1985, pp. 243–53.

Such multiple-dimension positioning often confuses target users because they won't spend as much time figuring it all out as the seller would like them to spend.

The new focus of positioning is surrogates (or substitutes). Positioning a product on a benefit attribute (for example, lose weight fast) is clear. But the product could also be positioned as "a dietary product created by a leading health expert." This says the product differs because of its designer (its manufacturer, actually). Specific reasons *why* the product is better are not given; the listener or viewer has to provide those. And, the theory says, if the surrogate is good, the listener will bring favorable attributes to the product.

The system is efficient because a one-sentence statement of surrogate positioning lets the listener bring perhaps four or five attributes to the product, the next listener can bring a different set, and so on. About a third of all positionings today are surrogate, and the percent is growing. See Figure 16–4 for recent examples of the various positioning alternatives.[5]

Surrogates Defined

The surrogates are discussed below in descending order. The claim in each case would be that "Our product is better than, or different than, the others . . .". Examples taken from 1985 usage are in parentheses.

Nonpareil: . . . because the product has no equal; it is the best (the Jaguar car and the Dysan diskette).

Parentage: . . . because of where it comes from, who makes it, who sells it, who performs it, and so on. The three ways of parentage positioning are *brand* (Cadillac or Citizen printer), *company* (the Data General/One or Kodak diskette), and *person* (*The Living Planet,* a book by David Attenborough).

Manufacture: . . . because of how the product was made. This includes *process* (Hunt's tomatoes are left longer on the vine), *ingredients* (Fruit of the Loom panties of pure cotton), and *design* (Audi's engineering).

Target: . . . because the product was made especially for people or firms like you. Four ways are *end use* (Vector tire designed especially for use on wet roads), *demographic* (Republic Airlines, now Northwest Airlines, specially designed for the business traveler),

---

[5] Ibid.

FIGURE 16–4 Representative Positionings for Selected Categories*

Consumer nondurable goods:
Vitalis — benefit: the neat look, well groomed.
Hanes Alive hosiery — indirect benefit: your support will be secret.
Chloraseptic — endorsement: recommended most by pharmacists.
Sunlight Wesson cooking oil — feature: 100 percent sunflower seed oil.
Fitting Pretty pantyhose — target, demographic: for the queen size.
Nuprin — experience: 100 million prescriptions strong.
Hallmark cards — nonpareil: the very best.
Jack Daniels whiskey — manufacture, process: charcoal mellowing.
Michelob — target, psychographic: for people on the way up.
Sunkist oranges — parentage, brand: the Sunkist name means quality.
Knorr Homestyle soup — manufacture, ingredients: fresh-cut flavor.

Consumer durable goods:
BMW automobile — manufacture: engineering and technical design.
Caravelle automobile — competitor: same as Century and Ciera.
Sharp calculator — rank: number one in sales.
Troy-Bilt tiller — target, end use: for persons with small gardens.
Econoline truck — rank: number one in sales.
Ford Thunderbird — predecessor: 30th anniversary of classic.

Industrial products:
Selectric 2000 — parentage, company: from IBM.
Tandy 6000 computer — benefit: value, lower cost.
RCA display — feature: high performance.
Hewlett-Packard office automation — benefit: productivity.
Tseng Labs multifunction board — nonpareil: only one that does it all.
Xerox office machines — indirect benefit: get home quicker, family.
Contel software — benefit: increases efficiency, especially speed.

Services:
Fortune magazine — feature: unique offering of the news.
Sheraton Hotel — target: especially good for business travelers.
Avis — benefit: we serve you faster, save you time.
Hertz — rank: number one in usage.
Jacksonville — experience, bandwagon: 50 big firms moved in.
Tulsa — target, end use: the city that is good for business.
K mart — feature: branded items carried.
Metropolitan insurance — feature: very competent agents.

*Ascertained from print advertising in 1985.

---

psychographic (Michelob Light for "the people who want it all"), and *behavioral* (Hagar's Gallery line for men who work out a lot, "fit for the fit").

Rank: . . . because it is the best-selling product (Hertz and Blue Cross/Blue Shield).

Endorsement: . . . because people you respect say it is good. May be expert (the many doctors who use Preparation H) or a person to be emulated (Farrah Fawcett shampoo).

Experience: . . . because its long or frequent use attests to its desirable attributes. Modes are *other market* (Nuprin's extensive use in the prescription market), *bandwagon* (Stuart Hall's Executive line of business accessories are the tools business professionals rely on), and *time* (Bell's Yellow Pages).

Competitor: . . . because it is just (or almost) like another product that you know and like (IBM PC look-alikes Compaq and Cannon).

Predecessor: . . . because it is comparable (in some way) to an earlier product you liked (Hershey's new Solitaires addition to the Golden line).

The Decision Process

Deciding exactly what a new product's positioning will be is somewhat systematic and somewhat artistic. The concept permits considerable creativity.

It begins with concept generation — where a need may have led to a product. It is enhanced when concept test and use test data show favorable user reaction to attributes. But the full set of options appears when competitive products are arrayed with their positionings. If the new item will compete with six others, we need to know how the others are positioned to see what gaps are available.

To do this, we actually use two variations on positioning: (1) the position an item's sellers claim for it and (2) the position consumers put it in. These often do not coincide. The analytical technique is the same gap (or map) analysis discussed in Chapter 6.

The positionings of competitive products are then compared with *the preference of potential users*. We simply look to see if current products have preempted the positions of the most preferred attributes. The Taylor Wine Company once used market research to find a small group of heavy wine users who offered new product potential; and surprisingly, no competitor was positioning its product to this segment on the basis of great taste. Taylor did, and succeeded immediately.

Usually, the preferred attributes are already taken and only offer us an option *if we meet needs better on a given attribute*. Cake mix A goes after cake mix B, even though B is positioned on taste and has the market, if A thinks it has data showing people prefer its taste to B's.

If (1) there is no open preference and (2) there is no preference where we score better than the firm there now, we can turn to option (3) and select an attribute (feature, function, or benefit) where there is less preference and *try to build it* (make people want a safer car, for example, even though they might not have wanted one before). This alternative is more questionable and more expensive.

The fourth approach — *skip the attributes and go to surrogates* — is where the art begins. How did Avis know it would succeed with "We try harder"? How did Savin know its positioning of copiers exactly on Xerox would work? It didn't, but each approach can be concept tested. The new product manager is advised to study the list of surrogates, see if any make sense in the current situation, select one or two, and give them a try. The purpose is to position the product in a way that permits the user to bring to the product the two or three attributes preferred by that particular person. The bundle of attributes must be unique or perceived as unique in the market.

Of course, the best positioning of all is an important, unmet need (such as Kleenex's disposability or Polaroid's instant pictures). Most new product marketers are not so lucky.

Cautions

A concept as powerful as positioning can be abused, so here are several cautions:

- A product will be positioned by the user. Why not at least try to make that positioning be one we like?
- Positioning drives the entire program — everything. Don't let dissonance exist between the cues given to the user.
- Every positioning, even an obvious one, should be tested with the intended user.
- Contingency positionings should be in place in case the one used flops. The departments involved in implementing the contingency positionings should be informed of the possible change.

MARKETING MIX

Early in this chapter, we saw that strategy for a new product contains the target market, the positioning for the product, and a marketing mix. The *marketing mix* is a name given to the particular combination of product–promotion–price–distribution actions selected for the product. Here are the tools we have at our disposal.

Product. We can improve its attributes, put a brand on it, package it, add a presale or postsale service to it, offer a warranty, develop a line extension for it, and so on. All these ways of winning customer support cost money. Which ones will be used? How much emphasis will be placed on them?

Promotion. Advertising, personal selling, direct mail, coupons, samples, free merchandise, in-store promotions, trade and consumer shows, publicity, contests, premiums, billboards, and scores more can be used. How much of each? What will be the lead effort?

Price. Should we skim price, meet the market price, or penetrate price? Offer discounts, promotional allowances, rebates, or trade-ins? Again, we have lots of options, all costly, and from which we must choose one or a few—plus, of course, decide just how important a low price is in the overall mix of activities.

Distribution. Only direct sellers do not need distributors (retailers, wholesalers, industrial distributors, supply houses, agents of all kinds, and more). But, a distributor is selling the manufacturer a service, for which there is a charge, often a very high charge (for example, office furniture dealers may take 70 percent of what the user pays for a new desk).

If the new products manager starts down through the above list of options, picking and choosing item by item, the list will be long, expensive, and not very well "packaged," much like a trip through a well-stocked cafeteria. It's far better to have a mix strategy, an understanding of which of the four horses will be the lead horse and which will be supporting. Then, we can spend whatever it takes to make the lead effort successful; if the supporting efforts fail for lack of funds, much less damage is done.

There is also the matter of *synergy.* Any two efforts can add up to the equivalent of three if they go well together. For example, every now and then a firm will select personal selling as its mix strategy but then opt for a low, penetration price. The low price cuts the firm's margins, so it may lack the money for personal selling materials, follow-up service, free merchandise, and so on.

Options in Marketing Mix Strategy

The new products manager has these strategic choices:

1. None—Strategy Is Given. In most industries, established firms really have no choice when it comes to marketing tools. Consumer packaged goods are almost always based on television, strong packaging, and distribution through mass outlet channels. The only option a new products manager has is to deviate from the standard, and that is very rare. Other examples include smaller hardware items, pharmaceuticals, caskets, and clothing. Newer industries (computer products and financial services) may lack established marketing mixes, and some industries are split into two categories based on marketing mix strategies – for auto parts, OEM and aftermarket; and for cameras, full service (Leica) and mass outlet (Polaroid).

2. Product as Lead Tool. Money goes to improvements and rapid line extensions. This choice often applies where there are technical breakthroughs and product is widely demanded. Promotion is supportive, and its role is primarily awareness.

3. Pull. This is the classical consumer packaged goods strategy described above, but it is also a key option in business-to-business marketing. Good distributors and agents are often in short supply, so a product innovator may opt to promote directly to the end user and allow end-user adoption to pull the item down through the reluctant channels.

4. Push. This is the opposite of pull. Distributors are the key members in the mix. Their margins are higher, and our personal selling supports them via missionary selling and training of distributor salespeople. As times change, it is interesting to note that the retail food chains are threatening to upset their traditional low level of importance in food manufacturers' marketing mixes by demanding "slotting allowances" on new products and otherwise exercising new muscle.[6]

5. Price. Remember that a new product was defined in Chapter 1 as a product *new to the firm*. And in Chapter 3, we saw that imitation is one strategic choice for degree of innovativeness. Thus, a seller may be marketing a me-too and decide on a marketing mix built around its low-cost manufacturing capabilities – a price strategy. If so, other tools suffer accordingly – few, if any, improvements and a pairing of some promotion and low trade margins versus no promotion and higher trade margins. The latter, for example, would be the marketing mix for a new line of so-called white labels in the grocery trade.

6. No Leader. Although not necessarily a good strategy, in some industries the marketing mix just happens to be a rather equal blend of all four tools. Automobiles are the prime example. This may be an option in all industries, but it is usually not recommended.

---

[6] See Richard Gibson, "Supermarkets Demand Food Firms' Payments Just to Get on the Shelf," *The Wall Street Journal,* November 11, 1988, p. 1.

In implementing these strategies, it is not uncommon to see certain pairings (for example, pull and price, push and price, product and pull). The mix depends on the resources available, strength of protection against copying, and so on. The situation analysis provides the answer.

But the point is, there should be *some* marketing mix strategy. With it, many of the decisions made by people doing the product, promotion, price, and channel management tasks are simple. And, the strategy decision should be made at the beginning of marketing planning.

SUMMARY

Part IV is studying commercialization. Chapter 16 presented a widely accepted outline of a marketing plan for a new product. It is thorough and probably as much as any firm would need, perhaps more than most need. The chapter then dealt with the three marketing decisions that are absolutely critical and central to success—selecting the target market, positioning the product, and picking a marketing mix strategy. These three decisions drive all of the marketing decisions to follow, and many of the nonmarketing decisions as well. They compose what we call *marketing strategy.*

We can now turn our attention to some special aspects of the four tools of marketing, the subject of the next chapter.

APPLICATIONS

1. "My daughter is a newly appointed assistant professor at a school in the South, and she recently was joking about how similar the development of courses is to the development of new products. In fact, she said courses have to be planned for and their marketing has to be just right. Even to using positioning as a concept. I wonder if you could take a new college course, say, one on the application of financial analysis to the operation of a retail store, and show me how you could position that course, using each of the various methods for positioning a new product."

2. "I read a fascinating story recently about the development of a Hanes product called Underalls. It seems Hanes had this idea of eliminating the need for panties by adding material to pantyhose. The new pantyhose would offer the wearer several advantages, and the company was worried about how it should be positioned. So, it tested four positionings:

   a. Appearance—the elimination of panty lines under slacks and dresses.

b. *Comfort*—fewer layers of clothing.

c. *Economy*—no need to buy panties.

d. *Logic*—no need to *wear* panties.

The first one won convincingly, so that's how the product was marketed, and you probably know it was very successful. But, my gosh, how in the world would you be able to test those four positionings? It's a new concept; many people would resist talking about panties to a stranger; and folks probably wouldn't even take the thing seriously. You have any idea about how Hanes might have tested that set of positionings?''

3. "The Wham-O Manufacturing Company tells a story about marketing its Super Ball that is interesting to me. You know that ball was the superbouncy thing that jumped all over a room if you tossed it fairly hard. It was developed by a rubber company researcher whose supervisors didn't think it had any practical application. Anyway, when Wham-O marketed it, the company allegedly bribed a messenger at the New York Stock Exchange to dump a carton of Super Balls on the trading floor. The resulting pandemonium created a news story that hit most of the evening papers. Great publicity. Why in the world do companies turn to gimmicks like this on these new toy products?''

4. "I read a while back about a cocktail party in Detroit where someone casually mentioned that a particular photographer (known to be a Ford favorite) was in Paris. This intrigued a Chrysler executive standing nearby because he wondered why Ford would send a top photographer to Paris. A wire to Chrysler's Paris office yielded the answer—Ford was photographing new models at the foot of the Eiffel Tower. The word was that Hong Kong was next on the schedule. Chrysler correctly concluded that Ford was planning to introduce the models under an international theme. Consequently, Chrysler quickly developed a campaign showing Chrysler models at American landmarks—places Chrysler believed the American auto buyer could identify with more quickly. Chrysler was right and got a big jump on Ford that year. To me, that's smart thinking.

"I heard about another company that rented a large training room in a Chicago hotel for a routine sales meeting. The room had been rented the day before to a direct competitor, one of whose salespeople had left behind a notebook containing details on a completely new product. These slips do happen. What would you do if you were the head of marketing for that competitor and found out that one of your salespeople had left that notebook behind? You're about four weeks from advertising break, and the product is a laxative headed for ethical promotion to doctors, drugstores, and hospitals.''

Case: Barstow Chemical Co.

It was pretty evident in the early 1980s that any firm heavily committed to chemicals was going to have to do something to escape the brutal price competition so prevalent on commodity-type chemicals. So, Frieda Fletcher, general manager of Barstow Chemical Company's Specialty Chemicals Division, asked her staff to suggest ways their resources could be used to come up with new product concepts that they could develop and with some modest help be able to market.

Barstow's home office was in Stamford, Connecticut, but Fletcher's group had been moved to Pittsburgh to "get away from the heavy chemicals mentality," as the chairman had put it. The move seemed to work because the Specialty Chemicals group now had four major projects under way: two in chemicals that could be sold to the automotive industry for undercar finishing, a fabric strengthener they weren't sure of a use for yet, and a shampoo.

The shampoo had actually been an accidental spin-off of the undercar treatment project. A chemist was working on chemicals that resisted cleansers of the type used in car washes and by car owners. He tried to find the strongest cleansers he could and even made up some new ones just to be sure the protectant really worked.

The surprise came when he tried a relatively simple concoction that cleaned everything he had been testing yet seemed very soft on the materials and on the hands of workers. (The firm would not comment on the chemicals used in the new concoction.)

By early 1986, Specialty Chemicals had a product and had tested it with all ages, sexes, and social classes of people. It worked about the same with all of them: not better than present shampoos, unfortunately, because all of the shampoos tested were about the same (except for smell, thickness, and so on), but certainly as well. It was also safe and had passed several government tests. So far, it had no added conditioners.

The problem, of course, was how to sell it. The firm considered (and rejected) selling the formula to another firm already in the shampoo business. Unfortunately, it had forgotten to bring up target/positioning early enough before testing, and the issue wasn't raised until four months ago.

The company actually didn't know too much about the shampoo market and would be undertaking market research soon; but in the meantime, Fletcher asked the new products manager to use his personal experience in the shampoo market to come up with some alternatives. He was to find four possible target markets (not currently being used as targets, to his knowledge) and then position the new product for each of them. The new shampoo, as stated, worked about the same as the current market leaders, but it did have two noteworthy features. One, the formula was usually in a very thick gel and, in fact, could be as thick as Vaseline. Two, its natural aroma was much like almonds. Fletcher said it would take some effort to get the chemical firm's management to begin thinking of targets and positionings, so she wanted to get some reasonable examples to begin the exposure. And, she hoped, at least several of them would be "off the beaten track" so people could see the possibilities.

Chapter 17

Tools of the Marketing Mix

SETTING

Chapter 17 continues the discussion begun in Chapter 16. The two chapters together comprise a discussion of the marketing planning process for a new product. Chapter 16 covered the overall plan, target market selection, positioning, and the concept of the marketing mix. Chapter 17 picks up at this point with further discussion of the tools of that mix. More time is given to the product tool because of its role in the new product operation.

PRODUCT AS A MARKETING TOOL

Sometimes, the excitement surrounding a new product and the convictions of its developers cause people to forget that the product itself is one of the four tools of the marketing mix. Price, promotion, and distribution can't do the whole job, even if the product is a 100 percent me-too. A better product lightens the jobs of the other three tools.

During the commercialization process, the new products manager focuses on three aspects of the product: (1) the physical good or the service sequence, whichever delivers the benefits; (2) the branding; (3) all other aspects of the product actually purchased by the buyer, including the packaging, the presale and postsale service, and the warranty. These items are pictured in Figure 17–1, where we see that the purchaser usually wants just one part of the core benefit set but instead gets the full set, some parts of which are not at all wanted. For example, to some people this means excess packaging, poor service, or a bad image.

Occasionally, the full set of things the buyer gets can be separated, or unbundled (such as today's employee benefit package), so the buyer can take only those parts actually wanted. Usually, however, the buyer gets

FIGURE 17–1   Purchase Configuration—What the Buyer Actually Buys

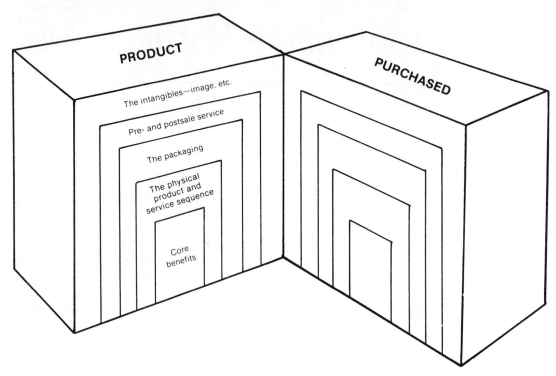

Explanation: One or more core benefits are wanted by the buyer; but to get them, the buyer must also take delivery on the physical product or service sequence, its packaging, its attendant service, and all intangibles that go with the brand and firm making/selling it. These other purchase "layers" may enhance the total value or detract from it, but they each offer opportunity for differentiation or opportunity for the core benefit to be destroyed or overpowered if not handled correctly by the new product manager.

the particular mix of things the new products manager has decided are best. This actually is the product *submix*. Let's look at the different parts.

The Physical Good or Service Procedure

Months before launch, the protocol stipulated what benefits the new product should deliver. New products managers then examined the prototype and concluded that the product did indeed deliver these benefits. That was followed by product use tests, where potential users agreed. But, deciding to make a particular product doesn't guarantee it will turn out exactly that way.

Ostensibly, the manufacturing people are responsible for *producing a quality product,* and they usually do a fine job. The new products manager, however, is responsible (as the "little president" discussed in Chapter 19) for seeing that they do so. Here is a case where he didn't: A firm in the dental supplies business had created a new impression material used in the making of crowns and other dental prostheses. But dentists had problems getting the product to work the way testing showed it should. After months of frustration, it turned out that the manufacturing department had been storing the finished product in an area of the warehouse exposed to the afternoon sun. The added "heat treatment" had ruined the product.

Besides quality, there must also be quantity — *timely production of the needed amounts.* Both quality and quantity are key aspects of the new product tool, and each has its price for the firm providing it.

Another issue is *product improvements,* ideas for which pop up during late-stage testing but too late to be incorporated into the marketed product. So, the good ones are scheduled for soon after launch as another way to strengthen the product tool. Some firms don't see their product as a pliable tool in this manner. For example, Lestoil, a heavy-duty liquid detergent for household cleaning, was the first product of its kind and leaped to dramatic sales volumes. However, the product had an objectionable odor, which the manufacturer did nothing to fix. A large detergent manufacturer used that weakness as a key improvement to support its launch of a similar product. Lestoil was doomed.

Line extensions constitute another area of product action. The best strategy here is to develop profitable line extensions before competitors do. As the first product is coming down the pike, the first couple of line extensions are already in development. Then, after launch, when competitors are casting around for ways to come out with better versions, we market them first.

Line extensions include new uses and applications as well as new versions for other segments of the main market. Each line extension is usually intended to yield a profit in its own right, but a loss operation (for example, cannibalization) can be defended if it steals an option from a potential competitor.[1]

Product action in the area of cost reduction is also high on the agenda. Some years ago, price competitors usually showed up later, during the early maturity stage of the product life cycle. But not today.

In sum, the product itself is not a given. It is a living tool of marketing and must be managed as such.

---

[1] For more on this defensive use of line extensions and product improvements, see C. Merle Crawford, "How Product Innovators Can Foreclose the Options of Adaptive Followers," *Journal of Consumer Marketing,* Fall 1988, pp. 17–24.

Branding

Every new product must be identified, and the accurate term for what identifies products is *trademark*. Under U.S. federal law, a trademark is usually a word or a symbol. That symbol may be a number (how many of the following products can you identify? 6, 21, 45, 57, 66, 76, 380, and 5000[2]) or a design (for example, the stylized lettering in GE, the golden arches of McDonald's, or the paint firm's Dutch boy). The law doesn't care how unusual the trademark is and just requires it to identify and differentiate the item using it.

Most businesspeople and their customers use the term *brand* instead of *trademark*. This book uses *brand* when talking about marketing strategy and *trademark* when talking about the legal aspects. A couple of other technical distinctions can be made (for example, services are actually protected with service marks, not trademarks).[3] And businesses have trade names, not trademarks. But these distinctions are not important to strategy.

Trademark Registration.[4]   Another definition, however, is very important: registration. Historically, and still today in most countries, the first user of a trademark had exclusive rights. But the United States now has a system whereby you can ask that your trademark be registered—that is, if you can get it registered, you can keep that trademark forever, even if another firm later displays proof of prior use. This is of immeasurable value in today's world of heavily advertised brand names. Can you imagine the loss to the MasterCard people if someone suddenly informed them that they had no right to use that mark? Or that any other financial operation could use the MasterCard brand?

The U.S. Patent and Trademark Office grants trademark registration under certain conditions. The three conditions important to a new products manager are as follows.

First, the trademark cannot be *too descriptive* of a product type. A court once found the brand Light too descriptive when used as the brand of a cigarette. The judges felt that Light identified all cigarettes with the

---

[2] If you want to guess their identities, they are, in order, a car, a restaurant, an ale, a line of condiments, a gasoline, another gasoline, a car, and a car.

[3] Services get special treatment in Leonard L. Berry, Edwin E. Lefkowith, and Terry Clark, "In Services, What's in a Name?" *Harvard Business Review,* September–October 1988, pp. 28–30.

[4] A good source for trademark legal information (though not current with the 1988 revisions of the act) is Dorothy Cohen, "Trademark Strategy," *Journal of Marketing,* January 1986, pp. 61–74. Many corporate legal departments have prepared in-house brochures on the topic.

lighter taste of a low-tar cigarette, not just the one firm's brand. Similarly, Overnight Delivery Service would not be acceptable as a competitor to Federal Express.

Second, the proposed trademark should not be *confusingly similar* to the marks of other products. This is the toughest requirement, given the huge number of goods and services on the market today. Here is an example. Quality Inns International, a nationwide motel chain, decided to develop a new economy hotel chain. Quality Inns wanted to name the new chain McSleep, capitalizing on the Scottish fame for wise spending. Reaction was prompt—a McDonald's lawyer said its use of the mark would not be tolerated. McDonald's felt that the "Mc" (called a *formative*) would lead people to believe the motel chain was part of McDonald's Corporation—using its good name and reputation to help Quality Inns. As a further confusion, McDonald's was at that time building a chain of truckstop-style operations called McStop, which offered gasoline, fast food, and lodging at one site.

A federal district judge ruled for McDonald's, and Quality Inns switched the new chain's name to Sleep Inns. The judge punned that his ruling was a McPinion. McDonald's also blocked a New York store from using McBagel.

Third, the trademark should not be *immoral or misleading*—it should not disparage people or institutions, and it probably should not be the name of a person.

In 1988, Congress passed an extended revision of U.S. trademark law. The key aspect for a new products manager is that the new product no longer has to be on the market when the registration is applied for. Companies now have three years to enjoy exclusive use of a trademark without making any sales. Prior to this act, the innovative firm had to actually market the product with the hoped-for brand on it and then wait for opposition (such as from McDonald's, above). A subsequent loss of brand rights and the costs of rebranding and repackaging can be disastrous for a highly advertised packaged good. Quality Inns had only built one or two inns, so the change was not very costly.

Keeping a Trademark Registration.   Getting a trademark registered and surviving the waiting period until it becomes uncontestable from lack of complaint doesn't mean the battle is over. The holder of a trademark must use it properly.

Proper use means we use it to describe our brand of something. A typical proper use is *Jello-O, General Foods' brand of gelatin dessert,* which tells the brand, the owner, and what it is a brand of—gelatin dessert. There are other brands of gelatin dessert, but this is a particular one.

"Gelatin dessert" is called a *generic*. It identifies a category or a class of goods. Automobile, cola drink, shirt, laptop computer, and so on are generics. If the new product being named is the first of a type, the producer has the task of selecting the brand *and* selecting an appropriate generic. Examples are Kleenex disposable tissues, (a common shortening of the full Jell-O branding given above), United airline, Embassy Suites hotel, and Gilbey's London dry gin.

But what happens if the maker merely refers to Escalator, or Thermos, or Formica? Do you know what types of products those are? If you do, as most people do, then the terms no longer just describe one maker's brand of something. Though starting out as brands, they became their own generics, and thus makers of other brands can begin using them. Alladin did so with its thermos (note no capital letter). Alladin was sued by the Thermos people—and won. *Thermos* became a generic. Over the years, so did aspirin, cellophane, brassiere, dry ice, shredded wheat, trampoline, yo-yo, linoleum, cube steak, RIP, corn flakes, kerosene, high octane, raisin bran, lanolin, nylon, mimeograph, and scores more. The multibillion dollars lost could all have been avoided if the marketers had been careful to meet the legal conditions.

Stating the full brand plus the generic at least once on every label and in every ad is one way. Putting the *R* in a circle is another. Using asterisks referring to the registration is yet another.

Perhaps the most critical is a watchful view over promotion materials, one reason why most firms want their advertising screened by a legal department. To squeeze advertising copy and give it more zip, product managers will occasionally use their mark possessively (Boppo's great taste), or as a verb (Boppo your letters), or in the plural (Boppos taste great). This type of use assumes customers think of Boppo as a generic, and if the owner of the brand feels this way, then others can too. A trademark is a proper (capitalized) adjective that modifies the generic.

Last, though it doesn't involve the new products manager directly, trademark owners must also watch the marketplace and complain any time they see their brands used as generics. Thus, if Johnny Carson tells a joke about using a Kleenex to blow his nose, you can be sure his staff will get a letter the following week that goes something like this: "Kleenex is Kimberly-Clark's brand of disposable tissue and should be used only in that manner. One blows his nose on a tissue, not on a Kleenex." American Express went so far as to run an ad in business publications showing a judge sitting on the bench, fully robed, under a headline that said, "Use our trademarks in your ads and you may have to answer to him."

What Is a Good Brand Name? Given all of the legal aspects, the new product manager still has to find a good brand. Today it's not easy, most good combinations of letters having already been taken. But, if Xerox can work out OK, and Clabber Girl too, then there is hope for all.

Experts have given us criteria to follow. Let's look at them.

What Is the Brand's Role or Purpose? Beyond distinguishing our brand from others and providing protection against encroachment, the brand may have some special purpose. For example, if the brand is purely for identification, then an arbitrary combination of letters will work well. This combination is called a *neologism,* and examples include Kodak, Exxon, Weejuns, and Nerf. But, if the brand is to help position the product, then we want to use letters that already have meaning, such as CareFree, DieHard, Holiday Inn, Rely, and Kno-draft air-conditioning units. The clearer the positioning, the less flexibility the firm has in changing that positioning or in adding new items to the line. Firms can't have it both ways.

Will this Product Be a Bridgehead to a Line of Products? If so, the name should not limit the firm, as Liquid Plumr did. Can you accept *Liquid* Plumr *crystals*? We did become accustomed to *Frigid*-aire ranges and *Hot*point refrigerators. Campbell Soup Company surprised many by marketing a new brand, Bounty Soups, but its critics did not know Campbell planned a line of Bounty products; Campbell (soupy?) Pudding would have made no sense. And, what started as Western Hotels had to change to Western International and, finally, to Westin.

Do You Expect a Long-Term Position in the Market? If so, a more general and less dramatic name is preferable; but if you're only going to be around temporarily, something like Screaming Yellow Zonkers can (and did) work.

How Good Is Your Budget? If you don't have the funds to put meaning into a meaningless combination of letters, better avoid that type of brand. Too, if the promotion budget is weak and the brand will have to carry some of the promotional load, this again argues for a brand that carries a message.

Is There an Image Conflict? If a firm has an image of stodginess or low tech or anything else that conflicts with the new product, a brand can be selected to help dispel this image.

Have You Remembered the Physical and Sensory Qualities of the Brand? Specifically, the brand name should be easy to pronounce, easy to spell, and easy to remember. It is strange how often these rules are violated (for example, Precis, Jhirmack, and Alegis). Some believe Honda did the ultimate when it chose Acura; phonetically, the spelling should have been *Accura,* and Americans would have had little trouble, but Acura works much better on an international scale. And, before we get too critical about pronunciation, we should remember Grey Poupon and Häagen-Dazs![5]

---

[5] This issue is discussed further in Ronald Alsop, "Firms Create Unique Names, but Are They Pronounceable?" *The Wall Street Journal,* April 2, 1987, p. 29.

Is the Message Clear and Relevant? Product characteristics should come forth clearly. For example, the meaning of *Isovis* motor oil to the engineers who named it probably was "equal or constant viscosity"; but to the average consumer, it was just a mix of letters. New products people are often too close to their developments to permit sound branding without careful testing, as might have been the case with Glasstex batteries, E-Z-Do wardrobes, and Hi-Low-Witchery bras.

Does the Brand Insult or Irritate Any Particular Market Group? For example, women told Bic that Fannyhose was objectionable, so the firm switched to Pantyhose. Yves St. Laurent's Opium offended Chinese because they thought of opium as something that had been forced on their culture by the British. And the French firm that marketed a drink under the name of Pschitt certainly thwarted the brand's extension to England and the United States.

Beyond these general principles, there is no end to the specific advice given by branding experts. See Figure 17–2 for some of their suggestions, and see Figure 17–3 for a summary of the new products manager's role in trademark management. Managers have much to think about when selecting a brand name for a new product, and there are many conflicting considerations. But the decision is often very important, and it can be botched or brilliant.

FIGURE 17–2   Collection of Practitioners' Suggestions about Branding

1. Use digitals for modernity.
2. Family brands are quick, cheap, and void of surprises.
3. Use "stop" letters (called *plosives*): B, C, D, G, K, P, and T.
4. Use geographic connotations: Rebel Yell, and Evening in Paris.
5. Do something ridiculous: P. Lorillard had Watchamacallits cigarettes.
6. Embellish an ordinary word: the vine leaf intertwined in "o" of Taylor Wines.
7. Put one odd letter in the name: Citibank, Toys 'R' Us.
8. Borrow clout: General Mills' Lancia pizza mix picked up the sports car image.
9. Use the word *The* with the brand for dignity: The Glenlivit.
10. Use personalities: Reggie Jackson candy bars.
11. Use an attention grabber: My Sin cologne.
12. Reinforce a low-price strategy with a name like Klassy Kut Klothes.
13. Play with the letters: *Serutan* is *Natures* spelled backward.
14. Add a symbol to reinforce the brand: Travelers' red umbrella, the rock of Prudential.

FIGURE 17–3   Role of New Products Manager in Trademark Management

1. Direct the original selection. Legal will make the next-to-last approval (just prior to top-executive approval), but product people lead the process.
2. Cooperate in the registration process. Legal needs certain things.
3. Closely inspect any revisions that come back from legal (either the inside legal department or any of the consultants). Minor changes to legal may be major changes to marketing.
4. Carefully monitor all original use of the trademark. Legal will do some of this too, but only the new products manager will see *every* use of the trademark. Correct all misuse immediately.
5. Monitor continued use: less pressure, fewer mistakes. But there is potential trouble at every turn of a label, a package, an ad, or a selling piece.
6. Take the lead in suggesting and directing any revision needed to keep the trademark current.

The Process of Selecting a Brand.   By the time a brand decision is to be made, a thorough situation analysis (competition, customers, and so on) will have been completed and some overall marketing strategy determined. From this will come the role for the brand.

Next, you probably should have some discussions with intended users (to learn how they talk about things in this area of use) and with phonetic experts, who know a great deal about such things as word structures. From all this, via brainstorming or other group activity, will come a large number of suggestions. Some people use computers to generate huge numbers of possible combinations.

This list must be screened down, through several stages, to a set of, say, 5 to 10 that would work and can be legally checked. The screening should include user interviews in which users are specifically asked what they think each proposed brand means and for what type of product it would be used. This is the stage where P&G caught Dreck (Yiddish and German definitions included garbage and body waste), so it was changed to Dreft. Unfortunately, the maker of Barclay cigarettes must not have done this screening, for it would have discovered that British smokers already had Berkely cigarettes, pronounced like Barclay.

Not all brand selection is this complex. Many new products are additions to a line, in which case the logical brand is almost obvious. In other cases, a product characteristic dominates. In still others, a powerful manager simply expresses a personal preference, and that's that. It's good advice, however, to keep two or three brands alive and approved, just in case an unexpected problem pops up.

Figure 17–4 tells a story about brand selection in the crazy real world; some managers find it too close to the truth to be funny.

Packaging

Many goods and most services have no packaging. But when packaging is used, it is apt to be very important. For example, packaging becomes a critical variable when the new item will be distributed through self-service environments, when the product category is already established and the new item will have to force its way in, and when many strongly entrenched competitors sit next to one another on a store shelf.

The original purpose of packaging was to protect the contents until the item was purchased and taken to the point of consumption. This is still one of its purposes today, but marketers are missing a bet if that is its only purpose. Most product developers are aware of the marketing value of L'eggs, pop-top cans, aerosol cans, the unique Coca-Cola bottle, and scores more.

Consequently, packaging gets lots of attention today, and decisions about it are often made at the highest levels in the firm. More money is spent on packaging food and beverage products than on advertising them.

What Is Packaging?   Three "containers" are usually included in the term *packaging,* and some variations exist on those. *Primary packaging* is the material that first envelops the product and holds it. The primary packaging may be a bottle for pills, a paper wrap for a candy bar, and a foil sack for film.

Secondary packaging gathers a group of primary packages and holds them for transportation or display. In some cases, secondary packaging may envelop only one primary package, as with the cardboard box that holds the pill bottle. The one-pound oleo package is secondary, as is the cellophane bag of candy pieces if they are individually wrapped.

Tertiary packaging is the bulk packaging that holds secondary packages for shipment—the large cardboard box or the pallet, for example.

Variations abound. Bales of box board leave box plants wrapped in immensely powerful plastic strips—that's packaging. For such products as bicycles, primary, secondary, and tertiary packaging are all represented by the large box in which the partially disassembled vehicle comes. Small hardware items are in cellophane primary packages inside the carton.

The Various Roles of Packaging.   The following roles have been assigned to packaging, although only rarely do they all operate for one product:

FIGURE 17–4   How to Develop, Market, and Identify a New Product: Horror Story or Unfortunate Reality?

1. Sales, research, and advertising meet to discuss new product's designation (generic) and trademark.
2. Research proposes "methyladenaliumenfluoropolydia."
3. Ad manager struck speechless. Points out pronunciation difficulty and suggests "liquid rock."
4. All present compromise. Settle on generic of "fabric."
5. Computer gives them 117,973 choices for a trademark.
6. Group pares choices down to 15. Computer's feelings hurt.
7. Group overrules using company founder's name spelled backward.
8. Compromise again. Decide on "DIGIR," which is *rigid* spelled backward.
9. Sales manager vetoes: was in North Africa in 72. Claims it is Arabic word for unauthorized pilgrimage to Mecca and therefore unsuitable. Suggests "diccalf," which is *flaccid* spelled backward. Overruled.
10. Group then selects "ZONKO" because it doesn't mean anything spelled any which way.
11. Legal vetoes. Discovers it is obscene word in Slobbovia.
12. Legal throws out five others. Already registered.
13. Bucked to higher authority. VP sales OKs (1) "ZIZ-BOOM," (2) "BIZ-ZOOM," and (3) "ZOOM-BIZ."
14. Company ships to Washington product bearing all three trademarks.
15. Proof of shipment to Patent Office with application for trademark.
16. Patent Office advises number one already registered; application rejected.
17. Patent Office advises number two too descriptive; application rejected.
18. Patent Office advises number three too similar to latest NASA rocket; application rejected.
19. Patent Office reverses itself. Approves number-two choice, "BIZ-ZOOM," company rejoices.
20. Advertising and public relations form their battalions and launch massive promotional attacks for "BIZ-ZOOM" fabric.
21. Orders for "BIZ-ZOOM" roll in. Sales manager measured for white hat and halo. SM smirks smugly.
22. Black hat appears. Millions using "BIZ-ZOOM" as generic term for fabric. Competitor has registered "BUZ-ZAM." If customers ask for "BIZ-ZOOM," they get "BUZ-ZAM." "BIZ-ZOOM" now completely generic; "BUZ-ZAM" isn't.
23. B.I.G. Daddi, company president, starts asking embarrassing questions like "Why wasn't trademark protected all along the line?"
24. Horse gone, company now locks barn door. Sends hundreds of letters to writers, editors, and retail advertisers asking them PLEASE to capitalize the trademark and use quotes and proper generic with it.
25. Company goes through travail of educating and orienting all employees to assure proper use of trademark.
26. Company goes to court. Litigates with trademark pirates. Contributes substantially to support of judges, bailiffs, and lawyers.
27. Massive advertising campaign instituted to instruct trade on proper use of trademark. Costs quite a bit and erodes budget more than somewhat.
28. Snoqualmie Indian in Pacific Northwest named Bizzoom sues company for using his name without permission.

Source: Unknown.

Containment—hold for transporting.

Protection—from the elements.

Safety—from the damage that the contents (acids) might cause and from danger to the contents (theft, glass).

Display and promotion—attract attention, inform, persuade, promote companion products, tie to the firm's overall line, and so on.

Usage assistance—partly with instructions and information (pharmaceuticals or food) and partly with mechanical aid (beer cans and deodorant dispensers).

Miscellaneous—permit reusability of the package, meet ecological demands on biodegradability, carry warnings, and meet other legal requirements.

These roles help many different people. Inside the firm, manufacturing wants containers, distribution wants protection and safety, and marketers want promotion and display. Users want some of those things, plus the usage assistance. Society wants most of the miscellaneous. Because these interests rarely mesh, the package can become a genuine problem.

Packaging Relates to Many Departments in the Firm. However, the package is usually not the responsibility of the marketing or new products planning groups because of the many diverse departments whose interests are reflected in it. Figure 17–5 shows those departments and how the packaging process focuses on a person most often called the director of packaging. The packaging function has three elements (also shown in the figure) providing the specialization needed to reach all of the diverse interested groups. This diversity of interest reflects the many dimensions of the packaging decision—size, shape, design, illustration, brand position and emphasis, materials, opening, reclosing, copy, reuse, disposal, safety requirements, and so on. No wonder the total packaging "decision" takes many months in most cases!

The Packaging Decision. Each company tends to develop a somewhat unique approach to packaging, but there are common steps. First, a packaging person should be involved early on and become familiar with the marketplace and its participants. Field trips are mandatory, as is access to the various market studies that have been made. A unique packaging approach for Pfeiffer's salad dressing was found when research noted that salad dressings were displayed in stores by type rather than by brand and that most competitive bottles were shaped like whisk brooms with flat iron heads.

FIGURE 17–5 Packaging Development Communications Network

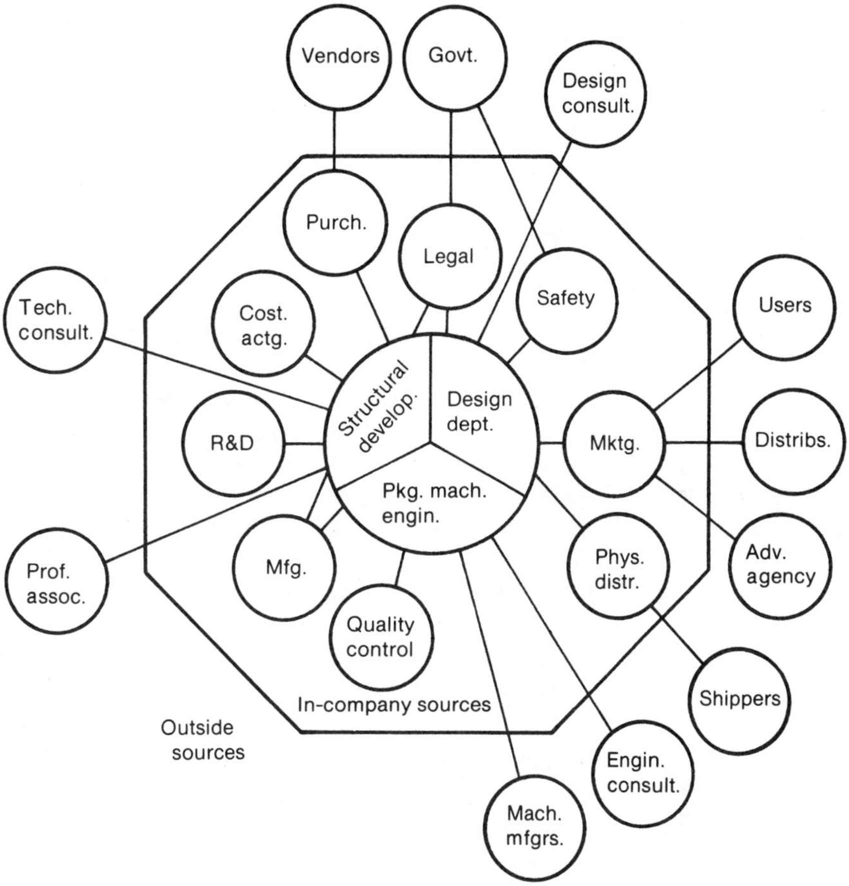

Source: Edmund A. Leonard, *Managing the Packaging Side of the Business,* AMA Management Briefing (New York: AMACOM, 1977), p. 14. © 1977 by AMACOM, a division of the American Management Association. Reprinted by permission of the publisher. All rights reserved.

Packaging copy is needed next and should be carefully checked for understanding. Then the physical work can begin. Size, shape, graphic design, special materials, and many other issues are involved.

Somewhere about this time field testing begins, and the process resembles that for the product itself. Tests include dummy packages, in-store displays, color tests, visual tests, psychographic tests, physical tests, distribution tests, and even some in-store selling tests. For example, 96 women out of 100 chose a pink cosmetic package over an otherwise identical yellow one. In another case, a cosmetic firm tripled sales when it changed from a blue package to a yellow package.[6]

Because packaging sits at the middle of manufacturing, distribution, and marketing, a market test is a dry run for the packaging as well as for the product. Most package design personnel are prepared at this stage to shift to a standby approach in the event of miscommunication, physical breakdown, or some other trouble.[7]

Other Aspects of the Product Tool

Besides branding, packaging, and the other topics just covered, many other dimensions of the product tool have to be considered during a development project. These other dimensions, however, tend to be rather specialized and cannot be covered here in any useful way. Warranty, for example, is a must and contains both legal and marketing dimensions. Service is yet another aspect, including both presale (such as design and configuration) and postsale (repair, exchange, training workers in use of equipment, and so on). But, service is so case specific that general discussion of it yields very little, and both service and warranty verge into promotion as a marketing tool.

THE OTHER THREE MARKETING TOOLS

So far, we have been working with only one tool of the marketing mix—the product. This emphasis came because the new products manager will be taking the lead in making product decisions. Other managers usually handle promotion, price, and distribution. Just as this book doesn't delve deeply into how to do field market research, technical product design, process engineering, and the many other specialized tasks, it will not spend time on how to do new product advertising, personal selling, pricing, and distribution. However, we do have to address several key issues of management on this topic, ranging from when to begin involving marketing people in the development to learning how to stay flexible as we roll the new item into orbit.

---

[6] Eberhard E. Schueing, *New Product Management* (Hinsdale, Ill.: Dryden Press, 1974), p. 176.

[7] A helpful summary of the packaging procedure is given in Richard T. Hise and James U. Neal, "Effective Packaging Management," *Business Horizons,* January–February 1988, pp. 47–51.

Relationships with Personnel from the Other Tools

When Involved? A question that comes up regularly is "When should marketers become involved in the new product project?" The answer depends on the nature of the new product strategy. If there is strong technical drive, then marketing is involved at the very beginning (PIC development) but not much more until R&D has something to show for its efforts. Otherwise, marketing gets involved at the beginning and remains so all the way through.

How soon each individual gets involved depends on how important that person's activity is in the impending product's development. An industrial firm developing new metal-grinding machinery will have downstream customer coupling, and by the time the project is ready for marketing, the sales department has been involved for a long time. Advertising people have not been. For consumer packaged goods, advertising people are involved early on, but the sales department usually is not.

The key is what any particular department can contribute to the decisions being made at any one time. Because the positioning of a consumer product is critical and often settled at the time of concept testing, advertising people are essential.

The involvement issue becomes especially critical regarding the sales department. Some say to keep salespeople away from product development (no need for them to know, we must continue selling today's products today, and we don't want to have customers start holding up their decisions for the arrival of a new item). Others say to involve sales from the start, especially because someone in sales may have sent in the idea in the first place.

The answer is to have sales managers involved, not so much the sales reps. Many firms have small groups of district or regional sales managers rotating on advisory teams.

Beyond this, the answer to the original question is still situational. Some firms have a trade relations manager, who must be involved if the distributors are to play a major role. Otherwise, involvement depends on whether the firm uses marketing product managers. If it does, these people represent all of the other marketing tools (promotion, pricing, and so on). If not, then those responsibilities are located in other people.

How to Motivate Them? Probably a more critical issue than involvement, however, is motivation. Because the new products manager is often from the marketing department these days, we sometimes forget that marketing support people must be sold on a new product every bit as much as technical and manufacturing people must be. A new product is an intrusion. It takes time. It disrupts schedules. It involves change and risk.

Take the typical salesperson, for example. Unless the new item takes the firm into a market that requires a new sales force, salespeople are not usually given reduced territories when asked to sell a new product. So, it is important to (1) *investigate* in advance any possible reasons why salespeople might object to the new product, (2) give them all the *training and materials* they need to be effective, and (3) make sure the product is *available,* in their territories, when they start seeking orders. A recent study turned up a new idea in incentive compensation—setting up a special pool from which salespeople are paid for success on the new product. This way, they can be protected for the added risk of effort on the new item and still get their regular incentives.[8]

Some new product managers forget or understate the role of salespeople in giving fast feedback on conditions during the launch period. This feedback may be formally collected (see the discussion of launch control in Chapter 18), but informal feedback is stimulated by field trips, 800 numbers for salespeople to use, and lots of phone calls to the most perceptive reps.

The same applies to any other marketing support people, including the distributors. Remember the reseller is partly our employee in pushing the product down the channel and partly the user's purchasing agent. Resellers are like real estate brokers: they need both sides of the bargain to be successful.

Their help is often so critical (especially in the push strategy) that a large set of motivating tools have evolved (see Figure 17–6). Someone has to develop a submix from this list. Incidentally, the same list (with word changes) could serve as a checklist for motivating any other group of people involved in the product launch.

Price as a Positive Marketing Tool

Unfortunately, many new product marketers do not see price as a tool of marketing. It is a decision to be made, but it is not seen as the strong force for sales it could be. Often, the pricing decision is made elsewhere in the firm (such as by the finance division); if so, price will not be seen as a marketing tool.

It is a marketing tool, however. The new product has at least three different price strategy options—skimming, meet the market, and penetration. As their names imply, *skimming* sets a higher price, accepts lower volume, and makes up for it by a large margin over costs.

---

[8] *Management Briefing: Marketing* (New York: The Conference Board, 1986), p. 5.

FIGURE 17–6   Alternative Tools and Devices for Motivating Distributors

A. Increase the distributor's unit volume.
   1. Have an outstanding product.
   2. Use pull techniques — advertising, trade and consumer shows, public relations, missionary selling.
   3. Give the distributor a type of monopoly — exclusivity or selectivity.
   4. Run "where available" ads.
   5. Offer merchandising assistance — dollars, training, displays, point of purchase, co-op advertising, in-store demonstrations, store "events," and repair and service clinics.

B. Increase the distributor's unit margin.
   1. Raise the basic percentage margin.
   2. Offer special discounts — e.g., for promotion or service.
   3. Offer allowances and special payments.
   4. Offer to *prepay* allowances to save interest.

C. Reduce the distributor's costs of doing business.
   1. Provide managerial training.
   2. Provide dollars for training.
   3. Improve the returned goods policy.
   4. Improve the service policy.
   5. Drop-ship delivery to distributor's customers.
   6. Preprice the merchandise.
   7. Tray-pack the merchandise or otherwise aid in repackaging it.

D. Change the distributor's attitude toward the line.
   1. By encouragements — management negotiation, sales calls, direct mail, advertising.
   2. By discouragements — threats to cut back some of the above benefits or legal action.
   3. Rap sessions — talk groups, focus groups, councils.
   4. Better product introduction sessions — better visuals, better instructions.

Penetration uses a low price, where the firm wants its new item to get in fast and establish a strong position before competitors enter. *Meet the market* is a decision that price will play a very little role in determining from whom customers buy. It only comes into play if the new item is substantially like competitive products; otherwise, there is no market to price to.

The point is, any price below skimming is actually a discount. It is a way of offering the customer cash rather than using that money to buy more of one of the other marketing mix tools. For example, when an airline enters a new route (market), it can offer extremely low prices to penetrate rapidly. Or, it can enter at a higher price and use the added money to do more advertising, pay for special in-flight menus or beverages, or give rebates to travel agents who book on the new flights. If you think about these options, you will see that they involve the other tools in the marketing mix—better meals is a product improvement, agent rebates is increased distributor margins, and more advertising is promotion.

Price should be viewed as a variable option, right along with the others.

Every Marketing Tool Should Be Given a Role to Play

It's strange, but the product manager who on the weekend understands why every member of a favorite football team is given a specific role to play will forget about it when putting together a team to introduce a new product. A pulling guard on a football team knows exactly what to do on each play, but the advertising manager is often told something like "We want you to help introduce the new product; give us some really great advertising." What would the guard do if told "Give us some really good guarding"!

Look at Figure 17–7, which shows some typical role patterns for advertising. Note the dramatic difference between consumer goods and industrial goods, and between one time period and another. We don't just need advertising; we need advertising of one type at the beginning, another type in the middle, and still another type late in the introduction period.

The same applies to the personal selling function, to price, and to the distributor. For example, distributors may be asked to handle all of the marketing (for example, a private brand deal with Sears). Distributors are more often asked to supply availability (stocking), and/or promotion through their sales force, and/or service. These three items can be put together into several totally different submixes. For example, Polaroid may introduce two new items:

Low-price disposable model: retailers are to provide stocking, aggressive in-store promotion, advertising in their weekly schedule, and very little service.

High-value model for use after dark: retailers are to provide some availability on a selective basis, very little promotion except to announce its availability, extensive in-store assistance in explaining the new model, and extensive first-line service when problems arise.

These two packages or submixes of effort show how the roles of other marketing tools must vary in tune with each other.

Now, it would be nice to say we have such clear roles for each tool in each new product introduction. We don't. We have no established playing

FIGURE 17–7   Typical Role Patterns for New Consumer and Industrial
Product Advertising

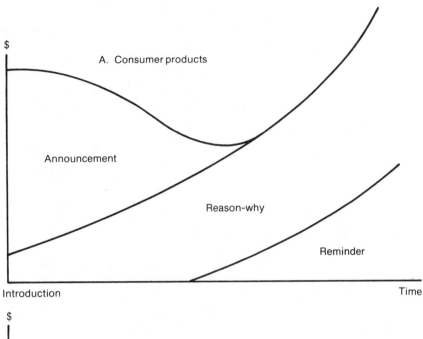

A. Consumer products

Announcement

Reason-why

Reminder

$

Introduction

Time

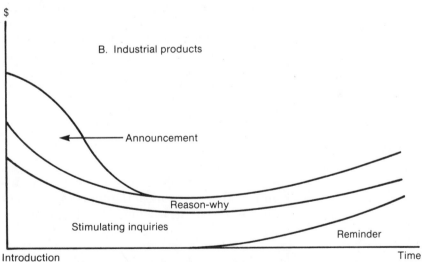

B. Industrial products

Announcement

Reason-why

Stimulating inquiries

Reminder

$

Introduction

Time

grounds and rules such as there are in football. Instead, we're supposed
to be creative. And we don't "play a game" every week, gaining
experience each time. However, the new products manager who thinks
like a team leader will get closer to putting together a more effective
package of efforts.

The Forgotten Tools

Mention of marketing mix brings forth visions of personal selling and advertising. We have been talking about product, price, and distribution as other strong members of the mix. Actually, different industries have other tools that are sometimes almost as important as those. For example, can you imagine introducing a new telecommunications product, a new employee moving service, a new packaging material, or a line of very expensive shoes without extensive presale service? Such an effort can even be the basis for a new product and run through the concept testing, use testing, and market testing procedures.

Another important tool frequently overlooked is samples (or, in some cases, actual free merchandise). Transportation companies often run a new service free for a period of time to let customers get acquainted with it. Samples of consumer packaged goods can be used in print advertising media, in direct mail, door to door as doorknob hangers, in product carriers on companion products, and in personal distribution in high-density locations or in stores. Such a flexible tool is used often and vigorously.

General Foods once used an outside sampling firm when it arranged to have 200,000 chicken wings baked with its then new Oven-Fry batter-mix coating. The 16-week operation, conducted in 20 supermarkets, required in-store propane ovens, tight scheduling of chicken parts arrivals, and careful cooking. The operation was credited with playing a major role in the product's successful introduction.

Another tool, often not even considered a tool, is publicity. Because new products are often newsworthy, a firm's public relations department can make a major contribution. It should always be given a chance to do so.

Changes during Launch

Just as the advertising role mix changes during the launch period (see Figure 17–7 above), so does the entire mix. A product that may have been a valuable tool in the beginning becomes much less so as soon as a major competitor enters with a similar or better product. A price starting out as skim may be forced down by new entries that are using penetration. Postsale service may have a little role at the start but become a major player as we establish users. A distributor may be compensated to play an educational role for a while, but most distributors won't stay in that mode for long.

And so on. The changes are sometimes planned, sometimes just prepared for, and sometimes made in surprised panic. If readers will permit another sports analogy, many coaches are heard to say, "We had to change our game plan when . . ." or "Our plan was to hit them hard in the beginning, load them up·with personal fouls, and then selectively play against the particular individuals in the greatest trouble." A new products manager should be able to make the same type of statement, and each tool manager on the team should know about it and be ready for it. A baseball team carries 25 people, and only 9 play at a time. Unfortunately, many product managers have to (or want to) use the entire team from the beginning.

Variations Abound

Here are some vignettes indicating the many opportunities for creative marketing mixes:

The trade show: Amtech Industries had a new, $90 electronic box that would let people operate portable radios through car speakers, which thieves usually leave behind. Lacking money, Amtech introduced the item at trade show exhibits, where it signed up manufacturers' reps, who in turn essentially handled the marketing.

Billboardlike ads on company trucks: Orval Kent Food Co. also lacked money to promote its new foodstore singles version of its traditional delicatessen salads. So, the firm painted the sides of its trucks to look like billboards and got free advertising everywhere the trucks went. The firm also leased the sides of other trucks.

Price and train posters: The Oak Tree Farm Dairy hired walking billboards (ice cream containerlike "sandwich boards") offering $1 off a trial purchase. This was combined with 5-by-6-foot posters in all Long Island Railroad trains.

In-store promotion: Abbott's of New England nearly went broke trying to get its new chowder products into supermarkets. So, it persuaded some of the stores' deli counters to offer single portions of hot chowder. The products were soon in 20 percent of U.S. supermarkets.

Price: A CT scanner company faced objections from hospitals over the product's necessarily high price. So, it put scanners on tractor-trailers and sold them to several hospitals, which shared the cost. In some cases, a hospital's radiologist bought a scanner and sold its service to his hospital.

Product change: Lazare Kaplan International uses a laser engraving process to imprint the firm's name on every diamond it sells. Though invisible to the naked eye, it can be seen by proud owners and dealers. The firm emphasizes product quality and charges more for it.

SUMMARY

In Chapters 16 and 17, we have seen that a product innovator must first develop an appropriate marketing strategy of target market, positioning, and marketing mix. Managers must then flesh out the strategy with decisions on each marketing tool in that mix. Each tool has many options, so not only do we have to decide the relative importance of each major tool class, we then must make submixes within each tool.

The major tool discussed here was product, and we looked at the new item itself (as a thing or as a service action sequence), then as a brand, as a package, and so on. We next looked at some problems of managing the other three major tools, especially deciding what each tool's role should be and how to motivate the "owners" of that tool to work as a team in the new product effort.

We also looked at price, not as a given but as a flexible marketing tool with lots of options. This was followed by how we need to stay flexible during launch and some of the forgotten tools that are available. Some vignettes demonstrated the creativity of new products managers who had to find some unusual way to introduce their products under less-than-desirable conditions.

During the launch phase of commercialization, something else is going on—managers are watching progress and making corrections in their actions. They are trying to manage the launch to success. This process of managerial control during launch is the subject of Chapter 18.

APPLICATIONS

1. "Now, on pricing, I have no doubts: 'Hit 'em high, and slide down the demand curve.' So help me, some of these new products people spend years and lots of money developing a product better than any on the market—and then they want to price equal or below competition. I call that being a coward—taking the easy way out. You can't lose—on volume, that is. But profits are another story. Just to be sure, I'm willing to put my thinking to a test. Can you name all of the possible circumstances when a penetration or meet-the-market price would be appropriate for a superior new product? Bet there aren't more than a half-dozen and that those are rare."

2. "Packaging must be terribly important today on lots of products. We spend a fortune on it. I read recently about a new detergent someone is developing that will have a thing called an 'overcap.' Apparently it goes onto a bottle, over the regular cap. It can be torn away and sent in for a refund, for example. Less likely to be cheated on than a

coupon. I think this is terribly creative and ought to be encouraged. For example, I'll bet you could think of 10 or 15 new packaging ideas for detergents if you set your mind to it. Good ones, that is, not just a bunch of foolishness."

3. "One of our divisions recently came up with a new way of testing new brand names (at least it was new to us). They have, say, a new shampoo that they are getting ready to market. So they narrow the list of possible names down to, say, five and then go to target consumers with just the names—asking the consumers to guess what the new product is. The guessing is easy if the name has a giveaway in it (keyed to specific usage, for example), but they learn the most when it doesn't. As the consumers guess the product type, the company is learning what the brand is saying—what message is being conveyed. You ought to try this approach sometime, after you get back home. Just make up a set of five brand names, and ask people to describe the generic products they are for, one by one. Then generalize on what you have learned. Our people say you will be surprised, especially if you have a generic type of product in mind for the brands."

4. "Sampling is another tool we like—really effective in getting awareness and trial among the people who are somewhat inclined toward a new product in the first place. But several of our divisions can't use samples per se because of the nature of their products. Could you tell me what might be a substitute for trial in the marketing of a new type of each of the following?
   a. Heavy industrial elevators.
   b. Coffins.
   c. Word processors.
   d. Diamond rings.
   e. Replacement tires.
   f. Milling machines."

Case: Chilled Foods*

In the first half of 1989, the American food industry was working feverishly to capitalize on a new technology and what it felt was a new consumer interest—chilled or refrigerated foods. The products were shipped and stored at

*Source: Some of the information in this case came from Barbara Toman, "Will U.S. Warm to Refrigerated Dishes?" *The Wall Street Journal,* August 18, 1989, p. B1.

retail under refrigerated conditions, not frozen. These prepackaged foods were ready to be taken home and heated or lightly cooked. The Industry activities were varied. For example:

Marks & Spencer.   A British firm based in London, Marks & Spencer was a large retailer, selling food under its St. Michael private label. Arrangements were being made to introduce chilled products under this label into the United States through a regional chain of supermarkets it had acquired. The firm had been a pioneer in prepackaged, refrigerated food and in the United Kingdom marketed a line of "yuppydom" foods, such as Salmon en Croute with cream sauce at $5.34 for two servings. Its reputation was for top-quality products, with a short, integrated farm-to-store distribution system.

Campbell.   After first trying to market its Fresh Chef line of refrigerated sauces, soups, and salads in 1987 (later withdrawn), Campbell was in 1989 test marketing Fresh Kitchen refrigerated sauces, entrees, and desserts.

Philip Morris.   A 1986 effort by its General Foods division to market a Culinova line of fresh entrees failed due to problems in distributing these chilled products. But in 1989, the new Kraft General Foods division was test marketing Chillery entrees, salads, pasta, and desserts.

Nestlé.   Nestlé's Carnation division was already national with a Contadina Fresh line of sauces and pastas, which are less temperature sensitive than entrees. In addition, another division (Nestlé Enterprises) was test marketing the FreshNes line of entrees and salads in Columbus and Cleveland.

The issues faced by these firms (and, according to industry insiders, by several others in early stages of planning) were (1) how to get the products delivered to the stores and maintained conveniently in those stores until sold, (2) deciding just where in the midscale/up-scale range these products would end up, (3) finding the product lines (such as entrees or salads) where the sales volume would be the best, and (4) making sure the new technology could work its way into a market already overloaded with deli offerings, precooked meals, and others. Less critical matters were how best to assure the buyer that the items had not spoiled, how spicy should these products be, and how to price them.

And, in the meantime, branding problems arose. Should these new items be tied to the strong family brands that these firms all had? If so, what secondary branding should distinguish them? In secondary branding or nonfamily branding, what image should be projected by the brand (that is, how up-scale)? Did retailers have the same branding problems when they developed their own lines of chilled foods? How could the essence of chilled foods best be communicated, or should the brand even try in a situation such as this? Or in other situations?

Post-Launch Control

SETTING

Once the new product is marketed, the long trek through the development process may appear to be ended. The people involved in the program are happy, satisfied, and anxious for a well-earned rest.

But, the group was charged with launching a *winning* product, not just a product. Just as managerial control over the *development process* was needed (checking actual progress against the plan and making adjustments where it appeared there would be trouble meeting the schedule), control over the *marketing of the new product* is needed. Launch control lasts until the new product has finished its assault on given objectives, which may take as long as six months to a year for an industrial good and commercial services or as little as a few weeks for some consumer packaged goods.

Managerial control is a difficult subject that becomes even more so when applied to the launch of a new product. Therefore, reviewing the introductory control material in Chapter 15 might help students get a handle on it.

WHAT WE MEAN BY LAUNCH CONTROL

Comparing a NASA space capsule to a youngster's slingshot will explain the subject of this chapter. After firing at a crow in the upper branches of a tree, the youngster quickly panics and runs if the rock sails well over the crow and heads directly for the kitchen window in the neighbor's house. That's when the youngster would rather be in the NASA control headquarters in Houston, Texas, because NASA scientists launch *guided* space capsules, not unguided slingshot rocks.

NASA would have anticipated that an in-flight directional problem might occur and thus would simply make an in-flight correction allowing the space capsule to continue its controlled flight. Not having in-flight corrective powers, the youngster must just continue the unscheduled "flight."

This analogy isn't as farfetched as it may sound. It literally offers the new products manager a choice—NASA or a run for cover. Good tracking systems make successful launching of new products more likely. The manager who has to run for cover simply wasn't a manager.[1]

Unfortunately, only a minority of firms systematically apply managerial control to new product launches. Historically, the day of launch presumably ended management's ability to control the fate of a new product. Prior to launch, management could pour overtime dollars into a project that was behind schedule, but there was no counterpart of overtime on the launch side.

That view is being rejected. If troubles are anticipated properly, and if contingency plans are thought out at least informally, then there is indeed time and opportunity to correct marketing troubles early—perhaps early enough to achieve original goals.

A Conference Board study of marketing plans reported that the majority of companies settled on a single set of objectives and action programs in their plans.[2] Some kept close-second rejected alternatives as contingency plans, in case the chosen one started to fail. One marketing manager said, "Our plan is not cast in bronze," implying that the door was open to at least a degree of flexibility. A later study reported the same majority position but found that about one fourth of the firms *were* using contingency planning.[3]

Apparently, most managements today are at least receptive to the concept of a "guided launch"; a few use such a system, some are experimenting with parts of systems, and the rest are watching what the others are doing.[4]

---

[1] People marketing new products are not the only ones using NASA-type systems today. Manufacturing quality control managers have the same problem—anticipating problems that might endanger product quality, watching to see if these problems are coming up, and being ready to do something if they do.

[2] David S. Hopkins, *The Short-Term Marketing Plan,* Report no. 565 (New York: The Conference Board, 1972), p. 16.

[3] David S. Hopkins, *The Marketing Plan,* Report no. 801 (New York: The Conference Board, 1981).

[4] For a discussion of contingency planning in general (not as applied to new products), see Robert E. Linneman and Rajan Chadran, "Contingency Planning: A Key to Swift Managerial Action in the Uncertain Tomorrow," *Managerial Planning,* January–February 1981, pp. 23–27.

THE LAUNCH CONTROL SYSTEM

A launch control system contains the following steps.

1. *Spot potential problems.*   The first step in getting ready to play NASA on a new product launch is to identify all potential weak spots or potential troubles. These problems occur either in the firm's actions (such as poor advertising) or in the outside environment (such as competitive retaliation). As one manager said, "I look for things that will really hurt us if they happen, or don't happen."

2. *Select those to control.*   Each potential problem is analyzed to determine its "expected impact." Naturally, only problems that would hurt us are on the list; but, some problems are more likely than others. *Expected impact* means we multiply the damage the event would cause by the likelihood of the event happening. The impact is used to rank the problems and to select those that will be "controlled" and those that won't.

3. *Develop contingency plans for the control problems.*   Contingency plans are what, if anything, will be done if the difficulties actually occur. The degree of completeness in this planning varies, but the best contingency plans are ready for *immediate* action. For example, "We will undertake the development of a new sales compensation plan" is no contingency plan. "We will up commission on the new item from 7 percent to 10 percent, by fax to all sales reps" *is* a contingency plan. It's ready to be put to work immediately.

4. *Designing the tracking system.*   As with NASA, the tracking system must send back usable data fast. We must have some experience so we can evaluate the data (Is the dealer stocking going too slow, or is this normal on products like ours?). There should be trigger points (for example, trial by 15 percent of our customers called on, by the end of the first month). These points trigger the contingency plan. Without them, we just end up arguing about whether the data coming in indicate we have a serious problem. Remember, money to execute a contingency plan has to come from somewhere (someone else's budget), and thus every plan faces opposition from people who want to delay implementing it.

If a problem cannot be tracked, no matter how important its impact may be, then we don't have it under control. For example, competitive entry usually cannot be followed like dealer stocking can, but we can have a contingency plan ready if it happens. This situation is not ideal, because managerial control tries to anticipate a problem before it gets here; then we implement the remedial action in time to keep it from ever occurring. (See Figure 18–1.)

On the following pages, we will look in depth at each of these four steps in a launch control system.

FIGURE 18–1   Graphic Application of the General Tracking Concept (with remedial action)

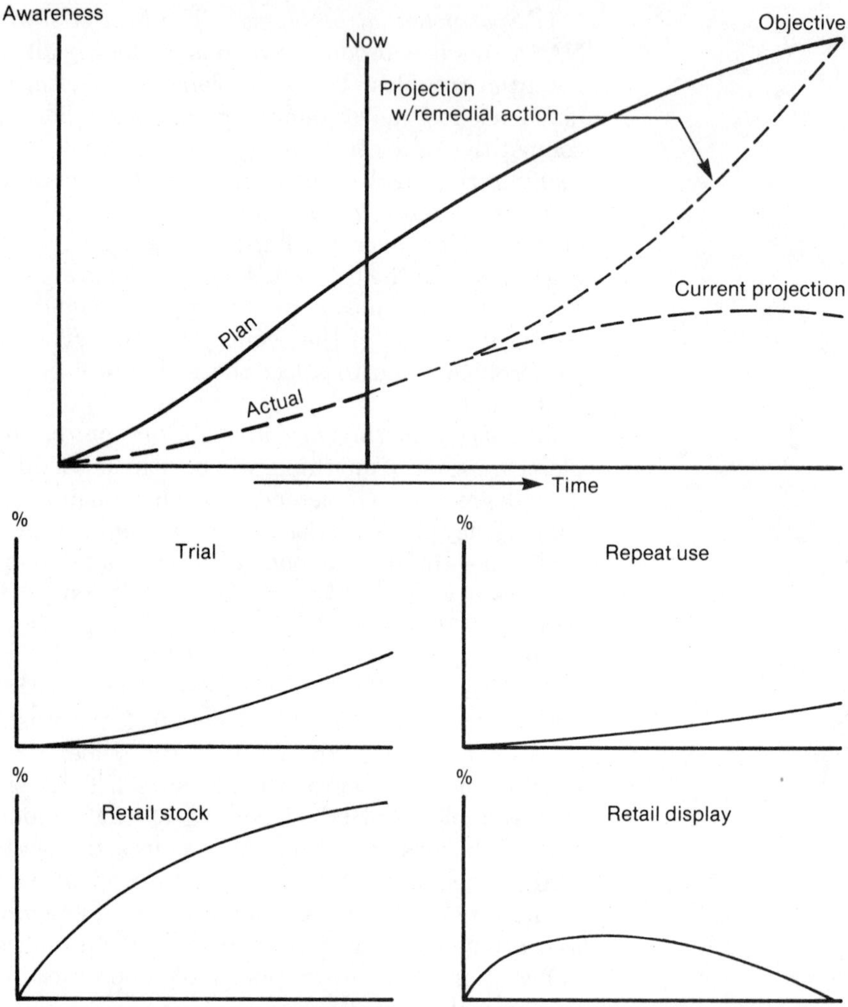

Step One: Spotting Potential Problems

Four techniques are used to develop the list of potential problems. First is the *situation analysis* made for the marketing planning step. For example, government lawyers may recently have criticized an ingredient used in the product. Or, buyers may have indicated a high level of satisfaction with present products on the market, suggesting trouble in getting them to try our new one.

As another example, the firm itself may not be prepared, skilled, or motivated to do certain things. This delicate (and politically dangerous) assessment, although difficult to do objectively and fairly, inevitably discloses potential problems, particularly in nonmarketing departments. The *problems* section in the marketing plan will have summarized most of the potential troubles from the situation analysis.

A second technique is to *role-play what competitors will do* after they have heard of the new product. Vigorous devil's advocate sessions can turn up scary options that competitors have open—far better that we think of them now.[5]

Third, we *look back over all of the data* accumulated in the new product's "file." Start with the original concept test reports, then the screening forms, the early Alpha testing, the rest of the use tests (especially the longer-term ones with potential customers), and records of all internal discussions. These records contain lots of potential troubles, some of which we actually had to ignore in our efforts to move the item along.

For example, a food product had done well in all studies to date, except when the project leader ran a simulated test market. The sales forecast from the research firm came out very low. Study of the data indicated that the research firm had gotten a "trial" of 5 percent in the test, whereas the agency and the developer had anticipated a trial of 15 percent. The difference was highly significant because success depended on which estimate would be right. The developers believed they were right, so they discontinued research and introduced the product. But, they made trial the top-priority item on the control list. Shortly after introduction, surveys showed that 15 percent was the better estimate, so the contingency plan was happily discarded. But, they were ready if action had been warranted.[6]

Fourth, it is helpful to start with a satisfied customer or industrial user and work back from that satisfaction to determine the *hierarchy of effects* necessary to produce it. This hierarchy is the same one used earlier in the awareness–trial–repeat triad.

But, the hierarchy of effects may vary in each situation. Thus, for example, the satisfaction point for an industrial drill may be "known, provable, substantially lower output cost." But reaching that point requires the customer to measure actual costs. It also requires the customer to have data on what the drills cost previously. These are like rungs on a ladder—the customer cannot get to the top (satisfaction)

---

[5] A new way of anticipating competitive actions is given in Carolyn M. Vella and John J. McGonagle, Jr., "Shadowing Markets: A New Competitive Intelligence Technique," *Planning Review,* September–October 1987, pp. 36–38.

[6] David Olson, "Anticipating New Product Problems—A Planning Discipline," unpublished manuscript in working paper form (Chicago: Leo Burnett, 1981).

without having stepped on the rungs of "know previous costs" and "know actual costs of the new drill." Both are potential problems, given that most firms do not have such sophisticated cost systems.

If a firm is developing a control plan for the first time, it will probably hold to a simple hierarchy and give attention only to the really critical and identifiable steps. Figure 18–2 shows the standard A–T–R hierarchy altered to fit the marketing of ethical pharmaceutical and nutritional specialty items. Note each product had a different problem and required different remedial action (contingency plan). All three items were marketed by one firm in one year.

A far more detailed and generic hierarchy of effects would be as follows:

Customer has the basic need of the category.

Customer is aware of the need.

Customer decides to do something about it.

Customer explores our alternative action.

Customer is exposed to our promotion.

Customer gives attention to our promotion.

Customer becomes aware of the new product – by name.

Customer becomes aware of the new product – by appeal or positioning.

Customer has occasion to use the product.

Product is available where customer shops.

Product is brought to the customer's attention in the shop.

Right form, package size, and price are available in the shop.

Customer buys the product.

Customer knows how to use the product properly.

Customer remembers how to use the product properly.

Customer actually uses the product properly.

Customer takes the time to assess the product's performance.

Customer has the knowledge to make a proper assessment.

Customer decides the product performed satisfactorily.

Customer decides the product performed at least as well as or better than product previously used.

Customer must find no major breakdown tangential to the product's performance – for example, a side effect.

Customer must decide to use the product again.

Customer must have the opportunity to use the product again.

FIGURE 18–2 A–T–R Launch Control Patterns (actual) for Three Pharmaceutical/Nutritional Products

Product A

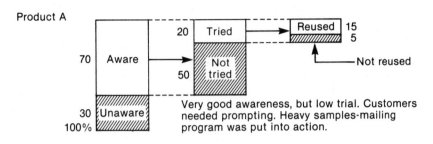

Very good awareness, but low trial. Customers needed prompting. Heavy samples-mailing program was put into action.

Product B

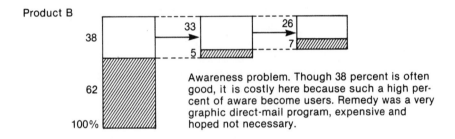

Awareness problem. Though 38 percent is often good, it is costly here because such a high percent of aware become users. Remedy was a very graphic direct-mail program, expensive and hoped not necessary.

Product C

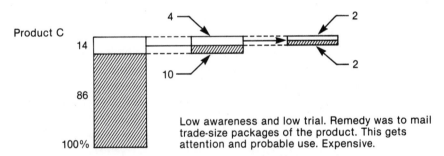

Low awareness and low trial. Remedy was to mail trade-size packages of the product. This gets attention and probable use. Expensive.

Comment: All of the above data were as of 10 weeks' time on the market. In each case, the firm had to decide whether there was a problem, what the problem (if any) was, and what to do about it.

Customer must be able to buy what is needed.

Customer must actually make the repurchase.

Use must again produce satisfaction.

Product must be put into the customer's use cycle.

Even this detailed list takes no account of the many variables outside the customer chain—for example, competitive action to thwart some item on the above list. But, it is a good checklist. Even so, some problems may not show up from any of the above searches; they relate specifically to the new item and are the creative concerns of smart developers.[7]

Oddly, one "problem" usually overlooked is the possibility of being *too* successful. It's kind of a happy hurt, but it can be expensive and should be anticipated if there is any particular reason to think it might happen.[8]

Last, note one item has not been mentioned — actual sales. We do not "control" sales and do not have tracking lines and contingency plans for low sales. It seems that we should, and most control plans put together by novices include sales. But, stop to think. If the sales line is falling short of the forecast, what contingency plan should be ordered into action? Unless you know what is causing poor sales, you don't know what solution to use.

Instead, we use the above efforts to list the main reasons why sales may be low and then track *those reasons*. If we have anticipated properly, tracked properly, and instituted remedies properly, then sales will follow. Otherwise, when sales lag, we have to stop, undertake research to find out what is happening, plan a remedial action, prepare for it, and then implement it. By then, it's far too late. Contingency planning is a hedge bet; it is a gamble, like insurance. Most contingency planning is a waste, and we hope it all will be.

Step Two: Selecting the Control Events

No one can control the scores of potential problems that come from the analysis in step one. So, the planner's judgment must cut the list down to a number the firm can handle. (See Figure 18–3 for a graphic representation of what follows.) Some people say never more than six, but a new televised shaving product would surely warrant more contingency planning than the launch of a new line of jigsaw blades.

The judgment used to reduce the list of problems is usually based on the potential damage and the likelihood of occurrence. Figure 18–4 shows how the two factors combine to produce nine different categories, of four types. Those with little harm and little probability

---

[7] Even in established markets (such as consumer packaged goods), the common measures vary. For example, a recent study in the United Kingdom cited three measures: number of first-time triers, their rates of repeat buying, and how their buying related to other brands in the market. See Dee M. Wellan and A. S. C. Ehrenberg, "A Successful New Brand: Shield," *Journal of the Market Research Society* 30, no. 1 (January 1988), pp. 35–44.

[8] Joshua Hyatt gives examples of this problem, including one successful firm that barely avoided bankruptcy from a too successful launch, in "Too Hot to Handle," *Inc.*, March 1987, pp. 52–58.

FIGURE 18–3 Decision Model for Building Launch Control Plan

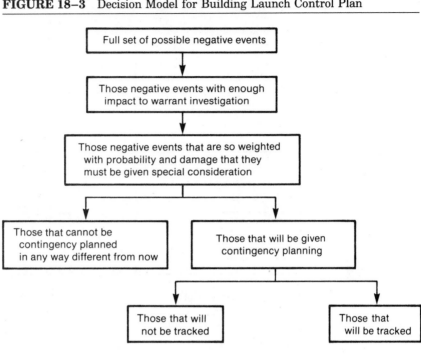

can safely be ignored. Others farther down the diagram cannot be. At the bottom are problems that should be taken care of *now;* they shouldn't have gotten this far. In between are problems handled as suggested by the patterns on the boxes. How they are handled is very situational, depending on time pressure, money for contingencies, the firm's maturity in launch control, and the managers' personal preferences.

For example, most new product managers have been burned on previous launches and so have developed biases toward certain events. They may have been criticized so severely for forgetting something on a previous launch that they never forget it again.

Step Three: Developing Contingency Plans

Once we've reduced the problem list to a size the firm can handle, we have to ask: "If any of those events actually comes about, is there anything we can do?" For example, although competitive price cuts and competitive product imitation are on many lists, there is usually nothing

FIGURE 18–4   Expected Effects Matrix for Selection of Control Events

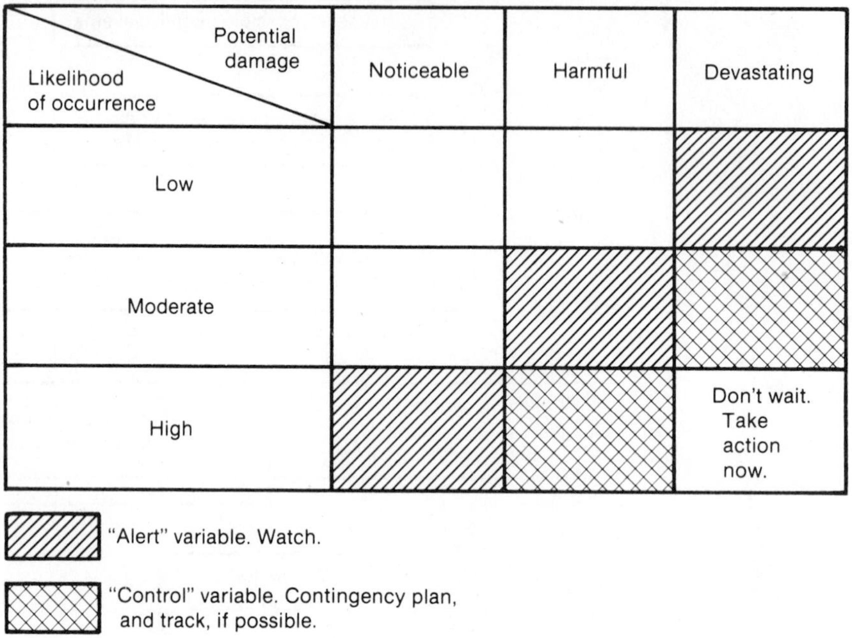

Likelihood of occurrence \ Potential damage	Noticeable	Harmful	Devastating
Low			/////
Moderate		/////	XXXXX
High	/////	XXXXX	Don't wait. Take action now.

///// "Alert" variable. Watch.

XXXXX "Control" variable. Contingency plan, and track, if possible.

the firm can do. The competitor is going to try to hold most of its share, and the developer is usually better off to ignore those actions and sell on the uniqueness of the new item.

For the other events, our planned reaction depends on the event. Let's take two different types: a company failure and a negative buyer action (consumer failure). The most common company failure is inadequate distribution, particularly at the retail or dealer level. Correcting the problem usually just depends on how high a price the company is willing to pay.

Retailers sell the one thing they have — shelf space exposure to store traffic. Shelf space goes to the highest bidder, so if a new product comes up short, the remedy is to raise the bid — special promotions, more pull advertising, a better margin, and so on. These were rejected options when the marketing plan was put together, so contingency planners usually have lots of alternatives from which to choose.

A consumer failure is handled the same way. For awareness, the plan had called for a particular action. If it turns out that awareness is low, we usually do more of the same action — increase sales calls, increase advertising, or whatever. If people are not actually trying the new item, we have ways of encouraging trial (such as mailing samples or trade packages as in Figure 18–2, or giving out coupons).

Many product developers have marveled at how easy good contingency thinking is while preparing to launch, compared to doing it under the panic conditions of a beachhead disaster.

Step Four: Designing the Tracking System

We now have a set of negative outcomes, for most of which we have standby contingency plans ready to go. The next step is developing a system that will tell us when to implement any of those contingency plans. The answer lies in the concept of tracking.

Tracking.   The tracking concept in marketing has been around for a long time but probably got its greatest boost when Russia launched the Sputnik satellite. This launch led to the absorption of the rocketry lexicon into American language. Though we had guided missiles for some time before that, they lacked the drama of a launch into outer space, especially with the spectacle of television.

The concept of tracking as applied to projectiles launched into space seems to fit the new product launch well. There is a blast-off, a breakout of the projectile into an orbit or trajectory of its own, possible modification on that trajectory during flight, and so on. The launch controller (whose title originated in the concept of managerial control) is responsible for tracking the projectile against its planned trajectory and for making whatever corrections are necessary to ensure that it goes where it is supposed to go.

Applying this tracking concept to new products was as natural as could be. Earlier, Figure 18–1 showed the graphic application of the basic concept to a new product.

Three essentials are involved: first is the ability to lay the *planned trajectory*. What is the expected path? What is reasonable given the competitive situation, the product's features, and the planned marketing efforts? Although it is easy to conjecture about such matters, setting useful trajectory paths requires a base of research that many firms do not have when they launch a new product.

The new product research department at Leo Burnett Company, a large advertising agency, studied all of the new product launches that the agency had participated in and plotted all of the actual awareness tracks and actual trial tracks.[9] From these scatter diagrams, the director of

---

[9] Olson, "Anticipating New Product Problems – A Planning Discipline."

research computed generalized paths that could be applied to future new product situations (see Figure 18–5). A firm that lacks experience can sometimes acquire the data it needs from such outside sources as advertising agencies, marketing research firms, trade media, or industry pools.[10]

Second, there must be an *inflow of actual data* indicating progress against the plan. This means quick and continuing marketing research geared to measure the variables being tracked.

Third, we have to *project the probable outcome* against the plan. Unless the outcome can be forecasted, we have little basis for triggering remedial action until the outcome is at hand.

The key is speed — learning fast that a problem is coming about, early enough to do something that prevents it or solves it.

Selecting the Actual Tracking Variables. Now we hit perhaps the toughest part of launch control. How will we actually measure whether one of our key problems is coming about?

If the problem is some specific step of action or mind, like awareness, then the answer is clear — find out how many people are aware of the new item. Trial is easy; repeat purchase is easy. What about trade support? Many new product marketers fear they will not get the push they need. But, does trade support mean stocking the product? Displaying the product? Advertising the product locally? Giving presale service? Gearing up to give postsale service? The launch planner has to decide.

We need relevant, measurable, and predictable tracking variables. A variable is *relevant* if it identifies the problem, *measurable* if we can get a statistic showing it is or isn't, and *predictable* if we know the path that the statistic should follow across the page.

Look back to Figure 18–1. The top graph displays awareness: "Have you heard of . . . ?" It is a percentage of all people in the target market. The track line, labeled *plan,* shows what we hope will happen. The broken line shows what we find is happening, and what we fear will happen if we do nothing. The tracking variable is relevant, measurable, predictable.

But, let's look at dealer support. At the bottom of Figure 18–1 is a track of retail stocking, the percentage of target dealers who have stocked the item so far. This too is relevant, measurable, and predictable (based on our past experience). But, what about shelf space? The height

---

[10] A source that may help some readers is Christopher J. Easingwood, "Early Product Life-Cycle Forms for Infrequently Purchased Major Products," *International Journal of Research in Marketing,* no. 1, 1987, pp. 3–9.

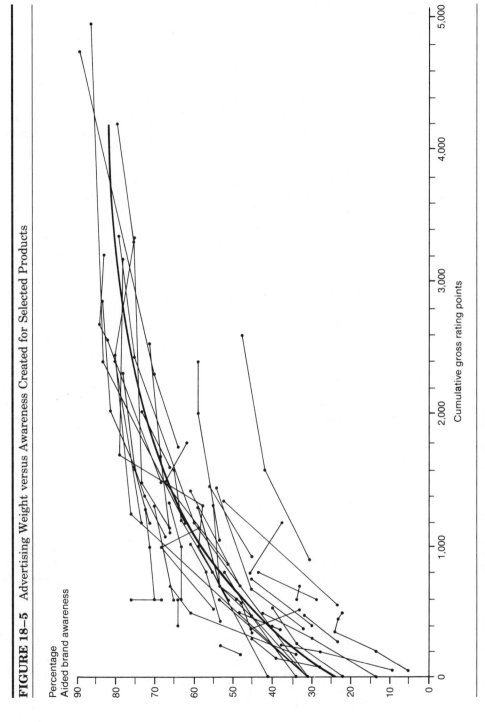

FIGURE 18–5 Advertising Weight versus Awareness Created for Selected Products

Percentage
Aided brand awareness

Cumulative gross rating points

Source: David Olson, unpublished working paper, Leo Burnett Company.

of the stocking, the number of facings, and the department in which it occurs are all aspects of shelf space. They differ in relevance, they are all tough to measure without actually calling on stores and looking at the shelves, and we are apt to lack the experience we need to predict them. Figure 18–1 also shows retail display, but such a track is mainly a guess.

Too, watch out for situations where even a fairly obvious variable may be tricky to define. Take awareness (perhaps the most common variable tracked), for example. Exactly what is it? Ability to recognize the brand name? Know the product's key differentiation? Ability to recall the brand, or spot it in a list? Or, does awareness mean consumers know enough about the item to evaluate it and decide whether they want to try it?

There is no way to settle this argument, so most firms just arbitrarily pick a definition that they can measure and use it every time.

Many developers shun launch control because of problems in finding good tracking variables. If they can't easily measure the emergence of a problem early on, the whole idea of controlling the way to success makes a lot less sense.

Selecting the Trigger Points.   Given that we have found useful variables for warning that a problem is coming about, the last step is deciding in advance how bad it has to be before turning the contingency plan loose. Say, for example, we have a low budget situation and are worried that customers may not hear of our new item — low awareness. If our objective for three months out is 40 percent of customers aware, and tracking shows we actually have only 35 percent, should we release the standby direct-mail program?

This is not an easy decision to make under beachhead conditions, for political reasons as well as for time constraints. Throwing the switch for direct mail admits that the original advertising has failed. This admission is not popular, and arguments will be made that the advertising is working as planned and the awareness will soon increase.

To avoid these no-win situations, agree in advance what level will be the trigger and put the triggering decision in the hands of a person with no vested interest. With this, the tracking plan is complete. With diligent implementation, the launch will probably be "controlled to success."

Nontrackable Problems.   But, what do we do when we have a problem that worries us but cannot be tracked because we can't find a variable for it, or because we don't have a track that the variable should follow, or because there is nothing we can do if the problem is found to be coming about? The answer is, very little.

Typically, management watches sales, and, if they are falling below the forecast, someone is asked to find out why. This means to interview salespeople, customers, distributors, and so on. It's a difficult inquiry because things are changing so fast and because most participants have vested interests—they may not reveal the true problem even if they know it.

When the cause is found, a remedy is devised. If it's not a fast-moving market, time may be available to get the new product back into a good sales pattern. If it's too late, the new item is dumped or milked for a while. The loss may be very little if the costs of launch were low, as they often are for small firms, for line extensions, and for products that were never expected to amount to much.

A SAMPLE LAUNCH CONTROL PLAN

Figure 18–6 shows a sample launch control plan. In it are samples of real-life problems, specific variables that were selected to track them, trigger points, and the standby contingency plans ready to go into effect. Note particularly that this was not a large firm, it had no market research department, and it was not then sophisticated in how to launch new products. Still, the plan covers the main bases, permits launch control to be in the hands of available managers, and provides effective action if any of the possible problems come about.

Larger firms with big budgets will have more sophisticated plans, but in principle they will be exactly the same—problem, tracking variable, trigger point, and remedial plan ready to go. Very small firms may have the energy to deal with only a couple of problems; the manager may use what we call *eyeball control* to move around the market and find if they are coming about, and then have in mind what will be done if they are.

But, whether in the mind, in the format of Figure 18–6, or in a sophisticated formal plan, the essentials are the same.

OBJECTIONS TO LAUNCH CONTROL

We saw earlier that many firms do not utilize this type of formal contingency planning. These firms may simply never have heard of launch control on new products; more likely, they do know about it and have specific reasons for not using it.

It Costs Too Much.   Launch control uses extensive market research, both before and after launch. And, like all insurance, the dollars spent getting remedial plans ready are wasted if the plans are not needed.

FIGURE 18–6 Sample Control Plan

Setting: This tracking plan is for a small or medium-sized industrial firm that is marketing a unique electrical measuring instrument. The device must be sold to the general-purpose (that is, factory) market, whereas past company products have been sold primarily to the scientific, R&D market. The firm has about 60 salespeople, but its resources are not large. No syndicated (for example, audit firm) services are available in this market.

Only a few parts of the marketing plan are presented here, but the control plan does contain the total set of control problems, a plan to measure those that could be measured, and what the firm planned to do if each problem actually occurred.

Potential Problem	Tracking	Contingency Plan
1. Salespeople fail to contact general-purpose market at prescribed rate.	Track weekly call reports. The plan calls for at least 10 general-purpose calls per week per rep.	If activity falls below this level for three weeks running, a remedial program of one-day district sales meetings will be held.
2. Salespeople may fail to understand how the new feature of the product relates to product usage in the general-purpose market.	Tracking will be done by having sales manager call one rep each day. Entire sales force will be covered in two months.	Clarification will be given to individual reps on the spot, but if first 10 calls suggest a widespread problem, special teleconference calls will be arranged to repeat the story to the whole sales force.
3. Potential customers are not making trial purchases of the product.	Track by instituting a series of 10 follow-up telephone calls a week to prospects who have received sales presentations. There must be 25 percent agreement on product's main feature and trial orders from 30 percent of those prospects who agree on the feature.	Remedial plan provides for special follow-up telephone sales calls to all prospects by reps, offering a 50 percent discount on all first-time purchases.
4. Buyers make trial purchase but do not place quantity reorders.	Track by another series of telephone survey calls, this time to those who placed an initial order. Sales forecast based on 50 percent of trial buyers reordering at least 10 more units within six months.	No remedial plan for now. If customer does not rebuy, there is some problem in product use. Since product is clearly better, we must know the nature of the misuse. Field calls on key accounts will be used to determine that problem, and appropriate action will follow.
5. Chief competitor may have the same new feature (for which we have no patent) ready to go and markets it.	This situation is essentially untrackable. Inquiry among our suppliers and media will help us learn quicker.	Remedial plan is to pull out all stops on promotion for 60 days. A make-or-break program. Full field selling on new item only, plus a 50 percent first-order discount and two special mailings. The other trackings listed above will be monitored even more closely.

It Takes Too Much Time.   Unfortunately, launch control demands the time of new product managers at their busiest period. The management that forces launch control over the objections of the new products manager will usually be disappointed.

Impossibility of Predicting Major Troubles.   A Kodak executive said there are contingency plans (such as those described above) and then there are *real-time plans*. Real-time plans require instant reaction to the unexpected. "For the most part, we at Kodak deal with real-time or sudden change alternatives. Our markets are such that we rarely encounter 'either-or' situations calling for true contingency plans."[11]

In some cases, this criticism is certainly valid; in others, it is not. At a recent seminar of new product executives, one group member cited unforecastable government intervention on a new chemical, but the others protested that anyone dealing with toxic chemicals should anticipate that problem.

Supporters of contingency planning have referred to (1) the expense and confusion of "turning on a dime," (2) the need to avoid "crisis management," (3) the desirability of more leisurely analysis, and (4) the advantage of dulling the shock of surprise.[12] Another said, "A crisis seldom offers the time required to develop sound plans. A panic-induced fire-fighting promotional effort is the result of not being sure-footed in the first place."[13]

Contingency Planning May Destroy Morale.   Some managements want their new product teams to be great project boosters. Indeed, the champion concept is inherent in most new product organizations, and significant opposition must usually be overcome. Asking the new product people, in the very midst of launch planning, to list all the major ways in which the project might fail is, to some people, unthinkable. The objection is understandable if unbridled enthusiasm is necessary to make the project fly.

A corollary to the view that contingency planning destroys morale is the view that contingency planning dilutes a manager's commitment to a plan by inducing "escape clause" thinking or fallback inclination. That

---

[11] Wylie S. Robson, "Market Plan Adjustments," in *Marketing Strategies,* ed. Earl L. Bailey (New York: The Conference Board, 1974), pp. 93–96.

[12] Rochele O'Conner, "Planning under Uncertainty: Multiple Scenarios and Contingency Planning," in *Strategic Planning for Growth Management,* ed. Michael V. Laric and Subhash C. Jain (Storrs: University of Connecticut School of Business Administration, 1978), pp. 59–76.

[13] Seymour Banks, "Promotional Adjustments," in *Marketing Strategies,* ed. Earl L. Bailey (New York: The Conference Board, 1974), p. 105.

is, contingency planning makes not achieving the original plan as written seem normal or expected.

Last, written contingency plans may create a morale problem because remedial action is often cost-cutting, and keeping job elimination plans secret is difficult. For this reason, some developers make it a point to keep contingency plans in a locked vault.

You Can't Launch Control without a Marketing Plan.   A surprisingly common complaint is that it makes no sense to include contingency planning on a marketing plan that was poorly constructed in the first place. This complaint is valid, of course, and if a firm finds that better launch planning doesn't pay, then it certainly shouldn't do it. But, the criticism begs the question.

NO LAUNCH CONTROL ON TEMPORARY PRODUCTS

Some products unintentionally live short lives. Occasionally, however, products are marketed that the managers know from the start will be on the market only a short time. Such products include fad products, temporary fillers of a hole in a product line, products keyed to a market participant's special needs, and *occasional* products. One producer of occasional products is Baskin-Robbins, which has a standing set of flavors always available, and another stable of flavors that move into and out of the line. A cereal producer is rumored to be planning the same approach as a way to get more variety in its store offerings without needing as many shelf facings.

Here are some suggestions for managing such products.

1. *Advertising and personal selling.*   Spend only the amount essential to achieve lift-off and to build the cooperation of distributors. There is no investment spending, therefore no new sales force.
2. *Sales promotion.*   These devices are used strictly to generate quick awareness and stimulate early trial.
3. *Distribution.*   Distributors are loaded up early. No out-of-stocks are allowed because such lost sales are usually lost permanently.
4. *Products.*   No line extensions or product improvements are planned. The new item is apt to be but part of a changing line.
5. *Production.*   Production is contracted out, if possible, or at least done only in flexible facilities. No new facilities are built.
6. *Inventories.*   Stocks in the possession of the company are moved to distributors as quickly as possible. Production is close to the reorder rate.
7. *Service.*   Essentially none; otherwise, the item should not be marketed.

8. *Pricing.* The plan is to cut prices early by using discounts. No need to change the basic list price.
9. *Market intelligence.* This is the critical activity. It is needed to spot the leveling off of sales if possible, or at least to catch the first downturn.[14]

Products marketed this way will have little, if any, launch control. By the time troubles are identified, the time to solve them is past.

PRODUCT FAILURE

Despite everyone's best efforts, products do sometimes fail or appear to be failing. When this happens, the firm has five general alternatives:

1. *Increase the spending.* This should have been part of the control plan, but sometimes it is not.
2. *Revise the strategy*—target and positioning. This drastic action requires everything to be put on hold while the changes (for example, advertising) are being made.
3. *Revise the product.* Again, this does not mean the minor changes of mind during launch control. It means to put things on hold until a major redirection in product character can be made. It is very high risk because everyone is in a hurry and will not have the time needed to do the job right.
4. *Pull the product temporarily.* This is still more drastic—and even less likely to succeed—unless the project is begun again from scratch. Chances are something is basically wrong.
5. *Abandon the product.* This means abandon the market opportunity. Most firms have many new product options and like to get their losers out of sight and out of mind.

Abandonment criteria are essentially the same as acceptance criteria, and a full financial analysis would be nice. But, the politics are bad, people are scurrying to escape the sinking ship, critics are reminding everyone how they predicted this trouble, and so on. Firms seem to follow the dictum: If in doubt, abandon it and get on to something else. This tactic does not work in situations where (1) major asset investments have been made (for example, the microwave oven or automated bank tellers) or (2) a major market change means either succeed or leave the business (for example, small cars, calculating machines, and black-and-white TV). In these two cases, alternatives 1, 2, and 3 will be tried for some time before a major write-off is taken.

---

[14] Chester R. Wasson, *Dynamic Competitive Strategy and Product Life Cycles* (St. Charles, Ill.: Challenge Books, 1974).

Action to Implement Abandonment.   The manager's job is not finished even when a firm decides to scuttle a new product. The manager usually must notify many people (including governments, distributors, and trade groups). A gradual stock-reduction program may be necessary, particularly if persons or firms have become dependent on the item. And, careful coordination is necessary within the firm to minimize the impact on schedules, personnel, and the like. Follow-on responsibilities may include stockpiling parts and offering a period of repair service.[15]

SUMMARY

This chapter brings us to the end of the commercialization process. Chapter 15 introduced the launch cycle and the general subject of managerial control. Chapters 16 and 17 then covered the marketing planning process, including the plan itself; the strategic decisions of targeting, positioning, and marketing mix; and then special attention to the product tool of that mix. Chapter 18 concluded the commercialization subject by showing that a new product manager's task is not ended until the new product is a winner, not just a marketed product.

Getting good launch control applies the same principles operating during pre-launch. The requirements are a plan, measurement of progress in the market, analysis of events to determine if prearranged contingency actions should be put into play, and continuing study to ensure that any problem becomes known as soon as possible so action can be taken to avert or at least ameliorate it.

Launch control and tracking are especially tough because most of the activity is out in the marketplace, too many variables can change, and measurements are difficult and expensive (not like walking through the factory in the eyeball control method). But, the methodology is available, and when the situation warrants this effort, a new products manager can certainly gain from it.

Chapter 18 also looked briefly at the temporary product and abandonment.

We can now return to one of the two "enabling conditions" of new products management. As Chapter 2 pointed out, a firm should (1) determine an appropriate new product strategy to guide the new products process and then (2) provide an organization to meet the conditions of the strategy. Chapter 3 covered strategy, and now that we have looked at the entire process, Chapter 19 will introduce the organizational options.

---

[15] For a recent study of product abandonment, see George J. Avlonitis, "Linking Different Types of Product Elimination Decisions to Their Performance Outcome: 'Project Dropstat,' " *International Journal of Research in Marketing*, no. 1, 1987, pp. 43–57.

APPLICATIONS

1. "Thanks for telling me about that launch control idea you were studying. But, look, I'm a bit mixed up on one thing. You mentioned (1) critical events, (2) control events, and (3) tracking variables. You say you have to list all three things? Isn't one event likely to be on all three lists? For example, take awareness of the new product's key determinant attribute. Not getting it is a critical event, selecting it for control makes it a control event, and tracking it makes it a tracking variable. Right? Help!"

2. "I've had occasion several times over the past year to see a new product land in trouble—great expectations and terrible sales. And the saddest part is that so many people try so hard to deny the inevitable—the product has bombed, and the quicker one gets away from it the better. Otherwise, it's just sending good money after bad. In fact, I'm going to make a speech to that effect at our next general executive meeting, and you could do me a favor. Would you please develop a list of all possible reasons why someone might want to string a loser along? That would help me be sure I've answered all of the objections before I give the speech."

3. "Don't get me wrong—I believe in contingency planning and in what you call launch control. If you have anticipated a problem and have an action planned in case it comes up, I'll buy going ahead, at least for now. But, a lot of companies don't necessarily agree with me. I noticed recently, for example, that one of the big electronics firms was in quite a dispute with its dealers over whether a new device would be successful. Dealers said no way. The company said it just takes a little time. They wouldn't be having this argument if they had done their contingency planning, right? They would have standby plans ready to go. Tell me, if a new product team neglects to do proper contingency planning and then hits trouble, what can they do then to get a handle on the problem as soon as possible? (Preferably before someone like me tells them to pull the plug.)"

4. "If I remember right, the whole idea of launch control depends partially on having a track or plan that each variable should follow if everything is going OK. I believe you showed me some figures with those plan lines on them. But, it seems to me those plan lines are just pure conjecture, at least in the case of really new products. For example, I was just reading about Arco Solar Inc. (that's a division of Atlantic Richfield). It has a solar-powered plate that can be set on a car's dashboard and feeds power to the car's battery. That power makes up for the natural self-discharge of a battery, the drain from electric clocks, and so on. Now, how in the world would they know what the normal path of awareness or trial would be? Are they unable to use launch control? Lots of our divisions are developing really new things like that."

Case: Interfoods, Inc.: Valley Butter

Interfoods, Inc., was a large international food company headquartered in Paris whose Colombian subsidiary was about to introduce a new butter product called Valley Butter. There were doubts about this introduction, so the product manager, Carlos Minago, wanted to be sure the launch went well.

Interfoods began its Colombian operation by acquiring a Bogota firm that had, among other products, a line of nonbutter products. These included a nonrefrigerated margarine called Planet, which sold nationally with around 80 percent of that market, and a refrigerated margarine called Dairy Planet, which was distributed only in the major cities (because of the need for refrigeration) and had a 90 percent market share. Planet made little money and was no longer being actively promoted. Dairy Planet was very profitable. The total spread market was about $4 million at the factory and at this time was divided 50 percent to butter, 30 percent to refrigerated margarine, and 20 percent to nonrefrigerated.

Moreover, that 50 percent share for butter had been achieved within the past three years, and almost all went to the Ahoy brand. Butter had previously been a very expensive import, but the Ahoy firm produced it locally and was rapidly gaining sales from Dairy Planet. Its price was now only about 30 cents against Dairy Planet's price of 19 cents.

The Valley Butter project had been under way for about a year and a half, although corporate management in Paris wasn't enthusiastic about it. They wanted the market to stay with margarines, where Interfoods dominated, and they didn't really think the Colombian Interfoods people knew much about butter.

General knowledge was that taste was the big thing in butter and that taste had been winning Dairy Planet customers to Ahoy. So, Valley Butter was supposed to taste better than Ahoy—and it did (though it took six versions; the previous five had flopped when tasted by employees). The most recent in-home, blind, paired-comparison use test showed Valley was preferred by a statistically significant 55 percent to 45 percent. To get this preference, the cost was unfortunately increased to the point that Valley would not be as profitable as new brands were supposed to be.

No test market would be undertaken because the butter market was essentially the three cities of Bogota, Medellin, and Cali. Colombia as yet had no research firms offering simulated test markets or scanner market testing. The strategy was to use fairly heavy advertising backed by four consumer promotions (two price-packs deals and two premium offers printed on the wrappers) to force trial. The advertising would be a three-month saturation drive on TV stations and in movie houses, plus radio and newspapers. The total budget for Valley advertising would be more than Ahoy had been spending but less than the firm would normally spend because of the higher product cost and the firm's basic desire for the market to stay with margarines.

The sales forecast called for a 10 percent market share after one year, but management made it plain they expected much more than that soon thereafter or it wasn't worth the effort. The target consumers were the top economic class—about 10 percent of all people in the leading cities.

The product was positioned as the "better-tasting butter," and the copy strategy was simply to communicate the positioning. Valley was chosen as the name because it connoted delicious-tasting butter and an image of quality. It came from a list prepared by the ad agency and was selected by consumers as easily remembered and pronounced and connoting a high-quality butter. The packaging would also be expensive (foil wrapper versus Ahoy's plastic wrap). A consumer packaging test confirmed that the package communicated a quality image. The price was to be the same as Ahoy's. Colombian Interfoods had a national sales force of about 55 people, but Valley would be handled only by the special 10-person sales force created just to sell Dairy Planet in the major cities. The sell-in by this smaller group would begin about two weeks ahead of advertising break.

It was company policy to have launch control plans, so Carlos now had the job of preparing a list of potential problems, narrowing them down to the ones he had to do something about, and then planning how he would track them and what he would do if any of them occurred.

Part V

Structure/Environment

Organizing for
New Products

SETTING

We have ignored the issue of how to organize for new products because
we had to know the task before we could organize to do it. Even now it's
a tough subject, partly because reliable decision rules are scarce and
partly because industry seems to be in a constant state of organizational
flux. Most new products managers joke about who reports to whom for
what.

But, within that turmoil, some key organizational concepts are
gradually gaining acceptance, and a strong trend is emerging toward a
reduced number of options. Chapter 19 will present the basic alternatives currently in use and show how a firm can select something from
that set for any particular situation. Beyond the basic alternatives are
several special aspects of the package, such as coupling with other firms;
these will also be discussed.

Then we go to Chapter 20, where we meet the "other half" of the
organizing decision—the process of management that turns the structures of Chapter 19 into a successful program. For example, in Chapter
19 we talk about teams, and in Chapter 20 we talk about how to staff
them and manage them for the best results.

Before getting to the options, however, we really should look at what
is going on in industry today relative to organization, including current
managerial philosophies and the role of strategy. Now might be a good
time to glance back through Chapter 3, because the biggest input to
structure is strategy.

THE SITUATION TODAY

Life is never calm in new products land. Product innovation is a major contributor to most firms' well-being, top management (corporate or divisional) is involved, and we spend lots of money. Ongoing operations management is also involved because everything we do touches some line activity—we're usually encroaching on their territory.

Specifically, today managements are doing (and thinking) several things that help determine organization:

1. *Cutting costs.*   This means all costs, including people. Particularly vulnerable are staff middle managers, the nucleus of new products operations. Intense pressure is exerted on us to find cheaper ways of doing our job.
2. *Cutting time.*   This means getting new products to market faster, partly to hold down costs and partly to capitalize on those windows of opportunity that open suddenly and disappear just as fast. Some situations call for slow development (for example, one of the leading new product firms today is Merck, a firm that must live with product development cycles of 7 to 12 years). But, most managements no longer permit the leisurely development cycles of the past.
3. *Getting smaller.*   Managements are learning that one good way to develop new products faster and cheaper is to have the work done in nonbureaucratic, smaller settings. Divisions now are getting far more new product autonomy than before, and we are seeing divisions of divisions of divisions. New and established small firms have played a major role in product innovation over the past 40 years, and managers of large corporations have been seeking (and finding) ways of emulating them. We will talk about those later.[1]
4. *Thinking entrepreneurially.*   A giant corporation cannot be run like a Silicon Valley start-up of 50 people. However, such corporations very much want more entrepreneurial spirit. An excellent current example is the work of John Sculley at Apple; he wants creative output, but he knows it cannot be gotten as Steve Jobs got it in Apple's early days. So, he is seeking new methods, and organization is a key area of search.[2]

---

[1] For good examples of this thinking, see "Is Your Company Too Big?" *Business Week,* March 27, 1989, pp. 84–94.

[2] A candid discussion of Sculley's thinking can be found in Brenton R. Schlender, "Apple Computer Tries to Achieve Stability but Remain Creative," *The Wall Street Journal,* July 16, 1987, pp. 1+. He was still working on it in 1990.

5. *Throwing out the rule books.* No two projects have to be organized the same way. Many firms used to have one accepted method of organizing, and everything had to fit it. Procter & Gamble is a classic case, and its basic brand management system made it not only rich but famous as well. Recently, however, P&G bought Vidal Sassoon; recognizing the unique requirements of the beauty aids market, P&G kept the new operation separate, without imposing P&G's regular brand management on it.

6. *Style over form, and results over activity.* Again (within limits, of course), managements are looking less at how operations are managed on a day-to-day basis and more at what is being accomplished. Many new products managers talk about what they are able to "get away with" as long as they produce.

All of this means one thing—we can install basic organizational options, but we then have to manage them in a way that makes them productive. This points to the importance of Chapter 20.

GETTING READY

We need several specific decisions and pieces of information to select from the following set of organizational options. Some of them will come up later when we talk about the decision process, but now, before looking at the options, we need several things:

1. *Organizing for what?* For ongoing product improvements that keep us competitive? Or for line extensions that hold our position in current markets? Or for line extensions that take us into new markets? Or is this a special operation, say, to solve a current market problem or to capitalize on some opportunity, such as an underutilized technology?

2. *Special management mandates.* Select from the above list (speed, cost, and so on) and find any others peculiar to our situation (risk limits, for example, and dollar investment limits).

3. *The product innovation charter* applicable to this activity. See Chapter 3. The new product strategy may be stated in many forms, but there should be one. And, all key players should agree on it.

4. *How well have we done in the past?* Not only is it good to stick with a winner, but a winning organization tells us the players are familiar with it and know how to make it effective.

There's no set list of this information, but the four items just given cover most of the bases.

THE OPTIONS

The five basic options for new products organization are shown in Figure 19–1. These options are five segments of a continuum, and, although quite different, they do have several things in common.[3]

Understanding those options requires several definitions:

Functional: People in the ongoing business departments (such as marketing or finance) are involved, and the product innovation activity must mesh with their work. The opposite of *functional* is *project* or *venture.*

Project: The importance or uniqueness of the product innovation activity requires people who think first of the project. They are project oriented.

Matrix: This standard organization term tells us that any particular piece of work being done is directed by two people: the project manager and the head of the line function involved. Thus, a decision to make a new package out of silver foil is probably keyed on someone from a packaging department. This person may *want* silver foil because it makes the product far more attractive in the store (project focus), but may *not want* it because it adds to manufacturing difficulty and cost (functional focus). Theoretical matrix thinking was 50/50 on this type of decision. See Figure 19–2 for a matrix diagram.

Putting these terms together gives us the five choices. The first, *functional,* means the work is done by the various departments, with very little project focus. There usually is a new products committee or a product planning committee. The work is usually low risk and probably involves the present line of products—improvements, new sizes, and so on. The ongoing departmental people know the market and the business; they can get together and make the necessary decisions easily and effectively.

Of course, not much innovation occurs that way. So, we have the other four options. Three of them (in the middle of Figure 19–1) are matrix variations. If the people on Project B (in Figure 19–2) get together to make some decisions, they may be 50/50, or they may lean toward the functional or toward the project. This leaning is called *projectization,* as defined in Figure 19–1.

---

[3] New product organizational options have been expressed in scores of ways. The listing here follows one that appears to be most useful and understandable, originally stated in David H. Gobeli and Eric W. Larson, "Matrix Management: More than a Fad," *Engineering Management International* 4, 1986, pp. 71–76. The only change is that what the authors called *project team* is here called *venture* to reflect recent preferences.

FIGURE 19–1   Options in New Products Organization

Options				
Functional	Functional matrix	Balanced matrix	Project matrix	Venture
With or without committee				Inside Outside
0%_____ 20% _____ 40% _____ 60% _____80% _____ 100%				
Degree of Projectization*				

* Defined as the extent to which participants in the process see themselves as independent from the project or committed to it. Thus, members of a new product committee are almost totally oriented (loyal) to their functions or departments; spin-out (outside) venture members are almost totally committed to the project.

The *functional matrix* option has a specific team, with people from the various departments (such as manufacturing, R&D, marketing, and finance), but the project is still close to the current business. It requires more focus than routine product improvements, but the departments call the shots. Team members think like functional specialists. On that foil package mentioned above, the marketing member would argue for it, and the manufacturing member would probably argue against it.

The *balanced matrix* option is for situations where both functional and project views are critical — neither ongoing business nor the new product should be the driver. This traditional matrix was for a long time held in disfavor for new products, because either the new product required push or it didn't. Using 50/50 thinking would just make for indecision and delay. Texas Instruments used balanced matrix for many years in its product innovation — and then discarded it for just this reason.[4] But, today's managers have apparently found ways to make it work.[5] See Figure 19–3 for recent data.

The *project matrix* option recognizes the occasional need for stronger project push. Here projectization is high. Team people are project people

[4] "An About-Face in TI's Culture," *Business Week,* July 5, 1982, p. 77. For more on this situation, see Bro Uttal, "Texas Instruments Regroups," *Fortune,* August 9, 1982, pp. 40–45.

[5] Erik W. Larson and David H. Gobeli, "Organizing for Product Development Projects," *Journal of Product Innovation Management,* September 1988, pp. 180–90. An earlier study by the same people gave slightly different success scorings, but the sample of firms in that study was only a fifth as many as the 1988 study. For the earlier study, see Gobeli and Larson, "Matrix Management: More than a Fad."

FIGURE 19–2   The Matrix Concept of Business Organization

Program or Project	Departments—Functions				
	Marketing	R&D	Manufacturing	Finance	Others
A Shilling	Thomas	Mansfield	Swaston	Statler	—
B Politi	Thomas	Hilger	Morrison	Richert	—
C Metz	Weirich	Hilger	Fedor	Dumont	—
D Anderson	Feldkamp	Mazrui	Swaston	Dumont	—
E Wiley	Berigan	Klein	Fedor	Grady	—
Others —	—	—	—	—	—

Explanation: For Program B (probably a new product), Politi is the manager (variously defined as leader, coordinator, and so on). Thomas is on the team representing the marketing department, Hilger represents R&D, Morrison represents manufacturing, and Richert represents finance. Functional people often represent their group on more than one team. If the company uses a functional format or a venture (see Figure 19–1), there is really no matrix. Here, Thomas reports jointly to Shilling and to her department director, thus creating the inherent issue of matrix: whose direction does she follow?

first and functional people second. The manufacturing member will be trying to sell the foil packaging idea to people in production. Department heads complain that their people have sold out to the project and are trying to drive the project even against the departments' best interests. And they are. Example: When IBM developed its original personal computer, the team manufacturing member argued for having outside manufacturers make most of the key pieces in the system. The new product had to be made fast, and IBM's manufacturing department was not set up to do the job that way.

The *Venture* option extends projectization to its ultimate. Team members are pulled out of their departments and put to work full time on the project. The venture may be kept in the regular organization, or it may be spun outside the current division or company. How far out it goes depends on how critical it is that there be no influence on the team from current departments, policies, and so on. IBM sent its PC team from Armonk, New York, to Boca Raton, Florida. Other firms have sent venture teams to another part of the city or to another part of the firm's

FIGURE 19–3 Performance Success of the Five Basic New Product Organizational Options

Organizational Option	Percent of Projects	Percent Successful	Percent Successful or Marginally So
Functional	20%	32%	63%
Functional matrix	34	41	79
Balanced matrix	23	58	88
Project matrix	20	62	92
Venture	14	62	94
Total	100%		
Total projects: 540			

Source: Erik W. Larson and David H. Gobeli, "Organizing for Product Development Projects," *Journal of Product Innovation Management*, September 1988, pp. 180–90.

building complex. The venture form also merges into the *joint venture* (where another firm cooperates in the activity), an approach that will be discussed in a moment.

A venture is expensive and has several purposes besides freeing people from the functional constraints of their departments. The purpose is often *focus,* a word we hear a great deal of these days. To do something new and really worthwhile may require freeing the mind of all other matters. Still another purpose is coordination, especially in very large and complex firms where communication is bureaucratically restricted. Ford, for example, was cited during the 1980s for its Taurus/Sable project, a venture format previously rare in the auto industry.[6]

But, don't think ventures are only for complex industries—Campbell Soup's president, Gordon McGovern, made headlines when he urged venture-type operations, complete with power to forge ahead and incentive compensation consistent with the risks. Of course, he was speaking of markets with odds of, say, 5 to 1, not 50 to 1. Thus, ventures are not for everyone, partly because strategies may not call for this much risk and partly because the firm may not be able to do what ventures require. For example, one study of ventures found that all but 1 of the 11 successes in the sample sold to established customers, used experienced market research personnel from the parent organization,

---

[6] For example, see "How Ford Hit the Bull's Eye with Taurus," *Business Week,* June 30, 1986, pp. 69–70. The article overflows with such phrases as "stealing a page from the Japanese," "the first step was to throw out Ford's traditional organizational structure," "normally the five-year process is sequential," "Team Taurus took a program management approach," "worked together as a group," and "the team took final responsiblity for the vehicle."

obtained market-experienced personnel from outside, and based the new product on market need, not technological capability. The 17 losers in the study almost uniformly did not.[7]

A more recent study of Exxon's failures in a series of ventures came to much the same conclusion—there must be major congruencies between the new venture and its market.[8]

The Hidden Power of the Team

At first meeting, this distinction between the functional view and the project view may appear strained or overblown. Does it really matter whether people think like team members or like functional specialists? Yes, it does, for a reason that we have just recently come to appreciate. Historically, product innovation has been conducted in a linear form, like a mile relay race. In fact, early texts on product innovation had charts showing that first we do the technical work, then we pass the baton to manufacturing people, who figure out how to make the new item. We then pass it to marketing people, who figure out how it will be priced, advertised, and so on. Last, it goes to salespeople, who sell it.

This practice came to a screeching halt in the 1980s when we realized that the more successful firms (particularly the Japanese) were managing product innovation more like a rugby match.[9] There was no baton passing—all of the players were involved at each stage. Marketing people helped work on desirable product characteristics (recall the discussion on protocol in Chapter 10). Manufacturing people were present when scientists began to configure product, so they could speak to its manufacturability.[10] Technical people were still present during marketing planning, because they understood some of the customers' problems and service needs.

In short, the team functioned as a team. A different phrase used to describe the operation is *parallel processing,* meaning the various parts

---

[7] Eric von Hippel, "Successful and Failing Internal Corporate Ventures: An Empirical Analysis," *Industrial Marketing Management* 3, 1977, pp. 163–74.

[8] Hollister B. Sykes, "The Anatomy of a Corporate Venturing Program: Factors Influencing Success," *Journal of Business Venturing,* Fall 1986, pp. 275–93.

[9] Getting most of the credit for sensing this change were Hirotaka Takeuchi and Ikujiro Nonaka, "The New New Product Development Game," *Harvard Business Review,* January–February 1986, pp. 137–46.

[10] See Daniel E. Whitney, "Manufacturing by Design," *Harvard Business Review,* July–August 1988, pp. 83–91. The subhead for this article was "The manufacturing engineer asks, 'What good is it if I can't make it?'" Unfortunately, many such managers are still asking.

of the work are done simultaneously. That is, manufacturing and marketing planning are begun at the start of the project, and technical work is not ended until the product is successful.

In fact, though too complicated to explain here, the whole complex of design–purchasing–manufacturing has jelled into a major player in much product innovation today. They are integrated in several ways, including by computer (design-aided manufacturing).[11]

Whether rugby, parallel processing, or some other term, you can see that the approach meets two of management's current concerns stated at the beginning of this chapter: speed and cost. And, working through teams fits with overall company thinking today, not just in product innovation but in regular ongoing management as well.[12]

Other Terms and Approaches

New products organization may involve many other terms and approaches:

New Product Committee (or Product Planning Committee).   This is used in the functional approach to do what the team does in the other options. All departments are represented, a large number of projects are covered, and the committee meetings are held, say, monthly for communication and coordination. The words heard most frequently at these meetings are "Project X is running late; why is that, and what should we do to get it back on track?" Though often tedious and political ("It's not our fault!"), the committee works well if the projects are, indeed, close to current operations and call for no disruptive innovation, and if the committee chair is a ranking executive and knows how to run a meeting. Unfortunately, many firms try to use the committee to handle all new product projects, and the innovative ones suffer.

Product Manager.   This common term is applied to people who manage ongoing products. A *new* products manager handles new products and may or may not also be handling ongoing ones. Both product managers and new products managers manage the teams in the various matrix and venture options, the choice of terms being based on industry practice and company preference.

---

[11] To understand the major new role for purchasing, see David N. Burt, "Managing Suppliers up to Speed," *Harvard Business Review,* July–August 1989, pp. 127–35.

[12] This broad view of team application is described in "The Payoff from Teamwork," *Business Week,* July 10, 1989, pp. 56–62.

Task Force and Project Team.   These terms apply to new product teams, and their use is so varied that they are virtually useless. The five terms used for the options (above) are much more descriptive and should replace these older terms.

Venture Group.   This term was formerly used to identify venture teams spun completely out from the firm. *Spin-out* is preferred today.

Spin-Out.   This is a venture team that has been detached from the regular organization. Allied Chemical recently began using spin-outs to develop what it calls orphan technologies—R&D developments that didn't fit the business when they appeared and sat around on shelves, sometimes for years. Another spin-out was Metaglas Products' work to develop lightweight alloys used in cores for electrical transformers.[13]

Another Look at Projectization

Anytime two or more people from different departments (functions) of an organization gather to work on a project, issues of priorities are raised. Should they put first priority on the project or on the function they represent? Legislators face this problem daily (well-being of the total versus well-being of the voters back home). So do student homecoming committees, civic development groups, and many others.

When a sales manager, for example, goes to a new products *committee* meeting, there is little doubt about priorities because committee members are engineers or marketers first and committee members second. The sales manager is "functionalized," not projectized. Committee members want the company to make profit; they are not disloyal. But, they have independent opinions about how any particular new product may contribute to profit. The sales manager may see a new package size as meeting customer demands and adding sales; the engineer may believe production costs will go up more than the sales volume; accounting objects to another line item that may just split customers' current purchases and add to cost; R&D says work on the new package size will pull a key person off a far more important project needed next year.

These are not idle concerns. They are the reality of new product life, and they are legitimate (ignoring the political problems that also arise).

---

[13] These and other spin-outs are discussed in Earl C. Gottschalk, "Allied Unit, Free of Red Tape, Seeks to Develop Orphan Technologies," *The Wall Street Journal,* September 13, 1984, p. 33.

Projectization is the way we handle them. If a project is important and faces lots of opposition of the types just mentioned, then we increase the projectization. We go to functional matrix, balanced matrix, or project matrix. If the opposition is very high (for instance, imagine the problems when steel firms first started making plastics products), then we move to the venture.

Caution

All business terminology is fragile, and the distinctions given above between different types of matrix are forced. Businesspeople think about what they want to do, do it, and then, when asked, name it. Too, consultants who work in new products organization are always seeking terms that distinguish their recommendations from those of others. This is not new—we still can't decide how to spell *catsup,* so why should anyone expect new product terms to be fully accepted and unchanging? But, think about the conditions, about what type of operation is desired, and then select a term that communicates this to other people.

Summary of Operating Characteristics and Making a Selection

Figure 19–4 summarizes how the five organizational options differ on various dimensions. How to choose among them? Much the same way a refrigerator is purchased. Begin with what you want the organization to do and then buy as much organizational power as needed to do the job. The more the power of the team, the more the "cost" to the firm in terms of personnel, disruption, and so on.

So, begin with the functional form and move up the ladder as little as necessary. Ventures are highly disruptive and tend to bring forth new products whether they are right or wrong (team members see to that). The form shown in Figure 19–5 sometimes helps. Other factors can be added to those, and the factors can be weighted (much as we did with the scoring model used for screening concepts in Chapter 10).

Most firms use most of the forms all the time because of the mix of ongoing new product work. People going to meetings have to reorient themselves continuously.

Is There an Ideal Organizational Form?

No. A form appropriate to the 486 or 586 computer chip technology would be quite inappropriate for a new flavor of soup. And vice versa. New products people often disagree, because they want an organiza-

FIGURE 19–4 Operating Characteristics of the Basic Options

Operating Characteristics	*Spectrum of Options*				
	Functional	*Functional Matrix*	*Balanced Matrix*	*Project Matrix*	*Venture*
Decision power of leader	Very little _____ Almost total				
Independence of group from depts.	None _____ Total				
Percent of time spent on one project by member	Very low _____ Total				
Importance of project(s)	Low _____ Critical				
Project(s) focus	Total list _____ One				
Degree of risk of project(s) to firm	Low _____ High				
Disruptiveness of project(s)	Low _____ High				
Degree of uncertainty in most decisions	Low _____ Very High				
Ability of team to violate company policies	None _____ Almost total				
Independent funding	None _____ Total				

Interpretation: This array shows how the various options of Figure 19–1 differ on each of several operating characteristics. The three matrix forms are at points between the extremes of functional and venture.

tional form that makes for the best and most frequent new products. They want action, not committee meetings. They seem to opt for the venture, or at least the project matrix, every time.[14]

---

[14] The only evidence we have on this came from Larson and Gobeli, "Organizing for Product Development Projects." In their study of 540 development projects, almost all of the participants said (after the project was finished) they would like to have had more projectization. This was regardless of format used, from functional to venturing.

FIGURE 19–5   Decision Rules for Choosing among the Five Basic
Organizational Options

Answer the following questions, giving each a score from 1 to 5, the 1 being
for such terms as low, little, not much:

Score	Factor
_____	1. How difficult is it to get new products in the firm?
_____	2. How critical is it for the firm to have new products at this time?
_____	3. How much risk to personnel is involved in this new products work?
_____	4. How important is speed of development?
_____	5. Will the products be using new procedures in their manufacturing?
_____	6. In their marketing?
_____	7. What will be the dollar profit contribution from each of the new items?
_____	8. How much training do our functional people need in the markets represented by the new products we want?
_____	Total score

If the score is below 15, then functional or functional matrix probably would work. From
15 to 30, the firm probably needs a balanced matrix. Situations scoring above 30 probably
require a project matrix or even a venture.

If they can't get what they want, chances are they have not presented
their case well enough, because their problem lies in strategy, not
organization. A firm that has not made a commitment to product
innovation (with its costs and risks) has little reason to use project
matrix and ventures.

COMPLEXITIES OF STRUCTURE BEHIND THE TEAMS

The five organizational options don't cover everything we need to know.
Let's look at some aspects that concern managers.

Small Is Good

We saw at the beginning of this chapter that managements today want
to gain the advantages of being small. Innovative new products have
often come from very small firms, for good reason. Such firms have few
people and no entrenched departments, so every new product project
uses the venture option. They want new products, and they get them. Of

course, the failure rate is high, because lots of those new products should never have come about.

Large firms want the advantages of both sizes and try to gain them by splitting up. GE says today it would not build Appliance Park, its huge set of plants in Louisville that employed 21,000 people at its peak. Experiments now show that economies of scale are often a mirage; economies of commitment by people are real.[15] This explains the current trend toward more projectization.

Roles/Participants

Product innovation is done by groups of people; within the group structure, however, we usually find certain people playing different roles. Figure 19–6 shows the full set. Although these roles are not always present (for example, an inventor often isn't needed if an invention is acquired outside), they usually are. Sometimes, who is playing which role isn't clear, and people often compete for the role they want.

FIGURE 19–6   Roles/Participants in the New Products Management Process

Participant*	Activity	Participant*	Activity
1. Strategist	Longer-range Managerial Entire program	4. Champion	Supporter Spokesperson Pusher Won't concede
2. Inventor	Creative scientist Basement inventor Idea source	5. Rationalist	Objectivity Reality Reason Financial
3. Project manager	Leader Integrator Translator Mediator Judge Arbitrator Coordinator	6. Sponsor	Senior manager Supporter Endorser Assuring hearing Mentor

*The participant's role may be either formal or informal.

---

[15] See *Business Week,* "Is Your Company Too Big?"

Strategist. This is the leader who spelled out the product innovation charter. It is usually an upper-level manager, someone not personally involved in the project, and rarely informal. It often is the CEO.

Inventor. Somewhere, inside the firm or outside it, there is a person who actually gets the idea that underlies a new product. The inventor may be an Edison stereotype, an establishment scientist, a lone individual in a basement laboratory, a thoughtful consumer, a product manager, or a creative copywriter in the ad agency.

Project Manager. This is the new products manager/team leader role; it is formally assigned to a particular individual when teams are used and is informally seen active on projects supervised by a new products committee. The various names given to it indicate its importance and its character.

Product Champion. This role varies a great deal but is important. Projects get hung up; people lose interest; political conflicts arise; volume and cost projections sometimes turn sour; technical breakthroughs aren't achieved. The product champion's role is to push past these roadblocks or, at least, try to. Champions can't win every time, but their task is to see that no project dies without a fight.

Some firms, such as 3M, make the project manager the champion. In fact, 3M has two champions: one during the technical development phase and another during the commercialization phase. 3M's commitment to innovation makes this desirable. (See Figure 19–7 for a story about one 3M champion.) Other firms want enthusiastic project managers but expect someone else to be the one who refuses to let an idea die. These champions are often self-appointed.

In most cases, the champion is expected to be vigorous and enthusiastic but play within the rules. Sometimes (less often today as managements become more supportive of new products), champions run roughshod over the rules. For example, a champion in a firm that made infant vitamin products surreptitiously charged a market research survey against the budget of a marketing research director who opposed a project the champion wanted. The survey proved the champion correct, and the product was successful, but that particular budget loophole was closed!

Merck uses product champions within its R&D department. One, active in the development of Mevacor, was specifically charged with selling the program to fellow scientists in various disciplines. He had to persuade such specialists as chemists and pharmacologists to pledge their own budgets to work on the project. And, one of his earliest "sales" was to the marketing department, which he won over nearly eight years before the new specialty became available for sale.[16]

Sponsor.   The sponsor is often confused with a champion. But, the sponsor is usually a more senior-ranking executive, perhaps even the president or (as in the story of Figure 19–7) the chairman. This person does not drive anything but is supportive and lends encouragement and endorsement to the champion. Champions are wise to develop sponsors, whom some call godfathers or mentors.

Rationalist.   Another essential role is that of the tough, show-me, unemotional team member typically, but unjustifiably, associated with the finance department. If champions sometimes push beyond reason, then rationalists drag beyond reason. In the same way a team can "go negative" on a project, it can lose touch with reality and get carried away.

Entrepreneurship

As is apparent from all the talk about product champions, venturing, and so on, firms today are seeking more than just organization charts and job descriptions. Some say they want *entrepreneurship,* the enthusiasm and commitment of those rare people who sell their homes, leave their families, and work 16 hours a day for three years—all to establish a new business. Because this entrepreneurship occurs inside an organization, some call it *intrapreneurship.*

To get such dedication, managements have occasionally used the spin-out method discussed earlier or, at least, an internal venture. Convergent Technologies used the latter with Matt Sanders when they kicked him out of his office, told him to go round up a staff of employees, find some working space around the company somewhere, and come back quickly with something that eventually would be called Workslate (a handheld computer). He did.[17]

Entrepreneurship is dramatic—glamorous, exciting, challenging, fun, and rewarding. Who wouldn't want the lifestyles we have come to

---

[16] See "The Miracle Company," *Business Week,* October 19, 1987, pp. 84–90. Oddly, however, another group of technical people at a special conference indicated that the concept of a product champion had been oversold, that any good project manager must do what champions are said to do. See William A. Fischer, Willard Hamilton, Curtis P. McLaughlin, and Robert W. Zmud, "The Elusive Product Champion," *Research Technology Management,* May–June 1986, pp. 13–16.

[17] Erik Larson and Carrie Dolan, "Thinking Small," *The Wall Street Journal,* August 19, 1983, p. 1.

FIGURE 19–7   The Saga of Donald Gorman: Champion

An abbreviated version of a story told by L. J. Thomas, senior vice president, Eastman Kodak Company, in May 1980.

"I will focus attention on a particular Kodak inventor, now retired, who was responsible for available light movies, Donald Gorman—an inventor and researcher of the first order . . . . He was uncompromising. He had absolutely no regard for anything short of total victory . . . . He is always looking for a better way . . . . It was in Gorman's allegiance to the customer, in his quest for picture quality, that the available light movie program began.

"He needed a camera with a rapid pulldown [after the program was well underway]. There was such a camera—the Wittnauer Cine-Twin. Gorman learned that the Kodak patent museum had a Wittnauer in its collection, and he asked that it be sent to the Research Labs. It was sent to him and without the museum's knowledge Gorman dismantled it to look at the shutter. He quickly saw that the mechanism was ideal for his experiments.

"Gorman had really begun to interact with other members of the organization, many of whom were trying to discourage him because he had what they thought was a crazy idea . . . . At this point in his work, Gorman was badly in need of support from the top. Enter Dr. Chapman, Kodak's chairman of the board and chief executive officer at that time . . . . On one particular Tuesday morning Gorman was projecting something from another projector for him on the screen. After that demonstration, Chapman said 'Mr. Gorman, come out from behind that projector and tell me what you are up to these days.' Gorman said, 'Dr. Chapman, I am glad you asked.'

"Of course Gorman hadn't gone through proper channels because he had gone right to the top. All of us know that this is not always the best way to proceed. One moral here, never underestimate the power of a quiet lunch with the right people.

"Good decisions were Dr. Chapman's great contribution, just as innovation and invention in research were Don Gorman's. The two work together—and are both essential."

P.S. This story also highlights the role of the sponsor.

Source: L. J. Thomas, "Available Light Movies—An Inventor Made It Happen," in *Living Case Histories of Industrial Innovation* (New York: Industrial Research Institute, 1981), pp. 5–9.

---

associate with the Silicon Valley firm (Friday afternoon social sessions on the company patio, shirt-sleeves, midnight creative sessions of dedicated teams of co-workers, and so on)? But, dissenting voices say this is almost irrelevant to most day-to-day product innovation. Who wants refrigerators designed by people who disdainfully reject traditional thinking on freon containment?

Harold Geneen, longtime head of ITT, said large public corporations are public trusts from which investors expect 10 percent annual returns, and entrepreneurship risks are inconsistent with that expectation. Corporate officers cannot "bet the company," and employees should never be compensated at the level of owners. Founders may function as entrepreneurs, Geneen said, but when the company is listed on the NYSE, the "headstrong mavericks will not be allowed or able to fly free."[18]

If these people are correct, most firms should not use much entrepreneurship. Most projects probably don't need it. P&G's technical development groups apparently do not get entrepreneurial support if one staffer's comment is correct: "I'm tired of throwing general managers, kicking and screaming, through the doors of success."[19]

Entrepreneurship implies a typical start-up fanatic running loose around an established firm. So, most managers opt for less dramatic approaches encouraging *manageable* change and innovation. For example, Eastman Kodak developed several unique approaches in the late 1980s that were not the start-up type but did, nevertheless, encourage innovative behavior. One thing Kodak did was to establish an incubator where in-house ventures could locate and get supportive services much like those in incubators established in many U.S. cities for local inventors.

Outside Service Organizations

Every function, task, or operation required for new products can be assigned to outside firms. Advertising agencies began adding new product services for their clients in the 1950s. But, technical work was being done by such organizations as Battelle Memorial Institute (which did the essential final work on xerography), Arthur D. Little, and Stanford Research Institute for many years before that. Marketing research firms and consulting firms are also frequently active in new product work today. Numerous such firms are actually full-time new products developers.

How They Work.   Outside firms span a full range of operations. Some take the initiative, develop a new product on their own, and then find a manufacturer to buy it. Others specialize at one or two points in the process (for example, idea generation, concept testing, or prototype creation). Still others do essentially everything, including the technical work. Foster Snell developed Arm & Hammer oven cleaner, New Product

---

[18] "Harold Geneen: Why Intrapreneurship Doesn't Work," *Venture,* January 1985, pp. 46–52.

[19] This quote appeared in G. Bettle, "Letters," *Fortune,* March 18, 1985, p. 15.

Insights developed Dunkin' Donuts coffee, and William Norton developed Crisp 'n Tender (for General Mills).

Some outside firms work on a fixed daily, monthly, or annual retainer fee, some on a negotiated project fee, and some on a small up-front fee followed by royalties based on sales. Usually, only small manufacturers will accept the last. Total costs vary from as little as $5,000 to several million dollars.

In most cases, the staff of outside firms have experience in the industry or operation they sell as their service.

Pro and Con.   Outsiders can be more objective and do not have the many internal "hang-ups" common in new product work. They can concentrate energy on a problem, work faster, and produce more creative approaches. They are highly motivated by the discipline of fees. Most times they truly are specialists and offer manufacturers a way to "buy experience" rapidly, without the problems and time of staff recruitment.

Yet, the inevitable "not invented here" syndrome creeps in — many company people cannot accept ideas from outsiders. (This is also one of the major problems in joint ventures.) Using outside firms means no product champion, training the outside firms, problems of security, and higher expenses (because outside firms have to assign overhead, whereas inside budgets do not). Consultants cannot assign their best people to all of their clients, outside firm personnel tend to move around more than manufacturers' staff, insiders often change proposed products without telling the outsiders, and so on.

It's doubtful that permanent use of outside firms is wise, except for such specialized services as market research. But, on a temporary basis when speed is important and experience is lacking, buying outside services makes a lot of sense.

Outside Coupling, Joint Ventures

A dramatic 1980s contribution to the new product 1990s was the opening of one firm's doors to cooperation with others in the business. (This is not the buying of particular services discussed just above.) This cooperation takes three forms:

Upstream coupling: BMW worked with General Electric to develop thermoplastic body panels for the ZL two-seater.

Downstream coupling: Owens-Illinois worked with a pharmaceutical company to develop a new concept in packaging for use on pediatric products.

Horizontal coupling: Several computer chip companies arranged a consortium to do fast development work on a particular technology.

In 1989, P&G had partnerships with Upjohn for a baldness remedy, with Syntex for anti-inflammatory analgesics, with Gist-Brocades for gastrointestinal medicine, with Alcide for a new technology in mouthwashes, and with Triton Biosciences and Cetus for a synthetic interferon. In each case, these ethical firms licensed P&G to use a technology in the consumer market.[20]

Today, although all forms of coupling tend to be called *joint ventures,* the variety is too great for one label. The nature of the coupling varies from the assistance an adhesive sales rep gives to a maker of refrigerator motors to the setting up of entire new firms (for example, Dow-Corning). For all vertical coupling, it is difficult to say whether the initiative came from above or below.

The simple fact is, most firms do not take advantage of the resources available to them outside their own walls. For example, research has shown over and over that the needs and desires of customers and end users are overlooked. A Stanford study contained the following quote:

> I asked the CEO of a $30 to $40 million company how often he saw customers. He said, "I really don't have time to do that, I have to represent the company to stockholders, I have to . . . . I leave it to my vice president of marketing." The VP of marketing said, "Well, I have a rather considerable staff. I have a sales force; I have advertising; I have promotions. So I don't really have the time. But we have a very highly trained sales force, and they are talking to customers all the time, bringing back ideas." Later, the salespeople said, "We get customer inputs and perceptions all the time, but nobody in management listens."[21]

The day is long gone when an organization could afford to "go it alone." More and more of them are beginning to treat vendors, customers, and competitors are parts of their organizations for product innovation.[22]

Global

Very few product innovators today think nationally. In almost every case, they see foreign markets as viable options and organize accordingly.

---

[20] "Can P&G Commandeer More Shelves in the Medicine Chest?" *Business Week*, April 10, 1989, pp. 64–65.

[21] "Why Products Fail," *Inc.*, May 1984, pp. 98–105.

[22] But, don't think joint ventures are easy. Research indicates most joint ventures fail, though this data was for all types of joint ventures. See "Corporate Odd Couples," *Business Week*, July 21, 1986, pp. 100–105.

Structurally, global product innovation can be handled in several ways:

1. Make no special arrangements. Export what is developed for the home market.
2. Keep structure the same, but develop versions of the new item to meet the needs of viable foreign markets. For example, if Gillette comes up with a new razor for the U.S. market, smaller, heavier, or safer versions may be developed for sale in Europe, Southeast Asia, and other markets.
3. Use the facilities of the home firm, but have separate projects directed by managers in each viable foreign area. These foreign managers learn of available technologies in the home firm, study their local markets to see how each might apply, and then set up projects to develop what is needed.
4. Assign the basic responsibility for product innovation to each foreign business large enough to have the resources for it. This usually means some local R&D, local manufacturing, and almost totally local marketing. The manager of each foreign business is a general manager and develops strategies and organizations according to technology and market opportunities. The people working in, say, Spain are free to "buy" service from the headquarters firm if they wish to do so.

Tough issues thread their way through these alternatives: (1) Is it better to have R&D in one place, or scattered around the world? (2) Can manufacturing be regionalized to capture advantages of both centralized and decentralized operations? and (3) Who decides which countries will market which products and with what strategies?

A firm should treat each foreign market in the life-cycle sense – at the beginning, it is strictly exported to; but as it grows and offers increased profitability, the structure gradually evolves to where the foreign market has the same structure as the headquarters division.[23]

Coupling and joint venturing tend to occur more often on the global scene. Vendors, customers, and competitors all differ in different countries, so you may joint venture with competitor A in China, with competitor B in Columbia, with customer X in France, and with a vendor in Italy. It makes for interesting discussions in airplanes and large hotels around the world.

---

[23] Evidence suggests that managements do not "life-cycle" their foreign operations. See Christopher A. Bartlett and Sumantra Ghoshal, "Tap Your Subsidiaries for Global Reach," *Harvard Business Review*, November–December 1986, pp. 87–94. These authors claim to have found two different approaches; but in either case, multinational firms treated all foreign subsidiaries alike. Note this was not strictly a study of product innovation.

Some consultants urge a total strategy of global product innovation. The Ford Escort, for example, was billed as the first "world car." If a firm "goes global" (anything it does is done worldwide), then the product innovation task may appear simplified. However, it actually becomes almost impossible, because the one product has to meet the needs of people from scores of cultures. Though there was a trend toward global product innovation in the 1980s, current preferences recognize country differences.

SUMMARY

Chapter 19 addressed the structural aspects of organization. We saw the five basic options, from the purely functional format to the venture. They lie on a scale of projectization, where members vary from a functional commitment to a complete project commitment.

No option is any better than the others. Nothing is inherently good about a venture or about a functional matrix. No one form can fit all of a firm's product innovation needs.

As with any kit of tools, we have to look at each situation, decide what our needs are, and then select the form that seems to fit best. Even on close fits, there are objections. Much depends on the people available. Many firms have tried to use ventures when they lacked the risk-taking managers that ventures require. Other firms had the risk-takers but lacked top managers willing to trust them.

These structure decisions are then complicated by current managerial desires for quicker developments, better-quality and lower-cost products, and a general atmosphere of entrepreneuring. And even then, various roles are needed in a project, whatever structure is selected. Plus, many opportunities arise to couple (joint venture) with vendors, customers, and competitors.

Now add the rest of the world! The result is a cacophony of structures, sometimes scores of them, each appropriate for its situation but in conflict with others. It's difficult for the project leaders and sometimes almost impossible for staffers around the firm who work on perhaps 10 or more projects.

Structure is only the start. It helps, but how the structure is managed is more important. This is the topic of Chapter 20.

APPLICATIONS

1. "Our foods division is now large enough to make a serious attack on worldwide markets, and for now it is committed to what it calls product line extension and adaptation from the United States to selected other countries. But, there is some question about how to organize this activity. Management plans to make the decisions on

adaptation in their St. Louis headquarters, and at least for now they will sell through importers or agents in other countries (occasionally through the marketing departments of other divisions). What thoughts would you have about assigning this responsibility? That is, should it be given to the test kitchens the foods division has, to the product managers in the marketing department, or to a separate group set up just to handle this international operation?"

2. "Several of our divisions say they get tremendous help from their vendors. But, to tell you the truth, I think they're just lazy. They've got good talent in those divisions, or darn well should have, and all they're doing is giving away some of their innovation profits. Most vendors don't pull their share in these funny partnerships. Do you see anything wrong with a simple corporate rule that we work ourselves out of these so-called coupling arrangements and go it alone in the future?"

3. "Actually, I'm not convinced that any particular organization formats are better than others. I've run into too many exceptions. For example, that great portable tape player, Walkman by Sony, was conceived and pushed through by Akio Morita, Sony's chairman of the board. He got the idea from seeing a past chairman wearing a headset in the office, and he personally directed the project through its technical phases, even over the opposition of his people in manufacturing and sales. Even gave himself the title of project manager. I'll bet that approach doesn't fit any of your academic formats. And, I'll bet you wouldn't discourage it."

4. "I recently visited the head of our major appliance division, and I told him he should consider using some of these venture teams I've been reading about. He said he probably would, but not until I had approved the division's new product innovation charter that he said he was about to send me. Why does his use of venture teams have to await that?"

Case: Marko Products

As a major and profitable division of a large conglomerate for the past seven years, Marko Products was one of those acquisitions that worked out well. It specialized in medical supply products (items bought by physicians for use in their offices, not medical products for the patient).

Marko's president, Bill Wong, was an aggressive executive who tried to keep his firm poised for maximum market impact. He had installed the product manager system three years ago and was pleased that it seemed to be working well. The product managers were in the marketing department, and, although they did not have the almost unlimited informal authority of their packaged goods counterparts, they were respected around the firm.

Marko had two manufacturing divisions: one for consumable supplies (such as bandages and rubber gloves) located in a different state, and another for equipment (examining tables, cabinets, ophthalmoscopes, and so on) located at headquarters. All R&D was physically centralized, but the VP for that function had divided her staff into six parts, each dedicated to a particular technology, such as rubber, laminated materials, or electronics.

One sales force sold the entire line, but in the more populated regions, the firm used separate salespeople for supplies and for equipment.

Top-management staff included a long-range planning group, an international marketing division organized by areas of the world, a governmental/public relations department, finance, human resources, and legal. Packaging and quality control were part of the manufacturing staff.

Marko Products' management chased tough goals in profit and market dominance. They planned to hold the number one or two spots in each major market or else would pull back promotional and R&D support.

Marko recently held a two-day planning retreat, which produced new product innovation charters for each of its businesses. It had been a productive session but not without controversy because most of the managers thought Marko should concentrate on what it did best: manufacture top-quality examining room furniture. They argued that furniture earned most of the profits and that supply was a commodity business Marko entered only because it came with the cabinetry business of Mainline Medical (a firm Marko acquired six years ago). Bill Wong was pleased that he had persuaded them to become more aggressive and to set their sights on bigger and better things.

Following are two of the charters:

Medical Office Equipment, Nonscientific:
Marko will actively develop any and all new products in what might be called the "furniture" category, for use in doctors' and hospitals' examining and consultation rooms. The items will typically (and desirably) utilize our skills in "metal bending" and our knowledge of examining room procedures. The goals of this activity are (1) to add $70 million profit contribution over the next four years and (2) to ensure that we dominate (actual or close) in each major market we enter.

To do all this, we will rely primarily on our marketing department for input on market needs, supported by input from knowledgeable technical staff who maintain market contacts. Each new product will be unique in at least one critical dimension, and we hope it will make a contribution to examining room procedure. We intend to continue our reputation as the leading light in this industry, and all new items will be of the highest quality ("absolutely no schlock," as Wong put it). Our major contribution will be in designing products that can be manufactured to the traditionally high standards of our operations group.

Disposables:
In recent years, the medical community has turned to disposables to solve many of their operating problems, and Marko wants to take advantage of this trend. Our two small lines of disposable gloves and disposable aprons will be the springboard for this activity. The key to dominance here is predicting what new

methodologies the medical personnel will agree to convert to disposability next. We want to develop products that extend disposability and are thus unique. Finding these product concepts will be difficult and will require a combination of office procedure knowledge, attitude study, and technical capability.

Profit goals are not clear for this operation, but we do want the program to get us into at least 10 new lines over the next five years, to dominate at least 8 of those lines (plus gloves and aprons), and to be the firm contacted by persons in medicine who see an opportunity for disposability. Minimum ROAs will be developed as the projects come along.

Some new disposable products will be reasonably nondifferentiated add-ons to capitalize on our position in a given market.

Wong now wondered what organizational structures would be appropriate for each of the PICs. If not possible now, toward which ideal could he work?

Chapter 20

Managing the Process

SETTING

Chapter 20 is a continuation of Chapter 19, which looked at the various *structure* options for product innovation. Here we look at the problems of managing whatever structure is selected. Because the team is at the heart of those options (in that we almost always need all functions of the firm to play a role in new products), Chapter 20 will focus on team management.

Of course, other issues are important too, in particular, choosing the overall style of management that will be used and defining the role for top management (general management). We will also look at techniques to address some special problems.

WHY MANAGEMENT IS IMPORTANT

In recent years, several studies have demonstrated the importance of how we manage the new product process.[1] New products are made by people, not machines or systems. The process is very personal, and people from many backgrounds are involved, often against their "druthers." Finally, the risks are very high—not only may individuals receive bonuses and promotions worth many thousands of dollars, but they may also be out of a job if the project aborts.

---

[1] Examples include Robert G. Cooper, "The Dimensions of New Product Success and Failure," *Journal of Marketing,* Summer 1979, pp. 93–103; Robert G. Cooper, "New Product Strategies: What Distinguishes the Top Performers?" *Journal of Product Innovation Management,* September 1984, pp. 151–64; William E. Souder, *Managing New Product Innovations* (Lexington, Mass.: Lexington Books, 1987), especially chaps. 7 and 9; Roger J. Cantalone and C. Anthony di Benedetto, "An Integrative Model of the New Product Development Process," *Journal of Product Innovation Management,* September 1988, pp. 201–15.

By now, you may be thinking this sounds like most management situations — what's so different about new products? The answer is in the concept of *nonauthority*. New products managers usually have no line authority over the people whose performance will make or break the operation.

Here are some of those people:

1. *Peers.*   People who head the departments from which you draw your workers.
2. *Peers' subordinates.*   The peer department head may ask a person to work directly with you, but you are not that person's boss.
3. *Temporary employees.*   They may be job-shoppers, or temps, or contract personnel, but they are gypsies.
4. *Vendors, subcontractors, suppliers.*   These people work for you through the purchasing department and must follow whatever policies that department has established. And, unless they own their own small firms, they have bosses of their own. Even the supplier's salespeople can only follow your suggestions so far.
5. *Customers, clients.*   The nonauthority role is clear here. You can ask, beg, persuade, cajole — but the customer can refuse to cooperate (say, in a product use test), and that's that.
6. *Your boss.*   Obviously, a nonauthority situation.[2]

Taken together, the new products manager may literally have not a single person over whom there is line authority. Every person on whom that manager depends has to balance new product needs against other job demands, especially those of the person who really does have direct authority.

So, we substitute nonauthority managerial modes, and we will see many of them in this chapter.

OVERALL STYLES OF MANAGEMENT

Chapter 4 discussed three styles of management. The *managerial* style is for noninnovative situations, the *collegial* style for somewhat innovative process situations, and the *entrepreneurial* style for those situations requiring in-house effort comparable to start-ups.

Here is a list of actions or policies that people have associated with the entrepreneurial style of management. Judge for yourself whether you

---

[2] Modified list from Murray J. Shainis and Kevin J. McDermott, "Managing without Authority: The Dilemma of the Engineering Manager and the Project Engineer," *Engineering Management International*, November 1988, pp. 143–47.

would like to be managed in this style and, perhaps equally interesting, whether you would enjoy managing others this way:

- Find persons who will accept lots of risk. They must be willing to lay their jobs on the line.
- Free them from oppressive administrative responsibilities. (To these people, that means virtually every administrative matter.)
- Make sure they have a risk-sharing manager who is willing to accept every risk that the team worker is asked to take. That is, whatever happens to the project, all people will suffer or benefit accordingly.
- Be prepared to move fast whenever these people ask for something. Barring some special reason, they should get whatever they ask for.
- Arrange to give these people constant feedback, which they crave.
- Be sure no analytical devices get in the way. No net present value calculations, no minimum margins over costs.
- Reward them all handsomely. Give them a percentage of the profits from the new product. Money talks. Let them invest personal dollars in the project. Don't claim all of the windfall for upper management and stockholders—those "freeloaders" risked very little, personally.
- Don't cut them off at the pass. Let them continue with the product all the way to market and beyond. Move them out only if they get bored.

This list sounds dramatic, which entrepreneurship is. That's why the popular style for product innovation management today is not entrepreneurial but collegial. This is the essence of a "team" of equals, or nearly equals. Collegial (sometimes called *consultative*) management will be discussed in a moment as good team management.[3] The entrepreneurial style is reserved for the rare venture that just won't move without it.

THE ROLE OF TOP MANAGEMENT

Probably the most common lament of product innovators is about their top management. (They mean top managers of the unit where the innovation is taking place—this may be the president of a smaller firm or the general manager of a division.)

The top manager is personally responsible for the actions that give product innovation its character in a firm. This means giving a clear charter to the team, not "Find some new products that I will like."

---

[3] A clear and concise statement of this subject is found in Sam McClelland, "The Consultative Style of Management," *Industrial Management,* January/February 1987, pp. 12–13. A much more complete presentation of a study of product innovation management styles is James Brian Quinn, "Innovation and Corporate Strategy: Managed Chaos," *Technology in Society,* 1985, pp. 263–97.

Providing focus also means funding, key staffing, and clearly committing the firm to product innovation and to excellence in it.

How is this type of commitment displayed for all to see? By appointing some of the firm's best managers to product innovation, by treating new products as longer-term investments, and by a stream of little things: lunching with product innovation people, welcoming occasional updatings, dropping by the laboratory once in a while, attending focus groups, writing memos of encouragement, and holding awards dinners.[4]

Top managements know that salespeople working in capital goods (such as new installations, new conveyor systems, and new power-generating systems) must work for a year or two before making a sale. It is easy to get discouraged, so they pump the salespeople up from time to time. The same attitude should prevail toward product innovation people.

Top management should be willing to market the new item when it comes along, not revise it to death. And, no formal postmortems should be held on products that didn't work out. Such finger-pointing sessions kill incentive.

MAKING TEAMS WORK

Managing formal and informal teams of people in business has been a focus of research for over 40 years. Most of this research has concerned *project management,* a popular form of team operation in new products.[5] This chapter cannot summarize what we know about project management. Instead, it will focus on special aspects of application to new products — some current problems and some new methods of team management.

Getting Started—Team Building

What Makes a Good Team.   What is a team supposed to do? What is it supposed to be? Recent research found that high-performing teams are characterized by the qualities shown in Figure 20–1. In addition, the following barriers impede team performance:

- Unclear project objectives.
- Role conflict and power struggles among team members.

---

[4] For more on the top-management commitment, see Thomas D. Kuczmarski, *Managing New Products* (Englewood Cliffs, N.J.: Prentice-Hall, 1988), pp. 50–53.

[5] There is a full supply of books titled *Project Management* in one way or another. A couple of the more recent are W. Alan Randolph and Barry Z. Posner, *Effective Project Planning and Management: Getting the Job Done* (Englewood Cliffs, N.J.: Prentice-Hall, 1988); and Harold Kerzner and Hans J. Thamhain, *Project Management* (New York: Van Nostrand Reinhold, 1986). There is also a periodical publication, *Project Management Journal.*

FIGURE 20–1   Characteristics of High-Performing Teams

Task-Related Qualities	*People-Related Qualities*
Oriented toward technical success.	High involvement, work interest, and energy.
Committed to the project, result-oriented attitude.	Capacity to solve conflict.
Innovative and creative.	Good communication.
Concern for quality.	Good team spirit.
Willingness to change project plans if necessary.	Mutual trust.
Ability to predict trends.	Self-development of team members.
On-time performance.	Effective organizational interfacing.
On-budget performance.	High need for achievement.

Source: Hans J. Thamhain and David L. Wilemon, "Building High-Performance Engineering Project Teams," *IEEE Transactions on Engineering Management*, August 1987, pp. 130–37.

- Excessive changes of project scope, specs, schedule, and budget.
- Lack of team definition and structure.
- Wrong capabilities, or poor selection of project personnel.
- Low credibility of project leader.[6]

The Team Assignment, Mission, and Charter.   A clear understanding by everyone involved as to what the team is for, its mission, and its strategy is critical. One manufacturer of reasonably technical medical care products wanted only the moderate risks of *innovative imitation,* so R&D was made responsive to the directions of marketing: new projects originated only in marketing, key product attributes were determined before R&D began, and a marketing manager ran each project. Another firm in an allied industry wanted to implement an *aggressive technical innovation* strategy, but two qualified R&D directors came and went before management realized the short-term focus of a dominant marketing department was totally misleading the teams.

Funny things happen when new product teams lack strategy, because they pick up whatever strategy they think is correct, and the result

---

[6] Hans J. Thamhain and David L. Wilemon, "Building High-Performance Engineering Project Teams," *IEEE Transactions on Engineering Management*, August 1987, pp. 130–37. A good summary of techniques used to achieve good team dynamics is Mohad Tushman and David Nadler, "Organizing for Product Innovation," *California Management Review*, Spring 1986, pp. 74–92. Another good source, written by a practitioner, is Ernest F. Totle, "Management Team Building: Yes, But!" *Engineering Management International*, 1988, pp. 277–85.

is technical people saying team success is measured by technical performance. The customer has a different opinion.

The IBM PC. The more important the team, the more important for all players to understand the strategic guidelines. A classic team was put together when IBM wanted to develop what became the IBM PC. That team was given one year to do the job, and its first action was to draft a statement of team guidelines that was sent to top management for approval. Without that list, the job could not have been done. Here it is. Notice how it clarifies and integrates.

1. Open architecture for the product—invite other firms to participate.
2. Encourage third parties (other computer hardware and software firms) to offer anything they have.
3. Have a panel of 12 employee computer hobbyists handy at all times.
4. Have personal computers (competitors' models) in managers' offices.
5. Use a product management team with minimum staff and maximum speed.
6. Review the process constantly and simplify everything. Get it "upstairs" fast.
7. Go for volume manufacture (no job shop), demand quality, handle as a routine stock item.
8. Ride past the obvious channel conflict by getting the product into the stores where it can be sold.
9. Develop a dealer support plan that will make them members of the team.

Change, Uncertainty. New product situations have four peculiar management requirements: uncertainty, knowledge intensity, competition with alternative courses of action, and boundary crossing.[7] Translate these into we don't know what's going to happen, we're going to use a lot of technical know-how, there are many Ys in the road, and we're going to be working with people we really don't know or understand.

Compound all that with management's seemingly unending changes in how it's going to be done. Even Procter & Gamble, the company that created the brand management system so long ago, has changed it. In 1987, P&G announced that it was going to adopt the team system. This came as a surprise to many who thought the brand system was already a team operation. Apparently not so. As one P&G brand manager said, "We thought of ourselves as the hub of the wheel. We didn't have much contact with manufacturing or purchasing. We'd go to research and ask

---

[7] Rosemary Kanter, "Support Innovation and Venture Development in Established Companies," *Journal of Business Venturing,* Winter, 1985, pp. 47–60.

for something and they'd say, 'That's impossible.' We'd say, 'Do it anyway.' "[8] The company is now reporting successes from incorporating the thinking of people from other departments, which wasn't considered before.

This is not to say that the change is for the good. Who can tell at this time? A former P&G brand manager objected, "With teams, it's difficult to make your own mark and see how good you really are. I wanted the opportunity to dig my own grave or build my own pedestal."[9]

Other Actions that Help.   Several specific actions should precede team operations. One is compensation. Management can't ask team members to take career risks without a clear (and big) reward. And, management should make its support clear when a team is set up. This helps ensure the team will have a good image around the firm. Company people sometimes come to doubt or fear a team, and they can isolate or ostracize it.

Some firms want to start a team off with an intensive two- or three-day training session for the team members. (At Digital Equipment, this pretraining is so critical that teams spend up to a month on it.) Other firms identify the team's *critical success factors (CSFs)*. CSFs are the conditions necessary for success, actually subgoals that if reached will permit the overall goal to be reached. They usually begin with "We must . . ." or "We need to . . . ." They are both strategic and tactical.[10]

Selecting the Leader

Sometimes, selecting the team leader is automatic—for example, the firm that uses a product manager system and the new product concerns an addition to a particular person's product line. Or if, as in the case of 3M, the project originates from a particular person's technology.

Members of the team represent the various functions (sales, manufacturing, and so on), so their supervisor must be a general manager, not one of them. This is not easy for the one chosen. In fact, a group of marketing and R&D heads at a recent training session debated whether any one of them could actually shuck off their functional biases and

---

[8] "P&G Makes Changes in the Way It Develops and Sells Its Products," *The Wall Street Journal,* August 11, 1987, p. 1.

[9] Ibid.

[10] IBM is one of these companies. See Maurice Hardaker and Bryan K. Ward, "How to Make a Team Work," *Harvard Business Review,* November–December 1987, pp. 112–19.

emerge as a team general manager. Some wondered whether they would even want to.

Still, they must if they are to be good team leaders. They lead without direct authority, and so must win personal support. Studies show that team leaders must have strong self-confidence (based on knowledge and experience, not just ego), have empathy (be able to look at things from another person's point of view), have a good self-awareness of how others see them, be enthusiastic without special effort, and be expert in personal communication.[11] A successful new products consultant says new product leadership should be young, bright, multifaceted, persevering, unflappable, diplomatic, and secure.[12] An even more interesting list of factors is shown in Figure 20–2.

FIGURE 20–2   Factors Associated with Project Leadership

1. General management skills.
2. Green thumbs: make little seeds grow into big things.
3. Blank-page vision: lead without a map.
4. One-man band: play all the instruments (at least to some extent).
5. "Miss-a-meal" pains: be hungry, impatient.
6. Christopher Columbus syndrome: explorers who can't sit in port.
7. Night sight: vision improves while others grope in the dark.
8. Lead from the middle: able to work in the trenches and cause change in the whole organization.
9. Velvet hammer: hit without inflicting lasting damage.
10. Stamina: physical and mental.
11. White liar: trick people into doing what they later will be proud they did.
12. Veterinarian: hear the clues, even when the situation is not speaking.
13. Ideaphile: love ideas—anybody's, anytime—store them, talk about them.
14. Biblical: "Let my people go," leave them alone, encourage them, praise little victories.
15. Audacious: Think big and bold.
16. Tinker, tailor, try: be able to try, try, try again.
17. Execution overkill: relentless, meticulous execution, with the job done right.
18. Manners matter: "thank you" and "please," 50 times a day.

Source: Larry Wizenberg, *The New Products Handbook* (Homewood, Ill.: Dow Jones-Irwin, 1986), pp. 212–15.

---

[11] Shainis and McDermott, "Managing without Authority." A newer perspective is that leaders should be "transformational." See Jeremy Main, "Wanted: Leaders Who Can Make a Difference," *Fortune*, September 15, 1987, pp. 92–102.

[12] Frederick D. Buggie, *New Product Development Strategies* (New York: AMACOM, 1981), p. 41.

Selecting the Team Members

Note one important thing about team members: each is on the team as the representative of a group of others "back home" in the department. Although the R&D team member can't do all the technical work, this team member stimulates, directs, and encourages others in R&D to do it, usually in the face of competition from many other team representatives who also are trying to win the lion's share of R&D time and energy for their projects. This makes them "little leaders," and all of the above attributes of team leaders fit team members too. It's just that we can't expect to find them very often. They are in training for team leader slots, but they're not ready yet.

So, we seek people who are knowledgeable in their respective areas, have the respect of their departments, and want to be on the team. If they have to be talked into the job, they will probably not do it well.[13]

In choosing team members, note that most people in a business are either integrators, receptors, or isolates. *Integrators* love to relate to people from other departments or other firms. They naturally give, and get, respect. *Receptors* respect others and welcome information from them but do not desire personal relationships. They are good contacts but not particularly good team members. *Isolates* prefer to be alone and left alone. They are deep specialists in their field and really want nothing to do with people from other functions. They are rarely able to play a role in new product team operations.

How many members should a team have? As many as there are key functions in the development. Usually, this means around 6 to 8; though in complex situations (such as a new car development), there may be as many as 30. Not all are active at one time.

Networking.   The issue of how many people to involve leads into networking, an important step on new products. Figure 20–3 shows a representative new product network.

A *network* consists of nodes, links, and operating relationships. *Nodes* are people important to the project in some way. *Links* are how they are reached and how they relate to others in the network. *Operating relationships* are how these people are contacted and motivated to cooperate in the project.

Who are the nodes? This is the toughest part. Any given project may enlist the support of hundreds (or even thousands) of people. Only

---

[13] This and several other good points are discussed in William J. Altier, "Task Forces—An Effective Management Tool," *Sloan Management Review*, Spring 1986, pp. 69–76.

FIGURE 20–3 Product Innovation Network, Abbreviated Version

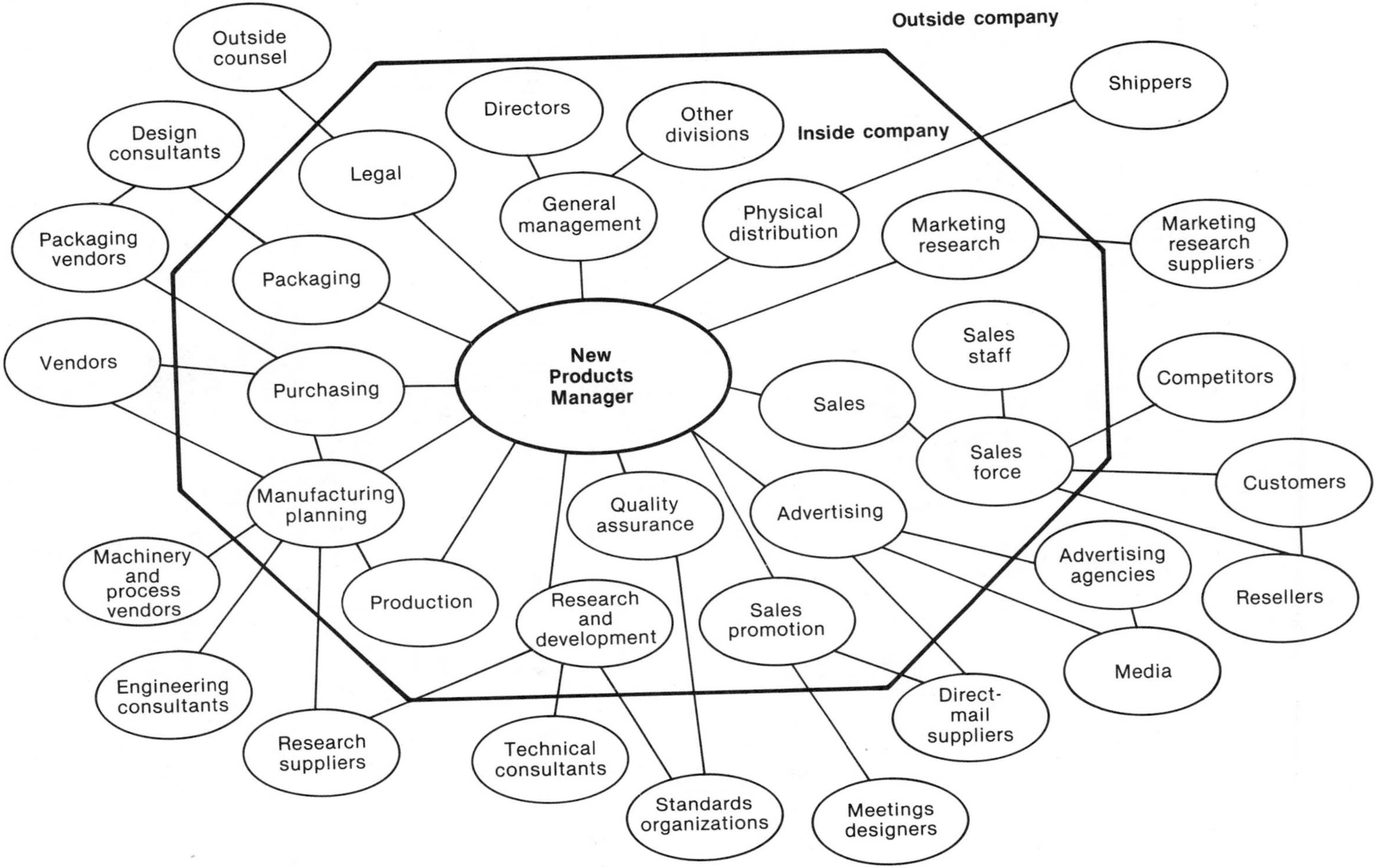

441

judgment can decide how many of them should be put into a formal network and managed.

Linking is not as big a question. The network maker merely studies current relationships and capitalizes on any links already established. If there are none, then they need to be created. Several key business functions are now being asked to play more participative roles— a good example is the purchasing department, but linkages to purchasing are weak, perhaps even broken. Network makers, unfortunately, admit it's a lot easier to draw linkage lines than it is to work them.[14]

Good project leaders are what network professionals call *fly-eyed,* because fly eyes are actually thousands of eyes able to see many things at once. Leadership is also said to be *polycephalous* (many-headed), because it takes many people to manage a network properly. One head simply cannot do it, with or without fly eyes.

Ongoing Management of the Team

Students sometimes ask, "Is there an analogue to the new product team manager's job?" There is, but it is disconcerting—the conductor of a symphony orchestra. On the one hand, conductors are music's famous people; yet on the other hand, we often hear that most orchestras could perform very well without a conductor. At least one well-known ensemble does—a violinist nods his head to begin the performance.

The members of an orchestra are artists, and most are accomplished artists. Each has a professional life beyond the orchestra and so does not wholly depend on it. They all have their own ideas about how their parts should be played, often at odds with the conductor's ideas. And, they are often unionized, fully capable of walking off the stage at any time.

Despite all this, the conductor must conceive interpretations, think about the problems with getting new views accepted, motivate big egos to even bigger ones, and get top performance out of each individual (or at least a performance that doesn't stand out in its poorness).

Each instrument section has its head (like a department manager). Some sections (percussion or brass) play hardly any role in some numbers, while others are absolutely critical. The analogy could go on and on, but the picture is clear. Novices must not think a new products

---

[14] An excellent source for network training is Jessica Lipnack and Jeffery Stamps, *The Networking Book: People Connecting with People* (New York City: Methuen, 1986) 192 pages.

manager just calls a group of people together and tells them what they will do.[15]

Special Problems. The most pressing problem probably involves keeping the group enthusiastic. As work goes on, as creative needs are not met, as efforts fail, as people get tensed up, it is imperative to give what one manager calls his pep talks. The innovation-derailing patterns of behavior that new products face are almost unbelievable: "the not-invented-here syndrome, the tendency to fight over turf, the rush to gun down any wild geese who challenge the system. What folks who have been pushing corporate innovation for the past few years have discovered is that organizations, and their denizens, have even more ways of resisting change."[16] Here is just one (others were mentioned in Chapter 4):

> *The ambassador syndrome:* On coming to the conclusion that more entrepreneurship is needed, management creates a team that will force its way past department blockades. But, the departments all appoint ambassadors to the team, not individuals free to, or interested in, bypassing department power.

New products people live with these problems, but they grow weary. That's why they need to be recharged.

Another special need, oddly enough, is for a perimeter defense. A recent research project disclosed that teams actually use two such persons. One, called a *sentry,* protects the team against well-intentioned suggestions—a product variation, a technology that just appeared, or a new advertising approach. These suggestions often come at the wrong time and are terribly distracting if not kept away from the team.

The other person, called a *guard,* prevents unnecessary interruptions from upper managements who are anxious to know what is going on and from units from around the firm that will need to know about decisions made but want to know too soon.[17]

Another aspect of the problem may appear trivial—the ability to run effective meetings. New product people seem to be in meetings continuously, partly because of the networking but also because so many people do not know how to run a good meeting. Some product innovators

---

[15] This has prompted some CEOs to take over. At Monsanto, CEO Richard J. Mahoney says, "But we demand milestones, and I'm the keeper of the milestones." See "Why Monsanto Is Plunking down Its Chips on R&D," *Business Week,* August 21, 1989, pp. 66–67.

[16] Walter Kiechel III, "The Politics of Innovations," *Fortune,* April 11, 1988, pp. 131–32.

[17] Deborah Gladstein Ancona and David F. Caldwell, "Management Issues in New Product Teams in High-Technology Companies," unpublished working paper no. 1840–86 (Cambridge: Alfred P. Sloan School of Management, Massachusetts Institute of Technology).

have caught on to this need and are now studying their own team meetings for ways to speed them up and improve the decisions.

Interface Management.   The most frustrating aspect of ongoing project management is the friction existing between the three key functions — marketing, R&D, and manufacturing. All functions have some troubles (people always complain about the lawyers, the accountants, and salespeople), but the key functions *must* cooperate often and effectively.

Most of the time, most people on these interfaces get along pretty well, some very well. But, as Figure 20–4 reveals, problems often exist. Whenever a problem occurs, the entire project is threatened, because if people cannot work well together, they cannot communicate.

Different Interfaces.   The three key functions create three interfaces (technical/marketing, and so on). Second, at least three levels are involved — department heads, key team members, and operating people within each department. Department heads get along the best, primarily because they have learned the value of repressing counterproductive differences. Key team members are often chosen for their ability to work across functions. But at the operating level, the big problems appear.

When a third-level scientist must deal with a third-level marketer, sparks may fly. The same applies to the other departments, and this

---

FIGURE 20–4   The Incidence and Consequences of Interface Problems

Incidence of Interface Problems

Condition	Percent of Projects with This Condition
Harmony	40.8%
Mild disharmony	20.5
Severe disharmony	38.7
Total	100.0%

Outcome of Projects Experiencing the Three Conditions

| Condition | Project Outcomes | | |
	Success	*Partial Success*	*Failure*
Harmony	52%	35%	13%
Mild disharmony	32	45	23
Severe disharmony	11	21	68

Note: This table seems to indicate that disharmony produces project failure, a reasonable assumption. However, we don't know which came first, disharmony or project problems.

Source: William E. Souder, *Managing New Product Innovations* (Lexington, Mass.: Lexington Books, 1987), pp. 168, 170.

problem often takes place out of sight from the brass and near-brass. The behavior is almost childlike and immature. It is often deliberately hidden.

The interfaces also vary by time, some continuing and others just flaring up in a crisis. The continuing ones are the most damaging, but the flare-ups are the most frustrating.

Why the Friction?   Scores of differences between the three functional sets of people have been identified by research studies over the years.[18] Some go deep into the psyche of stereotypes, while others are operational. For example, most new products people can identify with this complaint from manufacturing people: "Those marketers can't get through the day without a two-hour lunch at the most expensive restaurant in the area." Yet, a bedrock fundamental problem between these people is their different time frames (manufacturing people are medium-term, while marketing people are very short-term). Another problem is their measure of success (marketing people want sales, manufacturing people want quality, but R&D people want acceptance by other scientists and society at large, not the firm).

Such statements are, of course, dangerous. Although generalizations, they are so often true that new products managers must recognize them.

A second reason for the problem is that these personal differences are exaggerated by separation. Unless people work close to each other, full and open communication is difficult. Research long ago showed that communication goes down with the square of the distance between two people.[19] Yet, corporate size has led us to build huge research centers hundreds of miles from the offices of marketers and the production lines of manufacturing people. Problems caused by these separations have led today's managers to want smallness (see Chapter 19).

A third reason is found in the weaknesses of upper managements, both general managers and the heads of the three functions. Sometimes, these people are still fighting battles previously won or lost on their way up. Some are just careless. For example, the head of R&D in one firm gave

---

[18] Ashok K. Gupta, S. P. Raj, and David Wilemon, "A Model for Studying R&D–Marketing Interface in the Product Innovation Process," *Journal of Marketing,* April 1986, pp. 7–17. A second article by the same three authors covered one type of business: "The R&D–Marketing Interface in High-Technology Firms," *The Journal of Product Innovation Management,* March 1985, pp. 12–24. A summary of one author's research over a 10-year period is William Souder, *Managing New Product Innovations* (Lexington, Mass.: Lexington Books, 1987), especially chaps. 9 through 11.

[19] The research on physical separation was first reported by Jack Andrew Morton, *Organizing for Innovation: A Systems Approach to Technical Management* (New York: McGraw-Hill, 1971). Those findings were later confirmed by T. J. Allen, *Managing the Flow of Technology* (Cambridge, Mass.: MIT Press, 1977).

such a lashing to a staff scientist for telling marketing some bad news about a product test that the individual wouldn't even talk to marketing for over a year. Neither did the other scientists. Their stock answer was "Call the boss and ask him."

Managing the Interfaces.   Most interface management is straightforward, and any experienced manager knows a hundred things to do. Figure 20–5 summarizes the key findings of research over the years. If all the techniques were summarized into three statements, those statements would be:

> Top managers get the interfaces they deserve, because they can eliminate most of the problems anytime they choose to do so.

> Interface management primarily takes time, not brains or slick personal skills. One new product manager said he willingly gave at least 40 percent of his time to seeing that all key players spent a lot of time with each other, on and off the job.

> Participants who continue to be a problem should be taken out of new product team situations; they get some perverse satisfaction out of reactions to their behavior.

Closing the Team Down

Strong differences of opinion arise regarding when a new product team should be closed down and the product turned over to the regular organization. Some firms close out early, well before the item is marketed; they bring in operating people bit by bit. A second practice lets the team prepare for the marketing (for example, write the plan or train the people) but, at the last minute, the regular people launch it. When this is done, the key team people are usually kept close to the action to help solve problems. A third, and rarer, practice lets the team actually market the item and either become the nucleus of its standing management as a new division or turn it over to the regular organization after it has been successfully established.

No matter when the new people get the assignment, they should be brought into the action a few at a time. They serve as the linkage to the rest of the organization.

SPECIAL PROBLEMS AND ACTIVITIES

Battling Bureaucracy

Unfortunately, the nature of bureaucracy thwarts product developers. The hindrances take various shapes:

FIGURE 20–5   Conditions that Minimize Interface Frictions

Existence of the following actions and policies suggests the natural friction of the various functional interfaces in new products work will be softened, if not essentially eliminated. The list makes a convenient checklist for evaluating any given situation.

1. People who need to communicate are physically close to each other.
2. Where there is physical separation, management has constructed human, procedural, or policy bridges that bring people together as often as practical.
3. Product team managers "wander around" a lot.
4. For situations known to be potential problems, the project matrix or venture form of organization is used.
5. Technical and manufacturing people are welcome in the field and to meet with customers. Marketing people are welcome in the factories and labs.
6. Frequent social interaction occurs between the players, on and off the job.
7. Functional heads discourage misguided acts of "loyalty" by their staffers, fight clannishness and cliquishness.
8. Any flare-up in personal friction is immediately addressed by management and not permitted to continue.
9. Both sides of interfaces receive equal treatment, especially regarding celebration of successes, top-management attention and support, rewards, perks, and office furnishings and space.
10. Mistakes are tolerated, but incompetence is not. Everyone and every group will occasionally fail a task.
11. Goals are clear. Everyone knows what the new products team is to accomplish, and they are rewarded accordingly. Goals are common to the team, not to individuals on the team.
12. The firm has a corporatewide culture. People comfortable in that culture are attracted to it. Trust is part of that culture.
13. Management takes time to find out what the various participants think about the interface. They know people act on their perceptions of reality.
14. Special attention is given to ensuring that R&D learns of customer requirements, competitive actions, and feedback on product performance.
15. No attempt is made to deny the basic differences between people. Individuals can laugh off the marketing claim that there is a time in every product development when it becomes necessary to shoot the engineers and start production. And, all nod knowingly when a scientist laments, "I'm going to lunch. If my product manager calls, get the name."

---

1. Review and Approval.   Scores of pressures are on new product managers to avoid doing something wrong—product liability laws, environmentalists, public relations staff, the financial markets, investigative reporters, the Consumer Product Safety Commission, Federal Trade Commission rules on advertising, OSHA, and so on. Bigger firms pay the highest price for a major mistake (will we ever forget Exxon and the Alaskan oil spill?), so they are the most likely to set up technical staffs and review committees. Product developers can't avoid these screens, so they try to soften their effect by giving them information as soon as it's available, welcoming their inquiries, scheduling time for them to do their work, or, as a last resort, appealing to a higher power for relief. Fighting them directly is only for those who like to live dangerously.

2. Personnel Changes. We have to be prepared for the inevitable reorganizations and individual job switches. Some innovators fight for stability in the original assignment by demanding that none of the key players accept a change during the life of the project. This demand usually requires some financial promises. Team managers are also always on the lookout for backups to the key people, just in case.

3. Disinterest. As important as a new product project appears to its team, larger bureaucracies have scores or hundreds of managers who couldn't care less about it. They have their own agenda, often very rigorous ones, and they simply lack the time and energy to get to know everything going on. Therefore, the new products manager should view important internal people as customers or clients—study them, have strategies for them, cultivate them carefully and continuously, build informal ties, and be sure they are in the network. Among the most difficult to include are top managers, who tend to forget about the project no matter how interested they were at its beginning.

4. Overorganization. Bureaucracies breed the trappings of organization. Experts have suggested that we not draw up any chart of the new product's organization, slide past the usual steps of "business plan" and "financial review" by doing them informally and off track, get permission to give outstanding pay for outstanding performance, and try the "club" idea—letting the team find its own location, change the locks, create a few secrets, establish a lottery (for example, on the date of first sale), put a special name on the operation, and so on. As one consultant said, "Unorganize."

Last-Minute Changes

New products managers have a natural urge to make the new product as good as possible. Selling it will be difficult, so we supposedly don't want to market something if we know how to make it better. But this thinking has led to very bad habits—making last-minute changes that add time, confusion, and cost. The Japanese have traditionally "frozen the specs" months or even a year prior to introduction, thus allowing manufacturing, distribution, and other departments to finalize their plans effectively. The product marketed is not perfect in design, but it is well made and well serviced. Far better a well-made product that will be upgraded soon than a "superior" product that is poorly and inefficiently made.

Industrial developers now insist it is best to begin selling the new product as soon as possible, with all its warts, at least to selected customers. If the idea has merit, the customers will help improve it.

SUMMARY

Whereas Chapter 19 talked about the organizational structure for new products, Chapter 20 talked about management of the process. We looked at the various styles of management available and also at the role of top management, which some developers believe is more important than anything else we can do.

The majority of the chapter was devoted to the problems involved in making teams work. Almost all structures involve some type of team arrangement, even if only a committee, and managing these teams is one of the most difficult management tasks. First the team has to be built. Then it has to be staffed, which means selecting the leader and then selecting the team members. Both decisions are critical and dangerous, given the important roles of people in this process.

The chapter also discussed the ongoing management of teams after they have been set up, plus battling bureaucracy and the push for last-minute changes. An analogy between the new products team leader and an orchestra conductor was offered as a way to explain the team leader's unique position.

APPLICATIONS

1. "You say the new product team leader's job is a lot like the conductor's job? I understand it's also a lot like the job of a professional quarterback, or at least that's what the head of our sporting goods division recently said. What do you think he had in mind? Surely he didn't think the quarterback is a manager! He must not know those pro football coaches very well. Next thing you know, he'll be telling us college and high school quarterbacks have that type of job too!"

2. "I keep hearing arguments between our technical R&D staffs and their counterparts in the marketing departments. Seems as though a lot of them don't get along too well, and this doesn't surprise me too much. But what I can't understand is why these disputes seem to crop

up so often in some divisions and so rarely in others. Can you help me on that?"

3. "One of our most profitable divisions sells consulting service to smaller colleges of various types, not the big, state universities. At lunch the other day, Angela Lopez, the head of that division, was telling me that many of these schools are trying to develop new products—new (mainly adult) educational offerings that they can 'sell' to their communities and get some additional cash flow. You could help her and her staff by drawing up what you think one of those networks would look like. She said one of her consulting reps was approached by a college in Tennessee that wanted to develop a new program for educating people in how to earn a living while retired. Assume you were appointed leader of that team; what would your network look like?"

4. "I had to laugh when you mentioned the importance of top management. I've been president of two different divisions and now president of the corporation for several years. I've heard that line—just give us your support and we can get that new item to market quickly. Sure they can, and fall flat on their faces too. They do bad enough without our help; can you imagine what disasters would happen if I started telling people, 'I sure do like Joe Higgins; I'll support him all the way!' Listen, right now our Mountain States banking division has a team of people working on debit cards—they think there is a way to sell these cards, and make a profit, even if they wipe out half of our credit card interest income. What would you have that division president do if he were asked to give 'top-management support' to that project? I think the idea is that debit cards would be tied to long-term borrowing contracts and home mortgages, or something like that."

Case: P&G and the Great Team Switch

In August 1987, Lisa Rathburn and Walker Herrle were sharing a pot of coffee in the Northwest Lounge at Detroit's Metropolitan Airport. They had just finished reading a *Wall Street Journal* account of an organizational change at P&G. Lisa was a marketing consultant for one of the big general-management

---

Source: In this case the people and their activities are realistic but fictitious. The firm's actions are real, taken from various trade publications including "P&G Makes Changes in the Way It Develops and Sells Its Products," *The Wall Street Journal*, August 11, 1987, p. 1.

firms, and Walker worked with a small marketing consulting outfit in Atlanta. Although friends since undergraduate days at Bentley College, they were at odds on this one.

The article said classic brand management wasn't working any longer, that it was being buffeted by consumers who knew what they wanted and by sophisticated retailers who knew how to get it to them. The industry felt brand management wasn't dead, just not good enough any more.

Thus, P&G was doing several things. First, it was creating category managers to combine similar brands, like some of the detergents or the dental care products. Brand managers would work for the category managers now. Second, management was telling marketing research, manufacturing, purchasing, and other departments that their advice and participation were wanted now. The firm was even setting up a new position (supply manager) to supervise manufacturing, engineering, procurement, and distribution. Such a manager would have major responsibilities.

Technical people were no longer just to be told what to do. Brand managers were being assigned to teams, along with representatives from these other departments, and were to work equally with people they had previously ordered around like mini-czars.

Prior to this time, the brand manager's recommendations had to pass muster at several levels higher up but never in other departments. P&G apparently believed products had become complex and were getting more so; they required more than enthusiasm, drive, and dedication. New technologies would also get more attention (the article mentioned Olestra, the cholesterol-and-calorie–free fat substitute that had sat around the labs for almost 20 years before getting a full hearing).

Too, the old system let the brand manager take the time to do a good job – get a good product and market it smartly. But lately, the firm had been beaten by competitors who moved faster (such as Kimberly-Clark's refastening tabs on disposable diapers).

John Smale, P&G's chief executive at the time, was quoted as saying, "When you're going to address a problem, get the people who have something to contribute . . . together." A former brand manager said, "Working on a team with 12 to 20 others, it takes longer to reach decisions; but once that's done, you've got everyone you need in place to move a product to market faster."

The team was expected to avoid problems like that of the brand manager who rushed a promotional package to market and then found it wouldn't fit supermarket shelves.

Some of the many new teams would actually elect a leader, and at least one of them was deliberately holding its meetings on neutral ground away from company offices.

But, another P&G manager said, "Sharing authority is always painful." People in manufacturing and market research supposedly aren't under as much career pressure and thus don't move as fast as brand managers want them to. And, the new category managers were beginning to standardize packages and formulas, against the wishes of their brand managers. Some brand managers had already left for more familiar pastures.

To Lisa and Walker, these changes spelled opportunity. They hoped all firms would make this type of change – they saw their consulting services being in great demand. But then they began arguing. They had very different ideas of how they would go about retraining brand managers and people from the other departments. Lisa would call them together and have John Smale give them the new message. He would explain, inspire, direct. On the other hand, Walker argued for going underground—urging more open teams, letting brand managers see what nice things could happen if they had more interest and faith in other experts from around the firm. In about a year, he would let John Smale hold his meeting.

What do you think?

Chapter 21

Public Policy Issues: Product Liability

SETTING

The Way It Was

New products managers in the United States in the mid-1800s were free to create and sell virtually anything they wanted. A new shoe could be of any size or shape, made of any material, assembled in any manner, and described without limitation. It could wear for years—or for days.

Medicines could be poisonous and totally ineffective, and packaged foods could be unrelated to the package description. Wool coats could be of cotton; a gallon jug could contain three quarts; a dress could be explosively inflammable; and sausage could contain anything swept up from the packing-house floor.

Caveat emptor prevailed—let the buyer beware. Yet, the system functioned fairly well at that time for several reasons. New products were few and usually minor variations on previous ones. Buyers generally knew how to judge products at the point of purchase, partly from extensive experience and partly because critical product attributes could easily be determined in the store.

Patent medicines were a problem, and the young or less intelligent were regularly victimized, but no problems were great enough to question the new product system. Not, that is, until new products began to change. When typical buyers became unable to evaluate products accurately and thus the rate of mistakes or abuses accelerated, consumer concerns became political issues and we entered an era from which we have not yet exited—nor will we.

The Way It Is

Today's new products managers operate within a complex array of restrictions imposed by laws, pressure groups, and individual buyer attitudes. Product innovation charters and every step in the development and marketing process now reflect these new conditions and restraints. Chapters 21 and 22 address this subject and focus particularly on the issues of today. The discussion sorts the many charges, speeches, suits, and so on, into six major areas of concern and then probes behind the rhetoric to spotlight the real issues causing trouble. Because these issues are essentially unresolvable, they constitute the framework for understanding future new product pressures.

BIGGER PICTURE: A CYCLE OF CONCERNS

New products managers are not alone in reacting to the social changes that have been taking place, and the story of public pressures on new products is similar to the story of public pressures on any business front. All public pressure goes through a life cycle of the following phases (see Figure 21–1).

Phase I: Stirring

Individuals begin to sound off long before enough people have been injured or irritated to cause a general reaction. Letters to company presidents, complaints in newspaper or magazine articles, letters to political representatives, and tentative expressions of concern by knowledgeable authorities are typical of phase I. Looking back, such periods are easily identified, but most people ignore the stirrings while they are occurring. Consequently, this phase may last a long time— decades, in fact. For example, packaging of consumer products began in the 1900s, but the Fair Packaging and Labeling Act was not passed until 1966. Inadequate "fill" was probably a problem for a hundred years.

This phase is a genuine problem for new products managers because they don't know what will happen. Flare up, or die away? For example, a stirring is occurring at this writing on "fresh refrigerated" foods using an oxygen-free pouch. They get a heat treatment during packaging and are heated again before serving; is this double cooking harmful? And, food technologists are beginning to worry about the care the packages get in the home. Producers and the FDA are watching cautiously. Stirrings indeed.

FIGURE 21–1 Life Cycle of a Public Concern

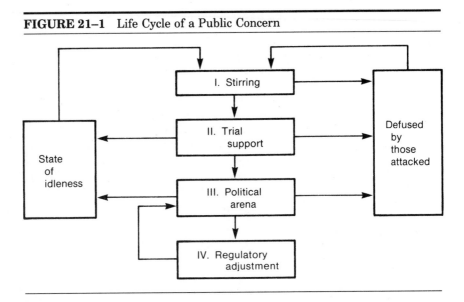

Phase II: Trial Support

As the stirrings over an issue increase, the point is reached when an individual or an organization decides to take on the issue as a *cause*. Often the individual is an unknown, as Ralph Nader was when he tackled auto safety and as Robert Choate was when he selected breakfast cereals. Estes Kefauver was a senator when he attacked unsafe and inefficacious drugs. So was Phil Hart when he decided to go after packaging. The potential leader of the new cause is usually attempting to marry the basic unrest in a situation with a personal desire for publicity, so the key question usually is "How widespread is the unpublicized unrest?" Or, "How dramatic can the headlines be made?"

In any event, phase II is a period when the would-be leader and the muted cause are on the stump, seeking a political base. If achieved, the action moves to phase III; if the industry being attacked can defuse the situation, or if the cause fails to capture broad support, the issue is allowed to die or, at least, enter a prolonged period of hold. Of course, the key individual in the situation is often quite reluctant to abandon the issue.

Phase III: The Political Arena

By the time an issue has acquired a political base and has aroused widespread active interest among the voting public, the opportunity for defusing has usually passed. Now, companies must gird up for political battle in state and/or federal legislatures or in the various regulatory arenas and courts. The issue is the content of new laws or regulations, and, although there is great smoke in the battle, the companies usually recognize the widespread consumer demands and are only trying to achieve the least costly and least restrictive mode of meeting them. Occasionally, companies feel the cause and its supporters are simply wrong and vigorously fight against them. The cereal industry did. The air bag, though now in wide use, is not a settled issue, and neither is the bicycle nor, especially, the all-terrain vehicle and the anti-acne drug Accutane. However, the political base is usually all the cause leader needs to force some modification in a practice, and the modification is usually severe enough to require legislation or a court ruling.

Phase IV: Regulatory Adjustment

New regulatory legislation is rarely precise, and this imprecision leads to a period of jockeying by the adversaries over its interpretation. The Fair Packaging and Labeling Act called for some "voluntary" programs by industry. The Consumer Product Safety Act directed a commission to order the seizure of "imminently hazardous consumer products," which began an extended argument over each of those four terms. The proposed Model Uniform Product Liability Act calls a product *defective* if it is "unreasonably unsafe in construction." Imprecision may well be a necessary, or even wise, approach in regulation, but it clearly governs the nature of this phase in the life cycle of a public concern. The phase often lasts for years, and sometimes the difficulties that arise during this period of regulatory adjustment cause the general issue to be pushed back to one of the earlier phases.

At any point along the way, the political base may erode or product redesign may voluntarily stay the concern. General shifts in a country's political thinking also cause various issues to move into or out of the idle state, a point dramatically underscored by the sharp decline in product-related political controversies in the Reagan administration.

All social issues of business go through these phases, not just new product issues. This chapter, however, will deal only with *product* problems, which are probably well behind employee relations as a source of social concern.

BUSINESS ATTITUDES TOWARD PRODUCT ISSUES

No research report has thus far professed to show exactly how the business community feels on the general issue of social responsibility for new products. But, individuals do speak out, and studies are often made on specific issues as they arise. We are therefore able to discern the following general views, which have considerable support among business leaders. These views guide and help explain business actions.

1. Products with *major, hidden* safety defects should be sold only under controlled conditions, if at all. Thus, there is no room for the anticonstipant that causes blindness, but industry can safely handle caustic chemicals, and homeowners should be able to use power mowers that require some caution in use.

2. Regulation generally hinders new product innovation and should be discouraged. Innovation is the greatest single source of material well-being, and it should be encouraged at every turn.

3. The marketplace should be the primary tool to punish and reward various firms for their new products activities.

4. Consumers can generally make decisions that in total maximize their well-being. No one should expect any consumer's decision package to be error free or based on complete information.

5. The business world is competitive, and not all countries share our concerns. Regulations should not hamstring American companies as they compete in other markets.

6. Regulation is costly, and all attempts to improve buyer decision making should be subjected to cost/benefit analysis. Controls on new-drug testing formerly caused a firm to lose half of its 17-year patent period. This forced higher prices during the shorter period of cost recovery.

7. Our political process gives the various self-appointed champions of causes far more clout than consumer concerns or needs warrant. These "cause" champions often, or perhaps usually, express *their own* value systems, not those of consumers.

The above are *general* beliefs, and they are waived as necessary in special situations. But the beliefs are strong, and they have been the basis for the patterns of new products activity we have seen in the past. They are the cause of the major new products issues of today (discussed later), and they dictate the internal new products innovation process used in industry. This chapter and the next deal with the problems arising as these beliefs clash with the contrary beliefs of persons outside business or, occasionally, of a few leaders within business.

SCOPE OF THE PROBLEM

Only a few major federal laws have been passed in an effort to alter the new products process, the new products themselves, or the presentation of new products to the public. The laws all relate to one or more of the six current areas of dispute that will be discussed in Chapters 21 and 22.

The problems caused by these major pieces of legislation are vastly overstated and overpublicized. Alone, they would fall rather heavily on only a minority of new products managers. The true scope of the problem becomes clear only when the following ingredients are considered.

1. *The constant threat of new laws.*   Each session of Congress sees hundreds of new bills on various aspects of the so-called consumer revolution and scores more that would impact industrial products and services.

2. *The scores of federal regulatory bodies trying to fulfill the numerous responsibilities perceived as their domain.*   A new technical product may well require contact with regulators on employee safety, environmental protection, the handling of hazardous products, special taxes, product measurement, and so on. A food producer, for example, must get Department of Agriculture approval on a label that includes a photograph of the product or ingredients. The *uncertainty* of which regulations are involved in new products perhaps causes the greatest concern.

3. *The control laws and regulatory groups of 50 states and an enormous number of cities or counties.*   Actually, enforcing all such laws would probably make introducing any really new product on a national scale impossible.

4. The numerous *individuals and groups* trying to get new laws passed or simply using their power to enforce the present laws as they feel those laws *should* be enforced.

5. Last, the strong feelings of *individuals within the firm.*   Every firm has employees who think the product line is wrong or products are being improperly presented to the marketplace. Such internal dissension has probably always existed, but it is now becoming much more vocal and moving up the organization—even to the top-mangement level.

Out of this complex situation have come many battles and today's problem areas.

CURRENT PROBLEM AREAS

New products managers face three major problem areas as they study the influence of social and legal pressures: (1) product liability, (2) quality of the purchase decision, and (3) product performance. Problem areas involving fewer new products or more nearly resolved questions are (4) morality, (5) monopoly, and (6) ecology. Product liability is discussed in this chapter and the other five areas in Chapter 22.

These issues are worldwide, though our discussion will mainly use American examples. Members of the European Economic Community are currently wrestling with the product liability question because of a

1985 directive stipulating that the Community will have what we call *strict liability*. Although going slower than it was supposed to, the directive will apparently be implemented.[1] European firms have less problems with the other five areas of concern. Most nations in the world have yet to face even the product liability issue.

PRODUCT LIABILITY

The issue here is simple: You buy a product and are injured. The injury may have come when you carried the product home, when you opened it, when you stored it, when you used it, when you disposed of it, and so on. If you were injured and if you think the maker or the reseller of the product did (or didn't do) something that caused the injury, then you have a product liability claim. If guilty, the accused party is liable for the cost and the pain of the injury, plus punitive (punishing) damages as well.

This issue is so general because courts apparently look first to see if there was injury and then to the nature of the product usage. If injury occurred and if usage appears normal or justified, then courts tend to feel the maker or the seller is probably at fault, and rule accordingly. If they find a ready law, fine, but if they have to search a while, or if plaintiff's attorneys have to be creative, that's OK. Justice is served, presumably.

As one expert said, "The courts are not always careful to distinguish which theory is being applied to produce liability in a particular case."[2]

A good example of the problem comes from services. Historically, product liability meant for goods, not services, and there have been many lost attempts to extend the law to cover services. Yet, services are products (both in fact and as we use the terms in this book); they are sold and bought in good faith, injuries do occur, and some redress should be possible. For example, right now there is much concern about expert systems, because such systems often tell the professional (say, a physician) what action to take. What if the advice is wrong (software glitch, or defective "expert," or poor manufacture of the software)?

As said just above, the courts are not always careful to distinguish. Physicians cannot escape responsibility for poor medicine by claiming they sell a service. Airline crashes are very expensive, whether due to pilot error or a poor engine. In 1986, the Detroit Tigers baseball club was

---

[1] A good summary of the European situation is Steven M. Schneebaum, Esq., "Products Liability in the European Community," *Food, Drug & Cosmetic Law Journal*, May 1989, pp. 283–89.

[2] George D. Cameron III, *Business Law: Legal Environment, Transactions, and Regulation* (Plano, Tex.: Business Publications, 1988), p. 327.

sued by a fan for "failure to warn." She was sitting in the front row of a box between home plate and first base and was hit by a foul ball.[3] And, a zoo had a problem when it sold a llama to a patron and the llama began biting him and his friends.[4] Product liability?

So, the new products managers should look to the logic in the situation and to the general process of law, without worrying about which particular theory is being used at any one time. The company's attorneys get to worry about that.

Status Today

Where are we today on product liability? The answer depends primarily on who is asked, because so many people have vested interests. Thousands of product liability suits are being filed (in federal and state courts), and many of them end in sizable verdicts against the firms (exact data are not available because the majority are settled out of court). Some people estimate that we spend more money in legal costs than we get in awards. But, the statistics are difficult to interpret because the large numbers on asbestos and a couple of pharmaceuticals make it appear that all industries are getting a flood of suits, and this is not true. At the end of this chapter, we will return to our current situation.

In the meantime, product liability is clearly a managerial problem.

Typology of Injury Sources

Here is a list of the ways we get into trouble, and most of them are double trouble on new products.

1. Many products have *inherent risks.*   For example, blood transfusion carries the risk of hepatitis infection, and dynamite will explode. This type of risk is a benefit in a sense because it cannot be avoided — and that fact sometimes wins more sympathy in the courts for makers of such products.

---

[3] An excellent summary of the thinking on services versus goods in the area of product liability is in Fred W. Morgan, "Strict Liability and the Marketing of Services versus Goods: A Judicial Review," *Journal of Public Policy & Marketing,* 1987, pp. 43–57. A key issue is that if the seller of the service can "control the process to render a predictable result every time," then strict liability will apply. If not, the charge will be negligence. The distinction makes a great deal of difference, but the new products manager wants to avoid both of them, and the same managerial techniques are used for both those theories and for other theories as well.

[4] Candace Renalls, "Man Wins Suit against City for Psychotic Llama," *Detroit Free Press,* December 7, 1987, p. 11D.

2. *Design defects* can cause the manufacture of an unsafe product in three different ways. First, the design may create a *dangerous condition*. One example is a large vehicle that must be backed up in normal use and may run over a person standing nearby because the driver of the vehicle cannot see immediately behind it. A rear-view mirror would have corrected the problem. Another example is a steam vaporizer whose center of gravity is so high that the unit is likely to be turned over accidentally. Second, an essential *safety device* may be *absent*. For example, a hair dryer may lack an overheat cutoff switch. Third, the design may call for *inadequate materials,* which perform their function at first but may eventually deteriorate and become dangerous. For example, a gearshift knob was made of material that became brittle after exposure to the environment. Many variations are possible on these three classifications of design defects.

3. *Defects in manufacture* have perhaps always been a new products problem. Inadequate quality control techniques may result in defective individual units even if the product is well designed. Ladders with poorly welded rungs and contaminated intravenous solutions are examples.

4. The manufacturer may produce an acceptable product but *fail to provide adequate instructions for use or warnings against particular uses.* These are often cited as different problems, but they are usually opposite sides of the same coin. For example, if used improperly, the power mower is a potentially dangerous device. The instructions should tell the user how to use it and how not to use it. But courts are much more interested in how strong the warnings are against misuse (even unforeseeable misuse). Thus, one firm was found guilty in a case where an owner used a mower on wet grass—against instructions—and lost part of a foot that slipped under the machine. The court ruled that the company's warning of possible injury should have been much more emphatic.

What constitutes adequate warning will never be known for sure, but here is what courts have used in recent years: The warning should be placed conspicuously on the product, it should be where the user most likely can be expected to see it, it should communicate the level of danger, it should instruct the user in how to avoid the potential hazard, sellers should not engage in marketing activities that vitiate an otherwise adequate warning, and it should not be accompanied by statements that the product is safe. Apparently, the user must be told what may happen, specifically, if the warning is ignored. Too, makers must be prepared to prove that the user got the warning, not just that they posted it.

An even more threatening aspect of this problem for some producers concerns products getting to the wrong market segment. For an example, take the case where a producer of an industrial- and professional-strength drain cleaner was sued by an injured consumer.

The product had been purchased in a *retail store* and was used in a manner inconsistent with the instructions on the label—in fact, the user was shown to be unable to even read the label.[5] Sellers of dangerous products should anticipate and guard against channel deviation. If it is logical to expect deviation, then product labeling, packaging, usage, and so on should be investigated for the added channels.

5. Finally, sometimes dangers appear *after use,* and the manufacturer's liability may continue into this period. For example, TV picture tubes can implode and result in serious damage to bystanders, and manufacturers of spray cans have to urge that the discards not be burned in fireplaces.

All of these categories must be included in planning for the new products process. Unfortunately, definitions of terms, degrees of responsibility, and modes of defense are highly variable. As an extreme case, for example, marketing research firms have recently become concerned about their own product liability in new product testing programs. If they use competitors' products, and if they remove instructions, repackage the products, or create any new usage patterns, they may be held responsible for the consequences. In fact, safety is questionable if a paired-comparison test is conducted blind or if any relabeling is done.

Caution

Before going into this further, note that the press has created many misimpressions around this topic. Product liability suits are newsy and often dramatic, thus leading to abuse. For example, it was widely cited that an overweight man with a heart condition who bought a Sears mower had a heart attack while starting the mower and was awarded $1.8 million. In fact, court records showed that the mower mechanism was defective and required an abnormally large number of pulls. The doctor, incidentally, did not have a heart condition.

In another case, a drunk driver rammed his car into a roadside phone booth and injured a man in it. Outcry greeted the decision that the manufacturer of the phone booth was liable. But, press reports did not make clear that (1) over 15 accidents had occurred in which cars rammed phone booths at other locations on that road and (2) 15 complaints had been lodged regarding trouble with this phone booth locking. We can't make court decisions here, and the decision made may or may not have

---

[5] William L. Trombetta and Fred W. Morgan, "Market Segmentation and Product Liability," *Journal of Marketing and Product Policy,* 1982, pp. 15–26.

been fair to all parties. But, casual readers of the press rarely have enough information to reach a good judgment, though they do form opinions. So approach this topic carefully.

The Four Legal Bases for Product Liability

The four main routes to liability for a product manufacturer are shown in Figure 21–2: negligence, warranty, strict liability, and misrepresentation. All cases require a basis for the claim, and the manufacturer has to have done something—at the very minimum, make, sell, or lease the product to someone.[6] See Figure 21–3 for some classic liability cases relating to the following discussion.

FIGURE 21–2 Forms and Sources of Product Liability

A manufacturer or reseller may be found guilty of product liability via these four routes:

	Negligence	*Warranty*	*Strict Liability*	*Misrepresentation*
Source	Common law, 1800s; Once required privity, but dropped in 1960.	Uniform Commercial Code; Enhanced by Magnuson/Moss Act.	Court decisions, 1960s.	Common law.
Conditions	Defective product, by design or manufacture, and with failure to warn.	Defective product: Implied warranty of merchantability or of fitness for particular purpose. Express warranty: Untrue claim.	Defective product: No requirement for negligence or privity, and no disclaimer is allowed. Reasonably foreseeable.	Untrue claim or misrepresentation that led to injury. User relied on it. No need for defective product.
Defense	Not negligent; product not defective.	Not implied by common usage; Not actually stated; Normal puffery.	Buyer knew, so assumed risk. Unforeseeable misuse. Product not defective.	Was truthful. Normal puffery. Buyer should have known better.

---

[6] A good general source on the following issues is Cameron, "Business Law." A summary of the product liability situation from the perspective of a person marketing a new product is Fred W. Morgan, "Marketing and Product Liability: A Review and Update," *Journal of Marketing,* Summer 1982, pp. 69–78.

FIGURE 21–3 Four Classic Product Liability Cases

Ford Motor Company: It has been alleged that automatic transmissions Ford installed in some cars from 1968 to 1980 slip from park to reverse if the engine is left running. These cars were claimed to have "chased" their owners for some distance when they stepped outside for some purpose. A consumer group claims 234 deaths and thousands of injuries have resulted. The total liability could exceed $500 million.

Firestone Tire & Rubber Company's Radial 500 tire: It was alleged that manufacturing defects caused premature wear resulting in 70 deaths. Firestone denied guilt in some 8,000 lawsuits but spent over $180 million to settle.

Procter & Gamble's Rely tampon: The super-absorbent product was linked to toxic shock syndrome, a disease believed to have caused at least 100 deaths since 1980. Over 200 suits have been filed so far (P&G won some and lost some) based on (1) the clear defect and (2) whether the firm should be responsible for what no one knew at that time. Millions of dollars are at stake.

Merrell-Dow's Bendectin: This antinausea drug had been on the market for 27 years but was now alleged to have caused birth defects. Though the firm won the first 2 of the 700 suits against it, the product was withdrawn because of the unprofitability caused by the high cost of liability insurance. Millions of dollars remain in potential liability.

Source: "Unsafe Products: The Great Debate over Blame and Punishment," *Business Week*, April 30, 1984, pp. 96–104.

Negligence. Prior to the Industrial Revolution (or, essentially, prior to the late 1800s), a manufacturer's liability for products was based in common law as derived from English law. The claim of injury required two things: (1) that the manufacturer's *negligence* in operations let the product become defective and thus injurious and (2) that there was a *contract* between the manufacturer and the injured user (privity).

Negligence is a tort (personal wrong), and liability in negligence requires fault. A duty was breached, and the breach of duty caused the injury. Before the Industrial Revolution, perhaps a wagon maker was careless and failed to attach a wheel securely to the axle. The wheel came off, the driver was injured, and negligence was easy to establish. The wagon maker failed to exercise "ordinary" care (the care that a reasonable person would use). Failure to use ordinary care can also be a mistake by salespeople, advertising, labeling, retailers and wholesalers, and so on, because one aspect of negligence is failure to warn.

Privity of contract was also relatively simple in the olden days because manufacturers were local craft industries that usually dealt directly with the buyer. Privity became an issue as the Industrial Revolution permitted large-scale manufacturing and the extension of markets made retailers and wholesalers necessary. In fact, the late 1800s saw few product liability suits because it was so difficult to prove negligence and because there was usually no privity of contract. Privity of contract was waived in instances involving *inherently dangerous* products, such as dynamite or firearms, or in instances where the manufacturer sold goods *known to be defective,* but these were rare exceptions.

In 1916, the New York Supreme Court ruled that manufacturers could be held responsible for defective products—even if these were sold through distributors—on the reasoning that a defectively manufactured product was "inherently dangerous" and thus void of the privity requirement. By 1966, every state had accepted this line of reasoning, and privity as a defense against negligence was useless.

Warranty. This still left injured consumers in a tight spot, however, because it was difficult for them to prove negligence. Thus warranty, another development of the first half of this century, is relevant. *Warranty* is a promise, and if a promise can be proved and is not fulfilled, the seller can be charged with breach of warranty, whether negligent or not. Therefore, depending on the definition of warranty assumed in a given sale, a manufacturer of a new product may be found guilty of causing injury even if great care was exercised in the design and production process.

Warranty is express or implied. An *express* warranty is any statement of fact made by the manufacturer about a product, whether made by salespeople, retailers, or others. The major issue with express warranty is the degree of puffing a court will allow, but express warranty is not the problem implied warranty is.

Implied warranty arises when a maker offers a product for a given use. An implied warranty of merchantability is part of the sales "contract" and means the product is of average quality and can be used for the purposes for which such products are customarily used. If the seller recommends and the buyer depends on this recommendation, the buyer then has a right to assume the seller (being an expert and knowing how people customarily use the items) is right.

Implied warranty has resulted in constant court bickering over such issues as who said what to whom or whether the distributor could have known as much as the maker. Our society was too complex for law that seemed to confuse more than clarify, so we next saw the development of the strict liability concept, which actually married negligence with warranty.

Warranties are also *full*, where the seller is required to remedy a defective product within a "reasonable" time without charge, or *limited,* where some or all of that requirement is disclaimed. Most sellers use a limited warranty and must say so on or around the product.

Strict Liability.   Under the concept of *strict liability,* the seller of an item has the responsibility for not putting a defective product on the market. If the product is defective in any of the categories listed in the typology presented above, the manufacturer can be sued by any injured party even if that party was only a bystander. There need be no negligence; there need be no privity of contract; and no statement by the seller will relieve the liability.

However, the manufacturer may be able to use three key defenses. The first is *assumption of risk*. If the user of the product learns of the defect and continues to use it regardless of the danger, a suit may not be sustained.

Second, the manufacturer has the defense of *unforeseeable misuse,* meaning the injury occurred because the user misused the product in a way that the seller could not reasonably have anticipated. This defense is particularly troublesome for new products managers because they often do not have the experience in new markets necessary to anticipate misuse, and yet courts expect them to be completely market-wise.

If one develops a new electric typewriter and markets it without knowing that typewriter owners can be expected to ignore instructions not to probe around inside the machine, liability is almost sure to occur. In an extreme example, Faberge, Inc., lost a case where a teenager poured a perfume made by the company over a lit wick. The perfume ignited, burned a friend's neck, and the friend sued Faberge. Even though the firm insisted it could not have anticipated such an eventuality, it lost the case on the basis of foreseeable misuse.

Third, the defense may be that the product, though causing injury, is *not defective*. For example, a man hit his eye on the pointed top of a small ventilation window on the side of his car. Though he leaned over and accidentally bumped the window, the jury held that this injury did not mean the window was defective. Presumably, the plaintiff should have been more careful. As another example, lawyers cite the impossibility of collecting for damage done to fingers stuck into electric pencil sharpeners.

Some manufacturers quickly point out that these defenses may not be as real as they appear. They cite the California *diethylstibestrol (DES) case* of 1980, which introduced the concept of "market-share" liability. If a consumer has clearly been harmed by a product that several manufacturers produced over a period of time, the liability is laid against them all. They share the penalties in ratio to their market shares.

This matter of suing groups has come up several other times. For example, a woman was burned when a smock caught on fire, but she couldn't remember whether she purchased the smock at one store or another, so she sued them both. They in turn sued their garment makers, who then sued their fabric makers. In the end, payments from them all met a settlement of $50,000 to the woman. Market-share thinking was not involved, however.

Misrepresentation.   Actually, a product itself doesn't have to be defective (as it does in the three other situations above) so long as an injury took place when the product was used on misrepresentation (intentional or not) by the seller. These cases are rare, but an example was the helmet manufacturer who made a helmet for motorcyclists and showed a motorcyclist wearing one in a picture on the carton. An experienced police officer bought one for use while riding on duty, but the helmet was not made to be used as a safety helmet. The court ruled there had been misrepresentation.

Other Legislation

Many industries have had unique problems leading to specialized legislation. The Food and Drug Administration, for example, was created in 1906. The most widely publicized product quality legislation in recent times was the Consumer Product Safety Act. Passed by Congress in 1972, the act established the Consumer Product Safety Commission (CPSC). Although the commission's direct impact has been much less than anticipated, the indirect impact has been substantial.

Congress gave the CPSC a large task, including the following assignments:

> To protect the public against unreasonable risks of injury associated with consumer products, to assist consumers in evaluating the comparative safety of consumer products, to develop uniform safety standards for consumer products, to minimize conflicting state and local regulation, and to promote research and investigation into the causes and prevention of product-related deaths, illnesses, and injuries.

In fulfilling these assignments, the commission has the power to establish standards for products, order the recall of products, issue public warnings about possible problem products, stop the marketing of new products, ban present or proposed products, and levy substantial civil and criminal penalties.

The major questions revolve around terminology because the act defines three types of product hazards: (1) unreasonable risk, (2) substantial product hazard, and (3) the immediately hazardous product. How much risk is unreasonable? How much hazard constitutes substantial? How severe must the hazard be for one of the more drastic actions to be necessary and warranted? Various procedures have been established to determine these things, including announcements, voluntary and mandatory standards, hearings, and appeals to courts, but it remains a fact that industry and its critics rarely agree on any of the CPSC actions.

Unfortunately, the CPSC had several false starts, its promise exceeded its ability to produce, and some of its actions caused undue harm to industry. One of the most glaring examples was the 2:00 A.M. Saturday morning notification of Borden and 3M that their spray adhesive products were being banned, based on a physician's report of chromosome damage. This medical finding was reversed seven months later, but the companies' images suffered irreparably. Another case concerned the Marlin Toy Company, which had two products recalled for redesign. When the revised products were issued to the marketplace, the firm was dismayed to find that a typographical error at the commission banned the *revised* products, not the original ones. A substantial successful suit for damages followed.

So, thwarted on the one hand by legal battles over the terminology of injury, hazardousness, and safety and on the other by the difficulty of writing specific standards, the Consumer Product Safety Act might appear to have had almost no effect. This would be a mistaken conclusion, however, for several reasons; the most important is the wide range of actions that manufacturers are taking to help guarantee that their products escape the clutches of the commission's system. Safer products are being made, internal procedures are being tightened, and so on, all of which is very much to the credit of the powers granted the commission.

Attempts at Standardization and Clarification

Throughout all this legal history, manufacturers have been particularly bothered by several things:

1. *Variations by states.*   Lacking a federal law, manufacturers must fight battles in 50 states, which vary a great deal in their laws, the nature of their judicial judgments, and the quality of their enforcement people.
2. *Their seemingly unending responsibility.*   Even when a product was produced 40 or 50 years ago, when entire technologies have changed, and when the product is worthless today, manufacturers may still be held liable.
3. *The pressure on them not to change a product whose original design is in court.*   Such a change, even if anticipated a long time before the case, suggests that the defendant manufacturer admits guilt. Plaintiffs have so claimed. For example, did Ford feel pressure not to change the Pinto gas tanks during the long trial periods?
4. *Alterations by the buyers, by their buyers, and so on.*   Some machinery manufacturers have been ruled against, even when an

injury was caused by the user's removal of safety devices put on a machine by the maker.

5. *Punitive damages.*   Punishing a company for committing a careless mistake, thus making it more careful in the future, may seem reasonable. But, one act may result in 100 suits. Should there be 100 punishments? What is a fair way of deciding how much punishment is appropriate?[7]

6. *State of the art.*   In some cases, manufacturers have been held responsible for making a dangerous product when, in fact, the state of the art at the time it was made offered nothing better. Later discoveries led to the bad verdict.[8]

7. *The discouragement of innovation.*   High-technology firms believe they must be very cautious in marketing products that, although rendering benefit to certain users, offer a risk of misuse and injury. Makers feel courts may decide the injury was too high a price to pay for the benefit. Pharmaceutical companies call it "drug lag" and cite scores of products that were delayed entering the U.S. market though welcomed in many other markets.[9]

Many in government agree with these concerns, and attempts have been made to pass federal legislation to settle them: first the Model Uniform Product Liability Act, then the Kasten bill, then others. One variation even included a fund, financed by manufacturers, to source payments for claims; the system would have arbitration, no trials by jury, and, presumably, no punitive damages. Opposition by consumer and trial lawyer groups have beaten these proposals back every year.

So, at this time, attention has turned to the state level, where manufacturers have been having better luck getting changes on most of their concerns. In recent years, 24 states have changed laws relating to punitive damages, 10 have set a limit on noneconomic damages, 22 have authorized courts to penalize frivolous suits, and 9 now place some limits on contingency fees of attorneys.[10]

---

[7] A 1986 settlement of an asbestos class-action suit gave 751 workers over $100 million. The settlement barred punitive damages, at least partly because the managers who made the decisions are long gone. "Thirteen Former Asbestos Firms Settle Class-Action Suit for over $100 Million," *The Wall Street Journal,* April 10, 1986, p. 4.

[8] This subject is extensively discussed in Kevin F. Cox, "Use of State-of-the-Art Evidence: Confusion, Inconsistency, and Absolute Liability," *Journal of Products Liability* 2 (1987), pp. 91–110.

[9] "Keeping the Genie in the Bottle," *U.S. News & World Report,* April 21, 1986, pp. 50–51.

[10] *Marketing, The Conference Board's Management Briefing,* June/July 1989, p. 6.

Current Situation

It is interesting that product liability produces thousands of cases, with awards of millions of dollars, and perhaps billions of words in the press, yet a Conference Board study of the topic concludes:

> The most striking finding is that the impact of the liability issue seems far more related to rhetoric than to reality . . . the so-called twin crises in product liability and insurance availability have left a relative minor dent on the economics and organization of the individual large firm or on business as a whole . . . . Product liability remains a part-time responsibility in most of the responding firms . . . . The findings refute the general contention of a severe and deepening crisis in tort liability.[11]

What does this mean to new products managers? That they have done an excellent job. The report just cited goes on to say that the problem has been solved in the trenches. Continuing to make products like we did in the 1960s would not have produced the manageable status we have today.

Granted, many suits are still filed, and the seven concerns cited above still exist. Moreover, a critical review of the Conference Board report claimed the problem is still serious indeed, with high and unreasonable costs, thwarted innovation, rampant uncertainty, and chaos among smaller firms (not in the cited study).[12]

People's views apparently depend on where they sit. The new products manager, of course, is not involved with many of the legal problems, insurance costs, and so on. But without doubt, they do know how to avoid many product liability problems. And, most company processes now involve the legal dimension, with which new product management must work.

Specific Actions.   A manufacturing professor/consultant recently said that when manufacturing firms lose product liability cases, it's often "because they don't have . . . [managers] aboard who can look at rational developments in product liability law and apply them to decisions in warnings and designs."[13]

First, manufacturers should anticipate how customers will use products; and, if that use looks like it will cause problems, then action

---

[11] Nathan Weber, *Product Liability: The Corporate Response,* report no. 893 (New York: The Conference Board, 1987), p. 2.

[12] Victor E. Schwartz, "Product Liability: A Crisis Well with Us," *Across the Board,* October 1987, pp. 14–22. Note this journal is published by the Conference Board, publisher of the Weber report that this article attacks.

[13] Richard Moll, quoted in Joani Nelson-Horchler, "Dodging the Liability Bullet," *Industry Week,* April 6, 1987, pp. 30–35. Major parts of the following section came from this article.

should be taken now, not after injuries mount. Anybody could have seen that the all-terrain vehicles would be problems. Power mower manufacturers knew full well that customers would get their hands and feet under the housings.

Second, the firm's top manager should be personally involved in potential liability developments as they progress. And, that person should strongly desire to make safe products. For example, makers of v-style accordian gates for children were finally forced into redesign, and they came out with something better and less expensive. Makers of chain saws found a way to set tough standards that are now being met. Many product categories are never mentioned in connection with product liability.

Third, follow the advice of the legal department to keep full records of actions taken and results achieved.

Fourth, prepare adequate warnings that take the approach suggested above. The Manville Corporation was defending against asbestos-death lawsuits as early as 1929. The firm's chief physician urged caution labels in 1953, but they didn't go on until 1964 and even then did not indicate the gravity of the risk. Almost 50 percent of federal product liability cases in the past 20 years have been on asbestos, pharmaceuticals, and automobiles.

Manage the marketing and distribution process with the same vigor you manage its design and manufacturing. If the product is unsafe in lay people's hands, ensure that it is sold only through professional channels and clearly marked "For Professional Use Only" with explanation of why.[14]

In general, these steps simply say the firm wants to market safe products. Most firms certainly do. What happens between the "wants" and the lost suits is very situational, and horror stories are indeed told. But, there should be fewer to tell in the future, and the odds are that will be the case.

SUMMARY

Chapter 21 presented the first part of the general subject of public policy. It introduced the subject, showed a general life cycle of concern, summarized how business thinks on the subject, and then explored the first of six specific topics: product liability. Chapter 22 will take up the other five.

---

[14] Another good general source of preventative actions to take is Marisa Manley, "Product Liability: You're More Exposed than You Think." *Harvard Business Review,* September–October 1987, pp. 28–41. This article cites the case of a hair bleach product from Curtis that was so marketed and labeled. When an injured customer sued, the court ruled she was responsible by buying at a beauty shop, mixing two products, and ignoring the labels.

APPLICATIONS

1. "I was in Chicago the other day and had a chat with a woman who told me a sad story. Her firm had developed a pillowlike gauge to measure the pressure of hits and squeezes on the chest, you know, the type where a person has a heart attack and someone has to beat on the victim's chest to start the heart going. Would prevent a lot of broken ribs and other damage. Well, she's an entrepreneur and wanted to get going on the product when she found that the only obvious supplier of the primary gauge said no. It didn't decline because of price or profit but because its lawyer said to. We didn't have a chance to finish the conversation, but maybe you can explain what might have been going on here?"

2. "Next, I must say I liked those seven basic views of business. They reflect almost exactly what I happen to think. But tell me, why is it necessary to state them in such a debating way? There is really no alternative position to those stated, as I see it. Even if you agree, I'd like to see you try to attack each of those positions—just to see if there is something about any of them that I've overlooked. Would you do it?"

3. "The worst thing about product liability is what they call strict liability. Now, I know it's hard to prove negligence against a typical large corporation of today, but that's no reason to go to the other extreme and say a company is guilty when there is no evidence it did anything wrong. We market thousands of products involving thousands of people. Strange things are going to happen. Employees are not robots—they make human errors. You've probably already made a mistake or two today, yet if you were a business, you could be sued, found guilty, and then hit with a punitive damages ruling like a common criminal. That's just not fair."

4. "We're currently about to market a new type of hair dryer. It's not a blower in the usual sense—there are no wires that get hot. Instead, we have combined two chemicals that tend to heat up if they are charged with an electrical current. The air is directed through the wire mesh container in which these chemicals are kept (they're solids, not liquids), and whenever there is electricity, there is heated air. If you feel you understand the moral and legal issues of product liability, would you please tell me what you think we should have done, and what we should do in the future, to conform with what the public generally expects of us and with what the law requires of us? We still have several months before we market the new dryer, but the product specifications are frozen and the item is currently about to be started through production."

Case: Hartz Mountain and Blockade Tick and Flea Spray

In 1987, Hartz Mountain spent $10 million to launch a product called Blockade, a tick and flea spray. After a rocketlike take-off, many dog and cat owners began to complain that their pets were either sick or dead. The Environmental Protection Agency ordered Hartz to perform toxicity tests. Late that year, because of the negative publicity, the company decided to withdraw the spray from the market.

When the toxicity test results were available, the company said the product was safe, left the chemical makeup of the product the same, relabeled the can with new dosage warnings (on which the EPA concurred), and relaunched the product in early 1989 with a new ad campaign.

The scene was not completely clear of concern. The Illinois Animal Poison Information Center (the largest such facility in the United States) had received more complaints after the remarketing and was doing some toxicity testing of its own. A dozen or so lawsuits were working their way through the courts, although a judge refused to grant class-action status to the complainants.

Naturally, some pet owners were outraged, especially those who believed their pets were killed by the original Blockade. The EPA apparently was supportive of the firm or, at least, was not currently pressing it to not market the product.

The remarketing efforts were based on the problem the firm faced. Bad publicity often responds to testimonial advertising, so Hartz featured Betty and Bob Dawson of Memphis, dog owners who talked about how pleased they were with the product. The TV commercials were appropriately nonslick (even a little grainy), the Dawsons' dogs were named Sugar and Honey, the scene with owners hugging dogs took place outside without background music, and a print campaign displayed pictures in the form of a TV scene.

Moreover, the firm started a mail campaign to veterinarians, with a toll-free number and an emergency EPA number that redirected callers to the Illinois poison center. Animal toxicologists at the poison center answered questions and kept records for possible follow-up.

Eight months later, the product relaunch had apparently been successful. Even competitors said it was selling well, perhaps as well as before it was withdrawn from the market.

Source: This case is based on public sources, especially columnist Mark Robichaux, under the title "Hartz Mountain Brings back Insect Spray Some Pet Owners Fear Is Fatal," *The Wall Street Journal,* September 6, 1989, p. B7.

Chapter 22

Public Policy Issues (Continued)

SETTING

Chapter 21 addressed the general question of public policy pressures in the new products field and delved into the first of the six problem areas — product liability. It is currently the most complex and difficult of the six, but the other five may surface at any time. Though easier to understand, they are often tougher to solve.

After looking at these problems, we will try to draw some conclusions about the unresolvable threads running through them and what new products managers are now doing to address them.

QUALITY OF THE PURCHASE DECISION

Many consumers (and their spokespersons) believe the development and marketing of new products is done in such a way that buyers make bad purchase decisions. At least, they do not make the decisions that these people think they *should* make.

Inadequate or Incorrect Information

> *Food companies are taking studies that favor the product and not telling the full story.*
>
> Statement by Stephen Gardner, *Texas assistant attorney general*[1]

---

[1] "The Great American Health Pitch," *Business Week*, October 9, 1989, p. 116.

First, some critics say, a large number of people are offered an *inherently risky purchase decision* because they cannot absorb whatever information is offered—for example, children who cannot read or understand product descriptions or older persons who are unable to hear, see, or understand such information. Also, some members of society lack the mental ability to understand product information. At the same time, new products are becoming more complex on electronic and other dimensions.

Too, consumers sometimes depend on *deliberately or unintentionally inadequate product information.* Manufacturers and retailers are accused of using deliberately deceptive promotion, designing products with deceptive packages, appending inadequate instruction labels, and using confusing warranties. The result of all this, we are told, is that consumers buy the wrong products—or products that are wrong for them. A recent cartoon cited a "new and unproved product." The mistake was attributed to a person who "screwed up and spelled it right."

Manufacturers refuse to accept responsibility for ensuring consumers will make the product purchase decisions felt to be the best or wisest for them. The essence of competition, they argue, is that each seller will present products in their most favorable and impressive light and that consumers will, by whatever means they desire, select from among the offerings.

The interface between these two positions has resulted in a series of legislative and regulatory actions that have, on occasion, seriously restrained new products managers—labeling acts, packaging acts, warranty acts, court decisions on strict liability, reviewing councils on advertising, new standards-setting bodies, trade association programs, and many more. The manager still must make the central decision of just how much information is to be provided (nay, actually communicated), and the task is one of striking a balance between the two opposing positions.

In the pharmaceutical industry, as an exception, this decision has been taken from the firm. New pharmaceuticals must be backed with *all* of the even remotely applicable information, and the information must be presented in a physical manner that equally emphasizes the bad and the good.

Consumers' Buying Habits Are Casual and Careless

> *[The health pitch has] got to be here to stay if it sells products. But it's really a mixed bag because the consumer is so foolable.*
>
> Statement by an unnamed food company executive[2]

---

[2] Ibid., p. 114.

> *Consumers felt their ignorance had been traded upon in a very unfair way.*

> Statement by Mona Doyle, *president, Consumer Network, Inc.*[3]

An extension of the first charge is that even when adequate information is provided, consumers will make their purchases in a way that ignores it. Only a small minority of American consumers regularly read *Consumer Reports*. Consumers still "kick tires" in the showrooms of automobile dealers, and auto manufacturers still work hard to build the right sounds into door closing because so many buyers depend on this sound for their overall judgment of manufacturing quality.

Developers of new products believe they are not responsible for mistakes caused by consumers' carelessness. Unfortunately for them, public policy has rejected this position. The essential element is foreseeability (see Chapter 21). If the purchase is important, if mistakes are being made or are likely to be made, and if the product innovator has good reason to suspect that careless buying behavior is frequent, then the firm will be *expected* to make special efforts in communicating the information about the new item. Look at the instruction materials on complex products to see what companies are doing on this front.

Although neophyte product developers are occasionally surprised, careless buying is rather easily anticipated if the proper market studies, concept tests, and product tests are performed.

Simultaneous Excessive Choice and Inadequate Choice

> *I don't own this place. When the chairman says "Why don't we have 87 products like this?" I'll roll them out as fast as I can.*

> Statement by an unnamed food company executive[4]

Another criticism is that manufacturers produce far too many products of a similar nature, products that unnecessarily obsolete other products, and products designed only to round out lines. Examples are legion — more cold products than even a drugstore can carry, far more models than brands of cars, and so on. In the pharmaceutical industry — an extreme case because of the great importance attached to health — current regulation will not permit the development of a true me-too chemical specialty.

---

[3] Ibid., p. 120.
[4] Ibid., p. 115.

The basis for the criticism is that *unnecessarily excessive choice contributes to mistakes in purchasing.* Developers counter that these mistakes are a small price to pay for an economic system that encourages innovation—innovation that brings not only imitation but also innovative imitation.

As our new products system ferrets out smaller and smaller market segments, and as changes in the world's income levels give economic strength to those tiny segments, products will be developed for them.

The second half of the "excessive choice" criticism—that industry fails to meet many market needs with new products—is equally debated. The person with rare physical dimensions or the person with an extremely unusual lifestyle will look at the shelves of essentially similar products and ask, "How about me?" Industry has provided a fruitful series of new product developments designed to meet the needs of narrow and uneconomic segments, an example being special formula products for babies whose digestive systems will not tolerate certain ingredients in the common products. But, these developments have obvious public policy (and thus public relations) overtones. Industry has not hesitated to claim the right to decide which products it will develop and which it will not.

As they see it, in the vernacular of President Harry Truman, the buck does not stop with them. So, they have been saying to government, if you want this product to be available, the public will have to bear part of the costs because we could never make a profit on it. In the pharmaceutical industry, these products are called *orphan drugs,* and the problem is so real that in 1983, Congress passed the Orphan Drug Act, which provides federal aid for the development and marketing of drugs that otherwise may not be commercially feasible because of the relatively small number of potential users. An example resulting from this law is a new drug for treating narcolepsy, which is the tendency to suddenly fall asleep regardless of place or action if the person happens to laugh or enjoy even a small bit of elation. Until now, 40,000 sufferers had to remain completely emotionless.[5]

Vaccines have also been a problem because of the high risks in producing them. In 1986, Congress passed the National Childhood Vaccine Injury Act, which has provisions to reduce manufacturers' risk and to motivate them to continue their development and production.[6]

---

[5] An odd case arose in 1987 when Genentech complained to the FDA that profits from its human growth hormone orphan drug were being threatened by an Eli Lilly product. A supposedly unprofitable orphan drug was so profitable that the company sought protection against Lilly. "Genentech' Custody over an Orphan Drug," *Business Week,* March 23, 1987, p. 39.

[6] A 1989 case reaffirmed the law. See "Drug Concerns Win Collective Liability Case," *The Wall Street Journal,* August 1, 1989, p. 84.

Twisted Priorities

> *We are not the sum of our possessions. We cannot hope only to leave our children a bigger car, a bigger bank account. We must hope to give them a sense of what it means . . . [for a citizen to leave] his home, his neighborhood, and town better than he found it.*

Statement by President George Bush in his 1989 inaugural address[7]

A clear understanding of this charge may come from the following:

> Mishan challenges the maxim that sustained growth offers hope for the betterment of the human condition. He sees several jeopardies, including the unexpected side effects of technological breakthroughs and the fact that heroin was originally introduced to the medical profession as a nonaddictive sedative derived from morphine.[8]

This argument has sometimes been labeled "tail fins versus parks" (from the famous tail fins on cars in the 1950–60s era); and in times of restricted resources, we have readily let government make such prioritizing decisions as the elimination of trouser cuffs and wide margins in books during World War II. Families do the same.

It is usually considered the task of product innovators to create ideas that can be turned into products wanted by enough of the marketplace to sell at quantities and prices yielding satisfactory net profits to the firm. But, in the process, is the innovator to be concerned with the possible drain of moneys from the support of museums or the possible effects of the product on the social attitudes and relationships of people?

If the public is concerned about such matters, it has the power of the pocketbook and the recourse of government, both of which it has used on many occasions. And, developers resist taking this decision into company hands. For example, they cite the automobile industry, which was rebuffed at great cost when it tried to sell safety through seat belts in the 1960s.

Some believe blaming industry for the public's love of wasteful products is like "blaming the waiters in restaurants for obesity." Industry defenders also note that producers don't invent desire for new products—that desire is already there. Even such unexpected new products as the automobile, television, the kidney dialysis machine, and the typewriter met existing needs. To credit Madison Avenue with generating unwanted or false demand is to ignore the Edsel, Corfam, and hundreds of other failures.

---

[7] Ronald Henkoff, "Is Greed Dead?" *Fortune,* August 14, 1989, p. 41.

[8] E. J. Mishan, "What Monsters Technology Hath Wrought," *Business and Society Review,* Summer 1978, pp. 4–8.

No one but diehard members of the Libertarian party holds to the literal position that the public should be given whatever it wants. Product developers don't believe that. There is no surge of support for slot machines, fireworks, or thalidomide.

But, and this seems conclusive, the function of new products management is not *currently* charged with making social value decisions. It is not expected to rule on the pleasure value of the hula hoop versus the wastefulness of the plastic used in its production or the diversion from their books of the players who use it. Some even insist that such decisions cannot ever be made and cite as an example the question of how durable new products should be during the rapid evolution of a new industry. Is the producer doing consumers a favor by saddling them with products that will still be very useful long after major improvements have been made?

PRODUCT PERFORMANCE

> *If I were a hospital administrator, I would never buy one of the first 20 to 50 instruments made unless the manufacturer could show me field test data—laboratories where the instrument was actually tested under normal conditions. Volume is small in that industry, and the first 20 to 50 instruments are still in the development stage.*
>
> Statement by Harvey Gittler, *former manager in that industry*[9]

We hear that American products—particularly automobiles, cameras, watches, radios, and TV sets, to the extent there are any left—are of poor quality compared to certain foreign products. We also hear that American products are frequently of poor quality even when there is no higher-quality foreign competitor—residential furniture is a major example. This charge has several facets:

1. *"Products are intentionally designed to be of low quality."* This viewpoint cites attempts to lower the costs of items by using cheaper materials that do not hold up and by eliminating features or attributes that contribute to long-term durability.

2. *"Product quality control is lacking."* Whether the problem is the physical system of production, the managerial motivation (or demotivation) system for employees, or just the poor attitude of today's workers (all of which have been accused), the fact seems to be that in some product lines, quality is "not what it used to be," or at least not what we perceive it to have been.

---

[9] Harvey Gittler, "Listen to the Whistle-Blowers before It Is Too Late," *The Wall Street Journal,* May 5, 1987, p. 18.

If we consider the technical complexity of today's television sets and single-lens reflex cameras, for example, their immediate and long-lasting performance is astounding.[10] *The Wall Street Journal* canvassed this subject in 1981 and reported a general feeling among both manufacturers and retailers that growing product ownership (for example, perhaps 15 electrical/electronic items in a home) and increased product complexity are the cause of consumer troubles. The "hammer and wrench" mechanic of 25 years ago simply cannot cope with an 18-cycle washer with 10 push buttons, three temperature settings, and so on.[11] New products managers must anticipate potential design and production problems and be sure to include testing provisions to control such problems and anticipated consumer attitudes.

3. *"Normal repairs and service are often unobtainable, even for products properly designed and carefully manufactured."* Service complaints are partly a function of personnel shortage at the retail level and partly a matter of economics. The new products manager, unfortunately, does not have much control over service unless the firm is getting into a new line of merchandise. New products have been designed on a modular basis (small appliances by Procter and television by Motorola/Quasar) in an (unfortunately, unsuccessful) attempt to help solve the service problem. Attempts along other lines will probably be made. In fact, the service problem is often studied as a new idea opportunity.

MORALITY

Nowadays, his 430 employees produce 7,000 satellite receivers a month. A recently acquired machine could triple that figure. But, in the meantime, Peter Drake does without a satellite receiver—he prefers that his children not have access to everything on the air waves.

Gist of statements by Peter Drake, *owner of R. L. Drake Company*[12]

Morality is the issue of whether society should be denied certain new products for its own good. Specifically, do consumers have a right to

---

[10] The service issue is sometimes almost beyond comprehension. Since 1975, people in and around the auto industry have been trying to figure out how to define a lemon, a necessary first step toward getting relief from the purchase of one. So far, they have failed. See Deirdre Fanning, "What Makes a Lemon?" *Forbes,* January 25, 1988, p. 86.

[11] "Repair People Struggle to Keep up with the Glut of Breaking Products," *The Wall Street Journal,* January 5, 1981, p. 1.

[12] George Stricharchuk, "Losing Sales, Radio Company Finds Success in New Product. Is It Too Late?" *The Wall Street Journal,* February 27, 1984, p. 23.

buy a product even if it may hurt them morally? Do sellers have a right to tempt consumers into buying a product that caters to a weakness? Shouldn't consumers be permitted a full choice? Can't the marketplace be the decision mechanism as to what should or should not be available?

One of the earliest problems of this type concerned the birth control pill, though the "public" in that case was the Roman Catholic Church. Scientists at G. D. Searle were themselves split on the issue, and the company went so far as to obtain a ruling from the Catholic archdiocese in Chicago that permitted Catholic employees at Searle working on the "pill" to request transfer to another phase of the business. But, the real problem came at marketing time. Did Searle have the right to market a product that permitted the practice of an act that Catholics considered sinful? Government did not become involved in this case, but the problem for Searle and other producers of birth control pills remained genuine for several years. Time played a greater part in settling it than did breakthrough wisdom.

Similar problems occasionally arise—for example, in connection with new alcoholic beverages, new gambling devices, and sex devices. Producers of radar-detecting systems like the Fuzz-Buster have been accused of aiding law violation. Anheuser-Busch was forced to withdraw a product from test market when the public complained that the level of alcohol in what was a "kid's drink" would "train" youngsters to like alcoholic beverages. The product might have been worthwhile for the company, but it was abandoned. A revised product was reentered into test, but the damage had already been done.

A current issue concerns the popular satellite TV dishes. They are now used in out-of-the-way places that would not have much TV otherwise, but they are also used in large cities, in apartment houses, and in bars. Their purpose is at least partly to capture program signals from satellites without paying for them. As of this writing, they have not been declared illegal, and the solution may be to have all signals sent to earth scrambled. But, in the meantime, what are the responsibilities of the manufacturer of electronic components, without which the satellite signal could not be used by the TV set? They merely sell to the satellite receiver firms.

A later, and perhaps more difficult, version of the satellite dish problem concerns digital audio taping and dual-drive VCRs. Both technologies were held up for some time because they permit (encourage?) the illegal behavior of taping from compact discs and prerecorded rental videotapes. The explanations given for their marketing have provoked much comment.

MONOPOLY

> *The essence of the competitive process is to induce firms to become more efficient and to pass the benefits along to consumers. That process would be ill-served by using antitrust to block hard, aggressive competition that is solidly based on efficiencies and growth opportunities, even if monopoly is a possible result.*
>
> Statement by David A. Clayton, *federal trade commissioner*[13]

The charge of monopoly is occasionally applied to new products. Some persons concerned with public policy and some economists believe market dominance or large market share constitutes harmful monopoly. The breakfast cereal industry, for example, was "on trial" for several years on the charge that product differentiation had enabled four companies to acquire monopolistic control, and the request was made that they be fragmented into smaller companies. Their new products managers had been too successful.

Apart from fringe exceptions, this country has not penalized successful product innovators. Even attacks on the patent system, which have been a direct consequence of this public concern, have not been very successful. One action, the Drug Price Competition and Patent Term Restoration Act of 1984, may indicate a turn in this history. The pharmaceutical industry was restored up to five years of patent life lost during their products' lengthy developments in return for letting generic drug producers get into action almost instantly when the patent does expire. We don't know if this suggests other actions in areas where patented products are in such demand.[14]

Bell and Howell once claimed that Kodak secretly developed some film products and introduced them before Bell and Howell had a chance to retool its own cameras and projectors. Consequently, Bell and Howell lost market share because its equipment was rendered instantly obsolete and the firm was stuck with useless inventories. Bell and Howell won the first round, but appeal overturned the first judge's decision that Kodak would have to inform competitors of its impending product changes well in advance of hitting the market with them.

Economic theory tells us that the best way to defeat a monopoly is to invent a product that replaces the one being monopolized.

---

[13] "The New Case for Monopolies," *Business Week,* December 15, 1980, p. 58.

[14] A thorough analysis of this law is Henry Grabowski and John Vernon, "Longer Patents for Lower Imitation Barriers: The 1984 Drug Act," *AEA Papers and Proceedings,* May 1986, pp. 195–202.

Putting a damper on product innovation in the name of avoiding monopoly would be ironic, and, fortunately, the courts have refused to do so. Some protests do arise when a firm buys potentially competitive patents and "deep-sixes" them, but no official action has been taken.

ECOLOGY

> *The airliner, in addition to plunging us into an era of shrieking skies from which it is virtually impossible to escape . . . has been responsible for a tourist explosion that has irrevocably destroyed all of the once-famed beauty spots of the Mediterranean coast and the natural beauty of inland resorts and lake districts the world over.*
>
> Statement by English economist E. J. Mishan[15]

New products are often criticized on the following ecological bases:

1. A new product is destructive to the environment if any of the *raw materials* used in its manufacture are scarce or will soon be scarce, or if they are needed in some other way. On these grounds, critics have faulted products utilizing copper, mercury, gold, silver, tungsten, and so on.
2. The *manufacture* of some products causes environmental pollution (the prime example is paper), and the use of great amounts of power in making some items may overtax power-generating facilities.
3. The *use* of other products causes environmental damage—prime examples are the automobile and insecticides. Here, the nature of the effect is slightly different: cars cause air pollution during their actual use, and insecticides cause pollution by their accidental ingestion or accumulation in streams, eggs, and so on.
4. Some products cause difficulties during the *disposal process*—the prime example is beverage containers. Honeywell asks buyers of its home smoke alarms to return them to the factory for disposal.

These four situations are relatively straightforward, but we face the problem of conflicting public policy interpretations and actions. In this shaky environment, you can see the difficulty of developing new product

---

[15] Mishan, "What Monsters Technology Hath Wrought," p. 6.

protocols and reliable testing procedures. It will become much more difficult for new products managers if the world-based Green movement succeeds in becoming a viable political party. Some observers believe business's past brushes with environmentalism are nothing compared to what is coming.

Environmentalism got a strong shot in the arm in 1990 by the rejuvenation of Earth Day and the sudden awareness that the United States was running out of landfill space. As of this writing, there is every evidence that makers of new products will need to deal with a new mentality in the market place. The shrill complaints of a trivial minority may have been ignorable in the past; today's loud shouts from all sides will not be.

Interestingly, the business world is discovering profit in environmentalism. Specifically, there is now evidence that being first in adopting less damaging packing materials and design not only increases demand but may actually cut costs. It is a safe bet that the environmental factor will join product liability as a common item on new product protocols.

Unfortunately, developers trying to respond to environmentalism must deal with underlying residual issues that are not easily pushed aside, and we will now look at five especially difficult ones.

THE UNDERLYING RESIDUAL ISSUES

Only a small number of genuine issues thread their way through the above confusions, and they must be understood because company action programs are built around them. Students may want to try writing out their own answers to each issue.

What Are Reasonable Goals for Action Here?

A risk-free existence is totally unreasonable. Zero-defect quality control is a goal for guidance, not achievement. With the complexity in most of today's consumer products, nothing short of government decree would stop consumers from making errors — and then only because they would not be making any decisions at all.

Lloyd Tepper, then an associate commissioner for science in the Food and Drug Administration, stated the problem this way:

> The fact that safety is relative is further illustrated by the statistical elements of every test, for the demonstration of no adverse outcome among 100 animals still leaves us with a 5 percent chance that the true outcome is not zero but rather 3 percent. If the number of animals is increased to 1,000, and there is

still an apparent zero effect, there is still a 5 percent chance that the true response is 0.3 percent. It is rarely possible to design experiments this large or larger, and yet 0.3 percent of the 200 million people in this country is 60,000 persons.[16]

Just how little risk is feasible to seek? The safety argument turns mainly on this question, especially when we have no accepted means of measuring the value of a human life.

Can the Market System Rule?

Some critics insist that consumers be given more and more information so they can make better decisions. But, even with almost total information, would the consumer choose wisely? Almost certainly not—with respect to what these critics think the consumer should buy. If consumers don't like liver, they won't buy it.

So, anytime we are asked to change the way we develop and market our new products, the question usually is "Will it work?" Far too often we just don't know—and neither does anyone else.

The Trade-Off Problem

Even when a particular situation seems to have a clear-cut guiding principle, we often find a contrary principle of equal merit. Which of two worthy options should be accepted?

For example (and we could pick any of several situations), there is logic in wanting the American physician to control the prescribing of medicines—to keep the healer free of the "selfish" influences of drug manufacturers that have product biases. On the other hand, when drug manufacturers produce medicines wanted by physicians, they are often accused of abrogating their responsibility to stop the careless or uninformed prescribing of useless or even harmful drugs!

In the same industry, an allied example concerns the role of the pharmacist. For safety and patient convenience, the pharmacist should control drug dispensing, but the manufacturer is blamed for the resulting "high costs" of such careful overseeing.

---

[16] Lloyd B. Tepper, "The Safe and Effective Issue: 1. A Regulator's View," *Research Management,* March 1976, pp. 7–9. The economic consequences of a zero-defects program are much more grave, especially when advocates of social action ignore the costs while overstating the benefits of improvements. Many current areas of controversy are discussed in Warren T. Brookes, "The Wasteful Pursuit of Zero Risk," *Forbes,* April 30, 1990, pp. 161–72.

The discoverer of DDT won a Nobel prize because the material would markedly enhance world crop productivity and thus reduce world hunger. Yet the discovery was ultimately banned in large areas because it produced undesirable effects.

The real issue is, How do we resolve these conflicts? So far, we have used the traditional American system of power, politics, and the courts. Don't view political activity and court suits negatively—they are the normal method of resolving conflicts between worthwhile positions in democratic countries.

How Should We Meet Needs that the Market Apparently Cannot Meet?

Much concern has been expressed about people whose needs are not met in the normal course of business—the special nutritional needs of children and the special needs of the senile elderly person, the low-intelligence buyer, the undereducated urban dweller, or the odd-sized person. These and many other groups are occasionally forced to make decisions that we can expect to be wrong. And, they are frequently denied new products that would be useful but, for one reason or another, cannot be made available.

Most attempts to meet the special needs of such groups have proved disappointing. Many projects have been established to develop special, low-cost food products, for example. Manufacturers have attempted to cooperate, but there are criticisms of restraint of trade. And, it's tough to get firms excited about this type of project when their motivating structure is profit. Perhaps someone else will have to do it.

Where Should the Costs Fall?

In many of the controversies that affect new products, the argument is not so much *what should be done* as *who should pay for it*. Assuming (1) no production system can ever make products perfectly and (2) no consumer group will ever use products with perfect wisdom, there will always be injuries and waste. Who should pay? Convenient soft-drink containers are a source of litter—who should pay to pick them up? Newspapers constitute a major component of urban waste—should their price include the cost of disposal?

Governments are already under pressure for tax reduction. Insurance companies know the negative reactions to inflated rates. So, the no-fault approach is becoming popular—or, as the manufacturer says, the total-fault approach. The manufacturer assumes all responsibility and is expected to pass along the costs somehow. This solution doesn't really solve anything, and the issue remains controversial, though some firms have privately begun to accept it.

WHAT ARE NEW PRODUCTS MANAGERS DOING ABOUT ALL THIS?

So far, we have talked about issues, problems, pressures, and regulations. Yet, despite the frustrating positions taken against product innovation, we have more of it than ever, and the track record on almost every front is improving. We have few crises now; when they do come up, firms know how to handle them. How have we done it? Let's look at actions in each phase of the product innovation process.

Strategy and Policy

Ciba-Geigy, Switzerland, has stated the following:

> Research and selection of new products is so directed as to favor those that contribute materially to progress and are ecologically irreproachable. In other words, we have deliberately chosen a policy of qualitative and not quantitative growth.[17]

Such statements have appeared in many corporate documents over the past 15 years, and outsiders can only presume they are serious attempts to address the question of social policy and new products. How sincerely and faithfully these policy statements are implemented is, of course, quite another question.

Dow Chemical Company has genuinely tried to implement such stated policy despite being in a business that keeps it in the ecological limelight.[18] Dow's action illustrates the essence of strategic response to public policy issues. Carl A. Gerstacker, then chairman, denied that Dow's new program was an attempt to be socially responsible or committed to a cause. He said the firm's goal was to make more profit. But, the Dow program—called Product Stewardship—was total, and it assumed full responsibility for how Dow products affect people.

Dow's strategy, like that of many other companies, takes the position that it should be managed so its actions optimize the balance between short-term and long-term positions. Sometimes this means *certain types of products will not be developed*. Dow, for example, did not develop a

---

[17] Brian Andrews, *Creative Product Development* (London: Longman, 1975), p. 37.
[18] "Dow's Big Push for Product Safety," *Business Week*, April 21, 1973, p. 82.

paint containing an organic arsenic for ship bottoms because of the paint's potential effects on the environment. Firms also make it their strategy to effect *socially desirable redesign of new or established products when this will enhance the product's longer-term position in the market.* Dow, for example, developed special cylinders to haul agricultural chemicals sensitive to shock hazards. Other firms have removed fluorocarbons from spray products and lead from paint and gasoline. Furthermore, overall strategies often call for *special marketing tactics* — such as Dow marketing an industrial cleaning chemical only to customers that agreed to special handling, and its positioning of a fire-retardant only for use on thermal plastics. *Special and vigorous market testing and revised warranties* are other examples in the marketing field.

The bottom line is that good strategy leads companies into developments where they have expertise and where errors are less likely.

Control Systems

Managements today want no surprises in the public arena, so they have tightened control over the whole process—setting tough standards, rigorous auditing at all points, good record-keeping, training and retraining of new product employees, and much more. They are serious, and everyone knows it. To be sure, many firms (such as Gillette and Monsanto) have appointed what are called *safety czars.*[19] Also sometimes called *watchdogs on a long leash,* these czars are officially often product acceptability managers. Quality is their assignment, and they carry a big stick. *Reader's Digest* called the Gillette czar Dr. No.

Disaster plans are one of the newest and perhaps most effective approaches. A good contrast in recent years was the action Campbell Soup took as compared with that taken by two other firms. When Campbell's routine checking program disclosed a can containing botulin, the company immediately canvassed 102,000 food outlets in a 16-state area, stopped shipments from the plant involved, and inspected 65 million cans. A new manufacturing process was abandoned, two dozen spoiled cans were discarded, and the firm was back on top of the situation. In contrast, when National Presto Industries and McCullough Corporation were criticized by the Consumer Product Safety Commission, they told the CPSC to "tell it to the judge." The CPSC did just that,

---

[19] Greg Johnson, "Product Watchdogs on a Long Leash," *Industry Week,* June 28, 1982, pp. 65–68.

and the firms had to negotiate a settlement before proceedings began.[20] Not every new product marketing program includes contingency plans, let alone contingency plans for public policy matters, but apparently the practice is increasing.

Many firms have also stopped gambling that a known product defect will not be discovered or that if discovered, the costs of adjustments will be much less than the costs of repairing or replacing the bad products in advance. Though outsiders never know for sure, it has been said that some of our most publicized product liability cases (autos and components) arose from this type of misjudgment. As the "cost" of bad publicity rises, the cost of anticipatory repair goes down.

Another useful control device is the 800 number. Procter & Gamble currently gets close to a million customer contacts a year, many of them on 800 numbers, of which there is one per product. The manager of this service said that without the early-warning signal of product problems, "we wouldn't find out about them for weeks or months. There's a whole lot of enlightened self-interest in this."[21]

The 800 number is just a peek at the new launch control systems gradually emerging (recall Chapter 18).

Control often raises questions of restraint. Are we adding to the "innovation lag" that public pressure can cause? Maybe; but, so far, the controls are being used sensibly and, apparently, in a way that satisfies management. The costs of poor control are just getting too high.

Product Testing

A totally inexcusable and tragic embarrassment arises when a firm simply neglects to test a new product under foreseeable conditions of consumer usage. So, even when a management honestly believes it knows how well a product works, a sound practice is to:

1. Test the item with all conceivable user groups.
2. Push the product to its limits—really know what it will do.
3. Be sure there is no opportunity for misunderstanding and misuse.
4. Be satisfied that there can be no reasonable charge of negligence or lack of concern over misuse or abuse.
5. Prepare the data in a form that regulators and juries can understand.

---

[20] Paul Busch, "A Review and Critical Evaluation of the Consumer Product Safety Commission: Marketing Management Implications," *Journal of Marketing,* October 1976, pp. 41–49.

[21] "Customers: P&G's Pipeline to Product Problems," *Business Week,* June 11, 1984, p. 167.

Market Testing

Knowing a product functions well under controlled test conditions is not enough. The *market* test, where some or all of the marketing plan elements are tested in conjunction with the product, can spot other miscommunications. Distributors may not understand promotion, discounts, instructions, or service. People who shouldn't buy it may be doing so. Competitors may be bad-mouthing it in a way that creates confusion.

Education

Various firms have decided that everyone in the act should be better informed, so we have seen activity on two fronts. First, efforts have been made to educate *company personnel* — through ombudsmen, consumer affairs officers, scientific advisory panels, environmental scanning, training programs, and generally any activity that helps ensure important decisions won't be made in ignorance. Second, *the consumer* is getting much more information — labels, instruction sheets, warranties, special company brochures and training programs, and more instructional advertising. *Advertising Age* ran four full pages of instructions on how to protect product users while not reducing the effectiveness of advertising.[22]

External Affairs

Actions have also been taken outside the firm's internal program of product innovation — the foremost is lobbying. Most industries now aggressively greet every legislative thrust on new products, and their winning percentage is rising. They are also learning how to deal effectively with such regulatory offices as the Consumer Product Safety Commission. And, vigorous public affairs programs, including joint advertising programs by trade associations, have been directed to all of the firms' publics.

In addition to public influence, more companies today are working with trade association and distributive personnel to establish standards or common policies on such matters as customer or store personnel education, product service, and product recall. Apparently, fewer firms

---

[22] Though dated, the advice still appears sound. "Product Advertising and Consumer Safety," *Advertising Age,* July 1, 1974, p. 47.

are deciding to "go it alone" and prefer to involve the entire business or industry teams—and even include consumer units on the team.

PERSONAL ETHICS

Before we leave the topic of public policy, you may be interested in knowing whether any problems exist regarding *personal* ethics. There are quite a few, and most of them involve differences in moral judgments on the many issues discussed earlier in this chapter. However, there are some others:

1. Ideation or concept generation often leads us to explore the minds of customers, to find something they want or will want when they hear about it. We often use *intrusive techniques,* such as observation or psychological question techniques. Is it ethical to trick people into telling us what they want?

2. Is a *purely imitative product innovation charter* really moral? Does the individual have a right to object when a firm markets something that is not new in any way, even a promotional gimmick?

3. How about hiring an independent market research firm to set up focus groups, and then letting company people *secretly sit behind the mirrors* as your customers tell their all?

4. You introduce a temporary product that will be replaced when a better one in development is ready a year from now. You are told *not to let distributors or your sales force know* it is only temporary.

5. You are in a consulting firm and are about to market a new seminar service for banks. Your firm, for a fee, will run seminars during which you will train bank personnel in investment counseling. But there is no product use test on the seminar, and *you don't know that the bank people will really learn how to counsel.*

6. You work for a detergents company and recently learned that over the years thousands of rodents have been force-fed each new product, including versions in development. The *force-feeding goes on until half of the rodents die* (the so-called LD50 test).

7. You are currently working on a patented item that schools will use for map displays. It is so good that virtually every K–12 school will buy several of them. You come across the cost figures and calculate that the *gross margin will run about 80 percent.* A co-worker comments that the price could be cut in half and the company margin would still be a healthy 60 percent.

These ethical situations only have answers on an individual basis. New products people are particularly hard-pressed to reach such individual answers because our activity takes in everything—strategy to post-launch, including all functions.

However, it is probably a good idea to think through some of the above situations and get practice dealing with them.

SUMMARY

This concludes our trip through a troublesome phase of the new products process. The pressures are very real, and the difficulties are at times almost overwhelming. The unresolved issues discussed in this chapter have no "answers," and new variations on the six general problems will continue to unfold.

New products managers, however, are finding they can manage under these circumstances *if* they do their homework well. Avoiding needless troubles requires that they understand the process, that managements support them at critical times, and that they follow up marketing with more aggressive launch control than ever before used in American industry. All temptations are to do just the opposite.

The Achilles' heel of new products management is time, as we have seen more than once. In 1985, Coca-Cola chose to go directly national with its new-flavor Coke based only on taste tests and without market testing; some people believe it committed one of marketing's all-time goofs. Developing and marketing new products are such high-pressure tasks that managers are continuously under the gun to skip this step or that. Most of the public pressure difficulty that firms encounter is a calculated risk, not oversight or stupidity. Firms today are increasingly less willing to take that risk.

APPLICATIONS

1. "One of our R&D directors was formerly with Xerox, and he told me about its troubles with patents. Most large firms get access to many patents, of course; people are always trying to sell what they have invented. And, we all buy up some of these—the few really good ones. Now, we don't always use them right away. They are kept for when we need them—when a competitor makes a potentially harmful move, or when we get new foreign competition, or when our current patents run out. But, the Xerox people got taken to court under the antitrust laws for doing just this. Managers of the SCM Corporation felt that Xerox should be required to license others to use patents Xerox held if Xerox wasn't going to use them. The trial lasted five years, and I'm glad to say that Xerox won. Could you please construct the legal argument that SCM and the government probably used in this case? I don't have access to the trial documents, but I'd like to hear their logic (if any!)."

2. "Two other firms I know about were less fortunate. Morton-Norwich Products introduced Encare, a vaginal suppository contraceptive, and American Home Products came out with a similar product called Semicid at about the same time. Both advertised that the products were safer than IUDs and that, unlike the 'pill', they had no hormonal side effects. They called the items a safe, medically tested, positive method of birth control, which they are. But, the Federal Trade Commission has ruled that the firms cannot claim a comparative advantage over other methods unless they also state that the new product is not as effective as the others. The FTC says the only novel aspect of the new products is the suppository form, and that has very little advantage to the consumer. Both firms now have to distribute a new pamphlet telling the advantages and disadvantages of all forms of birth control. All of this may be well and good — I don't know — but the aspect that bothers me is that the two firms were ruled responsible for telling consumers the *good* things about their competitors, not just the bad. Why do you suppose the FTC ruled the way it did, and is this a forecast of what we are all going to face? Since when am I responsible for helping potential customers choose a competitor's product?"

3. "Our electronics division had an interesting case history on the monopoly issue you studied. A man in Ottawa, Ontario, named Richard C. Foss was president of Mosaid, Inc., regarded by some as a premier engineering outfit. When a new integrated circuit for computer memories hit the market, Foss would buy one and then disassemble it to find out what made it tick and how it was manufactured. He then published this information in full detail. The consequence was that other chip makers could get into the new market much more quickly, thus reducing the advantage of the originator. But, the presence of this man also spurred firms to innovate constantly to avoid being caught from behind. He also claimed his work speeded up standardization and lowered costs to the ultimate market. He even offered what were called 'masks' to make it easier for a copier to copy.

   "At the same time, he was so competent that his technicians were often asked to make independent appraisals of chips that people were considering buying. He joked about being the *Consumer Reports* of that industry. As you can see from all this, Foss seemed to be helping competition, and he was rendering a service to the large firms as well. So, no one filed charges against him, and apparently the government was unwilling to do so. How does this example fit with your thinking about the pressures on innovators not to contribute to monopoly?"

4. "You know, you were telling me about those, what do you call them, public policy issues? I was thinking about our health industry group. It is rapidly developing a line of health maintenance organizations

(HMOs) by acquisition, primarily, and several by invitation of leading hospitals. Most of them are not-for-profit operations (they have other advantages for us), and it is pleasing to think that at least this part of our corporate family won't raise public policy issue problems. That's right, isn't it?"

Case: Trintex, by IBM and Sears

In early 1988, a new service called Trintex was about to be offered for sale in three markets (San Francisco, Boston, and Atlanta). As a joint venture of IBM and Sears ($350 million invested, 650 employees), it was an advanced version of videotex and followed in the failure footsteps of Warner's CUBE, Times-Mirror's Gateway, and Knight-Ridder's Viewtron. It was being billed as much superior to the others.

The system worked this way: A person (target market was dual-income, aging baby-boomers in their late 30s, especially working women) slipped a personal diskette into the PC (hooked up with a modem to the telephone line) and typed in a personal ID and password. A screen showed what was available. (Offerings would include home banking, travel reservations, news, business columns by Liz Smith and others, grocery products, clothing, brokerages, Buick, Procter & Gamble, Florsheim, Neiman-Marcus, Levi Strauss, a cruise line, and Fuji Film.)

From the central menu, the user selected categories and then went into subcategories, detailed information, action options (buying), and so on. The system, called Prodigy, was user friendly and used simple English commands.

Problems were several. High up-front costs for the PC and modem then ran over $1,000, and home banking was not yet available. More competition was coming.

The service had been in home use tests for over two years—500 households in the three cities targeted for actual selling effort at the end of the test. Further testing was going to be run, right up to and through the immediate introduction date.

The ad campaign was not yet public knowledge, but it was to be direct response and have a respectable budget. Roll-out would follow introduction in the three markets, scheduled to be national within two years.

In addition to the basic issue of whether the new service would be successful, there was the other matter of legal and social pressures. What would you advise about such matters as product liability, quality of the purchase decision, product performance, morality, monopoly, and ecology?

Source: Most of the material came from Rebecca Fannin, "The Last Great Hope?" *Marketing & Media Decisions*, February 1988, pp. 24–30.

Chapter 23

Conclusion: The Future and Other Thoughts

SETTING

We've now finished the product innovation process. What's left? First, you might be interested in how the future environment for product innovation looks and what changes we anticipate in the product innovation process. All forecasts have a margin of error, and these are no exceptions. You will probably enjoy pointing out where you think the forecasts are wrong, and it's good that you do. One of the new product manager's toughest tasks is evaluating the forecasts of others—from a date that some equipment will be in place to the amount of dealer reorders in the first 30 days.

After the forecasts come a couple of operational items—first, a set of complaints I have heard about product innovation people (not necessarily true, but probably with some merit), and second, a set of guidelines for evaluating a product innovation program.

FUTURE CHANGES IN THE ENVIRONMENT FOR PRODUCT INNOVATION

Most forecasts are extensions of current trends. If some exogenous variable enters to change a trend, then the forecast is wrong. A good example is glasnost, for which many people feel the equilibrium of progress is very unstable.

Positive Forces

Essentially, the positive forces spell out opportunity—to make things and to sell things.

A Better World.   Strong evidence indicates that we now want to stop world wars, that peace is attainable. Most of the world's major nations are now trying to achieve economic growth and personal freedoms, an effort that offers a tremendous opportunity for new products. Moreover, other evidence indicates that we may have learned how to control against depressions and even major recessions.

Business Is in Good Shape.   Not only are sales and profits in most industries good, but we are building capability for the future. Productivity will increase, the fund of capital will grow, we will have more capable managers than imaginable a generation ago, and a new cadre of top management will appear. Business downturns can always happen, of course, and some critics believe we are weakening ourselves internationally with budget and trade deficits. But, as of now, the economic condition must be viewed as a positive force.

Strong evidence shows that CEOs are increasingly opting for a quality operation—not just quality products, but quality people, quality behavior, and quality vendor/customer sets. They're saying they want to create and sustain a corporate environment that values better performance above everything else—cultures and value systems. Leading this trend have been Nike, Cray, Wal-Mart, Toys "R" Us, and Apple Computer.

Technology.   What can the future hold? We have only seen the beginning: computers, molecular biology and the other life sciences, fiber optics, surface ceramics, three-dimensional scanning, telecommunication, and more. Each five-year period yields more than the last. We have only sampled the technology of expert systems, which has exciting applications directly into the management of new products. Moreover, managements are again investing in R&D and are expected to continue.

Market Opportunities.   We are currently forecasting *increased sales* in virtually every market, based on what are excellent times in the developed nations of the world—more people, more families, more disposable incomes, more activities.

The word here is *international*. Nationalism will remain a strong political force, but the economic world is now an international one. We're told that Americans will soon begin thinking automatically in a larger geographical construct, as Europeans have always done. Can you imagine the richness and demands of a new products program that focuses on a world of 100 consuming nations? Some of these world markets are now flexing their muscles; we don't yet know whether Americans will gain from the European Economic Community's new energy.

Perhaps the greatest grower in these global markets will be *services*. Goods will remain important, but so much of what people in developed nations want comes from services, not goods — health, security, leisure activities, financial security and management, and so on.

In fact, the most interesting aspect of future demands is the extent to which they are based on *severe social needs*. If you take a new product view, you can see the almost immeasurable market opportunities in drugs, AIDS, crime, education, transportation, medical care, care of the elderly, and more. Then combine these needs with what many feel is a turn from the greed of the 80s (self-satisfaction) to the needs of people. This new interest is expected to stimulate growth in nonprofit organizations of many types. Although we often forget, governments themselves offer a huge market for new goods and services.

Courts and Regulation.   In recent years, American court decisions seem to be going business's way — joint ventures, trademarks, and employee rights on inventions, less so on product liability. Ten years of appointments by a conservative administration have perhaps led to a more conservative judiciary. Similarly, we can forecast that regulatory issues will still be in a conservative mode, though perhaps less so with Bush than was the case with Reagan.

Small Business.   We will be getting more start-ups, better start-ups, more and better assistance for those new firms, and a better infrastructure in general. More people will be interested in working for smaller firms that are well known for their output of new products.

New Role for Couplers.   Producers of goods and services will continue to make better use of vendors, distributors, and customers, all of whom are showing increased desire to play a role in product innovation. We are probably just seeing the beginning of vertical cooperative structures that may someday dominate.

A True Product Innovation Profession.   Ample evidence points to the birth of a general profession of new products management. We see a proliferation of positions with new product titles, a new association for such persons (the Product Development and Management Association), expanded college courses on the subject, an established journal (the *Journal of Product Innovation Management*), and widespread offerings of short courses through various private and university organizations.

A standing joke for many years has been that one rarely sees a grey-haired new products manager. (The same is said about product managers on established products.) People entered new product jobs, stayed for a while, and then moved back into the line organization. This situation is being corrected. Not only are we building a lower, entry position in new products management, but incentives are increasing to stay in this work. We hope to be able to send college graduates directly into new products and then see them stay in that work for many years as they progress up through several levels of management. Many, of course, go on with their products as they enter the market and stay there.

The conditions are ripe for the world's first undergraduate or graduate degree program in product innovation management. This would have to be a joint degree program between two or even three schools within a university.

Negative Forces

The future isn't all bright, of course, and you should keep your eye on several specific trends.

At the Market Level.   One negative force is *segmentation of markets* and the requirement of niche marketing. Every new product today is marketed to just one or more segments of a larger market. As time rolls by, segmentation slices markets into smaller and smaller pieces. Sometimes these slices become too small to make a profit, though an interesting current twist is the efforts of some people to market products specifically for tiny niches. This practice, called *micromarketing,* should thrive during the age of store scanners. The ultimate in niche marketing is a target market of one, another developing potential. For example, GM's Saturn automobile is designed so customers can essentially design their own model at the dealer's showroom, Honored Guests at Marriott can do the same, and a catalog company keeps records of individual families (based on what they buy) to follow their trek through the family life cycle. They are sent catalogs accordingly (for example, a school supply catalog five years after first purchase of baby clothing).

Going along with this is the *shortening of product life cycles.* In one new strategy, the innovator actively tries to obsolete a recent new entry before a competitor does.

Perhaps of more concern is the current suggestion of a *turn against materialism.* When a society turns from greed to need, product innovation will not gain if that need can be satisfied by noncommercial modes. If materialism goes out the window with greed, then we can expect some downturn in new products.

Distributors also pose a potential problem. A battle is currently raging between the traditional mass outlets and the narrow, specialized outlets;

if the mass channels prevail, then new products will be hurt (for example, K mart versus Toys "R" Us). We can't be sure either how that battle will turn out or what the new product attitude of the winner will be. One possibility is that the traditional outlets will (like the manufacturer) try to break up into smaller units that can be managed more innovatively.

Makers of packaged goods are already feeling the muscle of large chains. They are being charged special fees to stock new products (slotting allowances) and are being forced to divert advertising dollars into sales promotion dollars. All of this works against product innovation.

At the Business Firm Level. We can predict that the *costs of product innovation* will continue to increase. R&D will probably never be as low cost as it is now. New product introductions are already expensive and getting more so. Risks go up with the sales volumes discussed above. Right now, the thrust is on speed and quality, both of which can be costly depending on how much a better product cuts the costs of service, returns, and so on.

Another negative current trend is an *increase in employee disloyalty,* or perhaps just no loyalty. Over the past five years, we have seen massive downsizing, and many of those firms had to abandon their long-standing policies against firing people. Product innovation thrives on employee initiative and people willing to take large personal risks, confident that their efforts will be rewarded. And, they must do most of their work without close supervision.

Beyond loyalty, some people believe we are boosting a type of *built-in instability:* fewer people, all working harder, and less bureaucracy, efficiency, and fine-tuned operations. This instability may spell disequilibrium, or a tendency to breakdown. Bureaucracies, for all their weaknesses, rarely breakdown.

Last, we fret about information overload. In new products work, we thrive on information, especially information someone else lacks. But when we get too much information, we can't do our job; there isn't time to study it, yet we try. Computerized data bases help, but finding information is not our problem; rather, our problem is what we do with it. We may end up developing products at about the pace of the pharmaceutical industry.

Conclusion

Some of the negative factors are real, and just when we think everything is going perfectly, something falls apart. However, no one is forecasting that. It appears that the opportunity is there, if we can develop the process that capitalizes on it. That is what we turn to next.

FUTURE CHANGES IN THE PROCESS OF PRODUCT INNOVATION

Difficult as it is to forecast the environment, predicting within the new product system is harder. We know the system is growing more complex and expensive, at the very time management wants better products faster. Change is inevitable, at least change from the status quo. The techniques are already available, but they must be put into use. What this means is that you as a student have already studied well into the future—that is, for most firms. We will have continued process improvements, but a great increase in productivity can come just from using the tools we already have available.

The Process as a Whole

The techniques currently in favor will probably continue to be used. And, their application will continue to be company and project specific. We don't anticipate the discovery of a major new technique with universal application. But then, that's what we always think prior to breakthrough innovation.

We can forecast several things across the board. One is focus—only by focus can we achieve the intensity, the speed, and the performance demanded by today's managements. This means the full gamut—strategic focus, an appropriate organization, concentrated creativity, and so on. Think of how the laser can turn the light of a candle into a force that will burn a hole in concrete. Instead of thinking we lack people for the job, think of changing the job so our few people can do it.

This line of thinking leads to less rigidity in personnel assignments, overlapping of phases, and multilearning. An individual has to be prepared to do more things at the same time, a mind-boggling task given the rate of change in technology, psychology, the computer, and so on. Can we manage this?

In an attempt to get smarter, we will reach out for any technique that helps us do more, faster and better. Thus, we will read more, attend more university and private training programs, and lean more often on an increasingly capable force of consultants.

We will also give a premium to those who can manage people in this new milieu. Instead of computer-based critical path schedules and other control systems, it seems we will put our faith in people. With small, tightly focused teams, we don't need monthly control reports in 10 copies—we need people "walking around," with their minds turned on. And, we will probably be putting our faith in these people, even if they can't pass out net present value calculations on demand.

They will, of course, use technology—expert systems, planning software, perhaps some simulations, and very advanced forms of computer-aided design (CAD). But, this use will be selective, for a specific purpose.

Another change that appeared dramatically late in the 80s was the drive to cut time from the overall development process. Managements dearly want to get new products to market faster and are demanding changes to accommodate that desire. Here are some of the techniques being used; you can see how each might have implications for what you will be doing:

1. Cut the planning. Get better information to the right people, decide what to do, and do it.
2. Improve the design process. Computer-aided design of several types is now available. Stereolithography produces prototypes in days rather than in weeks.
3. Improve the manufacturing. Involve its managers at the beginning of a project, use design for manufacturing (DFM), do several jobs simultaneously, and build more flexible manufacturing systems.
4. Use fewer "clean sheet" designs; that is, revise, not start over.
5. Design products with fewer parts, products that can be assembled easily and only one way, and products that are easy to test.
6. Do it right the first time and avoid last-minute engineering changes.
7. Involve the customer from the beginning, so that less time is needed for product use testing and market testing.

Of course, anytime we rush things we have problems—in this case, product ready before the market planning is finished, low-quality product, products that don't meet customer needs, manufacturing that can't meet unexpected volumes, lags in product support, high product costs, and many more.

In the Strategy Phase

The change here will be strategies for smaller and smaller pieces of the business. This is part of focus, which we just discussed. We should see the end of companywide new product strategies, such as Gerber's 1930s strategy of "Babies are our business, our only business."

There will be more simulated entrepreneurship, or intrapreneurship. More risk, but better managed. More use of selective innovation, meaning that on one product line we may be pioneering, while on another we may be imitative.

And, most certainly, more and more firms will adopt dual drive: every major new product program or project will have a clear statement of (1) a specific market group and a major problem we know it has and (2) a specific technology on which we are very strong that will be used to solve that problem.

In the Organization Phase

Consistent with the strategy change will be the steady miniaturization of organizational form to match the smaller strategic arenas. We will see fewer overall organizations, fewer corporate research laboratories, and fewer corporate new product planners. Instead, we will see teams, of all sizes and shapes, but still teams. We know how to do it and will see it done more often, though the number of top executives who can run this type of shop and remain secure may be limited. Customers will more often appear as regular members of those new product teams.

There will be more ventures of all types, including joint ventures. The joint ventures will be with anybody and everybody—suppliers, competitors, customers, distributors, and other sources of technology or market.

The interface problem will be essentially solved. We know now how people can work together across functions; in time, managements will no longer put up with costly frictions.

In the Concept Generation Phase

Here we have an odd situation. On the one hand, we will see declining interest in ideation. In most cases, we already have more ideas than we can evaluate. Even a neophyte using a morphological matrix can come up with hundreds of new product ideas in half an hour. But, these are not what new products managers want or and seek with a passion.

They want great ideas—ideas that are problem based, truly original, easy to visualize to product form, and that communicate themselves. We hear a lot about the Polaroids, the Post-it notes, even the light bulb—the products that people didn't think would work and that had to be pushed against the grain of the firm. However, most good new product ideas looked good at the very beginning. (Of course, lots of bad ideas look good at first too, to their creators.)

The patent system will steadily improve, and it will become more responsive to the needs of the marketplace. Regulators have begun replacing broad, cover-everything policies and rules with special arrangements (such as the one giving the pharmaceutical firms a bigger piece of the 17-year patent life as a trade-off with letting generic firms get in faster at the end of the 17 years).

In the Evaluation Phase

Concept testing will continue and will grow. So will basic market studies and the full screen. The protocol, by whatever name, will grow in use as R&D people demand it and as marketing people become better prepared to write it. Product testing and market testing are more difficult to forecast. We have had good techniques for years and good arguments for using them. But in most firms, they gather dust; everyone is in such a hurry, and the new item looks awfully good anyway.

Evidence for product use testing is growing, however. In 1989, IBM announced that 1,700 units of a new minicomputer were produced and put into use in customer establishments for use testing. The company learned absolutely that the item solved customer problems and how to sell it when marketed—no wonder it chalked up over $3 billion of sales the first year. That type of evidence cannot be denied much longer.

On market testing, the roll-out is predicted to grow and assume various forms. We're also told that there will be more simulated test markets (the mathematical models) for nonpackaged goods—getting into clothing, appliances, even cars.

In the Commercialization Phase

We already know a great deal about how to market new products, and we will learn more. Fewer serious marketing mistakes will occur, partly because managements will no longer accept them as necessary. As everything leading up to marketing is done better, sound marketing becomes easier. Almost any reasonable form of market testing will spot the disasters.

The managerial side of the commercialization phase will be much easier and more fun. Using teams will involve other departments in the marketing phase, there will be less bureaucracy and fewer big meetings, more time will be spent with customers (remember we will be involving them a great deal more in the future), and market feedback will be far quicker.

SPECIFIC NEW PRODUCTS OR TYPES OF NEW PRODUCTS

In drawing to the close of a book on new products, it seems natural to make some forecasts about new products of the future. This was done in the first two editions of this book, and many readers felt they were not very helpful. Some forecasts were so general as to be obvious: "More products for the business sector," which students didn't consider particularly daring. Other forecasts were daring—and wrong!

But there is a challenge to you here. You have some special area of interest — some field you have studied, or worked in, or grew up in. A good challenge would be for you to find someone else who has the same interest, both make predictions of 10 new products that you anticipate, and then compare notes. The discussion might just bring into focus many of the things we have been discussing in this chapter.

CONCLUDING MATTERS

Complaints of CEOs about New Products Managers

Students often ask about the personal qualifications of people working in the new products field. Studying the material in this book has answered most of those questions. But, upper-level managers often comment on some more personal dimensions, things that some people in new products lack and that hinder their achieving their personal goals. Some of the most meaningful of those are the following.

1. *Not Street Smart.*   Some people don't fully commit to a project or to a business. They try to remain new product generalists and to avoid becoming flashlight specialists, or cork specialists, or office furniture specialists. One consumer products president, listening to a new product presentation on a mushroom soup, interrupted to ask what the product manager thought about the flavor and how it compared to other such soups. The answer was evasive, the soup actually hadn't been tasted, and neither had the competitive products. Reference was made to use tests. But, a new products person must soak up everything about the field, live with available products and with ours, get out to the stores, know everything that is going on. That's street smart, not academic smart. We need both.

2. *Unwilling to Take Personal Risk.*   Few CEOs put new products managers to the personal test, but they would like to: "Would you invest $30,000 of your own money in this project? Do you feel so strongly about this product that if we reject it, you will risk your job to show us we were wrong?" If we aren't willing to risk our own well-being, then we seem to lack faith in what we have done and are recommending. Or, at least, top managers sometimes think so.

3. *Not Team Players.*   Many people play on teams without being team players. They sit back a little, let the team make a decision, sandbag, and then, if it turns out wrong, step in to criticize. They are more worried about their personal success than about team success. They haven't accepted the idea that their personal success depends on team success. We all know of sports teams where people of just modest talents win because everyone committed to team success. Each person's attitude on this point is patently obvious to upper-level managers; they know who is a team player and who isn't.

4. *Fail to "Live" Innovation.* The best new products people welcome innovation in all phases of their lives—they like the new and the different. They look at every situation as an opportunity to improve something. On the other hand, some people are quite conservative and seek the vicarious fun of new products—being there without really participating. These people drag the operation down.

5. *Don't Walk Around.* It's been touted so much by followers of Peters and Waterman that it's become a cliché. But, it's still true that new products people need to walk around a lot. Get out of the office and into the shop, the lab, the freight dock, accounting, the boss' arena, and so on. Some new products people are naturally analytical and genuinely enjoy dealing with problems at their desk. They seek solutions in numbers or things, whereas many upper managers believe the answers are in people—and people are not there in the office. One vice president, in a state of frustration, told a product manager, "If I see you in your office the next two times I come by here, we will part company."

6. *Don't Try to Understand Other People.* We can all learn to listen pretty well, with some effort, but some people listen only to prepare a response. New products people work in such diverse and changing environments that they need to build the skill of actually understanding others. Learning what makes others tick. And this has to be practiced so sincerely that it becomes habit and instinctive.

7. *Failing to Remember that Products Evolve.* Too many people spend most of their time trying to force to a conclusion: finalize the product; set it in concrete. They even try to do this in the concept test. This weakness shows up especially at the time of management presentations; persons in the audience know nothing is final. Intuitive new products people stay open and active, trying to improve what is on the table at the moment.

8. *Judge Others by What They Do Rather than by Results.* New products work can be managed too closely. Sometimes we have to look the other way as a particularly good person tries out a new approach or cuts a corner. Sure, there has to be discipline, but it's tempered with some crossed fingers. We're cutting new paths, so we often simply don't know what to do—yet we have to do it.

9. *Getting into the Rut of One Approach.* Goods and services differ. Consumer and industrial products differ. Packaged goods and dresses differ. Car wax and toothpaste differ. No packages of technique are available for these different settings, though we sure wish there were. The minute we decide concept testing doesn't apply to dresses, we hit a situation where it does. So, we hate to see new products people with the sign "Have system, will travel." Instead, we like to see "Have techniques, will design system." It's not that various types of goods or services all differ; the overall product innovation process chart in Chapter 2 laid out a general approach. But, it's best to arrive at an approach for any specific situation by thinking, rather than by pulling something off the shelf.

10. *Forgetting that the Customer Is at the Center of the Game.* It's easy for new products people to get wrapped up in the product, its form, its package, or its positioning. Any decision that benefits us at the expense of customer satisfaction is danger. Working in the trenches, we sometimes forget that.

Evaluating an Ongoing Product Innovation System

Figure 23–1 offers a set of guidelines for evaluating an ongoing product innovation system. It is not just a list of steps or techniques taken from the preceding chapters. It is a list of the essentials, the really critical specifics that hurt a program if they are missing. Special effort was put into finding items often overlooked.

When using the guidelines, two cautions should be kept in mind. First, whether a company does something is often a judgment. Lots of grey areas exist in the list. Second, don't expect high scores—we are a long way from where we might be and where we would like to be. The real value of the guidelines lies not in an accounting-type audit, but in stimulating discussion about the various criteria and exploring possible new approaches.

FIGURE 23–1 New Products Management Guidelines

This is a rather unique checklist. Every point on the list is valid and it would be nice if the world worked this way. But, product innovation managers face a real world, so the list is designed to show you ways in which the operations being evaluated might be improved. It lists those matters that are potentially quite important yet either new or managerially difficult to do.

The list of guidelines is constructed for use in all types of firms and will have some points that don't apply to you. Too, watch out for unique definitions. Unfortunately, there is no authority for terminology in this field, so there will probably be some terms unfamiliar to people you are evaluating. On occasion, a second statement has been added for clarity, and the terminology meshes with that found in the glossary in this text.

A good approach is for two or more people involved in an operation to go through the list, checking any item for which there is no action, policy, or whatever. Then, these items can be discussed in a joint session to see if the check holds up, to determine whether action should be taken on the point, and if so, what action.

1. The senior managers of this firm or division (general manager plus top key functional heads) are committed to innovation in general. They want innovation in all phases of operation, including that of product line.

2. This management attitude toward innovation has been clearly and unequivocally communicated throughout the organization.

3. Senior managements, both at corporate and at division, have gone through a planning exercise that established the overall goals for the product innovation function in each division.

4. Outside directors know the future role for product innovation and support actions to achieve it.

5. We have an innovation reward system. It includes insulation against punishment for failure, and there is evidence for all to see.

6. The firm's or division's top executive has assessed the ability and inclination of each senior functional manager to generate innovation, particularly product innovation. This assessment has included input from persons reporting to those senior managers.

7. General managers have learned the art of delegating full authority on new product projects while still sharing fully in the responsibility for them. (This managerial approach is unique to the product innovation function).

8. New product project responsibility is nonfunctional. That is, project leaders report in such a way that they are free of functional constraints and biases. Specifically, responsibility for new products is no longer housed in R&D.

FIGURE 23–1   New Products Management Guidelines *(continued)*

---

9. Senior management attempts to assess the productivity of the new products program. Standards of measurement have been established and communicated.

10. If senior management is dissatisfied with the overall product innovation program, specific causes have been determined and remedial plans put into place. Continuing dissatisfaction is not acceptable.

11. The firm's new product failure rate is somewhere between 10 percent and 20 percent. Less than that suggests no commitment to innovation, and more than that suggests an inadequately managed program.

12. Senior management has studied the industry's new product situation and has shared ideas with other industry leaders. Work is under way to find industrywide solutions to obstacles hindering product innovation in this industry.

13. Specific people in each division have been charged with opportunity identification, the creative assessment of technologies and markets available to the division.

14. Senior management is aware of the fundamental conflict between process innovation and product innovation. Efforts are taken to keep either from dominating the other and to see that decisions at the interface are made at general-management levels.

15. The firm has an overall system for developing new items, and its steps are well known to participants.

16. Product innovators on each team know their group's focus, arena of operation, or turf.

17. They also know the general goal and specific objectives of their team.

18. Each project team is making use of both market drive and technology drive. That is, they are working to resolve one or more specific problems in a selected marketplace, and they are bringing to that solution one or more key technologies at which the firm is very good.

19. There are no hidden agenda on our new product projects.

20. New product projects are usually managed by the collegial style, and exceptions that use managerial or entrepreneurial style are defensible.

21. For every new products project, it is clear who is the one person heading up that project and responsible for its success.

22. Every project is assigned one of three projectization levels—functional matrix, balanced matrix, or project matrix. We try to avoid the purely functional approach and use a venture (in-house or spin-out) only when absolutely necessary. All players understand projectization.

FIGURE 23–1   New Products Management Guidelines *(continued)*

23. We actively use upstream and downstream coupling by building in roles for suppliers and other vendors as well as direct involvement of potential customer personnel. These people are almost like members of the team.

24. We have an overall concept evaluation system in place and use it to build a special system for each project.

25. We make a basic market or technology study of each strategic arena before ideation begins, and that study is updated as needed during the project's life.

26. We believe in building the marketing plan right alongside the building of the product. It is a twin-streams, or coincident, operation.

27. We accept the idea that new products come into existence only after they have been successfully established in the marketplace. Even after they go to market, they are still only concepts (being modified) until we meet the objective set for them.

28. Our technical/marketing/manufacturing people are close together physically. Preferably, they are no farther than a five-minute walk apart.

29. We use the concept of the rugby "scrum" rather than that of the relay team "hand-offs." All functions are represented at all phase points in the project, including project specification and post-launch.

30. Managers of new products projects understand that they are really nontitled general managers and that they should manage their team of people as a general manager would. They also understand what a network is and how it should be built and managed.

31. We have a proactive concept generation mode of operation. That is, we don't just wait for new ideas to come in from the field, the lab, etc.

32. Our technical people are familiar with what customers think about products now on the market, what they use, and how.

33. We use a specific scoring model for screening concepts prior to any substantial development expenditures.

34. After screening, we make sure the technical people have a statement of the benefit attributes the new product is to have. That is, not what the product should *be*, but what it should *do* for the customer (protocol).

35. We do user-based product field testing on every item we develop, whether a good or a service. At least part of the testing is with typical potential users who are not our friends.

36. We believe product use testing should measure whether the product actually works as we had hoped, and also whether it solves the problem we started with and is satisfactory overall to the customer. That is, if we have been using Beta testing, we want to do Gamma testing too.

FIGURE 23–1   New Products Management Guidelines *(concluded)*

---

37. We have a marketing plan for every new item and do at least one type of market testing on the combined product and plan.

38. When marketing a new item, we have identified each potential problem that would be very damaging and that has a reasonable probability of coming about. We have agreed in advance what we would do about each, if it occurs.

39. We use post-launch tracking systems for guiding the product to success. That is, we have set up measuring systems to track each critical problem and give us early warning. We have also agreed in advance about what will constitute evidence that each problem is actually coming about.

40. Marketing plans for new products are distributed in draft form to all persons who are key to the launch process. Certainly to the basic functions of technical, production, and finance.

41. Unless the new item is itself a line extension, we have at least the next two line extensions to it already on their way down the pike. Each follow-on item is intended to foreclose an option our adaptor competitors would find lucrative.

42. Our advertising, technical brochures, and promotional literature do not contain unintended express warranties. Our salespeople understand that their statements may result in warranty liability.

43. We try to anticipate ways in which customers will misuse a new product, we develop legally sufficient warnings for those misuses, and we keep records relevant to all aspects of product liability.

Sources of Ideas Already Generated

New product ideas come from many places, some of which are peculiar to particular firms or industries. Here are the more broadly used sources.

Employees

Many types of employees can be sources of new product concepts. Salespeople are an obvious group, but so are manufacturing, customer service, and packaging employees, and, in the case of general consumer products, any employee who uses the products. These people need to know their ideas are wanted, and special mechanisms must usually be constructed to gather those ideas.

Employee suggestion systems are not dependable ways to turn up ideas, and special idea contests have an equally disappointing record. Toyota ran an Idea Olympics for some time and in one year produced 1,300 employee-inventor entries. The firm did not comment on the quality of the ideas.

The most helpful suggestions come from employees whose work brings them in contact with customer problems. For example, a drill manufacturer's service department found that many drills were burning out because customers were using them as electric screwdrivers. Adding a clutch mechanism to the drill created a new product. Complaint-handling departments also became familiar with consumers' use of products. Salespeople know when a large order is lost because the firm's product is not quite what the customer wanted. Manufacturing and engineering personnel are frequently part-time inventors who should be encouraged to submit their ideas, but these ideas need to be handled with care: they require the attention of the legal department and a clear statement of policy.

Dun & Bradstreet has a fine new products track record and once reported that most of its new product ideas come from field personnel. Eligible D&B employees can receive $5,000 for suggesting an idea that goes national. Some firms have used an "idea miner"—an employee whose job is to scout around among other employees, encouraging and collecting their ideas.

Customers

The greatest source of new product ideas is the customer or user of the firm's products or services, although their ideas are usually only for product improvement or nearby line extensions. Some people believe the majority of all new products in certain industries originate with users. Because some specialized user groups are personally involved with devices, new product people occasionally delegate new product concept development to them. Similarly, most auto parts and components manufacturers look to their giant OEM buyers for new product initiatives. On the other hand, one firm solicited 2,800 ideas from customers and was not able to use a single one.

The most popular ways to gather consumer ideas are surveys, continuing panels, special focus groups, and the mail. Some firms get so many suggestions in the mail that they do not read them. Industrial firms usually take the more initiative approach of using personal contacts by salespeople or technical staffs.

Resellers

Brokers, manufacturers' reps, industrial distributors, large jobbers, and large retail firms may be quite worthwhile. In fact, some mass merchandisers have their own new products departments and invite manufacturers to bid on specifications. Many industrial representatives are skilled enough to be special advisers to their clients, and selling agents in the toy industry not only advise but actually take on the new products function if the manufacturer wishes.

One chemical distributor suggested using a low-cost polyethylene bag to line steel drums to prevent corrosion; and a millwork producer learned about a new competitive entry from a dealer and then suggested how the new item could be improved. Both suggestions were successfully implemented. Kroger once told manufacturers that its customers want more easy-to-cook, single-portion frozen dinners, and another chain suggested a low-calorie enchilada.

Suppliers/Vendors

Most manufacturers of plastic housewares are small and thus look to the large plastics firms for advice. Virtually all producers of steel, aluminum, chemicals, metals, paper, and glass have technical customer service departments. One of their functions is to suggest new products made of the firm's basic material.

Competitors

New product idea generators are interested in competitors' activities, and competitors' new products may be an indirect source for a leapfrog or add-on new product; but competitors are rarely (as with government-mandated cross-licensing of ideas) sources of new product ideas. The first firms bringing a new product to a particular market segment (such as the smaller city banks) do use their innovative competitors as sources, but this is effective only when market segments are insulated. At Ford Motor Company, once the engineers get their hands on a new competitive product, it is systematically torn down into its 30,000 parts. All are cataloged and then mounted on panels so others can examine them.

The Invention Industry

Every industrialized country has an "industry" consisting of a nucleus of inventors surrounded by firms and organizations that help them capitalize on their inventions. The auxiliary or supportive group includes:

Venture capital firms	Banks
Inventors' schools	Inventors' councils
Attorneys	Small Business Administrations
Trademark and patent offices	Technology expositions
Consultants on new business	Patent shows
Patent brokers and other	Inventors' newsletters
inventor assistance firms	State entrepreneurial assistance
Individual investors	programs
University innovation centers	

Currently, both the inventor and the potential manufacturer are frustrated by the communications, legal, and funding problems existing in this supportive network. Fortunately, this highly fragmented new "industry" is in the process of shaking down and should soon settle on several dominant organizational formats with which manufacturers can deal.

One example of this emerging format is InstanTechEx, a service provided by Dr. Dvorkovitz & Associates. Dvorkovitz sponsors an annual international technology exchange exposition where hundreds of firms and scores of governments display technological advancements that they would like to sell. The show is a supermarket of technology and an emerging format for standardizing the new invention industry.

Other new organizations are merging the financial, legal, and managerial consulting assistance that inventors usually require, either as venture firms that actually take over and develop the idea or as facilitator firms that reach out to established manufacturers. In the meantime, some firms have what they call "inventors' farm systems" to get both quantity and variety of invention input.

Miscellaneous

Among the many other sources of outside new product ideas are the following:

1. Consultants. Most management consulting firms do new products work, and some specialize in it — for example, Booz, Allen & Hamilton. Some consulting firms are devoted exclusively to new products work and include idea generation as one of their services. Unfortunately, the stigma of being "outsiders" is strong in the new products field, as exemplified by the not-invented-here syndrome. Companies report very favorable experiences but also many horror stories. One alternative is to bring industry experts to discussion sessions with company personnel. General Mills used a newspaper food editor, a trade journal editor, an advertising copywriter, a restauranteur, a division manager of a food chain, and four company junior executives.

2. Advertising Agencies.   This source of new product ideas is badly underrated. Most agencies have the creative talent and the product/market experience to generate new product concepts. Some agencies have full-blown new products departments, and some take their concepts all the way to market, including simulated test markets and roll-outs. Consumer product agencies do more new products work than industrial agencies do, although the West Coast agencies specializing in the computer industry render a wide range of services because their clients are usually small.

3. Marketing Research Firms.   Normally, marketing research firms get involved in the idea-generating process by assisting a client with need assessment. They rarely stumble across an opportunity that they pass along to a client. Some of the bigger marketing research firms also serve as management consultants.

4. Retired Product Specialists.   Industrial new products people, particularly those with technical strength, often retire from their firms and become part-time consultants to other firms. One company actually tracks the retirements of all qualified specialists in its industry. Conflict-of-interest problems may arise, and divulging competitive secrets is ethically questionable, but most arrangements work around these problems easily.

5. Industrial Designers.   Industrial design firms sometimes function as part of a team implementing a new product decision that has already been made. However, many industrial designers are extremely creative. Industrial design firms and individual industrial designers are increasingly capitalizing on their own new product strengths. Industrial design departments of universities are sometimes assigned by government and other service organizations to do original new products work.

6. Other Manufacturers.   Most firms have potentially worthwhile new product ideas that they do not want because these ideas conflict with the firm's strategy. These ideas are usually allowed to remain idle. One such firm, General Electric, established a Business Opportunities Program in the 1960s in which it offered its "spare" technologies for sale. Sometimes, the offering was just an idea; but other times, prototypes and even molds, dies, and finished goods inventories were offered, depending on how far GE had taken an idea before deciding not to develop it further. In recent years, GE has expanded this service by listing the technologies of others in its monthly editions of *Selected Business Ventures* and in annual compilations in its *New Product New Business Digest.*

7. Universities. Professors and students occasionally offer new product ideas, especially in schools of engineering, the sciences, and business. Dentists, physicians, and pharmacists are scientific groups that play a major role in new products work.

8. Research Laboratories. Most of the leading countries now have at least one major research laboratory that will do new products work on contract from manufacturers and that occasionally comes up with interesting new product ideas. The Battelle Memorial Institute in Columbus, Ohio, received millions of dollars for its role in getting xerography off the ground. Other leading research laboratories are the Illinois Institute of Technology, the Stanford Research Institute, and Great Britain's National Engineering Laboratory.

9. Governments. The Patent Office of the U.S. government offers several services designed to help manufacturers find worthwhile new product ideas. The *Official Gazette* provides a weekly listing of (1) all new patents issued, (2) condensed descriptions of the patented items, and (3) which patents are for sale or license. Patent Office reports and services also make known what government patents and foreign patents are available.

The military services have a want list of products that they would like to buy; the Department of Agriculture will help manufacturers with new products; and state governments have programs to aid industries.

One by-product of today's regulation of business is increased assistance from regulators for solving such problems as unsafe products and unsafe working conditions. For example, the Occupational Safety and Health Act stimulated several companies to develop first-aid kits.

10. Printed Sources. The hundreds of technical and scientific journals, trade journals, newsletters, and monographs are occasionally sources of ideas for new products. Most of the ideas indirectly result from accounts of new products activity. Some publications are more direct sources of new product ideas—for example, *Newsweek's* annual *New Products and Processes*, *New Technology* (London), the *Soviet Technology Bulletin*, and such compilations as *New Product News*. Though not new product ideas directly, there are now at least two on-line computer data bases of actual new products marketed: *Thomas New Industrial Products* and *Predicasts' New Product Announcements*.

11. International. Minnetonka executives got the idea for pump toothpaste while browsing in a West German supermarket. Powdered Tide was developed by scientists in Cincinnati, but Liquid Tide used a formula for surfactants from Japan and a mineral salts antagonist from Belgium. Unfortunately, few firms have systematic programs to find ideas from other countries. Some establish foreign offices to monitor various technologies, others ask their advertising agencies' foreign offices to gather ideas, and still others subscribe to one or more reporting services.

Managing These Idea Sources

These sources of ideas do not function without special effort. For example, salespeople must be trained how to find users with good ideas and how to coax the ideas from them. International markets must be covered on the spot by trained people. Studying the competition must be systematic to catch every change in competitors' products. Each special source is also a potential source for the competition, and the firm that utilizes these sources most appropriately will acquire the best ideas.

Other Techniques of Concept Generation

Chapters 5 through 7 presented the leading ideation techniques with the best track records and the greatest chance of producing valuable new product concepts. Perhaps hundreds of other techniques are available, some of which are proprietary (confidential to the consulting firm that originated each), and some of which are techniques given here but with different names.

Thirty-two of the other techniques have been selected for brief review here. They are probably not necessary, but different individuals have found them useful. Perhaps you will too.

Techniques to Aid Problem Analysis

Composite Listing of Needs Fulfilled. By simply listing the many needs met by currently available products, there is a good chance some otherwise overlooked needs will come to mind. This mechanical process is successful only if the listing is pushed to one's mental limits.

Market Segmentation Analysis. By using one segmentation dimension on top of another, an analyst can develop a hierarchy of smaller and smaller market segments. For example, bar soap segmentation could use sex, age, body part cleaned, ethnic groups, and geographic location. All possible combinations of these would yield thousands of groups—for example, elderly Jewish women washing their faces in New York City. Each combination is potentially a group whose needs are peculiar and currently unmet. (Psychographic and behavioral segments are especially useful today.)

Dreams. This approach analyzes the dreams of people who have the problem(s) under study. Dreams offer a greater range of insights, equitably involve other persons in the problem situation, and offer paranormal aspects of the dream itself. Various famous people, one of whom was Robert Louis Stevenson, have attributed part of their creativity to dreams.

Techniques to Aid Scenario Analysis

There are many techniques for finding meaningful seed trends (trends that could be extended). Some are discussed in Chapter 5, and here are nine more.

Trend People.   Many believe certain people have a predictive sense and should be watched. *Women's Wear Daily* is one publication that uses this method, and the people it watches are well known to regular readers.

Trend Areas.   Major changes in American life and practice traditionally begin on the West Coast and gradually make their way east. Although television and other mass media have reduced the time lag, some firms station personnel in California just to be closer to the changes going on there.

Hot Products.   The automobile, television, and the computer have had a dramatic effect on lifestyles in this century. Others that may do so include fiber optics, biogenetic engineering, condominiums, small cars, and VCRs. One way to gather meaningful seed trends is to study such products and their effects. But watch out for false prophets, such as the CB radio of the 1970s.

Newspapers.   Some persons like to read leading newspapers, particularly the *New York Times*, cover to cover and make note of every trend, activity, or idea around which significant scenario change might take place.

Hypothetical.   A few persons believe one should just use any seed trends to create arbitrary scenarios. The more hypothetical the better, because the exercise is to stimulate creativity.

Technological Changeover.   This approach predicts when one technology will substitute for another and seeks the implications of the substitution for all products and systems involving either the new or the old. Doing this involves time series analysis, graphic analysis, and forecasts by technical people.

Technical Innovation Follow-On.   This procedure analyzes the implications for technical breakthroughs across a broad spectrum of technology, not just the immediate technology in which the breakthrough came. For example, a breakthrough in solar heating could be analyzed for effect in plumbing, clothing, furniture, or even entertainment.

Technological Monitoring.   Some scientists keep journals of technological progress. Every meaningful event is carefully logged, and from time to time, the journals are studied for meaningful trends. The technique helps guarantee the analysis of events in the construct of other events.

Cross-Impact Analysis.   First, list all possible changes that may occur over the next 20 years in a given area of activity (say, transportation). Then, apply these changes to other areas of activity, much as is done in technical innovation follow-on above. The difference is that this method is not restricted to forecastable breakthroughs.

Techniques to Enhance Group Creativity

Synectics.   In its pure form, synectics does not differ much from brainstorming. Synectics provides more structure and direction by having the participants think along the lines of certain operational mechanisms — usually analogy and metaphors. The system has a forced sequence through these mechanisms and other steps — viewpoint, forced fit, and so on. However, in recent years the two individuals involved in creating this approach have led their respective creativity firms into use of many ideation techniques. Analogy prevails as a critical feature, but the term *synectics* has come to mean two businesses running creativity seminars.

Delphi.   Although occasionally touted for ideation, Delphi is really a method of organizing a forecasting survey. Panels of experts are compiled, they are sent a questionnaire calling for forecasts within a given area of activity (for example, hospitals or data processing), the questionnaires are tabulated and summarized, the results are returned to the panel for their reaction and alteration, new summaries are prepared, the results are sent out again, and so on. The iterations continue until conformity is reached or until impasse is obvious. The method is essentially a cop-out because the individuals still must use some method to make their own forecasts. But in certain situations, it has been deemed effective, and it can be used quite easily in modified format.

Think Tanks.   This too is more a matter of organizing people than a mechanism of stimulating creativity. Think tanks are centers of intensive scientific research. Xerox, for example, maintains a center in Palo Alto at which, among other things, scientists are working on artificial intelligence. What they are studying today may be meaningful 5 to 20 years from now. The key to success here is the environment, which is thought to be stimulating to creativity. If the people in a think tank are charged with converting their outlandish ideation into useful products for marketing, the term *skunk works* is often applied.

Techniques of Attribute Analysis

Benefit Analysis.   All of the benefits that customers or users receive from the product under study are listed, in the hope of discovering an unrealized benefit or unexpectedly absent benefit. The technique is closely related to the needs-based composite analysis.

Use Analysis.   Listing the many ways buyers make use of a given product is also sometimes revealing. Some firms, 3M among others, have spent large sums of money asking consumers to tell them of new uses. Johnson Wax got into the car-polishing business when it found that its floor wax was being used on cars. One must contact users, however — not just list the uses already known to the company.

Function Analysis.

In between feature and use is an activity called function. Thus, for shampoos, we know the chemicals and product features present, and we may know the full reasons for using shampoos. But, it is also creative to list all possible ways that shampoos function — scraping, dissolving, depositing, evaporating, and so on.

Attribute Extension.

Also called parameter analysis, this technique begins with any attribute that has changed recently and then extends that change. Thus, for example, bicycle seats have gotten smaller and smaller. Extending that idea, one might imagine a bicycle with no seat at all; what would such a bicycle look like, and what would it be used for?

Relative Brand Profile.

Every brand name is flexible or elastic, meaning it can be stretched to cover different product types. People can understand a Minute Maid jelly or Minute Maid soup. But people also tell us that they cannot accept other "stretchings" — such as Minute Maid meats. Various market research techniques can be used to make these measurements, and any stretch that makes sense to the buyer is a potential new product. Incidentally, this thinking applies to goods and services, industrial as well as consumer.

Pseudo Product Test.

By using an essentially psychological projective technique, one can ask consumers to evaluate what is presented to them as a new product but is actually an unidentified product currently on the market. They will typically find unique characteristics matching the needs they have. These attributes can then be the base for a new product.

Systems Analysis.

This is a technique for studying complete systems of activity rather than products. Standard Brands once studied food preparation systems that involved margarine. It noted that virtually every one included an instruction to "melt the butter or margarine, stir in flour," and so on. From that came a stick-form sauce base called Smooth & Easy.

Unique Properties.

This technique is primarily valuable in technological fields. The analyst seeks unique properties of any product or material currently on the market. To aid in this, one usually begins by listing all *common* properties because the unique ones quickly pop out.

Hierarchical Design.

Here an organization chart design is formed, with product usage at the top and material types fanning out below. One such design began with deodorants, followed at the second level by roll-on, sticks, and aerosol. The brands were listed under roll-ons. Under each brand could be package size or target market segment. Another design had light construction at the top, followed by wood, steel, and concrete. Wood was broken into metal roof, tar or shingle roof, and so on. The technique is mainly a way of forcing one to see all aspects of a situation, which is the essence of attribute analysis.

Weaknesses.   All weaknesses of a product or product line (the company's own and those of the competition) are identified. This primarily defensive technique identifies line extensions and flanker products. Every resolvable weakness offers a new product concept.

Achilles' Heel.   Some analysts prefer to prune the list of weaknesses to one or two that are so serious as to constitute a basis for competitive action that would seriously endanger the product.

Theoretical Limits Test.   Both opportunities and threats can be visualized by pushing a known apparatus or device to its theoretical limits. The technique works especially well on a reasonably new technology that appears to have exhausted its usefulness.

Techniques to Enhance Lateral Search

Free Association.   This approach begins when the ideator writes down one aspect of the product situation being studied — a product attribute, a use, or a user. The trick then is to let the mind roam wildly and jot down every idea that comes out. The process is repeated for other aspects of the product situation. The associations are usually quite direct in the early stages when creativity is being stimulated; but with time, they become much less related and much more valuable as insights.

Stereotype Activity.   Here one asks, "How would _____do it?" The blank is filled in with a stereotype. Particular individuals can also be used, and the question can be reversed to ask what the stereotype would *not* do. Thus, a bicycle manufacturer might ask "What type of bicycle would a senator ride? Loudspeaker on it? Pedal both ways?"

Cross-Field Compilation.   As scientific disciplines have become increasingly blurred, a creative technique has been developed to bridge the between-field barriers. If a firm works primarily in the chemical area, its product developers may systematically scan developments in, say, physics or biology. Scientists in those fields may not know that some of their ideas have applications in chemistry.

Key-Word Monitoring.   Closely allied to the big-winner approach is the tack of monitoring newspapers and magazines and tallying the number of times key words appear. One firm used this approach to spot increasing use of *zodiac*, and it promptly marketed a series of successful products featuring the zodiac symbols. Some take this approach with electronic data bases and call it "data base tracking."

Use of the Ridiculous.   Just to show that anything can be done, some ideators deliberately try to force themselves to use ridiculous approaches. In one session, participants were asked to write out the most preposterous methods of joining two wires together. One answer was, "Hold them with your teeth," and another was "Use chewing gum." Those present were astounded to realize they had just reinvented alligator clips, and they promptly gave serious consideration to the chewing gum. It turns out that some ingredients in chewing gum may sometime be marketed for use in wiring!

Study of Other People's Failures.   Any product that has failed offers a chance for the next trier to spot its problem. Robert McNath runs a firm called Marketing Intelligence Service Ltd. in Naples, New York, where he displays over 10,000 actual failed products in a barnlike store. The failures apparently stimulate creativity.

Small's Ideation Stimulator Checklist

1. Can the dimensions be changed?

Larger	Economy-size packages, photo enlargements, puffed cereals
Smaller	U.S. paper money, hearing aids, tabloid newspapers, pocket flashlight, microfilm
Longer	King-size cigarettes, typewriter carriage for bookkeeping
Shorter	Men's shorts, women's panties
Thicker	Rug pads, heavy edge on drinking glasses, glass bricks
Thinner	Nylon hose, seersucker suits, wristwatches
Deeper	Deeper pockets in work clothes and army uniforms, grooved battery plates
Shallower	Wading pools, children's drinking fountain
Stand vertically	Skyscrapers (to increase floor space on expensive land), upright piano
Place horizontally	Ranch-style homes (to avoid stair climbing)
Make slanted or parallel	Reading stands, car mirror, eyeglass frames
Stratify	Plywood, storage pallets, layer cake
Invert (reverse)	Reversible coats, soft shoes to be worn on either foot, inverted ink and glue stands
Crosswise (bias, counter)	Bias brassieres and slips, pinking shears
Converge	Mechanical artificial hands, ice tongs

Source: From Marvin Small, *How to Make More Money* (New York: Pocket Books, 1959). © Copyright 1953, 1981, Marvin Small. Reprinted by permission of Pocket Books, a Simon & Schuster division of Gulf & Western Corporation.

Encircle	Spring cake form, knitted coasters to slip on bottoms of highball glasses, Life-Savers
Intervene	Buffers used in drug products to temper a harsh active ingredient
Delineate	Contour lathe, Scotchlite reflective sheeting
Border	Mats for pictures, movable office partitions, room separators

2. Can the quantity be changed?

More	Extra-pants suits; three stockings — a pair with a spare
Less	Variety of 1-ounce boxes of cereals, ginger ale splits
Change proportions	Nested chairs or dishes, hot-cold water faucets
Fractionate	Separate packings of crackers inside single box, 16-mm movie film usable as two 8-mm films, faucet spray
Join something	Trailer, hose couplings
Add something to it	Cigarette filter tip
Combined with something else	Amphibious auto, outboard motors, roadable airplanes
Complete	Freezer unit added to refrigerator, Bendix washer and dryer single unit

3. Can the order be changed?

Arrangement	Car steering wheels left-handed in United States, right-handed in England; Dewey decimal system of filing
Precedence	Rear-drive automobiles
Beginning	Self-starter, red tab to open cigarette package, red string to open Band-Aids
Assembly or disassembly	Prefabricated articles, knockdown boat kits
Focus	Kellogg packages — Name placed in left corner instead of center; Hathaway shirts ads — man with eye patch

4. Can the time element be changed?

Faster	Quick-drying ink, dictating machine, intercom system
Slower	High-tenacity yarns for longer-life tires, 33⅓-rpm long-playing records
Longer	Jiffy insulated bags for ice cream, wood preservative
Shorter	Pressure cooker, one-minute X-ray machine
Chronologized	Defrosting devices, radio clocks
Perpetuated	Photographs, metal plating, permanent magnets
Synchronized	Uniform vacation periods, group travel tours
Anticipated	Thermostat, freezer food-buying plan
Renewed	Self-charging battery, self-winding watches

Recurrence	Switch clocks for lights and electrical appliances
Alternated	Cam drive, electric current

5. Can the cause or effect be changed?

Stimulated	Generator
Energized	Magneto, power steering
Strengthened	AC-DC transformer, Simoniz car coating
Louder	Volume control, acoustical aids
Softer	Sound insulator, rubber heels
Altered	Antifreeze chemicals, meat tenderizer
Destroyed	Tree spraying, breath and perspiration deodorants
Influenced	Legislation to permit sale of colored oleo, wetting agent catalyst
Counteracted	Circuit breaker, air-conditioning, filters

6. Can there be a change in character?

Stronger	Dirt-resistant paint
Weaker	Pepsi-Cola made less sweet, children's aspirin
Altered	Aged or blended whiskey, transit-mixed cement
Converted	Convertiplanes (for vertical or horizontal flights)
Substituted	Low-calorie salad dressing (made without oils)
Interchanged	Interchangeable parts, all-size socks
Stabilized	Sperry gyroscope, waterproof plastic bandage
Reversed	Two-way locomotives
Resilient	Foam-rubber upholstery, cork floors
Uniformity	Standards in foods, drugs, fuels, liquor
Cheaper	Coach air travel, paper cups
More expensive	Cigarettes in cardboard or metal boxes, deluxe editions of books
Add color	Color television, colored plastics
Change color	Variously colored toothbrush handles, automobiles, electric light bulbs

7. Can the form be changed?

Animated	Moving staircases, package conveyors
Stilled	Air brakes
Speeded	Meat-slicing machine
Slowed	Shock absorbers, gravel driveway
Directed	Flowmeters
Deviated	Traffic islands
Attracted	Magnetic devices
Repelled	Electrically charged fencing
Admitted	Turnstiles
Barred	Gate, fence
Lifted	Forklift truck
Lowered	Ship locks
Rotated	Waring blender, boring machine
Oscillated	Electric fan
Agitated	Electric scalp stimulator

8. Can the state or condition be changed?

Hotter	Electric hot plate, washed coal
Colder	Freezer, thermos jug, water cooler
Harden	Bouillon cubes, cream shampoo (instead of liquid)
Soften	Krilium soil conditioner, water softeners
Open or closed	Visible record equipment, electronically operated doors
Preformed	Prefabricated housing, prepared Tom Collins mixer
Disposable	Bottle caps, Chux disposable diapers, Kleenex tissues
Incorporated	Counting register on printing press, cash registers
Parted	Caterpillar tractors, split-level highways
Solidified	Bakelite and other plastics, citrus concentrates
Liquefied	Chemical plant foods
Vaporized	Nasal medication vaporizers
Pulverized	Powdered eggs, lawn mower attachment to powder leaves, Disposall garbage pulverizer
Abraded	Snow tires or chains
Lubricated	Self-lubricating equipment
Wetter	Hydraulic brakes
Drier	De-Moist for cellars, tobacco curing
Insulated	Fiberglas, Dr. Scholl's foot appliances (insulate feet against pressures)
Effervesced	Alka-Seltzer
Coagulated	Jell-O and Junket desserts
Elasticized	Latex girdles, bubble gum, belts
Resistant	Rubber footwear
Lighter	Aluminum luggage, automatic electric blanket
Heavier	Can opener with weighted stand

9. Can the use be adapted to a new market?

Men	Colognes, lotions
Women	Colored-tip cigarettes
Children	Junior-size tools, cowboy clothes
Old	Walking stick chairs
Handicapped	Chair lifts
Foreign	*Reader's Digest* foreign editions

Appendix D

Glossary[*]

A

abandonment The discontinuance of a marketed product. Also called product deletion or product elimination. Abandonment may occur at any time from shortly after launch (a new product failure) to many years later.

acquisition The purchase by one organization of people, technology (process, facility, or material), product rights (trademarks), or entire businesses from other organizations. Acquisition is a method of expanding one's product offering by means other than internal development.

adaptive product Also called adapted product, this market entry acquires its uniqueness by variation on another, more pioneering product. The degree of adaptation is more than trivial (to avoid being an emulative or me-too product).

adopter categories Persons or firms that adopt an innovation are often classified into five groups according to the sequence of their adoption of it: (1) innovators (the first 2 to 5%); (2) early adopters (the next 10 to 15%); early majority (the next 35%); late majority (the next 35%); and laggards (the final 5 to 10%). The numbers are percents of the total number of actual adopters, not of the total number of persons or firms in the marketplace. There is wide disagreement on the exact percentage in each category.

adoption of innovation The process by which an innovation spreads throughout a population. It consists of adopter categories (innovators, early adopters, etc.) and a specific process of adoption by each adopter.

Alpha test The testing of a new product in-house, not with potential users (Beta test). The testing may be in a laboratory setting or (as in the case of glues or computers) in some part of the developing firm's regular operations.

---

[*]In those cases where a product definition was included in *Dictionary of Marketing Terms*, ed. Peter D. Bennett (Chicago: American Marketing Association, 1988), those definitions were used here. All other terms involved in new products management were defined and assembled here for the first time.

announcement   Second stage of the product launch cycle.

applications engineering   A strategy of applying one's technical skills to new areas. Adhesives manufacturers have often followed such a strategy.

A–T–R (awareness–trial–repeat)   A paradigm consisting of three key steps by the intended user; the steps take the person or firm from a state of ignorance about a new product to the point of product adoption. (See *awareness, trial,* and *repeat*).

attribute   (See *product attributes*.)

attribute analysis   A bundle of idea-generating techniques built on the concept that any product improvement is a change in the attributes of its predecessor. Dimensional analysis and the checklist are the most popular techniques.

augmented product   The view of a product that includes not only its core benefit and its physical being but adds other sources of benefits, such as service, warranty, and image. The augmented aspects are added to the physical product by action of the seller, such as with company reputation or with service.

availability   A measure of the extent to which target customers can get a new product if they wish to do so. Often stated as a percent of outlets where the product is stocked.

awareness   A measure of the percent of target customers who are aware of the new product's existence. Awareness is variously defined, including recall of brand, recognition of brand, recall of key features or positioning, etc.

B

balanced matrix   An organization option that uses matrix in approximately balanced proportions between the project and the departments.

basic market description   Market research done before or immediately after selecting an arena for product innovation charter focus. Prepares the firm to innovate in that area.

beachhead   The third phase of the launch cycle. It comes immediately after announcement, is quite frenetic, and ceases when the product is withdrawn or moves into the fourth (growth) stage.

benefit   A product attribute expressed in terms of what the user gets from the product, rather than its physical characteristics (features). Benefits are often paired with specific features, but they need not be. They are perceived, not necessarily real.

Beta test   The type of product use testing that follows Alpha testing and takes place on the premises of intended market users. The procedure may only concentrate on whether the product performs as expected or on whether the performance meets the needs of the user, as perceived by that user, in which case it is called a *Gamma* test.

blind test   The type of product use testing in which the identity of the new item's producer is kept secret. Unbranded, in contrast to a branded test.

brainstorming   A group method of problem solving used in product concept generation. It is sometimes thought to be an open, free-wheeling idea session, but more correctly is a specific procedure developed by Alex Osborn, with precise rules of session conduct. Has many modifications in format of use, each variation with its own name.

brand   A name, term, design, symbol, or any other feature that identifies one seller's good or service as distinct from those of other sellers. The legal term for brand is *trademark*. A brand may identify one item, a family of items, or all items of that seller. If used for the firm as a whole, the preferred term is *trade name*. (See *trademark, family brand,* and *individual brand*.)

brand extension   A product line extension marketed under the same general brand as a previous item or items. To distinguish the brand extension from the other item(s) under the primary brand, one can either add a secondary brand identification or add a generic. A brand extension is usually aimed at another segment of the general market for the overall brand. (See *family brand* and *individual brand*.)

brand generic   The second half of a product's identifying title. Brand is the first half and identifies one seller's version, while the generic is the second half and identifies the general class of item. [Example: Jello (brand) gelatin dessert (generic).] Not to be confused with generic brands (such as on some low-price items in supermarkets) where there is no individual brand (see *generic brands*).

brand image   The perception of a brand in the minds of persons. The image is a mirror reflection (though perhaps inaccurate) of the brand personality or product being. It is what people believe about a brand—their thoughts, feelings, expectations.

brand name   That part of a brand that can be spoken: letters, numbers, or words. The term *trademark* covers all forms of brand (name, mark, etc.), but brand name is the form most often meant when trademark is used. (See *brand* and *trademark*.)

brand personality   The psychological nature of a particular brand, as intended by its sellers, though persons in the marketplace may see the brand otherwise (called brand image). These two perspectives compare to the personalities of individual humans: what we intend or desire, and what others see or believe.

brand positioning   (See *product positioning*.)

branding, family   (See *family brand*.)

branding, individual   Using separate brands for each product, without a family brand to tie them to other brands of that firm. (See *family brand*.)

business analysis   A term of many meanings, and in marketing is usually associated in some way with the evaluation of new product proposals. In format, it may consist of a five-year, discounted cash flow, net present value type of financial analysis, or it may be a more comprehensive analysis of the entire situation surrounding the proposed product. Chronologically, it may come early in the development process (when it is used to decide whether expensive R&D should be undertaken), and/or late in the product development cycle when the commercialization decision is being made.

C

checklist A memory-jogger list of items, used to remind an analyst to think of all relevant aspects. It finds frequent use as a tool of creativity in concept generation and as a factor consideration list in concept screening.

commercialization A stage (usually the last) in the development cycle for a new product. Commonly thought to begin when the product is introduced into the marketplace, but actually starts when a management commits to marketing the item. (See *new product development.*)

component testing The testing of various parts of the marketing program, separately. Market testing tests them in unison, but during the development process each item in the marketing mix may be put through separate testing. Copy testing is the most common form of component testing.

concept (See *product concept.*)

concept generation The act by which new concepts, or ideas, are created. Also the definition of the second phase of the overall product innovation process, during which the concepts are created. Sometimes called idea generation or ideation.

concept statement A verbal and/or pictorial statement of a concept (for a product or for advertising) that is prepared for presentation to potential buyers or users to get their reaction prior to its being implemented. Product concepts are followed by prototypes, advertising concepts by one of several forms of semifinished production.

concept statement commercialized A term used in distinguishing two types of product concept statements. A commercialized product concept statement is prepared in an advertising format, as a persuasive statement. A noncommercialized product concept statement is prepared in neutral, nonpersuasive format.

concept testing and development The process in which a concept statement is presented to potential buyers or users for their reactions. These reactions permit the developer to estimate the sales value of the concept (whether product or advertising) and to make changes in it so as to enhance its sales value.

contingency plan The action ready in standby that will be taken if a given state of affairs comes about during the new product launch. Usually tied to one or more triggers in the launch control process.

control Usually called managerial control. Refers to practices that result in a project or other activity achieving its objectives. Guided missiles are "controlled." Midterm correction and contingency planning are characteristics of managerial control.

controlled sale A category of market testing techniques in which the ability of the firm to obtain distribution is not tested. Distribution is forced (for example, by giving the outlets free product).

control over use A dimension of product use tests. Refers to the degree to which the product developers maintain control over how the user uses the new item.

copyright An exclusive right to the production or sale of literary, musical, or other artistic work or to the use of a print or label. Occasionally applied to a brand, but brands are usually protected by registration in the Patent and Copyright Office as a trademark.

core product The central benefit or purpose for which a consumer buys a product. Varies from purchaser to purchaser. The core product or core benefit may come either from the physical good or service performance, or it may come from the augmented dimensions of the product. (See *augmented product*.)

coupling The joining of efforts between the firm innovating on new products and other firms or persons. Coupling can be upstream (with vendors), downstream (with customers), or sideways (with competitors).

creative stimuli A method of ideation whereby one thinks of a problem or a product and then studies a set of words or phrases that research has shown to be stimulating.

critical path scheduling A technique of project control, now usually incorporated in various software programs. The technique puts all important steps of a given new product project into a sequential network.

cumulative cost curve The shape of a line that depicts a firm's cumulative costs of developing and marketing a new product. It is plotted against the cumulation of time, so it runs from zero (start of project) to 100 percent of time (launch). The curve necessarily runs from lower left to upper right.

customer service Identifiable, but essentially intangible, activities offered by a seller in conjunction with a product, such as delivery and repair. Not to be confused with intangible products (services), types of products for which the activity is the primary purpose of a sale. The sale of service products may be accompanied by the provision of customer services.

D

decay curve The curve representing death of concepts during the development stage. Begins on the left with 100 percent of concepts and ends up on the right with the percent actually marketed successfully. Usually declines rapidly. Also called the mortality curve.

decline stage of the product life cycle   The fourth stage of a product life cycle, in which sales of the product fall off from their levels during the maturity (third) stage.

deliverability   The extent to which an organization is viewed as being capable of actually delivering to the customer and adequately servicing a particular new product concept. The measure is an attribute of the concept, much as manufacturability is. (See *manufacturability*.)

demand-pulled innovation   Innovation caused or at least stimulated by the needs, wants, or desires of customers. Contrasts with supply-pushed innovation. Other terms for these two ideas are market- or customer-driven innovation and technology-driven innovation.

design   A term of many meanings. In product innovation, it usually means the activity of going from the product concept to a finished physical item. Includes conceptual work as well as actual making of the item. *Industrial design* is a term usually applied to this subset of a larger definition of design. Includes the R&D function in many people's minds. In Europe, is sometimes used to encompass the entire product innovation process. (See *engineering design*.)

determinant attribute   An attribute of a product category that (1) distinguishes such products from each other and (2) is important to buyers.

determinant gap map   A two-dimensional map that uses two determinant attributes to plot all brands in a product category. The plotting is done by an experienced analyst, not by the consumers themselves (perceptual map).

diagnostic information   Information obtained from any of the evaluative steps of a product's development that goes beyond the current evaluation to give guidance to later steps. A product use test, for example, rates the product's usefulness but also gives suggestions on packaging, positioning, pricing, etc.

diffusion of innovation   The process by which the use of an innovation is spread within a market group, over time, and over various categories of adopters. (See *adopter categories*.)

dimensional analysis   A technique of attribute analysis, whereby new concepts are generated from an exhaustive listing of the dimensions of products in a given category.

disciplines panel   A variation of brainstorming in which each participant represents a scientific discipline relevant to the problem under study. Typical panels have psychologists, chemists, engineers, lawyers, and others.

diversification   The act of adding diverse product(s) to a line to move the seller into new markets. The degree of diversification can vary greatly.

dual drive   The strategic combination of technology and market as sources for product innovation. Contrasts with market drive and technology drive. Innovations are based on at least one specific technical strength of the firm and at least one specific market opportunity.

E

early adopters   The second identifiable subgroup within a population that begins use of an innovation. They follow innovators and precede the early majority. (See *adopter categories* and *product adoption process.*)

early majority   The third identifiable subgroup within a population that adopts an innovation. Preceded by early adopters and innovators. The early majority like to await the outcome of product trial by the two earlier groups. (See *adopter categories* and *product adoption process.*)

emulative product   A new product that imitates another product already on the market. Is somewhat different than previous products (not a pure me-too), but the difference is not substantial or significant. (See *adaptive product* and *innovative imitation.*)

engineering design   A function in the product creation process where a good is configured. Specific form is decided. The activity is sometimes seen as a late step in the R&D process and sometimes as an early step in the manufacturing process. The design engineering department is therefore often independent of both. (See *design.*)

entry evaluation   The first evaluation done after a concept emerges. It may be by the person creating it, but usually involves others in the immediate "vicinity." Judgmental, experience-based, not with creation of new data or opinions.

evaluation   A set of activities scattered through the third, fourth, and fifth stages of the overall product innovation process. These activities measure the evolving worth of the new product being developed. Includes such steps as concept testing, product use testing, and market testing.

evolving product   Like a butterfly, a new product does not just emerge. It begins as a concept (or even just an opportunity), then goes through various stages, such as protocol, prototype, pilot plant product, and marketed product.

expected effects matrix   A matrix of two dimensions: damage and probability. Used to classify negative events that might take place during the launch of a new item. A high score on both dimensions increases the need for action.

expressed warranty   Spoken or written promises made by the seller of a product about what will be done if the product proves to be defective in manufacture or performance. Contrasts with promises that are only implied by common knowledge of the product or by customary practices in a trade. (See *implied warranty.*)

F

failure rate   The percentage of a firm's marketed new products that fail to achieve the objectives set for them. Should not be confused with the decay or mortality rate. The term *failure rate* should only be used on products that go to the full intended market target, not a trial or roll-out subset. (See *decay curve*.)

family brand A brand used on two or more individual products. The product group may or may not be all of that firm's product line. The individual members of the family also carry individual brands to differentiate them from other family members. In rare cases, family brands have other family brands as members, each of which have individual brands. Automobiles fit the latter situation, as with Oldsmobile (family) Cutlass (family) Ciera (individual). (See *branding, individual*.)

family packaging Using one design or other key packaging element to integrate the packaging of two or more individual items. The packages clearly belong to one set, but there are usually some individualizations, especially in brand name.

feature A product attribute that is an identifiable characteristic. Is usually physical (on goods) or a sequence step (on services). Contrasts with other type of attribute (benefit).

field testing A term sometimes used to describe product use testing. The word *field* separates this type of testing from in-house, laboratory-type testing.

first-to-market The first product that creates a new product category or a substantial subdivision of one. Distinguishes the pioneering product from those that follow.

focus group A market research technique where 10 to 12 market participants are gathered in one room for discussion under the leadership of a trained focus group leader. Discussion focuses on a problem, a product, or an activity. The group often meets in special facilities for observation and videotaping.

forced relationships A concept generation technique whereby creativity is stimulated when two or more separate things are brought together. The items are unrelated, and the mere combining of them shows new and unexpected patterns.

fortuitous scan A class of concept-generating techniques not based on the problem find/solve route. The techniques are many, usually logical, and tend to make variations in products currently on the market. Attribute analysis and relationships analysis are two categories of fortuitous scan approaches.

franchise extension New product that capitalizes on a firm's market strength. A franchise is a strength of relationship with customers and may be based on a brand, a sales force relationship, a favorable trade relationship, etc. The new item is often not unique but sells based on the favorable franchise.

full sale A class of market testing techniques where the marketing is complete and in the mode that would be used under total launch. No limitations on distribution, advertising, etc. unless planned in launch.

full screen A screening stage where all preliminary work is finished, a scoring model is usually used, and a favorable assessment is followed by a preliminary business analysis that releases the concept to development.

functional matrix An organization option in which the matrix leans toward the functions. Participants have dual reporting relationships, but the functional reporting is intended to dominate thinking and action.

G

Gamma test A type of product use test wherein the developers measure the extent to which the item meets the needs of the target customer, solves the problem(s) targeted during the development, and leaves the customer satisfied.

gap analysis A category of techniques based on the idea that if one can position all of a market's products onto one two-dimensional chart, they will not be spread around like butter on bread. Rather, they will clump in some places and be void in others. Any void (gap) thus offers an opportunity for a new product. The charting uses x- and y-axes and plots against such attributes as price, strength, speed, and ease of use.

generic brands Products named only by their generic class (such as drip-grind coffee and barber shop). Other products have both an individual brand and a generic classification (Maxwell House drip-grind coffee, Maurice's barber shop). This approach is usually associated with food and other packaged goods, but many other consumer and industrial goods and services are marketed as generics.

generic terms, as brand names (See *brand generic*.)

goods Products that have tangible form, in contrast to services, which are intangible. (See *services*.)

growth stage of product life cycle The second stage of the product life cycle, during which sales are increasing at an increasing rate, profits are increasing, and competitors enter the market. Product differentiation takes place, and price competition begins.

H

heuristic A rule of thumb, from trial-and-error experience, used to guide decisions when algorithms are unavailable. Commonly used in the new products field because solid experience data are rarely available.

hurdle rate Any criterion or test figure that a new product must meet or exceed as it goes through development.

I

idea generation (See *concept generation*.)

identity disclosure The issue of whether to release to the user the name of the firm making the product being tested.

imitative innovation A strategy of copying the creativity of others, but modifying each "copy" enough to give it originality and, hopefully, market value. The improvement is not enough to call it an adaptive strategy. (See *adaptive products*.)

implied warranty   A warranty (promise of performance) extended to the customer but unstated. It usually is assumed from common practice in the trade or suggested by statements made about the product by the seller.

individual brand   The brand identity given to an individual product, as separate from other products in the market and from other items in the product's own line. A trademark.

industrial design   (See *design*.)

informal selling   A type of market test in which one or a few salespeople make calls on intended market users and full presentations are made. There is actual request for the order. However, product has not been released to the full sales force.

initial reaction   (See *entry evaluation*.)

innovation   (1) The act of creating a new product or process; includes invention as well as the work required to bring an idea or concept into final form. (2) A particular new product or process. An innovation may have various degrees of newness, from very little to highly discontinuous, but that must include at least some degree of newness to the market, not just to the firm.

innovativeness   (1) When applied to the seller, it is the degree to which the firm has the capability of, and follows the practice of, being innovative. (2) When applied to a buyer, it is the extent to which that person or firm is willing to accept the risks of early purchase on an innovation.

innovators   Firms, or persons, that are innovative. The term is often applied (1) to those who are the first to create a new type of product or (2) to those who are the first to adopt a new product introduced to the marketplace. Innovators are often thought to be opinion leaders. (See *adopter categories* and *product adoption process*.)

interface   The point where different functions in a firm come together during the product innovation process. Usually applies to pairings of the major players: technical (R&D), operations (especially manufacturing), and marketing.

intrapreneurship   The practice of entrepreneurship within a large firm. Intrapreneurship is a style of management to be independent, risk taking, innovative, daring, and typical of the style used in successful start-up firms.

introductory stage of product life cycle   The first stage of the product life cycle. The new product is introduced to the market, sales are slow, promotion is usually heavy, costs are accumulated, and expectation is focused on determining when and if the product will soon enter the second (growth) stage of the cycle.

invention   A new device, process, etc., that has been created. Can be in either physical or conceptual form. Preexisting knowledge is combined in a new way to yield something that did not heretofore exist. Not to be confused with a product innovation, which is an invention that has been converted by further management and process development into a marketable product.

inventive creativity The creativity required for product innovation. Is thought to combine artistic creativity and engineering creativity, either of which alone can be very strong but not productive of new product ideas.

itemized response A unique process whereby one person hearing another person's new product idea is to (1) give a full statement of support by citing several advantages to the idea and (2) express any problems or concerns in positive (what's the best way to solve this) form.

L

laggards The fifth, and last, group of users to adopt an innovation. (See *adopter categories* and *product adoption process*.)

late majority The fourth group of users to adopt an innovation. (See *adopter categories* and *product adoption process*.)

lateral search A term applied to a category of fortuitous scan ideation techniques that are partly miscellaneous but tend to force the ideator to stretch mentally out of normal channels. They are forcing techniques, based on the idea that ideation can take place only when the mind assumes unique positions of viewing people or happenings.

launch A term signifying the marketing of a new product. Can be either in a full-sale form of market testing or in the final marketing stage.

launch control The process by which a management plans for and supervises the introduction of a new product; the product's progress is monitored against preestablished norms, variances are detected, and corrections made such that the original goals set for the product are achieved.

launch cycle The subphases of the innovation stage of a traditional product life cycle. The big step of innovation is broken into preparation (for marketing), announcement, beachhead, and early growth.

lead user Those people or firms who most need the innovation being worked on and who will most likely participate in the innovation process. The idea itself often originates with a lead user and may even appear in prototype form in the lead user's firm.

learning requirements Various types of learning that new products often require from their purchasers. Without that learning, the purchase, trial use, or satisfaction will be threatened.

leveraged creativity Working a lesser creativity off the major creativity of others. A strategy of pioneering whereby the innovations are technically new and unique but considerably less significant than the original.

licensing A strategy or practice of leasing or renting one's technology to others. Can go sideways (competitors), upstream (vendors), or downstream (customers, resellers). A way one firm gains the right to use the creations of another. May be exclusive or nonexclusive.

limited marketing   A type of market testing that follows test marketing and precedes full-scale availability. Often called a roll-out. Commitment has been made to full-scale marketing, but the marketing is tentative and based on limited geographic areas, specific firms (such as lead users), or specific applications.

line extension   A new product marketed by an organization that already has at least one other product being sold in that product/market area. Line extensions are usually new flavors, sizes, models, applications, strengths, etc. Sometimes the distinction is made between near line extensions (very little difference) and distant line extensions (almost completely new entries).

M

manufacturability   The extent to which a new product concept or prototype is figured to be capable of effective and efficient manufacturing by available resources. Question is frequently asked at time of pre–R&D screening, and again prior to authorizing production. Also is used during the design process, particularly when using computer-aided design. A similar term is *producibility*.

market development   A new sales volume opportunity that, strictly speaking, does not involve product innovation. Current products are taken to new customers or users. Market development often does involve some product modifications, however, and may sometimes approach diversification in nature.

market driven   A strategy whereby a firm lets the marketplace direct its product innovation. Consumer product firms tend to be the primary users of this strategy.

market roll-out   (See *limited marketing*.)

market testing   The phase of new product development when the new item and its marketing plan are tested together. Prior testing, if any, involved separate components. A market test simulates the eventual marketing of the product and takes many different forms, only one of which bears the name *test market*.

matrix organization   A method of arranging teams or groups of people representing various functions of a firm. Each member of the group reports both to the head of the group (say, a program manager or project director) and to the head of the function where housed (say, the VP of manufacturing).

maturity stage of product life cycle   The third stage of the product life cycle, when initial rapid growth is over and when sales level off (though there may be intermittent surges and declines over the years before final decline sets in).

minimarket test   A type of controlled-sale market testing whereby the outlets used are a small, nonrepresentative sampling of the market. Product is usually placed into the outlets (not sold), and promotion is much less than planned ultimately. Primarily tests just the willingness to spend some money for a product trial.

mission statement   A part of corporate or division strategy. It describes the essential character of the business and is a necessary input to new product strategy.

mode of reaction   Describes how product testees give their reaction to a product use test. Options include like/dislike, preference, and descriptive/ diagnostic information.

monadic test   A product use testing format where only the new item is tested. Contrasts with the paired-comparison method.

morphological analysis   A fortuitous scan ideation method. Is based on relationships and includes using a multiple set of product forms, attributes, uses, users, etc. in matrix format.

multidisciplinary   Often called multifunctional and refers to persons or operations where a multiple set of disciplines or functions are involved. Product innovation necessarily is one of those.

N

negligence   A source of product liability, more common many years ago. If negligence occurs in the design or manufacture of a product, the manufacturer is liable for the injuries that result.

network   The informal mix of people, departments, or firms necessary to implement a product innovation project. Goes well beyond the persons assigned to the team and includes everyone whose work contributes significantly to the project. A network is established and managed by the project manager. As a verb, networking describes the informal activities of a new products manager to relate personally with all of the players on the project.

new product   A term of many opinions and practices, but most generally defined as a product (good or service) new to the firm marketing it. Excludes products that are only changed in promotion, though some persons like to think of a repositioned product (such as new use) as a new product.

new product development   (1) The overall process of strategy, organization, concept generation, concept and marketing plan evaluation, and commercialization of a new product. (2) Restricted in meaning to that part of the process done by technical (R&D) departments. New product development concerns activity within an organization, in contrast to the acquisition of finished new products from outside.

new product failure A new product that does not meet the objectives of its developers. Depending on what those objectives are, a profitable new product can be a failure, and an unprofitable new product can be a success.

new product strategy Strategy that guides the product innovation program. Is unique to new products and is a spin-off from overall corporate or division strategy.

new products management Similar to product innovation management and refers to the overall management of a new product project or a total product innovation program.

new products manager A product manager with a new products assignment. May direct a single project team, or several teams, or an entire product innovation program. Is nonfunctional, or general management in perspective, regardless of department housed in.

O

operations A term that includes manufacturing but is much broader. All activities (after R&D or systems design) necessary to provide the thing or the service that produces benefits for the customer. Usually includes procurement, physical distribution, and, for services, management of the offices or other areas where the services are provided. One leading firm calls operations management "supply management."

P

package The container used to protect, promote, transport, and/or identify a product. May be primary (contains the product), secondary (contains one or more primary packages), or tertiary (contains one or more secondary packages).

paired-comparison A mode of product use testing where the new product is paired with (usually) the category leader, and direct comparisons are made. Contrasts with monadic testing.

patent The legal right of exclusive use and licensing granted by a government to the person who invents something. An invention is patentable if it is a useful, novel, and nonobvious process, machine, manufacture, or composition of matter.

payback The time, usually in years, from the point of full-scale market introduction of a new product until it has recovered its costs of development and marketing. The market testing stage is usually considered a part of the evaluation process (and not in the payback period); but if a roll-out is used, practice varies on when the payback period should begin.

perceptual gap A gap that appears on a mapping of products where the positions of the products are determined by user opinions, not necessarily fact.

PERT A method of project control similar to critical path scheduling but also including costs as well as times, and probabilities for each. Highly computerized. Letters stand for *p*rogram *e*valuation *r*eview *t*echnique.

PIC Letters stand for *p*roduct *i*nnovation *c*harter.

pilot plant A trial manufacturing facility where the new process of production is tried out and revised. Small-scale model of what will later be built. Pilot plant is usually thought of as a small manufacturing facility or arrangement of machinery, but it can also be a part of an office or warehouse. Systems can be tried out in pilot operations.

pioneering innovativeness A strategy of trying to be the first to market new types of products. The highest order of innovativeness (others are adapting and imitating), it is often based on technical breakthroughs.

pioneering stage A nonspecific period early in the life cycle of a new type of product, during which the pioneers are trying to build primary demand for the product type more than secondary demand for their particular brands.

portfolio A set of things. Most often applied to that group of projects currently active in a research laboratory but may apply to all new projects under way.

positioning (See *product positioning*.)

precedence In product innovation, this term refers to the order of market entry. A product is first to market, second, etc.

preference gap An opportunity first discovered on determinant gap maps or perceptual gap maps and then evaluated using maps based on customer preferences. Perceptual gaps often coincide with areas of no preference.

pre-launch The first stage of the launch cycle. Involves getting ready to launch the product, including getting distribution and building necessary field service capability.

preliminary market analysis A type of market research that follows ideation and entry evaluation. Often used to gain greater knowledge of a particular market prior to setting up a concept test plan.

prescreening Those evaluation steps that follow ideation and precede the full screen. Involves entry evaluation, preliminary market analysis, and concept testing and development.

problem analysis A part of the problem find/solve method of concept generation. Relates to finding the problems and involves study of users to learn their dissatisfactions and unmet needs.

problem find/solve A general method of concept generation, usually thought to be the best. Requires finding problems faced by customers and other users and solving them. In the solutions are found new product concepts.

problem identification The first stage of the problem analysis method of ideation. Involves finding, describing, and analyzing the problem(s) of targeted market participants.

producibility (See *manufacturability*.)

product (1) A bundle of attributes (features, functions, benefits, and uses) capable of exchange or use; usually a mix of tangible and intangible forms. Thus a product may be an idea, a physical entity (a good), a service, or any combination of the three. It exists for the purpose of exchange in the satisfaction of individual and organizational objectives. (2) Occasional usage today implies a definition of product as that bundle of attributes where the exchange or use primarily concerns the physical or tangible form; in contrast to a service, where the seller, buyer, or user is primarily interested in the intangible. Though to speak of "products and services" is convenient, it leaves us without a term to apply to the set of the two combined. The term for tangible products is *goods,* and it should be used with services to make the tangible/intangible pair, as subsets of the term *product*. (See *services*.)

product adaptation The strategy of developing new products by modifying or improving on the product innovations of others. Contrasts with the strategies of pioneering and imitation. (See *adaptive products*.)

product adoption process The sequence of stages that individuals and firms go through in the process of accepting new products. The stages vary greatly in usage but tend to include (1) becoming aware of the new product, (2) seeking information about it, (3) developing favorable attitudes toward it, (4) trying it out in some direct or indirect way, (5) finding satisfaction in the trial, and (6) adopting the product into a standing usage or repurchase pattern.

product attributes The characteristics by which products are identified and differentiated. Usually comprises features and benefits.

product champion A person who takes an inordinate interest in seeing that a particular process or product is fully developed and marketed. The role varies from situations calling for little more than stimulating awareness of the item to extreme cases where the champion tries to force the item past the strongly entrenched internal resistance of company policy or that of objecting parties.

product class The group of products that are homogeneous or generally considered substitutes for each other. The class is considered narrow or broad depending on how substitutable the various products are. For example, a narrow product class of breakfast meats might be bacon, ham, and sausage. A broad class would include all other meat and meat substitutes even occasionally sold for breakfast use.

product concept A verbal or pictorial version of a proposed new product. Consists of (1) one or more benefits it will yield, (2) its general form, and (3) the technology used to achieve the form. A new product idea becomes a concept when it achieves at least one benefit and either the form or the technology. Further work in the development process gradually clarifies and confirms those two and adds the third. A concept becomes a product when it is sold successfully in the marketplace; prior to that, it is still undergoing development, even if marketed.

product deletion (See *abandonment.*)

product development (See *new product development.*)

product form The physical shape or nature of a good or the sequential steps in a service. Form is provided by one or more technologies and yields benefits to the user; for example, many technologies go to make a front-wheel-drive form of an automobile. Products of the same form make up a group within a product class (for example, all front-wheel-drive automobiles). Differences in form of service separate discount and full-service stock brokers.

product hierarchy An organizational chart-type array of the products offered in a given market, breaking first into class, then form, then variations on form, then brand. There are various options within these product hierarchy dimensions, so the array can be designed to fit the needs of the analyst. The hierarchy concept fits services as well as goods.

product idea (See *product concept.*)

product innovation (See *innovation.*)

product innovation charter The summary statement of strategy that will guide a department or project team in their efforts to generate new product volume. Specifies the arena within which the people will operate, their goals and objectives, and the general approaches they will use.

product innovation gap The difference between a firm's projected sales/profit goals and what its current product line is expected to produce. The gap must be filled by some form of product innovation.

product introduction The first stage of the product life cycle, during which the new item is announced to the market and offered for sale. (See *product life cycle.*)

product liability The obligation a seller incurs regarding the safety of a product. The liability may be implied by custom or common practice in the field, stated in the warranty, or decreed by law. If injury occurs, various defenses are prescribed by law and judicial precedent. Sellers are expected to offer adequate instructions and warnings about a product's use.

product life cycle (From biology) The four stages that a new product is thought to go through from birth to death: introduction, growth, maturity, and decline. Controversy surrounds whether products do indeed go through such cycles in any systematic, predictable way. The product life-cycle concept is primarily applicable to product forms, less to product classes, and very poorly to individual brands.

product line A group of products marketed by an organization to one general market. The products have some characteristics, customers, and/or uses in common and may also share technologies, distribution channels, prices, services, etc.

product manager   Within an organization, a person assigned responsibility for overseeing all of the various functional activities (such as manufacturing, pricing, and research) that concern a particular product. Actual responsibility varies widely, but the common feature is a narrow, product focus on the part of the manager. In some industries, the term *brand manager* is used in place of product manager.

product/market matrix   A two-by-two matrix in which the column designations are current products and new products, and the row designations are current markets and new markets. The matrix thus defines four types of new product opportunities ranging from the upper-left quadrant of improved versions of "current products to current users" to the lower-right quadrant of "diversification."

product planning   A term of many meanings but generally used to designate a staff position charged with part or all of the task of managing product innovation within an organization. In some firms, it also includes acquisition of products or processes.

product positioning   (1) How consumers, users, buyers, and others view competitive brands or types of products. As determined by market research techniques, the various products are plotted onto maps, using product attributes as dimensions. (2) For new products, product positioning means how the innovator firm decides to compare the new item to its predecessors. For the new item, the mental slates of persons in the marketplace are blank; this is the only chance the innovator will have to make a first impression.

product use test   One of several key evaluation steps in the product development process. Involves giving some of the new product to persons or firms in the intended target market and asking them to use it for a time and report their reactions to it. The purposes of a product use test are to (1) see if the item developed by the organization has the attributes prescribed for it, (2) learn whether it satisfies the market needs identified during the ideation process, and (3) disclose information about how and by whom the item is used.

profile sheet   A form that displays the characteristics of a proposed product at the time of screening. Scores are plotted on a diagram for easier analysis.

project   A unit of activity in the product development process that usually deals with creating and marketing one new product. A project involves a multidisciplinary group of people and may often be part of a larger unit of work, a program, which delivers a stream of new products, one from each project.

projectization   The degree to which a group of people working on new product projects feel committed to the project as against being loyal to the departments where they work. On major innovations, a high degree of projectization is often essential to break through barriers.

project matrix An organization option in which the matrix leans toward the project. Participants have dual reporting relationships, but the project is intended to dominate their thinking and action.

protocol A statement of the benefits (not features) a new product should have. A protocol is prepared after the full screen and business analysis, prior to the project being assigned to technical departments. The benefits statement is agreed to by all parties, thus the term *protocol*.

prototype The first physical form or service description of a new product, still in rough or tentative mode. With complex products, there may be component prototypes as well as one finished prototype. For services, the prototype is simply the first full description of how the service will work.

prototype concept test A concept test done after technical work has produced a prototype. The prototype clarifies many aspects of the concept and leads to superior concept test reactions. May precede technical work if the prototypes are inexpensive to prepare (such as food products).

pseudo sale A category of market testing methods wherein the customer does various things to indicate reaction to the product and to its marketing strategy but does not actually spend money.

R

relationships analysis A category of fortuitous scan methods of ideation in which the essential element is bringing together things not normally so considered. Two-dimensional matrixes are the simplest, but morphological matrixes are more productive.

relevance tree A form of dynamic leap scenario whereby we first set the goal or desirable end point somewhere in the future, and then work back to the present by describing the intermediate steps that must be taken if we are to go from here to there. The near-term steps show us where to start work.

repeat use A stage in the basic A–T–R model where persons who have tried the product make a decision to like it, use it again, or adopt it in their practice set. Contrasts with rejection of further use.

repositioning Changing the product positioning, either on failure of the original positioning or to react to changes in the marketplace.

required rate of return A financial hurdle that is a firm's cost of capital adjusted for the risk of the project. Most new product projects have more risk than ongoing operations, so most required rates are well above costs of capital.

research and development The function of working through various sciences and technologies to design new products. This usually involves some basic research for creating new technologies and some applied research for converting those basic discoveries (and others) into specific new products. The applied (or developmental) phase begins after new product concepts have been screened and desirable attributes set up for them. It ends when scientific personnel deliver to manufacturing the necessary process specifications and finished product specifications. R&D departments also have many other duties, not so directly related to new products. In some firms, a design or design engineering function has duties that overlap R&D.

risk curve   Used to put probabilities onto the net present value output of a financial analysis. Is an array of outcomes, either in normal distribution or in some variance from it.

risk matrix   A matrix of the risks at any particular point in a new product's evaluation process. It shows the risk of rejecting a product idea that would ultimately succeed and the risk of going ahead with a project that would ultimately fail.

risk premium   The amount by which cost of capital is raised to reflect added risks of any particular new product proposal. Such addition yields the required rate of return.

roadblock   A hindrance to creativity. May be personal (a negative person), procedural (many approvals), environmental (distractive), etc.

roll-out   (See *limited marketing*.)

S

scanner market   A type of controlled market testing. Products are offered for sale in stores where scanners have been installed, and special arrangements made to gather all relevant information about them and their buyers.

scenario   Technically, scenario is an unfolding picture of the future. In new products work, it more customarily refers to pictures of some future time and place related to a firm's area of interest. The future scenario may be created by extending current trends (the dictionary form) or by leaping into the future and using other methods of deciding what will exist.

scenario analysis   Scenarios are used to study how firms and individuals will be living at some future time; from that, one can determine what problems they will have that they cannot tell us about now.

scoring model   A weighted-factor checklist used to screen new product proposals. Factors are scored, and the scorings are weighted and then totaled to yield a judgment on the concept.

screening of ideas   Evaluation steps prior to R&D and systems design in the product development process. They involve use of scoring models, checklists, or personal judgments and are based on information from experience and various market research studies (including concept testing).

seed trends   Current trends used to spot possible scenarios.

sensitivity testing   The practice of changing one or more of the factors in a financial analysis. The analyses are usually put up on spreadsheets, and what-if questions can be asked by making such changes. Settles issues on how sensitive the model is to errors in the forecast.

serendipity The ability to gain knowledge from accidental events. Many famous new products have been discovered accidentally, but many potential discoveries were overlooked because the observer was not serendipitous (having a prepared mind).

service (See *customer service.*)

service mark A trademark for a service.

services (1) Products, such as a bank loan or home security, that are intangible or at least substantially so. If totally intangible, they are exchanged directly from producer to user, cannot be transported or stored, and are almost instantly perishable. Service products are often difficult to identify, because they come into existence at the same time they are bought and consumed. They comprise intangible elements that are inseparable, usually involve customer participation in some important way, cannot be sold in the sense of ownership transfer, and have no title. Today, however, most products are partly tangible and partly intangible, and the dominant form is used to classify them as either goods or services (all are products). (2) *Services,* as a term, is also used to describe activities performed by sellers and others that accompany the sale of a product. (See *customer service.*)

simulated test market A form of market testing in which consumers are exposed to new products and to their claims in a staged advertising and purchase situation. Output of the test is an early forecast of sales and/or market share, based on mathematical forecasting models, management assumptions, and input of specific measurements from the simulation.

singularity The number of other products against which a new item will be tested. If one, singularity is monadic. If two, the singularity is paired comparison.

speculative sale A type of pseudo sale market test. Consists of a sales call (usually in commercial or industrial markets) where the full presentation is followed by a "Would you buy?" question rather than a "Will you buy?" request for the order.

spin-out A form of new product team organization in which the team is broken out from the ongoing organization. It is the ultimate in projectization and used only in cases where the project will have major barriers to overcome.

sponsor An informal role or participant. Is usually a higher-ranking person in a firm not personally involved in the project (compared to a champion) but ready to extend a helping hand if needed.

state of the art A term describing the current outer limit of any developing technology. It is as far as we have gone at the present time. The state-of-the-art limit will move out over time.

STM Letters stand for *s*imulated *t*est *m*arket.

strict liability   An extreme variant of product liability (in common practice today) in which the producer is held responsible for not putting a defective product on the market. Under strict liability, there need be no negligence, sale no longer has to be direct from producer to user (privity of contract), and no disclaimer statement relieves the producer of this responsibility.

styles of management   The different cultures wanted for product innovation situations have led to three recognizably different styles of management. The first is managerial or administrative, a bureaucratic style associated with conservative product strategies. The second is collegial, a midrange style that says "Let's work this out together, as colleagues." The third is entrepreneurial, taken from the styles made famous by some well-known high-tech start-ups.

sunk costs   Costs that represent expenses already incurred in the development of a new product. Have been written off, involve no capital asset, and no anticipated salvage value. For purposes of net present value, sunk costs are ignored. After the project is over, an overall recap will include all costs, whenever spent.

supply-pushed innovation   (See *technology driven*.)

surrogate positioning   Product positioning that eschews product features and benefits, turning instead to 1 of perhaps 8 or 10 substitutes, or surrogates. The two most popular surrogates are nonpareil (our product is simply the best available, no features or benefits cited) and parentage (our product is good because it was designed by the designers or producers of product X).

surrogate question   Any question to which the answer can yield an answer to another question that cannot be answered at this time, if ever. For example, if the key question is "What retaliation will our chief competitor offer to our new product?", a surrogate question that can be answered would be "What retaliation did that competitor offer to its most recent serious competitive threat?"

T

target market   The group of potential customers selected for marketing. A market segment. Combines with positioning and marketing mix to yield marketing strategy.

tastemakers   Those who are the first to adopt product innovations are often called tastemakers, recognizing their influence on followers.

team   That group of persons who serve as on-site managers for a new products program. Each team member represents a function, department, or specialty, and together they form the management for that product. Team members may be full time or part time, and persons may move on and off a team depending on the continuing need for their specialty.

technology Essentially, the power to do work. Technologies are one of two bases for product innovation (market strength is the other). Technologies take many forms, the most common being a process, a material, a piece of equipment, a special knowledge, a person, or a science. They may also be a building, a manufacturing facility or know-how, or even something outside technical departments, such as a distributor's bottling and delivery system, a brand manager system, or an order-filling system.

technology driven A new products strategy or operation based on the strength of a technology. Technology yields new products, which are then offered to the market. Market driven is the alternative form of thrust. Dual drive uses both at the same time and is the preferred form today.

test marketing One form of full-scale market testing. Usually involves actually marketing a new product in one or several cities. The effort is totally representative of what the firm intends to do later on national marketing (or roll-out). Various aspects of the marketing plan may be tested (such as advertising expenditure levels or, less often, product form variants) by using several pairs of cities. Output is a mix of learning, especially a sales and profit forecast. The term *test marketing* is sometimes stretched to include scanner market testing (where the marketing activity is less than total), but the term is best confined to the full-scale activity.

top-two-boxes In concept and product use testing, it is common to ask the question "How likely would you be to buy this product?" The answer set is traditionally Definitely would buy, Probably would buy, May or may not buy, Probably would not buy, and Definitely would not buy. Listed with boxes in front of each choice, the analyst is looking for the percent of people who checked either of the top two boxes. The statistic is a common measurement of overall acceptance.

tracking The act of checking on the progress of important aspects or issues in the marketing of a new product. May be comprehensive or casual.

tracking variable A specific variable used to track a specific phenomenon. Distribution can be tracked, for example, by measuring the "percent of outlets that have stocked at least one package."

trademark A legal term meaning the same as brand. A trademark identifies one seller's product and thus differentiates it from products of other sellers. If registered, the trademark obtains additional protection, mainly exclusive use, but special efforts are necessary to keep the registration.

trade name A trademark used to identify an organization rather than a product or product line.

trade secret In contrast to getting a patent on an invention, the inventor or firm can simply attempt to keep secret the new aspect of the product. The Coca-Cola formula is a famous trade secret.

trade-off analysis A type of study that measures users' utility scales for various attributes of a given product category. Given the determinant attributes, and the utility scale for each, one can assemble the perfect product, putting in an optimized set of attributes that yields in total the greatest value to the marketplace. Originally (and still often) called conjoint analysis.

trial   The second part of the A–T–R triad. Defined in some way to indicate target customers who have heard of the product and like enough about its story to warrant a serious trial of it. The trial must involve some cost or outlay of effort on buyer's part or else does not assure us of genuine interest.

twin streams of innovation activity   The innovation process is building a product and also a marketing plan. The two processes go on simultaneously, and, in fact, the marketing plan may originate first if the firm's strategy is to develop new products for specific target markets.

two-dimensional matrix   A simple form of relationships analysis using only two dimensions. Contrasts with the morphological matrix of several dimensions.

U

universal product code   An identification system involving a series of different-width vertical lines used to identify individual products sold at retail. The code is standardized and can be used on any product (or its package) that has physical form.

use testing   (See *product use testing.*)

V

value added   A measure of the contribution to a product's worth by any organization that handles it on its way to the ultimate user. Value added is measured by subtracting the cost of a purchased product (or the cost of ingredients from which it was made) from the price that the organization got for it. For resellers, this means the firm's gross margin; for manufacturing firms, it means the contribution over cost of ingredients. Presumably, whatever work that firm did is reflected in the higher price someone is willing to pay for the product, hence that firm's value added.

venture   An option of organization. The team is fully projectized and has left the matrix mode. People are usually working full time on the project. Venture may be internal, spun-out, or joint with another firm. Used when the project must be free of substantial restraints within the current organization.

W

waiver   The release signed by an inventor who wishes to get consideration of a nonpatented idea or product.

warranty   A statement or promise made to the customer that a product being offered for sale is fit for the purpose being claimed. The promise concerns primarily what the seller will do if the product performs below expectations or turns out to be defective in some way. The promise (warranty) may be full (complete protection) or limited (some corrective steps), under terms of the Magnuson-Moss Act of 1975.

Bibliography

This bibliography displays (1) general books on the product innovation subject, both business and college oriented, published since 1980 and (2) selected other publications frequently sought for their reference value or some unique contribution.

Bacon, Frank R., Jr., and Thomas W. Butler, Jr. *Planned Innovation*. Ann Arbor: University of Michigan, Industrial Development Division, 1981. (A business-oriented book emphasizing the screening task.)

Betts, Jim. *The Million-Dollar Idea*. Point Pleasant, N.J.: Point Publishing, 1985. (A collection of some of the most helpful ideas from past issues of *The New Product Development Newsletter*.)

Bobrow, Edwin E., and Dennis W. Shafer. *Pioneering New Products*. Homewood, Ill.: Dow Jones-Irwin, 1987. (A business-oriented book.)

Booz, Allen & Hamilton. *New Products Management for the 1980s*. Chicago: 1982. (A survey of industry practice.)

Buggie, Frederick D. *New Product Development Strategies*. New York: Amacom, 1981. (A business-oriented book.)

Choffray, Jean-Marie, and Gary L. Lilien. *Market Planning for New Industrial Products*. New York: John Wiley & Sons, 1980. (Focuses principally on advanced techniques of management science.)

Cooper, Robert G. *Winning at New Products*. Reading, Mass.: Addison-Wesley Publishing, 1986. (A business-oriented book based on recent research findings.)

Duerr, Michael G. *The Commercial Development of New Products*. New York: The Conference Board, 1986. (A study of new product development in firms that call it *commercial development,* primarily chemical firms.)

Fuller, Melvin L. *A Step-By-Step Guide to Success*. Tarzana, Calif.: ILMA Printing, 1984. (A guidebook for inventors, including the patent process.)

Goulding, Ian, and Anita M. Kennedy. "The Development, Adoption, and Diffusion of New Industrial Products." *European Journal of Marketing* 17, no. 3 (1983). (The entire issue is a one-article summary of the literature on the stated subject.)

Gruenwald, George. *New Product Development: What Really Works*. Chicago: Crain Books, 1985. (A business-oriented book especially for consumer packaged goods.)

Guile, Bruce R., and James Brian Quinn. *Managing Innovation*. Washington, D.C.: National Academy Press, 1981. (Collection of seven stories of successful product innovation in eight industries, from a parts catalog to a bridge construction service.)

Hisrich, Robert D., and Michael P. Peters. *Marketing Decisions for New and Mature Products*. Columbus, Ohio: Merrill Publishing, 1984.

Hopkins, David S. *The Marketing Plan*. New York: The Conference Board, 1981. (Basic compilation of marketing plans in survey of members.)

Jewkes, John; David Sawers; and Richard Stillerman. *The Sources of Invention*. New York: St. Martin's Press, 1959. (A summary of research on invention prior to that date.)

Kinnear, Thomas C., and James R. Taylor. *Marketing Research*. New York: McGraw-Hill, 1987.

Kotter, John P. *The General Managers*. New York: Free Press/Macmillan, 1982. (A research report that fits nicely with the new products manager job.)

Kuscmarski, Thomas D. *Managing New Products*. Englewood Cliffs, N.J.: Prentice-Hall, 1988. (A business-oriented book that emphasizes the management consultant's view of strategy and organization.)

Moskowitz, Howard R. *Product Testing and Sensory Evaluations of Foods*. Westport, Conn.: Food and Nutrition Press, 1983. (The ultimate in coverage of the use testing field for consumer products.)

Oakley, Mark. *Managing Product Design*. New York: John Wiley & Sons, 1984. (Industrial design integrated into the new products management function. U.K.)

Osborn, Alex F. *Applied Imagination*. 3rd ed. New York: Charles Scribner's Sons, 1963. (The basic brainstorming work.)

Pessemier, Edgar E. *Product Management*. 2nd ed. New York: John Wiley & Sons, 1982. (A management science approach to new products, based on computer models of the process.)

Pinchot, Gifford, III. *Intrapreneuring*. New York: Harper & Row, 1985. (By the creator of the intrapreneuring concept.)

Rosenau, Milton D., Jr. *Faster New Product Development*. New York: Amacom, 1990. (A business-oriented book focused as indicated by its title.)

Scheuing, Eberhard E. *New Product Management*. Columbus, Ohio: Merrill Publishing, 1989. (An approach emphasizing the marketing viewpoint and the marketing plan.)

Souder, William E. *Managing New Product Innovations*. Lexington, Mass.: Lexington Books, 1987. (Compilation of the author's research findings from 10 years of studies, mainly industrial.)

Tushman, Michael L., and William Moore. *Readings in the Management of Innovation*. Marshfield, Mass.: Pitman Publishing, 1982. (Emphasizes the technology side.)

Twiss, Brian C. *Managing Technological Innovation*. 2nd ed. New York: Longman, 1980. (A U.K. technical perspective.)

Urban, Glen, and John R. Hauser. *Design and Marketing of New Products.* Englewood Cliffs, N.J.: Prentice-Hall, 1980. (Based heavily on new advances in mathematical modeling for sales forecasting.)

Urban, Glen L.; John R. Hauser; and Nikhilesh Dholakia. *Essentials of New Products Management.* Englewood Cliffs, N.J.: Prentice-Hall, 1987. (A condensed and updated version of Urban and Hauser, *Design and Marketing of New Products.*)

Wind, Yoram J. *Product Policy: Concepts, Methods, and Strategy.* Reading, Mass.: Addison-Wesley Publishing, 1982. (Marketing research orientation.)

Wizenberg, Larry, ed. *The New Products Handbook.* Homewood, Ill.: Dow Jones-Irwin, 1987. (A business-oriented book.)

Index

L

M